What's the Use?

Editors
Nick Aikens, Thomas Lange,
Jorinde Seijdel, Steven ten Thije

Valiz, Amsterdam   www.valiz.nl
Van Abbemuseum, Eindhoven   www.vanabbemuseum.nl
University Hildesheim   www.uni-hildesheim.de
L'Internationale   www.internationaleonline.org

What's the Use?

Constellations of Art,
History, and Knowledge

A Critical Reader

Contents

Appendix

What's the Use?
Editor's Introduction

This reader on art, use, and history comes at the end of modernity's end, after its long goodbye from its postmodern deathbed.

Throughout the modern period the human subject was conditioned by a rigorous logic of cause and effect. Everything was defined by what came before, and knowing what came before was the central objective of any pursuit of knowledge. It was common to return upstream to a phenomenon's source, with writing linear histories as the natural outcome of this endeavour. All of history flowed in one direction and time ended when the two great rivers of late twentieth-century ideology met: democratic capitalism and communism. They battled untill the bitter end, both claiming to offer the natural expression of the way of the world. For the West the Cold War was the war that would end all wars, the war that would end history, as Francis Fukuyama was later to proclaim.[1]

In the wake of 1989, with the fall of the Berlin Wall, and the establishment of the Internet, a postmodern, manic-depressive zombie time was set in motion. Celebrating infinite growth in new 'liberalized' economies coincided with the perpetual mourning for the injustice that free-roaming, globalized capitalism induced. For some time Third Way new leftism believed it could marry the incommensurable forces of social security and global capitalism. This utopian, two-faced automaton wasn't meant to be and it too died amid the financial crisis of 2008. Fukuyama's proclamation of the end of history was in one sense, at least, correct. Neoliberal hegemony signaled the end of a certain conception of time—we were no longer able to look forward as modernism had bid us do for so long. Instead we became stuck, our wheels spinning in the quagmire of the continuous present.

In art, modernism's tunnel vision was epitomized by the idea of schools and movements that represented stages of a singular and ongoing development, the endless 'isms' of art history. Such categorizations involved viewing history from a particular perspective—namely Western and colonial— discounting discourses and inputs beyond the confines of its specific cultural and political parameters. But modernism also placed history within an interpretative straightjacket, unable to cut loose from its relationship to art that preceded it or came after. In essence, modernism exiled art to a place where it was unable to claim traction outside its own boundaries, whilst limiting its capacity to draw on history as a means to negotiate the present. Even more so than the modern subject, modern art was trapped due to being the representation of the force that produced it.

Such a mode of viewing art and its so-called 'development' has, thankfully, long been challenged. Postcolonial discourse succeeded in significantly reorienting, if not quite overcoming, the hegemony of a Western conception of the 'development' of its own field. With postmodern eclecticism, representation started to feast on itself, passionately exploring its own end. Now, as we reflect modernism on itself, we are forced to reconsider what value system art stands for or against—what, if anything, art represents. From this perspective, the role modernism ascribed to art, and its position of exile from the world, has itself to be fled. But where should we look for alternative roles? This reader suggests, through a variety of historical perspectives, theoretical positions, artistic practices, and curatorial models that one way out of the impasse might be through considering art's relationship to use.

The rich variety of texts and artists' contributions herein test the possibility of analyzing art through use. The case studies and material draw extensively from a new long-term programme organized by the museum confederation L'Internationale: *The Uses of Art – The Legacy of 1848 and 1989.*[2] Within this

---

1   For Fukuyama 'the end of history' meant the establishment of liberal democracy and capitalism as final and universal forms of government. See Francis Fukuyama, *The End of History and the Last Man* (New York: Free Press, 1992).

2   L'Internationale is a confederation of six modern and contemporary art institutions: Moderna galerija, Ljubljana; Museo Nacional Centro de Arte Reina Sofía, Madrid; Museu d'Art Contemporani de Barcelona (MACBA), Barcelona; Museum van Hedendaagse Kunst Antwerpen (M HKA), Antwerp; SALT, Istanbul and Ankara; and Van Abbemuseum, Eindhoven. L'Internationale works with complementary partners such as: Grizedale Arts, Coniston, United Kingdom; Liverpool John Moores University, Liverpool; Stiftung Universität Hildesheim, Hildesheim; and University College Ghent School of Arts, Ghent along with associate organizations from the academic and artistic fields. The confederation takes its name from the workers' anthem 'L'Internationale,' which calls for an equitable and democratic society with reference to the historical labour movement.

programme, four activities dealt specifically with the relation of art to use, even if there were differences in approach, sometimes profound ones. These activities were: the exhibition *Really Useful Knowledge*, organized by Museo Nacional Centro de Arte Reina Sofía, Madrid, curated by What How & for Whom/WHW, 2015; the exhibition *Confessions of the Imperfect, 1848–1989–Today*, organized by the Van Abbemuseum together with curator Alistair Hudson, 2014–2015; the conference 'The Uses of Art: History,' organized by Thomas Lange, Institut für Bildende Kunst und Kunstwissenschaft, University of Hildesheim, 2014; and the exhibition *Museum of Arte Útil*, also organized by the Van Abbemuseum and initiated by artist Tania Bruguera, 2013. Combined with several special commissions by writers and artists, this reader provides a timely overview of the uses of art that seeks to inspire debate in trying to collectively imagine a future after modernity's end.

Art's Relative Use

Use is a thorny term. Embedded in it are questions of effect, utility, and instrumenta-lization, notions long seen as anathema to the field of art production, critique, and presentation. Taken more broadly as we do here, usefulness appears as a transient, malleable category. What was useful once might be utterly useless or incomprehensible later. What is useful to one person can be useless to another. Here, use's transient nature defines its presence as a relative category. Some put forward that art's use is only achieved when one can see results. Others argue that it is precisely in the unseen and immeasurable that art's use presides. Many intermingle the two. Yet there is some common ground, because however usefulness is defined, it is never an inherent quality or a representation of use—it speaks to a set of relationships of use. This relativity of use, enabling use to provoke discussion, makes it a productive wedge with which to break open modernism's stranglehold on art.

What is useful is what is affective. Through analyzing affects one can retrace useful relationships. The study of use therefore involves looking at the texture of affective surfaces.

These surfaces are not the counterpoint to modernity's endlessly receding origin that asked the modern subject to always dig deeper. They are the composite outcome of impure genealogies: that is, the family tree of use is contingent and chaotic—how something is intended to be used is not how it can be really useful. When, for instance, workers in nineteenth-century Britain were offered education by their employers, it was not the skills desired by their masters they considered truly useful. The affect of being in an educational surrounding was that it inspired the workers to turn from being educated into becoming educators. Affective relations are a messy affair, which is not something to purify through modern hygiene, but they can be carefully traced and analyzed. Instead of an all-encompassing overview, what is gained through these analyses is a detailed insight into the dizzying yet exciting web of societal and cultural relationships that link one thing to another.

Looking within the frame of use profoundly affects the category of art. Works themselves may stay the same, though the manner in which one relates to them undergoes significant shifts. In the modern condition, art was isolated, often serving as a critical mirror for reality. This reflective relationship is not necessarily obliterated when looking at art through its use, only this moment of reflection is folded into societal and cultural relationships. Art finds its specificity in dialogue with other types of relationships. If use often follows conventional lines, in the context of artistic intervention and through its self-awareness as art, it quite deliberately veers off these lines introducing new forms of use. Art thereby repurposes, as Stephen Wright argues, how something is used. It is then not so much a thing, but a type of relationship that is sometimes more pronounced than others. Art is still a specific domain but its specificity lies in its ability to connect different social, political, and economic fields. By analyzing these hybrid relationships, we come to a new understanding of art's use.

Likewise, the notion of use and its transient nature opposes the modernist understanding of historical progress: one thing leading to the next. Instead of acting as an overarching frame for development, usefulness points to specific moments in time, to a series of different singularities and relationships of affectedness. How or why did something become useful to somebody? This simple question has great currency in our contemporary moment, defined as it is through fragmentation, fracture, and its multiple genealogies. In its simplest form, use helps us come to terms with a situation in which people from different regions, with very different histories, interact. Instead of offering a coherent master narrative that seeks to fold everything into one enormous play of modernity, use offers a way to consider dialogues without knowing their beginning or end.

Historical Montage versus Linear Progression
This reader seeks to reorient modernism's insistence on progress by engaging in multiple understandings, interpretations, and applications of history. It seeks to revisit the long modern period, tracing the bond between Art and History in relation to subjectivity and autonomy. It explores the changing definitions of history, culture, memory, and oblivion in relation to the individual and the collective as key topics of an unfinished modern condition that emerges in the early nineteenth century. Various contributions focus on the role art plays in producing ideas, theories, and reinterpretations of 'history' within the struggle between collective identifications and making sense of the world on an individual level. The reader therefore explores art's critical potential as producer of knowledge through the construction of relations between past, present, and future. It both deals with and addresses the industrial and social revolutions and reorganizations of the subject and the community—from the nineteenth century to today.

As such, these texts and projects aim to contribute not only to a historical understanding of this particular timeframe, but to thinking through expanded and interwoven layers of time that reveal multiple connections: thinking and working with and in constellations. Through thinking in constellations it is possible to dismiss the idea of a historical series of 'developments,'

enabling connections between things and incidents of very different origins and times. For Walter Benjamin the image and application of constellations enables a critical practice that the image of a progressive sequence does not allow; it takes the opportunity to open the eyes and minds of historians and artists to the interrelation of events across time and to understand history as filled by the presence of a 'now.' In his text 'On the Concept of History' Benjamin points out that what 'has been' comes together in a flash in the now to form a constellation.[3]

Together the contributions and overall composition of this reader suggest that thinking and practicing history in constellations is a much more fluid notion that can accommodate what the idea of 'progression' neglects: the synchronicity of the asynchronous. Considering history as a constantly changing creation of the present, periods appear also not to be fixed, but reveal their malleable quality because they are the subject of working minds, determined to put forward an understanding of the present through reflecting on the past appearing in the present. Seen in this light the task of an artist and a historian, as well as the use of art and the use of history, adopt different means but have the same methodological basis. It is the work of montage and therefore a constant struggle to write and rewrite, construct and deconstruct narratives that enable any present to understand itself through and with a past. Montage was for Benjamin the only justifiable method to gain access to history because it makes past occurrences, terms, opinions, deeds, images, etc., present. According to Benjamin the just method to do so is to imagine these things from the past in our own space, and with our own terms, opinions, deeds, and past things. The artistic and curatorial endeavours brought together here witness this work on and with history and seek to reveal how these narratives have been constructed.

---

3   See Walter Benjamin, 'On the Concept of History,' in *Gesammelte Schriften*, vol. 1, bd. 2 (Frankfurt am Main: Suhrkamp, 1974 [1940]).

A Polemical Toolkit of Usership

This publication is divided into three sections that focus on history, artistic practice, and exhibition strategies, exploring art's affects and relative use. As 'usership' is a contested term, instead of tying the material together in an all-embracing theoretical frame, art's relation to use is introduced provocatively through Stephen Wright's 'Toward a Lexicon of Usership.' The text was originally commissioned to coincide with the *Museum of Arte Útil* and functions as a rogue fourth section in the book. Wright's short publication has proved both a pivotal and divisive contribution to recent conversations on art and use for a number of artists, thinkers, and curators. The text is inserted here as a polemical toolkit with which to explore the implications of a turn toward use. The core radicalism in his proposal is that modern systems of value and quality are simply no longer able to grasp what is at stake in the relation between art, artist, user, and society at large. This requires us to make a double lexical move. Certain terms need to be retired from use, while new terms need to be unpacked and constructed so that art can be repurposed to different ends.

Constellating History

The first section revolves around history, presenting both a series of relevant constellations to redefine the contemporary moment and ways to understand these constellations as a methodological and subsequently political exercise. One of these constellations is drawn around the anachronistic figure of art critic and social thinker John Ruskin (1819–1900). The affective web of relationships that is spun out of his writings is a clear demonstration of how history forms constellations that can become legible through montage. Ruskin was an early agent who argued for understanding art through use. While his ideas foresaw repercussions in different fields of architecture and design, as Lara Garcia Diaz details in her essay, his ideas on art and use have been forgotten within the field of art itself. Tamara Díaz Bringas, for example, looks at practices and initiatives taking place in Fidel Castro's Cuba as a means

to understand the combination of impulses and methodologies behind Tania Bruguera's notion of 'Arte Útil.' Adrian Rifkin's text similarly constellates ideas of use, the really useful, and the 'útil,' crisscrossing back and forth between nineteenth-century Britain and today to explore and bend our understanding of these terms.

Practicing Art, Knowledge, and Use

The second and largest section focuses on artistic practice itself. Through a diverse set of examples, both the affective working of artworks themselves and associated artistic practice, are presented and analyzed. Here the notion of constellations reemerges through the groupings of artworks. Thomas Lange analyzes, for example, Christoph Schlingensief's controversial *Ausländer raus!* [Foreigners out!] project, which intermingles contemporary migration policy in Austria and reality TV in the heart of the cultural centre of Vienna. This complex project orchestrates a montage of social and political forms and discourses that reactivates aggressive racist scripts from the past, combined with the complexities of guilt and repression.

Within this section film and video emerge as mediums that have been deployed to produce relationships of affect. Perhaps more than any other medium these reveal the potential of montage to re-situate relationships between past and present, author and actor, image and affect. These films are constructed, as Georges Didi-Huberman analyzes in the work of Jean-Luc Godard, to bring forth an active response from the subject. The viewer is asked not to merely experience a story that exists outside him or her, but to reconsider, through affective strategies, one's position toward that which is presented. The section concludes with a look at a series of artistic practices whose production is not a work to be placed on pedestal, but exists out of real and active social relationships, such as the *Freehouse* project by Jeanne van Heeswijk in the Rotterdam Afrikaanderwijk. These practices link more directly to what Bruguera calls 'Arte Útil.'

Exhibiting and Instituting

The final section presents a series of reflections on the role of the museum and specifically the exhibition when used to present an affective montage. The museum is an unlikely site for such gestures. It is the architectural and institutional embodiment of modernism, a generator and gatekeeper of histories, understood most explicitly through its conservation of objects or its presentation of unfolding narratives of history through exhibitions. The contributions try to track, expose, and challenge this position. The means with which to do this are varied. Specific institutions, like the Museo Reina Sofía, are analyzed, as in Jésus Carrillo's text, or exhibitions that focus on use directly as in *1:1 Stopover* in Moderna galerija, Ljubljana discussed by Zdenka Badovinac. Historical events in exhibition making are likewise looked at, as in the exchange between art historians Alois Riegl and Alexander Dorner, revisited by Steven ten Thije. Reflecting on how the museum positions itself in relation to the fields of use and history is central to the perceived role of institutions today, as museum directors Charles Esche and Manuel Borja-Villel address in their conversation. This section also gives space to the three exhibitions that form the main source of inspiration for this publication and concludes with a substantial reflection on the framing and methodologies of these projects by curators involved.

At the end of the end one expects to find a new beginning. Turning the page so that a new chapter can start. Yet the beginning that is proposed here is not the next chapter in an unfolding story. When entering this terrain of relationships of use not one but countless chapters open up. Constellations do not follow each other in the numbing cadence of cause and effect, but appear unexpectedly and seemingly at random when the stars start to move, each with their own trajectory and speed. When reading the material, we imagine new constellations to appear, and hope it will provide inspiration and energy to appropriate and repurpose events in a meaningful montage. Our ambition is that these constellations might allow a greater sensitivity to the dense affective tissue of relationships embedded within our daily reality. This reality is one that holds present, past, and future all at once—and it is ours to use.

Pa

Conste

His

Part I

Oscillating

Theory.

Constellating History

Introduction
Thomas Lange

The texts in this section deal with *historical constellations*. They also form a *historical constellation* in contributing, from various angles and timeframes, past and present notions of the relation between art and use over the long period of modernity. In doing so they make visible the traces from historical conceptions, struggles, and solutions to ongoing and current problems addressed by artists, scholars, and theorists today.

Within modernity (1800–present) capitalism reveals itself as a timeless, adaptive, and assimilating organism that is key to the notion of connecting (not separating) past and present. To make this visible through art, a concept of critical analysis, of presentation, of exhibiting with and within constellations emerged at the transition from the nineteenth to the twentieth century as an appropriate tool to reflect, comprehend, and work with a notion of 'history.' A notion of history which is, as Walter Benjamin put it in his notations entitled 'On the Concept of History,' a present aware of the fact that it is addressed by a past which the respective present remembers in a brief moment, a flash of acute danger.[1] This was put in strong contrast to the always ready, accurate 'truth' of history the *historicism* claimed to achieve. Moreover, constellation was used by Benjamin as a strong counterpart and the only logical alternative to the narration of history as a linear progress.

Thinking of history in constellations is a much more plastic, formable, fluent, and dynamic notion. It takes into account what the idea of progression within a timeline of singular events neglects: the simultaneity of that which does not belong to the same time period, the anachronism and heterochronism, the layers of different 'historic' constellations (conventionally understood as periods of time) that are present in every present. Understanding a moment in history in its constellation is understanding the process which lives in it. Thinking in and within constellations is the key to reconfiguring our understanding of history as an ongoing process with no determined direction or aim. Constellations show the expanded and interwoven matrix of layers of time revealing multiple connections to later or previous, past and present times. Constellations are configurations, montages, interferences that enable us to look at a specific historic place or moment in history.

Benjamin pointed out that ideas relate to things like star constellations relate to planets. They are neither terms nor laws. Instead, they make sense only because of their relative positions. They exist only in the very place that emerges from a given montage. Thinking in constellations is working on the ability to understand the 'layers of time' in breaking the one-dimensional idea of timelines (of linearity) as well as the notion of cause and effect or cause and consequence relations.

Extending from the nineteenth century to the present, we open with a reprint of John Ruskin's famous lecture 'On the Relationship of Art to Use' (1870). Ruskin's text addresses some of

---

1   Walter Benjamin, 'Über den Begriff der Geschichte,' in *Illuminationen. Ausgewählte Schriften*, ed. Siegfried Unseld (Frankfurt am Main: Suhrkamp, 1977), see chapter VI, p. 253 and chapter XVII, p. 260.

the section's main topics including: the relation of the arts to capitalist production and labour; comparisons to artists' achievements of the past; and the relevance of historic knowledge in tackling demanding problems to work on future solutions that counter the conditions of capitalism—of which art is inevitably part. In this sense Alistair Hudson's contribution takes Ruskin's approach seriously, opening up a substantial reflection on and development of Ruskin's ideas in suggesting how to use a specific understanding of art's use under today's tighter conditions toward an ecology of aesthetics. Tamara Díaz Bringas focuses on the early traces of Arte Útil in Cuba from 1976, shedding light on understanding the struggles of art's use in a complementary socialist system. In doing so she develops a substantial contextualization of Tania Bruguera's work on Arte Útil from the perspective of radical pedagogic practice, with the desire to bring about social change by finding a use for art in society. Adrian Rifkin addresses the ambivalence and contradictions inherent in the terms 'useful art' and 'useful knowledge' within the fields of industrial and artistic notions of 'work,' from the restoration of trade after the Napoleonic Wars to the present day. This, too, is closely connected to concepts of education, either as an instrument of domination or of emancipation. His sharp observations offer—with history's unveiled lamp—cogent insight into today's discourse of 'qualification' (as the internalized oppression) and the potential antidote.

Lara Garcia Diaz takes on another dialectical tension that occurred with the rise of capitalism and urbanism forming the opposition between 'town' and 'country,' which affected architecture, town planning, and even society at large. In her lucid inquiry she focuses on two 'counter-measures' against the rapid spread of aggressive and speculative capitalism: the *urban utopias* of Ebenezer Howard's *Garden City* of the late nineteenth century and Le Corbusier's *Pla Macià* for Barcelona in the early twentieth century. In making a vital distinction between 'utopian' (transforming the economic base of capitalism) and 'ideological' (preserving the rights of the powerful class) she investigates

other perspectives in which utopia is a vital tool for acting upon social reality. Christina Clausen looks back at the rather complex politics behind German nineteenth-century urban landscape painting. In her substantial contribution she examines painterly depictions of the medieval cathedral as a vital means to design cultural memory. Understood as a political and cultural way of engaging with history, Clausen points out that these 'past projections of a future society' were based on ideas of a free, civic society as it seemed to emerge in the Renaissance in Germany in opposition to restorative forces that had followed the Napoleonic Wars everywhere in Europe. The urban landscape paintings were a tool that shaped the perception and notion of history for the generations that followed.

The final text of this section by John Byrne is a dense reflection on the use of history, use-value, and the contemporary work (or labour) of art in its relation to life. It comprises all of the previous texts' main concerns by analyzing a major and highly complex difficulty that has hounded Western culture since the early days of modernity: the dividing line and distinction between the autonomy of art and heteronomy of everyday life. Arguing with Hegel and Marx as well as T. J. Clark, Jacques Rancière, Fredric Jameson, and Franco Berardi, Byrne points out that an increasingly necessary reuse of history can function 'as a means of navigating between the Scylla and Charybdis of autonomy and heteronomy … to escape the strong gravitational pull of our own inherited structures of understanding.' In a distinct way this essay shows how the use-value of art incorporates the craft of history so much so that the use-value of art becomes 'a means to actively rework our histories as a political means to negotiating our alternative futures.'

This text is partially adapted from the author's entry 'Constellation' under the referential field 'Historicity' in *Glossary of Common Knowledge* (GCK), 11 August 2014, http://glossary.mg-lj.si/referential-fields/referential-fields/constellation?ref=constellation. GCK is a five-year research project by MG+MSUM in the frame of L'Internationale. It is curated by Zdenka Badovinac (MG+MSUM), Bojana Piškur (MG+MSUM), and Jesús Carrillo (MNCARS).

Historical text
John Ruskin

The Relation of Art to Use

97.   Our subject of enquiry to-day, you will remember, is the mode in which fine art is founded upon, or may contribute to, the practical requirements of human life.

Its offices in this respect are mainly twofold: it gives Form
to knowledge, and Grace to utility; that is to say, it makes
permanently visible to us things which otherwise could
neither be described by our science, nor retained by our
memory; and it gives delightfulness and worth to the
implements of daily use, and materials of dress, furniture,
and lodging. In the first of these offices it gives precision
and charm to truth; in the second it gives precision and
charm to service. For, the moment we make anything useful
thoroughly, it is a law of nature that we shall be pleased
with ourselves, and with the thing we have made; and
become desirous therefore to adorn or complete it, in
some dainty way, with finer art expressive of our pleasure.

And the point I wish chiefly to bring before you to-day
is this close and healthy connection of the fine arts
with material use; but I must first try briefly to put in
clear light the function of art in giving Form to truth.

98.   Much that I have hitherto tried to teach has been
disputed on the ground that I have attached too much
importance to art as representing natural facts, and too
little to it as a source of pleasure. And I wish, in the close
of these four prefatory lectures, strongly to assert to
you, and, so far as I can in the time, convince you, that
the entire vitality of art depends upon its being either
full of truth, or full of use; and that, however pleasant,
wonderful, or impressive it may be in itself, it must yet
be of inferior kind, and tend to deeper inferiority, unless
it has clearly one of these main objects—either *to state
a true thing*, or to *adorn a serviceable one*. It must never
exist alone—never for itself; it exists rightly only when it is
the means of knowledge, or the grace of agency for life.

99.   Now, I pray you to observe—for though I have said this
often before, I have never yet said it clearly enough—every
good piece of art, to whichever of these ends it may be
directed, involves first essentially the evidence of human
skill and the formation of an actually beautiful thing by it.

Skill, and beauty, always then; and, beyond these, the formative arts have always one or other of the two objects which I have just defined to you—truth, or serviceableness; and without these aims neither the skill nor their beauty will avail; only by these can either legitimately reign. All the graphic arts begin in keeping the outline of shadow that we have loved, and they end in giving to it the aspect of life; and all the architectural arts begin in the shaping of the cup and the platter, and they end in a glorified roof.

Therefore, you see, in the graphic arts you have Skill, Beauty, and Likeness; and in the architectural arts, Skill, Beauty, and Use; and you *must* have the three in each group, balanced and co-ordinate; and all the chief errors of art consist in losing or exaggerating one of these elements.

100. For instance, almost the whole system and hope of modern life are founded on the notion that you may substitute mechanism for skill, photograph for picture, cast-iron for sculpture. That is your main nineteenth-century faith, or infidelity. You think you can get everything by grinding—music, literature, and painting. You will find it grievously not so; you can get nothing but dust by mere grinding. Even to have the barley-meal out of it, you must have the barley first; and that comes by growth, not grinding. But essentially, we have lost our delight in Skill; in that majesty of it which I was trying to make clear to you in my last address, and which long ago I tried to express, under the head of ideas of power. The entire sense of that, we have lost, because we ourselves do not take pains enough to do right, and have no conception of what the right costs; so that all the joy and reverence we ought to feel in looking at a strong man's work have ceased in us. We keep them yet a little in looking at a honeycomb or a bird's nest; we understand that these differ, by divinity of skill, from a lump of wax or a cluster of sticks. But a picture, which is a much more wonderful thing than a honeycomb or a bird's nest— have we not known people, and sensible people too, who expected to be taught to produce that, in six lessons?

101. Well, you must have the skill, you must have the beauty, which is the highest moral element; and then, lastly, you must have the verity or utility, which is not the moral, but the vital element; and this desire for verity and use is the one aim of the three that always leads in great schools, and in the minds of great masters, without any exception. They will permit themselves in awkwardness, they will permit themselves in ugliness; but they will never permit themselves in uselessness or in unveracity. …

105. And now let us think of our own work, and ask how that may become, in its own poor measure, active in some verity of representation. We certainly cannot begin by drawing kings or queens; but we must try, even in our earliest work, if it is to prosper, to draw something that will convey true knowledge both to ourselves and others. And I think you will find greatest advantage in the endeavour to give more life and educational power to the simpler branches of natural science: for the great scientific men are all so eager in advance that they have no time to popularize their discoveries, and if we can glean after them a little, and make pictures of the things which science describes, we shall find the service a worthy one. Not only so, but we may even be helpful to science herself; for she has suffered by her proud severance from the arts; and having made too little effort to realize her discoveries to vulgar eyes, has herself lost true measure of what was chiefly precious in them.

106. Take Botany, for instance. Our scientific botanists are, I think, chiefly at present occupied in distinguishing species, which perfect methods of distinction will probably in the future show to be indistinct—in inventing descriptive names of which a more advanced science and more fastidious scholarship will show some to be unnecessary, and others inadmissible—and in microscopic investigations of structure. … In the meantime, our artists are so generally convinced of the truth of the Darwinian theory that they do not always think it necessary to show any difference between the foliage of an elm and an oak; and the gift books of Christmas have every page surrounded with labouriously engraved garlands of rose, shamrock, thistle, and forget-me-not, without its being thought proper by the draughtsman, or desirable by the public, even in the case of those uncommon flowers, to observe the real shape of the petals of any one of them.

107. Now what we especially need at present for educational purposes is to know, not the anatomy of plants, but their biography—how and where they live and die, their tempers, benevolences, malignities, distresses, and virtues. We want them drawn from their youth to their age, from bud to fruit. ... And all this we ought to have drawn so accurately, that we might at once compare any given part of a plant with the same part of any other, drawn on the like conditions. Now, is not this a work which we may set about here in Oxford, with good hope and much pleasure? I think it is so important, that the first exercise in drawing I shall put before you will be an outline of a laurel leaf.

108. Next, in Geology, which I will take leave to consider as an entirely separate science from the zoology of the past, which has lately usurped its name and interest. ... In geology itself we find the strength of many able men occupied in debating questions of which there are yet no data even for the clear statement; and in seizing advanced theoretical positions on the mere contingency of their being afterwards tenable; while, in the meantime, no simple person, taking a holiday in Cumberland, can get an intelligible section of Skiddaw, or a clear account of the origin of the Skiddaw slates; and while, though half the educated society of London travel every summer over the great plain of Switzerland, none know, or care to know, why that is a plain, and the Alps to the south of it are Alps; and whether or not the gravel of the one has anything to do with the rocks of the other.

109. Now, as soon as you have obtained the power of drawing, I do not say a mountain, but even a stone, accurately, every question of this kind will become to you at once attractive and definite; you will find that in the grain, the lustre, and the cleavage lines of the smallest fragment of rock, there are recorded forces of every order and magnitude, from those which raise a continent by one volcanic effort, to those which at every instant are polishing the apparently complete crystal in its nest, and conducting the apparently motionless metal in its vein; and that only by the art of your own hand, and fidelity of sight which it develops, you can obtain true perception of these invincible and inimitable arts of the earth herself; while the comparatively slight effort necessary to obtain so much skill as may serviceably draw mountains in distant effect will be instantly rewarded by what is almost equivalent to a new sense of the conditions of their structure. ...

113. Lastly, in Zoology. What the Greeks did for the horse, and what, as far as regards domestic and expressional character, Landseer has done for the dog and the deer, remains to be done by art for nearly all other animals of high organization. ... I have placed in your Educational series a wing by Albrecht Dürer, which goes as far as art yet has reached in delineation of plumage; while for the simple action of the pinion it is impossible to go beyond what has been done already by Titian and Tintoretto; but you cannot so much as once look at the rufflings of the plumes of a pelican pluming itself after it has been in the water, or carefully draw the contours of the wing either of a vulture or a common swift, or paint the rose and vermilion on that of a flamingo, without receiving almost a new conception of the meaning of form and colour in creation. ...

115. Now it is quite probable that some of you, who will not care to go through the labour necessary to draw flowers or animals, may yet have pleasure in attaining some moderately accurate skill of sketching architecture, and greater pleasure still in directing it usefully. Suppose, for instance, we were to take up the historical scenery in Carlyle's *Friedrich*. Too justly the historian accuses the genius of past art, in that, types of too many such elsewhere, the galleries of Berlin—'are made up, like other galleries, of goat-footed Pan, Europa's Bull, Romulus's She-Wolf, and the Correggiosity of Correggio, and contain, for instance, no portrait of Friedrich the Great—no likeness at all, or next to none at all, of the noble series of Human Realities, or any part of them, who have sprung, not from the idle brains of dreaming *dilettanti*, but from the head of God Almighty, to make this poor authentic earth a little memorable for us, and to do a little work that may be eternal there.' So Carlyle tells us—too truly! We cannot now draw Friedrich for him, but we can draw some of the old castles and cities that were the cradles of German life—Hohenzollern, Habsburg, Marburg, and such others—we may keep some authentic likeness of these for the future. Suppose we were to take up that first volume of Friedrich, and put outlines to it: shall we begin by looking for Henry the Fowler's tomb—Carlyle himself asks if he has any—at Quedlinburgh, and so downwards, rescuing what we can? That would certainly be making our work of some true use.

116. But I have told you enough, it seems to me, at least to-day, of this function of art in recording fact; let me now finally, and with all distinctness possible to me, state to you its main business of all—its service in the actual uses of daily life.

You are surprised, perhaps, to hear me call this its main business. That is indeed so, however. The giving brightness to picture is much, but the giving brightness to life more. And remember, were it as patterns only, you cannot, without the realities, have the pictures. *You cannot have a landscape by Turner, without a country for him to paint; you cannot have a portrait by Titian, without a man to be portrayed.* I need not prove that to you, I suppose, in these short terms; but in the outcome I can get no soul to believe that the beginning of art *is in getting our country clean, and our people beautiful.* I have been ten years trying

to get this very plain certainty—I do not say believed—but
even thought of, as anything but a monstrous proposition.
To get your country clean, and your people lovely—I assure
you that is a necessary work of art to begin with! There
has indeed been art in countries where people lived
in dirt to serve God, but never in countries where they
lived in dirt to serve the devil. There has indeed been art
where the people were not all lovely—where even their
lips were thick—and their skins black, because the sun
had looked upon them; but never in a country where the
people were pale with miserable toil and deadly shade, and
where the lips of youth, instead of being full with blood,
were pinched by famine, or warped with poison. And now,
therefore, note this well, the gist of all these long prefatory
talks. I said that the two great moral instincts were those
of Order and Kindness. Now, all the arts are founded on
agriculture by the hand, and on the graces, and kindness
of feeding, and dressing, and lodging your people. ...

117.   Now look at the working out of this broad principle in
minor detail; observe how, from highest to lowest, health
of art has first depended on reference to industrial use.
'There is first the need of cup and platter, especially of
cup; for you can put your meat on the Harpies',[1] or on any
other, tables; but you must have your cup to drink from.
And to hold it conveniently, you must put a handle to it; and

---

1   'Saved from the waves, I am received first by the shores of the Strophades—Strophades the Greek
name they bear—islands set in the great Ionian sea, where dwell dread Celaeno and the other Harpies,
since Phineus' house was closed on them, and in fear they left their former tables. No monster more
baneful than these, no fiercer plague or wrath of the gods ever rose from the Stygian waves. Maiden
faces have these birds, foulest filth they drop, clawed hands are theirs, and faces ever gaunt with
hunger. ... When hither borne we entered the harbour, lo! we see goodly herds of cattle scattered over
the plains and flocks of goats untended no the grass. We rush upon them with the sword, calling the
gods and Jove himself to share our spoil; then on the winding shore we build couches and banquet
on the rich dainties. But suddenly, with fearful swoop from the mountains the Harpies are upon us,
and with loud clanging shake their wings, plunder the feast; and with unclean touch mire every dish.
Once more, in a deep recess under a hollowed rock, closely encircled by trees and quivering shade,
we spread the tables and renew the fire on the altars; once more, from an opposite quarter o the sky
and from a hidden lair, the noisy crowd with taloned feet hovers round the prey, tainting the dishes
with their lips. Then I bid my comrades seize arms and declare war on the fell race. They do as they are
bidden lay their swords in hiding in the grass, and bury their shields out of sight. So when, swooping
down, the birds screamed along the winding shore, Misenus on his hollow brass gave the signal from
his watch aloft. My comrades charge, and essay a strange combat, to despoil with the sword those
filthy birds of ocean. Yet they feel now blows on their feathers, nor wounds on their backs, but, soaring
skyward with rapid flight, leave the half-eaten prey and their foul traces.' Virgil, 'Aeneas' Tale: "The
Voyage,"' in bk. 3, *Aeneid, Eclogues; Georgics; Aeneid I–VI*, trans. H. Rushton Fairclough, Loeb Classical
Library Volumes 63 and 64 (Cambridge, MA: Harvard University Press, 1916), p. 209.

to fill it when it is empty you must have a large pitcher of
some sort; and to carry the pitcher you may most advisably
have two handles. Modify the forms of these needful
possessions according to the various requirements of
drinking largely and drinking delicately; of pouring easily
out, or of keeping for years the perfume in; of storing in
cellars, or bearing from fountains; of sacrificial libation,
of Panathenaic treasure of oil, and sepulchral treasure of
ashes—and you have a resultant series of beautiful form
and decoration, from the rude amphora of red earth up
to Cellini's vases of gems and crystal, in which series,
but especially in the more simple conditions of it, are
developed the most beautiful lines and most perfect types
of severe composition which have yet been attained by art.

118. But again, that you may fill your cup with pure water,
you must go to the well or spring; you need a fence round
the well; you need some tube or trough, or other means
of confining the stream at the spring. For the conveyance
of the current to any distance you must build either
enclosed or open aqueduct; and in the hot square of the
city where you set it free, you find it good for health and
pleasantness to let it leap into a fountain. On these several
needs you have a school of sculpture founded; in the
decoration of the walls of wells in level countries, and of
the sources of springs in mountainous ones, and chiefly
of all, where the women of household or market meet at
the city fountain. …

120. Well, the gist of this matter lies here then. Suppose
we want a school of pottery again in England, all we
poor artists are ready to do the best we can, to show
you how pretty a line may be that is twisted first to one
side, and then to the other; and how a plain household-
blue will make a pattern on white; and how ideal art may
be got out of the spaniel's colours of black and tan. But
I tell you beforehand, all that we can do will be utterly
useless, unless you teach your peasant to say grace, not
only before meat, but before drink; and having provided

him with Greek cups and platters, provide him also with
something that is not poisoned to put into them.

121.   There cannot be any need that I should trace for
you the conditions of art that are directly founded on
serviceableness of dress, and of armour; but it is my duty
to affirm to you, in the most positive manner, that after
recovering, for the poor, wholesomeness of food, your next
step toward founding schools of art in England must be in
recovering, for the poor, decency and wholesomeness of
dress; thoroughly good in substance, fitted for their daily
work, becoming to their rank in life, and worn with order
and dignity. And this order and dignity must be taught
them by the women of the upper and middle classes,
whose minds can be in nothing right, as long as they are
so wrong in this matter as to endure the squalor of the
poor, while they themselves dress gaily. And on the proper
pride and comfort of both poor and rich in dress, must be
founded the true arts of dress; carried on by masters of
manufacture no less careful of the perfectness and beauty
of their tissues, and of all that in substance and design
can be bestowed upon them, than ever the armourers
of Milan and Damascus were careful of their steel.

122.   Then, in the third place, having recovered some
wholesome habits of life as to food and dress, we must
recover them as to lodging. I said just now that the best
architecture was but a glorified roof. Think of it. The
dome of the Vatican, the porches of Rheims or Chartres,
the vaults and arches of their aisles, the canopy of the
tomb, and the spire of the belfry, are all forms resulting
from the mere requirement that a certain space shall
be strongly covered from heat and rain. More than
that—as I have tried all through *The Stones of Venice* to
show—the lovely forms of these were every one of them
developed in civil and domestic building, and only after
their invention, employed ecclesiastically on the grandest
scale. I think you cannot but have noticed here in Oxford,
as elsewhere, that our modern architects never seem to

know what to do with their roofs. Be assured, until the roofs are right, nothing else will be; and there are just two ways of keeping them right. Never build them of iron, but only of wood or stone; and secondly, take care that in every town the little roofs are built before the large ones, and that everybody who wants one has got one. ...

123. Now, it is not possible—and I repeat to you, only in more deliberate assertion, what I wrote just twenty-two years ago in the last chapter of the *Seven Lamps of Architecture*—it is not possible to have any right morality, happiness, or art, in any country where the cities are thus built, or thus, let me rather say, clotted and coagulated; spots of a dreadful mildew, spreading by patches and blotches over the country they consume. You must have lovely cities, crystallized, not coagulated, into form; limited in size, and not casting out the scum and scurf of them into an encircling eruption of shame, but girded each with its sacred pomœrium, and with garlands of gardens full of blossoming trees and softly guided streams.

That is impossible, you say! It may be so. I have nothing to do with its possibility, but only with its indispensability. More than that must be possible, however, before you can have a school of art; namely, that you find places elsewhere than in England, or at least in otherwise unserviceable parts of England, for the establishment of manufactories needing the help of fire ... and to reduce such manufactures to their lowest limit, so that nothing may ever be made of iron that can as effectually be made of wood or stone; and nothing moved by steam that can be as effectually moved by natural forces. And observe, that for all mechanical effort required in social life and in cities, water power is infinitely more than enough; for anchored mills on the large rivers, and mills moved by sluices from reservoirs filled by the tide, will give you command of any quantity of constant motive power you need.

Agriculture by the hand, then, and absolute refusal or banishment of unnecessary igneous force, are the first conditions of a school of art in any country. And until you do this, be it soon or late, things will continue in that triumphant state to which, for want of finer art, your mechanism has brought them—that, though England is deafened with spinning wheels, her people have not clothes—though she is black with digging of fuel, they die of cold—and though she has sold her soul for gain, they die of hunger. Stay in that triumph, if you choose; but be assured of this, it is not one which the fine arts will ever share with you.

124. Now, I have given you my message, containing, as I know, offence enough, and itself, it may seem to many, unnecessary enough. But just in proportion to its apparent non-necessity, and to its certain offence, was its real need, and my real duty to speak it. The study of the fine arts could not be rightly associated with the grave work of English Universities, without due and clear protest against the misdirection of national energy, which for the present renders all good results of such study on a great scale, impossible. I can easily teach you, as any other moderately good draughtsman could, how to hold your pencils, and how to lay your colours; but it is little use my doing that, while the nation is spending millions of money in the destruction of all that pencil or colour has to represent, and in the promotion of false forms of art, which are only the costliest and the least enjoyable of follies. And therefore these are the things that I have first and last to tell you in this place—that the fine arts are not to be learned by Locomotion, but by making the homes we live in lovely, and by staying in them—that the fine arts are not to be learned by Competition, but by doing our quiet best in our own way—that the fine arts are not to be learned by Exhibition, but by doing what is right, and making what is honest, whether it be exhibited or not—and, for the sum of all, that men must paint and build neither for pride nor for money, but for love; for love of their art, for love of their neighbour, and whatever better love may be than these, founded on these. I know that I gave some pain, which I was most unwilling to give, in speaking of the possible abuses of religious art; but there can be no danger of any, so long as we remember that God inhabits cottages as well as churches, and ought to be well lodged there also. Begin with wooden floors; the tessellated ones will take care of themselves; begin with thatching roofs, and you shall end by splendidly vaulting them; begin by taking care that no old eyes fail over their Bibles, nor young ones over their needles, for want of rushlight, and then you may have whatever true good is to be got out of coloured glass or wax candles. And in thus putting the arts to universal use, you will find also their universal inspiration, their universal benediction. I told you there was no evidence of a *special* Divineness in any application of them; that they were always equally human and equally Divine; and in closing this inaugural series of lectures, into which I have endeavoured to compress the principles that are to be the foundations of your future work, it is my last duty to say some positive words as to the Divinity of all art, when it is truly fair, or truly serviceable. …

This text is an edited version by John Byrne of John Ruskin, 'Lecture IV: The Relation of Art to Use,' in *Lectures on Art: Delivered Before the University of Oxford in Hilary term, 1870* (Project Gutenberg eBook, 2006), www.gutenberg.org/files/19164/19164-h/19164-h.htm#Footnote_10_10.

Essay
Alistair Hudson

An Extended Lecture on Tree Twigs

TOWARD AN ECOLOGY OF AESTHETICS

Here he is. Ecce Homo. Caspar David Friedrich's *Wanderer above the Sea of Fog*, painted in 1818, is the box cover image for the software of modernity. It is a complex thing; simultaneously a picture of the individual's will to mastery over nature and also his insignificance in the face of it. *Wanderer* reveals the rift at the heart of the modern era from which we need to escape.

Here we see our mountaintop journeyman, distinct from the world below, defining himself apart from nature and the messy quotidian world beneath the clouds. His back is turned to us, although he is possibly with us or even *is* us. He faces the horizon and looks longingly to an imagined future that is pictured in his mind alone. This is the artist as super-seer, sovereign genius and truth seeker; taking us to places we otherwise would not imagine to go. This is the artist avant-garde at the start of a journey into the unknown, leading us with hope into the perfect light.

Friedrich's painting is the introduction into modern romantic art history, a history presented as an unfolding, sequential development of form and ideas operating, for the most part, in parallel to the day to day world of politics and economics, albeit indexed to the historical context, but all the while distanced from it, above it— a witness to it, a critic of it, but never an accomplice.

The software engineer behind this packaging is Immanuel Kant. Through the dual architecture of purposeless purpose and the disinterested spectator he transformed art into a bespoke aesthetic system, operating in an autonomous zone that reflects the world from a safe distance, a beautiful thought experiment which gave privilege to the eye above all else, and a tool that would be complicit in separating man from nature, art from daily life, for the next two hundred years.

As the nineteenth century progressed, art under this Kantian model was increasingly framed by the triangulation of artist-spectator-connoisseur and, combined with a rising capitalist, industrial economy and the withering away of religion, this architecture rose to form the twin temples of the art market and the museum. This ensured that art was maintained in a privileged system of representation, reflection, and consumption in opposition to the pre-modern concept of art as the enhanced utility and ritual of human activity (and the objects thereof now rendered obsolete in the museum itself).

Now we find ourselves at the tail end of the modern era, the twin edifices of market and museum look increasingly

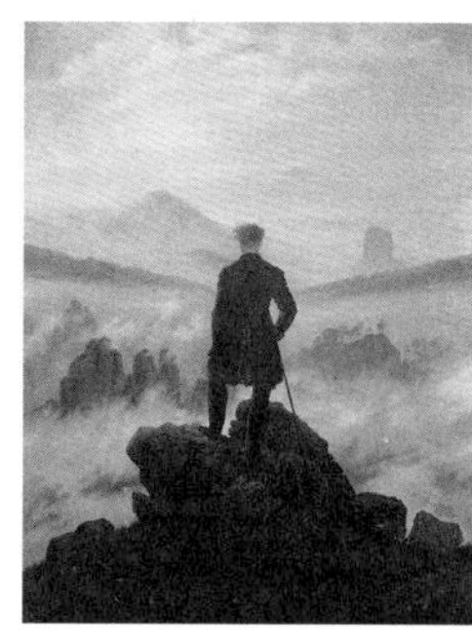

Fig 1 Caspar David Friedrich, *Wanderer above the Sea of Fog*, 1818, oil on canvas, 98.4 x 74.8 cm, Kunsthalle Hamburg, Hamburg

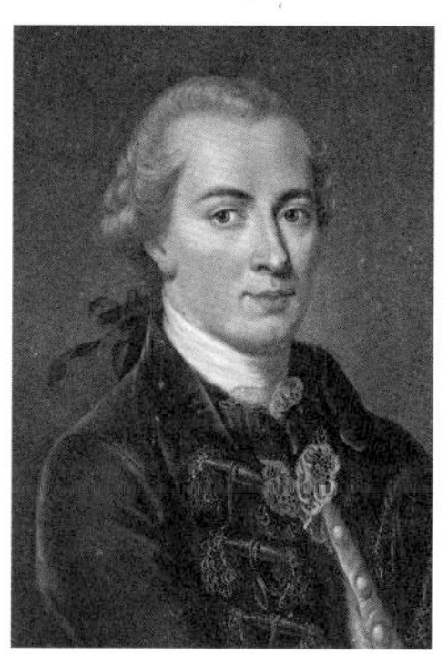

Fig 2 Unknown artist, 18th century, *Portrait of Immanuel Kant*

precarious within the unraveling of economics and politics in our late technological age. On a local level the public support of an art world that is by self-definition 'useless' and autonomous is faltering. The best claims for art now are made to us in terms of regenerative economics, numbers of hotel 'bed nights' sold, added value, our compliance in an attention industry, but increasingly this is less convincing as it becomes clear the true beneficiaries are somewhere else, not in our neighbourhood.

That art has found itself marooned in this way is for the most part a consequence of the compartmentalization of the arts initiated by the age of industry and capital. 'High index' user groups within our society have shaped art to their best advantage to create cultural capital and generate wealth. The market-driven spectacle economies of our major museums, whilst consumed widely, ultimately serve the highest percentiles. Elsewhere other arts, such as craft, architecture, and design have followed other trajectories, as we know 'demoted' to popular, folk, amateur, or functional arts. At various moments these arts (once referred to as low art) are absorbed into the higher index economy, but predominately at the behest of those higher up the food chain.

The bifurcation between High and Low is now apparently a thing of the past, but this has merely been replaced with a far more nuanced system of control, approval, and consensus commensurate with the complexities of the market. What not so long ago was termed High Art has mutated but maintained a trajectory away from common usership, continuing to serve the interests of its main stakeholders—although we might now describe it as cool, critically engaged, or important art.

This case is of course most acute in the world of the fine arts, which has become the one most removed from ordinary use (in part a requirement for its index of commercial value). For example, regardless of who controls the system, most people know how to regularly use music, film, or architecture in a way that most would not consider applicable to art. We can happily understand

that we can use music to stimulate a mood or to dance
to it within the ritualized behaviours of our culture, as
part of the way we live, at a wedding or on New Year's
Eve. The static gallery exhibition, art installation, or
performance is not accommodated into our regular
life patterns in the same way, though it can be done.
This would certainly mark out an individual as a culture
vulture of a particular metropolitan bent. Its forms are
constructed by a highly refined set of users, who for
reasons of money and power have a keen interest in
not allowing contemporary art to become too popular.

Subsequently art has drifted away from being
commonly understood as something of social value;
the wider populace have embraced art or rather applied
artfulness in other ways such as gaming, programming,
gardening, craft, selfies, Taylor Swift fandom, and creating
content for YouTube. It is noticeable that these forms
of art shift more toward the spectrum of prosumerism,
making, and usership, where meaning is generated
collectively, whilst still operating within a wider market.

There is a sense that something quite different is
beginning to happen, as the economic system that has
supported autonomous art for so long appears to be
collapsing, or at least under threat with the increasing
division between the haves and the have-nots becoming
vocalized. The cracks are also showing in the walls of
public art museums. These museums are not valued
enough by the majority and as the cuts come they are
first in line. The sector makes its claims on economic
grounds: regeneration, visitor attraction, added value,
but it is not enough. An art embedded in all our lives,
in consistent usership, would survive much better.

The compartmentalization of culture, division of
labour and society, has brought us seemingly to the
verge of annihilation: economic, political, and ecological.
It is in such times of high anxiety that we call upon
the idea of history to console us, but also to find tools
and stories that help us to think of a way out.

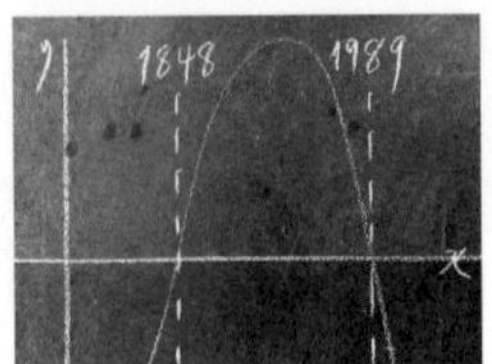

Fig 3 Graph showing a positive parabolic curve intersected by the x axis at 1848 and 1989

Let us picture a parabolic curve to represent modernity, in which the x-axis shows an unfolding linear time (or for that matter universal space-time) and the y-axis an index of power, certainty, and perhaps wealth. The curve rises from the start of the nineteenth century and descends toward a point we now occupy. We could draw a horizontal line across that intersects the rising curve firstly at the European revolutions of 1848 and meeting the falling curve in the year 1989, the moment the iron curtain falls, free market capitalism wins the day, the Internet begins to weave itself into our lives and very softly, the beginning of the 2008 crash is born. Its apex would sit somewhere around the time between Picasso's *Les Demoiselles d'Avignon* (1907), Einstein's Theory of Relativity, and the end of the First World War.

If we describe ourselves now on the tail end of the parabola, in some kind of transition between waves, somewhere in decline or somewhere before an uncertain something else, what is the narrative we construct to steer us through? What if we were to suspend the idea of linear, one-directional history and go back to Friedrich and 1818, look again around us, look under the clouds and on the ground, what would we find and what other routes could we discover?

John Ruskin was born in London in 1819, the year after Friedrich painted the *Wanderer*. Ruskin is an awkward character; his complexity, contrariness, and contradiction don't sit well with the single, linear story of art we have inherited. He appears more often as a kind of phantom or a series of cameo appearances: the eccentric and troubled critic who promoted Turner and the Pre-Raphaelites.

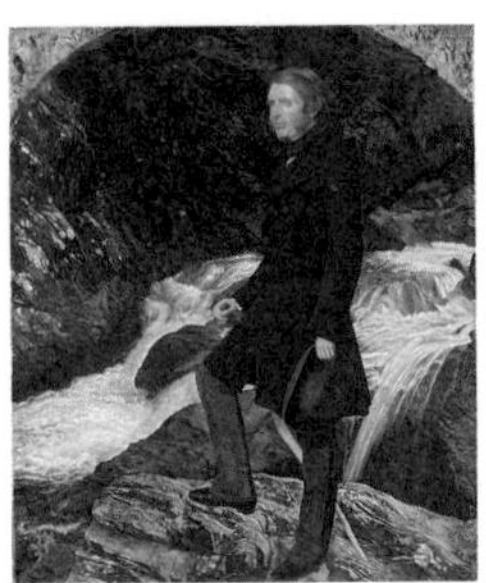

Fig 4 Sir John Everett Millais, *John Ruskin*, 1853, 78.7 x 68 cm, Ashmolean Museum, University of Oxford, Oxford

Growing up against the backdrop of the Machinery Question (the Industrial Revolution) Ruskin was the principle voice of conscience, calling for the humanizing of society through art and natural ecology.

Self-described as both Conservative and Communist (the curious movement of Anglican Socialism can be reserved for another day) he was prolific as a writer, artist, and social reformer, railing against the systematization and efficiency of society through the economic, social, and technological machinery of the industrialists. Unable to be constrained as simply a commentator on art, he gained wider fame for his fervent public critique against the inhumanity of the age in voluminous publications and highly performative public lectures. (Interestingly, as one of the first genuine celebrities of the modern age, his housekeeper would later sell his image rights for branded goods, souvenirs, and books.)

His vision was not the fashionable quest for an ideal future constantly remade by systematic growth, capital, and individual success, but a humanity based in living artfully, cooperatively, sustainably, and truthfully within an ecology of perpetual change. As such he insists we must understand art, not as an end in itself, but as process, the manner of work undertaken—as a tool to effect social, physical, and spiritual betterment. Throughout his life his work took him away from the limited field of art discourse, building a holistic view of the world in writing and also through teaching, action, lectures, social projects, painting, agriculture, architecture, and craft. In hindsight it isn't too hard to think of him as the world's first social practitioner.

His influence is still felt across our age within the best intentions of modernity, the moments when we have pushed art beyond the museum into traction with the world, inspiring the Arts and Crafts Movement, with all the twists and turns of its legacy from farming communes, the Toynbee Settlement to Frank Lloyd Wright and the Bauhaus. He established farms, education programmes, conservation projects, and instigated political and social reform. Through his texts and public lectures his influence is felt through education for all, the Labour Party, environmentalism, equal rights for women, the minimum wage, The National Trust, Welfare State, the preservation of Venice, Gandhi, and Rudolf Steiner.

Underpinning Ruskin's work is his holistic vision of culture as nature. Learning to see nature in all its truth was a first principle of a moral life, rather than succumbing to the idealized and perfect forms of the post-Renaissance.

This is the bedrock of this vision and the study of geology, flora and fauna, mountains, waterfalls and rivers—their constant variation and 'imperfection' is essential to constructing a humane and honest society. It is a scheme in which man and his actions do not operate above and beyond the natural world, but within it, contingent on it, subject to the same laws and conditions.

Fig 5 Portfolio illustration from John Ruskin's *The Stones of Venice* (1851–1853)

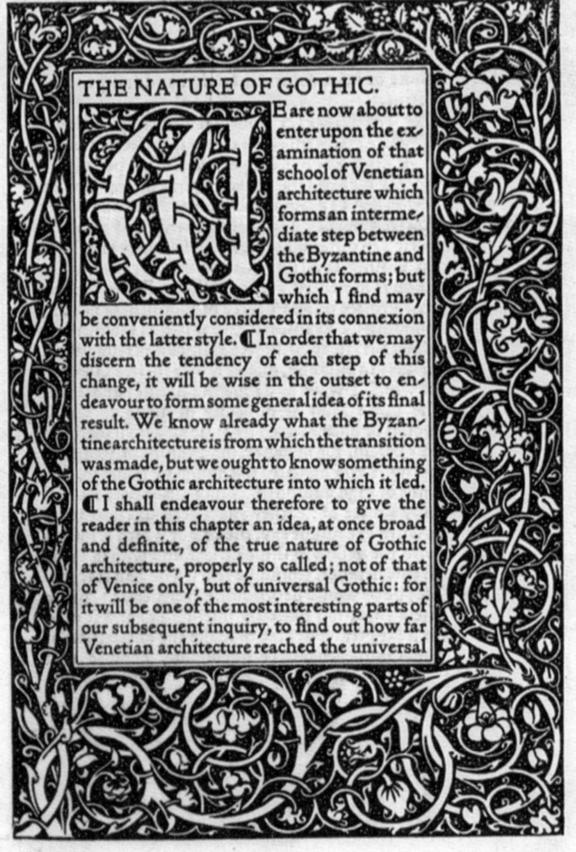

From 1851 to 1853 Ruskin published *The Stones of Venice*, his three-volume treatise on Venetian art and architecture as a commentary on society and labour conditions. Here he discusses the Byzantine, Gothic, and Renaissance periods as a parable of decline. Against the prevailing trend for building our civic architecture, homes, engine houses, and factories in the logical and mechanical forms of the Renaissance, Ruskin championed the highly unfashionable medieval Gothic, for its natural variations, ethical craftsmanship, and social conditions that supported it. In the chapter 'The Nature of Gothic' he forces the point home:

> We want one man to be always thinking, and another to be always working, and we call one a gentleman, and the other an operative; whereas the workman ought often to be thinking, and the thinker often to be working, and both should be gentlemen, in the best sense. As it is, we make both ungentle, the one envying, the other despising, his brother; and the mass of society is made up of morbid thinkers and miserable workers. Now it is only by labour that thought can be made healthy, and only by thought that labour can be made happy, and the two cannot be separated with impunity.

The Stones of Venice presented for the first time a complete view on the relation between art and life as a perpetual and necessary struggle with human imperfection.

> We may expect that the first two elements of good architecture should be expressive of some real truths. The confession of Imperfection and the confession of the Desire of Change.

You could not summarize the modern dilemma more succinctly than this. As we dream of a perfect world within reach through technological progress, this turns to out to be a dystopia that drives change anew.
His vision presents a critique of capitalist society's

ambition to resolve human imperfection through standardized production and government. However, Ruskin suggests that instead of worrying about a predetermined outcome we should focus on the process, aesthetics, and ethics by which we live and this will shape our society through responsive organic design as it grows and mutates. In this way we must live life artfully and experience our work not as toil for reward, but as an inherent part of a total social and ecological system of life and work.

In the Arts and Crafts Movement Ruskin envisioned such a system, yet inevitably the prevailing impetuousness and social conditioning of the market system meant that the movement was ultimately coopted into the emerging consumer lifestyle, exemplified by William Morris's ultimate fate as producer of luxury goods, rather than becoming an effective agent of reform.

We can contrast the development of an industrialized cultural machinery with Ruskin's persistent but somewhat flawed attempts to create genuine alternatives to those on offer. These include his education programme for Winnington School for Girls, museums for the working classes, road building projects for his Fine Art students at Oxford University, and the agrarian communes of the Guild of St George. In the Lake District village of Coniston, where he resided from 1871 until his death in 1900, he encouraged the development of the local mining and farming commu-nity around the Coniston Mechanics Institute as a hybrid centre for community, art, and education.

The Mechanics Institute movement was created to support the rapid technological expansion of Britain. It was to teach the workforce in the new emerging technologies, sciences and arts, toward building innovation, creativity, growth, and a healthier more contented population.

The institutes were conceived as both instrumental and altruistic. Whilst driving the nation forward as a global superpower through education, skills, cooperation, and entrepreneurship, they inadvertently created the crucible for true democracy: instigating voting rights for workers, unionization, equal rights for women,

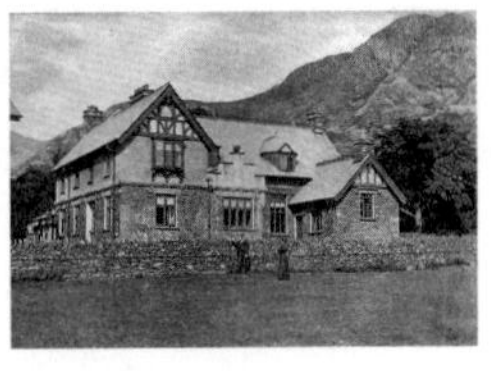

Fig 6 The Coniston Mechanics Institute and Literary Society, c. 1872

education for all, etc. The institute movement can
be cited as the reason the United Kingdom avoided
revolution, because this education for all instilled the
belief that they could bring progressive change through
their own evolution of the system from within.

By 1850 there were over 700 institutes in Britain
with equivalent numbers in the United States and the
Commonwealth Nations. In Ruskin's own Coniston Institute
he shaped local culture according to his philosophy of
art as living: a combination of hand, heart, and head.
The institute had a community bath house, library,
assembly hall, kitchens, collections of art, and artifacts
(for educational use not spectatorship) and workshops
which hosted Home Craft Industries—an Arts and Crafts
school for miners, farmers, and their families who learned
through making, drawing, wood carving, metal work, and
lace. Products of the school were humble, competent,
not especially refined but 'good enough.' This created an
internal sustainable economy for the village to supplement
and enhance their labour on the farms and in the mines.
In contrast to the publicized success of the Arts and
Crafts, this was a truer reflection of Ruskin's philosophy:
working in ordinary life for ordinary people, as a fellowship,
as part of the ebb and flow of daily living and learning.

Ruskin became an increasingly popular performer in
the 1850s, filling halls with up to 2000 people on national
lecture tours. He frequently used them to goad and provoke
the industrialists and politicians running the Victorian
empirical machine. For example a lecture on cloud forms
in painting could easily descend into a vitriolic attack on
the greed of the mill owners and the pollution of the skies.

Subjects were pointed. More often his talks were like
sermons: performative and illustrated with props and
numbered lecture diagrams drawn by himself, the artists,
and his household. These were thrown around the stage in
the manner of a wayward nineteenth-century PowerPoint.

In 1861 Ruskin was invited to give one of the
prestigious lectures at the Royal Institution, the
great theatre of science where luminaries such as

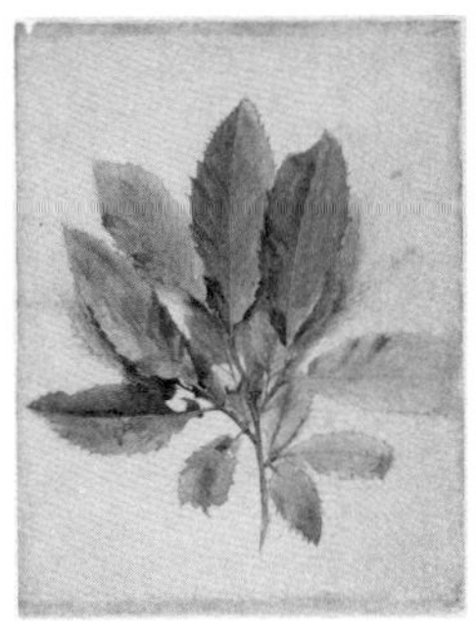

Fig 7   Horse chestnut leaf
from John Ruskin's 'Lecture
on Tree Twigs', 1861

Michael Faraday, Humphry Davy, and Henry Cavendish had presented their discoveries to the world.

However, on this occasion Ruskin chose to present on the apparently more humble subject of tree twigs. To the slight bemusement of such a refined audience, he proceeded to give an account of the growth of trees and their leaves, and in particular drawing attention to the unfolding development of the horse chestnut tree, describing in detail the extent to which each individual leaf in its individuality and imperfection, nonetheless finds its way to full growth in relation to a cohesive whole, in the interests of the complete tree.

The theme of the night is elaborated in greater detail in the chapter 'On Leaf Beauty' in the earlier pages of *Modern Painters* (1843–1860). Here on this night the real point is simply made: that man, his actions, and arts are not predetermined, universal, manufactured, and perfect, but an inherent part of a perpetual system subject to continual changes within the prevailing conditions, part of, and in dialogue with, the total ecology of nature. In this scheme the arts (including technology), are not distinct from nature, but a process intertwined within the very fabric of the universe.

In a wider context Ruskin speaks extensively about how to acquire, and how to employ art only for social effect, arguing that England had forgotten that true wealth is virtue, and consequently art is an index of society's wellbeing. As such individuals have a responsibility to consume wisely, stimulating beneficent demand. Economics is not simply fiscal, but in its original sense 'good housekeeping' and governance of the natural and cultural ecology over which we have custody. In this way we can look again at Ruskin as the first true environmentalist and a principle voice to untie the binds of spectatorship and division.

Arte Útil has become a quasi-movement that incorporates the group Asociación de Arte Útil initiated by artist Tania Bruguera. It has convened a growing international network of people who have the ambition

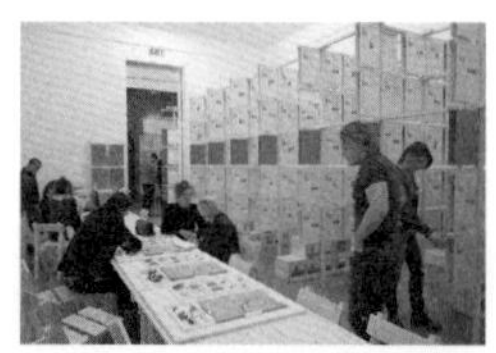

Fig 8 Exhibition *Museum of Arte Útil*, Van Abbemuseum, Eindhoven, 2013

to reintegrate art into society, away from an artist-centred, market-oriented paradigm, into an effectual manifestation of creative collectivity. This is a proposal of art beyond pictorial representation that works in the world, as part of the nature of the world, on a 1:1 scale. This, as Bruguera states, is art as a verb.

My involvement in this constellation of activity came through developing projects at Grizedale Arts in the English Lake District village of Coniston, where, serendipitously, Ruskin lived out the last thirty years of his life. The art projects conceived there came through a desire to reassert the idea of the artist as contributory citizen, working beyond the confines of the art world (Coniston is a place, like most, where the Art World has no currency) and to work in ordinary life, in this small rural community. Here we worked with artists and non-artists to make not art, but things more artful, to respond to the needs and urgencies of our fellow residents. The aim was not to give artists the freedom and space for individual expression, but contrarily utilize artistic competencies to the needs of our constituency. The results included a community shop, the restoration of the Coniston Institute, the annual harvest festival in the church, a new cricket pavilion, a farm, making cheese, running the Youth Club, a new public library—employing art processes to enhance daily life, rather than taking art from the autonomous realm and translating it into life. The results, for the most part not recognizable as 'art,' were welcomed by our community because they could be valued for what they did, what they contributed to conditions on the ground in tangible, useful ways. In the development of this way of working it became clear that the art did not lie in any particular object or thing, but in the way processes (a shop, festival, library, etc.) were changed by the application of artists' thinking. The key was how artfully something was done, rather than whether it was art or not.

This work drew us into working relationships with likeminded souls such as Bruguera, writer Stephen Wright, and the team at the Van Abbemuseum, all of us striving to escape the architecture of a system that was increasingly failing to take part in the evolution of society and merely looking to preserve the status quo, repeatedly, emptily acting out the rituals of the radical: 'Zombie Modernism.'

On the back of these conversations the criteria of Arte Útil were honed and used as a measure by which to asses projects that could be accessioned into the archive and *Museum of Arte Útil*—a repository of over 500 case studies that includes social enterprises, schools, therapy rooms, tools for illegal migrants, bullet-proof skin, and housing projects.

The common criticism of useful art or Arte Útil (or even *arte utile* as proposed by Pino Poggi in Italy in the 1960s) is that it is subservient to a neoliberal agenda, or even 'not art'—simply providing the services traditionally supplied by the state and now being withdrawn within a framework of a right wing ideology.

However, we could argue this view is mistaken on the grounds that Arte Útil comes from the ground up, creatively responding to urgencies within constituencies, more often as an anarchic critique of unfavourable social conditions. Furthermore it might be more strongly argued that nothing kowtows to the neoliberal agenda more than the idea of individual creative expression, reinforcing the sovereign artist, cut free of any moral obligations to operate within the complex ecology of our day to day grind.

At the same time this negative critique of Arte Útil also reinforces the system of division engineered two hundred years earlier that serves the market so well, polarizing positions into them and us, art and not art.

A more productive critique could be that Arte Útil in its current form is still quite divisive, separating art projects that are 'useful' from those that are not. For me one of the key propositions that comes out of the 'Lexicon of Usership' is that we can be liberated from the idea that art is simply a set of things in the world defined by the triangulate of artist, connoisseur, and spectator and move toward a more accurate and universal concept of art as way of doing something, in which we can talk of

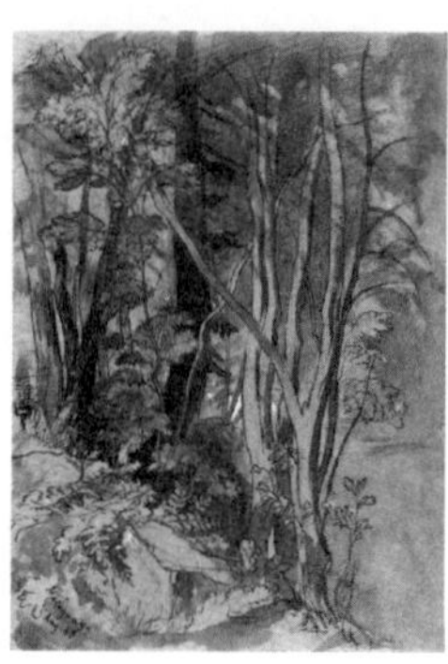

Fig 9 John Ruskin, *Rough Sketch of Tree Growth: Macugnaga,* 1872, pen and ink, watercolour and body colour over graphite on pale grey wove paper, 22.8 x 16.6 cm, Ashmolean Museum, University of Oxford, Oxford

the degree to which something is art, rather whether it is
art or not, art as coefficient not designated form.

Such a way of thinking where art is defined as a process
implicit in all human activity, to one degree or another (yet
still at times creates art products) would subsequently
allow us to reintegrate useful and useless, high and low art,
neo-conceptualism with folk art, music and architecture,
sculpture and craft. It would be a holistic system operating
in four dimensions, where the degree to which something
is art would be dependent on a complex of multiple factors,
which we could visualize as vectors between multiple
points within the matrix of all activity. Therefore Kew,
the Shanghai Yu Garden and seed bombing could all be
described as arts, in relation to traditions of gardening,
but occupy quite different coordinates within the frame,
albeit within the interconnected system we inhabit.

Criticisms of Arte Útil have also exposed the difficulty
that many have had with the idea of the word use,
which in itself has been misused with its negative
implications. However (as language clearly illustrates
that meaning is created by use), this is a word that
should be reclaimed, reused as, at present, the best
positive term to articulate a way of thinking art anew.

If Arte Útil can only exist in isolation, or as a counter
to the mainstream romantic conception of art, it limits its
chances of a wholesale impact that would reintegrate
and reclaim the value of art for broad society   and of
course maintain the danger that it could be re-captured
by the market system as a movement alongside
Futurism, Constructivism, and Pop—also movements
that strove like many to bring art back into life.

Therefore to negate this, it seems a vital project to
conceive a holistic theory of art that would accommodate
both Arte Útil and the post-Kantian history we have
inherited. This would mean a recalibration of 'aesthetics'
as a complete system of transformation, no longer an
idealized autonomous system based on the fallacy of
dis-interested spectatorship, and transform it into an
integral part of our way of living founded in the reality of

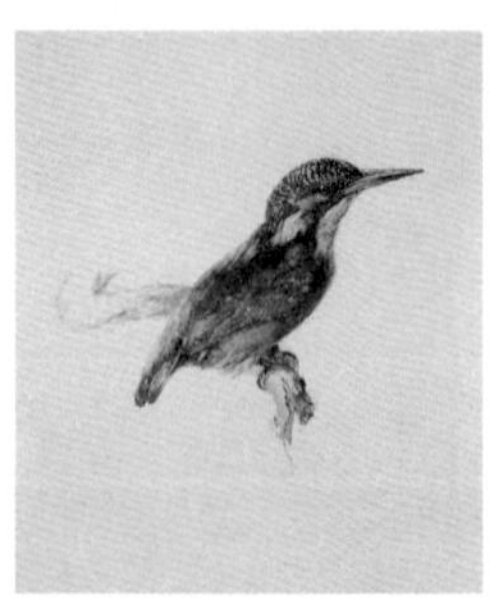

Fig 10 John Ruskin, *Kingfisher*, c. 1870–1871, pencil, ink, watercolour and gouache, 25.8 x 21.8 cm, Tate Britain, London

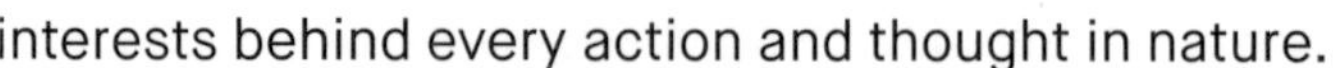

interests behind every action and thought in nature.

In such a rather bewildering and expansive conception we can also engage with the proposition that all art is, and has always been, useful to someone somewhere—even Kant himself provided the break clause of purposeless purpose, to acknowledge the necessity of function. Clearly the world of art before the market and industrialized production was one embedded in ritual, craft, design, architecture, and enhancement. But we can also articulate a matrix of usership around even the most traditional autonomous objects. This would include, for example, the manipulation of Abstract Expressionism in Cold War politics, museum education programmes to substantiate public value and funding, to the sensory stimulation and association triggered by the forms of a Mondrian or Morris. There are constellations of users around any given art process or object, which offer benefits in varying degrees. Even in a museum the broader usership encompasses the staff, the Friends Association, the school groups, the lovers' meeting, the aesthete or connoisseur, to the drug user who furtively finds his way to the top floor bathroom. To date it has been the wealthy who know how to use art best: for social status, wealth management, demonstration of power. Equally at other points in the ecosystem we might look at other forms of art as mechanisms to gain sociopolitical effect: graffiti art, union banners, amateur water colours. Indeed we could go way beyond the plastic arts to include music, theatre, cinema, horticulture, cooking, and in fact all human activity as constructions of interconnecting uses and users.

Confessions of the Imperfect was the companion exhibition to the *Museum of Arte Útil* held at the Van Abbemuseum one year later. Taking its title from Ruskin's *Stones of Venice*, the ambition was to begin to articulate a wider vision of aesthetics as part of an alternative history of art, from Ruskin and the French Revolution to the Arab Spring. It presented a story of the use-value of art, its application as a tool for social change and the ensuing network of organic, chance relationships laced

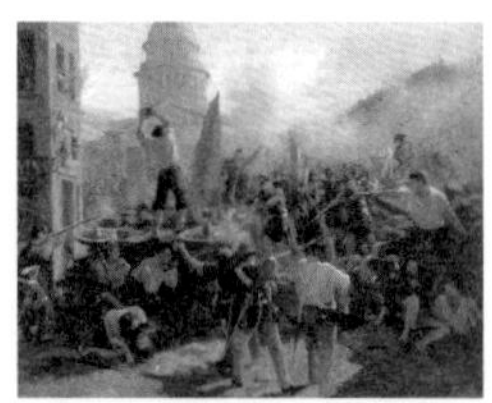

Fig 11 Horace Vernet, *Barricade on the rue Soufflot on 24 June 1848*, 1848

through our present understanding of modern times.

In asserting a history of use-value it also acknowledged the primary intention of many modernists to change the world, whilst proposing that these intentions have been downplayed by the dominant narrative of artistic form and content. Here we could say the emphasis is not on autonomy, but on the degree to which we can apply art to our day to day life processes, the degree to which something is artful: its coefficient of art.

As articulated earlier our inherited understanding of aesthetics is firmly rooted in the German philosophical tradition at the turn of the eighteenth and nineteenth centuries, creating the conceptual framework that sought to detach art from the animal instincts of self-interest. However, a reevaluation of the subject would inevitably go back through pre-modernity to times when art was more or less synonymous with general 'human activity' and 'technology' [*techne* in Ancient Greek].

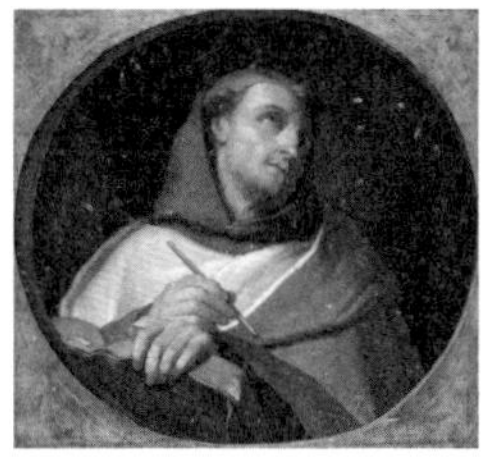

Fig 12 Portrait of Saint Bonaventure (1221–1274)

A key text in this story is *On the Reduction of the Arts to Theology* written by Saint Bonaventure in the thirteenth century. Although composed as a text to propose a path to a greater understanding of God, it may also be reread as a path to an understanding of the world through the senses. In it he presents a schema in which the arts, that is human action, is always situated in an ordered system of 'lights,' a matrix of sensory perception, process, and action, and in which art encompasses a complete spectrum of human activity, from seeing as an act itself, through to politics to armour making:

> Every mechanical art is intended for man's consolation or for his comfort; its purpose, therefore, is to banish either sorrow or want; it either benefits or delights.

Here is a view of the world that positions all human activity within an aesthetic regime, in which all actions, decisions, perceptions are contained within the flow of sensory data, and in which aesthetics now becomes the field of operation and transformation.

This is a proposal of art beyond pictorial representation that works in the world, as part of the nature of the world, on a 1:1 scale.

Quote
Alistair Hudson, *An Extended Lecture on Tree Twigs*
→ **See p. 43**

If 1:1 art seeks
to make an impact
on reality, we must
naturally ask:
Why does it still
strive to achieve
this impact as art?

Quote
Zdenka Badovinac,
Using Art as Art
→ **See p. 403**

Essay
Tamara Díaz
Bringas

I'd Like to Be Karl Ioganson… (But It Won't Be Possible)

CUBAN APPLICATIONS OF ARTE ÚTIL

Quisiera ser Wifredo Lam… (pero no se va a poder)
[I'd Like to Be Wifredo Lam… (But It Won't Be Possible)]
was the title of a Flavio Garciandía retrospective
held in 2014 in Havana. The Cuban artist uses the
same formulation—part parody, part homage—in
the title of other works, but in reference to Henri
Matisse and Piet Mondrian instead of Lam.

There are also works in which he 'insults' John Baldessari, Barnett Newman, Brice Marden, and Sol LeWitt. Although Garciandía has never mentioned Karl Ioganson— the most radical of the Constructivists founding the Productivist movement after he abandoned sculpture in 1923 to take a job as a metalworker in a Moscow factory—the desire (or the impossibility of the desire) to become a Productivist can help us to review some of the applications of Arte Útil in the Cuban context.

Garciandía was one of the participants and the main organizer of the groundbreaking 1981 exhibition *Volumen Uno*,[1] generally considered to have inaugurated the so-called 'New Cuban Art movement.' A generation of young artists was emerging at the time with the first batch of graduates from the Instituto Superior de Arte (ISA), founded in Havana in 1976. Garciandía was one of the first ISA graduates and began teaching at the school in 1981, becoming one of the key figures behind the changes that transformed art education at the ISA in the 1980s. In 1976 Garciandía began working as a specialist at the Ministry of Culture's Office of Visual Arts and Design, where he devised *Arte en la fábrica* [Art in the factory], a project that involved the participation of over forty artists in eight factories during the first edition in 1983.[2] The artists had to negotiate with the workers and make use of waste or other materials available on the industrial premises. Participants included artists who had taken part in *Volumen Uno* (José Manuel Fors, Gustavo Pérez Monzón, and Ricardo Rodríguez Brey), as well as younger colleagues such as Consuelo Castañeda, Sandra Ceballos, Marta María Pérez Bravo, and Tonel. Garciandía describes his own experience in the project as follows: 'They asked us to decorate a

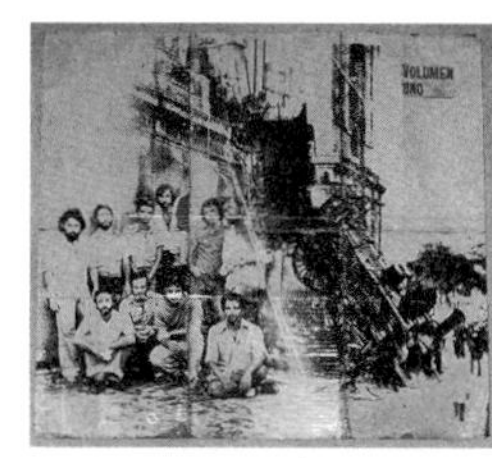

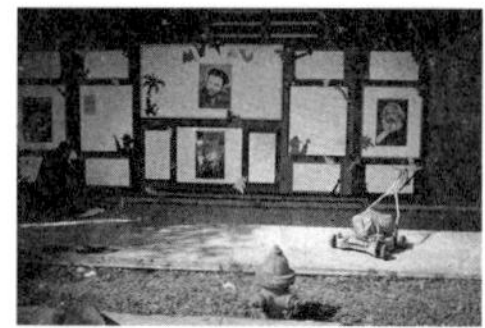

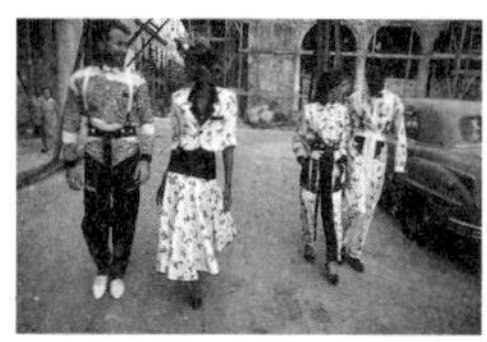

Fig 1   Exhibition *Volumen Uno*, Centro de Arte Internacional de Ciudad de La Habana, Havana, 1981

Fig 2   The project *Arte en la fábrica* [Art in the Factory] involved the participation of over forty artists in eight factories during the first edition in 1983. Mural by Flavio Garciandía at the 'Juan Hidalgo Valdés' Paper and Cardboard Recycling Factory, Havana, November 18-December 1983. Left to right: Ricardo Rodríguez Brey, Gustavo Pérez Monzón, Marta María Pérez Bravo, Lázaro Saavedra and Flavio Garciandía.

Fig 3   *Telarte VI Internacional* in 1989. People walking around Plaza Vieja in Havana using clothes designed by Madahui el Iraní and Sosabravo.

---

1   The exhibition *Volumen Uno* opened on 14 January 1981 at the Centro de Arte Internacional in Havana, with the participation of eleven artists: José Bedia, Juan Francisco Elso Padilla, José Manuel Fors, Flavio Garciandía, Israel León, Rogelio López Marín (Gory), Gustavo Pérez Monzón, Ricardo Rodríguez Brey, Tomás Sánchez, Leandro Soto, and Rubén Torres Llorca. A landmark exhibition noted for its formal experimentation and for including new subjects such as popular culture, kitsch, and Afro-Cuban religious practices, as well as for the intense critical debate that accompanied it. This exhibition is generally considered a symbol of the emergence of new Cuban art.
2   *Arte en la fábrica* was an initiative of the Ministry of Culture's Office of Visual Arts and Design, along with the 'Hermanos Saíz' Brigade of young artists. The first edition was held in 1983, and the project was repeated for a further two years.

damaged mural; they wanted us to make signs to label communal areas, to fix the ANIR (National Association of Innovators and Rationalizers) exhibition space, to retouch the painting of Che... .'[3] The artists placed their skills at the service of the workers, who considered them useful for ornamental types of tasks: decorating, fixing, retouching.

The changes that were already transforming the way art was produced and understood in Cuba in the early 1980s did not affect the factories, or at least not to the extent that they shook up the country's cultural and educational institutions. *Arte en la fábrica* officially billed itself as a 'salute to the 25th anniversary of the Revolution.' This initiative, similar in spirit to Soviet Productivism, did not grow out of the revolutionary changes that got underway in Cuba in the 1960s, but out of the push for institutionalization that reached its peak around 1976: the year in which the ISA and the Ministry of Culture were founded had begun with the enactment of the Socialist Constitution, which formally established the Cuban state under a legal framework along the same lines as that of the countries that became part of the Soviet Bloc after World War II.

In the 1980s, the Cuban Ministry of Culture implemented a programme of designs for the textile industry reminiscent of a 1920s Soviet avant-garde project organized by artists such Lyubov Popova and Varvara Stepanova. From 1983 to 1991, *Telarte* was the government's main project for the functional application of art, producing a substantial amount of fabric printed with artists' designs. The 150 participants produced fabric that included adaptations of motifs by Wifredo Lam and Amelia Peláez as well as designs specifically produced for the project by members of the Cuban avant-garde, and by artists, photographers, architects, and designers. In 1989, *Telarte* opened up to international participation, with artists such as Luis Camnitzer, Shigeo Fukuda, Julio Le Parc, and Robert

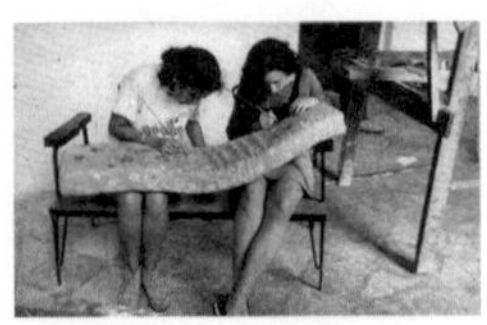

Fig 4 *Desde una Pragmática Pedagógica* [Based on Pedagogic Pragmatics], *La Casa Nacional*, 1990, organized by the artist and teacher René Francisco Rodríguez. 1ª Pragmática Pedagógica. Acela and Pila Reyes decorate the sofa of Mirtha Hernández's house.

---

3 Flavio Garciandía, quoted in Cristina Vives, '¡Bases llenas!... o, el arte en la calle (Una brevísima ojeada al arte público de los 80 en Cuba),' in *Trienal de Gráfica*, special issue, *Revista del Instituto de Cultura Puertorriqueña* (December 2004).

Rauschenberg. The commercially produced fabrics were shown at exhibitions under the oft-used title *Lo útil y lo bello* [The Useful and the Beautiful]. In the catalogue for the fifth edition of *Telarte* in 1988, the art critic Adelaida de Juan contextualized the project within a genealogy of relations between art and industry: John Ruskin, William Morris and the Arts and Crafts Movement, Art Nouveau, Russian Constructivism, the Bauhaus.[4]

In the early 1980s, Cuban artists and institutions shared the desire to imagine new functions for art. This convergence of interests explains the founding of ISA in 1976 and the Havana Biennial in 1984, which gave impetus to the New Cuban Art movement, and the experimentation promoted by the Ministry of Culture. But as Osvaldo Sánchez has suggested, this government support can also be read in terms of the political instrumentalization of art: 'Too often, we ignore the fact that this emergence in the eighties was not just a result of an art education system or of organizing a "third world" art biennial; it was also the expression of a new, post-Mariel political strategy:[5] the Ministry of Culture took it upon itself to lobby for a new international image for Cuba.'[6] The generation that came to be known as the 'Cuban Renaissance' emerged in parallel to the greatest mass migration and social crisis in the country's history, with the exodus of over 125,000 people. The Mariel exodus had an impact on Cuba's cultural policy, and even though the art of the time rarely refers to the migration crisis directly, it also influenced the artistic revolution insofar as artists sought new languages for a changing

---

4 See *Telarte V. Lo útil y lo bello*, exh. cat., Museo Nacional de Bellas Artes (Buenos Aires, May 1988).

5 Mariel is the port from which more than 125,000 people left Havana in 1980 in the biggest exodus in Cuba's history. The migration crisis and social divide resulting from what is known as the 'Mariel boatlift' began with the occupation of the Embassy of Peru by some 10,000 people in April that same year, and the Cuban government's subsequent announcement that anybody who wanted to leave the country could do so. Those who took the opportunity to leave from Mariel were publicly decried as 'scum.' They included the people who had sought refuge in the Peruvian Embassy and political prisoners, as well as people who were joining their families, who had criminal records, or who engaged in behaviour that was 'antisocial' or contrary to 'revolutionary morality.' (See Armando Navarro Vega, *Cuba, El socialismo y sus éxodos* (Bloomington, IN: Palibrio, 2013).

6 Osvaldo Sánchez, 'Los últimos modernos,' in *Cuba: la isla posible*, exh. cat., CCCB (Barcelona, 1995) reissued in *Antología de textos críticos: El nuevo arte cubano*, ed. Magaly Espinosa and Kevin Power (Santa Monica: Perceval Press, 2006), p. 151.

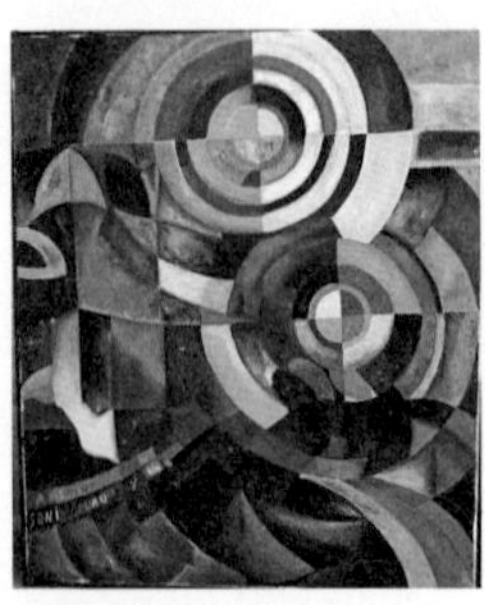

Fig 5 Sandra Ceballos, *Absolut Delaunay*, 1995, 132 x 112 cm, oil on canvas, The Farber Collection

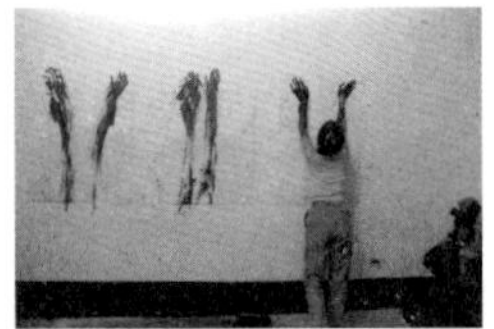

Fig 6 Tania Bruguera, *Tribute to Ana Mendieta*, 1985–1996, long-term, site-specific media piece

social reality and questioned the role of art in society.

The highly ambivalent relationship between art and the art institution gradually changed over a decade, culminating in several cases of censorship and the emigration of almost an entire generation of artists. But before the era drew to a close there were further attempts at the social integration of art, originating from artists themselves and from a certain overflow coming out of the institutions. One influential project in the late 1980s—a period unique for the profoundly collective nature of its debates—was called *Hacer* [Make]. Organized by a mixed group that included artists, musicians, and journalists, its aim was to 'connect art to socially useful labour, offering individuals new approaches and ways of understanding their work; to design an educational method for art schools geared towards professional activity; and to generate cultural wealth from the heart of communities, from their vital and spiritual nature.'[7] In another text, the artist Rubén Torres Llorca writes: 'Once the work of the *hacedores* had been separated from its creators, it took on a life of its own. It could no longer be judged on the basis of the individuality of the artist, but of its effects on society.'[8] *Hacer* encapsulated some of the pressing issues in Havana's cultural debates at the time, but the project was thwarted and its activities were restricted, so that it essentially became a theoretical proposal set down in a few documents.

In the middle of 1989, the group's main theorist Abdel Hernández concluded a long text also entitled 'Hacer' with circumspection: 'The possibility of institutional support must consider its own limits.'[9] When a group of *hacedores* (Lázaro Saavedra, Abdel Hernández, Hubert Moreno, Nilo Castillo, Alejandro López, and musician Alejandro Frómeta) decided to move to the village of Pilón at the eastern end

---

7   José Veigas, Cristina Vives, Adolfo Nodal, Valia Garzón, and Dannys Montes de Oca, eds., *Memoria: Artes visuales cubanas del siglo XX* (Los Angeles: California International Arts Foundation, 2003), p. 293.

8   Rubén Torres Llorca, 'Una mirada retrospectiva,' Centro Provincial de Artes Plásticas y Diseño (Havana, 1989), in *Antología de textos críticos: El nuevo arte cubano*, ed. Magaly Espinosa and Kevin Power (Santa Monica: Perceval Press, 2006), p. 294.

9   Abdel Hernández, 'Hacer,' mimeographed text, unpublished, Havana, June 1989, 55 pages.

of the island that same year, one of their initial principles
was to remain outside of official cultural institutions.
They agreed that their work would focus on the local
community, which Hernández described in the following
terms: '8,000 inhabitants, low educational level, Santeria,
spiritualism, large families, rapid spread of oral information
(myths, gossip, etc.).'[10] Poverty and disenchantment were
additional factors that emerged along the way, which was
probably why the project encountered resistance from
local political authorities and was eventually abandoned.

The artists in Pilón took on the challenge of living
side by side with the villagers so that their work would
spring from a genuinely collaborative process. Their
efforts to collectively identify the community's problems
and possible solutions ended up drawing attention to
areas of social conflict and political discord, such as
the indignation and disillusionment with the revolution
that the artists encountered when they moved to Pilón.
It appears that the project's success at bringing these
conflicts to the forefront also helped to hasten its end.
In a sense, art had been presented as an unauthorized
channel for the exercise of civil liberties that had been
curtailed by the Cuban Constitution, which restricted
freedom of speech and opinion to the social and mass
organizations designated by the state. Although the
Pilón project ended abruptly for the artists, their long
stay affected life in the village, and in particular their
own lives. In his account of his experiences in Pilón,
Lázaro Saavedra wrote: 'Many of my utopias crumbled,
it diminished me somewhat ... or I was a little more
realistic about the transformative capacity of art.'[11] The
ten months in Pilón oscillated between an idea of social
change and a practice of subjective transformation.

In *La Casa Nacional*, another project produced by a
group of students from the ISA in 1990, one of the aims
was for participants to become 'instruments' or 'bridge-

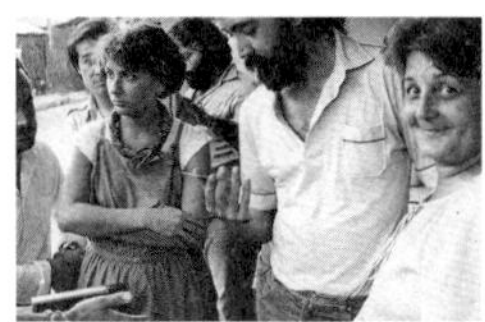

Fig 7 The opening of the
exhibition *Volumen Uno*, Centro
de Arte Internacional de Ciudad
de La Habana, Havana, 1981

---

10 Ibid, p. 3.
11 Lázaro Saavedra, interview with Rachel Weiss, Havana, 12 December 2002, quoted in Rachel
Weiss, *To and from Utopia in the New Cuban Art* (Minneapolis: University of Minnesota, 2011), p. 203.

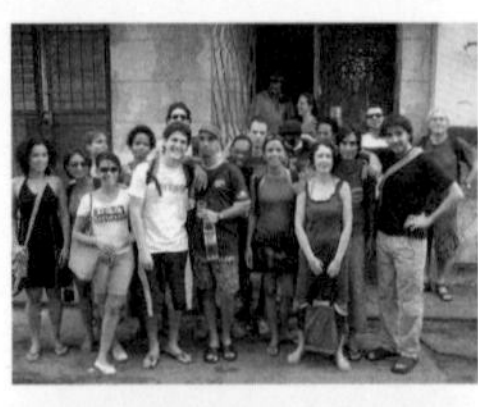

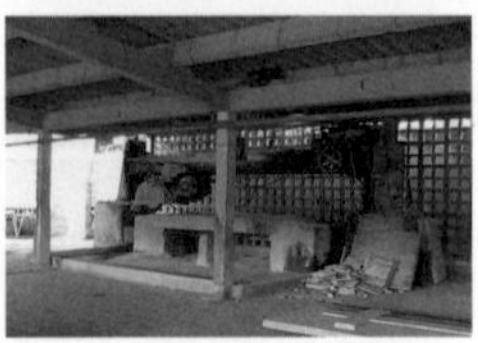

Fig 8 Workshop with Thomas Hirschhorn at Cátedra Arte de Conducta [Behaviour Art School], Havana, 2007
Fig 9 Adrián Melis, *The Making of Forty Rectangular Pieces for a Floor Construction*, 2008, video, dvd, colour, stereo, 5'30'' min.

tools.'[12] The project, an intervention in a tenement building in Havana, was one of the first actions of the educational programme *Desde una Pragmática Pedagógica* [Based on Pedagogic Pragmatics], organized by the artist and teacher René Francisco Rodríguez. For almost a month, the students lived with the building's inhabitants and carried out tasks entrusted to them. René Francisco wrote:

> … as if we had relegated ourselves to their 'insignificance', we set out to carry out their requests: repairing personal objects, refurbishing the building, providing paint for doors, numbers to label the apartments, tables for the dining room, paintings of martyrs for the common room, paintings of religious scenes with personal historical descriptions, a mural for committee announcements, a plaque to historically identify the building, and so on… .[13]

In this case, the question of the usefulness of art was addressed in terms of meeting the particular needs of a specific group of individuals. And it didn't take long for the scope of the project to adapt to the range of possible actions that were within reach of a bunch of art students, such as painting the image of a saint or decorating a wall. A year earlier, the artists in Pilón had brought to light a series of social and political problems, but *La Casa Nacional* seemed to narrow its scope to the economic sphere. The artists offered repairs and improvements on request, but failed to engage in a more radical questioning of the precariousness of living conditions. 'Pedagogic pragmatics' continued to work along the lines of the social integration of art that had been a key concern in the 1980s, but within the context of the then pervasive economic crisis.

The fall of the Berlin Wall and the overhaul of socialist thought in the late 1980s and early 1990s had significant

---

12 René Francisco Rodríguez, 'La Casa Nacional,' June 1990, in Danne Ojeda, 'Proyectos-Arte en acción de reescritura,' MA thesis, Universidad de La Habana (Havana, 2000), appendix III, p. 114.
13 Ibid.

consequences in Cuba, particularly as its economy had thus far depended on favourable transactions with the Soviet Union and other Eastern countries. Within Cuba, 1989 was also a year of deep-seated political tensions and crises that ended with the televised trial and subsequent execution by firing squad of senior military personnel accused of drug trafficking and other crimes. In the late 1980s, Cuban Socialism, and particularly the art world, was challenged ideologically and politically through a series of projects and debates initiated by artists and society at large. But the spirit of *perestroika* and *glasnost* were not welcome on the island, and attempts to engage in political debate through art were immediately suppressed. In Cuba, the political crisis, aggravated by the collapse of socialism in Eastern Europe, was interpreted primarily in economic terms, and was officially dubbed the 'special period in times of peace.' The 1990s began with a strong focus on the economic sphere due to the severe shortages of fuel and other resources, the pressing needs of a subsistence economy, and the introduction of an incipient market, but also due to a strategic emptying of politics from public debate.

La Casa Nacional played out against the backdrop of that tumultuous time, and by and large embodied some of its contradictions, such as the new (privileged) status of artists in an increasingly beleaguered social context.[14] Nonetheless, it also brought up many social concerns of the time, mainly to do with the social function of artistic practice. During the implementation of *La Casa Nacional*, participants wrote letters to each other as a way of sharing their thoughts and discoveries, and as a singular record of the experience. Over and over, the question of the usefulness of the art object echoes in their words ... 'many useful things are beautiful precisely because of the usefulness,'

---

14 In *To and from Utopia in the New Cuban Art* writer and curator Rachel Weiss wrote: 'In fact, the work seemed less adequate to the blurring of art and life than to the staging tableau vivant representing the dilemma of being privileged artists in a socialist system; the artists' genuine desire to "do something" with their work inadvertently to the spectacularization of poverty, and while the project empaneled them as Samaritans in the local context, it also aligned them with benevolent imperialism as the intervened into the local from the vantage point of the international.' Ibid., pp. 206–207.

wrote 'Dago' in one of the letters.[15] Another, addressed to
him by 'el Profe' [the teacher], says:
'… I started to read the book about Russian Constructivism,
guided by you and by the strange, mysterious intuition that
ends up leading us to the things we need. … This book
about the great utopians has arrived at the right time
to spread amongst us.'[16] Aside from Constructivism,
'pedagogic pragmatics' was also influenced by Cuban
political history through José Martí's *Campaign Diaries*:[17]
'That was the first book I read in all my classes. Martí
recounts the advance of a guerrilla army, but at the same
time he describes how a peasant woman places a
tablecloth, how she makes coffee…, *La Casa Nacional*
was a bit like that to me, it was about reducing ourselves
to degree zero and taking notes from there… .'[18]

The gesture of returning to degree zero became a
recurring strategy for artists in Cuba in the early nineties,
partly as a means to circumvent censorship through
the (real or fictitious) concealment of authorship. Some
artists carried out works 'commissioned' by fictitious
third parties. Fernando Rodríguez, for instance, presented
himself as the executer of works that had been ordered
by Francisco de la Cal, a heteronym with whom he has
shared authorship of his works ever since. Other artists
turned to intertextuality, such as Sandra Ceballos in her
1994–1995 series based on quotations from Lyubov
Popova, Alexandra Exter, Olga Rozánova, Sophie Tauber,
Sonia Delaunay, Nadeida Udaltsova, and others. And
Tania Bruguera in *Homenaje a Ana Mendieta* [Tribute to
Ana Mendieta] (1986–1996), which recreated objects
and performances by Mendieta—a Cuban artist who had
migrated to the United States as a teenager—in order
to claim her place in Cuban culture at a time when the

---

15 Letter from Dagoberto Rodríguez to Dianelis Pérez, February 1990, 'Correspondencia epistolar
efectuada durante la primera edición de la pragmática (fragmentos),' in Ojeda, 'Proyectos-Arte en
acción de reescritura,' appendix III, p. 135.
16 Letter from René Francisco Rodríguez to Dagoberto Rodríguez, 22 December 1989, ibid., p. 128.
17 José Martí (1853–1895) was a Cuban politician and writer. He was a prominent precursor of Latin
American modernism and one of the principal leaders of Cuban independence.
18 Interview with René Francisco Rodríguez by Danne Ojeda, November 1999, quoted in Ojeda,
'Proyectos-Arte en acción de reescritura,' p. 64.

issue of migration was both critical and silenced.[19]

Homenaje a Ana Mendieta, which is also Bruguera's first long-term work, offers a different way of exploring the notion of Arte Útil: through the connection between Bruguera's and Mendieta's work, and between their work and that of Juan Francisco Elso Padilla, Ricardo Rodríguez Brey, and José Bedia in the early 1980s. The practice of these artists was steeped in Afro-Cuban cultural and religious traditions such as Santería and Palo Monte, but also formed part of the Western artistic tradition in which they had studied. Some of Elso's works could be described as 'installations,' for example, but his use of materials laden with ritual meaning—such as his own blood—were closer to the elements of an altar or a Santería ceremony than to the formal and symbolic relations characteristic of the art world. Elso had grown very close to Mendieta after her first trip to Cuba, which coincided with the opening of the exhibition *Volumen Uno* in 1981. Also around that time, he was one of Bruguera's teachers at the Escuela Elemental de Artes Plásticas in Havana. Bruguera writes:

> I think I am strongly influenced by the work of a Cuban artist—the late Elso Padilla. My work is influenced by his work not because of the way it is seen, but because of the way art is conceived. He was my teacher, and I took from him the idea that art had to be completely linked with life   and not a fiction or a virtual reality, but as alive as possible. My art has to have a real function for myself, to heal my problems or to help other people to reflect and improve or think about certain subjects.[20]

The notion of art as therapy and the quest for a 'real function' of art ran through the 1980s and can be traced in many of the country's artistic and educational projects.

---

19 Ana Mendieta was born in Havana in 1948. At the age of twelve, she was sent to the United States by her parents through Operation Peter Pan, a collaborative programme run by the US government, religious charities, and Cuban exiles in which more than 14,000 children arrived in the US between 1960 and 1962. After her tragic death in 1985, Mendieta's work became an essential legacy for many art and feminist practices and narratives.

20 Johannes Birringer, 'Art in America (the dream),' *Performance Research Journal* 3, no. 1 (1998), pp. 24–31.

In the case of Elso, Bedia, and Brey, this function was also linked to Afro-Cuban cultural and religious practices, in which ceremonial actions or objects have the power to change reality. To some extent, the idea was also present in Mendieta's actions and in Bruguera's reenactments at the start of her research on performance, conceived as both representation and ritual. But the use of art as a tool is also echoed in many other works from the period. The exhibition that Bedia organized at the Museo Nacional de Bellas Artes in 1984, which summed up his research and interests at the time, was entitled *La persistencia del uso* [The Persistence of Use]. It presented a series of work tools from different cultures, placing equal importance on their utilitarian, magic, and religious aspects. In the exhibition catalogue, the curator and critic Gerardo Mosquera wrote: 'They are not axes and sickles from this culture or that culture, but artistic axes and sickles from the imagination, which are also "real" axes and sickles that can be used. Objects that are reality and metaphor at the same time.'[21] This ambivalent status—both reality and metaphor— could suggest other conditions for a 'useful art.'

But the notion of Arte Útil in Cuba can also be addressed from the perspective of pedagogic practice. Through their work as teachers, artists such as Garciandía, René Francisco Rodríguez, and Bruguera have played a pivotal role in linking several generations of artists. From 2002 to 2009, Bruguera ran the country's most radical educational project: the *Cátedra Arte de Conducta* [Behaviour Art School][22] for political and aesthetic change, collective discussion, and social impact. The work of some of the programme's participants resonates with avant-garde practices that connect the present with Soviet avant-garde experiments from the 1920s by way of the 1980s in Cuba. In 2008, while he was a student in the Cátedra programme, Adrián Melis carried out an action at a

---

21 *La persistencia del uso, José Bedia, Instalaciones y dibujos*, Pequeño Salón, Museo Nacional de Bellas Artes, Havana, 1984.
22 The *Cátedra Arte de Conducta* was conceived and produced by Tania Bruguera in Havana between 2002 and 2009 as a long-term artistic project in the form of an art school.

state-owned brick factory where production had ceased due to a lack of raw materials. Even so, workers had to continue to clock in each day and sit idly through the regulation eight-hour day. On one of those workdays, Melis suggested that they use their bodies and voices to imitate the sounds of the factory if it were operating normally. The result of that collective fiction was *Elaboración de cuarenta piezas rectangulares para la construcción de un piso* [The Making of Forty Rectangular Pieces for a Floor Construction] (2008). While in the 1920s Karl Ioganson had been more concerned with the intensification of work in the factory than with worker alienation,[23] at the start of the twenty-first century Melis engaged with the industrial world unconcerned with economic productivity, which by then seemed impossible. In his action, Melis and the workers harnessed elements such as play, noise, invention, and disobedience. Perhaps the oblique and vaguely useful functionality of this action in a factory should be read as one of those 'desiring machines' that 'interfere with the reproductive function of technical machines by introducing an element of dysfunction.'[24]

The juxtaposition, in the *Museo de Arte Útil*,[25] of a machine (Ioganson's) that increases labour productivity by 150 percent and another machine (Melis's) that produces on the basis of non-productivity, offers a lens through which to understand the complexity of Bruguera's notion of Arte Útil. I believe that these traces of desire and uselessness are precisely the point of tension at which Arte Útil resists merely instrumental art. In spite of Bruguera's insistence on achieving practical uses, results, and tangible benefits, the notion of Arte Útil defies translation strictly in terms of usefulness, and instead extends to the sense of art as a tool. The Cuban art projects that we have looked at in this text resonate with the ideas,

---

23 Maria Gough, *The Artist as Producer: Russian Constructivism in Revolution* (Los Angeles: University of California Press, 2005), p. 188.
24 Gilles Deleuze and Felix Guattari, *Anti-Oedipus: Capitalism and Schizophrenia* (London: Continuum, 2004), p. 34.
25 *Finishing Machine*, by Karl Ioganson and *Vigilia*, by Adrián Melis, are included in the online archive of the Museo del Arte Útil available at http://museumarteutil.net/projects/vigilia-night-wacht/ and http://museumarteutil.net/projects/constructivism-finishing-machine.

ways of doing, and terminology of Arte Útil: the functional application of art, measuring the value of works by their effects on society, art as a tool at the service of specific needs, the potential of artistic actions to transform reality. These concerns that ran through the Cuban cultural context from the early 1980s onward, and that echoed certain Soviet avant-garde movements, now seem to be missing from that same context, which is experiencing the retreat of the public into the private, the collective into the individual. Through her research and practice, from a 'state of emergency,'[26] Bruguera radicalizes the desire to bring about social change and to find a use for art within society. Likewise, the Arte Útil archive-in-progress suggest ways of imagining or experiencing other, more sustainable and socially committed, ways of living together.[27]

---

26 *Estado de excepción* [State of Emergency] was the title of a project by the Cátedra Arte de Conducta, Galería Habana, at the 10th Havana Biennial in 2009. Curated by Bruguera, it presented a new exhibition each day over seven days. The limited duration of each exhibition proved to be an effective way of avoiding censorship.
27 See http://museumarteutil.net/archive.

Essay
Adrian Rifkin

Really, Something?

Before 1.

When William Blake opened his poem 'London' in the 1790s with the lines 'I wandered through each chartered street, / Near where the chartered Thames does flow…' you might say that what we now call 'neoliberalism' had already had its dawn, the chill setting of the price and cost of everything, of people as of their habitation, of town and countryside alike. If we were to take together this poem of Blake's and just one of Francisco Goya's *Caprichos*, we could make them into a figure, a hybrid monstrosity showing what was, henceforth, to grow into the murderous implication of the ends and ultimate means of capitalist production.

O: Ironically William Morris's declaration at the opening of his essay 'Art under Plutocracy' (1883) repeats what capitalism or the Church had always known, but as critique, that there is nothing cultural that cannot be the instrument of domination. At least this irony draws attention to the ambivalence of 'usefulness' and therefore to uselessness as well. In Tania Bruguera's accounts of Arte Útil the ambivalence is sustained, in a new way, for what activism and critique has now become, in the suspense between the idea of art as a tool and the practices of art a ruse. Maybe in Bruguera's thinking one metaphor for art could be the lock picker's toolkit, instruments of burglary or evasion. Morris, differently:

> The carpenter makes a chest for the goldsmith one day, the goldsmith a cup for the carpenter on another, and there is sympathy in their work—that is, the carpenter makes for his goldsmith friend just such a chest as he himself would have if he needed a chest; the goldsmith's cup is exactly what he would make for himself if he needed one. Each is conscious during his work of making a thing to be used by a man of like needs to himself. I ask you to note these statements carefully, for I shall have to put a contrast to these conditions of work presently. Meantime observe that this question of ornamental or architectural art does not mean, as perhaps most people think it does, whether or not a certain amount of ornament or elegance shall be plastered on to a helpless, lifeless article of daily use—a house, a cup, a spoon, or what not. The chest and the cup, the house, or what not, may be as simple or as rude as you please, or as devoid of what is usually called ornament; but done in the spirit I have told you of, they will inevitably be works of art.[1]

---

1   William Morris, 'Art and its Producers,' lecture, first annual conference of the National Association for the Advancement of Art at the Rotunda, Liverpool, 5 December 1888, www.marxists.org/archive/morris/works/1888/producer.htm.

While for Morris, as Kristin Ross has recently shown in her *Communal Luxury: The Political Imaginary of the Paris Commune* (2015) his transmission of aspects of the thinking of the Paris Communards of 1871, the making of useful things, the being-artisan in a world in which art and utility are split, enables the recognition of the ideological power of the split. And, at the same time, the potentially revolutionary splitting of this split through its re-appropriation in a moment of the redistribution of the sensible, in the establishment of democracy as such:

> Yet from deep within his perception of the causes and effects of that degradation [of the 'lesser arts'] on the possibility of fellowship, creativity, and human happiness, Morris would derive the entirety of his political analysis.[2]

0.1: So there is already an irony in my construct, Blake + Goya, Poet + Painter; simply that it is itself built out of what Marx and Engels would soon enough come to see as the specialization of talent produced by the long-term elaboration of the division of labour:

> He (Stirner) imagines that the so-called organisers of labour wanted to organise the entire activity of each individual, and yet it is precisely they who distinguish between directly productive labour, which has to be organised, and labour which is not directly productive. In regard to the latter, however, it was not their view, as Sancho imagines, that each should do the work of Raphael, but that anyone in whom there is a potential Raphael should be able to develop without hindrance. Sancho imagines that Raphael produced his pictures independently of the division of labour that existed

---

2   Kristin Ross, *Communal Luxury: The Political Imaginary of the Paris Commune* (London: Verso, 2015), p. 62. See also French edition, *L'imaginaire de la Commune, Paris* (Paris: La Fabrique, 2015). This, along with the work of Caroline Arscott, is the most complete contemporary rethinking of Morris's aesthetic politics, but especially it resituates the Communard notion of 'communal luxury' as one that we can here re-appropriate as a missing link between Arte Útil and what I am calling 'arte inútil'.

in Rome at the time. If he were to compare Raphael with Leonardo da Vinci and Titian, he would see how greatly Raphael's works of art depended on the flourishing of Rome at that time, which occurred under Florentine influence, while the works of Leonardo depended on the state of things in Florence, and the works of Titian, at a later period, depended on the totally different development of Venice. Raphael as much as any other artist was determined by the technical advances in art made before him, by the organisation of society and the division of labour in his locality, and, finally, by the division of labour in all the countries with which his locality had intercourse. Whether an individual like Raphael succeeds in developing his talent depends wholly on demand, which in turn depends on the division of labour and the conditions of human culture resulting from it.[3]

Later this will give rise to the famous utopian assertion that:

The exclusive concentration of artistic talent in particular individuals, and its suppression in the broad mass which is bound up with this, is a consequence of division of labour. Even if in certain social conditions, everyone were an excellent painter, that would by no means exclude the possibility of each of them being also an original painter, so that here too the difference between 'human' and 'unique' labour amounts to sheer nonsense. In any case, with a communist organisation of society there disappears the subordination of the artist to local and national narrowness, which arises entirely from division of labour, and also the subordination of the individual to some definite art, making him exclusively a painter, sculptor, etc.; the very name amply expresses the narrowness of his professional development and his dependence on division of labour.

---

3   Karl Marx with Friedrich Engels, *The German Ideology* (1845-1846) (Moscow: Marx-Engels Institute, 1932), www.marxists.org/archive/marx/works/1845/german-ideology/ch03l.htm.

> In a communist society there are no painters but only people who engage in painting among other activities.[4]

And it is this space between the limitless injury inflicted by the division of labour and the need to envision its healing that the discussions around and demands for something called 'really useful knowledge' were enmeshed in the early nineteenth century. Art as such, as autonomous production, is both a symptom and possibly part of the cure—even if the notion of a useful knowledge and a useful art persists in being hard to match up or might match in some unexpected and damaging ways as well. How, after all, in an over-purposed time can one readily repurpose without either resuscitating the ill or resorting to a mechanistic view of class interest, or the interests of wounded forms of subjectivation as they become visible in our own times?

> [This] fact has naturally helped the victory of this machine-system, the system of the Factory, where the machine-like workmen of the workshop period are supplanted by actual machines, of which the operatives (as they are now called) are but a portion, and a portion gradually diminishing both in importance and numbers. This system is still short of its full development, therefore to a certain extent the workshop-system is being carried on side by side with it, but it is being speedily and steadily crushed out by it; and when the process is complete, the skilled workman will no longer exist, and his place will be filled by machines directed by a few highly trained and very intelligent experts, and tended by a multitude of people, men, women, and children, of whom neither skill nor intelligence is required.[5]

---

4   Ibid.
5   William Morris, 'Art under Plutocracy,' lecture, Russell Club at University College Hall, Oxford University, Oxford, 7 November 1893, www.marxists.org/archive/morris/works/1883/pluto.htm.

> The Manchester Mechanics' Institution is formed for
> the purpose of enabling Mechanics and Artisans, of
> whatever trade they may be, to be come acquainted with
> such branches of science as are practical application
> in the exercise of that trade. ... It is not intended to
> teach the trade of the Machine-maker, or of any other
> particular business, but there is also no Art which
> does not depend, more or less, on scientific principles,
> and to teach what these are, and to point out their
> practical application, will form the chief objects of this
> Institution.[6]

> Thus worthy work carries with it the hope of pleasure
> in rest, the hope of pleasure in our using what it
> makes, and the hope of pleasure in our daily creative
> skill... All other work but this is worthless; it is slaves'
> work—mere toiling to live, that we may live to toil.[7]

And so it was, in England, and in France, as the two
countries emerged from the long period of the Napoleonic
Wars and the restoration of trade in 1826, their different
forms of industrial skill and mechanization became
the one for the other the object of a phantasmatic
dread of actual or threatened superiority. Parliamentary
commissions, academic educationalists, and teachers
from the great schools of state, industrialists, and wealthy
members of the regional bourgeoisie went to work on
what it was that the worker should know to do his work,
the work that would accelerate the rate of profit. One
way or another, if the notion of 'really useful knowledge'
emerges amongst a section of the artisans it was a
response to the economically rational view—to put it
in as condensed a way as possible—that all the worker
needed was a capacity to recognize signs, so as to perform
tasks that required neither syntax nor grammar in their

---

6   'Statutes of the Manchester Mechanics' Institute,' in Mabel Tylecote, *The Mechanics' Institutes
of Lancashire and Yorkshire Before 1851* (Manchester: Manchester University Press, 1957) p. 131.
7   William Morris, 'Useful Work *versus* Useless Toil,' lecture, 1883, www.marxists.org/archive/morris/
works/1884/useful.htm.

execution: that is, to reduce their capacity for recognition to what would come to be the capacity of a robot or an advanced, automatic tool in the twentieth century.[8]

This is the stake between the bankers and industrialists, led by Sir Benjamin Heywood, who drew up the statutes of the Manchester Mechanics' Institute and the Owenite workers who set up the Hall of Science to establish their autonomy and independence from this hegemony. It is a struggle both for and against literacy, in which 'useful knowledge' is differentially either the mask of domination or the instrument of emancipation.

When Richard Johnson published his article 'Really useful knowledge: radical education and working-class culture 1790–1948,' in the volume of the Centre for Contemporary Cultural Studies (CCCS) entitled *Working Class Culture: Studies in History and Theory* in 1979 it was, for many of us, a moment of situating ourselves in a history in which we seemed still to be working. This is to say that it not only unfolded the complexities of a historical struggle for knowledge, the streams and tendencies of Co-operators, Chartists both of the Lovett and O'Connor schools, Owenites followers of William Cobbett, to name but a few, and their agreements and disagreements on political activism as well as the content of educational programmes, but it also seemed to allegorize our own situation.[9]

---

8   See Adrian Rifkin, 'Success Disavowed: The Schools of Design in Mid-Nineteenth-Century Britain: (An Allegory),' *Journal of Design History* 1, no. 2 (1988), pp. 89–102. This was first published as 'Les écoles anglaises de dessin: un succès contradictoire' in the final issue of *Les Révoltes logiques*, *Esthétiques du peuple* (Paris: Éditions La Découverte, 1985), pp. 113–129. My article deals with the deluded condition of classical economics in its relation to an aesthetics of profitable production and exploitation.

9   William Lovett (1800–1877), founder of London Working Men's Association in 1836 and secretary of the first Chartist Convention in 1839, a moral force Chartist rather than a violent revolutionary. Feargus O'Connor (1794–1855), Irish militant, member of the reformed parliament, and founder of the newspaper *The Northern Star* in 1837, as well as being originator of five of the six points of the 'People's Charter.' William Cobbett (1763–1835), critic of the Corn Laws, author of *Rural Rides* (1830), pamphleteer, and militant for Catholic emancipation. Robert Owen (1771–1858), utopian socialist and founder of the utopian industrial and educational project of New Lanark mill from 1810 and formulated the ideal for labour: 'Eight hours labour, Eight hours recreation, Eight hours rest.'

Even if the article came from the CCCS at Birmingham University—a major civic institution that had grown out of nineteenth-century colleges to be chartered in 1900—it was most often read in the new history or cultural studies departments of the polytechnics. These schools were only a decade into their development and themselves more open to radical experiments in syllabi than the established universities. Johnson's article was also a culminating example of the school of 'history from below' or 'people's history.' The piece was rooted in the writings of Edward and Dorothy Thompson, A. L. Morton, or G. D. H. Cole, that had grown out of the communist education movement on the one hand, and adult or continuing education on the other—and which had its counterpart in the popular scientific writings of J. B. S. Haldane and Lancelot Hogben.[10] That is to say that it seemed to be an article for us, and that our project in the polytechnics and art schools located within them after the reforms of higher education in 1969, had inherited that historical struggle.

'Useful knowledge' was another name for the struggle against worn out and conservative methodologies in the humanities, social sciences, and 'bourgeois' art practices as well. So the work of artists like Martha Rosler, Mierle Laderman Ukeles, Hans Haacke, PADD, *Anti-Catalogue*, Steve Willats, Loraine Leeson, Charles Parker and his *Radio Ballads*, or Conrad Atkinson would be the names for

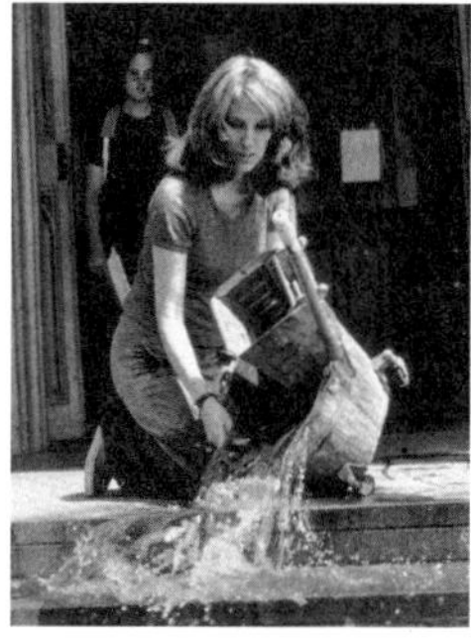

Fig 1   Mierle Laderman Ukeles, *Hartford Wash: Washing, Tracks, Maintenance*, 1973

10   For example, an overview of work aimed at a relatively popular market, written to encourage a post-Marxist world view: G.D.H. Cole and Raymond Postgate, *The Common People, 1746–1946* (London: Routledge, 1965 [1946]); J.B.S. Haldane, *Marxist Philosophy and the Sciences* (London: Random House, 1939) Lancelot Hogben, *Science for the Citizen: A Self-Educator Based on the Social Background of Scientific Discovery* (London: Unwin Brothers, 1938); A.L. Morton, *A People's History Of England* (London: Lawrence and Wishart, 1938); and Dorothy Thompson, *The Chartists: Popular Politics in the Industrial Revolution* (New York: Pantheon Books, 1984). For E.P. Thompson, in the context of this discussion, his most interesting work is probably 'Time, Work-Discipline and Industrial Capitalism,' *Past & Present* 38, no. 1 (December 1967), pp. 56–97, with its unpicking of the proto-robotics of post-machine time, rather than the more famous *The Making of the English Working Class* (1963).

some of those activisms that had become newly urgent.[11] But to say this is also to see that context was, and is now, a matter of projection, the projection of a desire to live decently through our practices, onto a screen of historical values that appear to lead back toward ourselves.

That world of embryonic movements of what would become the left, the early formation of a working class 'as-such,' of yearning for some self-directed usefulness in an over-purposed economy of which the phrase 'really useful knowledge' was then a counter slogan, is unavailable to us other than through a series of over-determined repetitions, of connections ruptured and remade.

Thus worthy work carries with it the hope of pleasure in rest, the hope of pleasure in our using what it makes, and the hope of pleasure in our daily creative skill… All other work but this is worthless; it is slaves' work— mere toiling to live, that we may live to toil.[12]

There is one excuse that is still made for the extra-vagance of the rich, and that is the excuse that *'The consumption of luxuries by the rich finds useful employment for the poor.'*

---

11 This list of artists or groups—PADD is Political Art Documentation/Distribution—is a fairly arbitrary choice of aspects of what one might now call activist aesthetics of the 1970s. These include the slightly earlier militant folklorism of the *Radio Ballads* in the United Kingdom that aimed to set working class speech and political issues (the imprisonment of Bobby Jackson, for example) to narrative in spoken and musical forms. It is interesting for me now, in light of Kristin Ross's rethinking of 'communal luxury,' to begin to unpick how we might see these kinds of art-working as the installation of a new form of such a commonality as a range of critical, affirmative, and decorative or environmental art practices. These we begin, then, to see in a new light, and as belonging to a more complex enunciative history that stands in the genealogy of Marx and Engels's *The German Ideology* (1845-1846), the artistic work of the Paris Commune, and William Morris. Very different from Jacques Rancière's later understanding of such generic relations in his *Aisthesis: Scenes from the Aesthetic Regime of Art* (2011/2013), nonetheless the space of this difference is itself one of theoretical and practical experiment. Here I would just like to suggest that, if we were to take Mierle Laderman Ukeles's *Touch Sanitation* (1977–1980) as an example we can suggest that her distribution of the sensible, her voicing of the sans-part that was the garbage worker, resituates service work of this kind, the most despised in the bourgeois economy, as an instance of communal luxury, and the work of art itself as being shaped by the search for such a new visibility.
12 Morris, 'Useful Work *versus* Useless Toil.'

It is a ridiculous excuse, and there is no eminent
economist in the world who does not laugh at it.[13]

If only ...

1: Let's begin here again, with this insistence: that
context is as well understood as the shape of a desire,
as a projection, rather than the trace of an origin,
of a genealogy, or a justification. Useful knowledge
then, in early nineteenth-century England, and now,
in the activist tendency of the international art world,
might only be commonly contextualized at the risk
of abuse and misrecognition. Albeit that abuse and
misrecognition alike can be thought of as the symptoms
of a desire: a desire to be of and in this world of art and
knowledges, but in a really decent way... one that is
useful, even really useful, to or for someone. ... to live...

Yet even at that very moment, around 1979, the basic terms
of association with past militancy were already being quite
radically questioned and transformed, through a philosophical episteme that has now become naturalized and
generalized in the languages of art criticism and in art
practices...

1.1: ... separated from the relations between capitalism
and war set behind in order to live a decent life; and is
still to be set behind, now it has grown to consume
continents, this dark side of enlightenment reason and
calculation aka finance capital. If I say 'to be set behind'
rather than 'fought' it is to suggest a great positivity as
such to the desire for an Other, useful knowledge to
inhabit as distinct from this monster's reasons and its
teleology.

---

13 Robert Blatchford, *Britain for the British* (London: The Clarion Press, 1902).

1.1(1): Coincidentally there is an interest in
St. Francis of Assisi, and Giorgio Agamben's
thinking of the 'highest poverty'...[14]

1.1(1.2): Yet for us who cannot set ourselves below,
nor afford the pretence, we can only choose not
to set ourselves above, which may be to become,
in some way, useless, merely parabolic, a story
about something other than what we refuse.

1.1: It is to understand that we need to turn away—
although to do so also seems to be the setting
aside of an historical struggle and the knowledge
that has come from it, for education, etc.

1.1(0): And, if what was one were, after all,
a poison a poison, that seems to have been
ingested as a right, but is really collateral
damage, its name must be 'qualification' and
the wish to seek it, ask for it, and pursue it.

1.1(0.0): The Art PhD is the case in point, the
subjection of a practice to a permission to exist,
even to think. Maybe an antidote to this is some
of the cunning that Arte Útil and *really useful
knowledge* might now come to share, though at a
certain cost to one another in the masquerade of
being-respectable: qualification as a masquerade.

... this shift was to be found in the pages of the French
journal *Les Révoltes logiques* (1975–1981), under the sign
of Arthur Rimbaud and in the early essays of Jacques
Rancière, who together set this desire in the frame of
misrecognition rather than that of a deluded epiphany of
recognizing oneself as being of the past in the mapping of

---

14 Giorgio Agamben, *The Highest Poverty: Monastic Rules and Form-of-Life* (Meridian: Crossing
Aesthetics, 2013), read at workshop at Casco – Office for Art, Design and Theory and at the
exhibition *Museum of Arte Útil*, Van Abbemuseum, Eindhoven, March 2013 with Christian Nyampeta
and Adrian Rifkin.

our future project. It is a misrecognition that we inherited
from the bourgeoisie who encouraged the worker poets
to write about work rather than landscape, and from the
traditions of radical folklore that made visible, but that
contained and constrained the cultures of the 'people.'
So, after the publication of *The Ignorant Schoolmaster*
(1987/1991), and then increasingly with *The Politics of
Aesthetics: The Distribution of the Sensible* (2004) and
The Emancipated Spectator (2009), it became unavoidable
that well-meaning identification did not bypass a radical
misrecognition of the desire of the worker-Other—
though it is still hard to take on how damaging this
understanding is for the terminologies of 'modernity.'[15]
As Rancière reworked the relation between the worker
and knowledge, or diverse cultural practices, through the
figure of the worker poets, a quasi-Kantian abstraction and
generalization comes to infuse this relation as the working
through of a still greater desire for the utter reversal,
the upturning of the relations of production, a disruption
even more imperious than the call to the barricades.

1.1(1.1): In this light Arte Útil will be quite unlike useful
knowledge, maybe as if it were rather a phenomenology,
a reaching out for a space in the world, but wised up
and critical, up to all the tricks of surviving. A tool-like
thing will not be quite the same as a knowledge that
avoids being purposed: unending subjectivation.
Something it will share with *arte inútil*, to really usefully
rename art for it's own sake, or Communal Luxury itself.

1.2: And also, here, a generalization; that really useful
knowledge is, more often than not, the detritus of what
is really useless, but that the really useless knowledge,
the ruses and algorithms of the financial markets, or
refinements of nuclear and chemical destruction, of

---

15 The earliest translations of the articles from *Les Révoltes logiques* are to be found in Adrian Rifkin
and Roger Thomas, eds., *Voices of the People: The Social Life of 'LA Sociale' at the End of the Second
Empire*, trans. John Moore, History Workshop Series, ed. Raphael Samuel (London: Routledge, 1988).
The most up to date collection in English is Jacques Rancière, *Staging the People: The Proletarian and
His Double*, trans. David Fernbach (London: Verso, 2011).

various theologies of oppression and the turning of the human hand into their instrument, for example, is really what makes the world go round the way that it does now. The ruse too risks its own undoing when ruse anyway is the rule.

1.2(1): The problem is to circumvent its experts— that is to say, the dead gravity of their uselessness and power of domination.

1.3(1): The desire to be qualified has become the internalized oppression of the commodity system, rather than commodities as such and it is to do with the marketing of the self and its *cursus*, its CV, before caring for subjectivation.

1.3(1.1): Two important tasks of our moment, then: to deal with domination and to escape from qualification.

2: That said, if this need, for an alternative way of coming to knowledge (something quite unlike its 'production') is to be well-enjoyed in the here-and-now, the desire fed and perpetuated, for better or even for worse, then... this for example might be just enough...

3: Aimons-nous, et quand nous pouvons
Nous unir pour boire à la ronde
Que le canon se taise ou gronde
Buvons ! Buvons ! Buvons !
A l'indépendance du monde ![16]
—Pierre Dupont, 'Le Chant des ouvriers,' 1846

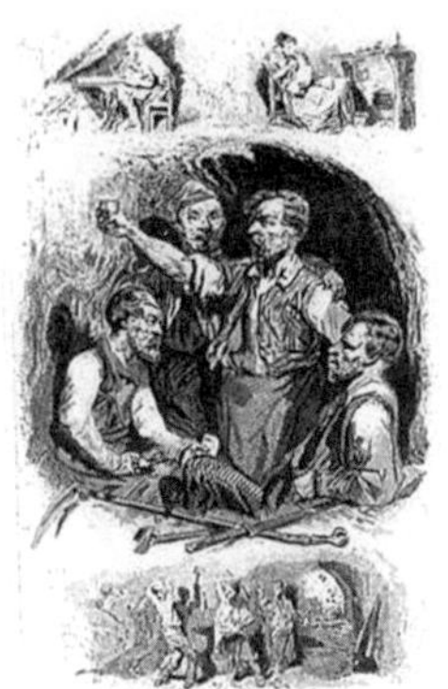

Fig 2 Pierre Dupont, *Le Chant des ouvriers*, 1846

---

16 Let us love one another and, when we can/ get together and drink a round/ Let the canon be silent or let it rumble/ Drink! Drink! Drink!/ To the independence of the world. Translated by author.

Essay
Lara Garcia Diaz

Pla Macià

THE GARDEN CITY MOVEMENT
AND ITS MODERN AFTERLIFE

There are in reality not only, as is so constantly assumed, two alternatives—town life and country life—but a third alternative, in which all the advantages of the most energetic and active town life, with all the beauty and delight of the country, may be secured in perfect combination….
—Ebenezer Howard, *Garden Cities of To-morrow*, 1898

Since the early nineteenth century analyses of the 'rise of capitalism' and theories on the duality of urbanism and capitalism have proposed that there is a dialectical tension or even opposition between 'town' and 'country.' This contentious relationship has affected concurrent developments in architecture, city planning, and even the functioning of society at large. Yet some sought to turn the tide. In a book titled *Tomorrow: A Peaceful Path to Real Reform* (1898), for example, English social reformer Ebenezer Howard declares that '[t]own and country *must be married*, ... and out of this joyous union will spring a new hope, a new life, a new civilisation.'[1] For Howard, the rapid development of industrial Victorian cities and the necessity

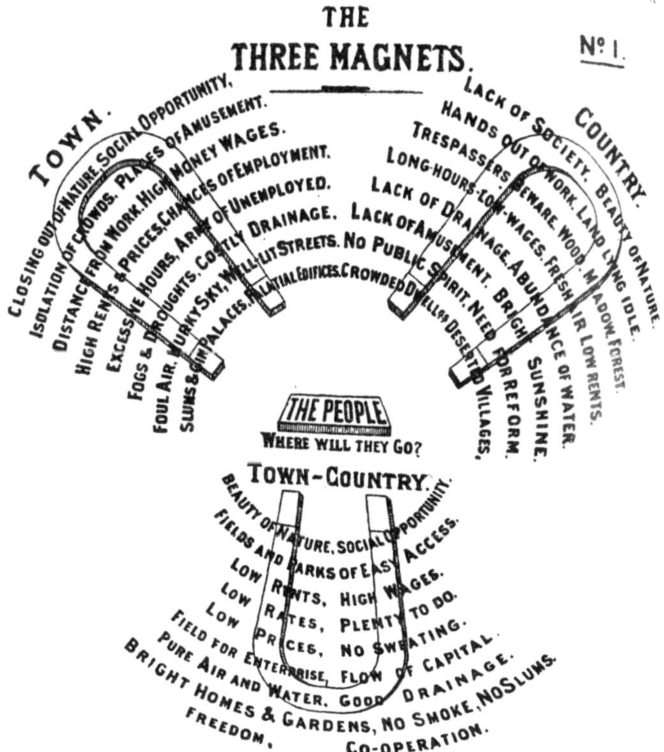

Fig 1 Diagram The Three Magnets, from Ebenezer Howard, *Garden Cities of To-morrow*

---

1 Ebenezer Howard's book *Tomorrow: A Peaceful Path to Real Reform* (1898) was republished in 1902 as *Garden Cities of To-morrow*. Howard's quotes indicated in this text have been extracted from this second edition, Ebenezer Howard, *Garden Cities of Tomorrow* (London: Swan Sonnenschein, 1902), p. 18.

to investigate alternative urban settlements was an unprecedented opportunity to experiment with urbanism as a facilitator of new social patterns. Against tendencies that romanticized and opposed town and country lifestyles, Howard envisioned a non-speculative, co-operative urban plan that reacted and responded to both the city's slum conditions and the countryside's lack of opportunities.

Although the practicality and sustainability of Howard's 'Garden City' could only be tested in Letchworth and Welwyn, the first garden cities planned between the 1910s and 1920s in England, its influence in the development of modern urban theory and practice must be noted. Indeed, it was during my research on urban utopias that I came across one interesting and controversial successor to Howard's Garden City, the Pla Macià [Macià's Plan]. This ambitious urban plan was developed for Barcelona at the beginning of the twentieth century by Le Corbusier and the Group of Catalan Architects and Technicians for the Progress of Contemporary Architecture (GATCPAC). The Pla Macià represented one of the most coherent and enticing urban developments of Barcelona thanks to advances in Catalonian local cartography, aerial photography, and demographic and economic studies since 1902. It was even adopted by the Congrès internationaux d'architecture moderne (CIAM) as one of the plans for the new twentieth-century city—or what Le Corbusier referred to as the Ville Radieuse [Radiant City].

Fascinated by the Pla Macià, I started to realize that both the Garden City and the Pla Macià were conceived as plans to counteract the rapid spread of aggressive and speculative capitalism. They were 'utopian' and not 'ideological,' to use a distinction introduced by sociologist Karl Mannheim, and later used to analyze city planning by architecture scholar Robert Fishman. In this context, urban utopias are conceived as 'programs of action to break the bonds' and urban ideologies are identified as plans for large-scale reconstructions that ultimately preserve

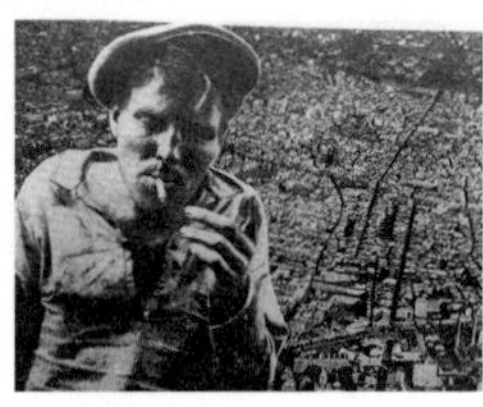

Fig 2 GATCPAC, illustration from *A.C. Documentos de Actividad Contemporánea* no. 6, Summer 1932

the rights of the powerful class.[2] In both the Garden City
and the Pla Macià, the improvement of the town or the
country had to first be anticipated by a transformation
of the economic base of capitalism.[3] Henceforth, it is my
intention to mobilize these words to provide a hypothetical
framework for the exploration of city planning beyond its
morphology, proposing the necessity to create parallel
historical and cultural analyses based on specific types of
planning that share utopian social characteristics. By doing
so, I seek to engage with other perspectives that foster and
disseminate utopia as a tool for acting upon social reality.

The Garden City Movement

Scottish political economist and moral philosopher Adam
Smith affirmed that in order to understand the transition
from feudalism to capitalism, it is necessary to recognize
the way in which the growth of the market in the nineteenth century fostered economic development. Indeed,
the explosion of industrialization, together with machinery's profound redefinition of labour, brought forth an
unprecedented and concentrated human conglomerate
that demanded new quantitative and qualitative dimensions to adapt the industrial city to its new demands. In
England, for example, the rapid development of London
was overcome by the even more rapid expansion of new,
northern industrial cities such as Manchester, Birmingham,
Leeds, and Sheffield. As the critic Raymond Williams points
out in *The Country and the City* (1973) these new industrial
cities started to be planned, between 1820 and 1850, in
both the physical and social terrain, as working places.[4]

---

2 Karl Mannheim distinguishes two kind of Ideologies, 'particular' and 'total'. However, what he
finds common to both is that what a person says/creates/designs is a result or a function of their
position in society. It is from this perspective that Robert Fishman determines the inclusion of Stalin's
totalitarian plans for the Soviet Union, Hitler's reconstruction for Berlin or Linz, and Mussolini's plans
for Rome in a category he calls 'urban ideologies.' Robert Fishman, *Urban Utopias in the Twentieth
Century: Ebenezer Howard, Frank Lloyd Wright, Le Corbusier* (Cambridge, MA: MIT Press, 1982) p. 13.
3 Here I recall Karl Marx and Friedrich Engels's assurance that 'any attempt to envision an ideal city
without waiting for the revolution was futile and, indeed, that any attempt to improve the cities
significantly was doomed as long as capitalism endured.' Quoted in Fishman, *Urban Utopias in the
Twentieth Century*, p. 17.
4 José Gorostiza Ramos, 'El descontento frente a la ciudad industrial: reformismo social y "ciudad
jardín" en España, 1900–1923,' in *Revista de Historia Industrial* (Madrid: Universidad Complutense,
2008), p. 87.

Planning new forms of settlements characterized by the expansion of a new understanding of urbanization, social thinkers such as John Ruskin attacked the industrial cities of the nineteenth century for their ugly and rigid aesthetics and production of alienating social relations. Ruskin situated the misery of capitalism in the division of labour: according to him expression depends on the existence of forms of labour—gothic craftwork for instance—that allow for the development of people's capacities for excellence.[5] He states that 'life requires imperfection for change and growth, to banish imperfection [in labour] is to destroy expression, to check exertion, to paralyze vitality.'[6] Ruskin's influence on figures such as William Morris, an active promoter of the early revolutionary organization the Socialist League[7] in the United Kingdom, member of the Pre-Raphaelites,[8] and initiator of the Arts and Crafts Movement,[9] is important and undeniable. In his utopian novel *News from Nowhere* (1890), for example, Morris imagined a clean and decentralized urban ideal, mixed with nature and carefully designed, recalling Ruskin's ideals and furthermore preconfiguring the development of Ebenezer Howard's Garden City.

In a broader sense, Howard's Garden City was a plan that rejected capitalist speculation by proposing the development of a city in which land could be owned collectively to the benefit of the community. Indeed,

---

5   John Ruskin, *The Stones of Venice*, Volume II, chapter VI, section 16, Project Gutenberg edition, p. 154. Original Source: *Fors Clavigera: Letters to the Workmen and Labourers of Great Britain, in The Works of John Ruskin 29*, ed. E. T. Cook and Alexander Wedderburn (London: George Allen, 1907).
6   Quoted in David Melville Craig, *John Ruskin and the Ethics of Consumption* (Charlottesville: University of Virginia Press, 2006), p. 99.
7   The Socialist League was a political and revolutionary organization that included Socialists, Fabians, and anarchists. Although their political impact was never extraordinary, the Socialist League gained respect and admiration among British political and intellectual groups through their newspaper *The Commonweal*. William Morris's utopian socialist and soft science fiction work *News from Nowhere*, for example, was first published in *The Commonweal* in 1890.
8   The Pre-Raphaelites were an English group of poets, painters, and critics founded in 1848 in the United Kingdom that rejected the machinist approach to art adopted for example by Mannerist artists, and pushed for a return to the abundant detail and the imitation of nature as the central purpose of art.
9   The Arts and Crafts Movement was a fine arts and decorative movement that flourished firstly in the UK and spread into North America between 1880 and 1910. The philosophy of John Ruskin was crucial, relating the qualities of architecture to the moral and social health of the nation. Craft production was preferred over Industrial production, and bold and strong colours and forms were some of the main aesthetic characteristics. In 1861, William Morris founded the company Morris & Co., producing furnishing and decorative arts with a clear medieval-inspired aesthetic symbolic of the movement.

as Howard notes, in the Garden City 'plots [would be leased] to inhabitants, for residential, commercial or other uses.'[10] Following a circular structure, and placing the public buildings, services, and park at its core, the city's cooperative factories were located on the exterior perimeter, to avoid bothering the rest of the community.[11] Next to the factories, a circular 'agricultural belt' had to be tended to collectively so as to provide the community with enough food. However, far from rejecting exterior contact, the circular town was linked to the rest of the world by a railroad, making it possible to enjoy rural as well as urban advantages, and combining as many activity sectors as possible. This combination would produce a Garden City that is 'not a suburb but the antithesis of a suburb: not a more rural retreat, but a more integrated foundation for an effective urban life.'[12]

Importantly, both freedom and voluntarily cooperation had to be combined through 'associative individualism.' Howard envisioned the existence of communal cooperatives flourishing next to private enterprises;[13] he advocated that every man be guided by individual interests as well as by a natural cooperative spirit and a tendency toward combined effort.[14] In other words, Howard's idea of communitarian propriety did not set aside individual action, but rather celebrated individual initiatives as well as communitarian proposals. It is therefore important to differentiate Howard's 'associative individualism' from Victorian capitalism or state socialism, as its direction points more, as economic historian and academic José Luis Ramos Gorostiza proposes, to an anarchic model such as that proposed by philosopher and anarchist Pyotr Kropotkin.[15] While based on a communist society reliant

---

10 Kiki Kafkoula, 'On garden-city lines: looking into social housing estates interwar Europe,' in *Planning Perspectives* (London: Taylor & Francis Journals, 2013), p. 171.
11 'It is not good to waste two hours daily in trains and buses and trams to and from the workshop, leaving no time nor energy for leisure or recreation. At Welwyn Garden City a man's house will be near his work in a pure and healthy atmosphere. He will have time and energy after his work is done for leisure and recreation.' Howard, *Garden Cities of To-Morrow*, pp. 56–57.
12 Lewis Mumford, preface, *Garden Cities of To-morrow*, p. 35.
13 Gorostiza Ramos, 'El descontento frente a la ciudad industrial,' p. 94.
14 Howard, *Garden Cities of To-Morrow*, pp. 56–57.
15 Gorostiza Ramos, 'El descontento frente a la ciudad industrial,' p. 94.

on voluntary associations between workers and free from central government, Kropotkin's model had a faint relationship to capitalism as his proposed auto-governed communities could communicate with each other and exchange goods. A crucial difference, however, was that collective cooperation would remain their foremost tenet. Similarly, it is important to notice how Howard proposed a cooperative vision that could nonetheless adopt a market economy, while preventing social conflicts and aiming at a specific model of 'municipal collective ownership.' By the time Howard's book was in its second edition in 1902 under the title *Garden Cities of To-morrow*, these ideals were spreading around Europe. In 1904 several Garden City associations from eleven different countries[16] were invited to discuss Howard's urban model in its first International Congress celebrated in London.[17]

Cebrià de Montoliu and the Civic Society Garden City
In Spain, and more concretely in Barcelona, Catalonia, it was thanks to the single effort of town planner and social reformer Cebrià de Montoliu that a Garden Cities association was inaugurated in 1912.[18] Since its inception, the Spanish Civic Society Garden City envisioned the reconstruction of a new Barcelona capable of equating English and German models of progress. Howard's theories, and those of Ruskin specifically with respect to his ideal of the transformative power of education, were great influences on Montoliu and manifest in the Civic Society Garden City. Yet these ideas also appear in Montoliu's previous Barcelona-based institutions Institut Obrer Català [Catalan Institute for Workers] and Museo Social [Social Museum]. Montoliu's efforts to create the Catalan Institute for Workers, which opened in 1902, crystalized his interest in workers' education, proposing

---

16 Later to become the Town and Country Planning Association or TCPA.
17 By 1904 countries such as Great Britain, Germany, France, United States, Belgium, Russia, Italy, Netherlands, Austria, and Sweden counted among those with City-Garden associations.
18 The Spanish Civic Society Garden City (1912–1923) was made helmed by: Cebrià de Montoliu as its secretary; politician, historian, and collector Joan Antoni Güell i López as its president; and architects Pere Falqués i Urpí and Guillem Busquets i Vautravers as its associates.

a form of self-organization in which the workers taught and learned from each other. Seven years later, in 1909, Montoliu began collaborating as a librarian in the Social Museum until its closing in 1920 with the intention to stimulate and foment initiatives and activities designed to improve the life conditions of the working classes.

In spite of these clear advances in Catalonian awareness of the necessity to concentrate on the less affluent social classes, by the early 1920s the Social Museum and the Civic Society Garden City were closed. After spending years propagating an invaluable understanding and practical application of Ruskin's and Howard's ideals in Catalonia, Montoliu emmigrated to the US, where he died in 1923.[19] It was also at this time that many Spanish urban planners concluded that to effectively organize modern industrial cities did not mean 'to totally abandon the machine but to design environments with which it could be compatible.'[20] The proclamation of the Second Spanish Republic in 1931 provided a ground for a suppressed Catalan regionalism, which centred its focus on making Barcelona flourish in a new and 'modern' direction. Though the pioneering figure of the Modern Movement in Spain[21] in the 1920s was Madrid-based architect Fernando García Mercadal, by 1932, Barcelona had become the more energetic site. Much of this was due to the Catalan architect Josep Lluís Sert, who was invited to assist at the second CIAM congress in Frankfurt in 1929, and who joined García Mercadal the

---

19 Around that same time, the anarchist movement was extinguished in Catalonia and other intellectuals such as the writer and philosopher Eugeni d'Ors i Rovira also migrated to the US.
20 Fishman, *Urban Utopias in the Twentieth Century*, p. 181.
21 It is especially important when referring to the historical developments of Barcelona or wider Spain to make a distinction between Catalan modernisme, Castilian modernism, and English modernism. The first two terms refer to a variety of influential aesthetic and literary movements that arose in the late nineteenth century, best understood as variations of the French and Belgian Symbolist movement, Art Nouveau, and of the British Arts and Crafts Movement. For that very reason, the word *Racionalismo* or *Modern* (or even *Noucentista* in Catalonia) is used in Spain to designate the school of architecture and town planning promoted by the Bauhaus and architects like Mies van der Rohe and Le Corbusier. It is indeed also relevant to notice the existence of a different Catalan and Castilian architectural terminology, as it points to the different modernization processes among the cities. Barcelona and Bilbao, for example, constitute unique case studies as they were industrialized much earlier and faster than other Spanish cities. The nineteenth century witnessed the growth of an important textile industry in the province of Barcelona, which together with the ensuing massive immigration and urban growth gave the city its modern and industrial character. Ramachandra Guha and Juan Martinez Alier, *Varieties of Environmentalism: Essays North and South* (London: Routledge, 1997), pp. 129–130.

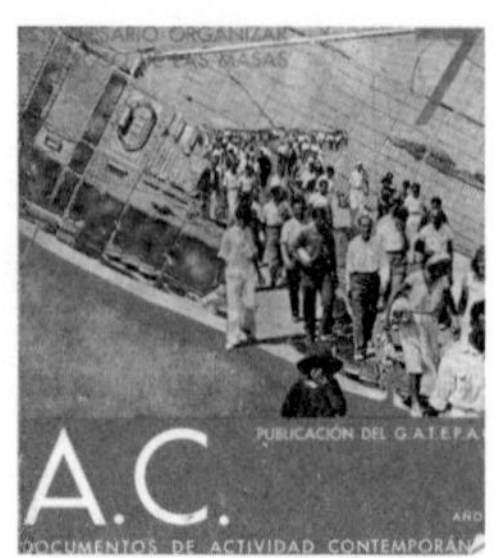

Fig 3 Cover *A.C. Documentos de Actividad Contemporánea* no. 7, November 1932

following year as a Spanish representative at the third CIAM congress in Brussels. It was also in 1930 that Sert and architect Josep Torres Clavé founded GATCPAC and the magazine *A.C. Documentos de Actividad Contemporánea* [Documents of Contemporary Activity], which recollected different reviews on art, interior and graphic design, and photography and cinema, mixed with extended reports from CIAM congresses, always giving a sense of 'another way of living.' Artists such as Hans Arp, Alexander Calder, Joan Miró, and Pablo Picasso were featured in the magazine. This established a close relation with the group of artists and poets Amics de l'Art Nou (ADLAN) [Friends of New Art], who worked in parallel with GATCPAC on the organization of exhibitions, and the edition of a parallel magazine entitled *D'Aci i d'Allà* [Here and There].

Pla Macià

It was in 1928, when Sert and Clavé invited Le Corbusier to visit Barcelona for the first time and began conceptualizing a possible model for a 'future Barcelona.' Adhering to the parameters of a modern 'functional city,'[22] the main aspiration was to allocate space 'by needs and by plan rather than by economic status.'[23] Three years later, next to Le Corbusier and Swiss architect Pierre Jeanneret, GATCPAC presented the ambitious urban plan, the Pla Macià.[24] Then president of Catalonia Francesc Macià i Llussà showed great enthusiasm in his meeting with Le Corbusier in 1932. This display demonstrated the institutional will of Barcelona to embrace an urban model capable of reorganizing a city that was already

---

22 Term coined by architecture historian and critic Sigfried Giedion, and used in CIAM's congresses to broaden the scope of architecture to include urban planning. Based on an analysis of thirty-three cities, CIAM proposed that the social problems faced by cities could be resolved through strict functional segregation and the distribution of the population among tall apartment blocks at widely spaced intervals.

23 Fishman, *Urban Utopias in the Twentieth Century*, p. 181.

24 Without much change in its largely Catalan membership, GATCPAC was renamed GATEPAC—the 'E' standing for *Españoles*—at the March 1932 CIRPAC meeting in Barcelona, and was accepted as the Spanish CIAM group. GATEPAC comprised three different groups: one located in Barcelona (GATCPAC) and the other two in Zaragoza and Bilbao. *A.C.* magazine was a common platform to collect their different ideas. However, the Pla Macià was developed mainly by the GATCPAC, meaning the GATEPAC collective based in Catalonia. However, to avoid confusion, I will continue referring to the collective with the acronym GATCPAC.

exceding the limits of Cerdà's Eixample—the largest town-planning project in Spain in the nineteenth century.[25]

In a broader sense, the Pla Macià synthesized Le Corbusier's ideas in his urban report for the reconstruction of Moscow in 1931. Along with the functional categories developed by Dutch architect Cornelis van Eesteren in Amsterdam, Le Corbusier concentrated on the centralized metropolis of Barcelona.[26] Barcelona's main problems were defined by the need to modify the city's existing chaotic construction, replacing old architectural materials with ones that could keep and meet both technical and societal needs. In 1932 GATCPAC presented the Pla Macià in an exhibition which '[oriented] the citizens of Barcelona, making them aware of the serious defects of the city in its actual state, as well as the huge possibilities that lie on Barcelona given its location and privileged climate … .'[27] The plan incorporated a business centre along the waterfront, constituted by skyscrapers set against the mountains behind the city.[28] Moreover, the plan envisioned two new districts made out of superblocks that were linked to a new superhighway bisecting the city, connecting the port facilities, the industrial areas, and the Ciutat de Repòs i de Vacances [City of Rest

25 The Eixample of Ildefons Cerdà i Suñer (1815–1876) is characterized by its grid pattern, consisting of square octagonal blocks of houses that are surrounded by long straight streets crossed periodically by wide promenades. In the first issue of GATCPAC's *A.C.* magazine, published in 1931, it is noted how Barcelona, like the industrialized cities in England, doubled its population from 1850 to 1900 (in 1850 Barcelona had 175,000 citizens, growing to 530,000 by 1900, and 1,000,000 in 1930).

26 It was after Le Corbusier's personal trip to the USSR in 1928, and after being approached by the head of Soviet trade who proposed he design Moscow's headquarters, that Le Corbusier started working on a fifty-nine-page urban report titled 'Response to Moscow' (1931). His initial response is unfortunately still hidden in private Russian collections, but many architects and scholars have highlighted how Le Corbusier's 'Response to Moscow' has a strong resemblance to the Green Town model presented by the Constructivists. Each shared a desire to deconstruct the historical center of Moscow and create a rectilinear organization of the city with communal facilities. Although Le Corbusier's 'Response to Moscow' was never carried out, he adapted the project and presented a modified version to CIAM as a theoretical basis for what would become the Ville Radieuse [Radiant City]. Indeed, the fourth CIAM congress was supposed to happen in Moscow, but the rejection of Le Corbusier's 'Response to Moscow' in 1933 could indicate how the Soviet Union decided to abandon CIAM's principles. That's why the fourth Congress was held in Athens, which concentrated on the 'Functional City' and broadened CIAM's scope from architecture to urban planning.

27 Salvador Tarragó i Cid, 'El "Pla Macià" o "la nova Barcelona": 1931–1938,' *Cuadernos de Arquitectura y Urbanismo*, no. 90 (July–August 1972), p. 25.

28 It is important to stress that, in GATCPAC's plans, much of the existing city was to be preserved, conserving the narrow medieval streets and the ramblas, clearing only interiors of the blocks and some limited areas identified as especially notorious slums. The cleared areas were to be turned into squares containing small community facilities such as branch libraries and kindergartens, and were later described as 'green islands' in a sea of densely constructed space. The remaining old streets and buildings were described as forming an 'archaeological promenade.'

and Vacations]. It is important to highlight that it is especially in the City of Rest and Vacations that traces of the urban utopia of the Garden City resurfaced.

The City of Rest and Vacations

Highly inspired by Le Corbusier's emphasis on the relation between city, nature, and human rest, the City of Rest and Vacations was conceived as a group of small houses situated on different parcels of land, which, oriented in three parallel lines, followed the coastline. It was meant to be located between the municipalities of Castelldefels, Gavà, and Vilafranca, a few kilometres away from Barcelona, and aimed to solve the problem of the lack of space in which to rest on non-working days. The first time the project was made public was in an article in *Mirador* in 1931,[29] in which journalist Màrius Gifreda quotes the GATCPAC as stating that 'Barcelona is, in all its manifestations, a worker's city.'[30] Furthermore, GATCPAC used the seventh issue of *A.C.* to print a thorough analysis of the project, pointing out on the cover that 'it is necessary to organize the rest of the masses.'[31] Later, writing on one of the canvases presented in an exhibition in Barcelona's main square Plaça Catalunya titled *La Ciutat de Repòs, futura platja de Barcelona* [The City of Rest, the future beach of Barcelona] in March 1933, they highlighted how urgent it was 'for the health of the inhabitants of Barcelona to organize the exodus from the crowds towards other beaches in better conditions.'

The City of Rest and Vacations was equipped with several sports facilities as well as cultural, technical, sanitary, and administrative services on the border between the City of Rest and the open country. They sought to avoid constructing huge buildings next to the coast and respected the natural landscape. GATCPAC's City

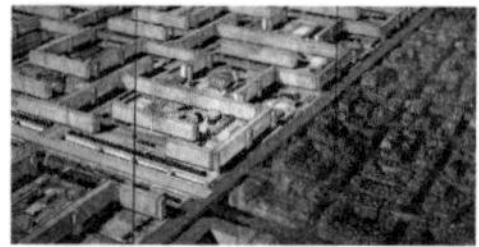

Fig 4 GATCPAC, detail of a canvas explaining the change in the pattern of 400 x 400 m and the arrangement introduced by the Pla Macià, exposed in the exhibition *New Barcelona*, Plaça Catalunya, Summer 1934

---

29 Màrius Gifreda, 'Actualitat arquitectónica,' *Mirador*, 1 January 1931, p. 7.
30 GATCPAC quoted in Roger Sauquet LLonch, 'La ciutat de repos I vacances del GATCPAC (1931–1938). Un paisatge pel descans,' dissertation, Architectural Projects Department, Universitat Politècnica de Catalunya (Barcelona, 2012), p. 20. Translation by the author.
31 A.C., 'Es necesario organizer el reposo de las Masas,' *Cuadernos de Arquitectura y Urbanismo* no. 7, 1932. Translation by the author.

of Rest and Vacations was highly influenced by the Soviet contest The Soviet Garden-City, to which the first issue of *A.C* magazine in 1931 dedicated an entire article. It is also relevant to highlight the influence of the book *Russland* (1930) by El Lissitzky in which the Soviet architect exalted the values of a new socialist society through the use of architecture and city planning. Indeed, Lissitzky allotted one entire chapter to 'The New City' where he envisioned the dissolution of the frontiers between countryside and city recalling Marx and Engels's famous 'Point 9' of *The Communist Manifesto* (1848): '[The c]ombination of agriculture with manufacturing industries; gradual abolition of all the distinction between town and country by a more equable distribution of the populace over the country.'[32]

Many architects and scholars, such as economic historian Eduardo Masjuan i Bracons, have contributed to thinking through these varied motivations in bringing together the city and countryside. In his book *La ecología humana en el anarquismo ibérico: urbanismo "orgánico" o ecológico, neomalthusianismo y naturalismo social* [Human Ecology in Iberian Anarchism: 'Organic Urbanism' or ecological, Neo-Malthusianism and social naturalism] (2000) Masjuan i Bracons underscores how divergent GATCPAC's and Le Corbusier's models in fact were.[33] GATCPAC's model of urban decentralization strove to make contact with the exterior, to overcome differences between town and country and avoid ground speculation. Le Corbusier, however, had in mind a more rational distribution that did not include the City of Rest and Vacations, and which was motivated instead by more industrial and functional ambitions. As Masjuan i Bracons observes, 'on the one hand, [we can include] Ruskin-Morris-Howard-Geddes, and in Barcelona, Cebrià de Montoliu and perhaps some anarchists, while on the

---

32 Karl Marx and Friedrich Engels, *The Communist Manifesto* (Moscow: Progress Publishers, 1969 [1848]), p. 26. Furthermore, it is important to stress that the relationship between the GATCPAC and the Soviet panorama found its nexus in the magazine *Sovremennaia Arkhitektura*, with Moisei Ginzburg and Alexander Vesnin its directors.
33 See Eduardo Masjuan i Bracons, *La ecología humana en el anarquismo ibérico: urbanismo "orgánico" o ecológico, neomalthusianismo y naturalismo social* (Madrid: Fundación de Estudios Libertarios Anselmo Lorenzo, 2000). Translation by the author.

other hand, [we can find] Cerdà and Le Corbusier with an increasingly industrialized and dehumanized line.'[34]

In sum, it is surprising that the figure of Montoliu remains quasi-invisible in Spain and elsewhere in studies on organic models of a city that dreams of being linked to the rural environment. Indeed, the efforts of my arguments here have been to acknowledge Montoliu's role in bringing Ruskin's and Howard's models to Catalonia, and thereby making the important introduction of a more egalitarian and organic understanding of city planning. Moreover GATCPAC's City of Rest and Vacations suggests that the collaboration among both this group of architects and that of Le Corbusier was restricted to the urban area of

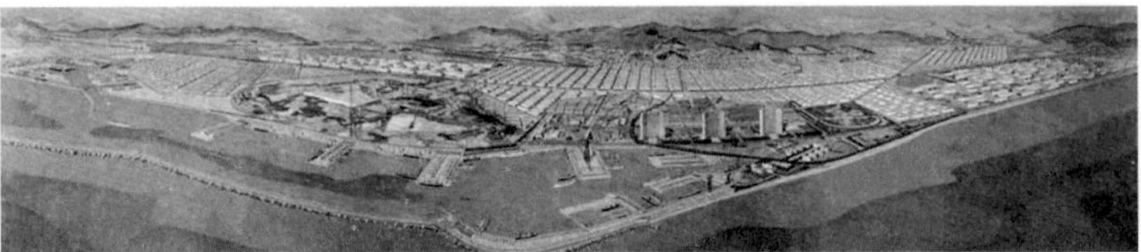

Fig 5 GATCPAC and Le Corbusier, diorama Pla Macià, 1934

Barcelona, excluding, from Le Corbusier's side, other sub-plans proposed for the countryside. This 'making invisible' of Montoliu prevents a wider embrace of GATCPAC's attention to the problems associated with a rise in big industry and urban concentrations, and necessity to consider how a city connects to its region.

Another important thing to consider is that the Pla Macià's utopia was, for a while at least, within reach. As Catalan architect Roger Sauquet Llonch notes, the City of Rest and Vacations was favourably viewed by politicians of the time such as the Socialist Minister of Public Works Indalecio Prieto Tuero, the President of Catalonia Francesc Macià, and the President of Barcelona Jaume Aiguader i Miró, the latter two both from the Republican left-wing party who vaunted the project's social-economic vision. It would be intriguing to assess the effects that

---

34 Eduardo Masjuan i Bracons, *Urbanismo y Ecología en Cataluña* (Mostoles: Nossa y Jara Editores S.L, 1992), p. 21.

the project would have had in present-day Barcelona if it would not have lost the central government's backing once General Francisco Franco took power in 1939. After the Spanish Civil War, Franco's preference for nationalistic, classical kitsch sadly suppressed all modern and progressive architectural innovation.

Surprisingly, utopian approaches are rarely discussed in current urban official programmes. Perhaps this is because these hypothetical urban plans would dangerously hover between the difficulty of actualizing an ideal utopia and the materialization of dystopia. They would have to confront, as geographer, social theorist, and political economist David Harvey argues, how '… materialized utopias of social process have to negotiate with spaciality and the geography of place and in so doing they also lose their ideal character, producing results that are in many instances exactly the opposite of those intended.'[35] Hopefully, however, these words help direct attention to the necessity to enhance the role of town planners, who, contrary to many of our contemporary architects, have dedicated their careers to respond to political and social necessities.

The City of Rest and Vacations outlines a migratory path of ideas and ideals of urban utopias that reimagine social transformation through a rupture in the social-economic ordering of city and country. Reflecting on the Pla Macià as response to the economical, ecological, social, and political crisis of the 1930s, one might wonder what the urban response to our contemporary crisis could be. As introduced in the very beginning of this text, it would be important to start deciding if these contemporary urban utopias should be plans that are 'incongruous with the immediate situation, [that] … when passed onto actions, tend to shatter the order of things,'[36] or urban capitalist ideologies.

35 David Harvey, *Spaces of Hope* (Edinburgh: University Press, 2000) pp. 179–180.
36 Karl Mannheim, *Ideology and Utopia: An Introduction to the Sociology of Knowledge* (London: Routledge, 1936) p. 341.

Essay
Christina Clausen

Designing Cultural Memory

THE MEDIEVAL CATHEDRAL AS A 'MONUMENT TO HISTORY' IN NINETEENTH-CENTURY PAINTING

Current research into representations of architecture tends to primarily focus, as it always has, upon drawings and models that belong to the creative design process. But across all ages, even before the triumph of photography, visual media have served as the primary basis by which buildings have been conveyed and received.

Therefore, it follows that the novel interest in retaining medieval buildings that arose in the eighteenth century, and the stylistic pluralism of architecture since, could not have been possible without the existence of a reciprocal exchange with painting and printed graphics.[1]

Beginning in 1771/1772 with Johann Wolfgang von Goethe's paean to the Strasbourg Cathedral, *Von deutscher Baukunst* [On German architecture], medieval structures in Germany began to be reappraised and increasingly treated as national monuments. What came to be called the *Altdeutscher Stil* [Old German style], equated rather simply at first with gothic and medieval architecture, was embraced after the eighteenth century as the national style of Germany. It bore the association of an architecture that was transcendent, spiritual—qualities that seemed appropriate for the new and explicitly sacred task of constructing national monuments.

In its new role as a carrier of symbolic meaning, the *Altdeutscher Baustil* was refined and developed through new architectural designs and, in particular, plans for monuments. Meanwhile, it was also being excavated within existing structures. As history and historic structures were interpreted from the subjective perspective of the present, a culture of monument preservation began to emerge that unabashedly made idealized interventions into existing monuments. In this context, architectural painting exerted a decisive influence on the ideal of gothic stylistic purity that architects and their clients strove to achieve. In the first half of the nineteenth century, the development of this aesthetic occurred throughout Europe and manifested itself in countless depictions of medieval architecture, that are both the cause and effect of a new civic sense of history as well as a pride and awareness of the importance of urban landmarks.

While in cities like Munich and especially Düsseldorf, this genre of painting emerged from an established

---

1   Johannes Grave, 'Architektur ohne Grund und Raum: Caspar David Friedrichs Kathedrale,' in *Zwischen Architektur und literarischer Imagination*, ed. Andreas Beyer, Ralf Simon, and Martino Stierli (Munich: Wilhelm Fink, 2013), pp. 317–339.

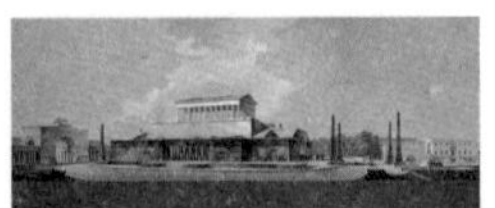

Fig 1   Friedrich Gilly, *Design for a monument to Friedrich II*, 1797, opaque colours on paper, 59.8 x 135.2 cm

tradition of landscape painting, the architectural painters of Berlin embraced the aesthetic of scenic paintings, dioramas, and panoramas. Equally influential were the painterly representative works made by Berlin architects. These were recognized for their intrinsic artistic value at least as early as 1797, when Friedrich Gilly exhibited his design for a monument to Friedrich II at the *Berliner Akademie-Ausstellung* (fig. 1). Largely due to the key figure of Karl Friedrich Schinkel, among other reasons, the tradition of architectural painting in Berlin has historically been in close communication with theatrical culture, contemporary architecture, and the new efforts toward monument preservation.

As medieval structures were restaged and interpreted in painted form, a process of transformation took place that documents a political, cultural, and religious reappraisal of medieval architecture. While this process can, on the one hand, be understood as a way of engaging with history, on the other, it also helped create and shape the perception of history for its own era as well as for the generations that followed.

The Identification Value of Medieval Architecture
Until well into the eighteenth century, princely residences were stylized and perceived as the architectural embodiment of dynastic rule. Since the French Revolution, however, churches and communal buildings have taken over this role; they have been transformed and reinterpreted as symbols of civic pride. Medieval buildings especially have been imbued with a new symbolism and iconic status, blending together to form emotional and mythical narratives involving history, city, and populace.

When the German Confederation was reorganized in the aftermath of the Napoleonic Wars, the city of Magdeburg—formerly occupied by the French—was reincorporated into Prussia's domain and named capital

of the province of Sachsen.[2] The restoration of the
Cathedral of Magdeburg, undertaken between 1826
and 1834, thus became an important prestige project
in the effort to lend a positive connotation to this new
relationship of sovereignty. Under the patronage of the
Prussian King Friedrich Wilhelm III, the chief aim of this
project was to suggest a continuity of traditions and
to shape the collective historical consciousness.[3]

In 1829, three years after restoration work on the
Cathedral of Magdeburg was begun, an issue arose that
allows us to analyse this objective: Should the finial on
the southern tower of the cathedral's west facade be
reconstructed? Although such a reconstruction would
likely have accorded with the nineteenth century's
general preference for symmetry, it was decided to
leave the southern tower in its incomplete form.[4]
An exchange of letters pertaining to this question
between the Governor Wilhelm Anton von Klewiz[5] and
the Prussian king from 1829 reveals the reasons for
this decision. Klewiz began by describing how the
towers appeared at the time, recounting a folk legend:

> It is claimed that this missing crown was shot down by
> Tilly during the occupation of Magdeburg [1631], and the
> city and its environs therefore treasure its absence as
> a historical reminder. Through looking at the Cathedral
> and looking at pictures of it, people's eyes have become
> accustomed to seeing one of the dome's towers with
> a crown, the other without one. Nothing in the older

---

2   Even today, the struggle against Napoleonic occupation is referred to as the *Befreiungskriege*
[Wars of Liberation] in Germany. The term still harbours the problematic political implications of the
years following 1815, which also find expression in the era's culture of monument preservation.
3   See Rita Mohr de Pérez, *Die Anfänge der staatlichen Denkmalpflege in Preussen: Ermittlung und
Erhaltung alterthümlicher Merkwürdigkeiten* (Worms: Wernersche Verlagsgesellschaft, 2001).
4   Peter Findeisen, *Geschichte der Denkmalpflege: Sachsen-Anhalt von den Anfängen bis in das
erste Drittel des 20. Jahrhunderts* (Berlin: Verlag für Bauwesen, 1990), pp. 59–60; Rita Mohr de Pérez,
'Die Anfänge der preußischen Denkmalpflege und der Domreparaturbau in Magdeburg 1826–1834,'
*Der Magdeburger Dom im europäischen Kontext: Beiträge des internationalen wissenschaftlichen
Kolloquiums zum 800-jährigen Domjubiläum in Magdeburg vom 1. bis 4. Oktober 2009*, ed. Wolfgang
Schenkluhn and Andreas Waschbüsch (Regensburg: Schnell und Steiner, 2012), pp. 124–125.
5   Wilhelm Anton von Klewiz was appointed governor of the province of Sachsen by the king.
For information about the background and function of the office of governor, see Thomas Nipperdey,
Deutsche Geschichte 1800–1866: Bürgerwelt und starker Staat, 2nd ed. (Munich: C.H. Beck, 1984),
p. 332.

reports mentions the crown being shot down. However, a handwritten chronicle of the city of Magdeburg from 1629/31 says in the copied excerpt attached here: that the Holy Roman Empire and Catholic League troops fired heavily at the Cathedral towers, and that one tower in particular was destroyed by this, and left in bad shape.[6]

We can glean telling insights into the background behind the restoration measures from this report, as it not only proves that the construction managers consulted historical sources and chronicles[7]—and even sent copies of these back to Berlin—but that they also took the memories of the city's citizenry into account. These citizens perceived the building's lack of symmetry less as an imperfection than as a cherished idiosyncrasy, which reminded them of a significant episode in the city's history. In order to preserve this local legend and thereby increase the cathedral's identification value—despite the fact that he doubted the authenticity of the folk legend—Klewiz recommended preserving its seemingly imperfect condition:[8]

> It seems to me, this damaged shaft should be left as it is, as a monument of history, and not be furnished a crown. However, as I am tasked with the complete restoration of the Cathedral structure, I submit the matter to Your Royal Majesty's sovereign decision.[8]

---

6   Original text of the quotation (German manuscript and quotations translated by Rob Madole): 'Die Volkssage behauptet, daß diese fehlende Krone bei der Belagerung Magdeburgs durch Tilly herabgeschossen sei, und insofern wird dieser Mangel von der Stadt und Umgegend als eine geschichtliche Denkwürdigkeit werth gehalten. Das Auge hat sich daran gewöhnt, am Dom selbst und in den Abbildungen davon einen Thurm mit, den andern aber ohne Krone zu sehen. In den ältern Nachrichten findet sich über ein Herabschießen der Krone nichts. Jedoch sagt eine handschriftliche Chronik der Stadt Magdeburg von 1629/31 ... in der abschriftlich beiliegenden Stelle: daß die Kaiserlichen und Ligistischen Truppen von einer Batterie hinter der Sudenburg heftig nach den Domthürmen geschossen und besonders der eine Thurm hierdurch zernichtet und übel zugerichtet worden.' The exchange of letters was printed and thereby advertised in 1835 in the volume *Moments in the History of the Cathedral Repair Project*: J.H.B. Burchardt, *Momente zur Geschichte des Dom-Reparatur-Baues in Magdeburg 1826–1834* (Magdeburg, 1835), pp. 52–53.

7   Pérez, 'Die Anfänge der preußischen Denkmalpflege und der Domreparaturbau in Magdeburg 1826–1834,' pp. 125–126.

8   'Nach ... meiner Ansicht möchte daher dieser beschädigte Schaft, als historisches Denkmal, ganz so wie er ist, zu belassen und nicht mit einer Krone zu versehen sein. Indeß macht die vollständige Herstellung des Domgebäudes mir zur Pflicht, Ew. Königl. Majestät Allerhöchste Entscheidung und Befehl darüber mir zu erbitten ...,' Burchardt, *Momente zur Geschichte des Dom-Reparatur-Baues in Magdeburg 1826–1834*, p. 54.

Only ten days later Friedrich Wilhelm III backed the opinion of the construction manager and decreed that no finial should be added:

> In accordance with the assessment contained in your report of March the 9th, I desire that the southern tower of the Cathedral be left without a crown, as a monument of history.[9]

The mythologizing of the cathedral's history and its identification value was successfully directed in lasting fashion, even outside the bounds of the city, as can be attested by a passage from Franz Kugler's *Kleinen Schriften und Studien zur Kunstgeschichte* [Small Texts and Studies on Art History] printed in 1853:

> Indeed, when it comes to restoring such a structure, I might prefer to retain some of those features that, even in contradiction to the laws of beauty, have become emblems of the city and its history. In particular here I am thinking of that missing flowery crown upon one of the towers, which was shot down during the catastrophic occupation of Magdeburg under Tilly in the year 1631. The history of this occupation has exerted an almost fairytale-like grip upon our imaginations since boyhood, like the fire of Troy, or the sacking of Rome by the Gauls, and I do not know whether the awakening of such a memory through an eye-catching memorial is not worth more than the abolishment of any and every disharmony.[10]

---

9   'Einverstanden mit dem in Ihrem Bericht vom 9ten d. M. enthaltenen Gutachten will ich, daß der südliche Thurm des dortigen Doms, als geschichtliches Denkmal, ohne Krone bleibe,' ibid., p. 23.

10   'Ja ich möchte, wenn es sich um die Restauration eines solchen Bauwerkes handelt, die Erhaltung selbst manch eines Umstandes wünschen, der, vielleicht im Widerspruch mit den Gesetzen der Schönheit, einmal ein Wahrzeichen der Stadt und ihrer Geschichte geworden ist. Ich meine hier insbesondere jene mangelnde Blumenkrone des einen Thurmes, die demselben in der verhängnissvollen Belagerung Magdeburg's unter Tilly im Jahre 1631, abgeschossen ist. Die Geschichte dieser Belagerung haftet aber seit unsrer Knabenzeit märchengleich, wie der Brand von Troja, wie die Eroberung Roms durch die Gallier, fest in unserm Gedächtniss; und ich weiss nicht, ob das Erwecken solcher Erinnerung durch ein so augenfälliges Denkzeichen nicht mehr werth ist, als das Aufheben all und jeder Disharmonie,' Franz Kugler, *Kleine Schriften zur Kunstgeschichte* (Stuttgart: Ebner & Seubert, 1853), p. 126.

Apart from Kugler's call to handle traces of history with care, he ennobles the history of Magdeburg by comparing it to the fire of Troy or the sacking of Rome. His remarks testify to how the decision to leave the building's figure seemingly incomplete serves to make its history visual in the present day. As a kind of scar, the missing finial is meant to symbolize the city's shared tragic history, and thereby endow it with a common identity. The decision to leave the finial unfinished points to a new understanding of the Cathedral of Magdeburg as an 'appellative carrier of mythological significance.'[11]

This new way of appraising medieval architecture had already diffused and taken root before the advent of photography, and to a predominant extent through campaigns supported by images. One of the earliest and most well-known examples of this is Gilly's campaign to preserve the Malbork Castle near Gdansk. In multiple instalments between 1799 and 1803, Gilly's drawings of the medieval castle were made into nineteen aquatint prints, which received widespread acclaim and established a perception of the structure as a national monument (fig. 2, 3).[12]

The Prussian architectural painter Carl Georg Adolph Hasenpflug is the central artistic figure in the case of the Cathedral of Magdeburg. Unlike the established Rhine romantics of the 1820s, Hasenpflug dedicated himself to the medieval cathedrals of central Germany.[13] He granted the Cathedral of Magdeburg a special place in his oeuvre, producing more than eleven different images of the

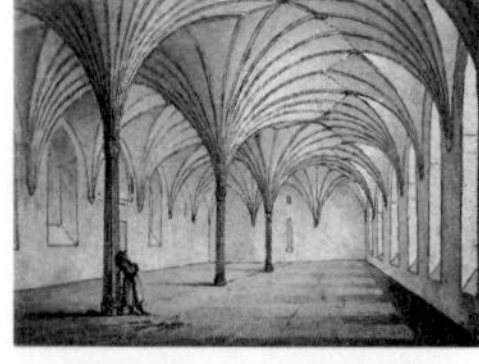

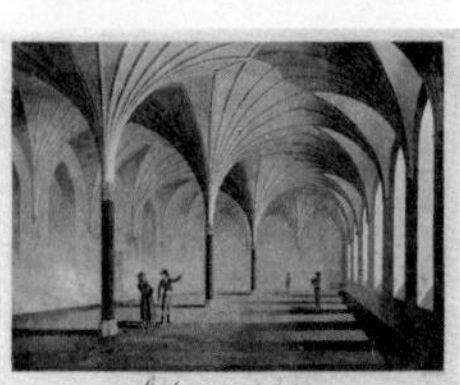

Fig 2 Friedrich Gilly, *Malbork Castle near Gdansk*, 1794, watercoloured pen drawing on paper, 25.7 x 35.3 cm
Fig 3 Johann Friedrich Frick after Friedrich Gilly, *Malbork Castle near Gdansk*, from *Schloß Marienburg in Preussen, nach seinen vorzüglichsten aeußern und innern Ansichten dargestellt*, Berlin 1799

---

11 Wilfried Lipp, *Natur, Geschichte, Denkmal. Zur Entstehung des Denkmalbewußtseins der bürgerlichen Gesellschaft* (Frankfurt am Main/New York: Campus Verlag, 1987), p. 24.
12 Hartmut Boockmann, *Die Marienburg im 19. Jahrhundert*, 2nd ed. (Frankfurt am Main/Berlin/Vienna: Propyläen, 1992), pp. 12–13 and 106–107; Maciej Kilarski, 'Schinkel und Marienburg (Malbork). Schinkels Erbe im Wandel der denkmalpflegerischen Anschauung,' *Zeitschrift des Deutschen Vereins für Kunstwissenschaft* 35 (1981), pp. 97–98; in 1794, Friedrich Gilly accompanied his father David Gilly on a trip to Marienburg. The elder Gilly was meant to document the building for renovation and removal measures. Friedrich Gilly's drawings were made at this time; in 1795 they were shown at the Berlin Bauakademie and later reproduced by Frick. Michal Woźniak, 'Die Wiederherstellung der Marienburg an der Wende vom 19. zum 20. Jahrhundert: Vorstellungen einer mittelalterlichen Burg zwischen wissenschaftlicher Restaurierung und nationalistischer Sehnsucht,' in *Bilder gedeuteter Geschichte. Das Mittelalter in der Kunst und Architektur der Moderne*, ed. Otto Gerhard Oexle, Áron Petneki, and Leszek Zygner (Göttingen: Wallstein, 2004), pp. 296–299.
13 In addition to the Cathedral of Magdeburg, he painted the Cathedrals of Erfurt and Halberstadt multiple times.

church (for example fig. 4).[14] Because these paintings are dealing with actual structures, his depictions of the cathedral are perfectly suited for exploring what happens when a mental image of history is rendered in concrete, painted form. Through the act of painterly idealization, he transformed the concrete building into an idea of a monument—a prototype, a model—thereby creating suggestive templates for conservationists and architects.[15]

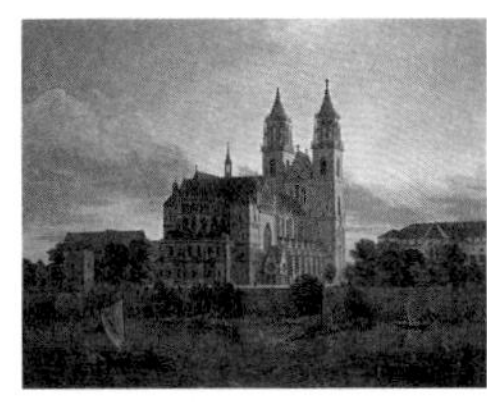

Fig 4 Carl Georg Adolph Hasenpflug, *Magdeburg Cathedral*, 1832, oil on canvas, 96 x 126 cm, Kulturhistorisches Museum, Magdeburg

To enhance his detailed precision and the persuasiveness of his painted architectures, Hasenpflug required an education in architectural history, which he acquired while apprenticing at the Gropius studio in Berlin. From 1820 until about 1826, he was educated there to be a scenic painter for Berlin theatres under the guidance of Carl Wilhelm Gropius.[16] Hasenpflug's most important advocate at this time was the general director of the Royal Theatre, Carl Friedrich Moritz Graf von Brühl. He had already hired the young architect Karl Friedrich Schinkel as a decorative painter in 1815, and in 1818 he paved the way for Gropius's appointment as superintendent of the Royal Theatre.[17] Gropius and Brühl described what was expected of the contemporary scenic painter in the following terms:

Comprehensive knowledge of the general and specific history of the constructive arts, across all ages and all peoples; the highest proficiency and precision in rendering perspective; knowledge of archaeology; precise acquaintance with all branches of painting,

---

14 Due to war damages and the fact that their retention in private collections can only be tracked down in rare instances, the number of paintings cannot be reconstructed with precision. However, as early as 1828, Wilhelm Körte reports of six different views of the Cathedral of Madgeburg in nine paintings. If we include the paintings produced subsequently that can be identified today, at least thirteen views must have been produced. Wilhelm Körte, 'Auszug aus einem Briefe an Dr. Sulpiz Boisserée in München vom 25 October 1828,' *Kunstblatt* 9, no. 94 (24 November 1828), p. 374.
15 For more on the relationship between anticipatory architectural images and the completed buildings, see the 'Planbilder' issue of the magazine *Bildwelten des Wissens*, tentatively scheduled for winter 2015.
16 *Carl Hasenpflug (1802–1858); Wahrheit und Vision*, ed. Antje Ziehr, exh. cat. Städtisches Museum in Halberstadt (Halberstadt: Städtisches Museum, 2002), p. 21.
17 Ulrike Harten, *Karl Friedrich Schinkel: Die Bühnenentwürfe* (Munich/Berlin: Deutscher Kunstverlag, 2000), p. 50.

> especially landscape painting; yes, and even botany. ...
> All these are indispensible requirements of the ideal
> decorator.[18]

Schinkel's teaching awarded the highest status of all to depictions of architecture, 'as the scenic painter should paint nothing that could not actually be built, and thus would not be feasible at least by appearances.'[19] To meet these demands, a student was expected to undertake a comprehensive study of the history of architecture and art, which was facilitated by the vast collection of engravings and templates at Gropius's studio.

In multiple letters to the Prussian king, Brühl advocated for financial support for Hasenpflug's travels, including his first stay in Magdeburg. Considering the general director's personal engagement, one can assume that Hasenpflug conformed to Brühl's expectations of a scenic painter, and that he identified with Brühl's educational policy and program. The imprint of these standards defined Hasenpflug's artistic output even after he attained artistic independence in 1826. It is to this program that his lifelong fidelity to accurate perspective and his studied approach to historical building styles and costumes can be attributed.

Layers of Time: The Liberation Movement in Historical Costume

The conception of medieval stylistic purity in the nineteenth century was not clear-cut; on the contrary, rival conceptions of historical preservation—and the perceptions of history associated with them—competed with one another. Hasenpflug positioned himself within

---

18 'Gründliche Kenntnisse in der allgemeinen und speciellen Geschichte der Baukunst aller Zeiten und Völker, die grösste Fertigkeit und Genauigkeit in der Perspective, selbst archaeologische Kenntnisse, genaue Bekanntschaft mit allen Zweigen der Malerei, vorzüglich der Landschaftsmalerei und des wahren Colorits, ja selbst Pflanzenkunde ... sind unerlässliche Erfordernisse für einen Decorateur, wie er seyn soll,' preface to first volume of *Decorationen auf den beiden Königlichen Theatern in Berlin*, ed. Karl Friedrich Moritz Paul Graf von Brühl (Berlin: Wittich, 1819–1824), cited in Harten, *Karl Friedrich Schinkel*, p. 63. Helmut Börsch-Supan believes Carl Wilhelm Gropius to be the author of this text. Helmut Börsch-Supan, *Karl Friedrich Schinkel. Bühnenentwürfe*, vol. 1: Kommentar (Berlin: Ernst & Sohn, 1990), p. 60.
19 Preface to the first volume of *Deorationen auf den beiden Königlichen Theatern in Berlin*, ed. Karl Friedrich Moritz Paul Graf von Brühl cited in Harten, *Karl Friedrich Schinkel*, p. 64.

these debates over national and ecclesiastical policy through the way he historicized his depictions of architecture, by inserting additional layers of time into the medieval structures. His portrayals were not limited to a reconstruction of some pure, originary condition; instead, they also incorporated later phases of the buildings' history and usage—for example, those of the sixteenth century.

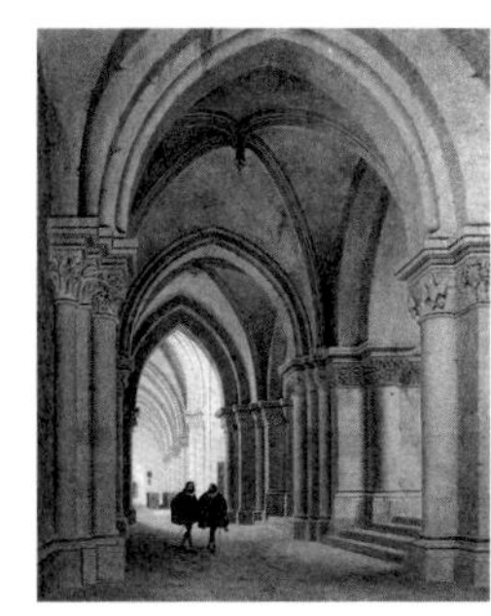

Fig 5 Carl Georg Adolph Hasenpflug, *Interior view of the Magdeburg Cathedral*, 1835

For a small-scale interior view of the Cathedral of Magdeburg from 1835,[20] Hasenpflug chose a vantage point at the southern end of its ambulatory, so that the view traverses two choir bays before reaching the pillars of the southern aisle in the background (fig. 5). The interior seems to have been purified of nearly all furnishing, and the walls of the aisle in particular almost look to have been whitewashed. The emphasis on the stark architecture gives the impression that what is being imagined here is not a medieval, Catholic church, but rather the interior of a reformed church. The personnel in the painting, decked out in historical costume, support this impression. Approaching the viewer are two men in sixteenth-century attire, deep in discussion. Because of the uniformly grey- and ochre-coloured composition of the architecture, their black-and-brown clothing contrasts sharply with their environment. Their cloaks extend to the thigh and their collars are lined with fur. Attached over the collars are white ruffs, which, paired with tight trousers and so-called 'cowmouth shoes' clearly evoke the fashion of the sixteenth century. One of Hasenpflug's contemporaries described similar men in a painting of the Cathedral of Halberstadt as 'well-drawn figures in Old German attire.'[21]

Much like the designation Old German building style,[22] the concept of Old German attire had undertones

---

20 Antje Ziehr dates this painting to 1836, but the signature reads 1835. Ziehr, *Carl Hasenpflug (1802–1858)*, p. 246.

21 Wilhelm Körte, 'Excerpt from a letter to Dr. Sulpiz Boisserée in Munich from 25 October 1828,' *Kunstblatt* 9, no. 94 (24 November 1828), p. 373.

22 Since the 1980s, numerous studies have been dedicated to the reception of the medieval era in Germany, to Old German building style, and above all their political and ideological implications. A good overview, focusing on the political developments, is offered by Thomas Nipperdey's 1983 work *Deutsche Geschichte 1800–1866: Bürgerwelt und starker Staat* (see note 5). It was translated into English in 1996 by Daniel Nolan: Thomas Nipperdey, *Germany from Napoleon to Bismarck: 1800–1866* (Princeton: Princeton University Press, 2014), pp. 490–493.

of national politics and identity formation in the nineteenth century. The issue of a homogenous German national attire had developed into a hotly contested matter since the mid-eighteenth century. The issue intensified after the French Revolution and especially after the Napoleonic Wars, as advocates sought to define a collective identity and cultural distinction from France through forms of dress.[23] Many of the designs for a national attire published in contemporary fashion periodicals made reference to clothing from the sixteenth or seventeenth centuries, which had been reconstructed through paintings and prints. Ernst Moritz Arndt, in his 1814 publication *Ueber Sitte, Mode und Kleidertracht* [On Customs, Fashion, and Clothing], also suggested the model of the sixteenth century:

> To discover what is fair and becoming, it is not necessary to turn to the Greeks, or to copy off Roman statues; rather, if you journey back two or three centuries to the attire of your ancestors, you might well discover something that both simply and nobly befits our German gravity and demeanour—that altogether befits a free people.[24]

The Reformation era, a cultural golden age closely associated with the ideal of an 'empowered German citizenry'[25] seemed a perfect frame of reference for a German national attire. All the way up until the Congress of Vienna, such clothing had the status of a 'confessional dress'[26] among those who advocated for a unified German nation and a constitution.

---

23 Eva Maria Schneider, 'Herkunft und Verbreitungsformen der *Deutschen Nationaltracht der Befreiungskriege* als Ausdruck politischer Gesinnung,' PhD dissertation, University of Bonn, Bonn, 2002, p. 23, pp. 35–36, and p. 76, available at: http://hss.ulb.uni-bonn.de/2002/0083/0083.htm.
24 'Du bedarfst aber nicht zu den Griechen zu gehen noch die römischen Bildsäulen abzuzeichnen, damit du findest, was schön und wohlgefällig ist; sondern wenn du zwei drei Jahrhunderte zurückgehest zu den Trachten deiner Vorfahren, magst du wohl finden, was zugleich leicht und stattlich deutschem Ernst und Sinn und überhaupt einem freien Volke wohl stehet,' ibid., p. 39.
25 Ibid., p. 54.
26 Ibid., p. 205.

But the people did not attain a political voice after the Napoleonic wars, and the individual states reasserted their sovereignty.[27] Due to these restorative developments after 1815, the insistence among students and members of students' associations on adhering to a national attire (which, after 1815, was exclusively designated as Old German attire)[28] received a new 'political charge.'[29] Following the Carlsbad Decrees of 1819, the outfit was forbidden, condemned as the 'clothing of demagogues' and the 'symbol of a subversive party.'[30] After 1826, the ban on student associations was relaxed, until the second 'persecution of demagogues' that followed the Hambach Festival of 1832, which could be described as the 'last pinnacle for the political significance of Old German attire.'[31] Notwithstanding this political backdrop, Hasenpflug still painted his background figures in sixteenth-century attire into the late 1820s, as this example of the Cathedral of Erfurt from 1827 shows (fig. 6, 7).

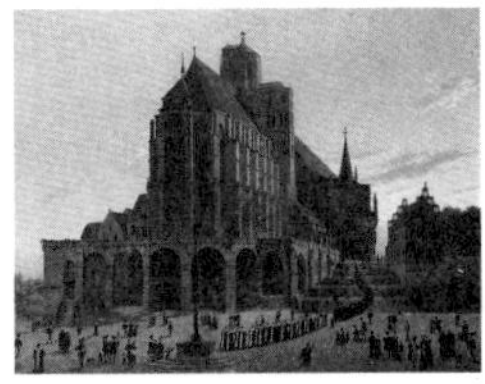

Fig 6 Carl Georg Adolph Hasenpflug, *Erfurt Cathedral*, 1827

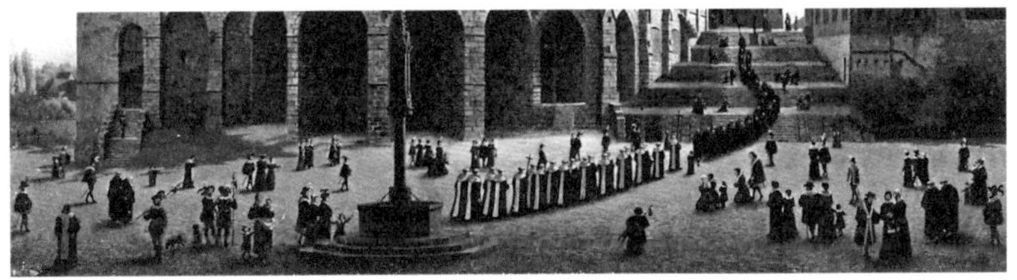

Fig 7 Carl Georg Adolph Hasenpflug, *Erfurt Cathedral*, 1827

While there is certainly a significant difference between the historical costumes carefully reconstructed by Hasenpflug and the clothing of the politically organized students, which was adapted to practical limitations, the shared model nevertheless invites us to speculate on possible similar motives.

---

27 Ibid., p. 108. For reactions to the failed constitutional settlement, see Ferdi Akaltin, *Die Befreiungskriege im Geschichtsbild der Deutschen im 19. Jahrhundert* (Frankfurt am Main: Verlag Neue Wissenschaft, 1997), pp. 137–143.

28 Schneider, 'Herkunft und Verbreitungsformen der *Deutschen Nationaltracht der Befreiungskriege* als Ausdruck politischer Gesinnung,' pp. 108–109.

29 Ibid., p. 111, 205.

30 Ibid., p. 163, 207.

31 Ibid., p. 173.

The Social Utopic Dimension of Architectural Painting in the Nineteenth Century

While the Prussian king was one of Hasenpflug's most important patrons at the beginning of his career, Hasenpflug's later historicizing architectural paintings were exclusively commissioned and acquired by bourgeois collectors. Although the sixteenth-century costume motifs in the paintings do obliquely refer to Prussia's political situation, and thereby contain a subtle critique, they nevertheless cannot be classified as revolutionary or anti-monarchical. Many bourgeois art collectors advocated for the cultural emancipation of the citizenry through channels like Kunstvereine or art publications.[32] Such a disposition may very well contain an 'ideal of freedom positing the equality of the educated over and against all estatist constraints,'[33] but nevertheless not aim at altering the foundations of the existing political system.[34] A famous passage from Friedrich Schiller's 1805 drama *Don Carlos*[35] epitomizes this tempered bourgeois yearning for reform in the wake of the savage course taken by the French Revolution—a yearning for reform that was still widespread among bourgeois liberal circles in the Age of Metternich, prior to the March Revolution of 1848: 'hand in hand/ The subjects' welfare and the sovereign's greatness/ Will walk in union.'[36]

Similar ideas also underlie the 'social utopic city

---

32 See Joachim Grossmann, *Künstler, Hof und Bürgertum: Leben und Arbeit von Malern in Preußen 1786–1850* (Berlin: Akademie Verlag, 1994), pp. 91–145; Nipperdey, *Deutsche Geschichte 1800–1866*, p. 267.

33 Michael Brix and Monika Steinhauser, 'Geschichte im Dienste der Baukunst: Zur historistischen Architektur-Diskussion in Deutschland,' in *Geschichte allein ist zeitgemäss: Historismus in Deutschland*, ed. Michael Brix and Monika Steinhauser (Gießen: Anabas-Verlag Kämpf, 1978), p. 236; for more on these middle-class aspirations, see Nipperdey, *Deutsche Geschichte 1800–1866*, p. 264.

34 Nipperdey, *Deutsche Geschichte 1800–1866*, pp. 270–271. Nipperdey describes the relationship between the liberal bourgeoisie and the state in the Age of Metternich in the following terms: 'In the liberal struggle against feudal, estatist society, the state – as weak as it might have been – was a potential ally for liberals. ... This was due to the continuousness of state reforms.' Ibid., p. 289.

35 Earlier versions of the drama were written as early as the late 1780s, but the last version to be authorized by Schiller was published in 1805.

36 'Bürgerglück wird dann versöhnt mit Fürstengröße wandeln.' Friedrich Schiller, 'Don Karlos Infant von Spanien: Ein dramatisches Gedicht' (1805), *Schiller: Sämtliche Werke in zehn Bänden*, ed. Hans-Günther Thalheim, et al., vol. 3: *Don Karlos Briefe über Don Karlos: Körners Vormittag*, ed. Regine Otto (Berlin: Aufbau Verlag, 1987), p. 477.

landscapes'[37] of the first half of the nineteenth century. Bernhard Maaz has used this designation to describe a sub-category of architectural painting that originated in Schinkel's pictures of cathedrals.[38] Before the backdrop of a fantasized medieval architecture, a panorama of bourgeois life in historical costume unfolded within these paintings. They adopted the free imperial cities of the fifteenth and sixteenth centuries as models for an idealized relationship with the state, embodied by the union of rulers and autonomous citizens.[39]

In the foreground of his 1815 painting *Medieval City on a River*, Schinkel developed an allegory for this unity by depicting the festive arrival of a ruler (fig. 8). The ruler approaches a cathedral, accompanied by the city's population. By drawing an analogy between the cathedral's unfinished tower (fig. 9) and the project to complete the Cologne Cathedral, which was discussed around the same time,[40] Schinkel articulates, in programmatic fashion, a call for societal completion similar to that of Joseph Görres, who wrote in 1814: 'In its fragmentary state of incompletion, in its abandonment, it [the Cologne Cathedral, CC] has become an image of Germany. So too, then, shall it become a symbol of the new Reich which we hope to construct.'[41]

This social utopic orientation might also underlie Hasenpflug's idealized vision of the completed Cologne

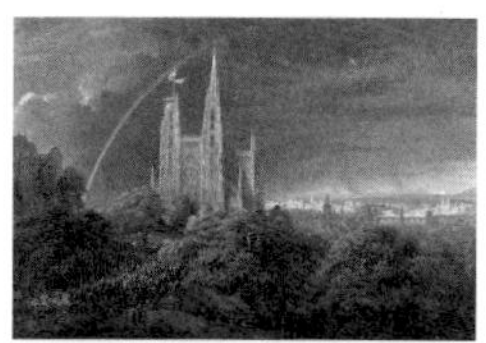

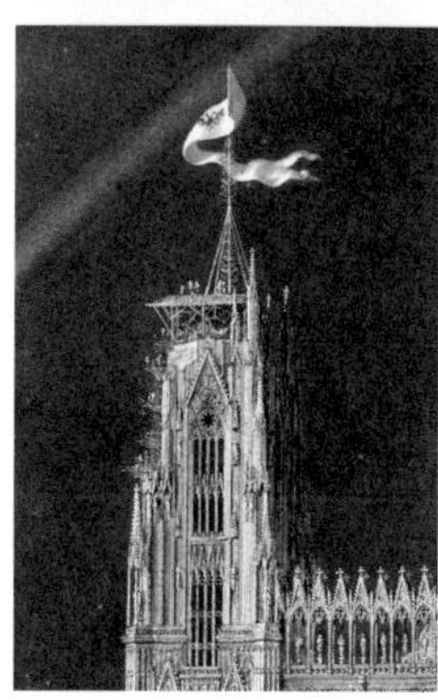

Fig 8 Karl Friedrich Schinkel, *Medieval City on a River*, 1815
Fig 9 Karl Friedrich Schinkel, *Medieval City on a River* (detail), 1815

---

37 Bernhard Maaz, 'Sozialutopische Stadtlandschaften: Schinkels Architekturmalerei, Bedeutung und Folgen,' *Klassizismus – Gotik: Karl Friedrich Schinkel und die patriotische Baukunst*, ed. Annette Dorgerloh, Michael Niedermeier, and Horst Bredekamp (Munich/Berlin: Deutscher Kunstverlag, 2007), p. 113.

38 Ibid., pp. 113–116.

39 Ibid., p. 114.

40 Thomas Nipperdey, 'Der Kölner Dom als Nationaldenkmal,' *Historische Zeitschrift* 233, no. 3 (1981), pp. 595–596; Gabi Dolff-Bonekämper aptly describes the towers of the Cologne Cathedral as 'icons of the German gothic.' Gabi Dolff-Bonekämper, 'Wahr oder falsch. Denkmalpflege als Medium nationaler Identitätskonstruktionen,' *Bilder gedeuteter Geschichte: Das Mittelalter in der Kunst und Architektur der Moderne*, ed. Otto Gerhard Oexle, Áron Petneki, and Leszek Zygner, vol. 2 (Göttingen: Wallstein, 2004), p. 237.

41 'In seiner trümmerhaften Unvollendung, in seiner Verlassenheit ist es [der Kölner Dom] ein Bild gewesen von Deutschland …, so werde es denn auch ein Symbol des neuen Reiches, das wir bauen wollen,' Joseph Görres, 'Der Dom in Köln,' *Rheinsicher Merkur* no. 151 (20 November 1814). Around 1815, societal completion was not only conceived in parallel with the completion of the Cologne Cathedral, but also with the new invention of the *Old German building style*, whose 'full completion is reserved for the time to come.' Karl Friedrich Schinkel wrote this in his *Denkschrift zum Entwurf eines Doms als Denkmal für die Befreiungskriege* in January 1815. Cited in Paul Ortwin Rave, *Karl Friedrich Schinkel: Berlin: Erster Teil: Bauten für die Kunst, Kirchen, Denkmalpflege: Nachdruck von 1941* (Munich/Berlin: Deutscher Kunstverlag, 1981), p. 196.

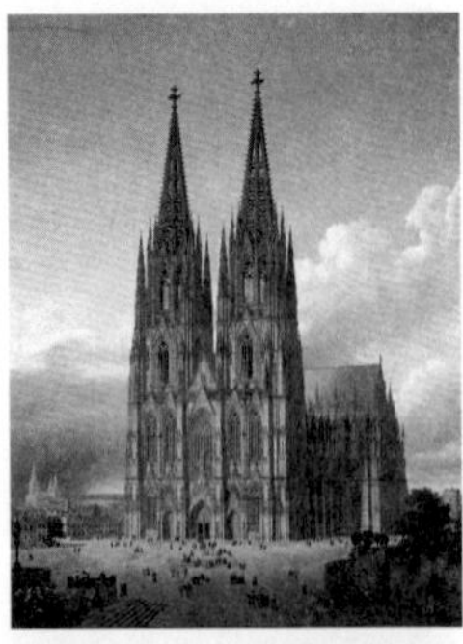
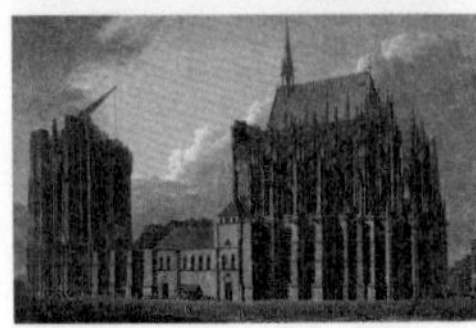

Fig 10 Carl Georg Adolph Hasenpflug, *Idealized vision of the completed Cologne Cathedral*, 1834–1836
Fig 11 Adolph Barnstedt, *Cologne Cathedral at the end of the Middle Ages*, 1809

Cathedral from 1834–1836 (fig. 10).[42] His first trip to the Rhein can be dated with certainty to 1832. At this point in time, completing the cathedral had been under discussion for many years, but no actual construction measures would be taken for another decade. The cathedral, and its western tower in particular, was only a fragment at this point (fig. 11). In contrast to the existing structure at this time the cathedral's twin tower facade and southern transept in Hasenpflug's painting are completed. The architecture rises above a low-slung horizon and is rendered precisely down to the minutest detail. It is likely that he also factored in the medieval sketch of the facade and prints by his contemporaries.[43]

Apart from his architecturally precise rendering of the finished cathedral, the time period selected by Hasenpflug and his portrait of society are noteworthy in connection with the *social utopic city landscape*. In the spacious square before the cathedral, Hasenpflug depicts a number of citizens dressed in sixteenth-century attire, talking with one another, walking about, or gathering around a fountain in the foreground.[44] Hasenpflug's picture fantasizes the cathedral being completed in the sixteenth century[45] and is once again making use of the idealized society of the Reformation era, despite the fact that—or *because* of it—*Old German attire* had been associated with a desire for political reform for many years now.[46]

---

42 Most scholarship on Hasenpflug assumes that he knew *Medieval City on a River*, although Schinkel kept the painting at his official lodgings until his death, where it wasn't accessible to everyone.
43 Herbert Rode, 'Eine Idealansicht des Kölner Domes von Karl Georg Hasenpflug 1834–36,' *Kölner Domblatt* 21/22 (1963), p. 91.
44 The fountain motif appears in many of Hasenpflug's historicizing depictions, for example in his *View of the Erfurt Cathedral* from 1827 (fig. 7). Both fountains are inventions on the part of Hasenpflug, who perhaps hoped thereby to symbolize a bourgeois place of assembly. Jörg Trempler has investigated the significance of the fountain motif in Schinkel's work; see Jörg Trempler, *Schinkels Motive* (Berlin: Matthes & Seitz, 2007), pp. 69–122. Its multiple appearances in Hasenpflug's work could be inspired by this model. As the fountains in Hasenpflug's work are always employed within historicizing depictions, it's conceivable they might serve, for example, as references to the course of history. Helmut Börsch-Supan, 'Carl Hasenpflug, ein Maler im Dienst der Dome,' in *Es Thun Ihrer Viel Fragen: Kunstgeschichte in Mitteldeutschland*, ed. Reinhard Schmitt (Petersberg: Imhof, 2001), p. 209.
45 Hellmuth Allwill Fritzsche, 'Der Architekturmaler Carl Georg Hasenpflug (1802–1858): Ein Wegbereiter der Denkmalpflege,' *Jahrbuch der Denkmalpflege in der Provinz Sachsen und in Anhalt* 6 (1937/1938), p. 106.
46 In his epic poem *Germany: A Winter's Tale* from 1844, Heinrich Heine even hails the cathedral's incomplete state as an accomplishment of Luther and the Reformation. Michael Brix and Monika Steinhauser explain that Heine greeted the 'historical caesura of the Reformation as an advance,' and that for him, 'the Protestant confession [was bound up] with the liberal idea.' Michael Brix and Monika Steinhauser, 'Geschichte im Dienste der Baukunst,' pp. 247–248.

The Suggestive and Anticipatory Quality of Architectural Representations

Hasenpflug's visual projection of the finished Cologne Cathedral numbers among a large body of images of the cathedral produced in the first half of the nineteenth century. These images were widely disseminated, in no small part thanks to printed reproductions. The decades-long discussion about the completion of the Cologne Cathedral was highly dependent on images. Indeed, broad public interest in the project was launched by the rediscovery of the original medieval architectural sketches between 1814 and 1816.[47] By 1817, Georg Moller had produced true-to-scale facsimiles of these original planning sketches.[48] As the Berlin Kupferstichkabinett's example demonstrates, the print could be mounted on canvas and shadowed in afterwards (fig. 12). In a letter of 1819, Goethe alludes to the suggestive power of this extremely large-scale, almost sculptural-seeming print. He describes how he begins to visually anticipate the completion of the cathedral:

> Through the remoteness required to assess the whole, an image lodges itself in the imagination, supplanting reality—which makes for a very pleasant gratification for the eye and the senses.[49]

When the representation of architecture exceeds the scope of a 'mere silhouette of lines,'[50] the structure is accordingly completed by the imagination of the viewer. The resulting mental image is on equal footing

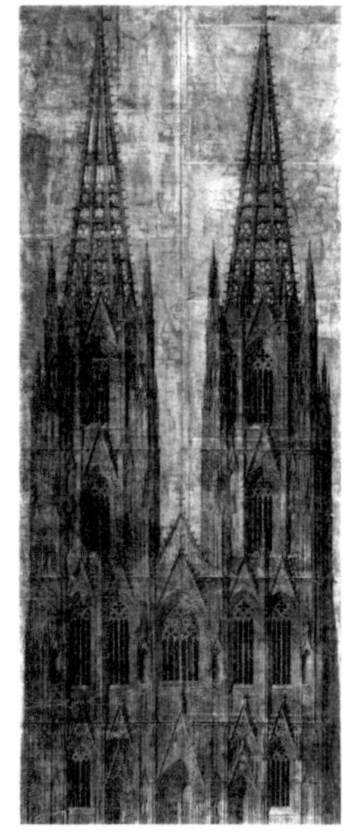

Fig 12 Karl Friedrich Schinkel, *West façade of the Cologne Cathedral*, 1817, 400 x 170 cm

47 Gertrud Klevinghaus, 'Die Vollendung des Kölner Doms im Spiegel deutscher Publikationen der Zeit von 1800 bis 1842,' PhD dissertation, University of Cologne, Cologne, 1971, pp. 36–37; Klaus Niehr, 'Ansichten, Risse und einzelne Theile: Abbildungen des Kölner Doms als Dokumente früher Kunstgeschichte,' *Kölner Domblatt: Jahrbuch des Zentral-Dombau-Vereins* 55 (1990), p. 169.
48 Ibid., p. 171.
49 'In der Entfernung, in der man das Ganze übersehen muß, macht es gerade ein Bild, das sich in der Einbildungskraft an die Stelle der Wirklichkeit setzt, woraus eine sehr angenehme Befriedigung für Auge und Sinn sich hervorthut,' letter from Goethe to Boisserée from 7 August 1819. Sulpiz Boisserée and Johann Wolfgang von Goethe, *Briefwechsel/Tagebücher*, vol. 2, facsimile reproduction of the first edition from 1862 (Göttingen: Suhrkamp/Insel, 1970), p. 249.
50 Johann Wolfgang von Goethe, 'Über Kunst und Alterthum, Band 2, Heft 2' (1820), *Johann Wolfgang Goethe: Sämtliche Werke: Briefe, Tagebücher und Gespräche*, ed. Friedmar Apel et al., vol. 20: *Ästhetische Schriften 1816–1820*, ed. Hendrik Birus (Frankfurt am Main, 1999), p. 405.

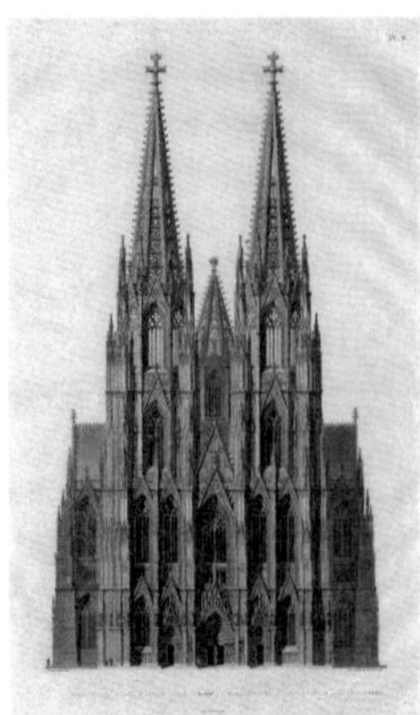

Fig 13 M.H. Fuchs/Mauchert,
*Idealised vision of the west
façade of the Cologne
Cathedral*, 1823, engraving

with one's visual perception of an actual structure.

Sulpiz Boisserée also made use of this suggestive power of persuasion in his own work on the cathedral from 1821, positioning the irregular, fragmentary condition of the building's body against an idealized, completed vision (fig. 11, 13). Both these engravings and Hasenpflug's paintings can be interpreted as a form of 'materialization of fiction,'[51] imprinting themselves upon the viewer due to their 'qualities of creating, shaping—that is, through their iconic potential,'[52] and thus contributing to and helping shape the viewer's perception of the structure.

While orthogonal parallel projections convey the idea of a building within a flat symbolic system of true-to-scale lines, the sculptural quality of Boisserée's and Hasenpflug's depictions delivers them from the surface of the medium that bears their image. We could make a differentiation here between the two properties of an image along the lines of Lambert Wiesing's reflections on phenomenological reduction—the property of being representational and the property of being a representation.[53] The image as a representation makes it possible that 'the viewer regards the image not to see the attendant material circumstances—the canvas, the paper—but to see the absent, represented circumstance, the so-called "image object."'[54] Conveying this theory of the image to the medium of architecture, one could argue that the architectural depiction rendered in perspective is the strongest generator of this effect. On the other hand, the linear architectural sketch, usually complemented by annotations and indications

51 Winfried Nerdinger, 'Vom Bauen imaginärer Architektur,' *Zwischen Architektur und literarischer Imagination*, ed. Andreas Beyer, Ralf Simon, and Martino Stierli (Munich: Wilhelm Fink, 2013), p. 172.
52 Gerhard Paul, *Bilder, die Geschichte schrieben: 1900 bis heute* (Göttingen: Vandenhoeck & Ruprecht, 2011), p. 8. Paul defines the iconic potential of an image on the basis of, among other things, 'formal design elements like composition and perspective, light and colour, contrast and depth of field,' and emphasises that images with an iconic quality have the 'possibility' to 'convey interpretations and meanings that are not exhausted by their character as reproductions.' While he is primarily referring to media icons that reach a far greater audience than architectural representations, I believe his thoughts on the imperative persuasive power of images can also be applied to this iconographic genre. Ibid., p. 13.
53 Lambert Wiesing, 'Phänomenologische Reduktion und bildliche Abstraktion,' *Einfühlung und phänomenologische Reduktion: Grundlagentexte zu Architektur, Design und Kunst*, ed. Thomas Friedrich and Jörg H. Gleiter (Berlin: LIT, 2007), p. 314.
54 Ibid.

of scale, functions as a representational medium for architecture—less a mimetic simulation than a symbol.

This effect of evoking spatiality that is inherent to architectural depiction—the effect, in Goethe's words, of 'lodg[ing] itself in the imagination, supplanting reality'— is of crucial significance for the genre of architectural painting.[55] This is particularly true in the case of Hasenpflug, whose architectural representations were so exhaustively and learnedly composed that the register in the 1840 *Kunstblatt* listed him as an 'architect and painter.'

This makes it possible to compare the construction of buildings to the imaginary construction of architecture in images. Without depreciating the physical significance of actual structures, this approach frees architectural painting from a purely servile function within the process of conceiving and conveying built structures.

In conclusion, it can be said that nineteenth-century architectural painting was a crucial component of the contemporary culture of monuments, with a hand in shaping early efforts toward monument preservation and with an active role in the process of establishing monuments. Architectural painting, as the materialization of an imagined history, shaped how built monuments were received, and thereby shaped the perception of the national past. On the one hand, architectural painting supported identification with the state in the interests of the Prussian king;[56] on the other hand, a bourgeois perspective also came to inform the new appraisal of medieval structures. In particular, after the Napoleonic Wars, the reference back to the sixteenth century resonated among those hoping for a political right to self-determination for an increasingly emancipated citizenry.

In Hasenpflug's idealised vision of architecture, in his reconstructed monuments, and above all in his views of cities populated by citizens, Hasenpflug's

---

55 Letter Goethe to Boisserée from 7 August 1819. Sulpiz Boisserée and Johann Wolfgang von Goethe, *Briefwechsel/Tagebücher*, p. 249.
56 Dolff-Bonekämper, 'Wahr oder falsch. Denkmalpflege als Medium nationaler Identitäts-konstruktionen,' p. 236.

work expresses a vision of the past oriented toward the future that cannot be characterized as 'Biedermeier' or 'Restoration era.' They have neither a purely objective-representational nor a nostalgic-reconstructive character. Rather, these works are meant to formulate an independent, future-oriented interpretation of history. By firmly establishing a subjective representation of the past, they shape a particular collective perception of history. Kurt Forster formulated pointedly that 'only portrayals of buildings assure them a chance to survive in the collective consciousness, as memory will always reduce what it pries from experience to icons.'[57]

Transferred to nineteenth-century architectural painting, this means that the staging of medieval structures in paint contributed to their establishment within the collective memory.

And beyond this, the way in which cathedrals were iconized in the nineteenth century influenced the perception of medieval architecture in such lasting fashion that, over the course of the nineteenth and twentieth centuries, and above all in the period of reconstruction following World War II, these very structures often began to resemble the shape originally anticipated in the image.

---

57 Kurt W. Forster, 'Bau, Bild und Bühne: Wie Schinkel seine Architektur veranschaulicht,' *Karl Friedrich Schinkel: Geschichte und Poesie, Das Studienbuch*, ed. Hein-Th. Schulze Altcappenberg and Rolf H. Johannsen (Berlin/Munich: Deutscher Kunstverlag, 2012), p. 72.

The use of minimum means—human bodies alone—attempts to downscale and de-monumentalize history by reconstructing it on a human scale.

Quote
Alexandra Pirici, *Actualizing History in the Living Body as Subject-Object*
→ **See p. 209**

Artworks allow viewers in the present to grasp past constructions of temporality different from their own—grasp them not as utterly foreign, but as both familiar and distinct.

Quote
Steven ten Thije quoting
Michael Gubser on Riegl
→ **See p. 365**

Essay
John Byrne

History, Use-Value, and the Contemporary Work or Labour of Art

Until relatively recently, asking 'what kind of work is the work of art' would immediately open up a well-rehearsed discourse surrounding a range of familiar and received wisdoms. More often than not, these romanticized clichés and sedimented forms of common sense depended, almost exclusively, on the deployment of a set of key terms and conditions that framed the specific role and function of art and artists in Western culture and society: alterity, aesthetic autonomy, artistic vision, and an almost messianic commitment to the ideology of the artist as secular shaman.

Likewise, to ask 'what is the use-value of the work or labour of art'[1] would, more often than not, open up an alternative set of debates and assumptions about utility, function, purpose, and instrumentalized culture. It also followed that these two kinds of debates pointed toward a fundamental schism or divide within Western culture, between the autonomy of art and the heteronomy of everyday life, which it was the sole purpose of the historical avant-garde to somehow bridge or reconcile. In doing so, it was also assumed that the historical avant-garde might be able to also offer us both aesthetic and political alternatives that would help us to imagine ways of living otherwise.

However, over the last decade or so it has become far more common for those involved in the art world to propose that art occupies both the spaces of autonomy and heteronomy. To put this another way, it has now become safer to assume that art's use-value and/ or purpose (or useless use-value and purposeless purpose if you prefer) is that it allows us to keep both the seemingly irreconcilable opposites of autonomy and heteronomy in a kind of useful tension. Coinciding roughly with the 2002 publication in *New Left Review* of Jaques Rancière's 'The Aesthetic Revolution and its Outcomes: Emplotments of Autonomy and Heteronomy'[2] the idea that a broader 'politics of aesthetics' represents an overarching metanarrative (within which the very struggle for meaning is played out through complex forms of shifting interaction) has allowed for a radical rethink of the role, function, and purpose of art within the terms and conditions of of globalized neoliberalism. At its weakest, this way of thinking has led to a form of pseudo-radicalism

---

1   I use the phrase 'work or labour of art' throughout this essay as a means to both identify, separate (and re-conjoin) three common and problematic senses or distinctions concerning our understanding of art: first, the 'work of art' seen as either an autonomous entity to be experienced as an isolated phenomena; second, the idea of the work of art as an autonomous entity which is imbued with, or somehow embodies, the work (as craftsmanship and skill) and labour (as time and effort spent) on the production of the art object itself—this idea is usually synonymous with the ideology of authorship; and third, the idea of the labour of art as either an individual or collective process, often 'open-ended' which is separate to, and usually bracketed off from, the art object (or work of art) in senses one and two.
2   Jacques Rancière, 'The Aesthetic Revolution and its Outcomes: Emplotments of Autonomy and Heteronomy,' *New Left Review* 14 (March–April 2002), pp. 133–135.

whereby art is seen as a collective noun that can somehow string together a range of practices and experiences that combine both the concrete and the ephemeral—the luxury commodity form of the art object sold at auction on the one hand and ground-up forms of collaborative social intervention on the other. At its best, this possibility has led to a range of projects, practices, and initiatives, undertaken by artists, museums, and galleries alike, which are attempting to renegotiate the Western split between art and life. This, in turn, is opening up the possibility of fundamentally renegotiating the existing structures of accepted institutional relationships that make art possible—artist, artwork, audience, museum, gallery, etc., through practices of constellation thinking, coproduction, and a commitment to active forms of usership.

At the same time as this, it also becomes clear that the more art as we know it (or knew it) changes, the more the old boundaries blur, the harder it becomes to tell what or where art is anymore.[3] Usually, the two answers to this difficulty are quite extreme—either hold on fiercely to what we already know to be art, or let art finally merge, unrecognizably, within the all-encompassing texture of everyday life. Such polarities, of course, return us directly to the bifurcatory logic of autonomy (where art is seen to provide a rebuff against instrumentalized culture) and heteronomy (where there no longer exists a case for art as a useful category in itself). Because of this, I would argue that it is becoming increasingly necessary to reuse history as a contemporary means of navigating between the Scylla and Charybdis of autonomy and heteronomy and to help us imagine alternative forms of future.

An example of this reuse of history was recently given to us by art historian and philosopher Georges Didi-Huberman in his article 'The Supposition of the Aura: The Now, The Then, and Modernity.'[4] Here, Didi-Huberman

3   See John Byrne, 'Critical Autonomy: Inside Out – Outside In,' *The Autonomy Newspaper # 1: Positioning* (Onomatopee 43.1 2010), pp. 14–21.
4   See Georges Didi-Huberman, 'The Supposition of the Aura: The Now, The Then, and Modernity,' in *Walter Benjamin and History*, ed. Andrew Benjamin (London: Continuum, 2005).

argues against an over-simplistic use of Walter Benjamin's work, specifically his 1936 text 'The Work of Art in the Age of Mechanical Reproduction,'[5] as a means to inscribe the 'death' of the 'aura' of an artwork. Instead, Didi-Huberman advocates convincingly for a more sophisticated and dialectical sense of the 'aura' which is embedded in Benjamin's work as a 'falling away': a 'supposition' of the auratic quality of an artwork which subsequently haunts any attempt to rethink the 'loss of originality.' This idea of a history as decline, of a history which haunts the present—rather like the barely visible calligraphic inscriptions that always lurk beneath any attempt at palimpsest—implicates history as the imperfect negotiation of erasure in order to rewrite. In this sense the lessons of history, for Didi-Huberman, are never simply there to be learnt, as if they somehow present an archival index of a future that was yet to be. Instead, the act of history is always a process of becoming. As Didi-Huberman, via Benjamin, puts it 'decline … is part of the "origin" so understood, not the bygone—albeit founding—past, but the two-way flow of a historicity that asks, without respite, even to our own present, "to be recognized as a restoration, a restitution, as something that by that very fact is uncompleted, always open."'[6]

Such an active use of history, of literally allowing ourselves to go back to the future and to remind ourselves of a time when art functioned in very different ways, would allow us to begin actively recuperating the period circa 1848. This was a period of radical thinking, of John Ruskin and Mechanics' Institutes, a period in which art still occupied a useful role in the production of new forms of citizenship. Crucially, this was a time before art and utility, autonomy and everyday life, had gone their own seemingly irreconcilable ways. An active use of this history would, I would argue, provide us with the means to begin reimagining our own current

---

5   Walter Benjamin, *The Work of Art in the Age of Mechanical Reproduction* (New York: Penguin, 2008 [1936]). There are also many versions of this essay which can be found online including www.marxists.org/reference/subject/philosophy/works/ge/benjamin.htm.
6   Didi-Huberman, 'The Supposition of the Aura,' p. 4.

situation. This would also allow us to begin the task of rethinking art and the kind of work, or labour, that the work of art has become (and is still becoming).

I.   In my own research, this operation of returning to the future has led to an ongoing analysis of use-value and exchange-value, in relationship to contemporary art, via Marx.[7] More specifically, I have become interested in Marx's insistence on a bodily/mental split between use-value and exchange-value as a means to re-imagine the shifting and complex relationships between autonomy and heteronomy within our increasingly networked and globalized neoliberal economy. In the early pages of *Das Kapital*, for example, Marx attempts to separate out use-value from exchange-value in any consideration of the commodity form. However, as Fredric Jameson has recently pointed out in his book *Representing Capital: A Reading of Volume One*,[8] this separation also belies a more fundamental and metaphysical distinction in the work of Marx between qualitative materiality and quantitative abstraction. By arguing that use-value does not matter to the capitalist who wishes to sell commodities for profit, Marx simultaneously proposes that use-value in the commodity form is, at best, subsidiary to its potential as exchange-value. One could go as far as to say that, for Marx, the supposition of use-value by exchange-value and profit was the defining condition for the development of the commodity form under capitalism. In doing so, Marx both externalizes use-value from the quantitative and abstract procedures of the commodity form (and its purpose as a vehicle for profitable exchange). At the same time he privileges use-value as something qualitative and material, something that both precedes and becomes lost from the commodity form under capitalism. To put this another way, use-value comes to be seen as the

---

7   John Byrne, 'Back to the Future: Grizedale Arts, Use Value and the Work of Art' available at *Grizedale Arts New Mechanics Institute Library*, www.grizedale.org.

8   See Fredric Jameson, *Representing Capital: A Reading of Volume One* (London: Verso, 2011), pp. 19–20.

bodily and socially produced necessity to satisfy basic human needs and to ensure the continued development of the means of production. It could also be argued that Marx's attempt to separate use-value (as qualitative bodily physicality) from exchange-value (as quantitative mental abstraction) ensures that any subsequent consideration of the commodity form is haunted, at every turn, by the absence of that which it can never fully be.

Marx presents us here with a now familiar ethical and moral hierarchy which clearly places qualitative bodily materiality above quantitative mental abstraction and, ultimately the productive over the ideological. His separation of use-value and exchange-value in the commodity form also marks a historical juncture. This is the point at which any calls for a future beyond capitalism begin to be predicated on use-value and, more often than not, on the valorization of ethical forms of non-alienated work and labour as an inalienable human right. We must, however, remember that the work of Marx was itself also formed and conditioned by this very same historical separation—a division between real and material forces and the abstraction of work or labour, within the growing mechanisms of capitalism, into the mental and judiciary formulation of structures which govern and contain us.[9] It is precisely at this historical moment—roughly the mid-nineteenth century—that we begin to witness the opening up of the familiar gap between art and life. Within this gap the possible complexity (and the potential use-value that the work or labour of art could embody or represent within this complexity) begins to get lost. It is also from this point onward that it becomes possible for the development of a European avant-garde which can imagine its job or work to be that of reuniting art and life. As we also know, it is under the aegis of this unificatory logic that both art's autonomy (as a resistance to the onslaught of

---

9   For example, as Raymond Williams pointed out in his 1977 book *Marxism and Literature*, Marx's own ideas were themselves determined by, and have to be read against, the tumultuous conditions of the Industrial Revolution and its concomitant faith in empirical science. One of the key examples Williams uses here is Marx's assertions that the economic conditions of a determining base of material forces could be read with the accuracy of a science.

mechanized industrialization) and art's utility (as a means of harnessing the power of mechanized industrialization as aestheticized revolutionary potential) begin to be offered up as possible avant-garde solutions to this division.

By returning to the past in this way, it becomes clearer to see the complexity of legacy that we have inherited from this period—a complexity which is obfuscated by the overly simplistic notion of an autonomy/heteronomy divide. On the one hand, the future of art carries with it the possibility of conceiving both autonomy and heteronomy, via use-value, as complex forms of interaction. On the other, the existing infrastructures of art that we have inherited from this period, predicated as they are on the narrow conception of an autonomous art that is capable of staving off the alienating horrors of industrialization, would seem to militate against the very idea of such complex interaction.

II.   However, to bring us sharply back to our present cultural condition, we might well ask what happens to the role and function of art when, as theorist and activist Franco Berardi argues, the hallmarks of modernist avant-garde resistance have long since been co-opted by the rhetorics of financial capitalism, and, more specifically, by the economically driven model of the culture industries.[10] If this is the case, then artists, or for that matter art institutions which see themselves as progressive progenitors of artistic possibility, can no longer simply reach out to the well-rehearsed mantras of artistic autonomy and cultural alterity. As both left and right increasingly occupy the same territory of rhetorical discourse surrounding freedom and community, the implications for our traditional understandings of the work or labour of art would appear to be stark.[11]

Berardi offers one way of thinking and working ourselves out of this melancholic dead end. In his recent

---

10 See Franco Berardi, *After the Future* (Oakland: AK Press, 2011).
11 For a stark account of the artist as 'at best the ultimate freelance knowledge workers and at worst barely capable of distinguishing themselves from the consuming desire to work at all times,' see Liam Gillick, 'The Good of Work,' *e-flux journal* 5, no. 16 (2010), www.e-flux.com/journal/the-good-of-work.

book *The Uprising: On Poetry and Finance*,[12] he argues that the radical deregulation of neoliberal capital is predicated upon the increasing abstraction of language from the body. Deregulatory logic, he suggests, relies on the possibility of endlessly connecting and reconfiguring language into regulated, recombinable and meaningless components. This, he points out, runs counter to the open, porous, and poetic use of language as a fluid form of conjunction—as an endlessly open means of understanding ourselves and each other through evolving forms of communication and growth. In light of this, Berardi proposes that the new job of the artist or poet is to return non-alienated forms of porous, mutable, and productive language to the physical and social body. By recombining language, autonomy and production in this way, Berardi also allows us to go back to the future. We can then begin rethinking the potential of radical alternatives while at the same time, returning to the social and historical bifurcation of use-value and exchange-value.

More specifically, Berardi insists on the distinction between abstract and connective forms of language from material and conjunctive uses of language. In doing so he consciously replays Marx's struggle with the codependency of use-value and exchange-value and its development, through the imposition of capitalism, of abstracted forms of use-value as an ideological means of measurement and calibration. In this way, we can see clear parallels beginning to emerge. On the one hand, between connective forms of language and the quantitative abstraction of exchange-value. On the other, between conjunctive and productive uses of language with the bodily necessity of use-value. Here, the use of language provides a material means to challenge the established status quo of economic predicates and determinates through the material production of new social meanings, and autonomies. These are themselves capable of escaping the gravity of power and its reliance

---

12   See Franco Berardi, *The Uprising: On Poetry and Finance* (Los Angeles: Semiotext(e), 2012).

on increasingly interchangeable, centralized, and regulated forms of connectivity. In this scenario, the job of the artist or poet becomes the work or labour of keeping language alive when there are no longer any simple distinctions between autonomy and heteronomy. If this is the case, then it also follows that the work or labour of art is no longer to unite, bridge, or combine the seemingly irreconcilable— it is to operate as a form of autonomous and social possibility, or use-value, within an already networked and saturated world of deregulatory and delusory logic.

III.   Berardi begins to offer us a useful resource for strategically rethinking what kind of work, or labour, the work of art has now become within a globalized and networked neoliberal economy; that of returning an instrumentalized and abstracted language, reconfigured as a porous and mutable form of poetry, to the physical and social body. But how, we might then ask, is it possible to imagine (let alone effect) such a strategy within a dispersed and networked society that is already predicated upon forms of alienation, instrumentalization, and abstraction on every level? And how can we even begin to imagine forms of resistance and organization, based upon the use-value of art, when all forms of traditional organization and resistance (class, race, gender, religion, sexuality, party affiliation) seem to be collapsing into each other under the weight of flexibilization and the exploitation of precarious labour? How does one radicalize, collectively or individually, when all faith in the mechanisms of inherited political affiliation would seem to be lost?

One way of beginning to think this conundrum through, I would argue, is again offered by Rancière. However, I'm not thinking of Rancière's suggestion of a metapolitics of aesthetics here—as a means of usefully rethinking the interconnectedness and emplotments of political and aesthetic activities that are, fundamentally, made of the same stuff (of a politics and aesthetics that are both, in essence, mechanisms for the re-distribution of the sensible, or of making 'sense of sense and sense' as Rancière puts it). Instead I'm thinking here of the Rancière of 'The Nights of Labour: The Workers' Dream in Nineteenth-Century France,'[13] of the Rancière who looks back to the future at the historical struggle of artisans, workers and craftsmen who used writing—and the growing availability of ground-up political publications in the 1840s—as a means to reuse and challenge existing languages of power and control. In doing so, Rancière consciously avoids the trap of projecting a revolutionary and proletarian class who is yet to be—a mythologized class somehow standing at the ready to free itself from the shackles and yoke of capitalist oppression (when, and only when, it is brought to the full consciousness of its own servitude by enlightened bourgeois revolutionaries). Instead, he weaves a more plausible picture of everyday micropolitical dissent—a rhizomatic reuse of the existing languages of mastery made by a class that is already fully conscious of its own fixed position within the hierarchies of power. For Rancière, this already existing class of fully conscious workers, who are willing to reuse a language that is always too mutable and porous to be owned completely by the hand of their masters, contains within it more revolutionary potential than an idealized and abstracted proletariat to be:

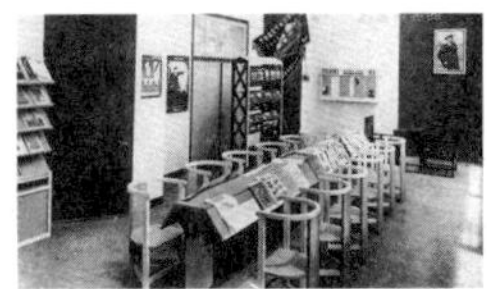

Fig 1　Alexander Rodchenko, Soviet Workers' Club, 1925

> A worker who had never learned how to write and yet tried to compose verses to suit the taste of his times was perhaps more of a danger to the prevailing ideological order than a worker who performed revolutionary songs. ... Perhaps the truly dangerous classes are not so much the uncivilized ones thought to undermine society from below, but rather the migrants who move at the borders between classes, individuals and groups who develop capabilities within themselves which are useless for the improvement

---

13　See Jacques Rancière, *The Nights of Labor: The Workers' Dream in Nineteenth-Century France* (Philadelphia: Temple University Press, 1989).

of their material lives and which in fact are liable to make them despise material concerns.[14]

This kind of work or labour, this continual reuse and reconfiguration of the possibilities offered by language, technology, and existing architectures and protocols of power is now, I would contend, the kind of work, or labour, that the work of art has now become. It is epitomized by the struggle for meaning that is the root of collaborative propositions such as Arte Útil and the new Museum 3.0,[15] and which resides at the heart of projects such as Grizedale Arts's Office of Useful Art.[16]

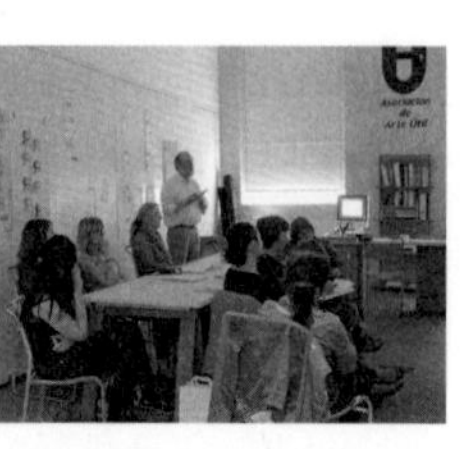

Fig 2 Grizedale's Arts's Office of Useful Art, Grizedale

IV. However, in a sense, this leads us straight back to the key difficulty I pointed to earlier on: How might we envision a useful work or labour of art based around the use-value of conceiving both autonomy and heteronomy as a complex emplotment through which the struggle for meaning is played out? More specifically, how is it possible if to do so would seem to decisively re-invoke a traditional bifurcation between art and life? Again, I would argue that it is now more necessary than ever to reuse history as a means to navigate between the Scylla and Charybdis of autonomy and heteronomy. Additionally, it is equally important to do this through using the past as a means to imagine our possible futures, to escape the strong gravitational pull of our own inherited structures of understanding. Another

14 See Jacques Rancière, 'Good Times or Pleasures at the Barriers,' in *Voices of the People*, ed. Adrian Rifkin and Roger Thomas (London: Routledge & Kegan Paul 1988), pp. 51–58. This essay appeared originally as 'Le bon temps ou la barrière des plaisirs,' *Les Révoltes logiques* 7 (Spring–Summer 1978), pp. 25–66.

15 In his book *Toward a Lexicon of Usership* (which is available as a free .pdf at the Arte Útil website, www.arte-util.org/tools/lexicon/www), Stephen Wright argues that museums and galleries have already adopted elements of Web 2.0 culture insofar as they are relying more heavily than ever on audience participation, feedback, and knowledge production. Wright goes on to speculate that a more radical shift toward the Museum 3.0 may be underway, one which will see the complete breakdown in the museum/audience divide. Instead, we will see the development of coproduced/open-source museums as both online and offline shared resources.

16 The Office of Useful Art is a vehicle for developing ideas of an open source and user-led museum and gallery experience which is coproduced through the active making of art. I have described one of the first iterations of this mechanism, which took place in 2010 as part of the São Paulo Biennial, in my article 'Back to the Future: Grizedale Arts, Use Value and the Work of Art,' cited previously. Since then the Office of Useful Art has amalgamated with artist Tania Bruguera's Association of Arte Útil and has manifested itself in Tate Liverpool and Ikon Gallery, Birmingham. There is now a permanent Office of Useful Art at Middlesbrough Institute of Modern Art (under the directorship of Alistair Hudson) and also further plans to continue developing this project.

key example of (or 'blueprint' for) this kind of historical methodology that helps us understand the problematic bifurcation of autonomy and heteronomy—and its potential use-value for radical change—is found in T. J. Clark's *Farewell to an Idea: Episodes from a History of Modernism*.[17] In his discussion of the Abstract-Expressionist painter Jackson Pollock, Clark makes an astonishing assertion: 'Modernism is Craftmanship' he declares 'even in its wildest moments.'[18] Here, Clark refers to a particular outtake of a Hans Namuth film in which Pollock appears to be using two brushes that have been fused together by dried paint. He uses this as a tool for carefully dripping his own paint at a consistent and variable speed onto a floor-based canvas. By making this assertion, and by using this particular example, Clark usefully confronts a complex process here. In doing so, he studiously avoids any attempt to normalize it. In the act of Pollock's making, Clark suggests that 'there had to be built in a whole series of obstacles to aesthetic freezing and framing. Aesthetic decision-making had somehow to be ingested into the act of manufacture, the de-skilled address to the surface from above.[19] Perhaps even more interestingly, Clark then goes on to quote from Hegel's *The Unhappy Consciousness* by identifying this decision-making moment as 'the positive moment of practicing what it does not understand.'[20]

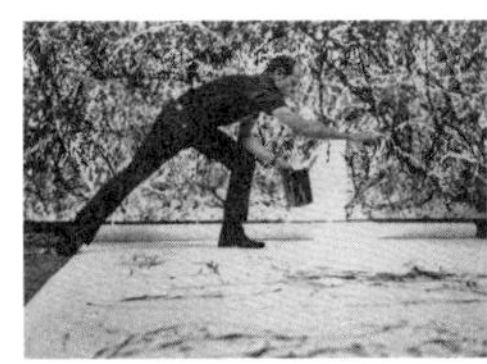

Fig 3 Hans Namuth, Jackson Pollock painting in his studio at Springs, Long Island, 1950, gelatine silver print

By analyzing Pollock's methodology in this way, Clark takes us right back to Hegel's identification of modernity as a moment in which both self-sameness and contingency (or, for the sake of our argument, autonomy and heteronomy) tragically confront one another as opposites. 'The "Simple Unchangeable" on one side, the "protean Changeable" on the other,'[21] as Clark succinctly puts it. At this point in history, absolute individuality (undividedness) and the endlessness of difference confront each other in

---

17   See T. J. Clark, *Farewell to an Idea: Episodes from a History of Modernism* (New Haven: Yale University Press, 1999).
18   Ibid., p. 328.
19   Ibid., p. 328–329.
20   Ibid., p. 329.
21   Ibid., p. 329.

what, for Hegel, is the essence of Spirit or Consciousness: the being together of the both in one. But the essence of modernity, for Hegel, was also its failure to grasp this—and this, of course, is also the root of our bifurcatory logic. The unhappy consciousness knows this bifurcation but simply cannot accept it. These two sides of self-consciousness are, for the 'unhappy consciousness,' alien to each other.

So far, so familiar. However, Clark also goes on to remind us (regarding Hegel) that, because the unhappy consciousness is itself the product of this division—brought into being, if you like, by the very friction of this opposition—it sides with the changeable consciousness (heteronomy) and 'takes itself to be the unessential Being.' Therefore, the real problem for Clark (again, regarding Hegel), lies in the inability of the unhappy consciousness to 'lay hold of mere difference and embrace it as its Truth because difference turns on indifference, and contingency on essential nature.'[22] As a consequence of this (and through, as Hegel defines it, a series of 'movements of surrender'—first of all the right to decide for itself, then of the right to decide its property and enjoyment and, finally, through the positive moment of practicing what it does not understand) the unhappy consciousness 'truly and completely deprives itself of the consciousness of inner and outer freedom, of the actuality in which consciousness exists *for itself*. It has the certainty of having truly divested itself of the "I," and of having turned its immediate self-consciousness into a *Thing*, into and *objective* existence."[23]At this point, Clark usefully reminds us that the movements of surrender that Hegel had in mind are those of modern religion and its forms and, for Clark, the way in which 'the religious surrenderings have been extended and amplified by those of art.' Clark then goes on to conclude this remarkable section of his book by stating that: "this would be the level on which even the self-satisfied Leftist claptrap about 'art as a substitute

---

22 Ibid., p. 329.
23 Ibid., p. 329.

religion' might be reworked so as to have some critical purchase … . To investigate why *God is not Cast Down*."[24]

This return to Hegel, via Clark, as a means to re-understand the necessity of Modernity's bifurcatory project, as well as its own essential misunderstanding of the conditions of its possibility as a bringing together of those bifurcatory opposites is, I would say, crucial here. If the self-sameness of identity (of autonomy, of a God who is not cast down) thereby underpins the very means of our surrender to an endless difference (and eventual indifference) of heteronomy, in which our self-identity is just one objectifiable contingency amongst others, then, by proxy, the endless fractalization through which neoliberal logic would alienate us from our own bodies does not, indeed cannot, guarantee the inevitability of our total surrender to this logic.

In this sense, the return of language to the body, which Berardi would advocate was now the job of the artist, would also depend (dare I say for its revolutionary success) upon the aesthetics of decision making being 'somehow' ingested—as we have already seen Clark put it in his analysis of Pollock—'into the act of manufacture, the de-skilled address to the surface from above.' A willful act, if you like, of re-inscribing precisely that line of bifurcatory distinction which modernity, and by proxy the avant-garde, sought so hard to ameliorate and undo. However, this time the re-inscription of this bifurcatory line would not be a decisive act of foreclosure or censure. Instead, it would be to allow, once again, the conjunctive 'working through' of art and life, use-value and exchange-value, as a means to reopen the possible dynamic of real social change, as the being together of the both in one. This sense of a reframing manufacture, as we have also seen, is for Hegel 'the positive moment of practicing what it does not understand.' It can also help us to repurpose Rancière's historical identification of a worker who attempts to reuse the available languages of mastery

---

24 Ibid., p. 329.

as a means to create alternative possibility. In so doing, they might keep alive a sense of agency within the all-encompassing confines of global neoliberalism. We can then, again, imagine that it is those migrants who refuse their place, who move between and across the fractalized borders of our endlessly networked culture, who are most effective in the production of real social change.

However, it is at this point, above all, that we must not fall back into the romantic trap of reinvesting the familiar object with the magical ability to negatively resist the ravages of the culture industry. Instead, if we are at the point where it is possible to reimagine our future through a revolutionary participation in a period of true change, then we must also allow our notion of art—what it can be, who can make it, where it can gain visibility, and how it can be used—to radically mutate. As such, the artwork now belongs as but one nodal point within a network of choices and refusals. In light of this, the craft of history is, of course, no longer the act of bearing transparent witness to ontological certitude. The use-value of art has now become the work of tracing a strategic pathway back through those rhizomatic networks of choice and refusal. It has become the collaborative use of art as a means to actively rework our histories as a political means to negotiating our alternative futures.

Pa
Practic
Know
and

Part 2

Making Art,
Knowledge,
Use

Practicing Art, Knowledge, and Use

Introduction
Nick Aikens

The contributions in the following section offer a means to navigate the varied terrain of this reader from the perspective of artistic practice. 'Practicing Art, Knowledge, and Use' is approached through a series of essays and conversations in which artists reflect on specific projects or modes of working, and artistic contributions that revisit and reconfigure existing works. The mode of address through which 'practice' is mediated deliberately moves across registers, echoing the varied methodologies and relationships at play.

A primary motivation for conceiving this reader is a shared belief that the role ascribed to art—particularly in Western modernism and its accompanying capitalist economy—and the means by which it increasingly turns in on itself has never, historically speaking, been a *fait accompli*. In considering alternative roles for art, we wanted to examine art practice that faced out into different societies and histories, absorbing them, mirroring them, or acting within them as a way to open up new cultural, discursive, and social spaces. Specifically within this section we were interested in considering how this mode of working is approached today.

Where were these practices facing socially, temporally, politically? And what methodologies and strategies were being deployed?

Whilst the structure of this section (and the reader) works against establishing a fixed trajectory or set groupings, a few key fields have become pronounced. The first involves the strategies deployed in film and video in providing an aesthetic and conceptual framework within which to address history. The film works presented here allow for different references, images, and modes of address to interlace. Their construction often uses techniques of montage, revealing the capacity of these works to incorporate and speak to different temporalities. Second, the use of actions, performance, and intervention as modes of working that disrupt the relationship between past and present also emerge as a strand within the section. Interestingly, these make available a means to address different forms of institutionalism (cultural, economic, or media) and processes of historicization. The section closes with a series of practices that deliberately blur boundaries between art and community, activist, or even commercial projects. Taking place over long periods of time and necessarily involving a range of protagonists, such practices aim to move beyond a position of criticality in order to think how art can act in the world today.

Viewed together, these essays and conversations explore how politics is articulated through the methodology of artistic practice—the use of image, history, or by leaving the framing of art altogether. The methodologies within different practices variously draw on, mine, and flee modes of representation and aesthetic strategies. None of them are concerned with representation and aesthetics per se. Rather, they show a drive to explore what role they can adopt in mediating particular historical and political impulses. Perhaps they are best summarized as showing art's possibilities, means, and scope to *resist*: outspokenly as part of a political act of resistance; strategically, in order that it might resist and overcome the limits of its domain, reappearing elsewhere; or nimbly, as a way to resist fixed meanings or temporalities.

Understanding the evolving relationship to its own modes of (re)presentation is to recognize that these methodologies and debates are never usurped or replaced. Like Walter Benjamin's historical constellation, the range of practices discussed here are always, in part, a result of preceding methodologies as well as the given conjuncture at which they appear.[1] That these methodologies have taken place in varied guises and contexts, within and outside artistic practice, is a measure of art's porous, contingent relationship to the surroundings from which it emerges.

To understand this range in trajectory we could begin with a distinction made by Jean-Luc Godard and used by Georges Didi-Huberman in his essay on the use of montage in the filmmaker's work. Godard famously talked of the distinction between 'making political films' and 'making films politically,' arguing that only the latter 'is to understand the laws of the objective world in order to actively transform the world.'

Indeed, Didi-Huberman's premise is that in the work of Goddard 'the sterile dichotomy of form and content can be overcome.' Montage, according to Didi-Huberman is dialectics, and that is how images can punctuate different perspectives in relation to history.

A different form of montage and quotation emerges in Yael Bartana's *And Europe Will Be Stunned* (2007–2011), analyzed by Sarah Stehr. Stehr looks at the trilogy of films that follows the fictional Jewish Renaissance Movement. She argues that the means by which Bartana mines different histories (from early Zionists films to Stalinist propaganda) and intermingles these with the present (its poignant locations in Warsaw for example) is also a form of montage that presents 'kaleidoscopic-like representations of antagonistic worldviews and history within the twentieth century.'

In Catarina Simão's research project and film, *Effects of Wording* (2014), the Portugese artist delved into the history of the first FRELIMO school in Dar es Salaam during the liberation movement of Mozambique. Reflecting on the project here, Simão reveals that her interest in the school came from how it served as a radical form of pedagogy as part of the militant FRELIMO movement. As Simão scoured archival material across three continents, specifically a textbook from and documentary film about the school, her interest settled on the indexical nature of the stills she saw, the way in which language was repurposed as a radical pedagogical device, and how she as a filmmaker could use word and image to generate readings and interpretation. In *Effects of Wording* 'making political films' and 'making films politically' seem to converge.

In the first of the artistic contributions Wendelien van Oldenborgh's *Beauty and the Right to the Ugly* (2014) similarly merges a narrative of a past social project with the methodology of the film's construction. Taking the history of the multi-functional building 't Karregat in Eindhoven, Van Oldenborgh constructs her three-part film as a collective process between herself, the building, and her protagonists, past users of the building. Here, Van Oldenborgh revisits the project,

---

1   See Thomas Lange, 'Constellating History' in this reader, pp. 16–17.

using the format of the publication as a means to bring in different different research and presentation methodologies such as press clippings, film stills, and installation shots.

In the two contributions by Manuel Pelmuş and Alexandra Pirici they reflect on their work *Public Collection of Modern Art* (2014), a series of live restagings of historical works that took place in the central gallery for the exhibition *Confessions of the Imperfect, 1848–1989–Today*. Pelmuş and Pirici discuss how history becomes replayed through performance. Yet, unlike in Bartana's trilogy, this consideration is literally embodied with images manifest in movement that continually resists aesthetic capture. Taking place over the three months of the exhibition, history becomes durational in new ways, 'claiming,' as Pelmuş writes, 'a temporality that becomes permanence.'

If history is reflected or refracted through *Public Collection*, mirroring is central to Thomas Lange's interpretation of German film and theatre director Christoph Schlingensief's *Bitte liebt Österreich – Erste Europäische Koalitionswoche* [Please Love Austria — First European Coalition Week], the seven-day public action that took place outside the opera house in Vienna from 11–17 July 2000. By initiating this project in all its varied, appropriated forms (from reality TV show to populist tabloid newspaper to xenophobic zeitgeist then haunting Austria) and the deluge of responses that it created, Lange argues that Schlingensief showed history in a nightmarish playback loop. This was a Benjaminian constellation of history simultaneously reemerging in the present—the past revealing itself as 'latent' and 'undead.' Significantly Schlingensief's work shows how artist moves from author or even collaborator in a project to initiator of a series of unfolding events and relationships in which he or she can only become a bystander.

In Li Mu's *A Man, A Village, A Museum* (2010–2015) we are presented, through drawings and the Chinese artist's letters to Van Abbemuseum director Charles Esche, with the story of Li Mu's wish to bring the history of Western modernism into dialogue with rural China. Constructing copies of works from the Van Abbemuseum, by artists such as Dan Flavin, Sol LeWitt, and Andy Warhol, Li Mu worked with local artisans to install the pieces in the streets and on the buildings of his home village of Qiuzhuang, 800 km from Beijing. Here quotation resurfaces across continents and cultures, similarly proposing new ways in which the museum might rethink and reuse the remnants it holds from modernism's past.

Quotation is equally central to Trevor Paglen and Jacob Appelbaum's *Autonomy Cube* (2014), which I discuss with him in this section. The work, which formally appropriates Hans Haacke's *Condensation Cube* (1963–1965)—in which a square of thick glass is presented on a white pedestal—houses a modem that is part of the Tor network, allowing users to surf the Internet without being tracked. *Autonomy Cube*, whilst positioning itself within the history—and development—of institutional critique, seeks to move, as Paglen states, into the realm of 'institutional enhancement.' Significantly, Paglen talks about how his interest lies in reclaiming the political traction of autonomy from the interpretive limitations imposed on it through modernist art criticism. With *Autonomy Cube* we see a shift occurring from the representational realm to the actual, into what Stephen Wright has termed the 1:1 scale artwork.

The forerunner to Wright's notion of the 1:1 scale artwork is perhaps Allan Kaprow's term 'non-art' referred to in artist's text 'The Blurring of Art and Life.' Kaprow, as George Yúdice emphasizes in his essay on the collective Static Gallery, was also an important reference for these British artists. Yúdice points out that Static's projects 'surf financial, publicity, and institutional flows,' instituting different micro-economies as a means to infiltrate cultural and art world circuits. These projects, which here include Noodle Bar (2008–2009) and Paul's KIMCHI Co. (2014–present), often quote and mimic commercial enterprises, as Yúdice claims, to 'ensure the generation of contradictions.'

Seemingly moving further away form the known domain of art, Christina Aushana and Melinda Guillen reflect on Tamms Year Ten,

an art project by Laurie Jo Reynolds that over
a decade campaigned and succeeded in
closing a maximum security prison in Illinois,
Chicago. Reading Aushana's and Guillen's
texts, the affinity Reynolds's approach has
with both feminist and durational practices
are striking. Here, it is no longer a question
of distinguishing between making political
art or making art politically. Rather, Reynolds
seems to suggest how we might practice
politics artfully. Significantly, Aushana's
and Guillen's contributions also signal the
need for alternative forms of interpretation
and criticism to address such practice.

Jeanne van Heeswijk's *Freehouse*
(2008–present), represented here through
a sequence of graphic maps, diagrams, and
illustrations, is another example of practice
fleeing museums and galleries. Her project,
begun in 2008 in the Afrikaanderwijk district
of Rotterdam, the Netherlands, was initiated
as a means to empower local residents
in the face of a regeneration programme
threatening the status of the local migrant
population. *Freehouse* recently formed a
workers' co-operative, meaning they are in
a position to self-organize as well as lobby
local politicians on issues affecting them.
Translated graphically, her contribution allows
us to conceptualize the different networks,
spaces, and interests implicated in *Freehouse*.

Both Tamms Year Ten and *Freehouse* were
included in the exhibition *Museum of Arte
Útil* at the Van Abbemuseum. The section
concludes with the first part of a conversation
between Annie Fletcher and Tania Bruguera,
the Cuban artist who initiated the Arte Útil
project. Prefaced by Bruguera's manifesto on
Arte Útil, the conversation reflects on the need
for artists to form collective agency that could
counter different forms of institutionalization
and commercialization that she feels has left
us with a sense of uselessness. Interestingly,
Bruguera sees Arte Útil as having the capacity
to harness 'desire': 'let's put desire on
track,' she says, 'in action and let's do it.'

Art exists rightly only when it is the means of knowledge, or the grace of agency for life.

Quote
John Ruskin, *The Relation of Art to Use*
→ **See p. 19**

An ecology of
knowledge can only
be based on the fact
that all knowledge is
always inter-knowledge,
a knowledge based
on the relationship and
antagonism of ideas.

Quote
Manuel Borja-Villel, *Use,
Knowledge, Art, and History*
→ **See p. 416**

Essay
Georges
Didi-Huberman

Between Hysteria and History

DIALECTIC OF MONTAGE IN
JEAN-LUC GODARD'S WORK

Are images symptoms or are they syntheses?
When asking that question you inevitably start
wondering about montage practices and the degree
of importance of the images. Because in the first
place—like words in a language—they coexist.

But how? In what form? That's the whole question. Here we might start from the striking ideas of Bertolt Brecht and Walter Benjamin on the arts of montage, seen as a way of effectuating—dialectically, poetically, and politically—certain *standpoints* vis-à-vis history.[1]

In two excellent texts, dating from 1931 and 1939, relating to Brecht's epic theatre, Benjamin did not fail to unite various fundamental motifs that Jean-Luc Godard literally implements in his own montage practices: 'quotable gesture' inherent in every Brechtian scene is said to be obtained by 'interruptions in action'—a series of 'jerks,' 'shocks,' 'breaks in action' (as Benjamin also says)—which play the formal role of authentic 'cuts' or frames that can be used as inseparable elements, of monads destined to be combined with one another. These are authentic *dialectical images*, 'dialectics at a standstill' integrated in the dynamic of a montage, 'comparable as such with the images of a cinema tape.'[2] Quotations, framing, interruptions, all contribute to producing what Benjamin calls an 'experimental arrangement' in which the famous Brechtian 'alienation' encounters its own form.[3]

In this way the forms position themselves. 'Forms that think,' Godard will soon say. Forms that, in their very poetics, bring about a conception of history and a political practice. It would not be very difficult to recognize in Godard's choices—with the exception of a few slight, but decisive differences, as we shall see—the appearance of this new artist figure from 1934 onward whom Benjamin termed the 'author as producer' [*Der Autor als Produzent*]. It certainly is not the film director of *Passion* (1982) who would consider Benjamin's premise to be wrong. The question related to the 'right of the poet to exist' in the context of the contemporary political and social struggles of the world (Benjamin's text was presented as an address to the Institute for the Study of Fascism in Paris on 27 April

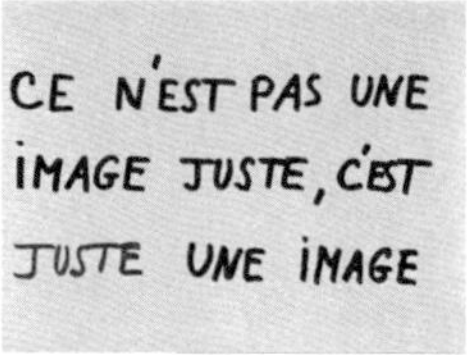

CE N'EST PAS UNE
IMAGE JUSTE, C'EST
JUSTE UNE IMAGE

Fig 1 Intertitle from the film *Vent d'Est* (1970) by Jean-Luc Godard and the Dziga Vertov Groupe

---

1   See also Georges Didi-Huberman, *Quand les images prennent position: L'œil de l'histoire, 1* (Paris: Éditions de Minuit, 2009).
2   Walter Benjamin, 'Qu'est-ce que le théâtre épique?' (1931), in *Essais sur Brecht*, trans. Philippe Ivernel (Paris: Fabrique Éditions, 2003), pp. 30–32 and 41–45.
3   Ibid., pp. 21–24.

1934).[4] When, a few lines further on, Benjamin sought to convince his interlocutors that 'a political work is likely to function in political terms only if it also functions in literary terms.'[5] He anticipated in his way the 'Godardian' manifestos from the end of the 1960s, for example 'Fighting on two fronts,'[6] or else the famous texts entitled 'What is to be done?' in 1970:

1   We must make political films.
2   We must make films politically.
3   1 and 2 are antagonistic to each other and belong to two opposing conceptions of the world … .
17   To carry out 1, is to understand the laws of the objective world in order to explain the world.
18   To carry out 2, is to understand the laws of the objective world in order to actively transform the world.
19   To carry out 1, is to describe the wretchedness of the world.
20   To carry out 2, is to show the people in struggle.[7]

Certainly, do show the people in struggle, but show them in the freedom of these 'experimental arrangements' in which the artist, far from being subjugated to the unadulterated messages dictated by some 'party line' or other, energetically refuses to separate form from content—proving that the 'living social contexts' (again in Benjamin's terms) never cease to question forms and transform our languages.[8] We know the author of *Einbahnstraße* [One-Way Street] (1928) saw, in connection with technique (via the famous question of reproducibility, but not only that) the potential scope for all these connections: 'The concept of technique represents the dialectical starting-point from which sterile dichotomy

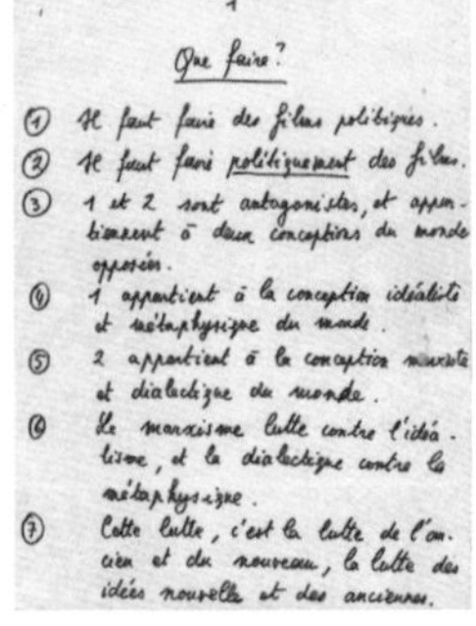

Fig 2 First page of the 39-point manifesto 'What is to be done?' ('Que faire?') written by Jean-Luc Godard for *Afterimage* no. 1, April 1970

4   Walter Benjamin, 'L'auteur comme producteur' (1934), in *Essais sur Brecht*, p. 122.
5   Ibid., p. 123.
6   Jean-Luc Godard, 'Lutter sur deux fronts' (1967), in *Jean-Luc Godard par Jean-Luc Godard*, vol. 1, 1950–1984, ed. Alain Bergala (Paris: Cahiers du cinéma, 1998), pp. 303–327.
7   Jean-Luc Godard, 'Que faire?' (1970), in *Jean-Luc Godard: Documents*, ed. Nicole Brenez and Michael Witt (Paris: Éditions du Centre Pompidou, 2006), p. 145 and 147.
8   Benjamin, 'L'auteur comme producteur,' p. 124.

of form and content can be surmounted.'[9] What is an 'author as producer' in that context other than an artist, capable—as Godard certainly was in the long course of his work—of transforming the conditions for producing his objects, of implementing the 'functional transformation' [*Umfunktionierung*] advocated by Brecht at all levels of creative work, including the economic?[10] Does Benjamin's reflection on '*the "polytechnic" of the author as producer*'— notably with respect to relations between artists who paint and those who photograph, people from the theatre and musicians, poets and journalists[11]—not cover a new field extending to the energy Godard displayed in the cinema, such as typography, sound editing and video engineering, historical research, as well as advertising techniques?

And, lastly, is it not striking that the focus of Benjamin's appeal aimed at this new way of being an artist is none other than what proved to be one of the greatest original aspects of Godard's work, that is, the intimate interweaving of image and language? Taking the example of John Heartfield's photomontages, in the 1920s and 1930s, Benjamin called for 'pulling down these barriers [of the bourgeois production system], overcoming one of the conflicts that oppress intelligent production. In the present case, the barrier between the written word and the image. We should ask the photographer (while also bearing the film producer in mind) if he could add to his shot the intertitle wresting him out of the confines of fashion and valorizing revolutionary practice. We will emphatically make that demand if we—the writers—embark on photography. There again, technical progress, for an author seen as a producer, is the bedrock of his political progress. In other words: within the spiritual production process, to overcome the competences required for production in keeping with bourgeois ideas—that is what makes such production valuable politically. Actually, the competence barriers thrown up between the two productive forces to

---

9   Ibid., p. 125.
10   Ibid., p. 132.
11   Ibid., pp. 126–136.

keep them apart should be broken down. The author as a producer experiences immediate solidarity with other producers, who previously meant little to him (at the same time as experiencing solidarity with the proletariat).'[12]

Does Godard not add intertitles to his 'shots'—I'm not saying 'information,' but 'intertitles': things 'to be read,' removing the images from possible 'weakening' from familiarity? Does he not consider head-on 'technical progress' (video montage, for instance) and 'political progress' (the possibility to reflect on the history of cinema in connection with history itself)? Does he not experience, quite obviously, that 'immediate solidarity with other producers' when, in *Film Socialisme* (2010), for example, he summons people around him by digital video camera and mobile phone. They include Patti Smith with historians from the Comintern, the philosopher Jean-Paul Sartre, by way of a quoted text, with the philosopher Alain Badiou by way of a filmed lecture, the face of Claude Simon with a chanson by Barbara, the intertitle by André Malraux with the famous intertitle from Euronews (with its black screen ending the film): *No comment*?

That is perhaps the primary use of montage for Godard: to *convoke* all possible exuberance of image and language—written and spoken, painted and mimed, Semite and Indo-European, whatever—to *provoke* something resembling paralysis or passion, or acceptation, or distance—again, whatever. *No comment*. It's his personal dialectic, his way of saying 'see, there' [*vois, là*] (which supposes a lengthy focusing process, of proposed relations) and 'there is' [*voilà*] (which supposes to some extent the suspense of a séance à la Zen or Lacan, or else the terse indication of artistic freedom, so to speak: 'period, take it or leave it.')[13] In the Godardian dictionary compiled by Jean-Luc Douin, the word montage ('the art of producing a form that thinks, the art of giving the image

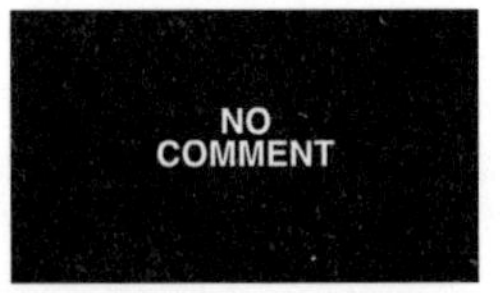

Fig 3 Euronews displays segments of breaking news on live television under the banner *No comment*, which has been the Euronews channel's signature program since its launch

---

12 Ibid., pp. 134–135.
13 For a less terse interpretation, see Suzanne Liandrat-Guigues and Jean-Louis Leutrat, *Godard, simple comme bonjour* (Paris: Harmattan, 2004), p. 13.

a dialectic meaning') is grouped with the, often esoteric, content of *associations* (why and how to combine Manet with Goebbels, via Zola, etc., etc.?) and even with the 'couldn't-care-less' side, the accepted *false connections*.[14]

It was in 1956 that *montage* became a key word for filmmakers, indeed a magic word: 'Montage, my beautiful concern.' It seems highly instructive that this already imposing concept—Sergei Eisenstein devoted thousands of pages to it, from La *non-indifférent nature* (1975) and *Cinématisme* (1980) to manuscripts on his 'Theory of Montage' and 'Method'—was addressed by Godard in the two or three pages of his article by way of a situation that perfectly characterizes his use of speed—both emotional and intellectual—in montage:

> If mise-en-scène is a glance, montage is a heartbeat. Anticipation belongs with both; but what one person tries to anticipate in space, the other seeks in time. Let us suppose that you see a young girl you like in the street. You hesitate about following her. For a quarter of a second. How do you convey that hesitation? Mise-en-scène would reply 'How do you approach her?' But to make the other question explicit: 'Will I love her?', you are obliged to attach importance to the quarter of a second when the two questions come about …. In this example it is clear that to speak of mise-en-scène is automatically to speak again, and already, of montage. When montage effects surpass those of mise-en-scène in efficacity, the beauty of the latter is doubled, the unforeseen unveiling secrets by its charm in an operation analogous to revealing something unknown in mathematics. Anyone succumbing to the attraction of montage also succumbs to the temptation of a short shot. How? By focusing on the main part of the action. Connecting up with a glance—

---

14 Jean-Luc Douin, *Jean-Luc Godard: Dictionnaire des passions* (Paris: Stock, 2010), pp. 40–41, 157–158, and 259–261.

that is pretty well the definition of montage.[15]

At the same time, it is best to mention the decisive importance and fatal fragility of montage: everything passes in a 'locking of eyes,' in a short scene, in the rhythm of a heartbeat. A montage would, therefore, always be on a knife edge: on one side there is the *knowing* of the strategist. Godard expresses it well, it is about 'foreseeing' everything in the dimension of time, the way in which something is revealed, by an algebraic calculation, what he calls an 'unknown.' On the other side there is the *not-knowing* of the lovers: How can you foresee that a girl will be walking in the street, that you will like her, that you will know how to approach her, that you will realize you are capable of loving her? In 'connecting on a look' the filmmaker risks the improbable, charm or failure of an encounter with *the one* whom he calls an 'unknown person.' In short, between the mathematical unknown and the erotic unknown, Godard once more plays on words better to reveal the dimension of montage that is both calculative and poetic, somewhere between a passion of science and a science of passion. Let us not forget that, in this text, the filmmaker would want to quote a well-known line of poetry—yet, as usual, hijacking it—by François de Malherbe, that great calculator of phrases, on the misfortunes of love—that is, the ebb and flow of 'connecting looks':

> Beauty, my beautiful concern for
> which the uncertain soul
> Has, like the ocean, its ebb and flow ...[16]

A compelling example of montage as a process developing on the two fronts of 'passion of science' and 'science of passion' is found in chapter 1(b) of *Histoire(s) du cinéma*.

---

15 Godard, 'Montage, mon beau souci' (1956), in *Jean-Luc Godard par Jean-Luc Godard*, vol. 1, pp. 92–93.
16 François de Malherbe, 'Dessein de quitter une dame qui ne le contentait que de promesse' (1600), in *Œuvres*, ed. Antoine Adam (Paris: Gallimard, 1971), p. 21.

It is even possible to witness its birth in a television sequence shot in December 1987 by Guy Girard and Michel Boujut for the *Cinéma cinémas* programme. There we see Godard at his *desk*—covered with papers, files, photographs, open books—which looks the complete opposite of his *editing table*. The filmmaker shows a famous shot by D. W. Griffith in which we see the body of a woman, apparently Lillian Gish, lying on an ice floe (the image is an extract from the 1920 film *À travers l'orage*). Then he looks for a paper in a file and begins to recite, as if it were a poem, what he maintains are the first texts written for the coming film, the text will in fact be found in the final version of *Histoire(s)*:

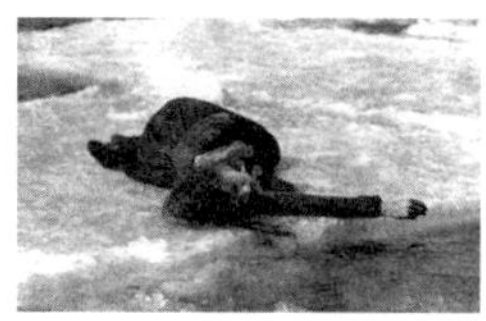

Fig 4   Jean-Luc Godard shows a famous shot by D.W. Griffith in which we see the body of a woman, apparently Lillian Gish, lying on an ice floe. Extract from the 1920 film *Way Down East.*

> and it's the evening of the nineteenth
> these are the beginnings of
> public transport
> and it's the dawn of the twentieth
> these are the beginnings of the treatment
> of hysteria
> it's old Charcot
> who opens to young Freud
> the gates of the dream
> he must find the key to the dreams
> but what is the difference
> between Lillian Gish
> on the ice floc in the storm
> and Augustine at the Salpêtrière Hospital[17]

So there was Gish as the embodiment of the 'unknown revealed' by the embodiment of the primitive master of the glance, of power, of close-up, of montage, etc., who, in Godard's view, continues to be the great D. W. Griffith. There will, as a reverse shot, be the other 'unknown person revealed' by Jean-Martin Charcot, including the scandalous sexual intimacy of an attack of hysteria. Then

---

17   Jean-Luc Godard, *Toutes les histoires — Une histoire seule*, vol. 1 of *Histoire(s) du cinéma* (Paris: Gallimard-Gaumont, 1998), pp. 241–243.

Godard turns toward the bookshelves of his library and extracts a book—published around five years earlier—on the photographic iconography of the Salpêtrière Hospital, a book which, on its cover, depicts graphically the convulsed body and face of the young hysteric.[18] The filmmaker's hands bring together these two images, these two 'fronts,' giving what seems to constitute their dialectic linchpin, which he terms 'public transport'—a well-known metaphor for the progress in urban communications and amorous passion, even the sexual act itself:

> Close-up [Lillian Gish]…
> close-up [Augustine]…
> It's the same image.
> And besides, it's public transport.
> And what is cinema?
> It's public transport,
> in the emotional sense.
> There it is.
> Well, that's it, work.

So is that what Godard means with montage? Might that be the work of 'two thinking hands'[19] setting in motion the convergence of the two images—and the two temporalities, a filming of actors, and medical photography, an artistic story and a scientific document—heterogeneous, as they can in fact be found in the final version of the *Histoire(s)*? If we express it like that it is to emphasize the heuristic plenitude, the potential exuberance of all montage. It is to perceive a *centrifugal movement* of associations producing new ideas, hypotheses, imaginative fantasies, but also authentic knowledge: a gesture with which to multiply the figures, to combine them in 'phrases' endowed with severity regarding *knowledge* (Griffith, Charcot's contemporary,

---

18 Georges Didi-Huberman, *Invention de l'hystérie: Charcot et l'Iconographie photographique de la Salpêtrière* (Paris: Macula, 1982 [revised, adapted, and amplified edition, 2012]).
19 See also Jean-Luc Godard, *Le contrôle de l'univers: Les signes parmi nous*, vol. 4 of *Histoire(s) du cinéma* (Paris: Gallimard-Gaumont, 1998), p. 45.

Charcot close to cinematography, via Albert Londe) and the intensity regarding passion or, at least, *desire* (Gish exposed to the wind in relation to her film-lovers, Augustine exposed to *aura hysterica* in relation to her doctors).

So montage is felt to be a royal road to the requisite union of the desire for knowledge (the algebraic 'unknown') and the knowledge of desire (the erotic 'unknown'). That is no doubt why the key character in the dialogue between Charcot and Griffith would appear to be Sigmund Freud, unless Godard is not comparing himself with old Griffith as he compares Freud with 'old Charcot.' What is this transition from 'old masters' to 'moderns' about? It's about a prelude to the actual idea of mastery linked to the hypothesis of the unconscious. Leading to a prelude to transference, associations, ideas, suspended attention, over-interpretation and, in fact, all the inexhaustible plenitude of the working of the unconscious: the metaphor and metonymy, synthesis and displacement, slip of the tongue and witticism. Last but not least, it is about recognizing and experiencing the powers of figurability in which, according to Freud, all exchanges and conversions proliferate between verbal forms and visual forms. That, in Godard's work, is the seat of the 'metapsychological' legitimacy of his own play of images and word mixtures. That is where the inexhaustible multiplicity of his figures of speech is fully explained: questions, provocations, false slips and real witticisms, portmanteau words, sophisms, going off at a tangent, maxims, aphorisms, chiasms, tautologies, truisms, comparisons, paradoxical formulas, logical arguments, trenchant judgements or, on the contrary, casual refusal to judge...[20]

It is hardly surprising that, in such conditions, Godard expresses his ideas on image and montage far more through quotes from poets than cinema theoreticians

---

[20] See also Jean Collet, *Jean-Luc Godard* (Paris: Éditions Seghers, 1963), pp. 14–37; Jean-Louis Leutrat, *Des traces qui nous ressemblent* (Seyssel: Éditions Comp'Act, 1990), p. 36; Liandrat-Guigues and Leutrat, pp. 7–16 and 73–100; Dominique Chateau, 'Godard, le fragment,' in *Godard et le métier d'artiste*, ed. Gilles Delavaud, Jean-Pierre Esquenazi, and Marie-Françoise Grange (Paris: Harmattan, 2001), pp. 13–14; and Douin, *Jean-Luc Godard*, pp. 263–265 and 294–295.

or actual filmmakers do. This, for example, is the way the great leitmotif comes about inspired by a phrase (itself reworked) by Paul Reverdy about the poetic image:

> an image
> is not strong
> because it is brutal or unreal
> but because the association
> of ideas is distant
> distant, and just …
> if there is any truth
> in the mouths of poets
> I will live[21]

Nor is it surprising, in this perspective of omni-figurability, that Godard's 'poems' function exactly in the same way as his montages of images, as these can function as pure play on words. That is evident in *Les enfants jouent à la Russie* (1993)—from among a good many possible examples—when the succession of single words 'Rome/ the Capitol/ Washington' is constructed to associate the Roman Empire—which we know fell—with American Imperialism.[22] Or else, in *Allemagne année 90 neuf zéro* (1991), Godard unites the 'Roads that go nowhere,' i.e., Heidegger's famous book *Holzwege* (1950), with the *Topographie des Terrors*, the title of a permanent exhibition in Berlin about the occupation of the city by the Nazi administration.[23]

In this way, montage—the thing that, in general, *we do not see* in films, according to Godard—is exactly what links things *so we do see them*.

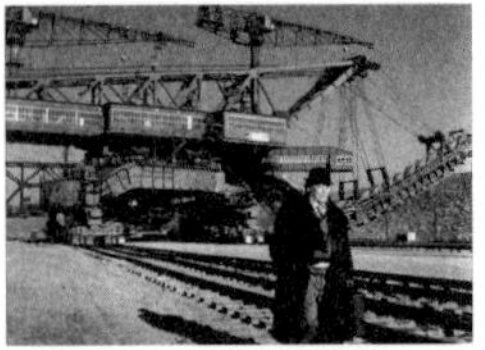

Fig 5 Actor Eddie Constantine, as Lemmy Caution, seeks the West in Jean-Luc Godard's *Allemagne année 90 neuf zéro*, 1991

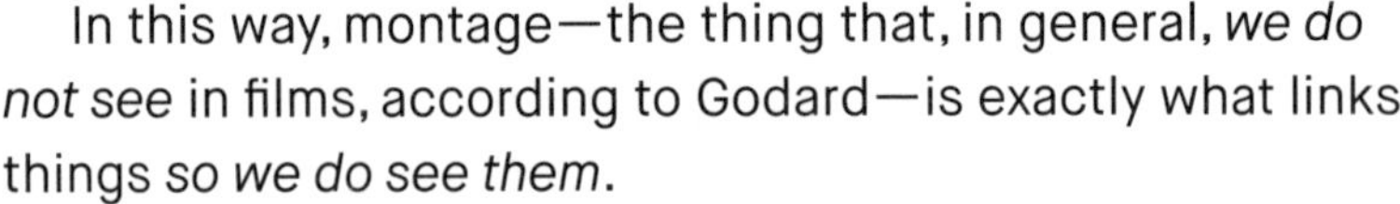

21 Jean-Luc Godard, *JLG/JLG: Autoportrait de décembre. Phrases* (Paris : P.O.L, 1996), p. 21 and 77. See also Godard, *Histoire(s) du cinéma*, vol. 4, p. 259. Two possible variations of this phrase can found in Reverdy: 'Une image n'est pas forte parce qu'elle est brutale ou fantastique—mais parce que l'association des idées est lointaine et juste.' Paul Reverdy, 'L'image,' *Nord-Sud* no. 13 (1918), p. 74. And also: 'Le propre de l'image forte est d'être issue du rapprochement spontané de deux réalités très distantes dont l'esprit seul a saisi les rapports. … L'image montée en épingle est détestable. L'image pour l'image est détestable. L'image de parti pris est détestable. … Il ne s'agit pas de faire une image, il faut qu'elle arrive sur ses propres ailes.' Paul Reverdy, *Le Gant de crin: Notes* (Paris: Flammarion, 1968 [1927]), pp. 32–33. For the concept of the image in Godard's work, see in particular Michael Witt, 'L'image selon Godard: Théorie et pratique de l'image dans l'œuvre de Godard des années 70 à 90,' in *Godard et le métier d'artiste*, pp. 19–32.
22 Jean-Luc Godard, *Les enfants jouent à la Russie: Phrases (sorties d'un film)* (Paris: P.O.L, 1998), p. 32.
23 Jean-Luc Godard, *Allemagne neuf zéro: Phrases (sorties d'un film)* (Paris: P.O.L, 1998), p. 41.

The main aspect in the cinema is what is called
montage—though people do not know what it is. It must
be hidden because it is rather powerful, it is connecting
things and making people see things... an obvious
situation... I mean... A guy who is cuckolded, in as much
as he hasn't seen the other guy who is with his wife:
he who does not have two photos, the man's and his
wife's, or his own and himself, has seen nothing; you
must always see twice... That is what I call montage,
merely a bringing together. That is the extraordinary
power of the image and of the accompanying sound,
or of sound and the accompanying image.[24]

But things come to light, and if you think about that a
little, they appear far more complicated than suggested
here by the Godardian assertion. The paths from *see,
there* to *there is,* are many and are even susceptible
to violently contradictory effects. There is a degree of
naivety—real or feigned, I don't know—in making *montage*
the magic word of the great cinematographic *revelation*.
Montage will remain a 'beautiful concern' as regards its
visual and temporal form, will respect the interplay of
centrifugal associations which constantly allow the work
of figurability to stream forth, engendering so to speak
a state of 'permanent revolution,' in which each image
will be capable of criticizing all that have gone before.
At all events, it is the 'beautiful concern' of what never
wants to end (does a desire which really finally ends not
cease as a desire?). But you can show, you can edit things
differently and for different stakes: even Leni Riefenstahl
also discovered montage to be a basic tool for cinematic
revelation—'montage her beautiful gun,' as it were.
      The dividing line which comes about here should
not, therefore, be sought in content alone but in
ideologies. It is found in the practices themselves and
in the different types of 'playing'—in the Structural

---

24 Jean-Luc Godard, *Introduction à une véritable histoire du cinéma* (Paris: Éditions Albatros, 1980),
p. 22 (see also pp. 175–176).

sense Wittgenstein attributed to that word—they allow or evoke. So we discover that, once more, it is a matter of different *linguistic conventions* from which the handling of images on the one hand, and the horizon of intentionality on the other, both stem. So from now on, the Godardian *No comment* could be interpreted in two absolutely opposite ways: is it a collection of *suspension points* or ellipses denoting something that momentarily is without words, as when a beautiful stranger passes by and one does not yet know how to look at her, how to approach her, if one might be able to love her or not? Or is it a *full point* or full stop, denoting the exact opposite: evidence of something permitting no other word, no explanation—evidence that interrupts you and, algebraically, 'resolves the unknown' in a formula without alternative? Is that the *poem* in which all possible multiples would again flourish, or else the *formula* in which all the multiples, all the possibilities, would be dogmatically reduced to something resembling an ultimate truth?

Godard likes fine phrases, he also likes bons mots. But, in actual fact, they do not say, definitely do not *do* the same thing: because fine—that is, poetic—phrases tend to be open (figurability, multiplication of possibilities, whatever hinders conclusion). Whereas bons mots, however witty they may be, tend to be closed (reducibility, exhaustion of possible options, whatever enables conclusion). So we need to know if, in a particular montage, it is a matter of putting the world into poetry or else into a formula. If Godard manages to confuse the two—and this is exactly the area where his linguistic ethic needs examining—it is undoubtedly because his poetic/political development took a decisive turn at the end of the 1960s—the period of *La Chinoise* (1967) or *Le Gai Savoir* (1969), the period in which he was quite well informed about reconciling Rimbaud with Mao. It was the period of the Dziga Vertov Group (1968–1972) when political watchwords were being chanted like poems and poems recited like watchwords, for example in the pro-Palestinian film *Jusqu'à la victoire* (1970), reworked in *Ici et ailleurs* in 1976.

A substantial part of Godard's work, including his most recent creations or standpoints (I'm thinking specifically of the link he forges between *Ici et ailleurs* and *Notre Musique* [2004], thirty years later) will probably not be included to the very end, just as an intellectual history of French Maoism will not be conducted in a precise (and critical) way.[25] It will be an outline of the Godardian language—or way of thinking—of the those years, following, in his 1970 'Manifesto,' the way in which the work of montage was introduced and developed:

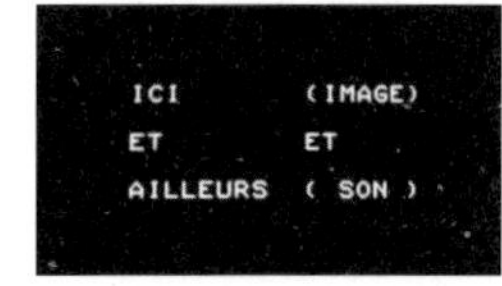

Fig 6 Footage of *Jusqu'à la victoire* (Dziga Vertov Group, 1970) was reworked by Jean-Luc Godard and Anne-Marie Miéville in the documentary *Ici et ailleurs*, 1976

Mao Zedong has said good comrades go where the difficulties are, where the contradictions are at their peak. Make propaganda for the Palestinian cause, yes. With images and sounds. Cinema and television. To make propaganda is to place problems on a carpet. A film is like a flying carpet that can go anywhere. There is no magic. It's political work. One has to study and search, record this research and this study, and then show the result (the montage) to other fighters. … For example: show an image of a fedayeen crossing the river, then an image of a Fatah militiawoman teaching refugees in a camp to read; then the image of a 'lion cub' in training. What are they—those three images? They are a whole. None is of value on its own. Possibly a sentimental, emotional or photographic value. But not a political value. To have a political value each of the three images must be linked to the other two. Then what becomes important is the sequence in which the three images are shown. Because they are parts of a political whole; and the sequence in which you arrange them represents the political line. We are on the Fatah line. So we arrange the three images in the following order: 1. Fedayeen during operations; 2. Militiawoman working in a school; 3. Children training. That represents

---

25 However, apart from the accounts in Robert Linhart, *L'Établi* (Paris: Éditions de Minuit, 1978) and Jean Rolin, *L'organisation* (Paris: Gallimard, 1996), we draw attention to two chronicles on French Maoism: Michèle Manceaux, *Les Maos en France* (Paris: Gallimard, 1972) and Christophe Bourseiller, *Les Maoïstes: La folle histoire des gardes rouges français* (Paris: Plon, 1996).

> 1. Armed struggle; 2. Political work; 3. Protracted
> people's war. In the end, the third image is the result
> of the other two. It is: armed struggle + political work
> = protracted people's war against Israel. But also: man
> (initiating combat) + woman (transforming herself,
> undergoing her revolution) who gives birth to the child
> who will liberate Palestine: the generation of victory.
> It is not enough to show a 'lion cub' or a 'flower'
> and say: 'This is the generation of victory'. You must
> show why and how. An Israeli child—you can't show
> that in the same way. The images that produce the
> image of a Zionist child are not the same as those for
> a Palestinian child. Incidentally, one should not refer
> to images, but to sequences of images. ... In other
> words, you compare, connect and finally conclude.[26]

We are quite far with this type of 'montage-gun' waiting impatiently for the conclusion (taking *sides*) of the first Godardian 'montage of concern' waiting impatiently for desire (actually taking a *stand*). The 'unknown' has certainly changed character. And that at the expense of a double reduction. In the ethical context, when commitment becomes segregation with respect to the 'Zionist child,' the idea of which seems to derive from some category of pure propaganda.

However, reduction also takes places in the logical context. So, the legitimate structural principal, according to which *relations* override terms that are harshly reduced to a question of *order* and political 'line,' i.e., a mandatory sequence, of the 'man + woman = child' or 'war + politics = victory' type. It is as if the will to conclude, for Godard, had, at that point, immobilized every ability to desire and associate freely.[27] It is as if poetic exuberance had to find its watchword in a schematism of formulas, clearly loved by Godard for their efficacy, the 'speed' and percussive

---

26 Jean-Luc Godard, 'Manifeste' (1970), in *Jean-Luc Godard: Documents*, pp. 138–140.
27 For a historical account of this crucial period, see David Faroult, *'Never More Godard:* Le Groupe Dziga Vertov, l'auteur et sa signature,' in *Jean-Luc Godard, documents*, pp. 120–129 and 'Du *vertovisme* du Groupe Dziga Vertov: With regard to an unappreciated manifesto and an unfinished film (*Jusqu'à la victoire*),' in ibid., pp. 134–138.

force (as demonstrated, to start with, in his repeated use of the acronym 'JLG' with which he, the artist—how complex and complete!—seems to want to simplify what he is for others, or permanently 're-initialize' himself).

Montage is a skill, a technique, a great art of dialectics. But which dialectics do we actually mean? Godard seems to have kept his Maoist idea from his 1970 'Manifesto,' published at that time in the *El Fatah* journal but not included in the canonical compendium *Jean-Luc Godard par Jean-Luc Godard* (1998)—the Maoist idea according to which 'a good comrade goes where … the contradictions are at their peak.' Undoubtedly this is a more illuminating remark than any attempts at psychological explanations both infantalizing and clearing Godard of any ethical or political responsibility when, for one of his 'limiting' arguments or one of his dubious wisecracks, all you want is to speak about the 'agitator' in him (a quality to which many artists have laid claim since the nineteenth-century poets and painters decided to 'épater les bourgeois'). In actual fact, Godard retained from Mao (who himself had it from Lenin) the lesson according to which—as we read in the *Little Red Book*—every area has its contradictions. Take 'the + and the − in mathematics, combination and dissociation in chemistry, productive forces and the relations of production, the class struggle in the social sciences, attack and defence in military science, idealism and materialism, metaphysics and dialectics in philosophy.'[28]
Whether it be in *Ici et ailleurs* or in *Film Socialisme*, the cinema does offer a 'concrete solution' in which it is a matter of 'placing the problems on the carpet' and 'placing them where the contradictions are at their peak,' according to a Maoist principle formulated in the classical text 'On Contradiction':

---

28 Mao Tse-Tung, 'On Contradiction' (1937), in *Five Philosophical Essays* (Peking: Foreign Language Press, 1971), pp. 69–70.

> In contradictions, universality exists in particularity.
> [From which] it is important, for guiding the course of
> our revolutionary practice, to study the particularity
> of contradictions inherent in the concrete things
> and phenomena facing us. ... To understand each
> aspect of a contradiction, is to understand what
> specific position each aspect occupies, what
> concrete forms it assumes in its interdependence
> and in its contradiction with its opposite, and what
> concrete methods are employed in the struggle
> with its opposite, [and] it is the concrete analysis
> of concrete conditions [that alone permits it].[29]

In short, what Godard wants from an image is that
it appeals to our gaze (*see, there*) and appears like
'the concrete analysis of concrete conditions' (*there
is*). And for it to accept a particular regulation, it
must, of course, be made in the frugality of montage
which will deliver its essentially dialectic content:

> There is no image, there are only images. And there is
> a certain method of assembling images: as soon as
> there are two, there are three. That's the bedrock of
> arithmetic, it's the bedrock of cinema. ... What is at the
> basis is always two, always at the start presenting two
> images rather than one—that's what I call the image,
> that image comprising the two, so the third image...[30]

So montage is dialectics, according to Godard, in as
far as it, firstly, makes the entire image into *the relating
of two images* at least, the link should be located as
much as possible 'where the contractions are at their
peak.' Secondly, in as far as montage reveals from the
implementation of the contradiction, *a third term*, possibly

---

29 Ibid., p. 58 and pp. 76–77.
30 Jean-Luc Godard, 'Jean-Luc Godard rencontre Régis Debray' (1995), in *Jean-Luc Godard par Jean-Luc Godard*, vol. 2, 1984–1998, p. 430. Jean-Luc Godard and Youssef Ishaghpour, *Archéologie du cinéma et mémoire du siècle* (Tours: Farrago, 2000), p. 27. In the film *Je vous salue, Marie*, there is a more 'theological' expression of the same idea: 'Mettre deux images côte à côte, cela s'appelle la Création, mademoiselle Marie.'

called 'the image' as such. It appears, in this regard, that something is never absolutely clear in the eyes of the interpreters: does Godard favour *two* (as when Jean Narboni, commenting on *Film Socialisme* once recalled Godard's 'trenchant word' in all things) or *three* (as, in the same text, Narboni recalls that Godard 'prefers the uneven in all things'?)[31] In other words, with Godard, does the idea of dialectics—stemming from his use of montage—favour the suspense inherent in all tension (*see, there*) or, rather, the third term, as the conclusion to be drawn from every contradiction (*there is*)?

So perhaps there are two possible uses of dialectics—very different ones as regards their procedure and their results—in the area of images: on the one hand, the practice that is dedicated to *syntheses*. It works with *order* and focuses on a moment of conclusion ('war + politics = victory') because from the start it is driven by political or aesthetic axioms. On the other hand, there is the practice dedicated to symptoms,[32] the *rhythm* of which can be reduced to neither a 'tempo' nor an 'order,' even less to a 'line,' and focuses solely on something unpredictable, let's call that the suspense of desire ('Lillian Gish, Augustine: so what does a woman want?'), because this practice right away rejected axioms, taking place entirely in the open dimension of a heuristic method of images. Since all my examples derive from the same corpus, you will have understood that the art of montage, for Godard, often hesitates between these two types of practices. In fact, Godard never ceases to 'play on two images,' which does not fail to produce many effects of *profusion*, indeed of *confusion*.

Profusion: Godard wanted the lot, he wanted the thing and its opposite, *and...and*, as, for example, Alain Bergala observed, concerning the maker of *Numéro deux* (1975), the wish to keep together a

---

31 Jean Narboni, '*Film Socialisme* de Jean-Luc Godard,' *Trafic* no. 80 (2011), p. 53 and 61.
32 I have tried to develop the idea of a 'symptomal' not 'synthetic' dialectic starting from Georges Bataille—but also Sergei Eisenstein, Aby Warburg, and Walter Benjamin—in *La Ressemblance informe, ou le gai savoir visuel selon Georges Bataille* (Paris: Macula, 1995).

phenomenological principle à la Bazin, and the structural principle inherited from the 'moderns':

> [Godard] refuses to lose from the cinema side what it is he knows he can gain from the other, [he] refuses to renounce Méliès, regardless of his love for the Lumières, and thinks about Hitchcock's plans when he films alongside Rossellini. He wants both ontology and language, just as he desires both the world and, at the same time, noise and chaos and the purity of music, the tremor of the unique moment and the nostalgia of repetition. Godard has [thus] been practising from the outset cinema with the greatest divergence between assumptions about his art that are considered contradictory. [He] does his utmost … always to hold up both ends of cinema *at the same time*, yet without denying their intractability. On the contrary, deploying the greatest divergence.[33]

This divergence can undoubtedly be extended considerably—munificence, profusion—like a fully opened fan to cover all manner of cinematographic possibilities. But a negative aspect also clings to that ambition, when plenitude becomes ambiguity or when profusion becomes confusion. That is apparent in Gilles Deleuze's analysis (could that be why Godard harbours resentment against the maker of *L'Image-temps*?) – in which the theme of *between* emerges, which, indeed, 'does away with all cinema of the One' when imposing its 'interstice' of immeasurabilty.[34] But that also means, according to Deleuze, that 'we no longer believe in this world, [that] we do not even believe in things that happen to us, love, death, as if they only half concerned us,' as seen, he suggests, in a film like *Bande à part* (1964).[35] Now, on the basis of that kind of 'break in the ties between man and

---

33 Alain Bergala, 'Godard ou l'art du plus grand écart' (1989), in *Nul mieux que Godard* (Paris: Cahiers du cinéma, 1999), pp. 84–85.

34 Gilles Deleuze, *L'Image-temps: Cinéma 2* (Paris: Éditions de Minuit, 1985), pp. 234–238.

35 Ibid., p. 223.

the world' as conveyed to us in Godard's films, the outcome
is a veritable 'dislocation' of language which Deleuze
qualifies as 'theorematic'[36] (though, with Pier Paolo
Pasolini, it would be 'problematical'), i.e., axiomatic or,
worse, dogmatic. But what is a dislocation turned axiom?

Such would seem to be Godard's great paradox when
using montage as well as when using plays on language:
to produce watchwords, trenchant forms, images without
discussion (*there is, no comment*), but based on a
fragmented language and an intense hesitation which
transforms the dialectics of the images (*look, there*) into
paralogism or confusion. When Godard boldly insists 'I like
to *confuse* things,'[37] does he not actually create a shift in
genres? Since he is saying he *judges by set confrontations*
('confusing' is said of the prosecutor handling a legal
case on this point of methodical precision and argued
dichotomies in which the offender will be irrefutably
blamed) and at the same time, *plays with risky amalgams*,
as he does when, on the subject of the child, he shifts
from the fact that he has a nationality (Israeli) toward
what he would personify a (Zionist) ideology, although a
child? The ethical question arises from this: the logical
paradox through which play-acting presents itself to be
judged, a confrontation is built by way of amalgams.

---

36 Ibid., pp. 225–228.
37 Cited by Douin, *Jean-Luc Godard*, p. 96.

The social body is the producer of this art and it is its object.

Quote
Thomas Lange, *History at Present*
→ **See p. 228**

This whole project should be concentrated on people and their stories.

Quote
Li Mu, *A Man, A Village, A Museum*
→ See p. 262

Beauty and the Right to the Ugly

Wendelien van Oldenborgh

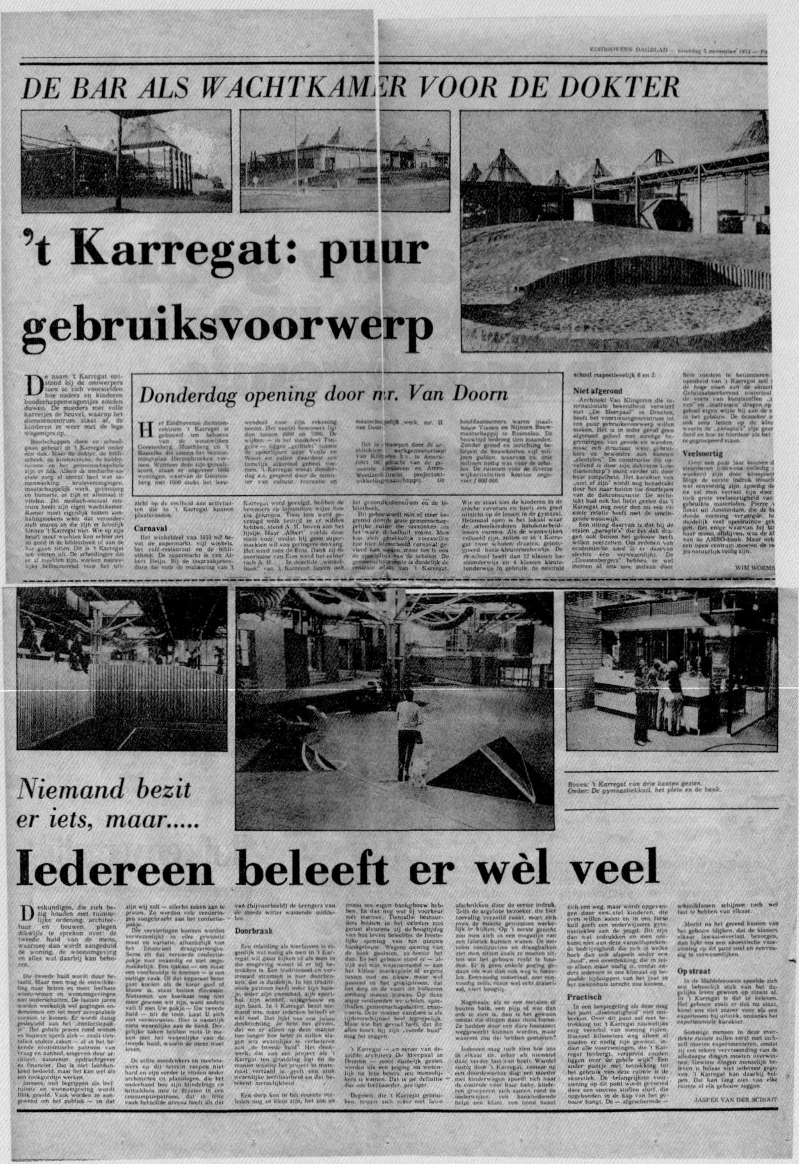

DE BAR ALS WACHTKAMER VOOR DE DOKTER

't Karregat: puur gebruiksvoorwerp

Donderdag opening door mr. Van Doorn

Niemand bezit er iets, maar.....

Iedereen beleeft er wèl veel

Boven: 't Karregat van drie kanten gezien.
Onder: De gymnastiekkuil, het plein en de bank.

Notes to chapter 1:
Newspapers from the 1970s

EINDHOVENS DAGBLAD
Saturday 3 November 1973

THE BAR AS DOCTOR'S WAITINGROOM

't Karregat: purely an object for use

No-one owns anything here, but…
Everyone experiences a lot

If after completion of the building it turns out that the classes suffer from each other's noise, it seems that an acoustic accommodation can be easily realized.

On the streets
In the Middle Ages a significant part of life took place on the street. In 't Karregat we experience exactly that. As it appears to us now, the building doesn't strike us as an experiment, despite its experimental character.

In this covered public space, some people will have to experiment with themselves first, since they will have to overcome a certain alienation from everyday things. To experience normal things in a human way, is unfortunately not a given for everyone. 't Karregat can be a help in that. And this cannot be said of each space or building.

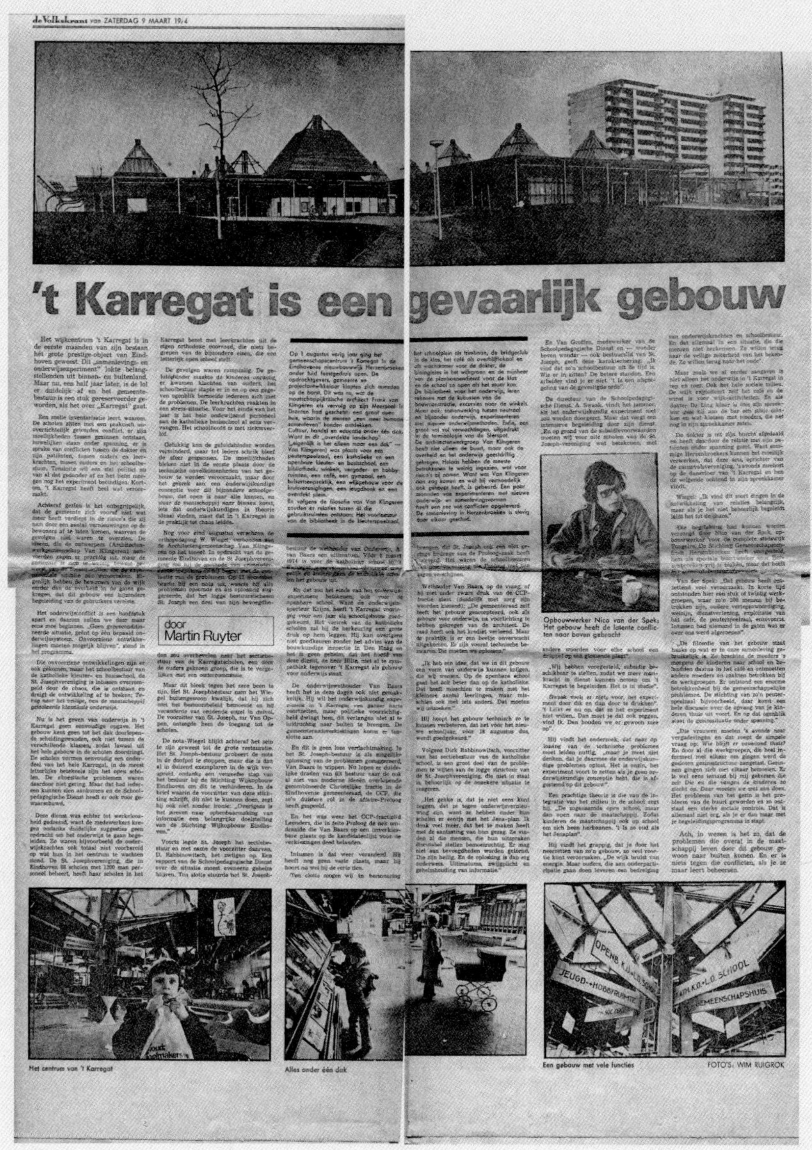

de Volkskrant van ZATERDAG 9 MAART 1974

't Karregat is een gevaarlijk gebouw

door **Martin Ruyter**

Opbouwwerker Nico van der Spek

Het centrum van 't Karregat

Alles onder één dak

Een gebouw met vele functies

FOTO'S: WIM RUIGROK

DE VOLKSKRANT
Saturday 9 March 1974

't Karregat is a dangerous building

Social worker Nico van der Spek: The building has brought latent conflict to the surface.

The building has caused a number of things. In a very short time some twenty voluntary teams were formed, in which about 200 people are active.

The women have to attend the meetings in the evenings and that raised the simple question: *Who is staying with the kids tonight?* And because of these many work teams where the conduct was very informal, the closed family unit has been challenged.

Families started to interfere with each other. A family problem has become a neighbourhood problem and so a very strong social control has developed.

Oh well, in essence, the problems which occur everywhere in society are expressed through this building. There is nothing against all these conflicts, if you learn how to dominate them.

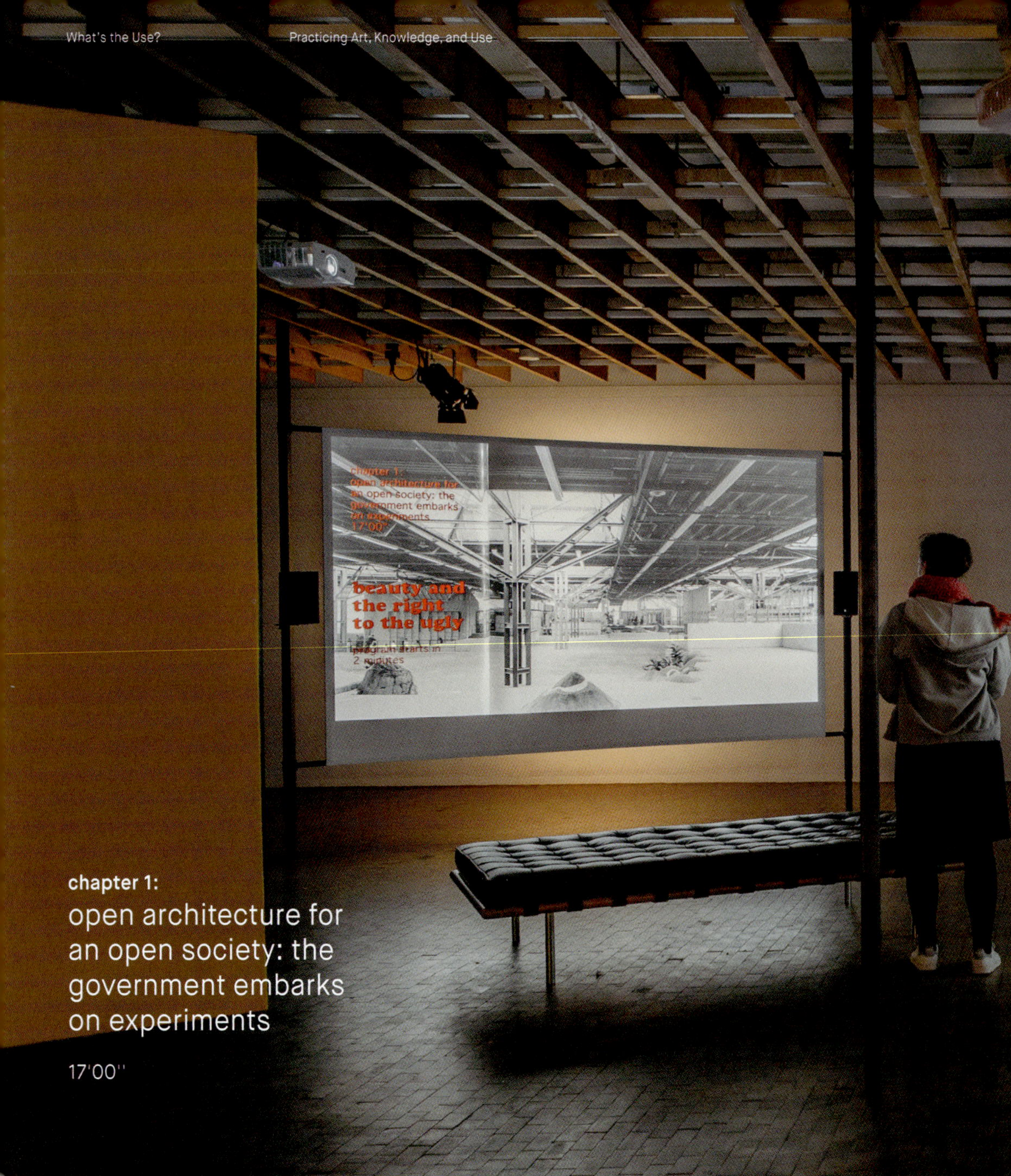

chapter 1:

open architecture for an open society: the government embarks on experiments

17'00"

Prelude to chapter 1
Romeo K. Gambier wrote and
sings:

/tc 00:00:01:14 00:00:04:18
At first everything was open
and now it is closed,

/tc 00:00:06:07 00:00:11:17
Noticed by many, and for many
people really started there

/tc 00:00:18:23 00:00:21:08
In her deep middle a pit,
about which one then slyly
whispered:

/tc 00:00:22:04 00:00:25:00
"They swap partners there"

/tc 00:00:25:08 00:00:29:15
The experiment was beautiful
And until today you feel it:

/tc 00:00:29:20 00:00:33:05
once 't Karregat was
powerful, if only as a
concept

/tc 00:00:15:19 00:00:18:20
People from far away

/tc 00:00:18:23 00:00:21:08
came to see the groundbreaking
idea.

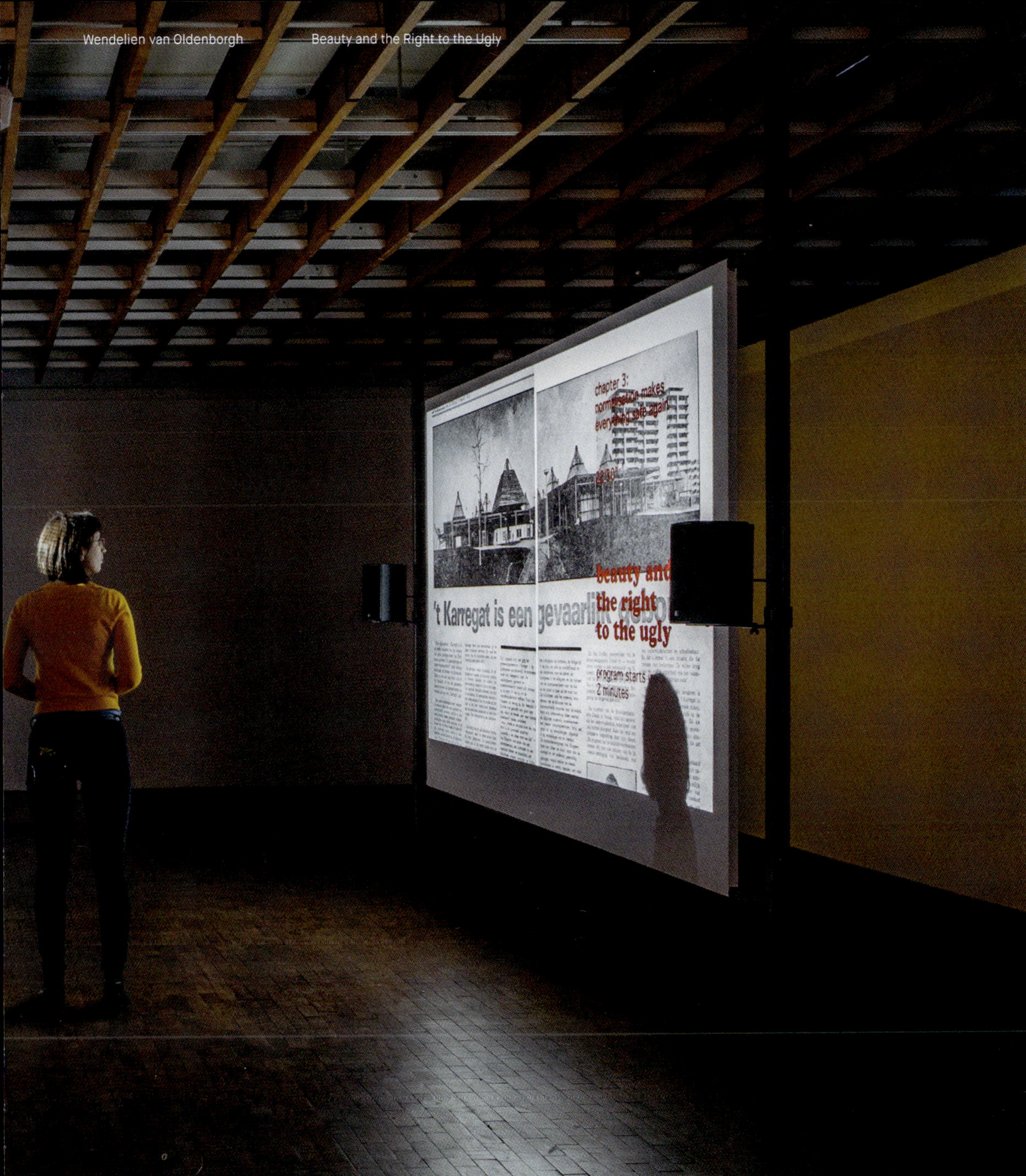

/tc 00:00:22:04 00:00:25:00
Architecture as a society
re-builder.

/tc 00:00:25:08 00:00:29:15
Nuisance and decluttering,
in Brabant in the south
there was a racket.

/tc 00:00:29:20 00:00:33:05
'Dust biters' and Chocoprince
lived there.

/tc 00:00:33:09 00:00:37:19
But nobody remembers what a
party it really was.

/tc 00:00:38:11 00:00:40:11
What people just did at te
time,

/tc 00:00:40:14 00:00:43:19
turned into what they expect
of us now.

/tc 00:00:44:04 00:00:47:19
Once, the idea of
't Karregat was mighty.

/tc 00:00:48:06 00:00:52:07
Now it doesn't seem more
than a questionable collection

/tc 00:00:52:10 00:00:55:08
of glass pyramids on a roof in
Eindhoven.

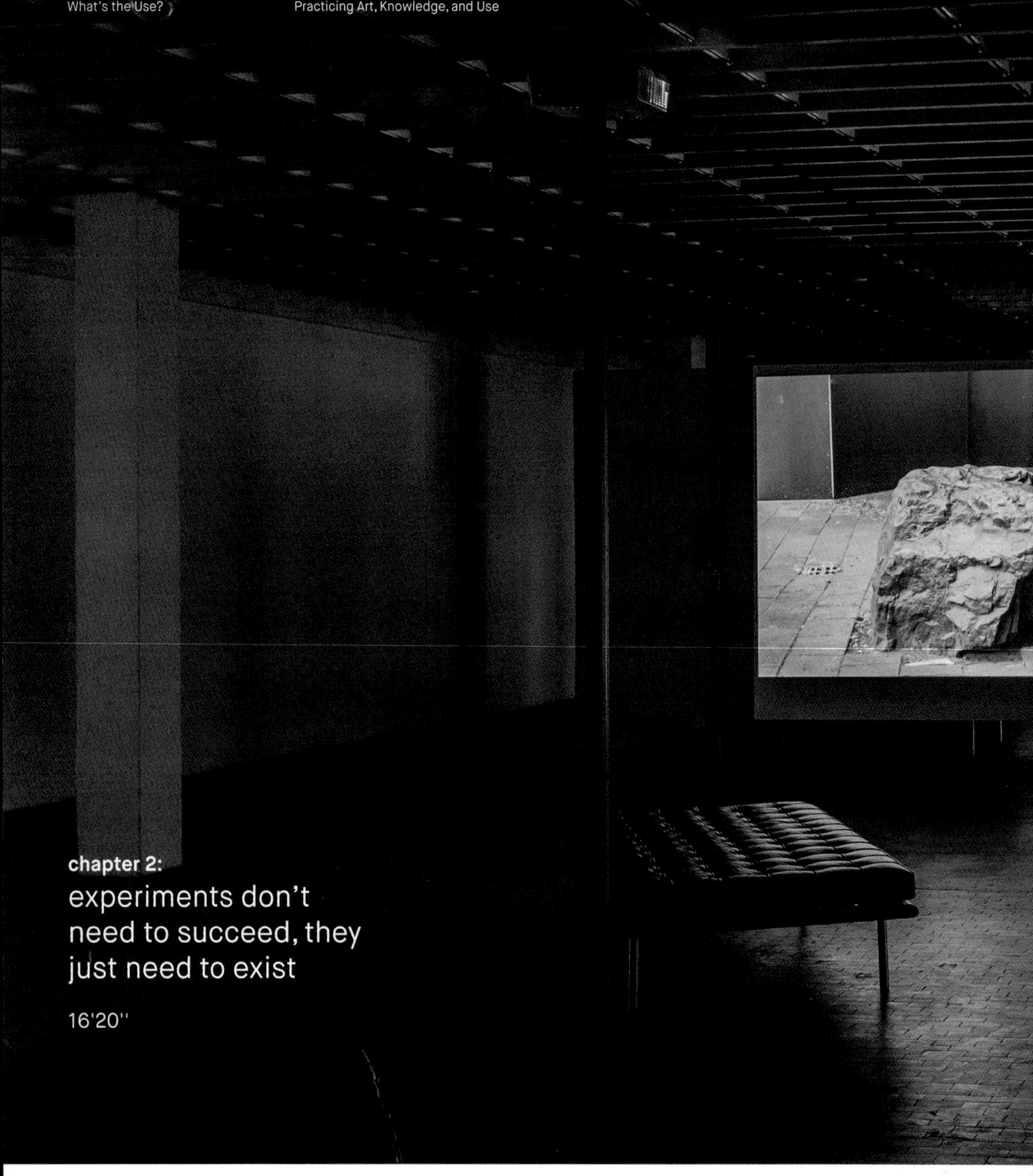

chapter 2:
experiments don't need to succeed, they just need to exist

16'20''

Prelude to chapter 2:

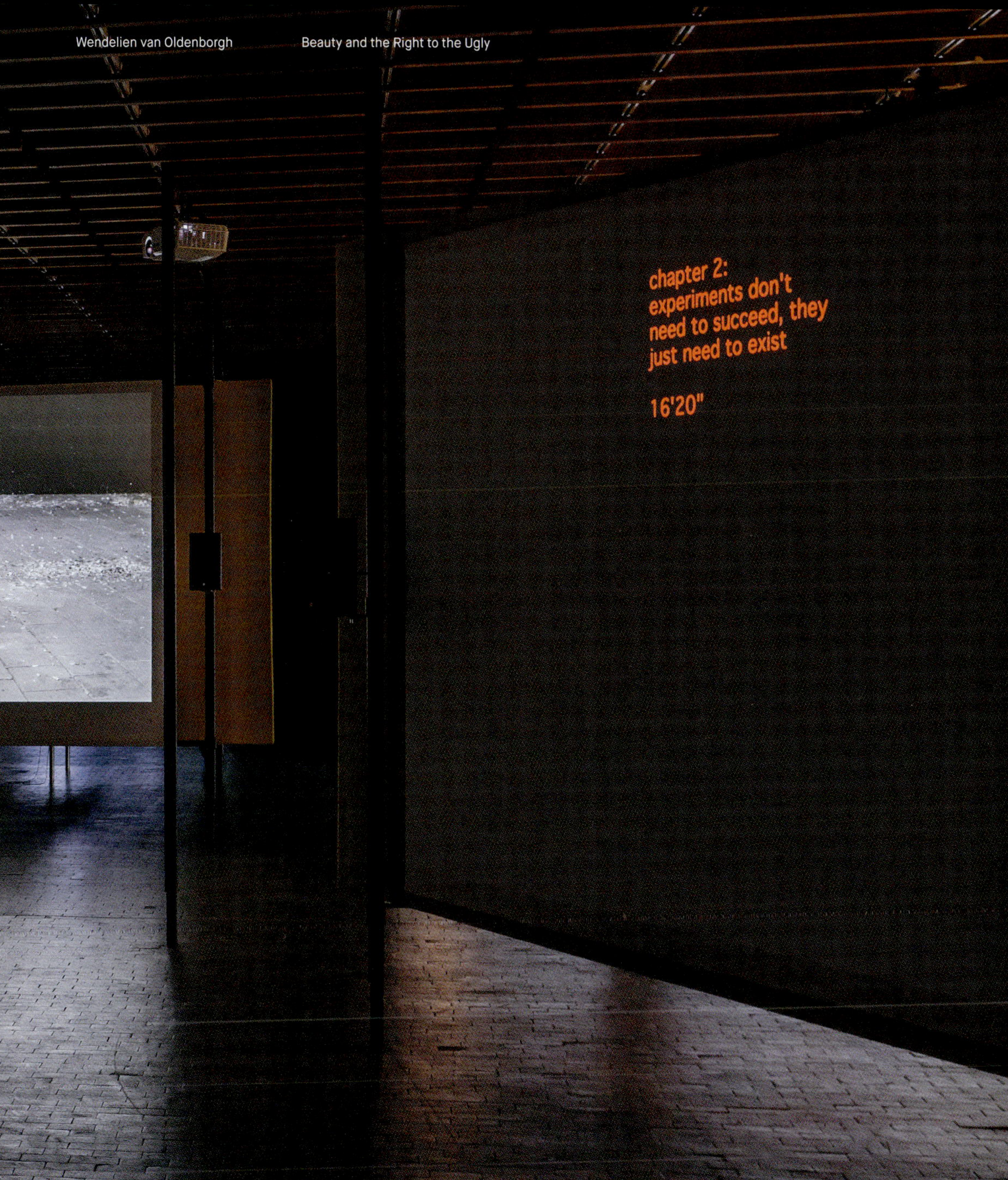

/tc 00:15:38:10 00:15:41:20
Covered in dust and noise,
it all happened

/tc 00:15:42:07 00:15:44:10
her fame was widespread.

/tc 00:15:45:02 00:15:47:06
Prestige, danger and humane,

/tc 00:15:48:06 00:15:51:07
how did all of this come
together?

/tc 00:15:51:20 00:15:54:24
What did Mr. Van Klingeren
ever think?

/tc 00:15:55:18 00:15:58:08
Or was this an experiment
where everyone

/tc 00:15:58:11 00:16:01:12
expected too much too soon?

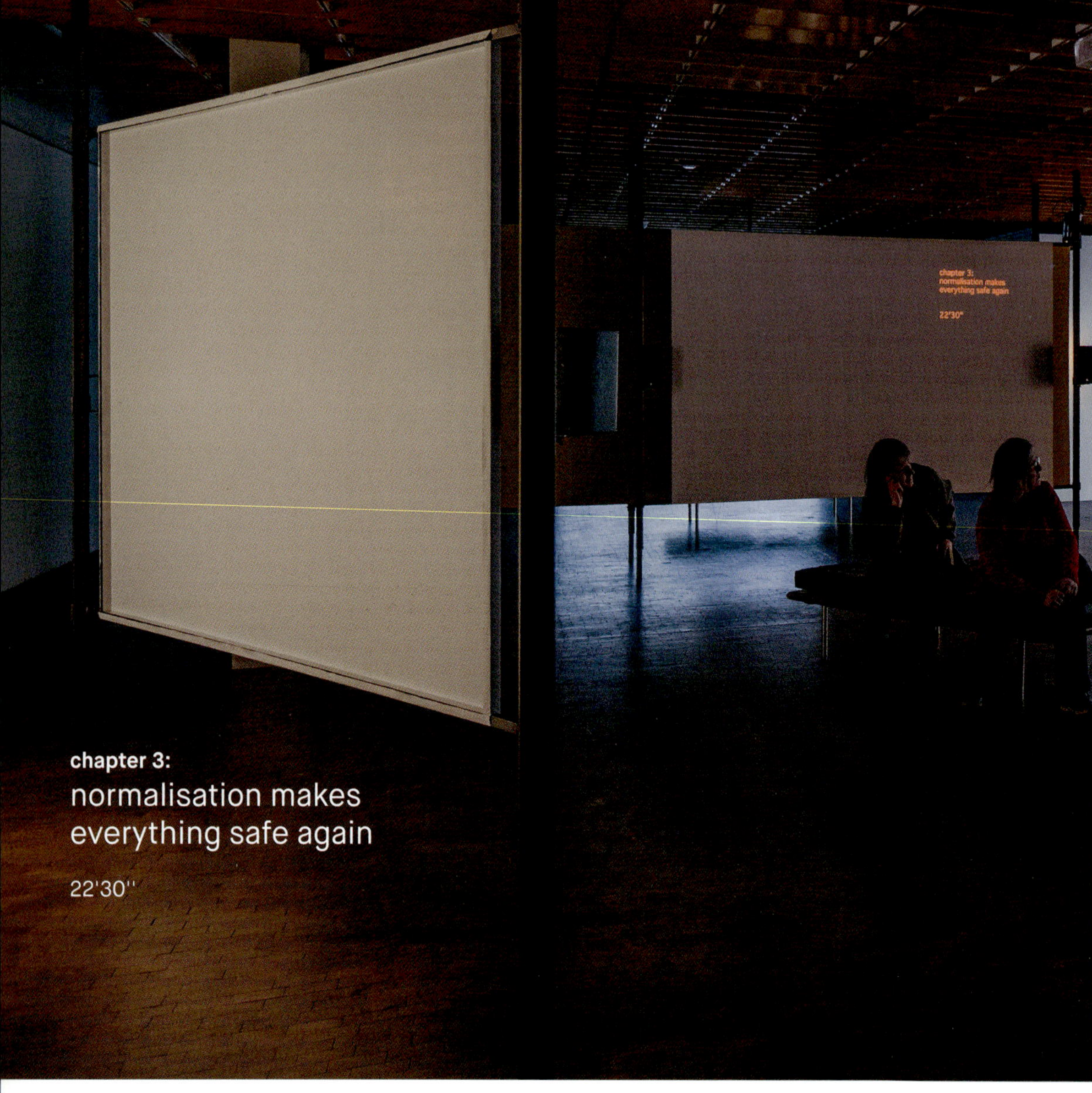

chapter 3:

normalisation makes everything safe again

22'30"

Prelude to chapter 3
Romeo:

/tc 00:34:07:03 00:34:08:18
Experimentally social

/tc 00:34:08:24 00:34:13:00
to neoliberal, as if it's
normal. That's what happened.

/tc 00:34:13:04 00:34:15:09
From striving to more humane

/tc 00:34:15:12 00:34:18:23
it turned into driven by
money.

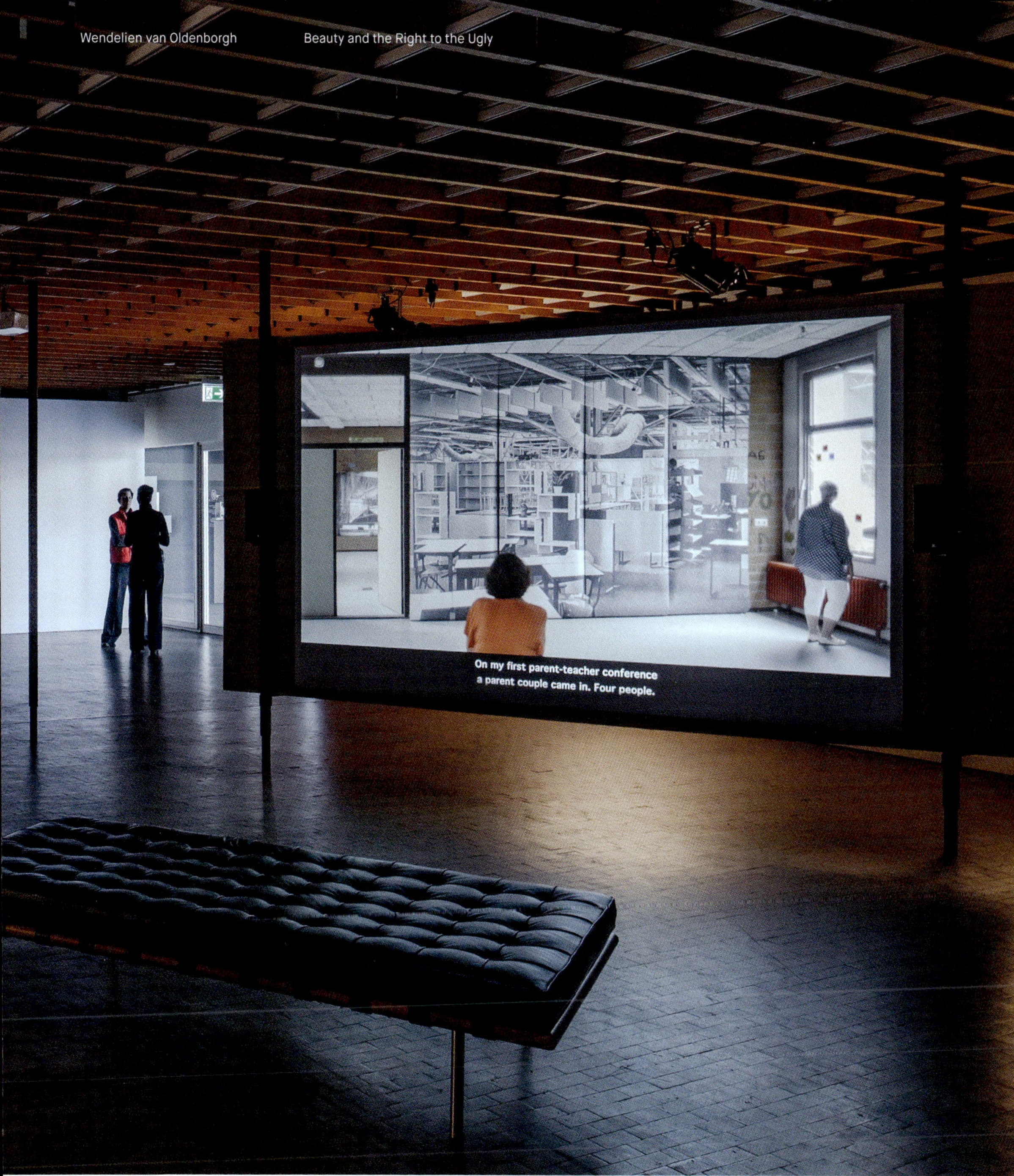

Postscript: /tc 00:54:34:20 00:54:38:10
Can we speak of preventive
neighbourhood initiative?

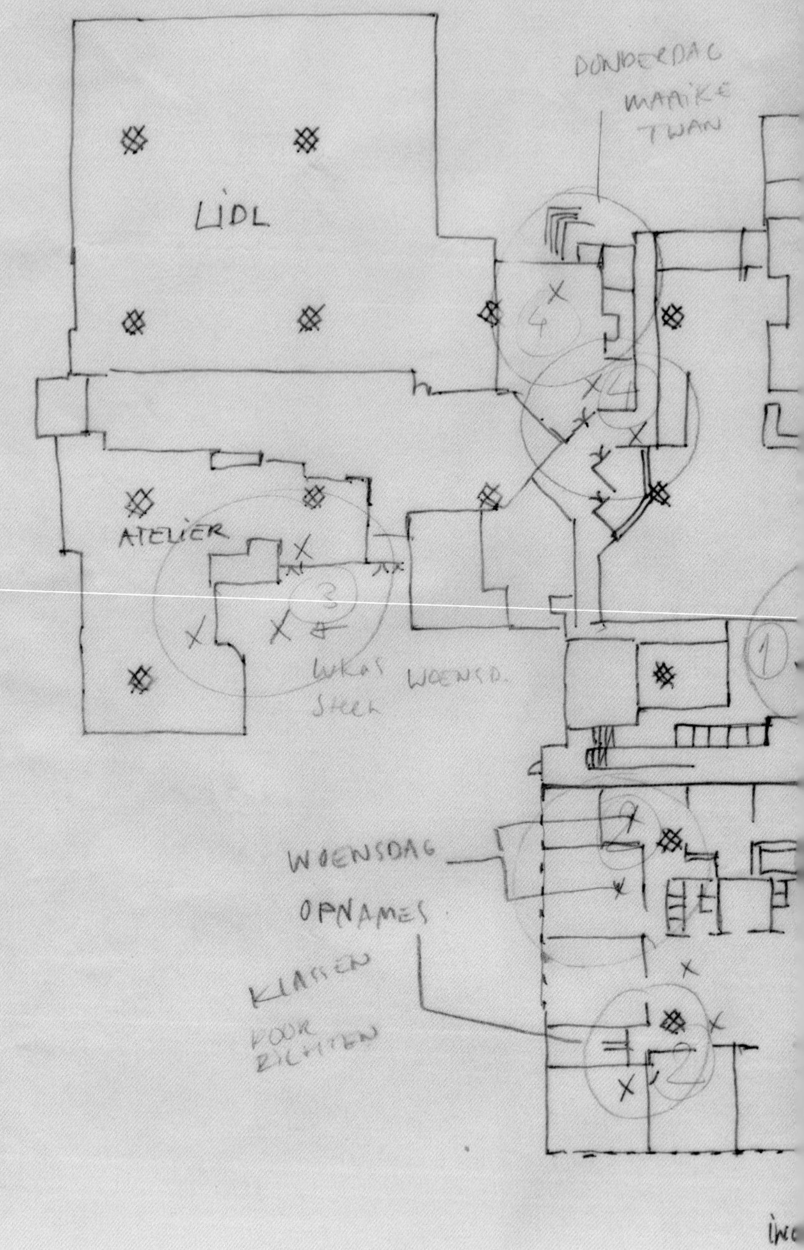

Notes for shoot 3 — May 2014

WEDNESDAY MORNING
Shots located in and around
Lidl and designers' atelier.
Scenes developed with Lukas,
who has his studio on an
anti-squat arrangement in the
former library.

—scenes according to route 3
(if experiments would succeed
they are dangerous (to a
conservative society)

WEDNESDAY AFTERNOON
Spatially located in the
school. Scenes developed with
Maria and Mirjam, teachers at

the school since the 1970s.
—scenes according to route 2
(experiments are not properly
executed/experiments don't
need to succeed—they just need
to exist)

THURSDAY MORNING
Shots located in the former

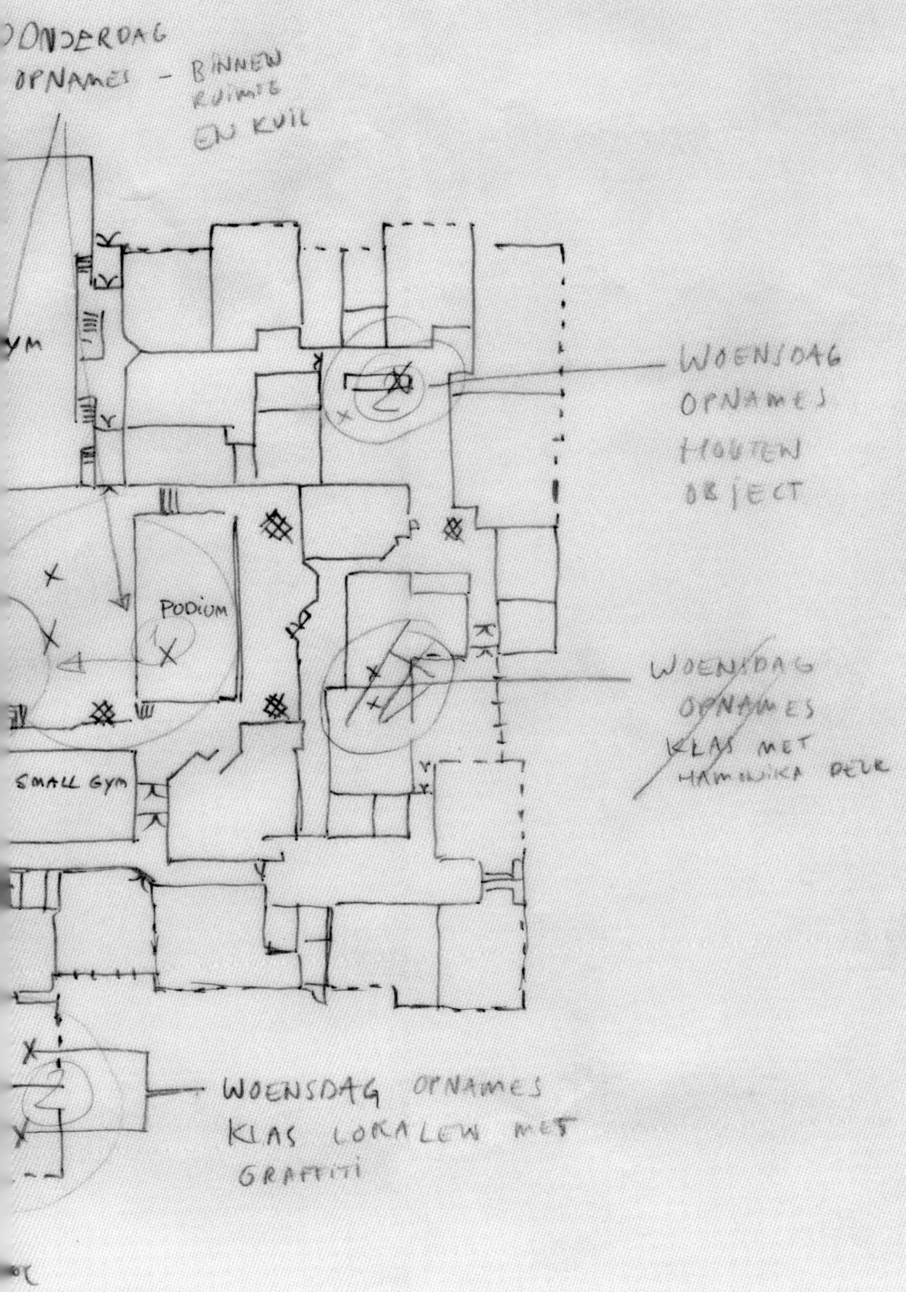

cafe and the area around Lidl.
Scenes developed with Maaike
and Twan, currently living on
an anti-squat contract in the
former cafe.
—scenes according to route
4 (normalization of the
experiment makes it safe
again)

THURSDAY AFTERNOON
Shots located in ex-washing
machine space (was Bruce
& Nick's anti-squat until
recently) and out into the
Kuil (skate hall). Scene
developed with Romeo and
Hans. Romeo samples Hans's
percussion rhythms. They carry

Romeo's words inspired by
Hans who has lived around
't Karregat since the
beginning and has been the
barman for twenty-five years.
—scenes according to route 1
(to hide its conservatism,
the Netherlands embarks on
experiments)

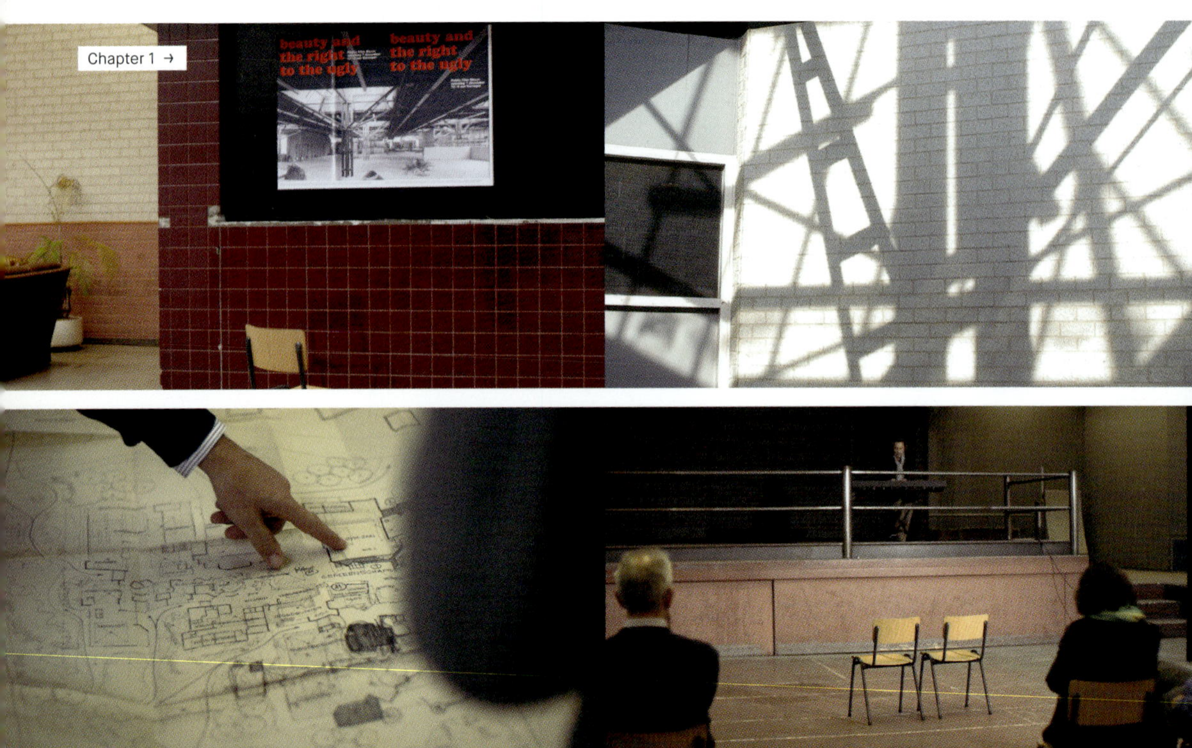

Beauty and the Right to the Ugly

Emily Pethick

***Beauty and the Right to the Ugly* is the title of an exhibition that the Italian-Brazilian architect Lina Bo Bardi presented at her seminal building SESC Pompéia in São Paulo in 1968. Organized in collaboration with INAMPS employees, it took a stand against bourgeois taste and values.**[1]

SESC Pompéia, a non-governmental organization that was developed out of a defunct factory by Bo Bardi from 1977 to 1986, still remains a popular and inclusive social space, housing diverse activities—football, swimming, theatre, dance, art, health services, and sunbathing decks (some of which were already taking place on the site informally before it was developed)—coexisting without hierarchy. As an architect who worked with Bo Bardi described, it was 'intended to foster conviviality as an infallible formula for cultural production.'[2]

The potential of such a project to cut across divisions of class, gender, and age, and to allow different people and activities to connect also lay at the heart of another architectural experiment, 't Karregat, a community centre in Eindhoven. Designed by architect Frank van Klingeren in 1970, it housed social, cultural, health, and educational facilities under one roof in an open-plan setting. Van Klingeren was concerned about the demise of the public domain as a meeting space and was interested

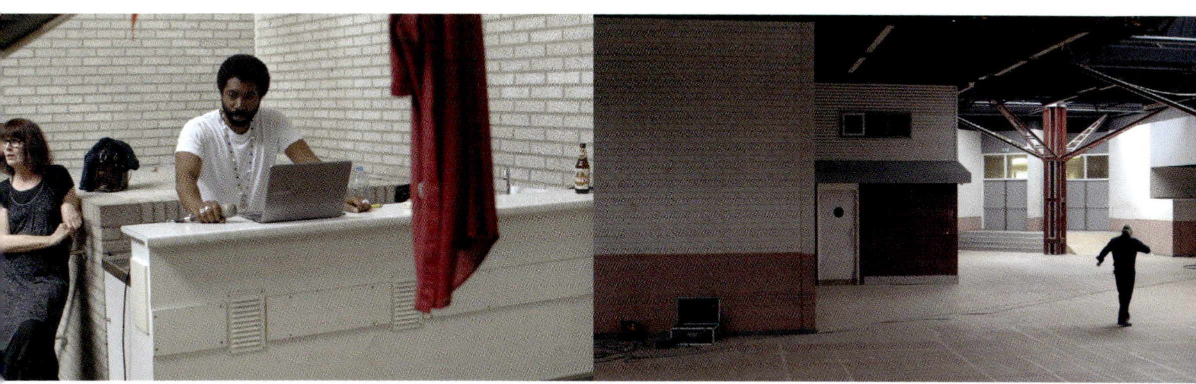

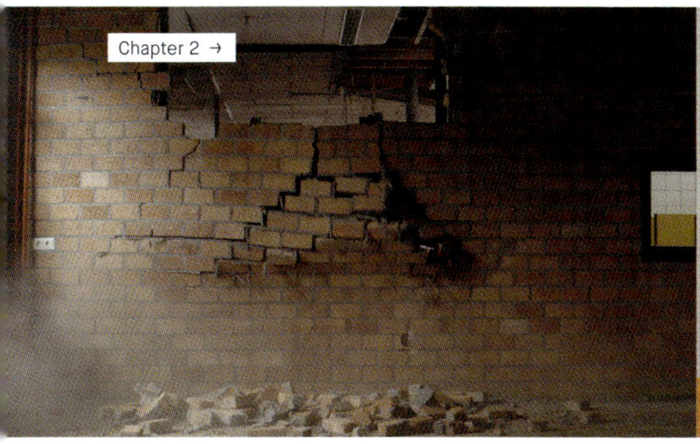

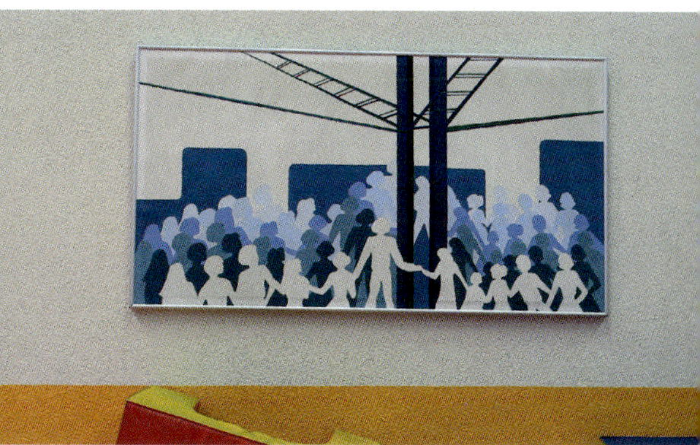

in what kinds of spaces could be produced through social interaction. He believed a space without walls would allow diverse people and activities to coexist and cross-pollinate, working with the philosophy that: '…if you group people so closely together that they initially hinder one another, some understanding will ultimately result. This can take the form of friendship or animosity, or anything in between.'[3]

Both Bo Bardi and Van Klingeren saw social interaction and the encountering of difference as a productive force, something that is also central to artist Wendelien van Oldenborgh's filmmaking, which often involves the forging of relations and dialogue between diverse players who would not ordinarily meet one another. Her work has frequently addressed unresolved histories, using the film as an open framework through which the complexities of these can surface. New scripts are formed via conversation, allowing voices that have not been acknowledged in more official accounts to be made visible.

1   Instituto Nacional Assistência Médica Previdência Social [National Institute for Medical Assistance and Social Prevention].
2   Marcelo Ferraz, "The Making of SESC Pompéia," Lina Bo Bardi: Together, http://linabobarditogether.com/2012/08/03/the-making-of-sesc-pompeia-by-marcelo-ferraz.
3   From "'t Karregat' community center in Eindhoven: Schoolwork in the supermarket," NAI, Rotterdam, http://en.nai.nl/collection/view_the_collection/item/_pid/ kolom2-1/_rp_kolom2-1_elementId/1_102977.

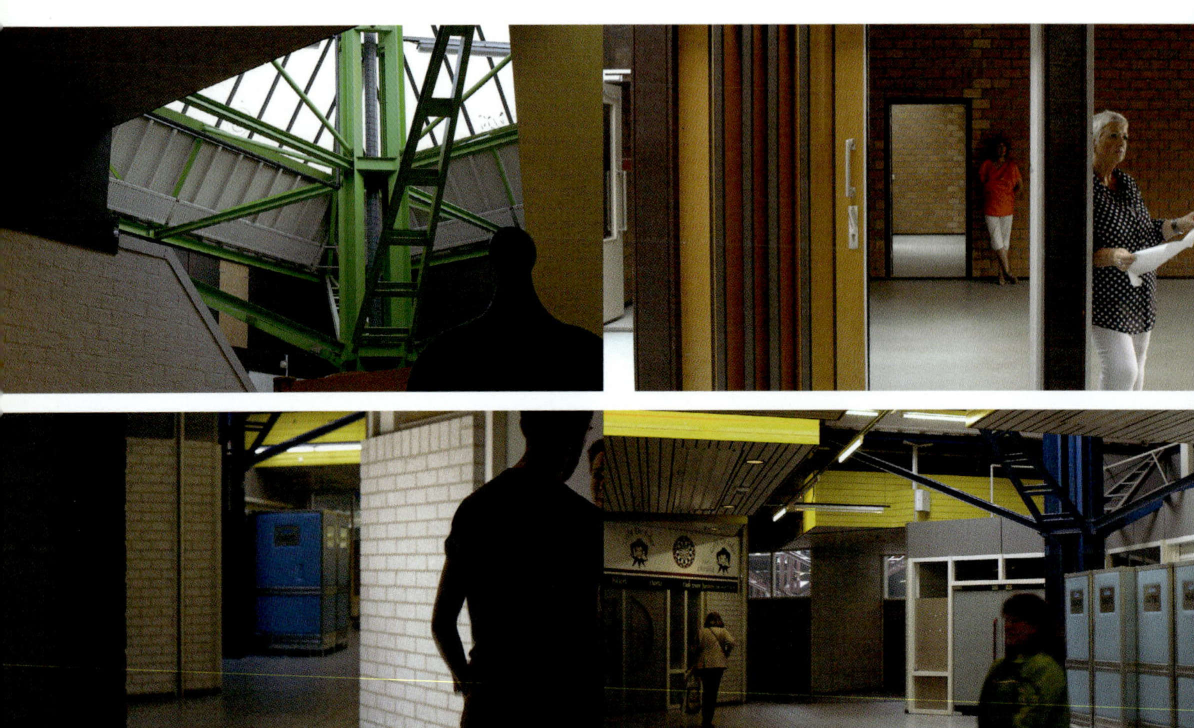

Produced through a series of shoots at 't Karregat, including one large, open, public shoot and smaller, focused sessions with invited participants, *Beauty and the Right to the Ugly* creates a performative space, where, like Bo Bardi's and Van Klingeren's architecture, a film unfolds in a live situation. Inhabiting the building with a range of people with differing relationships to it—a number of whom have been users at different times, including a doctor, barman, and architect— the camera and microphone move through a number of conversations happening simultaneously. These are interspersed with improvised musical interludes, composed by the building's former barman, Hans Muskens— a centrally present character throughout the film—and rapper Romeo K. Gambier, which are performed with live sampling and riffs from Hans's percussion kit, through which some of the core concerns of the building's story are posed. Together these form a multifaceted picture of the building, which emerges as both a space of possibility as well as of conflict.

The film is structured in three chapters referring to different phases in the building's history. *Open Architecture for an Open Society / the government embarks on experiments* explores the origins of the building as initiated by the city, stating how central to its early popularity was that 'the municipality did not tell us what to do,' where 'people who didn't know each other did things together.' The second chapter, *Experiments don't need to succeed, they just need to exist* reveals how this freedom— complete with love-ins, unruly children, and unorthodox family structures—presented challenges and tensions between autonomy and dependency. The relationship with the municipality, questions of economy, sound clashes, and a lack of a standardized educational structure, all contributed to its eventual division. Throughout the film the building itself looms as a player itself, not as an open space, but as an enclosed warren of stark, uniform, grey brick walls. Protruding in odd places, the original

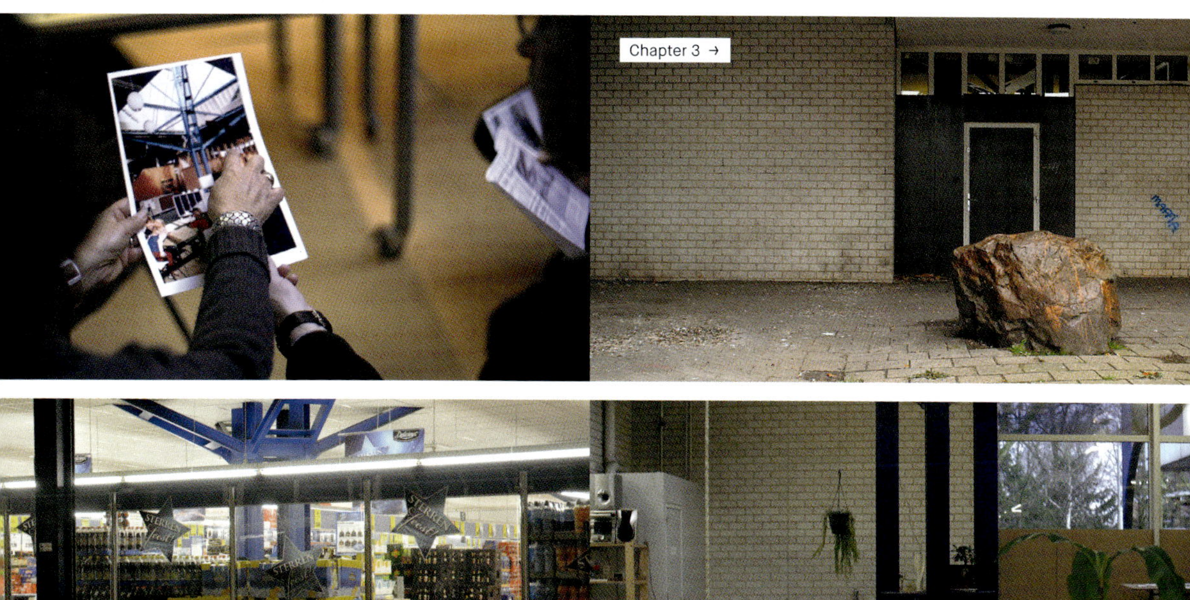

steel tree-like posts appear as buried links
to its more radical past.

In the final chapter *Normalisation makes
everything safe again*, one participant describes
how 'when you split it up the heart is gone …
when you build a wall you divide,' and the
territorialization reveals a clear reflection of
a more general shift in society toward the
privatization and competition of a capitalist
society. One former user discusses how as a
child at 't Karregat he learned to 'work without
limits,' and how he has brought some of these
ideas into his current business, setting up
flexible working structures, such as hot-
desking, which, as another participant points
out, is more about maximizing resources.

Both directing the participants, and in part
letting them take the lead, the film takes on the
tensions present in relational situations, as with
any building, between the architect/director and
user/ participant, and the negotiations that come
with this. However, through working together
an exchange takes place that enables each to

reach beyond their own limitations and produce
something they could not have done alone,
and like the building, create a situation that is
unpredictable and open to change. The rewards
of giving space and seeing what emerges is
clear in the enthusiasm of those participating to
discuss the building and the philosophies behind
it, which makes the question of failure that hangs
over it seem irrelevant and rather as chapters in
the life of a building that still has a future. As is
demonstrated by Bo Bardi in her experiment at
SESC Pompéia, which still has much life today,
there is a place for centres that bring disparate
people and spheres of activity into contact,
creating imaginative non-standardized spaces
and approaches to the production of culture
and everyday life, whatever this might include.

Text commissioned by Collective Gallery in conjunction with the
exhibition of *Beauty and the Right to the Ugly* in January 2015.

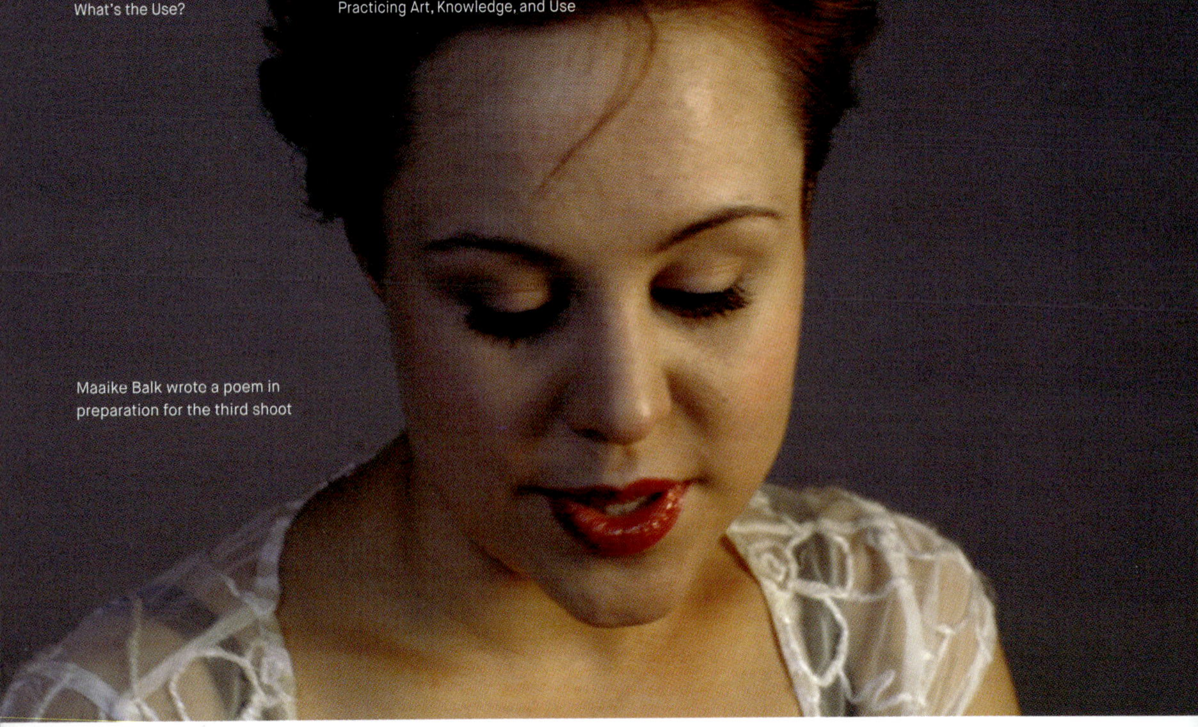

Maaike Balk wrote a poem in
preparation for the third shoot

A love letter to my walls

I'll be fair and give credit where credit is due
My dear walls, I've come to love you

Ever since the first day I walked within you
I just really wanted to stay there

You make me feel safe
and give me a space of my own

In the years we have been together
I've gotten to know you and I feel
like I can trust you with myself

I've really come to see you as my own
The borders you create for me are
more than I need, and that makes
me feel free to say the least

I can be myself around you

The way you stand so proud and tall
It teaches me a lesson in life
I feel much safer with you around me

And come to think that you were
never meant to be here
I become filled up with joy
that we did meet after all

My dear walls,
I can't even imagine a life without you

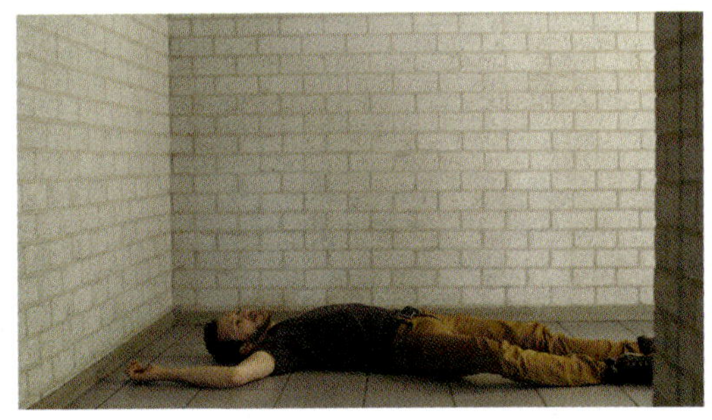

Essay
Sara Stehr

From History to Imagination

YAEL BARTANA'S TRILOGY
AND EUROPE WILL BE STUNNED

Yael Bartana's trilogy *And Europe Will Be Stunned* was
filmed in Warsaw between 2007 and 2011. The artist's
story of the fictional 'Jewish Renaissance Movement
in Poland' (JRMiP) advocates for three million Jews to
return to Poland and consists of three parts filmed at
two-year intervals: *Mary Koszmary* (*Nightmares*) (11 min.)
introduces the movement by way of its Polish leader;
Mur i wieża (*Wall and Tower*) (15 min.) shows the founding
of a kibbutz in Warsaw; and *Zamach* (*Assassination*)
(35 min.) entails the continuation of the movement
after the assassination and burial of its leader.

With this movement as the dominant narrative thread, Bartana deploys a variety of anachronistic motifs and stylistic devices derived from twentieth-century European history; these motifs and stylistic devices, serving as propagandistic *Schlagbilder* for political movements, have worked their way into our collective memory and have a productive impact on the film's plot.[1] While the motifs are recognizable, they are decontextualized in order to be re-contextualized within the new artistic narrative of the present-day JRMiP. *And Europe Will Be Stunned* has received a great deal of media attention and incited controversy, primarily because it invokes a painful chapter in Jewish-Polish history using images that have a partially propagandistic aesthetic. In 2011, Bartana was invited to represent Poland at the 54th Venice Biennale with *And Europe Will Be Stunned*. This not only garnered her worldwide attention, but also represented a unique distinction: Bartana became the first artist allowed to represent the nation who was not a Polish citizen. In light of the theme of her trilogy, her selection also had political and symbolic significance since it portrays the socio-cultural state of contemporary Poland.

Prior to the Venice Biennale, the work had been exhibited at internationally notable museums and galleries, and added to various museum collections.[2] The project also includes a variety of activities and accompanying material, including—but not limited to—a website, manifesto, and three-day JRMiP conference conducted in Berlin on the occasion of the Berlin Biennale in 2012. It is worth noting that the films are screened as large-scale projections, though

---

1   The concept of *Schlagbilder* was introduced by Aby Warburg in 1919 in the essay surviving in fragments, 'Heidnisch-antike Weissagung in Wort und Bild zu Luthers Zeiten.' Developed based on the example of leaflets from the era of Martin Luther, *Schlagbilder* is a term that describes compacted images with wide dissemination used to serve a purpose, 'whose language, additionally, was internationally comprehensible.' Aby Warburg, 'Heidnisch-antike Weissagung in Wort und Bild zu Luthers Zeiten,' *Sitzungsberichte der Heidelberger Akademie der Wissenschaften, Philosophisch-Historische Klasse* 26 (1919), p. 3; see also Michael Diers, *Schlagbilder: Zur politischen Ikonographie der Gegenwart* (Frankfurt am Main: Fischer, 1997).
2   Including Moderna Museet in Malmö, PS1 in New York, and 7th Berlin Biennale for Contemporary Art. Additionally, the work has been added to various museum collections, such as those of Tel Aviv Museum of Art, Van Abbemuseum in Eindhoven, and Zachęta National Gallery of Art in Warsaw. The artist's curriculum vitae along with a chronological list of her exhibitions and participations in exhibitions, as well as an itemization of her reviews, can be accessed at www.yaelbartana.com.

the form of installation and the accompanying material have varied. Three projectors running simultaneously are often employed to present the entire trilogy (including at the Venice Biennale presentation), deconstructing the conventional black-box concept by allowing spatial cross-views and audio overlays to define the character of the installation. A red neon sign announcing the title was hung over the entrance to the Polish pavilion; in addition, visitors were offered the opportunity to fill out a certificate of entry to the JRMiP.[3] When presented at Berlin's Martin-Gropius-Bau, the three parts were projected in chronological order, in combination with printed posters of the JRMiP manifesto meant to be taken home.[4] For an exhibition at the Van Abbemuseum in Eindhoven, in addition to the trilogy and posters, Bartana also exhibited archival material alongside her work that demonstrated her sources and inspirations.[5] Along with these exhibitions a number of reviews and catalogues have been published.[6]

My focus is on how Bartana situates and visualizes history and representations of history within the plot of *And Europe Will Be Stunned*. For this purpose exemplary scenes and motifs from the trilogy are submitted to iconographic analysis, although little has been published about the final segment, *Zamach*. In addition to the overlaying of anachronistic motifs within the contemporary framing story, on a meta-level the trilogy offers a critical approach to the

---

3   *… and Europe will be stunned*, Polish Pavilion, 54th Venice Biennale, Venice,
4 June–27 November 2011.
4   *The Century Mark: Tel Aviv Museum of Art visits Berlin*, Martin-Gropius-Bau, Berlin,
27 March–21 June 2015.
5   *Yael Bartana–…and Europe will be stunned*, Van Abbemuseum, Eindhoven,
24 March–26 August 2012.
6   The most significant publications on the work thus far are the monographic exhibition catalogues:
Joa Ljungberg and Andreas Nilsson, eds., *And Europe Will Be Stunned* (Berlin: Revolver, 2010); James
Lingwood and Eleanor Nairne, eds., *Yael Bartana: And Europe Will Be Stunned: The Polish Trilogy*
(London: Artangel, 2012); Secession, ed., *Yael Bartana: Wenn ihr wollt, ist es kein Traum/If you will it, it
is not a dream* (Berlin: Revolver, 2013), which also includes material pertaining to the aforementioned
conference in Berlin. The publication *Cookbook for Political Imagination*, published by the Zachęta
Gallery in Warsaw for the 54th Venice Biennale in 2011, also serves as a comprehensive anthology,
featuring contributions from both artists and academics: Sebastian Cichocki and Galit Eilat, eds.,
A Cookbook for Political Imagination (Berlin: Sternberg, 2011). Lastly, two interviews given by Bartana
in which she speaks extensively about her work form a fruitful source for academic engagement:
a conversation she conducted over multiple days with Galit Eilat and Charles Esche, two long-time
collaborators: Bartana et al., 'A Conversation between Yael Bartana, Galit Eilat, and Charles Esche,' in
And Europe Will Be Stunned, pp. 47–50, 75, 94–95, 115–117, and 166–169; and the interview with Doris
von Drahten, 'Yael Bartana. Die Gründung des Mouvements [*sic*] vollzieht sich im Kopf,' *Kunstforum
International* 210 (2011), pp. 256–261, quotations from which are translated by Rob Madole.

relationship between art and politics (and historical representation). Following the trajectory of the films, I end with a consideration of what potential the artist salvages from history in order to develop the vision she introduces at the end of the third segment, a vision of transnational society as a place of asylum for the weak, discriminated against, and dispossessed.

History is already implicated in the first part of the trilogy, *Mary Koszmary*, through the central plotline: the restoration of Jewish life in Poland through the JRMiP. In the setting of contemporary Poland, the narrative grasps far-reaching Jewish roots in Poland as well as the consequences of Germany's annihilation of the Jewish population between 1939 and 1945. A young man, Sławomir Sierakowski—a real-life sociologist, political activist, and co-founder of the liberal network and magazine *Political Critique* in Poland[7]—gives an emphatic speech inside the empty Stadion Dziesięcioleciam (described in the captions as Warsaw's 'Olympic Stadium'), its seats dilapidated and overgrown, calling for three million Jews to return to Poland (fig. 1). Sierakowski represents the engaged intelligentsia and stands for a pluralistic society in Poland. His involvement in *And Europe Will Be Stunned* as the leading figure of the JRMiP underlines the credibility of the idea of restoring Jewish life in Poland—he even wrote the speech himself with a colleague.[8] The appeal for Jews to return to Poland is not only stated verbally in the first section, but reinforced visually through lettering. Boys and girls in Young Pioneer uniforms, Sierakowski's only audience in the stadium, outline the following message in the grass with chalk: '3,300,000 Jews can change the lives of 40,000,000 Poles.' The numerical divergence between the spoken and written word goes uncommented on in the film; both figures, however, refer to historical estimates—the Jewish population of Poland amounted to 3.3 million before 1939, while 3 million Polish Jews

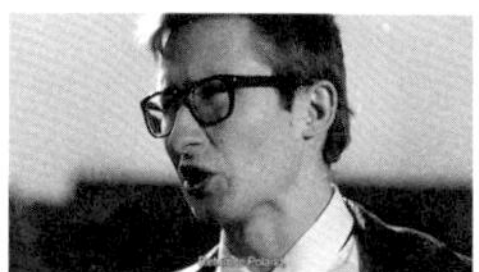

Fig 1 Yael Bartana, *Mary Koszmary* (*Nightmares*), 2007, 2'09"

---

7   See the *Political Critique* website at www.krytykapolityczna.pl.
8   See Bartana et al., 'A Conversation between Yael Bartana, Galit Eilat, and Charles Esche,' p. 116.

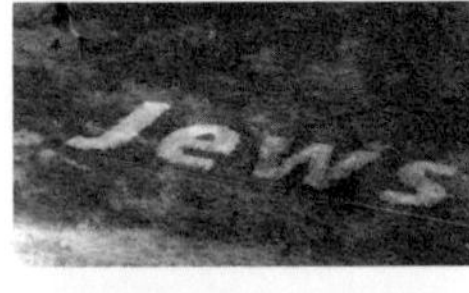

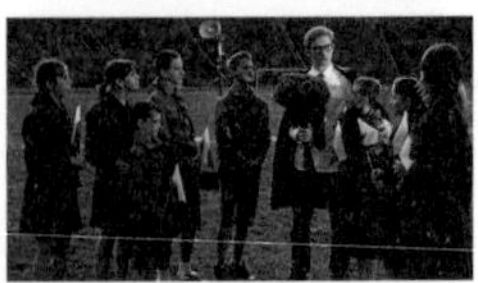

Fig 2   Yael Bartana, *Mary Koszmary (Nightmares)*, 2007, 3'50"
Fig 3   Yael Bartana, *Mary Koszmary (Nightmares)*, 2007, 9'09"

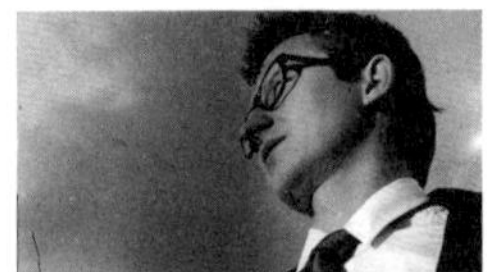

Fig 4   Yael Bartana, *Mary Koszmary (Nightmares)*, 2007, 3'21"

were victims of the Holocaust between 1939 and 1945. Sierakowski's appeal is irreconcilably confronted by the irreversibility of history, a fact which is also reinforced visually in different ways in *Mary Koszmary*: Sierakowski aims his appeal 'not to the dead but to the living,' which is contradicted by the absence of any audience in the stadium's empty rows; a crossfade between the word 'Jews' and the sky embodies Paul Celan's famous metaphor of a 'grave in the skies' from the poem *Todesfuge* [Death Fugue] (fig. 2). While the idea of a Jewish Renaissance in Poland serving as a leitmotif for the trilogy's plot may well have 'its roots in the imaginary,' as art historian Juli Carson has written, the real possibility of this renaissance is vividly embodied in the concrete figures of children dressed as Young Pioneers with their red scarves (fig. 3).[9]

But more than the uniforms, it is primarily the cinematographic staging and the theatrical presentation of the first part of *Mary Koszmary* that evokes associations with twentieth-century political propaganda with its strategies and potentials of affecting. 'I wanted viewers to feel addressed not only on a political level, but at an emotional level,' Bartana stated in 2011.[10] For instance, a discomforting feeling is evoked within the viewer through the occasional employment of a worm's-eye view from a diagonal vantage point and the over-emphasis on the gestures and facial expressions of the single male leader figure; the simple rhetorical structure of the appellative speech has the same effect (fig. 4). We see the contradictions between the topics that Sierakowski introduces in his speech and its staging and setting. In discussing *Mary Koszmary*, however, Bartana cited Israeli Prime Minister Menachem Begin as an historical reference for this kind of speeches. Critic and curator Joshua Simon sees a parallel in the work of German filmmaker Leni Riefenstahl, whose *Triumph of the Will* (1935) and *Olympia*

9   Juli Carson, 'Art of the Impossible: The Jewish Renaissance Movement in Poland (JRMIP),' in *Yael Bartana: Wenn ihr wollt, ist es kein Traum*, ed. Secession, p. 29.
10   Bartana and Von Drahten, 'Yael Bartana: Die Gründung des Mouvements [*sic*] vollzieht sich im Kopf,' p. 259.

(1938) are iconic propaganda films.[11] It's a thought echoed by Bartana who mentioned her grappling with Riefenstahl during a conversation on her film *Summer Camp* (2007).[12]

In the backdrop of the stadium, the artist has described seeing it as a type of building that is freighted with National Socialist ideology: 'Speeches in stadiums are connected with Nazi propaganda.'[13] Simon too makes reference to the setting of the stadium, citing the study 'National Socialist Weltanschauung' by Israeli historian Boaz Neumann, who argues that the stadium, as an Aryan space, forms the antithesis to the camp, the Jewish space.[14] In *Mary Koszmary*, the building type and its ideological determinacy stand in contrast to the specific materiality and individual condition of the Stadion Dziesięciolecia; in 2007, when part one was filmed, the stadium was still a ruin, leasing space to a Vietnamese market that Bartana incorporates into the frame multiple times in *Mary Koszmary* (fig. 5).[15] There is a further historical dimension to the Stadion Dziesięciolecia when one considers its material iconographic aspects—first erected from the rubble of a Warsaw destroyed by Germany following the Warsaw Uprising of 1944, it became a highly symbolic memorial to Polish resistance during the Second World War and attestation to the Manifesto of the Polish Committee for National Liberation, known as July of that same year. Thus, already in *Mary Koszmary*, Bartana not only intermixes history and the present, but also overlays motifs in such a way that they become kaleidoscope-like representations of antagonistic worldviews and depictions of history within the twentieth century. By producing such an effect, her trilogy is also formally reminiscent of an artistic strategy

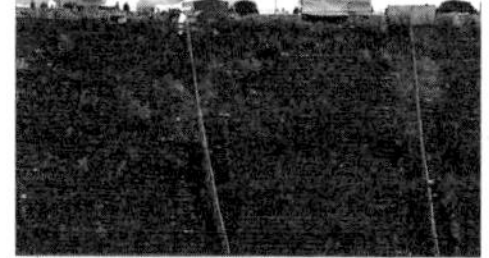

Fig 5 Yael Bartana, *Mary Koszmary* (*Nightmares*), 2007, 2'33''

---

11   On the significance of emotion in Leni Riefenstahl's film *Triumph of the Will* see Kristina Oberwinter, *'Bewegende Bilder': Repräsentation und Produktion von Emotionen in Leni Riefenstahls Triumph des Willens* (Munich and Berlin: Deutscher Kunstverlag, 2007).

12   See Bartana et al., 'A Conversation between Yael Bartana, Galit Eilat, and Charles Esche,' p. 95 and 116.

13   Ibid., p. 116.

14   Joshua Simon, 'Spaces of Appearance: Strategies of performative articulation, fictionalism and anachronisms,' in *And Europe Will Be Stunned*, ed. Ljungberg and Nilsson, pp. 108–109; see also Bartana et al., 'A Conversation between Yael Bartana, Galit Eilat, and Charles Esche,' p. 116.

15   See Riefenstahl's prologue to the first part of the two-part propaganda film *Olympia*, which begins with images of the ruins of the Acropolis.

of the last century: the collage. Bartana doesn't employ historical source material as 'artistic research' but rather uses artistic 'image-productions' that were created toward political ends and which live on today in our collective memory. In this way, her films introduce a level of reflection about artists and the role they play in the mechanism of writing history, just as she herself seems initially to be using her films to disseminate a vision of sociopolitical utopia.

In 1935, in the afterword to his essay 'The Work of Art in the Age of Its Technological Reproducibility,' Walter Benjamin wrote about the 'aestheticizing of politics' through the mass media of film and photography. Specifically he referenced the mass rallies common to fascism:

> The logical outcome of fascism is an aestheticizing of political life. The violation of the masses, whom fascism, with its *Führer* cult, forces to their knees, has its counterpart in the violation of an apparatus which is pressed into serving the production of ritual values. All efforts to aestheticize politics culminate in one point. That one point is war.[16]

While Bartana's artistic confrontation with this (historical) aestheticizing of politics also works with the mass media of film, she only involves herself with the fragments of a lost time, whose resuscitation in the present lacks the visual stringency and homogeneity of her source material.

The second part of the trilogy, *Mur i wieża,* reveals the practical implementation of the appeal. Beginning with a flashback to part one carries on this blending of anachronistic motifs into the contemporary narrative, common to each film and giving the trilogy as a whole structure. Following this entry point we are brought within the grounds of the former Warsaw Ghetto, in immediate proximity to sculptor Nathan Rapoport's work *Monument to the Ghetto Heroes* (1948). A group of men and women

---

16 Walter Benjamin, 'The Work of Art in the Age of Its Technological Reproducibility,' in *Walter Benjamin: Selected Writings, Volume 4 (1938–1940)*, ed. Michael W. Jennings (Cambridge, MA: Belknap Press, 2003), pp. 251–283.

in bright white clothing build an old-fashioned wooden kibbutz. Its most eye-catching features (from which the part two's title is derived) are a tower and a high wall topped with barbed wire that runs around the perimeter. The construction process is accompanied by different interpretations of the Polish national anthem. Having also been used in part one, we can consider the anthem as another leitmotif and atmospheric tool. The song's progressive character, typical of the genre, corresponds with the dynamic revolutionary attitude of the end of part one and beginning of part two. When the kibbutz is finished, Sierakowski appears and presents the builders with a red flag with an emblem of the Polish White Eagle and the Star of David. Two actors take the flag and affix it to the tower, while the group gathered below applaud, their gaze riveted upward—a staged sequence that Bartana accentuates by using the slow motion effect and playing a clip of the Israeli national anthem *Hatikvah* backwards.

This sequence represents the climax of the second film (fig. 6). On the one hand, the raising of the flag affirms the restitution of the Jewish community in Poland through an official act. On the other hand, territorial claims are traditionally designated with flags, a consideration that lends the euphoric JRMiP settlers the character of foreign intruders, as does the musical employment of the distorted Israeli anthem. Before it was an anthem, *Hatikvah* was embraced by the Zionist movement and stood for early nationalist efforts. Playing it backwards intensifies the impression of an inverse Aliyah. At the same time, its solemn, melancholy character forms a counterpoint to the progressive rhythm of the Polish anthem; here, emotional *overpowerment* is both represented and reception aesthetically produced.

A night scene follows in which a floodlight is used to symbolically link the kibbutz and the *Monument to the Ghetto Heroes*; the effect is to tilt the formerly festive mood toward a more threatening one. The kibbutz portrayed in the film is in fact an historical replica of a specific settlement erected by Zionists during the Arab

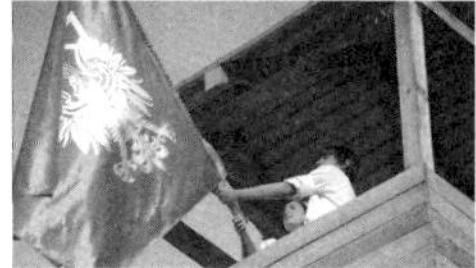

Fig 6 Yael Bartana, *Mur i wieża (Wall and Tower)*, 2009, 9'29"

revolt of 1936–1939, suited for defensive purposes.[17] An architecture whose first concrete application was to defend against the non-Jewish population of Palestine, becomes, due to its location in the former Jewish Ghetto of Warsaw—and particularly in light of a scene in which Bartana's characters continually sweep over the figures in *Monument to the Ghetto Heroes* with floodlights—a protected space against deportation. It becomes an image of remembrance, updated for a contemporary narrative via the continued threat of anti-Semitism (fig. 7). Simon points out the associations with the concentration camp, arising from both the structural qualities and the history of Poland, even though in this case the barbed wire is directed outward. Additionally, Simon mentions the archetypal character of this specialized form of the kibbutz, drawing a parallel between it and the Israeli barriers on the West Bank and the forms of settlement there, which, like the kibbutz, were once developed due to fear of the outside.[18]

Bartana's primary source of inspiration for the staging of settlers in *Mur i wieża* is Helmar Lerski's 1935 film *Avodah* (*Work*), especially its chapter *Building the colony*.[19] *Avodah* was already an important reference for *Summer Camp*, which was shown at documenta 12 among other venues.[20] Against the backdrop of growing anti-Semitism in the 1930s amid increasing demands for a Jewish nation, Lerski's *Avodah* became an epic monument to the early Zionist movement and its ideal of a socialist Jewish state. Featuring impressive images accompanied by a Paul Dessau composition played by fifty musicians from the Budapest Symphony Orchestra, *Avodah* depicts the collaborative erection of a kibbutz and the sourcing of life-giving water to make the land fertile

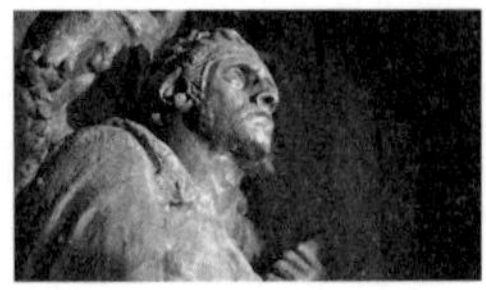

Fig 7 Yael Bartana, *Mur i wieża* (*Wall and Tower*), 2009, 11'33"

---

17 Joa Ljungberg, 'A Dizzying Appeal for Reconciliation,' in *And Europe Will Be Stunned*, Ljungberg and Nillson, p. 17; Simon, 'Spaces of Appearance,' p. 143.

18 Simon, 'Spaces of Appearance,' p. 143.

19 *Avodah*, 1935, directed by Helmar Lerski, 50 min., black and white, music with English subtitles, http://www.jewishfilm.org/Catalogue/films/avodah.htm, accessed 28.5.2015. See also Joanna Mytkowska, 'The Return of the Stranger,' in *Yael Bartana: And Europe Will Be Stunned*, Lingwood and Nairne, p. 132.

20 See Bartana and Von Drahten, 'Yael Bartana: Die Gründung des Mouvements [*sic*] vollzieht sich im Kopf,' p. 258.

(fig. 8).[21] Bartana describes her ambivalent perspective toward Lerski's film in the following terms: 'Avodah was just a fascinating film, so beautifully made but with a brutal relationship to the land. You see the influence of German and Soviet cinema as well, which might lead you to question the uniqueness of the whole Zionist movement and how much it is connected to other movements at the time.'[22]

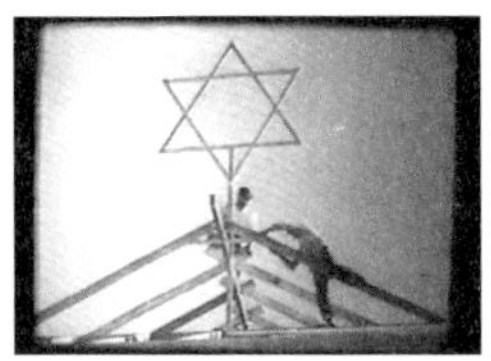
Fig 8   Helmar Lerski, *Avodah* (*Work*), 1934, 22'38''

The archetypal depiction of pioneers within a collective body as the foundation for forming an active Jewish nation grounded in joint work and effort was the central message of *Avodah*, as Ariel L. Feldestein makes clear in his study *Cinema and Zionism: The Development of a Nation through Film* (2012):

> These utopian images present a cooperative, healthy and happy society rather than the classic nuclear family with a father, a mother and children. The images do not reflect specific family relationships and the viewer realizes that the group provides a mutual guarantee and communal attachments to all members. The group, the collective, labouring together side by side—these are the secrets of the imminent revolution's success.[23]

Like the pioneers filmed by Lerski, Bartana's male and female actors remain nameless. With their white shirts, sailor caps, and headscarves, they wear clothing typical of early settlers. Hopeful faces that appeal emotionally to the viewer and engender empathy are captured in the frame of the camera zooming inward, a method also used by Lerski. And motifs that are encoded as socialist from *Avodah*, like human chains, the dividing of drinking water, or group listening to harmonica playing—which reinforce the image of a collective body—are also employed to great effect in Bartana's *Mur i wieża* (fig. 9, 10). The artist

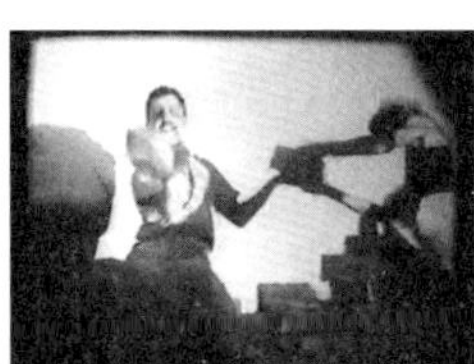
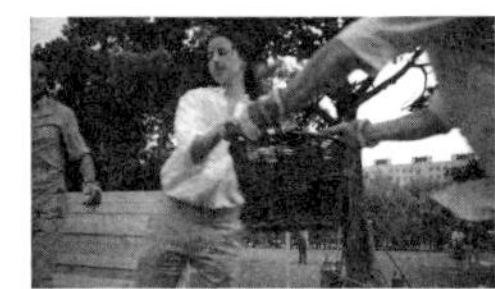
Fig 9   Helmar Lerski, *Avodah* (*Work*), 1934, 21'50''
Fig 10 Yael Bartana, *Mur i wieża* (*Wall and Tower*), 2009, 6'07''

---

21 Ariel L. Feldestein, *Cinema and Zionism: The Development of a Nation through Film* (London and Portland: Vallentine Mitchell, 2012), p. 153.
22 Bartana et al., 'A Conversation between Yael Bartana, Galit Eilat, and Charles Esche,' p. 95; for more on the German (Fritz Lang) and Russian (Sergei Eisenstein) influences on Lerski's filmic work, see Feldestein, *Cinema and Zionism*, p. 153.
23 Feldestein, *Cinema and Zionism*, pp. 149–150.

makes reference to the myth of the romantic, heroic era of the Zionist movement, which was created by filmmakers like Lerski, popularized through the medium of film, and still dominates the Zionist film canon into the present.[24]

However, Bartana re-encodes this myth; though she knows how to replicate its habitus to cinematographic perfection, the shared goal of the pioneers is no longer to construct a society in 'the promised land,' but rather in a Poland in which the history of both Jewish resistance and the Holocaust is deeply inscribed. The artist explains:

> What does it mean to build a kibbutz in the area of the former Warsaw Ghetto today? The new kibbutz was erected on the site where the future Jewish Museum of Warsaw will be build [the Polin Museum that opened in 2014]. But for me, this project is not about memory and creating a museum out of something, but about establishing a relationship to contemporary Israeli politics. Jews coming to Poland today would not constitute a diaspora anymore, but would be closely linked to a specific nation-state, to the militaristic rhetoric and politics of Israel. … The film juxtaposes reality and fiction, encouraging the viewer to reexamine constructed ideas of historical events. For me, it has actually become more and more interesting to create proposals rather than counter existing narratives.[25]

Whether the film actually relativizes the issue of a culture of memory must be questioned above all on account of the setting.[26] With *Mur i wieża* and its narrative of an inverse Aliyah, Bartana carries forward the history of cultural and

---

24 Galit Eilat addresses the phenomenon of a Jewish canon that exclusively consists of images of the settlement of Palestine by European Jews, and excludes in the collective memory the immigration of Arab Jews to Palestine. Galit Eilat, 'My Heart is in the East, and I in the Uttermost West,' *A Cookbook for Political Imagination*, pp. 102–110.

25 Bartana et al., 'A Conversation between Yael Bartana, Galit Eilat, and Charles Esche,' pp. 166–167.

26 In October 2014, the Polin Museum in Warsaw opened, featuring a permanent exhibition about the one-thousand-year-long history of Polish Jews at the site where Bartana also had a kibbutz built for the filming of her second film. The seven chronologically ordered sections of the exhibition, which encompass the span from the tenth century to the present, are opened by a 'poetical forest' as 'a space of historical imagination, inspired by legends that Jews told themselves about how they came to Poland and why they stayed.' Barbara Kirschenblatt-Gimblett and Anthony Polonsky, *POLIN: 1000 Year History of Polish Jews* (Warsaw: POLIN Museum of the History of Polish Jews, 2014), p. 27.

political Zionism. She seems to challenge Israel's status quo as a benighted land and destination of the Jewish diaspora, insofar as resuscitating Zionism's status in the present as a (historical) phenomenon, but conceives of it according to its origins as a socialist utopia, as has been done by filmmakers like Lerski, or even before that, by writer Theodor Herzl.[27]

Herzl's 1902 novel *The Old New Land* described the emancipation of the Jews into a tolerant, free, and egalitarian nation in the promise land. In Bartana's narrative, Poland is the utopic 'old new land' of the present day, where the dream of a pluralistic, tolerant, and open society seems more real than ever. As a daily routine comes into play, part two arrives at a prosaic end: the settlers learn Polish, plant flowers, and the residents of the surrounding buildings begin to inspect the settlement with curiosity, invited by a welcome sign at the entrance.

The third part of the trilogy, *Zamach*, relates most immediately to the present. By the first scene the assassination inferred in the title has been carried out with Sierakowski, dying the simultaneously tragic and stereotypical death of the visionary politician (fig. 11). In a later eulogy scene, the viewer learns that three shots were fired, which can be interpreted as both a reference to the assassination of John F. Kennedy and that of Yitzhak Rabin.

Iconographically, *Zamach* is dominated by bold motifs, primarily in service of a Stalinist aesthetic: pallbearers of various ethnicities conjure the image of Stalin as father of nations; a painting inspired by Boris Vladimirski's *Roses for Stalin* (1949) hangs behind the condolence book for Sierakowski, showing the politician surrounded by Young Pioneers with red carnations in their arms—a reference also to part one—recalling the origins of the JRMiP (fig. 12). The examination of art in service of a political worldview continues through the third section in which Bartana addresses the architecture, painting, and sculpture of Socialist Realism. The movement's growth and high status is illustrated through the number and composition of the

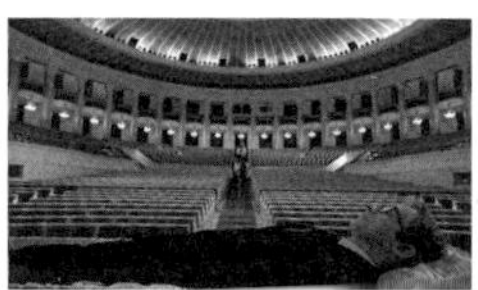

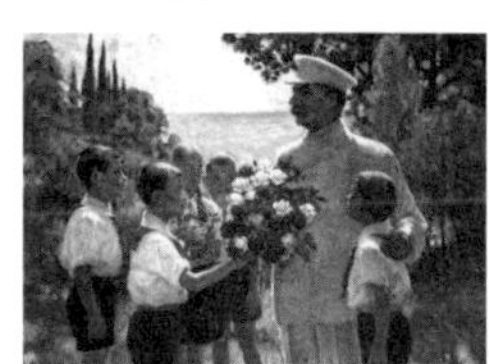

Fig 11 Yael Bartana, *Zamach (Assassination)*, 2011, 3'47"
Fig 12 Boris Eremeevich Vladimirsky, *Roses for Stalin*, 1949, oil on canvas, 100.5 x 141 cm, private collection of Patrick and Werner Horvath

---

27 See Bartana et al., 'A Conversation between Yael Bartana, Galit Eilat, and Charles Esche,' p. 169.

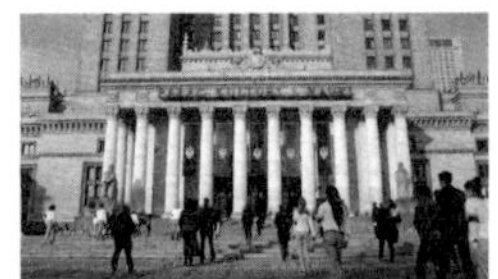

Fig 13 Yael Bartana, *Zamach* (*Assassination*), 2011, 3'10"

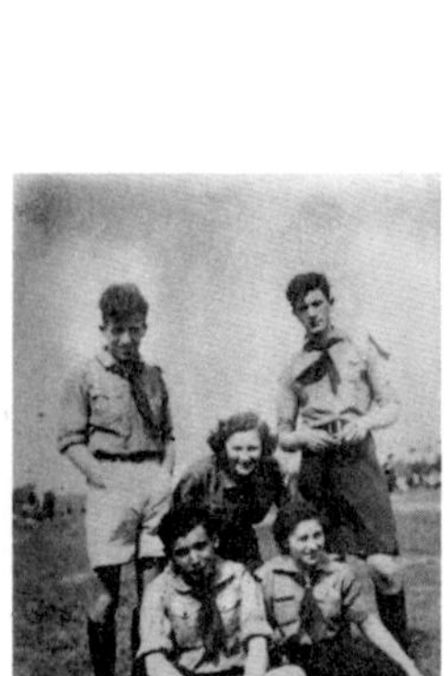

Fig 14 Group portrait of members of the Hashomer Hatzair socialist Zionist youth movement, Warsaw, Poland, 1938, United States Holocaust Memorial Museum, Washington

mourners attending Sierakowski's open coffin in the richly decorated Palace of Culture and Science in Warsaw (fig. 13). The palace was built between 1952 and 1955 in the style of Socialist Classicism as a gift from the Soviet Union to the Polish People's Republic. The monumentality of its architecture to this day calls to mind the Communist dictatorship. Incorporating primarily Stalinist motifs evokes the sorrowful chapter in Poland's history beginning with the Molotov-Ribbentrop Pact and the Soviet invasion of 1939, and continuing through the Communist foreign rule from 1945 to 1989 before the land became its own country.

While some of the mourners wearing contemporary civilian outfits pay their respects to the dead, the young members of the JRMiP pay their final respects in Young Pioneer uniforms. In their white shirts and neckties they don't only recall Stalin youth organizations, but also the members of the Socialist-Zionist youth organization Hashomer Hatzair, which was particularly active in Poland in the years between the First and Second World Wars (fig. 14).[28] Bartana provocatively and pointedly challenges the 'uniqueness of the whole Zionist movement'[29] with this hybrid depiction of JRMiP members. Alongside the contemporary context, irony also serves as a means of refraction: the stick figure drawn by Israeli journalist Yaron London in the condolence book, or a plump-looking concrete bust of Sierakowski that is displayed. However, it is particularly in the last third of *Zamach* that Bartana undertakes a programmatic turn, expanding the circle of those addressed by the JRMiP to include a transnational perspective—detaching her narrative from the specific circumstances of Jewish and Polish history and tying it instead into the contemporary political situation in Europe, and the hopes of a young generation looking toward the future:

28 See Kirschenblatt-Gimblett and Polonsky, *POLIN*, p. 281.
29 See, as above, Bartana et al., 'A Conversation between Yael Bartana, Galit Eilat, and Charles Esche,' p. 95; for more on the German (Fritz Lang) and Russian (Sergei Eisenstein) influences on Lerski's filmic work, see Feldestein, *Cinema and Zionism*, p. 153.

> I belong to the third generation since the Shoa. For us, the history is far in the past, even if the memories are still alive. But I feel so strongly in my generation that we all want to break with the status quo and live in a different society, a better society, a society finally freed from national divisions and brutality. I think—the world can change itself, and it's already doing so.[30]

Various figures contribute what at first seem to be contradictory personal views on the idea of a Jewish renaissance. The people, as with Sierakowski, are figures from public life or the cultural/political sphere: 'among the commentators is an avowed Zionist; then liberal Jews step up; finally, the far-left journalist and actor Yaron London,' is how Bartana characterizes the speakers.[31] A contradictory tension remains between the ongoing reality of anti-Semitism, and the proposed utopia of the movement—neither can the one be denied, nor the other disavowed as naive.

Lastly, two youths from the JRMiP step onto the podium (fig. 15), repeating the appeal originally made by Sierakowski, just as emphatically. Over the course of the speech, they extend it significantly, directing it toward all those 'for whom there is no place in their homeland, the expelled and persecuted.' They end their appeal with the words: 'We shall be strong in our weakness.' The utopia of a Jewish return to Poland transfers over to a global perspective, in which all victims of the political status quo can find refuge; the particularities of Jewish-Polish history and identity are synthesized into a sense of multinational universality. Bartana's trilogy thereby becomes a parable, one that no longer derives its reference points from twentieth-century history and thereby the past. It rather surveys the backdrop of the present day—with its restrictive refugee policies, intensifying nationalism, and racially, sexually, or religiously motivated persecution and discrimination—and breaks away from it.

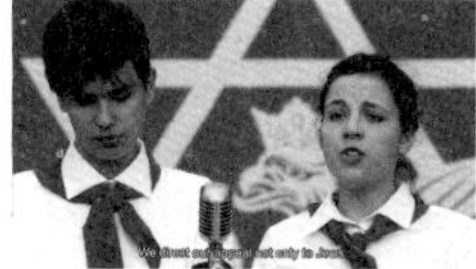

Fig 15 Yael Bartana, *Zamach (Assassination)*, 2011, 28'30"

---

30 See Bartana et al., 'A Conversation between Yael Bartana, Galit Eilat, and Charles Esche,' p. 260.
31 Ibid., pp. 258–259.

The Mozambique Institute Project

A Montage of Affect

Catarina Simão

I

In 2014 I was involved in a research project on nascent signs of a radical pedagogy in the context of Mozambique's struggle for independence. The war that pitted the Mozambique Liberation Front (FRELIMO) against the Portuguese colonial army lasted from 1964 to 1974. At stake was control of the 'Liberated Zones,' the entire northern region of Mozambique, bordering Tanzania, a staunch ally of the freedom movements.

The project lasted for over a year and resulted in research (on three different continents) on the history of the first FRELIMO school in Dar es Salaam. It was there, on the other side of the border, that the conditions to enable a new generation of Mozambicans to pursue their studies were envisaged and a new pedagogical system was founded, breaking away from the colonial system.

As early as 1962, while he was preparing the armed insurrection, the first president of the FRELIMO, Eduardo Mondlane, was fundraising to build this school. The first grant was offered by the American Ford Foundation, which enabled the school to function for its first year. The United States government did not oppose the support because, despite the agreements for an alliance in relation to Portuguese colonial policies, the Kennedy administration believed that supporting the education of African youths would increase US influence and prevent communists from gaining power in countries that were on their way to gaining independence.

American support for the Mozambican freedom movement strained US relations with Portugal and resulted in a controversy that was in large measure fuelled by the international press. At the American Ford Foundation archives in New York, the main elements of this controversy are revealed in letters exchanged between the foundation's president, Henry T. Heald, and Alberto Franco Nogueira, the Portuguese foreign minister at the time. This correspondence describes how the logic behind this educational project in fact concealed international political action, irrespective of the terms used to classify it as being a neutral or humanitarian act, and this was the case both on the US side as well as for the Mozambican Nationalist Movement.

In Lisbon I discovered a text written by Eduardo Mondlane, which played a decisive role in shaping my research. To be precise, what I read was a Portuguese translation of the memorandum sent in 1963, on behalf of the FRELIMO, to the African Liberation Committee. In it Eduardo Mondlane explained how he and Janet Mondlane, his American wife, had conceived of an educational project for young Mozambicans in Dar es Salaam, which they had called the 'Mozambique

Institute.' The idea emerged during a journey across Mozambique from 1960 to 1961, while Eduardo Mondlane was still working under the aegis of the United Nations. During the visit the couple met dozens of African youths wanting to pursue their studies, even though they were hindered by economic constraints and the system of racial stratification, which unofficially controlled the black population's access to higher levels of education.

The memorandum had originally been written in English but the text nonetheless transmitted Eduardo Mondlane's vivid capacity to communicate, reflecting his visionary mind, which felt the urgency for ambitious, emancipatory acts. In this text even the most elaborate ideas were circumspectly translated into impeccable Portuguese and words referring to concepts of emancipation were carefully underlined in pencil. One might think that the meticulous translation and the underlining in pencil were the work of an enthusiastic reader. However, this was not the case. This text was part of the archives of the Polícia Internacional e de Defesa do Estado (PIDE) [International and State Police], i.e., the Portuguese security agency, and is currently preserved at the Portuguese National Archive of Torre do Tombo in Lisbon. It was thus a document that had been intercepted by informers or spies and subsequently translated and examined by trained PIDE/DGS staff.

Eduardo Mondlane's text continued to explain the measures implemented to obtain additional funding to build the Mozambique Institute, for which the American Ford Foundation had provided the first important contribution. During this phase, Eduardo Mondlane was probably unaware that the initial support would be stopped due to allegations that the FRELIMO was involved in an armed struggle, with which the US administration and the American Ford Foundation ostensibly did not wish to be involved. Portuguese diplomacy had won the first battle.

This intelligent text, with its inspiring vision, was carefully examined and rewritten in Portuguese. However, it was interpreted in a manner that was radically different from its intended meaning. Can this contradiction be explained aside from the obvious ideological distortion? Why is it that expressions of emancipation, which nowadays resonate with our common sensibilities, could not be articulated fifty years ago? Perhaps the fascist mentality, so carefully structured in Portuguese, was not prepared to understand such a radical essay on a commitment to the future.

It is therefore revealing to learn that the expectations for transforming the Portuguese language were not formulated by those who opposed the Portuguese fascist regime, but rather by the freedom struggles in Africa. The decision to use Portuguese during the freedom struggle in Mozambique provided linguistic unity in the Liberated Zones and military training camps whilst also solving the problem of having to choose which African language would become the official tongue after independence. However, Portuguese soon ceased to be simply the language of the enemy. The FRELIMO adapted the Portuguese language to its own combatant culture. New songs were created, poetry and literature were appropriated and transformed. History books were rewritten. Literacy was freed from the logic of the mechanical memorization promoted by colonial education. Textbooks were reinvented based on revolutionary concepts; mathematics was now taught on the basis of oral learning, as compared to being taught on the basis of texts, which similarly corresponded to the European-colonial model. The Portuguese language acquired a new sonority, unknown outside the Liberated Zones. Words such as 'comrade,' 'responsible,' and 'engaged' were used with the connotation of social participation, self-discipline, and emancipation.

II

Initially, Eduardo Mondlane was determined to do everything in his power to achieve independence by peaceful means, using diplomacy and influence to try and convince the Portuguese government to negotiate. These efforts were in vain and by the time of the first FRELIMO congress, held in September 1962, he had abandoned diplomacy. He became convinced that an armed insurrection was necessary. In his theoretical plan for the struggle, Eduardo Mondlane defined his vision to legitimize the use of violence: 'Formal independence only substitutes the colonial with the neo-colonial. True freedom can only emerge from actions of empowerment and cultural emancipation.'

These sentences, proffered by an intellectual who was also the leader of an armed movement invested in achieving independence for his country, articulate the way in which the same revolutionary concept generated both culture and war. In his writings, struggle and culture are complementary tools to emancipate the Mozambican people. They have a common theory and share the same terminology.

Acts of emancipation which do not shed their violent impulse are part of an overarching experience and are hence difficult to translate when transposed to other contexts. This is particularly the case with the FRELIMO's international politics and their relationship with the West, since socialist countries were clearly interested in supplying arms in order to implement a type of international socialism in Africa. In keeping with the evolution of its political aims and depending on interlocutors, whether internal or external, socialist or capitalist, the FRELIMO skillfully promoted or eliminated references to violence in its discourse.

This dexterity made it possible to separate the war effort from educational initiatives, allowing the world to turn a blind eye to the situation's violent implications. This was how the Mozambique Institute managed to garner the support of the World Council of Churches and was the basis for support from the governments of other countries too. Denmark and Norway were members of the North Atlantic Treaty Association (NATO) and, along with Sweden and Finland, were also members of the European Free Trade Association (EFTA). They provided support to the Mozambique Institute at the same time as supporting Portugal's colonial policies.

The Mozambique Institute enshrined this ambiguous and singular model, which allowed it to inhabit a schizophrenic world: the vision of those who based their support on a channel of moral and purely humanitarian action and those who viewed the freedom movements as a necessary violence to achieve freedom from the yoke of capitalism. This was the case of the Angola Comité, in Holland, which regularly provided the FRELIMO with official Portuguese army reports, sent to Amsterdam by army officers in Lisbon who opposed the colonial wars. The FRELIMO also received foreign support from independent organizations that appeared during the struggle against US aggression in Vietnam and the anti-apartheid solidarity movements. These groups sought, above all, to attract support among civil society and pressured their respective governments to stop supporting Portugal's colonial policies.

In the long term the Mozambique Institute's objective was to enable some of its students to continue their higher education abroad—in European or Soviet countries or in the US—thus creating a generation of personnel who could take responsibility for building a nation: 'Serving the evolving needs of the free Mozambican people.' In the short term, however, the idea was to mobilize Mozambican youths for the movement and prepare them for the struggle's immediate objectives by imparting knowledge in areas such as geography, sciences, and mathematics. Learning the Portuguese language was a key element of the Institute's educational system, since it promoted a greater capacity to understand and apply military strategy. The guerrilla concepts taught by Chinese, Cuban, Soviet, and Algerian instructors could not be translated in the Bantu languages—which the majority of the young students spoke.

My film *Effects of Wording* (2014) shows documents, photographs, and excerpts from films derived from the data compiled during my research in the US, Holland, and, subsequently, in Mozambique. It includes oral testimonies by a former teacher and a student at the FRELIMO school, transmitting the voices and experiences of those who witnessed this era. This text takes the form of a more theoretical and descriptive interpretation of the lexical battle which became an integral part of the struggle. *Effects of Wording* also reveals my fascination for the principles of a militant structure and for organizing the struggle's matrix according to implicit rules, which need to be deciphered. This matrix was reinforced by the distribution and transcription of these operations within various other figurative strategies: the colours of the flag, the content of school textbooks, clothes, songs, and other procedures associated with the constant official representation of the struggle. The formula which transformed education into a strategy for war and emancipation is essentially transmitted via the experience of the film's visual and sound editing.

It was not possible to access the official FRELIMO archives on the Mozambique Institute. Nevertheless, I imagine they recreate the propaganda mechanisms to manage external relations and not only that. Other elements, which I saw described in other sources, corroborated the question of the specific juncture, which in many ways resisted the implementation of Eduardo Mondlane's plan for independence. This plan did not achieve a consensus from the foundation of the movement itself. Eduardo Mondlane's proximity to the imperialist front was used to discredit him as a leader of the movement. Internal and external subversive actions combined and took advantage of generational conflicts, instigating a revolt among students studying abroad, and, as a result, among the students at the Mozambique Institute. The students rebelled and became involved in violent actions. This crisis forced Tanzanian authorities to take steps and the Mozambique Institute's school was closed in 1968. The group of white teachers whom students had accused of being spies were expelled from the country; the details and main protagonists of this episode within the movement have been carefully studied by FRELIMO historians because the crisis had immediate consequences: the elimination of some elements of the movement and the assassination of the FRELIMO president Eduardo Mondlane in February 1969.

In order to ensure continuity and to

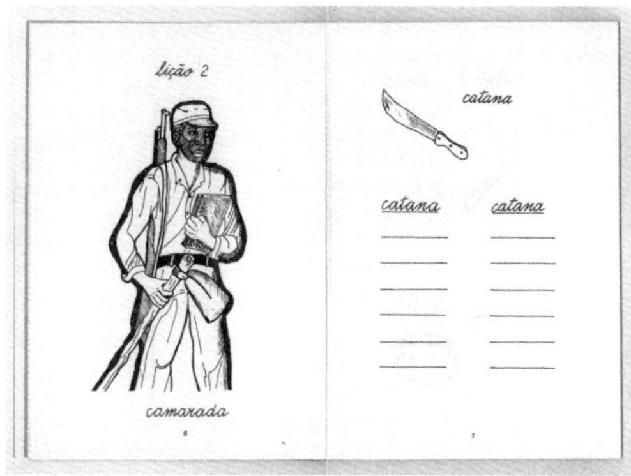

Fig 1   Lesson 2, *Livro da alfabetização 1* (Literacy Textbook 1), Bagamoyo, 1972

facilitate the restoration of relations with the organizations that supported the FRELIMO, a new strategy was formulated that did not focus on the violent episode of 1968. The Mozambique Institute survived the closure of the school, albeit only in name, becoming a fundraising entity that strove to maintain a set of diverse social structures. It established a new school, which opened two years later. The new school opened in a former training camp situated 70 km from Dar es Salaam, in Bagamoyo. Away from the city's disturbing influences, the FRELIMO sought to correct the 'vices and defects' of the past. Students arriving at Bagamoyo to attend the school had to have already lived in the Liberated Zones or undergone military training.

III

Even if the involuntary memories of the archives are imperfect sources for writing history they nonetheless served as a powerful simulation of experiences. It is known, for example, that in the archive's terminology, index signified a brief description, a shortcut to a larger cache of information. The index is a technical solution to reduce and create distance from that to which it refers. However, this shortcut quickly generates other new forms of affection and ties to these contents. In other words, there is a lag between the word and the universe this word evokes, leading from an initial state of detachment to that of a new attachment. Since it proved impossible to access the official FRELIMO archives, I asked myself which mechanisms would store the memory of this transformation, of this interval, where the same expressions (carefully translated and underlined) which clashed with the interests of the Portuguese fascist regime evoked gestures of emancipation for those who sought to defeat the colonial system?

'Lesson 2' of *Literacy Textbook* 1 occupies the two sheets that can be seen in the figure reproduced. On the right side there is a drawing of a machete. On the left is a guerrilla fighter, carrying a book, a hoe, and a rifle. In the terminology associated with the struggle the weapon signifies combat and sacrificing one's body, the hoe signifies production and autonomy, and the book signifies raising awareness in the future. 'What is important is to go to school, to harvest coconuts and to fire against the Portuguese,' said Samora Machel in the film *Dieci giorni con i guerriglieri nel Mozambico libero* (1972), 'The two things go hand in hand; one lives if the other lives.' What the guerrilla fighter is carrying are the tools of his own emancipation.

You can see the word 'comrade' [*camarada*] in the caption of the drawing and can say it while understanding its significance. This means that we are far from decoding the cognitive relationship between the image and its caption. We have to go back.

From the perspective of Paulo Freire, the famous Brazilian pedagogue, the process of literacy was also based on ties of affection between the thing, the way it was vocalized, and the way it was written. In experiments begun in 1960s Brazil he sought to identify the subjects and concerns that were of most interest for oppressed communities. These themes were then summarized into a single word. The word that was identified by this process was '*favela*' [slum]. In Freire's methodology, students began to read, write, and build new words on the basis of the phonetic units 'fa,' 've,' and 'la' only after a dialogue and after analyzing what their experiences of living in a slum meant for the community. Learning the word

corresponded to a progressive awareness of the world it evoked. Each of its syllables allows this awareness to create other words based on the same syllables. Freire called this formula 'reading the world before reading the word' and developed it in his theories on critical pedagogy.

At the new FRELIMO school in Bagamoyo, preparations for literacy campaigns brought literacy students together around problems that were similar to those described by Freire. Students and teachers continued to experiment and test methodologies. Working with a group of students who came from different regions in the interior it was found that the word 'machete' was something 'everyone knows and uses,' a work tool that was part of everybody's daily life. The 'R' sound does not exist in many Bantu languages; those who spoke Shimakonde, for example, found it difficult to pronounce, read, and understand the word 'comrade.' It was a word that was difficult to work with directly. The purpose of 'Lesson 2' was to link the sounds of the Portuguese words for machete [*catana*] and comrade [*camarada*]. This was a cognitive process based first on the affective ties with the machete tool and the subsequent transfer of this bond to a word that had phonetic similarities in Portuguese: comrade.

The comrade has a hoe
The comrade has a weapon
The comrade has a book
The comrade carries the old man
The comrade builds a house

These textbooks served as auxiliary material for the literacy campaigns promoted among the population in villages and training camps in the 'interior,' i.e., in the Liberated Zones. Many of these materials were lost while fleeing from attacks or left behind as they were considered subversive. However, since searches of white Europeans could be problematic depending on the official alliances their countries had with Portugal, some did survive, preserved among the belongings of European anti-colonial activists who had come to Tanzania to support the FRELIMO cause and who contributed as instructors.

Dutch teachers who had taught at the Bagamoyo school told me that this literacy textbook, apparently more politicized than previous works, had been conceived after Freire's visit to the FRELIMO school in 1972. This, combined with an approximate calculation based on correspondence between the Mozambique Institute and the heads of the World Council for Churches in Geneva, means it is possible to date this manual (*Literacy Textbook* 1) to 1972. This is a cyclostyled and stapled reproduction, undoubtedly produced in Dar es Salaam, at the Institute, which FRELIMO continued to use after the crisis for various purposes, such as a structure to host refugees. It also served as a printing workshop for the Department of Information and Propaganda to replicate the movement's propaganda texts and magazines.

Freire had been invited by representatives of the FRELIMO and the Mozambique Institute to visit the school in Bagamoyo. After a previous meeting with members of the Movimento Popular de Libertação de Angola (MPLA) in Zambia, Freire was keen to become better acquainted with the nature of the new educational methods that were being developed, particularly in the Liberated Zones, where the struggle was a pedagogical practice. His meeting with individuals who, holding weapons in their hands, were testing the conditions developed in his theories, must have impressed Freire. However, the story told by those who hosted him differed. Some spoke of the 'coincidence' between the tasks they were already implementing for literacy and the method put forward by Freire. Former Dutch teachers at the school spoke enthusiastically about his stay but feared that in the literacy manual that was prepared after his visit pedagogy had been sacrificed in favour of ideology.

Freire's visit can be viewed in different ways, but what is clear is how from lesson to lesson texts and images transmit a reality inextricably intertwined with life and experiences in the Liberated Zones. The meeting with the literacy students at Bagamoyo resulted in the tools for a radical indexation of the struggle.

IV

A short film made on Super 8 in 1967 with no sound shows everyday scenes from inside the training camps and the Mozambique Institute. This is an unexpected discovery, a break with the habitual FRELIMO militant cinema I found during research, where voiceovers and discourses are dominant. Domestic formats of films would only be tested for professional production in Mozambique after independence was achieved, meaning such images would most likely have been filmed by an amateur: the intimacy with which it is filmed means viewers imagine they could have shot those images—discarding the express function of describing a new vision within the one that is being observed. Instead, these images seem to intuitively describe the landscape, the building, the situations associated with its functioning, the reading room, the chemistry laboratory, a mathematics class, the playgrounds, and other activities. The core of the film is a sequence recording rehearsals for a play on the terrace of the Institute's building. A white man guides a group of black youths. One can sense the affection among them. The footage has a slow and amiable tempo in stark contrast to the scene being portrayed: an inert body is forced into surrender, pushed against a wall. Coconut trees can be seen in the background of the landscape and a sign staked to the ground clearly reads: 'Mozambique Institute.'

This film documenting everyday life at the Institute was made by Jacinto Veloso, a general and former combatant in the national struggle for independence, who is also a historical leader of the FRELIMO party and former minister for state security in Mozambique. Veloso was a pilot with the Portuguese army when he deserted in 1963, using the plane with which he was going on a mission to join the Mozambique Liberation Front in Tanzania. After various episodes resulting from this radical act Veloso returned to Dar es Salaam in 1966 and became a teacher at the Mozambique Institute. He taught geography, adapting the programme to include reconnaissance of military maps.

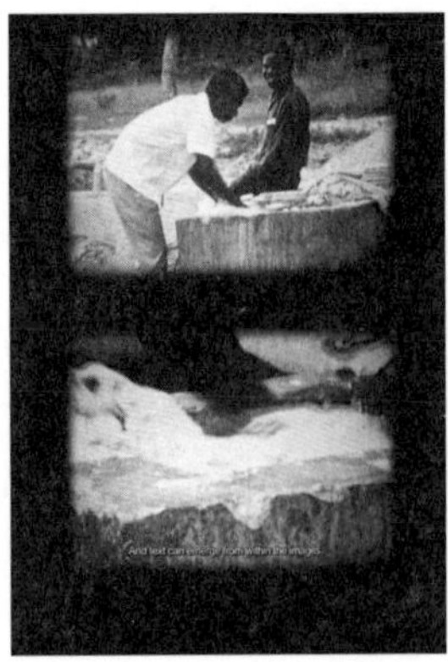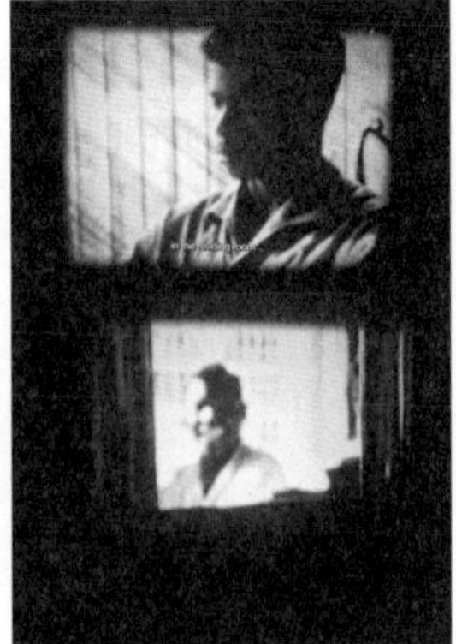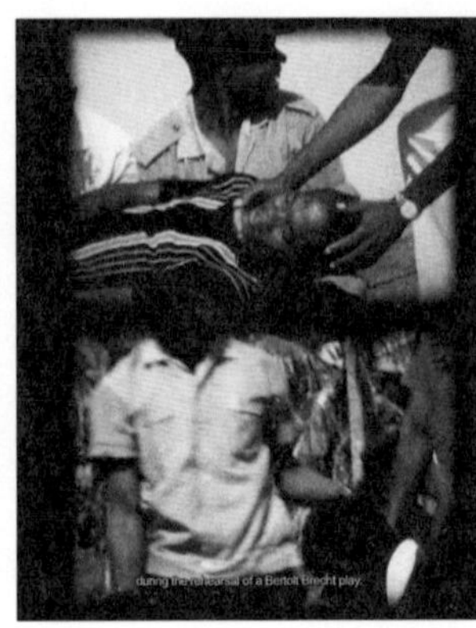

Fig 2–4
Jacinto Veloso, *Tempo de Luta* (Time of Struggle), 1967–1968, screen captures

I used this film in my research to identify the students and teachers who appeared in the images. Between adults and children those who were the easiest to identify had later assumed a public role in the political and cultural reconstruction of Mozambique and were part of the structure, at the university, in diplomatic circles and ministries. Other youths who could be identified were involved in the violent crisis of 1968, others died during the struggle whilst others fled to Kenya for fear of retaliation, not returning to Mozambique after independence. Veloso recalled that the play, which was being rehearsed on the Institute's terrace, had been a radical communist work by Bertolt Brecht.

As this concrete information became progressively articulated with the images I discovered they took on an inherently indexical quality, which accompanies an unexpressed text and causes the camera to linger at precise points. By examining the images that describe the history of the Mozambique Institute, I started to question them precisely in relation to the instructions that are implicit to the system of image/unexpressed text.

Two key moments reversed the way in which these images were initially interpreted by me— so that they no longer pertain definitively to the category of biographical memory. First, in the sequence showing the play, in which I discern the didactic and predictive functions of repeating gestures of violence. This frees the entire sequence from the need to imagine an audience for the play, with the exception of Veloso's camera-witness. The participants are the ones who are learning. By instituting the idea of a function associated with the staging of gestures, this also shakes off the initial signs of its being an amateur film, now imbued with meanings that have precise purpose. While capturing the preparation, staging, and repetition of the action, the film transmits the militant nature of the actions. The Mozambique Institute was a part of the project and efforts to achieve Mozambique's political independence. What narrative could these images reproduce if not that of being a constant witness to the various phases of its struggle?

Later, individuals holding photography equipment appear surprised. In one of these situations (at the Bagamoyo training camp), Veloso's camera follows the photographer, recording the moment when the guerrilla fighters pose and how they relax after the shutter clicks. It is this silent 'click' that diverts the eye from the discipline that has moulded these youths. Here, spotting this moment is like touching the moving image, or like turning over a photograph in your hand to read what the caption says on the reverse.

The ways of occupying spaces, the capturing of everyday tasks, how the youths

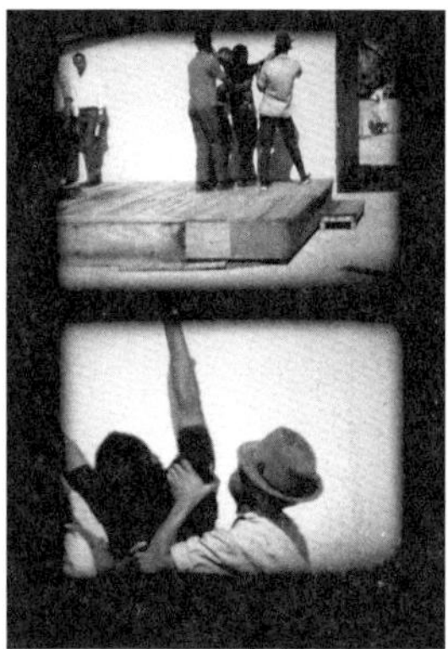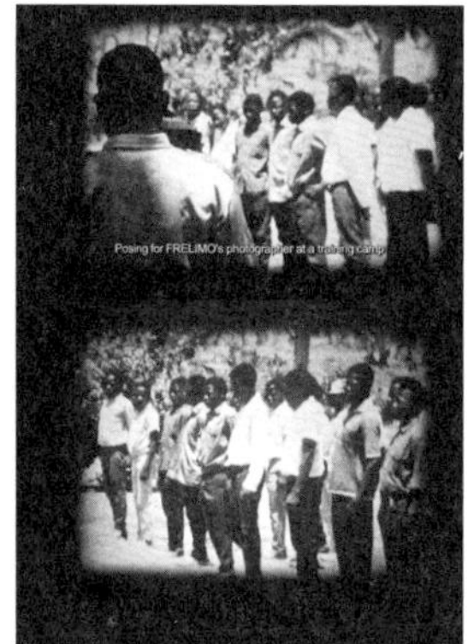

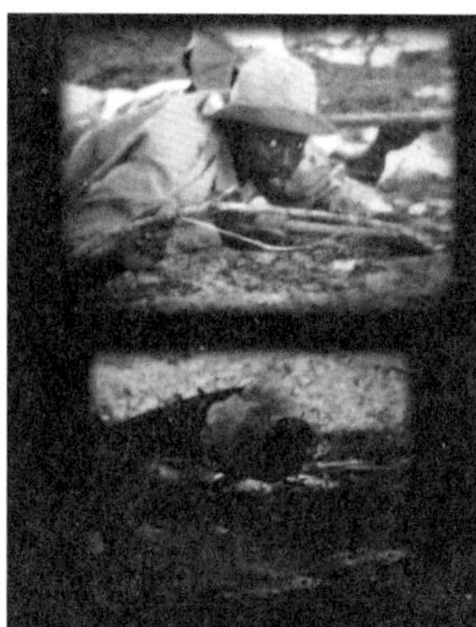

Fig 5–7
Jacinto Veloso,
Tempo de Luta
(Time of Struggle),
1967–1968, screen
captures

are encouraged to exercise both autonomy and discipline shows revolution as the resolution of different technical problems. Insurgency is shown as the outcome of both scientific and pedagogical advancement with the school serving as a proto-state. This is in fact the condition of the entire movement, at the site where the performance of the students and the organization itself unfolds and is tested, with a view to leading the country in the future.

I realized that the images in the Super 8 film and in *Literacy Textbook* 1 are complementary in the way they produce meaning through the montage process. Just like in 'Lesson 2' the contents of the Super 8 film are captured indexically. In both, indexation speaks to a common universe of ties of affection, where the tools for struggle and emancipation are being forged. It is the images' ability to instigate these ties of affection at the moment they are viewed that gives them this indexical quality.

The incorporation of the Super 8 images in *Effects of Wording* meant to provide clues to another story that is being told; firstly, using a strategy of impressions and contagion: surrounding them with conventional records such as archival documents and using an 'image-caption' logic. I added a voiceover which dubs the flux of images and duplicates its 'factual' interpretation. This echo of excess or gratuitous amplification seeks to bring the

experience of the reception specifically to the forefront. My intention was to form a circle of exchanges in which each of the 'image-fact' systems are freed from the burden of fixing a single protocol to describe the images.

…
In the reading room
…
During the interval
…
In the classroom
…
During the rehearsal of a
play by Bertolt Brecht
…
Posing for the FRELIMO
photographer, at the training camp

This echo becomes a new effect in which viewers could recognize themselves as being aloof observers, as though it would never really be possible to grasp these images. Like in 'Lesson 2,' its mode of operation escapes us as we might be too far advanced in our reading skills. These Super 8 images are pioneers in the context of a chronology of militant films that expanded shortly thereafter, with the arrival of foreign directors to the Liberated Zones. However, control of these images clearly belongs to a militant political group.

Public Collection of Modern Art

Alexandra Pirici & Manuel Pelmuş

Fig 1 Alexandra Pirici &
Manuel Pelmuş, *Public
Collection of Modern Art*, 2014,
enactment of *Luncheon on the
Grass* (1863), oil on canvas, by
Edouard Manet

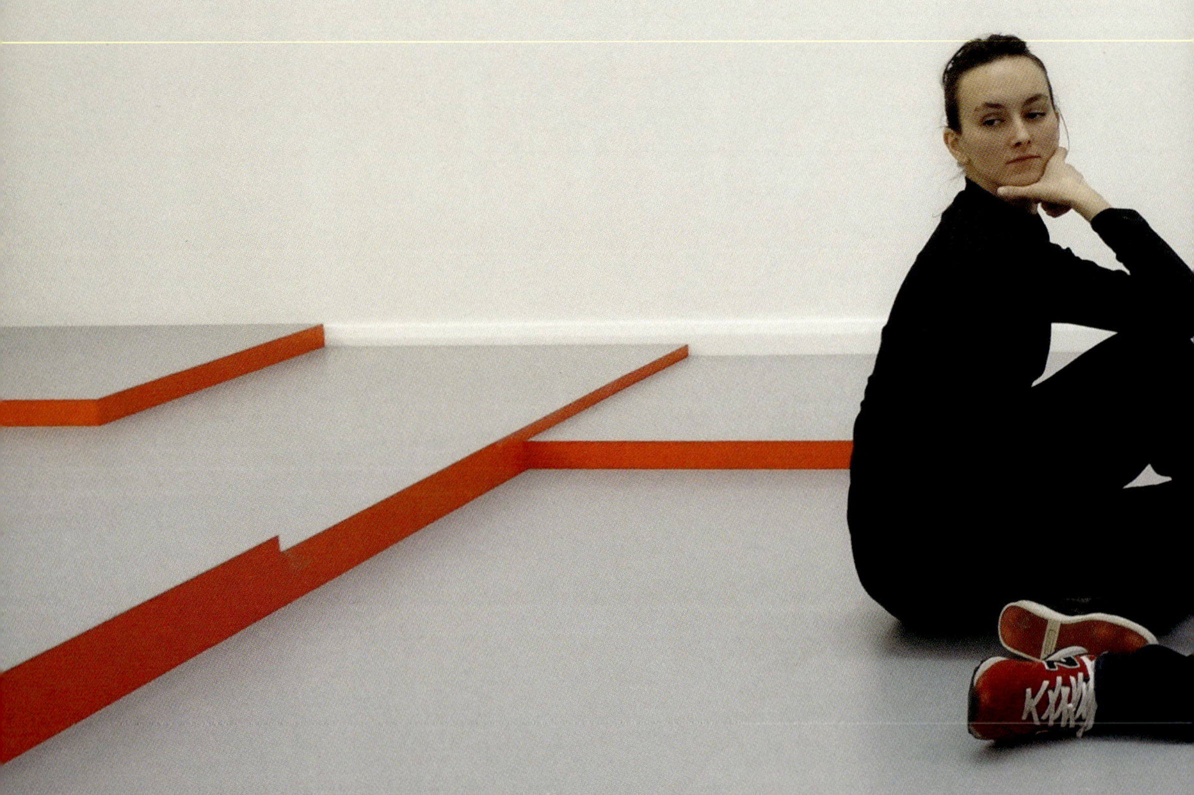

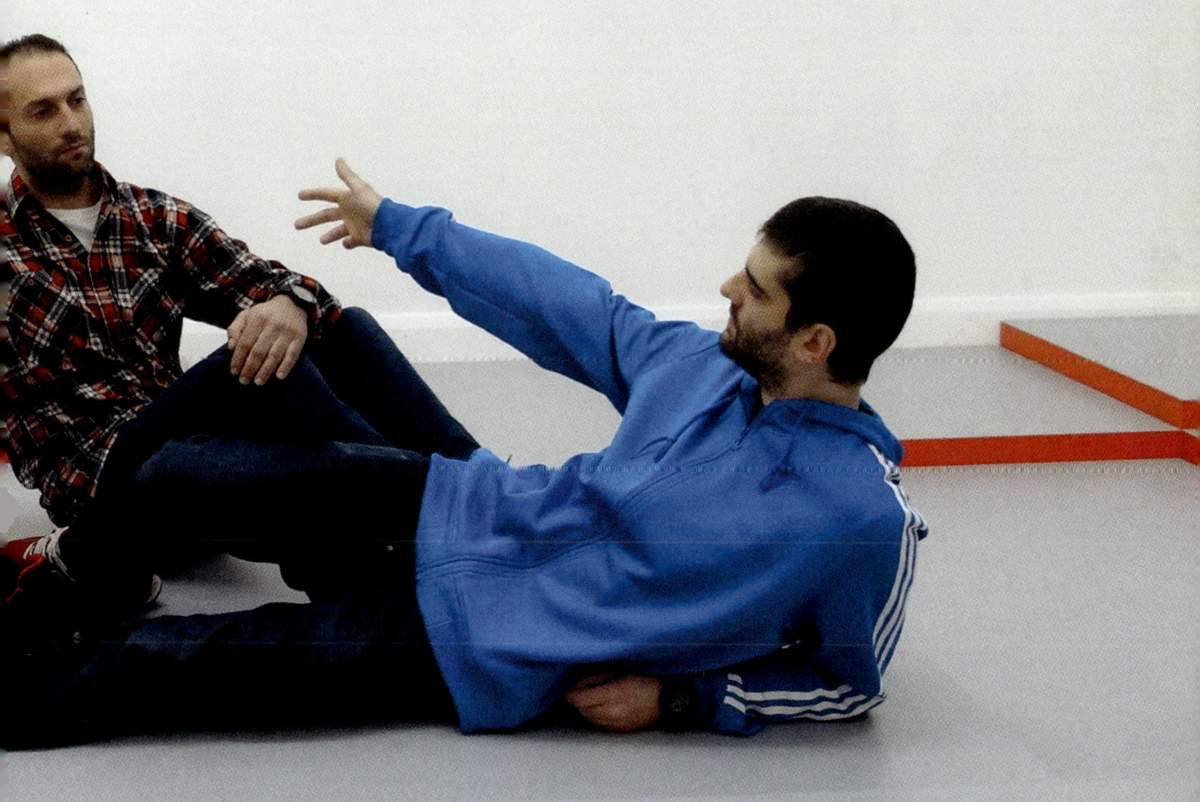

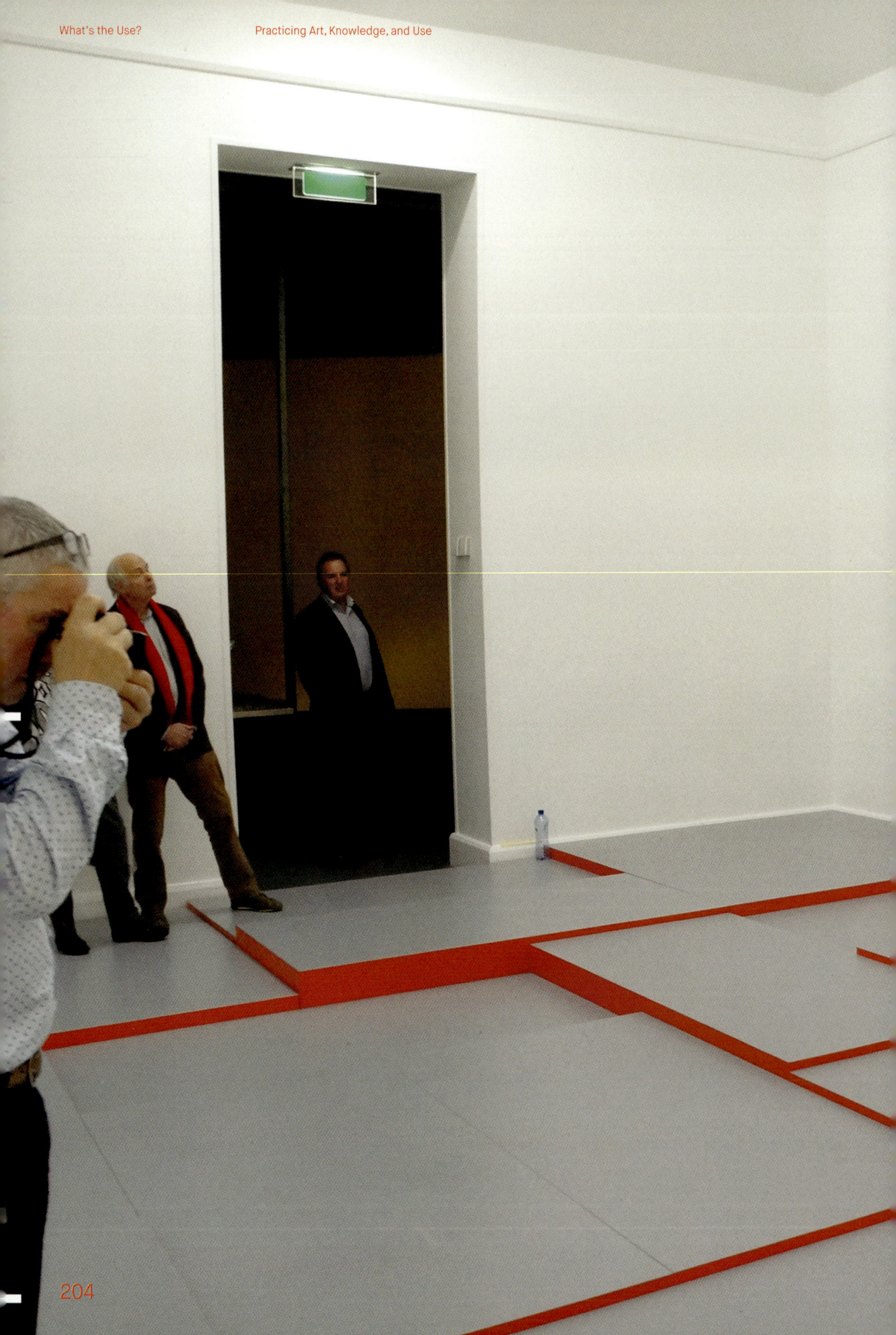

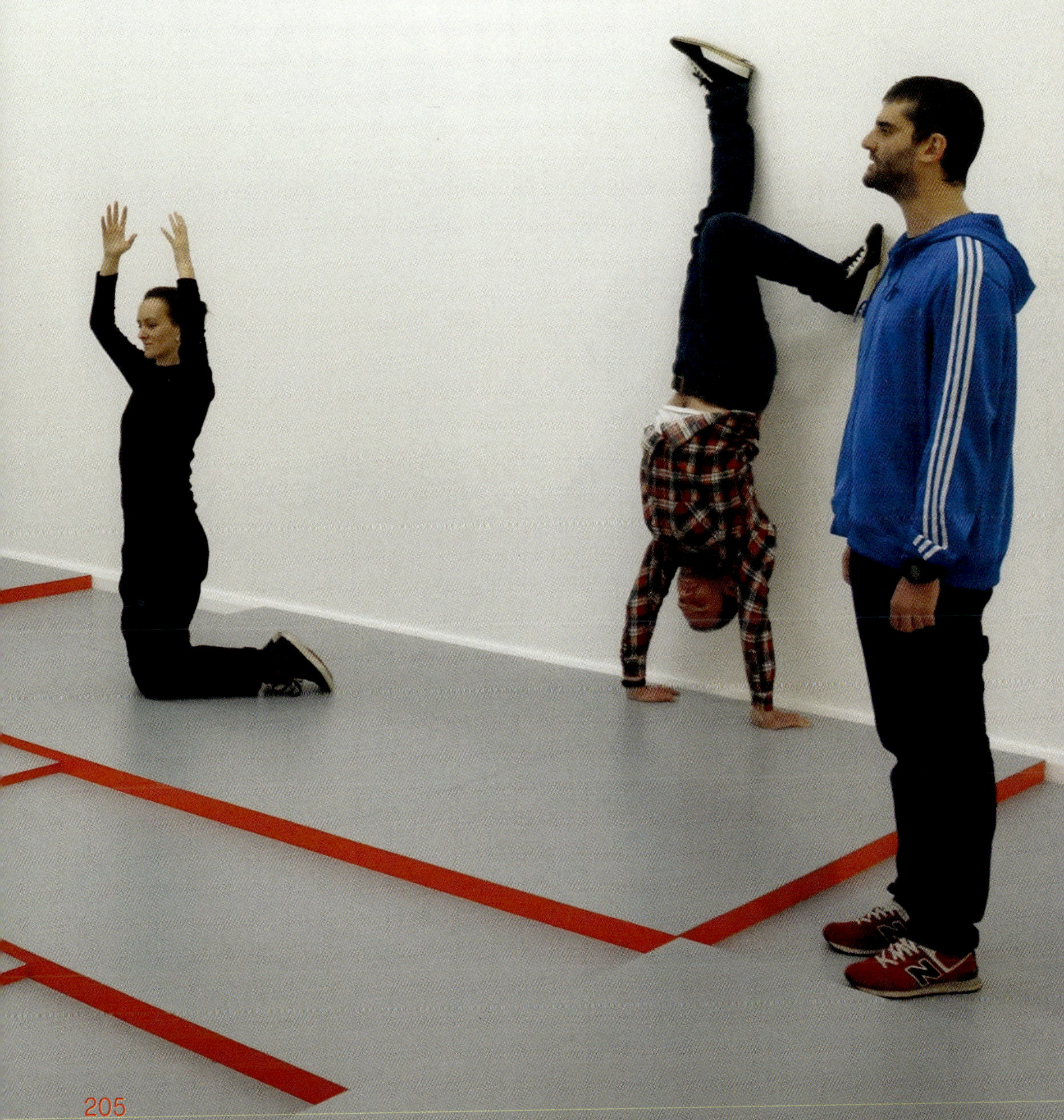

Fig 2   Alexandra Pirici & Manuel Pelmuş, *Public Collection of Modern Art*, 2014, enactment of *The Beach* (1927), oil on canvas, by Max Beckmann

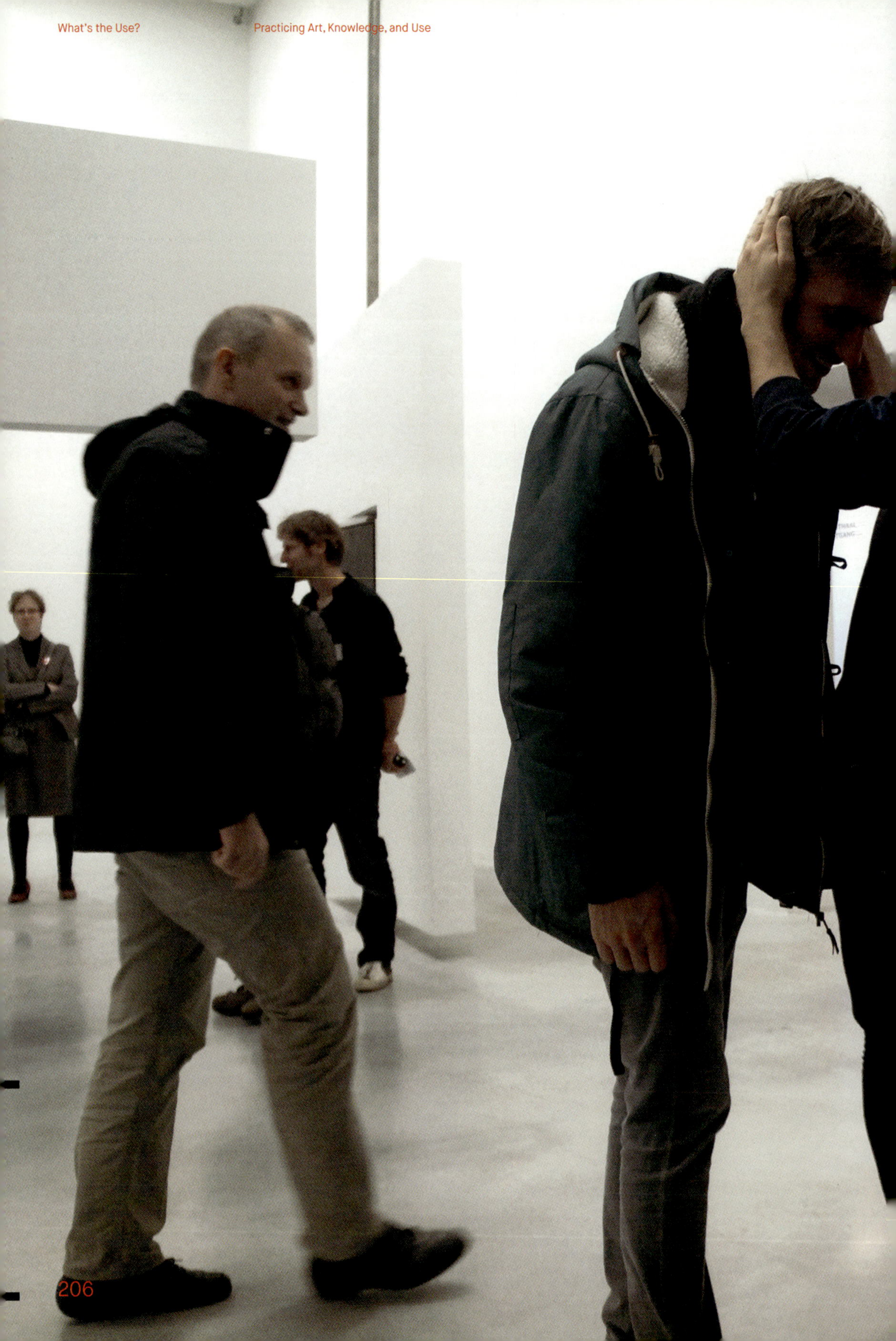

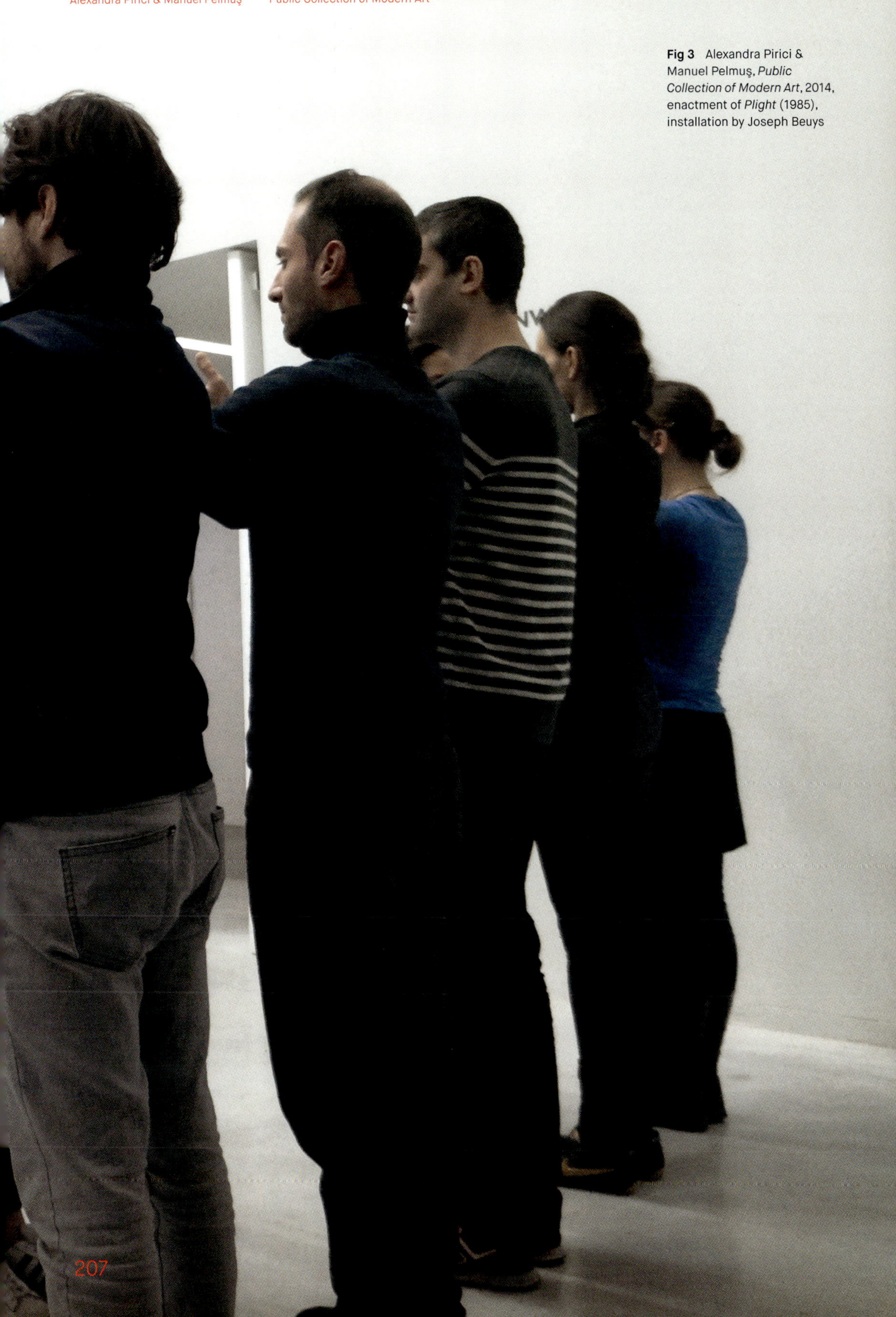

Fig 3 Alexandra Pirici & Manuel Pelmuş, *Public Collection of Modern Art*, 2014, enactment of *Plight* (1985), installation by Joseph Beuys

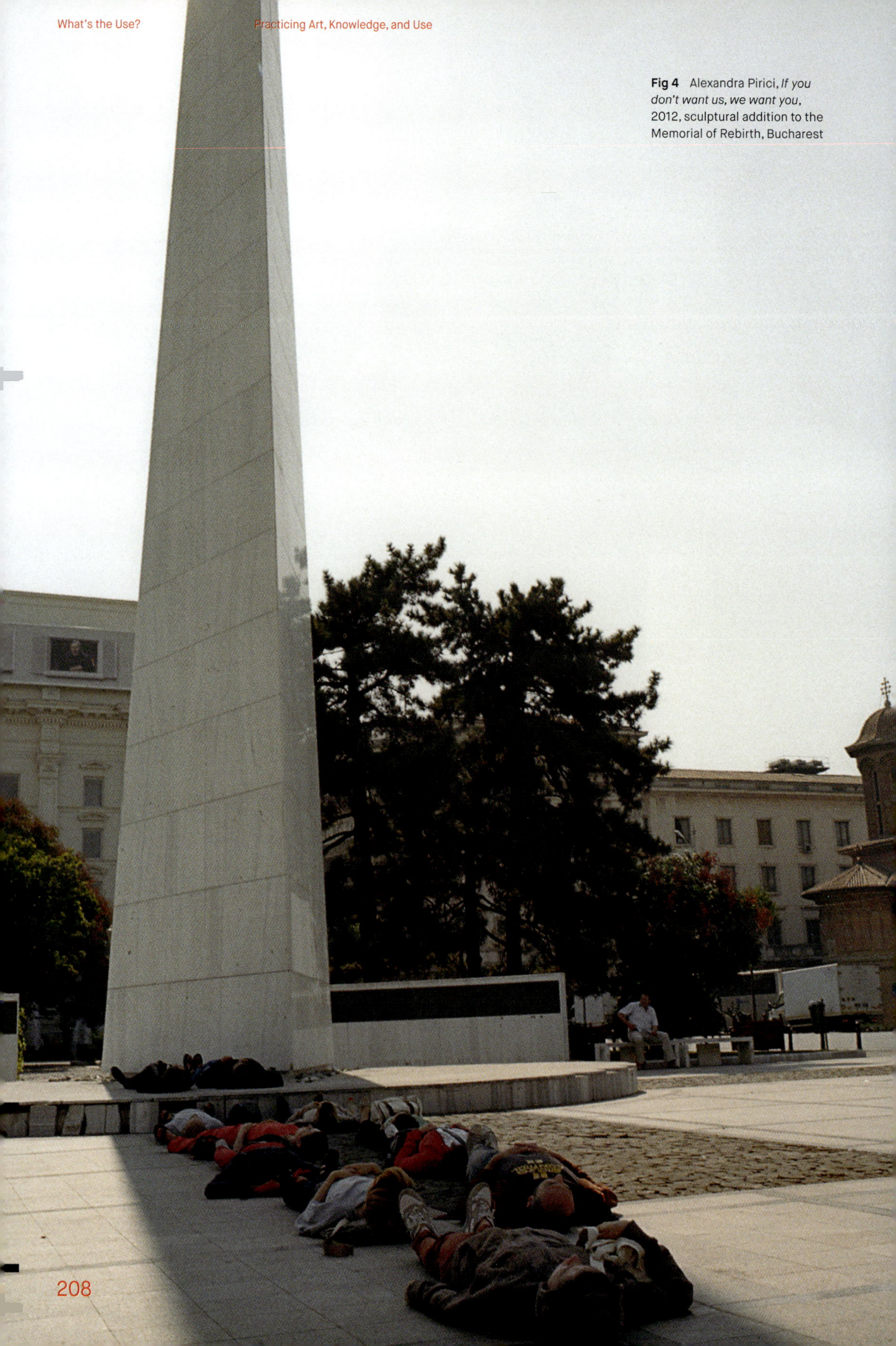

Fig 4   Alexandra Pirici, *If you don't want us, we want you*, 2012, sculptural addition to the Memorial of Rebirth, Bucharest

Actualizing History in the Living Body as Subject-Object

Alexandra Pirici

Public Collection moves toward building up a more specific immaterial collection of artworks, events, and manifestos that relate to the history of modernity and which also leak into the present (fig. 1 and 2).

Public Collection is more than a collection of translations, however. The enactments become new works brought into existence by living bodies/human material. Previous artworks are used as starting points. Yet they sometimes also evolve into formally different constructions, situations, or actions in the process of trying to function along the same lines, maintain the same course, or produce a similar experience (fig. 3). Thinking of what embodiment produces within the museum space and the exhibition ritual, we could maybe trace some links to art, use, knowledge, and history.

To begin with, the use of minimum means—human bodies alone—attempts to downscale and de-monumentalize history by reconstructing it on a human scale. This practice draws on a former one of mine, which I still continue, of embodying public monuments (fig. 4, 5). One of the aims of this process is to question the monument's symbolic function, its détournement and its confrontation with the human scale. There is a sort of 'reality check' where reality is not seen as a realm of existence fundamentally opposed to the virtual or symbolic. Reality is instead that which is already manifest in—not projected onto—the world; it is a 'ground' which, however, is never a sort of correspondent to a tabula rasa.

In a similar but less confrontational manner, these enactments of sometimes 'monumental' artworks in the gallery space aim to bring the living work both in tension and in alliance with the reference—these can be homages as much as a somewhat critical reconstructions.

On a more general level, the performers claim (parts of) art history for the present: they actualize it and bring it back into flux. The performers allow the present to remember history in a subjective and playful way, providing access through manifesting history in their bodies. Still or in action, these bodies invite the viewer to think of art history differently, as a living, porous, changing entity rather than an

Presented in the exhibition *Confessions of the Imperfect, 1848–1989–Today* at the Van Abbemuseum, *Public Collection of Modern Art* is structured on the basis of a 'public collection.' The work is an 'immaterial' collection of artworks enacted by performers that refer to the museum's history as a public institution whose cornerstone is its 'material' collection.

immovable collection of formally fixed objects or classified events. To relate to the idea of 'use' (understood both as concrete use and 'uselessness as use' as in Immanuel Kant's 'purposiveness without a purpose'), one could maybe say that these bodies take the liberty to maximally use art history and the past. These bodies cannibalize it and reproduce it or let it emerge anew into the present moment. They retrace and reaffirm the relevance of art history, bringing it back into the social, cultural, political, and economic fabric of contemporary life (fig 7).

Yet the work does not depart completely from the convention of an exhibition space and the (different) material objects it usually references. *Public Collection of Modern Art* remains close enough to this context to make the comparison possible thus trying to expand and alter the format from within. Placing the work within the exhibition ritual and the white (or grey) cube is also an attempt to create an ambiguous and potentially different experience. A potentially different affective field can thereby emerge. That said, following art historian and curator Dorothea von Hantelmann, the very principle of an exhibition is the principle of separation:[1] the viewer cannot completely separate herself from the exhibitions, she cannot totally extract herself from this arrangement and observe it *objectively* as the sameness of material—the living body/ live presence of the *subject-objects*—she encounters within this convention should make it difficult to completely *dis-identify*.

At the same time, *Public Collection of Modern Art* doesn't attempt to engage the viewer through simulating interaction, or asking for (complete) identification, or trying to produce emotion by stimulating her to a point of constant excitation. This practice, relatively common in performative or participative works, might fit very smoothly into today's fully spectacularized experience economy, where the depth of experience is replaced by speed and the imperative to (shortly) engage.

This collection of living works simply appear and allow the audience to take its own time in experiencing them, while the slow pace of the ongoing-action invites more time to be spent with them. It is possible to notice how one constructs and deconstructs the self, occupies space and time, breathes, speaks, sings, or sounds in movement. This presence, in between subject and object, tries to avoid both the problematic claim of human body as object or sculpture by reproducing the dynamics of stone, bronze, steel, or other material, and the constant over-stimulation of the spectacular, participative event. It doesn't play out the fast, spectacular animation as envelopment and attention-capturing device for more 'still' exhibitions. Neither is it fixed, easily bought and sold as decoration. Although collectible, the work proposes a different idea of 'ownership' or 'use,' one which is more related to taking up the responsibility to keep alive, take care of, and restage the work rather than speculate on its price over time.

The possible different use of the art object might also relate to a potential construction of knowledge as a more flexible process, one that is under constant self-reflection.

In this scenario, embodiment would also imply a different 'human' body might enact the works in the future. How would this body look, how would a cyborg body play out an enactment of *Guernica* (1937)?

Without depending on a precise forecasting of the future, such a public collection might be one way to make us notice the sensible and playful manifestation of knowledge and history in the material of the living body, however that material—or the definition of the 'living'—would change.

---

1   Dorothea von Hantelmann, 'The Exhibition,' lecture, *Demonstrations*, Haus der Kulturen der Welt, Berlin, 17 October 2014.

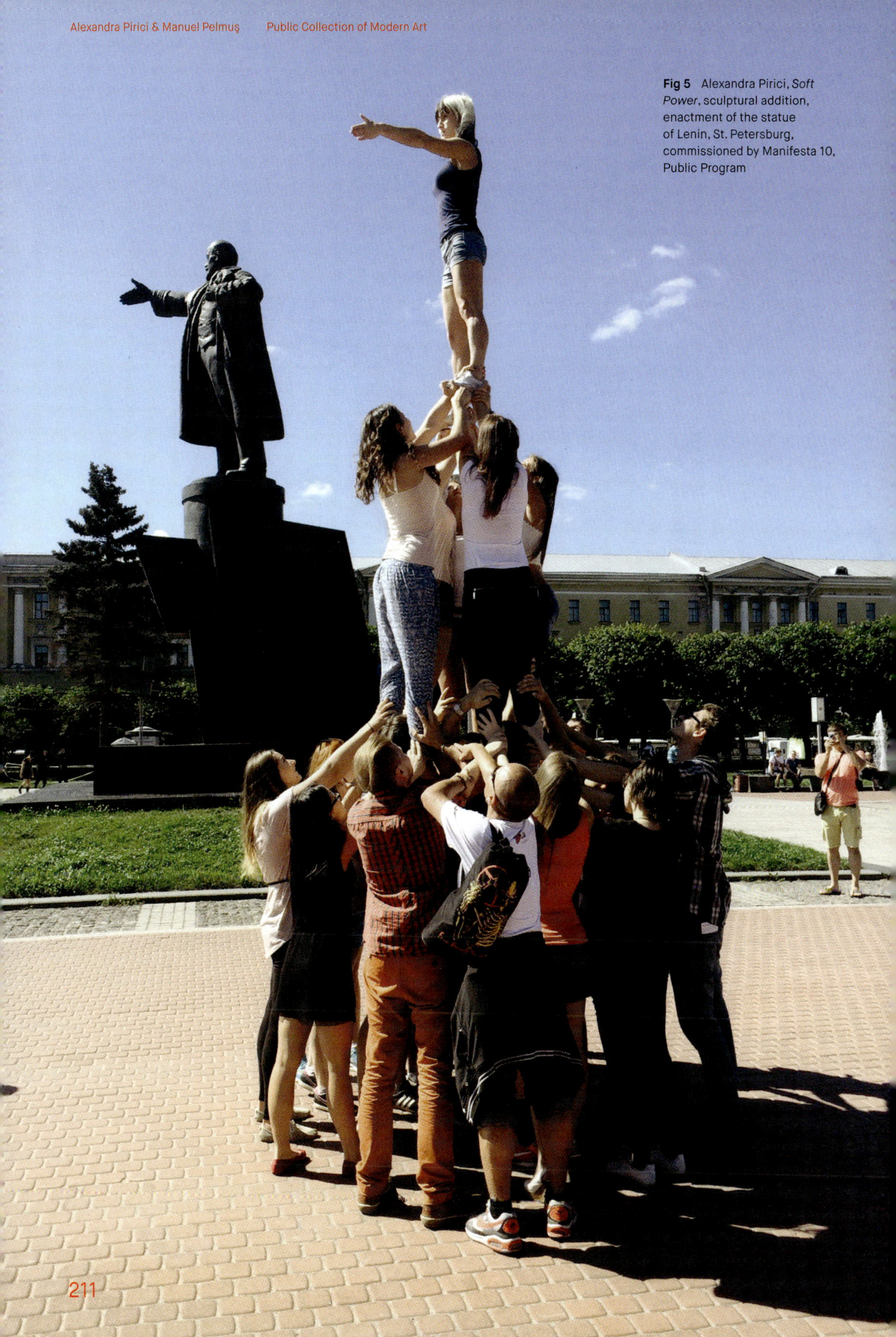

Fig 5 Alexandra Pirici, *Soft Power*, sculptural addition, enactment of the statue of Lenin, St. Petersburg, commissioned by Manifesta 10, Public Program

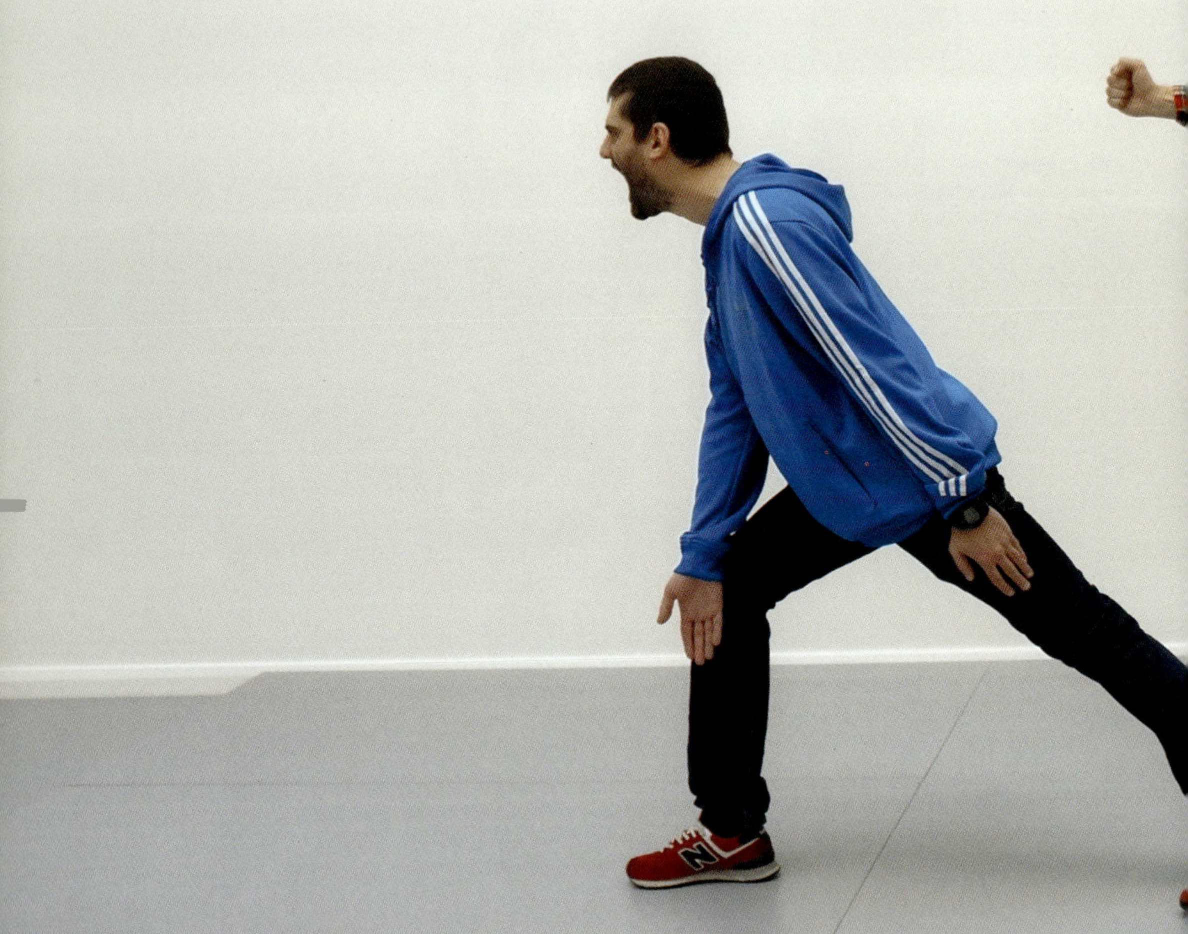

Fig 6 Alexandra Pirici &
Manuel Pelmuş, *Public
Collection of Modern Art*, 2014,
enactment of *Guernica* (1937),
oil on canvas, by Pablo Picasso

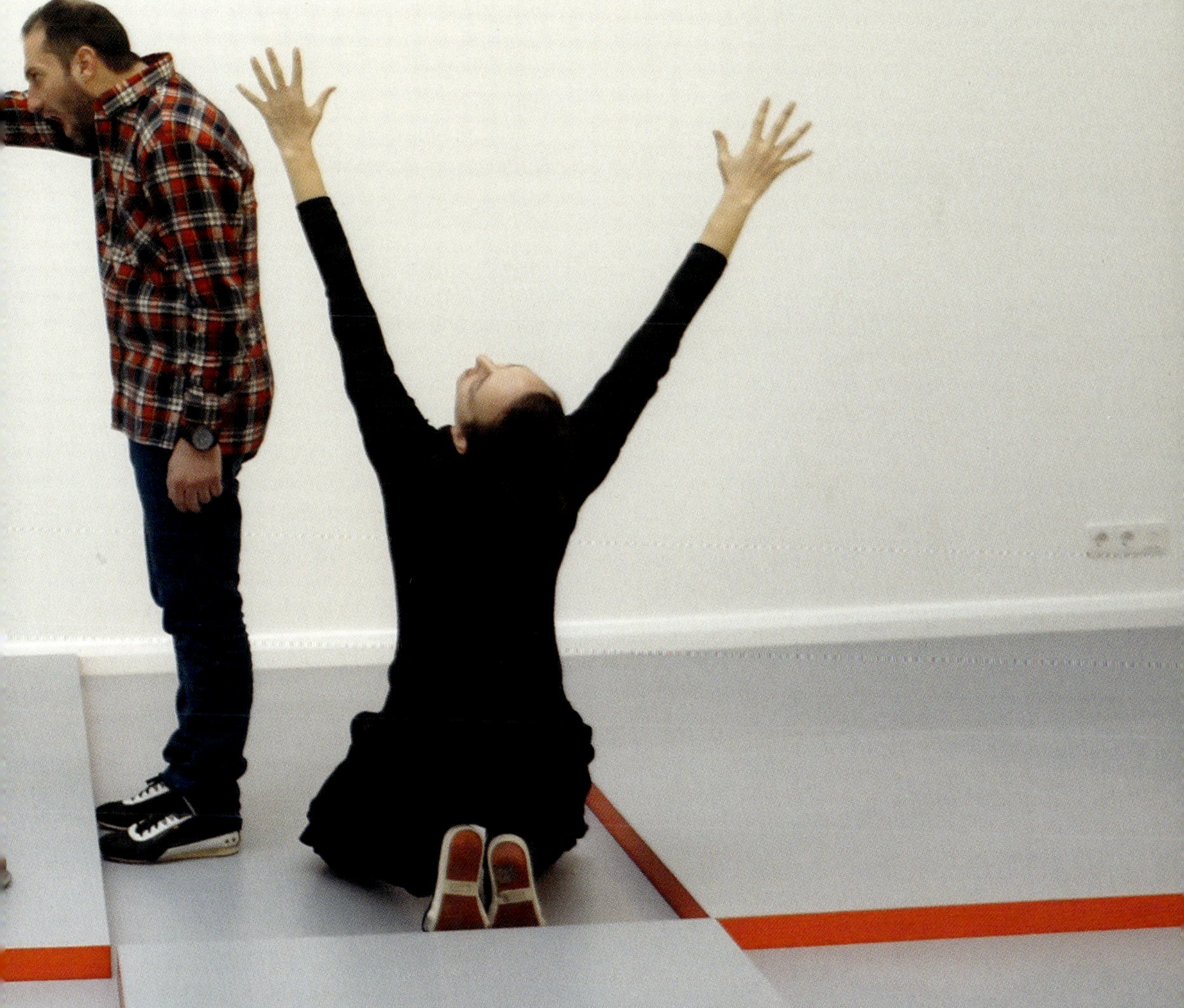

History, Time, Economy, and Museums of the Future

Manuel Pelmuş

My work with Alexandra Pirici is set in relation to the wider yet specific history of the museum as a place for producing and distributing knowledge and one in which long-term politics are played out. If we agree that the museum reflects the kind of society that has produced it and its economy, then it should now reflect—and address—the profound shifts in society and economy.

These range from technological change to rather radical adjustments in the production of subjectivity, as well as an overall move toward immaterial production. Much of today's so-called 'political art' operates on the level of content, producing representations of the political or denouncing the neoliberal status quo. I believe that the content of a work is not sufficient enough to offer a critical position. As such we are interested in questioning the modes of production and formats of today's museum. Besides history and memory, economy and value become pressing issues.

Currently almost everyone in the field of visual arts speaks about the 'performative turn.' Live events—dance, concerts, and so on— regularly appear in today's exhibitions, biennials, and museum programs. While it is not the first time that 'performance' has entered the museum, live events are more intensely present in the circuit of visual arts, taking centre stage. This development of course corresponds to the concurrently widespread 'economy of experience and attention,' where immaterial production has also become central and subjectivity is constantly put at work. Therefore the performative turn is often criticized as a capitulation of critical art in front of spectacle and the demands of neoliberal society. It is also accused of emptying performance of its critical edge—which it supposedly once possessed—by commodifying performance. Making performance participate in the art market thereby causes it to lose its formerly radical attitude.

I do not think that things are that easy to classify, however, especially with regard to a wider discussion concerning the 'museums of the future' and their relationship to present-day society. Live events being more and more in demand can also be an opportunity to address and redefine the context of institutions and their politics.

Historically speaking performance artists emphasized the uniqueness of their performances, the fact that they could not be repeated meant they resisted circulation within the market, rendering them risky and radical. But the reality of that claim, in most cases, was that the majority of performance artists had to sell documentation or objects related to their performances in order to survive. This situation is, perhaps, best described in a random quote from artist Mladen Stilinović when confronted with the general perception that his famous photographic series entitled *Artist at Work* (1978), was originally a performance: 'In the 70s when I did this. I was thinking about performance. What is it? When it is finished you must have a video or a photography. So why do performance in the public space?'[1]

One could say that instead of subverting the art market, the body and performance practice of that period, mainly the 1960s and 1970s, was just very cheap and did not really challenge the traditional formats of the exhibition. This is not meant to dismiss or mock the legitimate concerns and practices of performance artists then (many of which I do admire) but to revisit their claims from the perspective of today, almost fifty years later. I do not think that the performative turn in the visual arts is, *a priori*, a good or bad thing, but one has the opportunity to reflect on and set the limits of one's participation in the economy of the museum and to push those limits by challenging institutional frames and demanding a different economy for 'immaterial' work. I also see a chance to contribute further to an ongoing debate about the museum of the future, in which live events are not instrumentalized at very low cost to merely animate events, but are valued as equal elements in an exhibition display of the future, challenging the established hierarchies of visual art that prioritize the material object.

In our work we try to address issues related to the economy, and the experience economy specifically, as well as what and how the work is valued inside the museum format. One way we do this is by using a different time frame than is expected from live works. We install our ongoing-action for longer periods of consecutive days, so that we don't reproduce a 'one-time-only' event logic. We insist on a structure that invites the visitor to spend and invest time in

following the development of the work, which often takes more hours to unfold, so that it is not easily viewed and consumed. The fact that the work has no beginning or end (as in a theatrical performance) offers the possibility for the visitor to return and spend more time with it. We claim a temporality that suggests permanence. This should translate into bigger budgets for the live events demanding a more equal distribution of the existing economy.

History and memory play an important role in our work. It is a specific practice which proposes an embodied history (in the bodies of performers). The aim is to, perhaps, produce knowledge about the past together with the visitor, both by claiming history and hopefully proposing a reading of the future. One could argue that the work functions as a display for sharing knowledge in action; it is activated by performers, as opposed to a stand-still display, raising questions about immaterial production and also about what an object could be/become in an imagined museum of the future. It's not a fixed history but one that tries to engage the viewer on several levels of perception. By claiming, de-monumentalizing, and setting history to a human scale, we seek to produce a certain tension between the fixed and big history to open up the possibility for transformation. In that sense one is invited inside a frame which can be used for transmitting knowledge through bodies and on a scale (the human body) to which the viewer can relate. We produce a different kind of object that also invites an encounter. By encounter I mean a more hybrid exhibition display that makes space for works that shape an embodied experience, but an experience that does not shy away from meaning, criticality, discourse, and embracing a historical dimension.

In a museum that takes into consideration the recent shifts in society and economy, I think that experience, inter-subjectivity, and embodied history should have a place. That is, as long as the possibility remains to reflect on one's own participation, and to question and push the institutional frames which one has been offered.

---

1   Mladen Stilinović, artist talk during *It May Be That Beauty Has Strengthened Our Resolve,* exhibition, Para Site, Hong Kong, March 2013, https://vimeo.com/62851903.

Fig 7　Alexandra Pirici &
Manuel Pelmuș, *Public
Collection of Modern Art*,
2014, enactment of *Wonderer
Above the Sea of Fog* (1818),
oil on canvas, by Caspar David
Friedrich

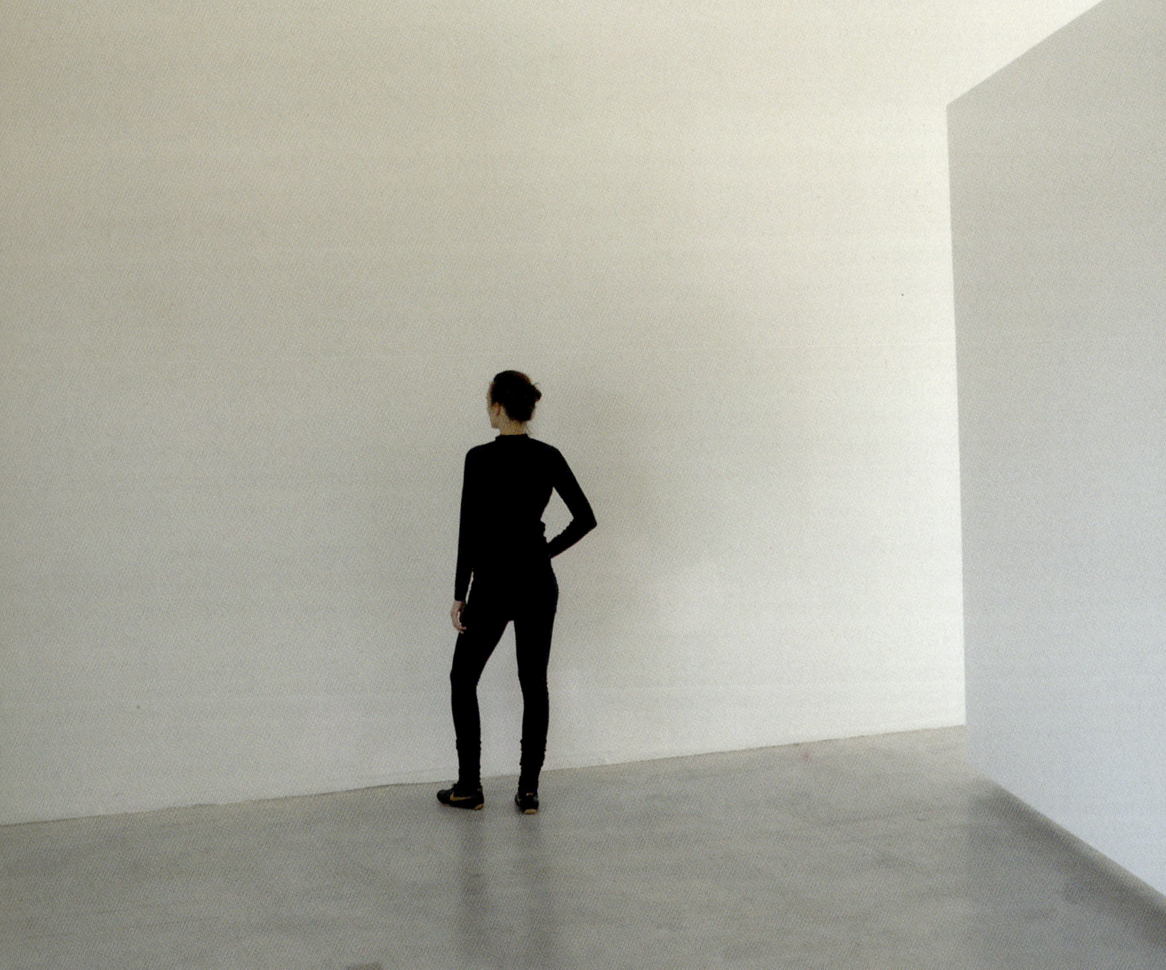

Essay
Thomas Lange

History at Present

THE REVEALING VOID OF CHRISTOPH SCHLINGENSIEF'S CONTAINER

From 11 to 17 July 2000, Christoph Schlingensief initiated a project in Vienna called *Bitte liebt Österreich – Erste Europäische Koalitionswoche* [Please Love Austria—First European Coalition Week].[1] It soon came to be known as *Ausländer raus!* [Foreigners out!], a title taken from the slogan placed on top of the construction of containers Schlingensief had positioned in front of the Vienna State Opera.[2]

---

1   All translations from German to English in this essay by author.
2   *Bitte liebt Österreich—Erste Österreichische Koalitionswoche*, *Wiener Festwochen*: director: Christoph Schlingensief; stage design: Nina Wetzel; coordination: Claudia Kaloff; dramaturgy: Matthias Lilienthal; production: Gabriele Kalba, Attila Láng, and Hannes Sulzenbacher; assistant director: Mario Rauter; production assistant: Katharina Gruber; sound: Ernst Zettl; technicians: Reinhold Hoffmann and Martin Kindermann; stage designer: Elisabeth Steger; patrons: Paulus Manker, Elfriede Jelinek, Luc Bondy, Josef Bierbichler, and Daniel Cohn-Bendit.

The primary material arising from this temporary event—and one of the main sources of reference for this essay—is a documentary film made by Paul Poet in 2002. Using footage from various cameras filming the event outside and inside the containers, it is cut with interview material from Schlingensief among others involved, alongside filmed discussions that accompanied the event.[3]

Shortly before Schlingensief's *Aktion*, the radical right-wing party Freiheitliche Partei Österreichs [Freedom Party of Austria] (FPÖ) had been elected into the government via a coalition with the Österreichischen Volkspartei [Austrian conservative party] (ÖVP). After Wolfgang Schüssel of the ÖVP became chancellor in February 2000, there were worldwide protests and the governments of the then fourteen member states of the European Union reduced correspondence with Austria to a minimum.

Every Thursday demonstrations took place in Vienna against this new government. In 2002 the coalition broke and Schüssel's ÖVP could alone govern Austria with a comfortable majority.[4]

Schlingensief's concept (commissioned by the Wiener Festwochen [Vienna Festival]) was this: twelve asylum seekers would live inside shipping containers in the middle of Vienna's touristic heart. Imitating the so-called reality TV format of *Big Brother*, the asylum seekers would be surveyed by cameras and two would be thrown out through daily online voting. Instead of being voted out of the show, however, the candidates were to be voted out of the country and the winner would receive a residence permit.

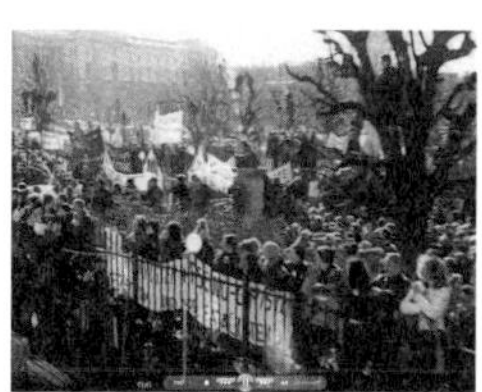
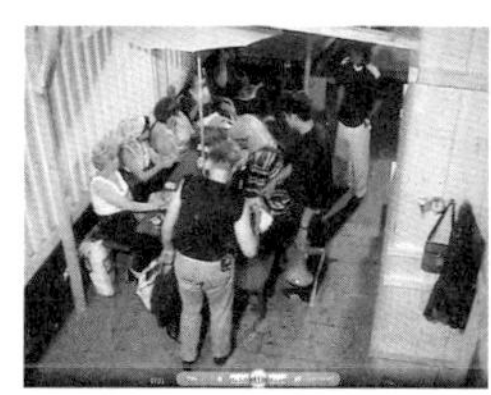
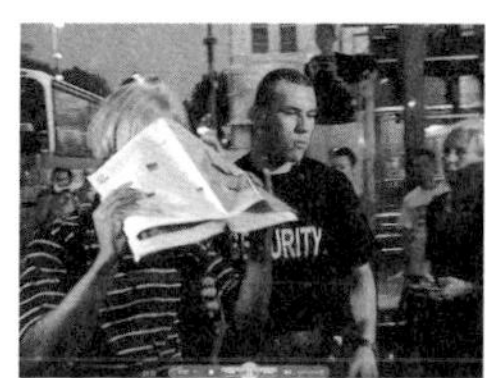

Fig 1–4 Christoph Schlingensief, *Ausländer raus. Schlingensiefs Container. Chronik einer Kunstaktion*, Paul Poet (director), 2000, screen captures

---

3 Key references include *Ausländer raus. Schlingensiefs Container. Chronik einer Kunstaktion*, directed, script, and music compilation by Paul Poet, camera by Robert Winkler and Mario Sternisa, graphics by Oliver Neumann (Vienna: Eine Produktion der Bonus Film GmbH, 2002); citations throughout essay follow the film's time sequence (hour:minute:second). Another main source is *Schlingensiefs Ausländer raus: Bitte liebt Österreich*, Dokumentation von Matthias Lilienthal und Claus Philipp (Frankfurt am Main: Suhrkamp, 2000) and a conversation between Peter Sloterdijk and Christoph Schlingensief moderated by Sven Gächter, 'Gespräch zwischen Sloterdijk und Schlingensief zur Wienaktion,' transcript, 17 June 2000, www.schlingensief.com/downloads/schlinge_sloterdijk_wien.pdf.

4 Poet's film *Ausländer raus. Schlingensiefs Container* opens with a brief history of Austria, beginning in 1945 with the country's transformation into a democracy. This is contrasted by his then chronological account of the recent development that lead to the situation Schlingensief takes on in the work: 00:00:41–00:03:04.

Schlingensief's work involves three aspects of imitation that copy contemporary elements which have a frequent media presence.

First, the format of reality TV with its active public as users, the European-wide and very popular elimination game that promises the viewer transparency and a certain power and control as an active part of the show.[5]

Second, the imitation, the mimicry of tabloid journalism's headlines and phrasing, especially of the very popular *Kronen Zeitung*.[6] This implied that the tabloid had sponsored the action that seemed to have been initiated by the new party in government, the FPÖ (its flag had been raised above the container). This move occurred despite Schlingensief stating 'this is a *Wiener-Festwochen-Inszenierung* … it is an actor [the first asylum seeker that had been voted out of the country] … it is absolutely the truth.'[7] He takes on various possible positions, e.g., asking passersby why they think the coalition does nothing against the incriminating slogan 'foreigners out' on top of the container construction, highly visible to onlookers and the cameras of the world's press agencies alike. This overlaying and merging of different positions is not so much a provocation ('provocation is for the dumb')[8] but a multiple ongoing reflection of the breadth of opinions among the people.

Third, these elements are implemented in a functioning interactive website, copying and using design elements of both the *Kronen Zeitung* and the FPÖ, combining them into a convincing *look* which alludes to colour and form elements of various non-particular European Neo-Nazi groups. On this website Schlingensief

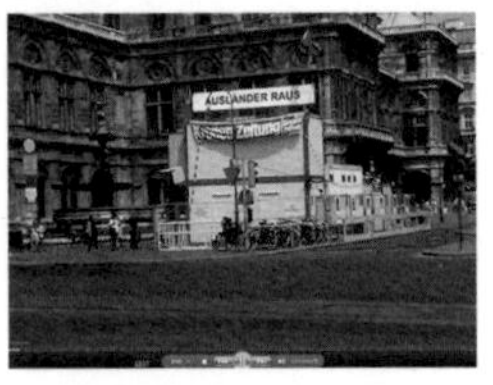

Fig 5 Christoph Schlingensief, *Ausländer raus. Schlingensiefs Container. Chronik einer Kunstaktion*, Paul Poet (director), 2000, screen capture

---

5 For a general analysis of the *Big Brother* format in German (and European) entertainment TV see Jens Roselt, 'Big Brother: Zur Theatralität eines Fernsehereignisses,' in *Schlingensiefs Ausländer raus: Bitte liebt Österreich*, Dokumentation von Matthias Lilienthal und Claus Philipp (Frankfurt am Main: Suhrkamp, 2000), pp. 70–78.

6 An Austrian tabloid paper with a very high distribution of 1 million copies (total population: 8 million) according to Poet, 00:16:01–00:16:13.

7 Poet, 01:15:47–01:15:49 ('We are from the FPÖ and we say *foreigners out*') and 00:22:14–00:22:25.

8 Schlingensief, in Poet, 00:39:36–00:39:38.

introduces himself as a German *Aktionskünstler*.[9]

A blog was also offered, and frequently used by tens of thousands to comment about, rave in appreciation for or hatred of, express their thoughts, or release feelings on the show and the emerging occurrences.[10]

Schlingensief points out that he had the idea to work with a mirror technique: to *create a situation* (rather than an artwork, a play, or a performance) in which people mirror themselves. It was an attempt to find an answer to 'the question of resistance' and the possible role of art in this situation: 'At the beginning there was this unanswered question of what this is, theatre, positioning in media?'[11] The attempted solution was to question the surfaces, the role of the media, the role of the public, the people in Vienna, and wider Austria and Europe. To question (in an open way, not with an affirmative or a negative prejudice) the structures and images of the complex of doubts, concerns, considerations, questions, and objections on the surface.

To do so, Schlingensief produced an image that was meant for the centre of Vienna which became a 'projection plane/surface': the image that he found was a container construction with the ambivalence of an entertainment show and internment (if not concentration) camp.[12] In doing so, he used the high level of reflection of a surface that was all beauty, Vienna, Kärntnerstrasse, Herbert-von-Karajan-Platz, Stephansdom, where all the tourists arrive to see the beauty and glory of the past. Precisely here, the other image has been served, with its potential to cause damage: appalled, horrified

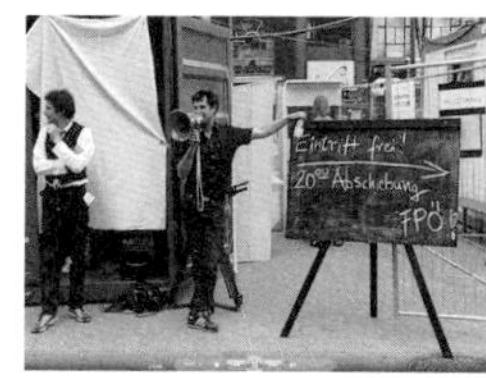

Fig 6 Christoph Schlingensief, *Ausländer raus. Schlingensiefs Container. Chronik einer Kunstaktion*, Paul Poet (director), 2000, screen capture

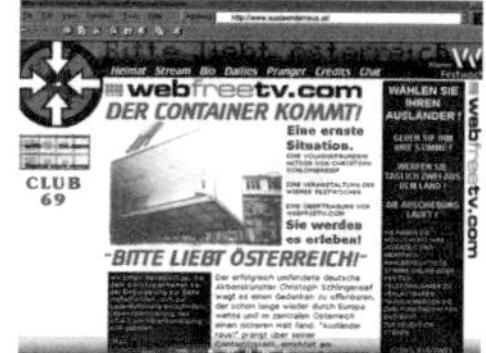

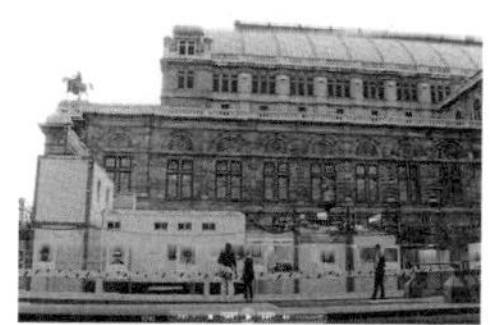

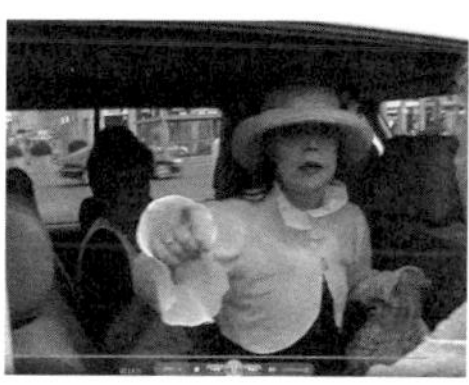

Fig 7–9 Christoph Schlingensief, *Ausländer raus. Schlingensiefs Container. Chronik einer Kunstaktion*, Paul Poet (director), 2000, screen captures

---

9 In collaboration with www.webfreetv.com. On activated 'voting pages' and via TED-telephone number (Mass-Calling Service) Austrians and Europeans (www.auslaenderraus.web) could actively take part in the 'elimination mechanism' of this 'elimination game,' terms used by Sloterdijk, in Poet, 00:36:56 and Schlingensief and Sloterdijk moderated by Gächter, 'Gespräch zwischen Sloterdijk und Schlingensief zur Wienaktion.' 'Elimination game' is also used by Schlingensief in 'Freiheit für Alles: Gespräch zwischen Alexander Kluge und Christoph Schlingensief,' in *Schlingensiefs Ausländer raus: Bitte liebt Österreich*, Dokumentation von Matthias Lilienthal und Claus Philipp, pp. 136–149.
10 Schlingensief: 'We calculated 50000 hits per day—in the end we had 80000 per hour.' *Schlingensiefs Ausländer raus*, p. 148.
11 Schlingensief, in Schlingensief and Sloterdijk moderated by Gächter, 'Gesprach zwischen Sloterdijk und Schlingensief zur Wienaktion.'
12 *Projektionsebene* [projection plane or projection surface] from Schlingensief, in ibid.

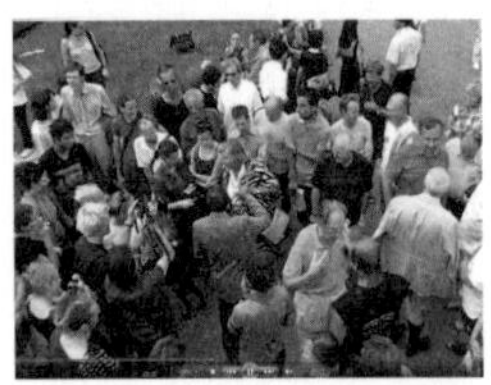

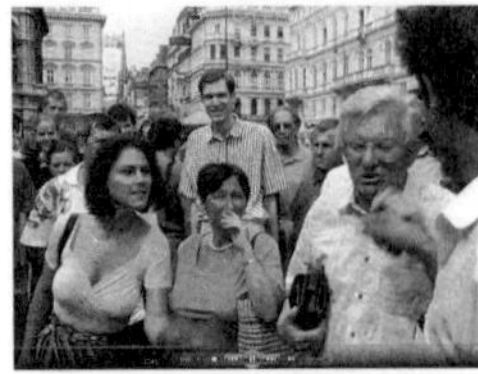

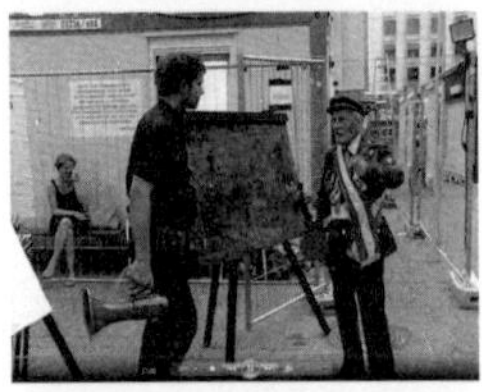

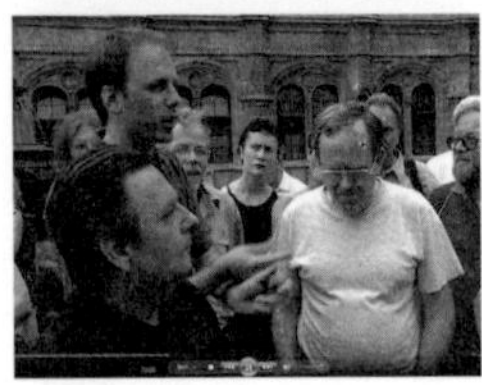

Fig 10–13 Christoph Schlingensief, *Ausländer raus. Schlingensiefs Container. Chronik einer Kunstaktion*, Paul Poet (director), 2000, screen captures

tourists exclaiming: 'Let's get the hell out of here.'[13]

Schlingensief's work began 'like an image on the wall … then spread out, grew like dough in all directions,'[14] everywhere, non-stoppable and—this is important—more and more autonomous, on its own. Autonomous means here: without being steered, commanded, controlled *so much* by an author.[15] Schlingensief was not governing, controlling the process, but he was fuelling it. Its author changed into the role of initiator; the work, the image turned into a powerful machine that accelerated in force. In fuelling it Schlingensief used a technique that mirrored the emotional, affirmative, irrational elements used in the language, gestures, and images of the extreme right-wing party—as well as of the conservatives' arguments to justify a coalition with it. And with this, of course, the whole range from an analytical to a polemical use of language in the press and media that accompanied and commented on this election and its result.

By repeating, *miming* the slogans of the FPÖ's election campaign against foreigners or those of the opposition, he propelled this machine: mirroring the noise, hate, exaltation, the overly emotional discussion, as well as the attempts to rationalize the irrational. This operation did not need to follow a *plan*, being ticked off box by box but needed only a constant reaction within the flow of what happened, what emerged out of the heated situation over the seven consecutive days it took place.

In a comment on the event included in Poet's documentary, dramaturge Carl Hegemann recalls his initial doubts on whether the project would work and how surprised he was when it became apparent just how well it did: 'one thought such a cheap mock-up would fizzle out, fall flat—but the people joined in, played along.'[16]

---

13 Schlingensief, in ibid.
14 Schlingensief, in Poet, 00:23:28–00:24:09.
15 See Michel Foucault's '… not to be governed by such an extent' in answer to the question 'what is critique?' *Was ist Kritik* (Berlin: Merve-Verlag 1992), p. 12. See also the French edition, Michel Foucault, *Qu'est-ce que la critique?* [Critique et *Aufklärung*], Bulletin de la Société française de Philosophie, vol. 84 (April–June 1990).
16 Poet, 00:27:20 – 00:27:51.

The people who joined in were part of a social body
that constitutes itself from subjective feelings and
opinions. They were immediately affected, absorbed
or repelled, contradicted and altered by the other. This
overall comprises the dynamics of a body made out of
many bodies, of feelings made out of many feelings, of an
opinion made out of many opinions, of an action fusing into
many actions. Such a body creates situations that are not
clearly determinable or easy to characterize. The situations
that evolve from this mirroring technique are in no way
determined or controlled by one position, opinion, or
standpoint, nor by a clearly definable aim or motivation with
the anticipation of a result. 'This is why you can't say: here
we demonstrate what fascism is. It is not that simple.'[17]

In Poet's documentary philosopher Burghart Schmidt
points out that we could concur with Walter Benjamin who
referred to Austrian writer Karl Kraus as an early twentieth-
century example of applying such a technique: '*critique
does not need to commend.*'[18] The pure citation is sufficient
(at the right moment, at the right place); the pure citation
that you take up is self-revealing.[19]

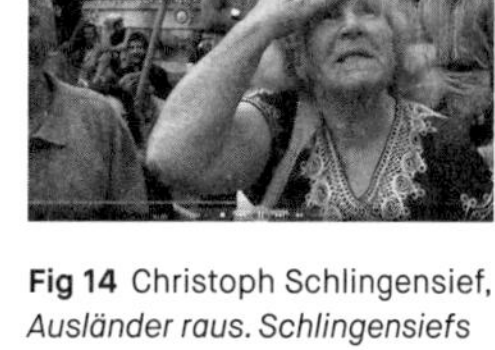

Fig 14 Christoph Schlingensief,
*Ausländer raus. Schlingensiefs
Container. Chronik einer
Kunstaktion*, Paul Poet
(director), 2000, screen
capture

Benjamin's analysis of this technique—invented and used
by Kraus—reveals the work of a polemic that consists
of three elements: to remain silent, to have knowledge,
and to have presence of mind. To remain silent allows the
collection and accumulation of knowledge. The presence
of mind then enables the deconstruction of the situation,
to discover the real question behind it, to present it, to
mirror it back (instead of attempting to answer it) to the

---

17 Carl Hegemann, in Poet, 00:31:24 – 00:32:14.
18 Poet, 00:31:47 – 00:32:14.
19 Karl Kraus (1874–1936), one of the most famous Austrian writers of the early twentieth century
and important satirist, founded in 1899 the journal *Die Fackel* [The Torch]. Since 1912 he was the only
author of this feared and respected critical instance. In his essays, glosses, aphorisms, poems, and
epigrams he pursued and tracked the stupidity, dullness, and malice found in literature, journalism,
and politics of his time. In his Essay *Die Sprache* [The Language] published posthumously in 1937
he enlarges upon the grounds of his technique of *Sprachkritik* [critiques of language] as pointed
out by Walter Benjamin (see the following references in this text). Kraus is also well known for his
anti-war theatre piece *Die letzten Tage der Menschheit* [The Last Days of Mankind], 1919. The book
edition published in May and December 1922 at 5000 copies each, and in 1926 the third edition
with 7000 copies was published. *The Fackel* is digitalized and provided with online access by the
Österreichische Akademie der Wissenschaften (ÖAW), Austrian Academy Corpus AAC Fackel Gate,
http://corpus1.aac.ac.at/fackel.

opponent.[20] This sheds light on the vital meaning of the critical (and artistic) technique of using the quotation to criticize something which escapes comment but reveals a critique out of itself through the mirror technique of quoting. Schlingensief's use of mimicry, of miming, can be further understood by looking at the importance of not representing an opinion, be it personal or public. According to Benjamin, Kraus considered opinion a false subjectivity that could too easily be detached (withdrawn) from the person to be entered into the 'circulation of commodities.'[21]

With Benjamin we can say that like Kraus's operation, Schlingensief's unmasking technique is intertwined with an art of self-expression that operates with archaic means and which creates ambiguity: self-expression and unmasking merge into self-unmasking. With this, following Benjamin's observations of Kraus and drawing strong parallels to Schlingensief's operation, the mirror technique allows both to assign their own vanity its legitimized place within the mime, within the actor.[22] To become a mime or an actor is needed for this operation which is in itself one of mimicry: mimic exposures created by the one who quotes. Benjamin points out that here we become aware of the 'unhuman' of an actor, that an actor is 'cannibalistic' in that with every role he devours a human.[23] In doing so—and this is important to realize—his language is freed from all moments of empowerment, is not a medium of government nor a medium of fortune telling. The mimetic use of language frees it from a—bourgeois— assumption that it is a means to communicate that what is (the conditions under which 'reality' is understood) produced and governed by those who own the power

---

20 Walter Benjamin, *Karl Kraus*, in *Gesammelte Schriften*, vol. 2, bk. 1, 2nd edition, ed. Rolf Tiedemann and Hermann Schweppenhäuser (Frankfurt am Main: Suhrkamp, 1999), 339. Paraphrased in English by author.
21 Ibid., p. 343.
22 Ibid., pp. 346–347. Schlingensief has been confronted by some critics as being vain in assuming he could enlighten (and maybe solve) the situation in Austria. He admits rightfully that an artistic action has to do with vanity, as a motivation, as a force or energy you can use *to show*—but not to solve. Solving problems is not the task of art or artists. Vanity can be a means if it's powerful (and dangerously self-destructive) force is used wisely, e.g., non-selfish. Comments on that in Poet, 01:17:25 – 01:17:48.
23 Benjamin, *Karl Kraus*, pp. 334–367. Paraphrased in English by author.

of the language they had formed to be in power.[24] All hierarchical moments of language have been abandoned by Kraus. It is no longer a medium of the visionary nor of regimen. The mimetic use of language reveals its other being: to be a *name* first of all, and within a name the human being communicates itself to God. And with this, naming reveals itself as the inner being of language.[25]

For our thinking it is necessary to understand that this is the key to freeing language—and its use—from opinion on or description of an understanding (manipulation of or comment on) of political power. From this 'language-area of the *name*' Kraus's as well as Schlingensief's polemical operation of quotations can be understood: to quote a word means to call it by its name.[26] According to Benjamin this operation enables Kraus to make even the press quotable; for Schlingensief the same operation is still valid to make the flood of opinions quotable (be they private, public, or, in the age of modern communication media, indistinguishably private and public). In doing so he is able to 'rescue the gossip [of public opinion, of the newspapers] from its night' and to reveal its nature.[27]

This operation is necessary to overcome the flood of opinions and to distinguish his own operation from it: not by an intellectual operation of refined analysis, but by using the mimicry of quoting *to call out the name.* This is, according to Jacques Lacan, what constitutes an object.[28] To constitute a chaotic, ambivalent, contradictory situation of raving affects or dulling loss of orientation, an accumulation of fear, hate, anger, or the will to do the right thing, to be good, *as an object*—as something that is standing in front of you to be seen first and for all. Only through naming, it comes into existence for a subject. Benjamin as well as Lacan refer to the book of Moses. After the *fall* (and after gaining the knowledge to distinguish

---

24 Benjamin, *Über Sprache überhaupt und über die Sprache des Menschen*, in ibid., p. 144.
25 Ibid.
26 Benjamin, *Karl Kraus*, p. 362. Paraphrased in English by author.
27 Ibid., p. 363.
28 See Jacques Lacan, *Das Seminar, Buch 11: Die vier Grundbegriffe der Psychoanalyse*, (Olten: Walter, 1978).

good and evil) humans become similar to God. With this, they have to carry the burden of judgment. This is the task (and the curse) of the reviewer of society as well: to rule over the things and beings of the world in giving them a name. This is Schlingensief's work of objectification, of keeping distance, of ruling and revealing: within this mimesis which is inherent to the quotation, the social body reveals itself. And this only works via and with bodies— it is a bodily action in itself. All that we do and understand is bound to this, is being perceived by this and is revealed and understood by our bodily condition. In this sense Schlingensief's operation in front of the Vienna opera house is a work with and within the social body.

Not commentated on nor explained or facilitated what happened around and in response or reaction to Schlingensief's *Aktion* reveals, above all, that societies are bound by strong emotions. Societies are not associations of apathy. But this drive of emotions is complex: part of society plays a game of elimination for entertainment (e.g., *Big Brother*, World Cup); part of it forms protest, brings out strong opinion *against* or *for* the situation in Austria; and a smaller part tries to make sense of what this situation and what this mirror image Schlingensief confronts them with, actually is. The effect of this mirror image is to show what these energies are, the status of this energy flux. The effect of what had happened was accompanied by the media who were also producing images, comments, and opinions of the event. In doing so, no clear image could be retrieved but it became apparent that—despite the struggle to say what was real and what was play—it was impossible to make a distinction between (the surface of) the media (as *virtual reality*) and (the surface of) the occurrences in front of the opera (as *actual reality*).

Schlingensief observed and concluded: 'It became apparent that this *reality* is constantly and strangely enough not being questioned at all. One is not questioning reality and this is so because we can't grasp, we can't

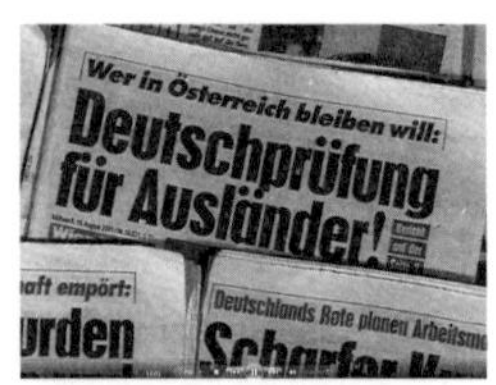

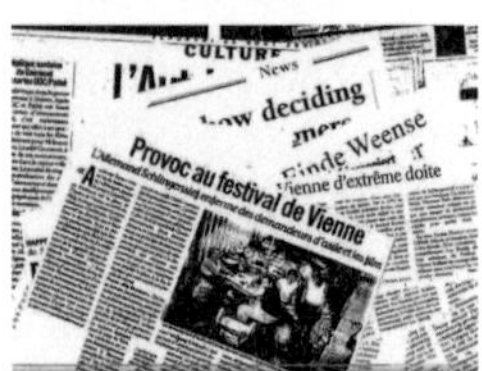

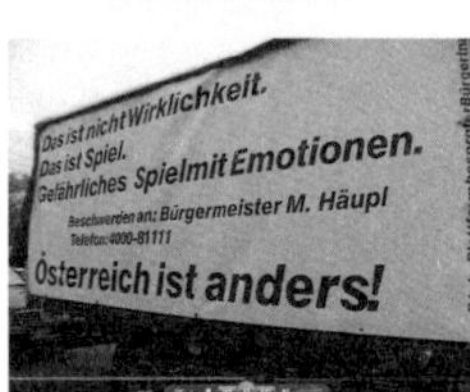

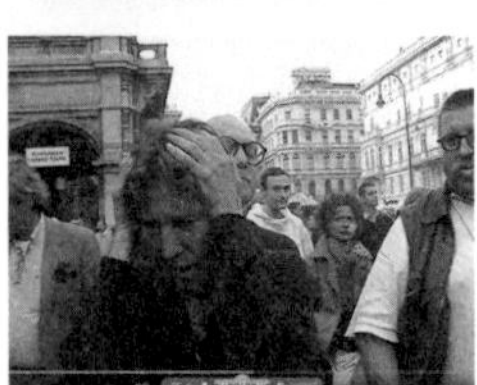

Fig 15–18 Christoph Schlingensief, *Ausländer raus. Schlingensiefs Container. Chronik einer Kunstaktion*, Paul Poet (director), 2000, screen captures

take hold of reality.'[29] The image of the container in front of the opera house is the manifestation of a dilemma: practically there is something that is not. Therefore it is actually there, but it is nevertheless unbelievable, incomprehensible. It is a different reality, a 'hyper-reality.'[30]

Everything seems to be real and unreal, for example, the asylum seekers: the newspapers say they are actors (when they need them to be actors); and they say they are real asylum seekers (when they want to show that these poor people are being disparaged). 'The whole thing was a sole rupture. Every point of stabilization (for instance, I know exactly that this works and that this does not work anymore) had been nullified.'[31]

Reality was made experiential through an art that opened a possibility-space and the new experienced reality was a different, strange, unknown reality.

The world appeared out of joint. To understand this effect, Schlingensief recalls the avant-garde:

'Once it was stated that the only true surrealistic deed is to take a gun and shoot randomly into the crowd. Here: Nobody heard a shot but you can see many people tumbling around wounded, screaming or you see people who suddenly start to scream.'[32]

For example the woman in a flowery dress, screaming her head off: 'Foreigners in, *Piefkes* [Austrian slang for Germans] out!' Later, in an astonishing progression: 'You German pig, you … artist!'[33]

The seeming closeness to mass culture phenomena becomes apparent as unrealistic and using it deprives us of a sense of what is real. But in being used Schlingensief's art will produce and provoke a different perception of what is real. The social body as *acting and interacting,* becomes

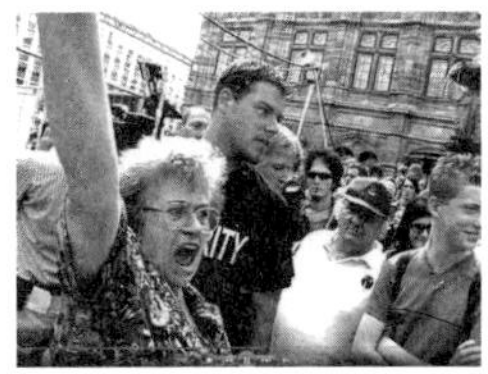

Fig 19 Christoph Schlingensief, *Ausländer raus. Schlingensiefs Container. Chronik einer Kunstaktion*, Paul Poet (director), 2000, screen capture

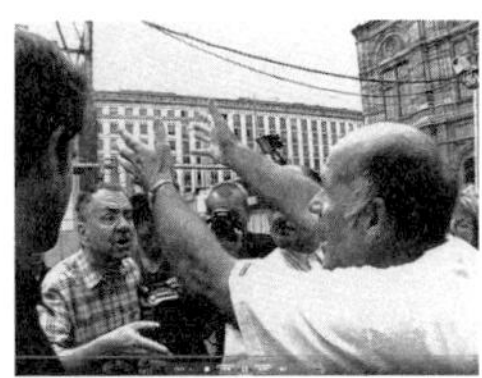

Fig 20 Christoph Schlingensief, *Ausländer raus. Schlingensiefs Container. Chronik einer Kunstaktion*, Paul Poet (director), 2000, screen capture

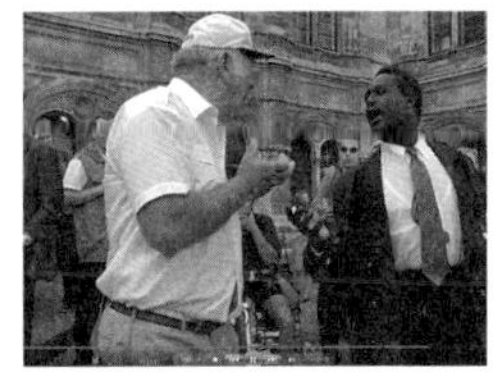

Fig 21 Christoph Schlingensief, *Ausländer raus. Schlingensiefs Container. Chronik einer Kunstaktion*, Paul Poet (director), 2000, screen capture

---

29 Schlingensief and Sloterdijk moderated by Gächter, 'Gespräch zwischen Sloterdijk und Schlingensief zur Wienaktion.'
30 Ibid.
31 Ibid.
32 Poet, 00:46:48–00:47:08, with reference to André Breton, 'Second manifeste du surréalisme,' 1929.
33 Poet, 00:47:35–00:47:40 and 00:51:12–00:51:15.

the object of this art. It becomes the object of this art and it is the driving force, the elixir that makes this art. The social body is the producer of this art and it is its object. The mirror technique is inherent to the dynamics of the social body and being alive, a living being of many bodies, emotions, and opinions the social body reveals itself as this energy. Schlingensief's work with the social body enables it to reveal itself as a conglomerate of manifold and very heterogenic perceptions, reflections, reactions, opinions, emotions, passions, neuroses, sane or insane (clear or disturbed) visions in and from which the *afterlife* of ancient social conflicts and solutions emerge and express themselves in that *superlative excess* (*Übersteigerung,* a term used frequently by Aby Warburg) in powerful images.[34]

The increasing acceleration of actions: discussions, verbal threats, violent actions (against the fence and the containers, against Schlingensief) culminated in what Claudia Kaloff (Schlingensief's project manager) called: 'The hippie-idea: we free the asylum seekers from the container' (and from whoever keeps them prisoners). This is the result of a lack of reflection on what is really going on: not knowing that it was serious what was at play, they played their part in the revelation of destructive frenzy.[35] Here the entanglement of argumentation, views,

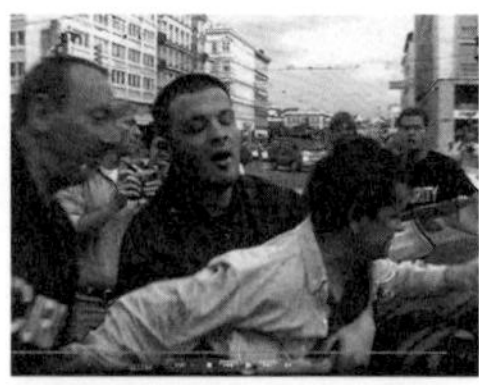
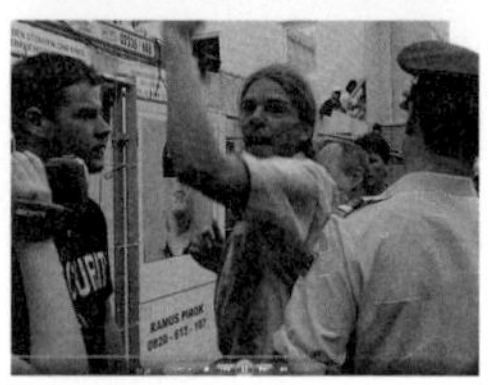

Fig 22–23 Christoph Schlingensief, *Ausländer raus. Schlingensiefs Container. Chronik einer Kunstaktion*, Paul Poet (director), 2000, screen captures

---

34 The art historian Aby Warburg (1866–1929), founder of the Kulturwissenschaftliche Bibliothek Warburg in Hamburg, since the emigration of the library and its leading staff in 1933 The Warburg Institute Library, University of London), considered himself as a 'psycho-historian' who developed a notion about art and culture based upon an—in principle—unfinished past which forms and haunts every present. In and with works of art the phantoms and ghosts of former centuries reappear as that which has not overcome. The long and ongoing clashes between culture and barbarism are contained, stored, and readable as the 'Leidschatz der Menschheit' [Treasure of the Sorrows of Mankind] in works of art. These dark affects of suffering are readable within works of art as well as transported through the centuries by works of art; the famous term 'Pathosformel' is an attempt to grasp this way of expressing, preserving, and passing on within works of art in 'superlative gestures.' (First analyzed in his PhD dissertation *Sandro Botticellis 'Geburt der Venus' und 'Frühling': Eine Untersuchung über die Vorstellungen von der Antike in der italienischen Frührenaissance* (Hamburg: Leopold Voss, 1893). Essentially this is about the perception of the past in its present effects, primarily and first of all with all the senses, bodily, emotional. It is about the suffering, joy, grief, euphory, and melancholy in light of history that addresses and concerns us because it is human. Violence and sorrow is not the topic of history but its substance—made, adulterated, suffered by human beings, not occurrences. The violence and sorrow stored over centuries in works of art are transformed via the works of art into forms of expression. Therefore it is possible to perceive this (with our senses, with our reason) and therefore it is effective in the perception of the following generations. It forms memory and experience likewise which enables preservation and work on culture with the consciousness of the constant endangerment of this thin layer of culture being wiped away, to fall back into barbarism. See for a profound interpretation of Warburg's method in general Georges Didi-Huberman, *L'image survivante: Histoire de l'art et temps des fantômes selon Aby Warburg* (Paris: Éditions de Minuit, 2002).
35 The whole storming of the container in Poet, 00:53:51–00:58:15 and 00:53:18–00:53:49.

aim, goodwill, and evil becomes apparent. Left-wing demonstrators wanted to take down the flag of the right-wing FPÖ because they wanted to show a clean Austria. They did not realize, however, that they were fulfilling the demands of the FPÖ and arguing and acting exactly alongside (and indistinguishable from) the *Kronen Zeitung* that also wanted a clean Austria. Their action revealed—as Armin Thurnher, editor of the *Wiener Stadtzeitung Falter* remarked—a blindness to where and what they were, how their public role changed when they stepped onto a stage or appeared on the screen in the media.[36]

Schlingensief points out:

> And this was for me the most beautiful [the most revealing] moment, when the Indians [left-wing activists] stormed and captured the fort. And in doing this they are generating this movie image: a revolution takes place; this is the image they and the media and the public want and appreciate the most; they are storming the fort, get in, stand inside it and suddenly: wait a minute, the Asylum Seekers are really afraid, they are getting scared, and then the Red Indians realize in the middle of playing Cowboys and Indians, in the middle of this Red-Indian-Resistance-Play: that this is really real! This came to the people who were inside (asylum seekers as well as left wing resistance-group) as a shock. And the name of this shock was: reality.[37]

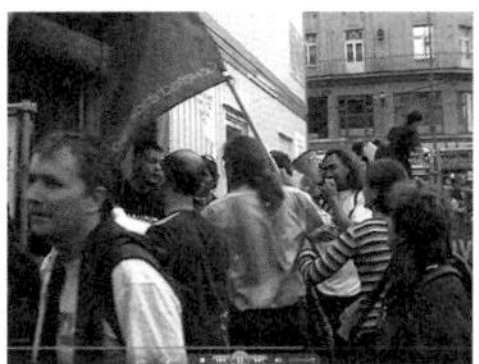

Fig 24 Christoph Schlingensief, *Ausländer raus. Schlingensiefs Container. Chronik einer Kunstaktion*, Paul Poet (director), 2000, screen capture

And this was revealed as something they never thought of, because what they thought of as reality was revealed as something entirely different, a game, playing around with images, an imagination; what was really real was the unknown, that of which they were totally unaware, clashing with them while they were entirely unprepared. The people who were inside were in shock. This was real.

---

36 Ibid., 00:55:44–00:56:12.
37 Schlingensief and Sloterdijk moderated by Gächter, 'Gespräch zwischen Sloterdijk und Schlingensief zur Wienaktion.'

This also created an image copied from collective memory. Six members of the left-wing activist group stormed the container, telling the asylum seekers: 'We want to liberate you, bring you freedom. We are from the anti-fascist front.'[38] This is history at present with a twist: the image of Americans liberating Europe, seen through the looking glass of Hollywood movies as well as newsreels.

To befall, to come up, to take place, to happen, to become a reality through a shock reveals that we can't specify from which point we grasp something. Schlingensief was interested in the *Big Brother* format, because of the pretended or supposed transparency: 'here everything seems to become transparent … that is the argument of the makers of the show; that is what the public has been served.'[39] In front of the Vienna State Opera during the Wiener Festwochen, in parallel with Austria's political situation, this produces confusion: because it seems to be transparent it is understood likewise as authentic and truthful. The aesthetic difference between art and reality seemed to collapse, indistinguishable for many who were involved be they 'ordinary' people or experts.

But analyzing in retrospect, this very difference was always there, it was even visible. It became invisible whenever the affects took over, blinding the rationale. The intense perception was exaggerated by an imagination that was—unaware to those involved in such a moment—nourished by their own fear. This affective take-over thereby triggered the power of that dark side of fantasy that enables the worst nightmares to become real. Blindness was enabled because the event was fueled by historical knowledge that suddenly seemed to apply to the situation. People became captured by and wrapped up in the ongoings having no access to their critical abilities that would allow them to see through

---

38 Told and quoted by *Bitte liebt Österreich—Erste Österreichische Koalitionswoche* dramaturge Matthias Lilienthal, in Poet, 00:56:47–00:56:53.
39 Schlingensief, in Schlingensief and Sloterdijk moderated by Gächter, 'Gespräch zwischen Sloterdijk und Schlingensief zur Wienaktion.'

the traps and disguises of Schlingensief's action.

To comprehend the whole of the situation is difficult because this form of art is brought to life through the personal involvement and responsibility of every single person passing by, stopping or reacting in whatever way they might. It demonstrates and reveals the difficulties of a complex conglomerate of behaviour that arises from the need to cope within such a situation; taking a critical distance to analyze what is happening (as in classical theatre, where the public is not responsible for what happens on stage) is highly challenged and is nearly made impossible. Yet Schlingensief counters this confusion by pointing out that truth takes place covertly: 'I look at this temple in the city centre, I assume seeing the untruth, I can't grasp this, but inside, however, there might be the truth.'[40]

During a television conversation between Schlingensief and philosopher Peter Sloterdijk the moderator Sven Gächter asks: 'But Christoph Schlingensief was the only one who had the privilege of this moment of truth?' Schlingensief counters by saying, 'It might be revealed to others too. That is not to be guaranteed, not to be planned, not to be assured, it's not my wife, my yacht, my nurse. It's more like my grease, my felt, my hare....' With this Schlingensief alludes to a then popular commercial with an affirmative, undisguised capitalist (and macho) attitude of two men (so-called 'best agers') who compete with their life's achievements (wife, yacht, nurse— easily comprehensible to a majority of consumers) to confront this with something quite the opposite, the key materials of Joseph Beuys's art. These are but interesting, valuable, and comprehensible to only a small minority. Schlingensief thereby opens up and counters the objection by reminding us that, after all, this is about art and what one can achieve with and through it. Moreover, Beuys is used as a convincing example for the rather sad fact that even being hugely popular as he has become, does

---

40 Ibid.

not at all mean that his work is understood by many.

In a conversation between filmmaker and writer Alexander Kluge and Schlingensief a comparison is made between Beuys's coyote performance *I Like America and America Likes Me* (1974) in New York City and Schlingensief's container.[41] Kluge points out that Beuys, as a German artist in the US realized, exhibited, and ran a [social] experiment with a native inhabitant (an animal) over the course of a week. Then Beuys was transported— blindfolded —back to his home country (as the coyote was likewise transported and released back into the wilderness).[42] It recalls Schlingensief, a German artist in Austria, who realized, exhibited, and ran an experiment with the 'social body' to then return to Germany. Both artists let things develop, don't interfere with the concept or aim at a result. They go along with the actual developments, take part, react, and interact but do not comment; they do not wish to let their own opinion, behaviour, and understanding dominate the action. Both mirror what occurs or happens and which—necessarily within such an artificial, experimental situation—comes to a point of culmination and therefore is clearly revealed. The metaphor of being blindfolded alluded to Justitia (the task of judgment recurs again) who must be blind to the parties in conflict and their opinions to be able to do justice, to let justice happen. Blindness as premise, or, the blind seer, who has not that which is present in front of his eyes, but who unveils that which will happen from that which has been. The blind seer is the poet or artist, able to make this blind spot where past flips over into future a place of revelation of the past and the future. And therewith shows how both productively fuse with each other, beyond the good and the evil and herewith again independent. Without taking a position. In doing so all four—Justitia, the blind seer, Beuys, and Schlingensief—reveal a moment of truth. It is always about these surfaces. But when does this clarity occur?

---

41 See 'Freiheit für Alles,' pp. 141–142 and p. 147.
42 See Caroline Tisdall, *Joseph Beuys: Coyote* (Munich: Schirmer & Mosel, 1980).

One could object, like Sloterdijk did in a conversation with Schlingensief, that the '*age of the shock*' is gone, that it made way for the '*age of excitation.*'[43] That what happened during the seven days could very well be described like this, which again describes a surface that could be received through the media or by any observer outside the container. But he misses the entire point of the very moment of truth Schlingensief indicates that took place inside the container between the few people involved.

Sloterdijk refers to the avant-garde who worked with surprises, direct attacks on an unprepared nervous system. In his view, our society is now politically vaccinated.[44] But Schlingensief *uses the reality (the self-exposure of reality)* as something against which no vaccine can be found. The operation of his art is the attempt *to enable (at least some) to perceive* an historic situation which emerged from the nineteenth century, raged in the first half of the twentieth century, had been buried in oblivion in the second half, and reappeared as strongly concerning the present.

Yet it is possible to perceive this as an historical constellation with its elements of building identity via strong nationalism, fear of foreigners, and an idea of culture as an enclosed field bound to its own time and space and protected against 'the Other.' The mirror technique of quotation helps reveal this constellation as not bound to a specific time-frame, but as something that obviously moves through the last two centuries at least and is still alive today. Quoting from history is a form of deconstruction as elements are being taken out of their context. This shows initially what Benjamin notes is always at work within the task of an historian: the occurrences surround-ing the historian and in which he takes part underlie his account as a text written in 'sympathetic ink.' The story he presents to the reader forms as it were the quotations in this text and only these will be received. To write history,

---

43 Schlingensief and Sloterdijk moderated by Cächter, 'Gespräch zwischen Sloterdijk und Schlingensief zur Wienaktion.'
44 Ibid.

Benjamin concludes, always means to quote it. But to quote history means a quote mining of the historical object.[45]

Schlingensief takes on this task operatively and changes a *malum* into a *bonum*: he uses quotations and their deconstructive power in a passive way (as Kraus had). He mirrors the disrupted elements that reflect back from the social body and its fragments of knowledge, phrases, and dark emotions. He then lets the survival, the afterlife of a certain historical constellation, show itself in the present. This method is called *montage* and it is found throughout the arts. It is Benjamin's preferred method in *The Passagenwerk*. It is likewise an adequate description and solution to the problem of quotation that the historian faces all the time. Like Benjamin, Schlingensief insists upon the fact that he has '*nothing to say. Just to show.*' He will not take away what is valuable and he will not arrogate brilliant formulations, comments, or conclusions. He uses the 'rags and the garbage' not to make an inventory. But, again following Benjamin, to let them come into their own right in the only possible way: to *use* them.[46] In doing so, 'a *télescopage* of the past through the present' takes place and via the quoted the past, or better, the afterlife, of a certain historical constellation enters the time and space of the present—as a rejuvenation, as an agglomeration, a concretion.[47]

There is another intriguing parallel to Schlingensief's method of mirroring a surface to Benjamin's method of montage, which for Benjamin is the only justifiable method to gain access to history: to make the things (past occurrences, terms, opinions, deeds, etc.) for oneself *present.* Again in his notations to *The Passagenwerk* Benjamin points out that the just method to do so is to imagine (for oneself) the things in our own space—not us in the space of the things (like the collector, the anecdote

45 Walter Benjamin, *Das Passagen-Werk*, Aufzeichnungen und Materialien, in *Gesammelte Schriften*, vol. 1, N 11, 3, p. 595. Paraphrased in English by author.
46 Ibid., N 1a, 8, p. 547. Paraphrased in English by author.
47 Ibid., N 7a, 3, p. 588. Paraphrased in English by author.

does).[48] Things imagined in this way do not allow an intermediating construction out of 'big contexts.' Like the sight of great things of the past, Benjamin concludes, the sight of the Cathedral of Chartres for example or the temple of Paestum, is in truth (and when it succeeds) this: to welcome them in our space. It is not that we project our thoughts into them—they enter into our life.[49]

On that note, with the coyote and Beuys something archaic and pre-cultivated that animal and human have in common entered modern capitalist New York. It is likewise something that haunts Europe at least since its time of colonialism and the idea of the national state, and which entered with Schlingensief's operation Vienna and Europe once again and became suddenly apparent. The nationalistic and racist past of Germany and Austria enters the democratic system of a state that is a member of the EU, dark emotions rekindled by extreme right-wing ideology enter the social body of a democracy on the occasion of the Wiener Festwochen and generate *auto-immune* reactions, cause sudden breakdowns and outbursts. The past reveals itself as latent, as *afterlife*, *undead*. The unresolved past has merely been repressed, with its spread and ramifications overlooked—until now. So from mid-week Schlingensief is no longer in the focus of the media attacks. Instead, Austrian politicians and the director of the Wiener Festwochen are. Schlingensief explained that because of this mirror plane, this 'in-transparency fort,' everybody who was ever involved suddenly had responsibility.[50]

Besides the polemical dimension there was an underrated enlightened dimension at play. Sloterdijk pointed out that an appropriate distinction between the polemical and the enlightened dimension is not applicable anymore: 'the enlightened and the polemical

---

48 Ibid., H 2, 3, p. 273. Paraphrased in English by author.
49 Ibid. Paraphrased in English by author.
50 Schlingensief and Sloterdijk moderated by Gächter, 'Gespräch zwischen Sloterdijk und Schlingensief zur Wienaktion.'

dimension are the same.'[51] He explained that the affront is being worked out with the material provided by the media—unclear, dark material, with affects for or against foreigners, with the Big-Brother-affects of transparency and democracy-founded elimination; with the mechanisms of the mass-media. This creates the polemic effect. According to Sloterdijk the enlightened dimension is there when the whole suddenly reveals itself as the society game that is, will and has always been played like that with those dark social affects. That is the mirror effect of this spectacle: to reveal that societies are huge plastic processes made of affective material, affective behaviour, and affective disorders. Today this material has been mystified through the transmission of affects and emotions through communication and information tools. But these affects don't have informative or communicative meaning. Societies have chaotic group dynamics and artistic realization is in depicting and mirroring them.[52]

Schlingensief remarked on the closeness he felt toward the people that enabled him to feel a presence of schizophrenia, to be at a complete loss as to what shall happen next and the growing fear that comes out of this.[53] Like the raw material suddenly reveals that what underlays all societies and cultures, that can break up any time and that is bound in artworks and has been vital in artworks as afterlife since the beginning of civilizations (according to Warburg, see footnote 34).

In an artistic sense it was necessary to make an important decision. After the 'Indians' had stormed the container, the asylum seekers were freed, the campaign/action *was ended*—at least it seemed so. At this point Schlingensief realized that it would have been a massive mistake to allow a demonstration-society that deceives itself, *the final image*. And so, with the re-establishment of the banner (*Ausländer raus*), the addiction to the action

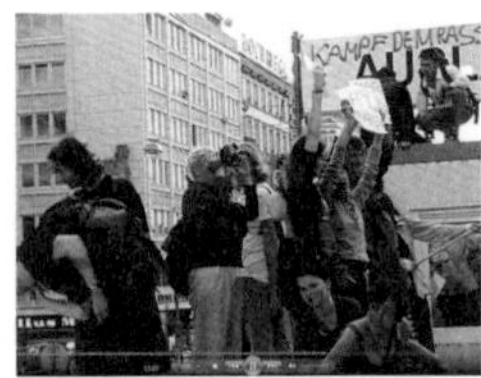
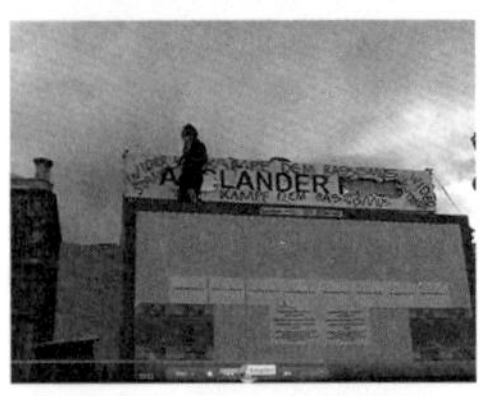
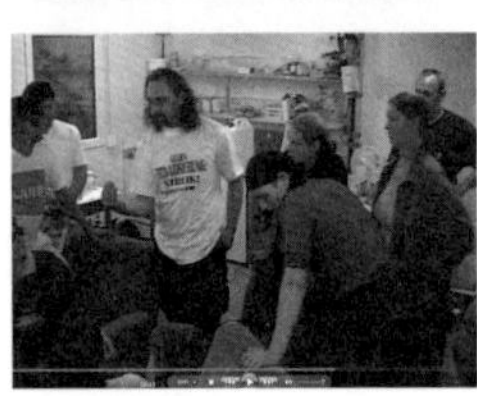

Fig 25–27   Christoph Schlingensief, *Ausländer raus. Schlingensiefs Container. Chronik einer Kunstaktion*, Paul Poet (director), 2000, screen captures

51   Ibid.
52   Ibid.
53   Ibid.

became apparent: immediately the heat went on.[54] 'That was the nuclear power plant, the fast breeder reactor, the fuel rod—they [the people] did not want to shut it down.'[55]

This sheds some light on a common misunderstanding concerning art, society, and politics. For example, politician Daniel Cohn-Bendit is misled by saying with excitement:

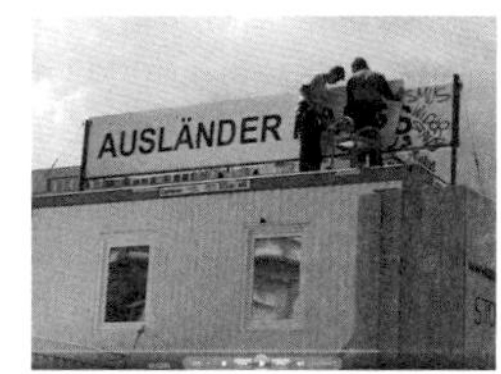

Fig 28 Christoph Schlingensief, *Ausländer raus. Schlingensiefs Container. Chronik einer Kunstaktion*, Paul Poet (director), 2000, screen capture

> ... I think one is dreaming. It's like being in the 1950s again. Art is becoming central again in the political dispute, with an artistic idea that is related to reality. And these are real people, real asylum seekers and these are real illegals ...[56]

Schlingensief corrects this view:

> What appreciation of art is this, that believes that art appears, changes the world and then everything is good—or bad. If this would be possible, I am asking myself: Why hadn't politics long ago gone into the arts? Why is politics not by now substituted by art? ... Against this I am interested in: *to ask different systems to dance*—and this, then, is the image (picture), and this image is there for six days, it stands there; and there it is still in 10 or 100 years. But whether it changed the world or even individual people is irrelevant ... Resistance is passé—you have to bring out contradictoriness/discrepancy.[57]

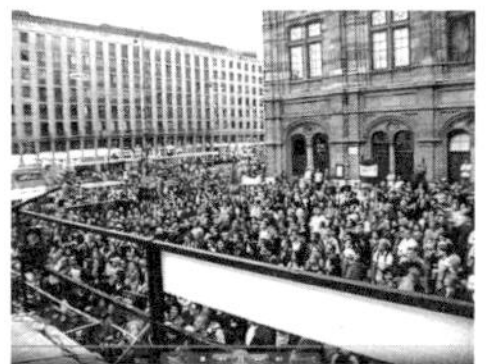

Fig 29 Christoph Schlingensief, *Ausländer raus. Schlingensiefs Container. Chronik einer Kunstaktion*, Paul Poet (director), 2000, screen capture

'To ask different systems to dance.' With this statement the social power of art comes into view because reception and production of the work is intertwined: 'To bind extremism to art. Here art is so wonderfully assimilated where art is so brutally nonconformist.'[58] Schlingensief finds a strong metaphor for this operation: for a short period of time to bring the patient out of his lie to face

---

54 Schlingensief, in Poet, 01:01:35–01:01:41 and 01:02:31–01:03:11.
55 Ibid., 01:03:12–01:03:21.
56 Cohn-Bendit, in ibid., 01:07:52–01:08:16.
57 Schlingensief, in ibid., 01:14:39–01:15:39 and 01:18:26–01:18:27.
58 Carl Hegemann, in ibid., 01:19:03–01:19:08.

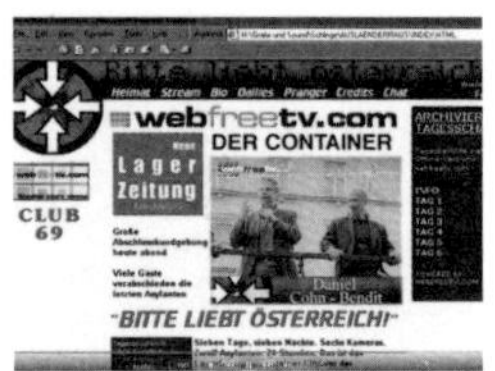

Fig 30 Christoph Schlingensief, *Ausländer raus. Schlingensiefs Container. Chronik einer Kunstaktion*, Paul Poet (director), 2000, screen capture

his real condition and there we can have a look at him.[59]

The generated images and acts have nothing in common with aesthetic objects, they turn into evidence within an historic process. As Schmidt concludes, nothing has been explained, nothing has been rectified—only something has been revealed. But this is what we have to be satisfied with.[60] Schlingensief's frequent reference to the twentieth century, to the avant-garde as the constant attempt to insert reality into art is a historic reflection, a reflection of a past that is present at present. In contrast, Cohn-Bendit's assumption about art and politics is an un-historic utopia. Schlingensief is constantly creating an awareness of an historic process, carrying on a debate that goes back to the art and media discussions of the nineteenth century, and the broad problematics of the twentieth century. To reveal rather than explain, to create a state of fruitful disorientation that alone allows one to escape the rhetoric machine of self-deceit and addiction to a comfort. These only give the sensation things are transparent or that one has power, when in actuality they are meant to disguise mechanisms of empowerment.

The revealing void gives us brief insight into the heart of the social integrative, the power of the plastic process, as a *heteronomy, inconsistency* (not dissolved in a homogeneous aesthetic that appeals to all and produces mass-identification). This insight into the conglomerate of emotion, memory, history, and imagination, from which nevertheless might emerge the reflective work of a mind that—by nearly drowning in a sea of self-contradictions—perhaps gains a moment of truth. In this we can realize that reality is a shifting presence fueled by a past that haunts us as unsolved, un-comprehended to avoid *nostalgia* and a future that we haunt as unachieved, un-thought of possibilities to avoid *utopia*. With this realized, the work of art is understood as a more and more demanding work on *reality*.

---

59 Schlingensief, in ibid., 01:19:20–01:19:27.
60 Burghart Schmidt, in ibid., 01:19:45–01:19:49.

Nick Aikens in Conversation
with Trevor Paglen

Autonomy Cube

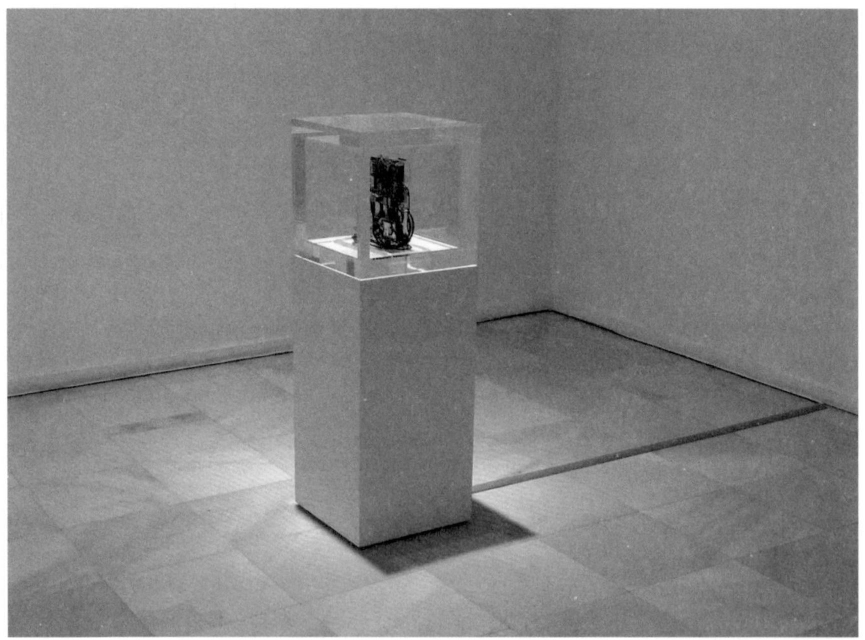

Fig 1 Autonomy Cube installation shot, 2014

Nick Aikens (NA) One of the areas we have reflected on in 'The Uses of Art' programme is the relationship between aesthetics, representation, and use. I felt it was important to include *Autonomy Cube* (2014, produced with Jacob Appelbaum) within this discussion as it both embodies and addresses this relationship, as well as implicates the art institution in a really intelligent way. Before discussing the work directly, I'd like to talk about the role of images, representation, and the visible in your work. You often address images from a particular vantage point— namely in relation to the invisible or the unseen.

Trevor Paglen (TP) In my image-based work there are two sides: one plays with representation and the second is the process that gave rise to the image and the politics within that process. I have a lot of sympathy for the avant-garde argument for abstraction. It was saying that as an ethical or political gesture abstraction was images that do not speak themselves. They are powerful precisely because a refusal to speak can also be a form of political speech. On the other hand it creates a relation between the viewer and the artwork whereby the viewer has to contribute something. In other words, the artwork does not speak itself but asks you to engage with it in a more empowered way. Now this is a good argument to make in 1942 but it's not a good one to make in 2015 because it completely ignores the economy of art objects these days. But the kernel of that argument is that I'm interested in images that don't speak themselves, images that you look at and can't really get much information from.

There is also the work that I do to make the image which in many cases involves things like tracking spy satellites or trying to figure out where different NSA infrastructures are, or infrastructures associated with covert actions. There is a politics in that process: first, ascertaining where those places are, second insisting on my right to take that photograph, and then third introducing—in this kind of elliptical, metaphorical way—these images and their associations into the world. So, a basic example would be that before I started studying spy satellites I never really even thought about the fact that they existed very much. And I think that by putting an image in a museum or magazine and saying 'this is a kind of spy satellite' you put it on the cultural agenda. You ask people to think about the fact that it's there.

NA But you are still using the language of aesthetics and a certain opacity that allows you to address representation in a specific way. With *Autonomy Cube* these relationships and references become more pronounced. Could you describe *Autonomy Cube* physically, the references it draws on and then what it does, its use?

TP *Autonomy Cube* is usually a forty-centimetre-thick Plexiglas cube. Inside that cube are several Novena motherboards, which are open hardware, open source computers. That entire cube generally sits on a plinth with a power cable and an Ethernet cable going into it. What the cube does is plug into the host institution's Internet connection and it does a couple of things with that. The first thing is it creates an open Wi-Fi network throughout the museum, an open network called *Autonomy Cube* that anybody can access. Instead of being a normal kind of Wi-Fi hotspot that you would find in an airport or in a cafe, it is a special kind of hotspot in that it encrypts and anonymizes all the data that goes over it. So it's the exact opposite of the hotspot you'd find in a cafe or airport, where the whole point of providing the free Wi-Fi is to spy on you. It makes it impossible for people to spy on you by routing all the traffic over something called the Tor network. The Tor network is a kind of alternative infrastructure for the Internet, although you access the same Internet over Tor that you do through your ISP or whatever. Now normally the way that the Internet works is that if you connect from your house for example, you have an IP address that is specifically assigned to you. Let's say you want to visit Wikipedia and let's pretend the server is in Palo Alto. Normally I would connect from my house here, in Berlin at the moment, through a local service provider. The local ISP would say okay, here is Trevor at this address and he wants to send a request to Wikipedia so we are going to send that over to the Internet exchange in Frankfurt and then it's going to go over to the Internet exchange in London and then it's going to go across the ocean

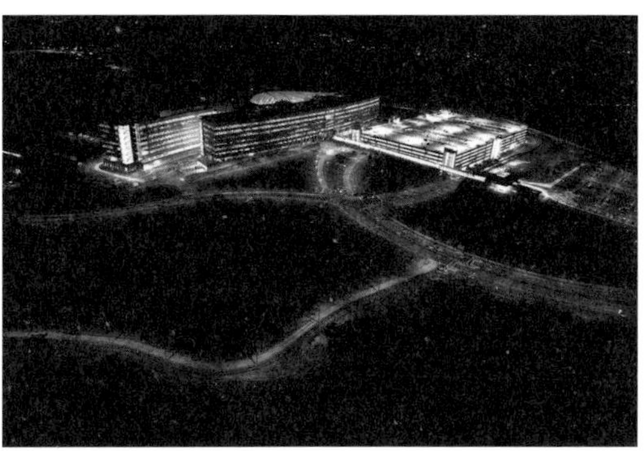

Fig 2 National Geospatial-
Intelligence Agency,
Springfield, Virginia, 2012

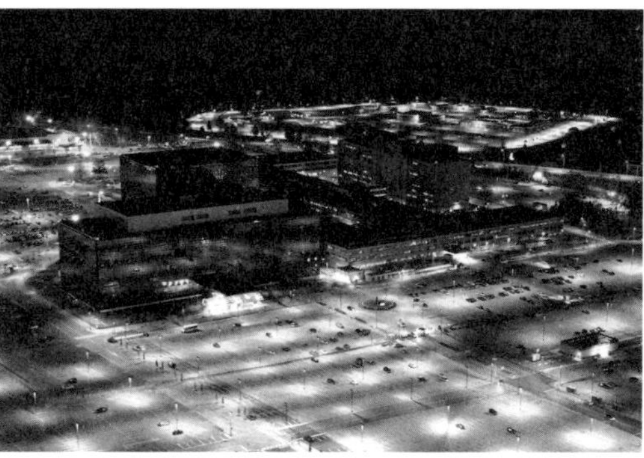

Fig 3 National Security
Agency, Ft. Meade, Maryland,
2012

through a transponder cable to the US and connect with
the server in Palo Alto. Now that whole process is
entirely transparent, anybody can look at exactly who
I am and what I want to do. Anybody on that network
who is looking at the traffic can see that and it's all
in the clear. The Internet was designed for all of
these devices to trust each other and be transparent
with each other. In part because of the very openness
of it, this is why the Internet is an incredible tool
of global communication, but also the greatest tool
of surveillance that humankind has ever created, Tor
is a way of using Internet differently. When you
download Tor, connect to it, and you want to go from
my apartment in Berlin to Wikipedia, the first thing it
does is encrypt all the traffic. So it makes all the
traffic look quite noisy and it only gives each stop
on the network enough information to move that data
packet to the next location. But your local ISP can't
see what the traffic is, it will only say, I have a
request to go somewhere else. Instead of taking a kind
of direct route to the Wikipedia server for example,
it bounces the traffic around to a random network of
what are called Tor relays around the world. So that
signal might go first to Japan, then it might go to
South Africa, and let's say it then would come out in
Poland and connect to Wikipedia. Anybody looking at
that circle can't see what's going on because it's
encrypted traffic. And then at the end at Wikipedia the
only thing they can see is that you are an anonymous

user from Poland, so it's a way of anonymizing my
identity and my location. It's a tool designed for
people living in countries where the Internet is
censored, for example, China or Iran, to get around
state censorship, or for people who are in countries
that have very bad human rights records to anonymize
their traffic and engage in political activities or
discussions that might otherwise land them in prison.
The tool was created to circumvent state censorship
and state surveillance. And now these Tor nodes, these
relays I was talking about, like the hypothetical one
in Japan or South Africa, are run by a network of
volunteers around the world, about 2000 people who
donated bandwidth to be a relay and to allow people
to anonymize themselves by routing traffic through
their own hardware. Now our *Autonomy Cube* is also
one of these relays: it creates a free open network
that anybody in the vicinity of the museum can use to
anonymize their Internet traffic but it also allows
people from around the world to use the museum's
Internet connection to anonymize their traffic, so it
helps anonymize people all over the world. If you
install the piece, it very literally becomes a part of
the institution.

It transforms the politics that are built into the
institution's infrastructure. In this way the piece
is thinking about a couple of different things that
in my mind descend from a series of conversations
that artists began to have with the late minimalism
of Robert Morris, for example—thinking about
phenomenology and relationality within artwork
rather than representationalism. This move away from
representation was using phenomenological philosophy.
I am thinking about relationality as a more robust
way of thinking about that, and that you see through
artists like Hans Haacke, with his systems work (1970-
present) and legacy of institutional critique, which
tried to look at institutional conditions that give
rise to something called art and, in a way, expose it.
Autonomy Cube isn't actually exposing anything but it
is descended from that tradition in the sense that it
is intimately integrated within the nuts and bolts
of the institution. But instead of being critical it
tries to help the institution become more of a civic
space as well as contribute to a more civic version of
the Internet. If we understand infrastructure is how
politics is imbedded in a kind of social and political

script, this is a proposal for an object that has different social and political scripts associated with it that as a result feed into the institution.

NA It also allows for a different type of knowledge production within the museum.

TP Historically, intellectual exploration has gone hand in hand with privacy and anonymity. But right after 9/11 the FBI in the US wanted to create a law that would allow them to check people's library records, because it would give them a record of what people were looking at and therefore a record of what people were thinking about. And librarians fought this, rightly so, opposing the idea that we are not free politically or intellectually when we are subject to surveillance and state oversight. So fast forward from 2001 to 2015: imagine you want to explore something, politically, culturally, or sexually. Where will you go? The main tool that we all use is the Internet and the Internet is one of the most surveyed things in the world. In many respects it has a dual use. The way it is constructed now is as an instrument of knowledge but at the same time it's also an instrument of mass surveillance. So, an infrastructure like Tor and a piece like *Autonomy Cube* are attempts to try to keep the part of being able to explore, intellectually and politically, and at the same time try to circumvent the ways in which mass surveillance of the Internet is conducted.

NA I think it is crucial that it reinvests the notion of autonomy with political meaning.

TP There's of course a double understanding of autonomy, particularly within the art context. The first is very much pointing to a history of the autonomous art object. There's something really liberating about the idea of an autonomous art object, of engaging in practices and making things that do not have to conform to the rules of the economy, society, or culture. It's an idea of undertaking practices that embody and propose forms of freedom that are not otherwise available. It's a beautiful idea, but it doesn't work. Or rather, it's a theoretical argument that's hard to actualize. The world doesn't work that way. So autonomy is a reference to a history of wanting to make autonomous objects as a gesture that points to a certain kind of freedom.

Within autonomy there is the idea of self-determination. Self-determination is something that's very difficult to engage with in an environment of mass surveillance and political repression, like the conditions we live in today. In a small way a tool like Tor—and this is why Tor was invented—is a way to try and give marginalized people or oppressed people a means to circumvent structures of oppression, with the goal of promoting self-determination and autonomy.

NA One of the essays in this reader, 'Museos del Sur', by Jesús Carrillo, talks about how the institution addresses subjects through a sense of lack. And artists and museums locate this lack by focusing the endless contradictions and problems of the world through a critique of the institution. If we expose the institution it somehow allows us to understand the dynamics of private interest and public good for example. But essentially, we are left with this sense of lack. What I like about *Autonomy Cube* is that it moves from a focus on the institution that is not only critical or even propositional, to something that functions as an alternative in real time.

TP That is absolutely crucial. I think for me—and especially in the way I was educated—critique was the be all and end all. I think that's ridiculous. Critique can be easy and it doesn't necessarily get you anywhere. So I'm definitely thinking about projects that instead of critiquing the existing infrastructures and institutions, try to make them better. Instead of 'institutional critique' we can think about 'institutional enhancement.'

A Man,
A Village,
A Museum

Li Mu

12 December 2012

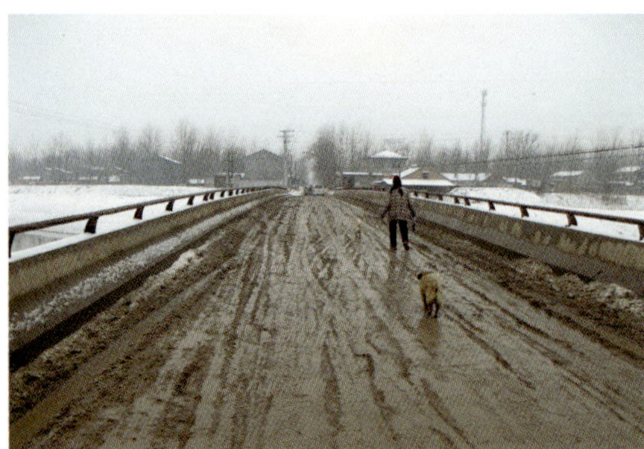
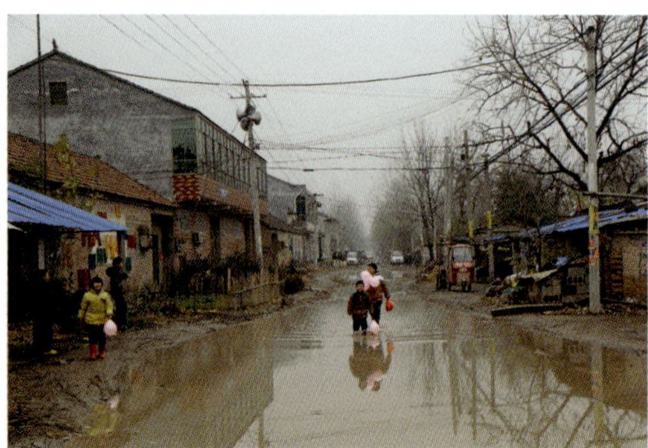

Dear Charles,

I am so excited that we can start the
project, which we prepared for more than
two years. Though we are still short of
money, this fund enables us to start. Last
night, I left Shanghai and came back to my
home in Suzhou. I was totally worn out.
My wife Fang looked at me seriously and
asked: Mu, did you ever think about this:
Why do you want to be an artist? I went
silent for quite a while and didn't know
how to answer.

This seems to be a simple question, but
for a full-ime artist like me, it's much
more complex. Because I want too much—
I want to create great artworks, I want
to become a great artist, I want to change
the world, I want to fulfill my life. But
did I ever ask myself: What is the real
purpose of doing art. Is it that important
to me? I had nothing when I was born;
I will bring nothing with me when I leave
the world. So, if I claim to be great will
it still mean that much to me?

Back to this project, I think I should
return to my original intention. I was
born and grew up in a village. But I
left it while my family and relatives
still lived here. Now I have come back
to the village with my art, knowledge,
and experience. I want to build up a new
relationship with the village, to figure
out whether there is a possibility for

me to get along with it and to influence
it or be influenced by it. Maybe I can find
the lost me, what I really want and my
direction by doing this project. I think,
no matter how big or complicated an art
project is, it should always be about
humans. It should have the temperature of
humans.

This summer I visited Cai Guo-Qiang's
studio in New York. I mentioned this
project to him. He said, no matter how far
a person goes from where he is born, he
can never cut himself off from that place
mentally. It's where his life starts and
will be the source of it for his whole
lifetime.

This project lasts from this winter to the
spring of next year. It will end in May of
next year when the weather is turning warm
and the flowers are in bloom. I invite you
and Davide to come to my village at that
time. You and Davide are the curators of
the project. I wish to keep in touch with
you all the time. Let's get this project
done together.

The recording of the project is very
important. I am looking for an assistant
to film and take pictures of the whole
process.

All the best,

Li Mu

17 February 2013

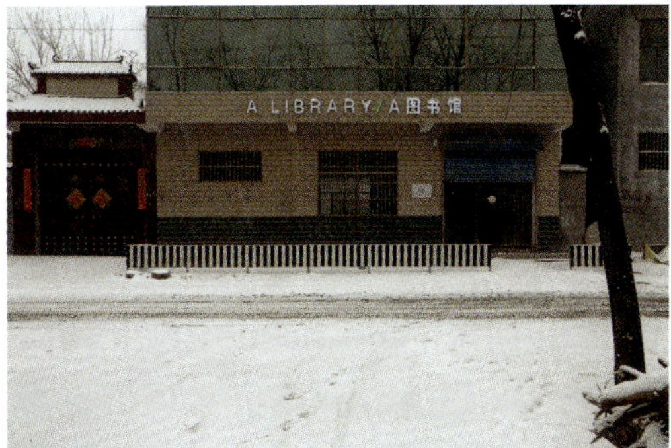

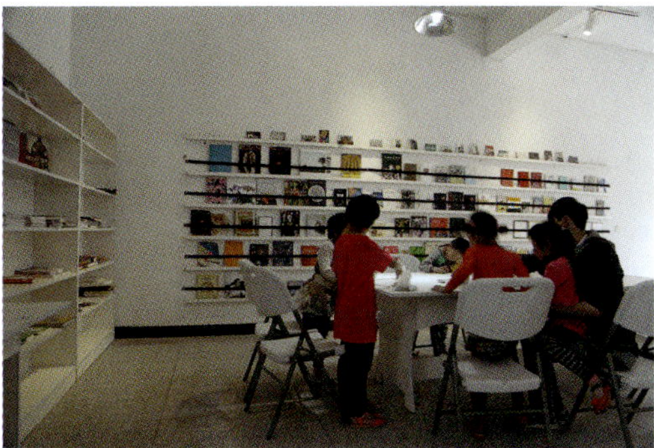

Dear Charles,

Time flies! I've been in Qiuzhuang for more than a month. It's the coldest winter in twenty-six years. There are few sunny days. Most of the time, it's overcast, foggy, and snowy. I wear a warm hat to go to sleep at night, because there is no heating system in the room. I got some chilblains on my hands. It reminded me of my childhood. I had chilblains on my hands and feet and I never had them after I left the village at the age of seventeen.

A Library was opened on the first day of the lunar year. I set off firecrackers. Lots of villagers came to the library with curiosity. They kept asking me, 'Non-profit library? Why do you do this?' Some people said to me, 'The peasants never read, don't waste this resource. You should move the library to the city.' They've already defined themselves as illiterate people. And they don't have the habit of reading and have no interest in new things. But the children are very happy, because they have sweets to eat and books to read.

A Library is open to the villagers every Saturday and Sunday. There are only about 100 books on the shelves. There is no rule here. And there is nothing but books. I do not want to define the library. It's more like a public space and I want to dig out its possibilities in the village. People here can't understand the books. I will play the role of a bridge to build up the connections between them and culture.

The village is just like any other village in North China. You can't see its history and future on the surface. All that you see is its endless change. It's no different from any other village, if you see it in terms of lifestyle, life values, and landscapes. However, it's the epitome of the problematic Chinese villages.

Na Yingyu, a video artist based in Beijing, came to my village before Spring Festival and started recoding the project. My assistant Zhong Ming also arrived here and started filming and taking pictures of me doing this project.

Before I am able to really start this project I still have a lot of problems: first of all, I'm still short of money. The Dutch consulate in Shanghai isn't sure about giving me the sponsorship. I almost used up the 5000 Euros. Secondly, I haven't received the detailed documents and pictures of the works in this project from the Van Abbemuseum.

I haven't heard from you for quite a long time. I wish you all the best.

Li Mu

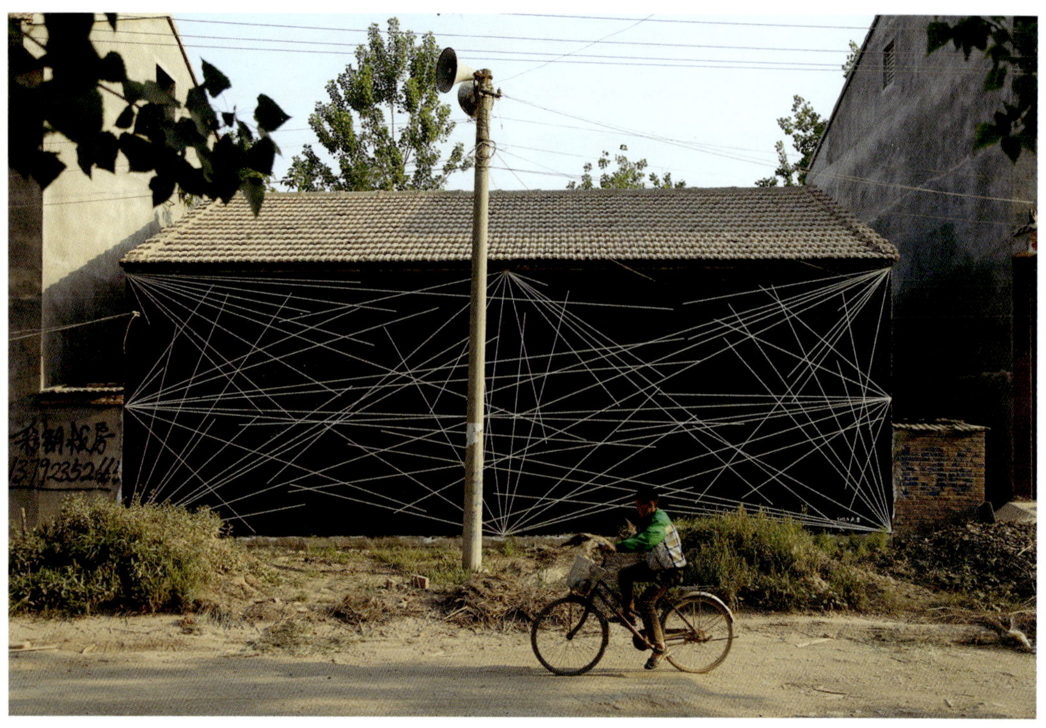

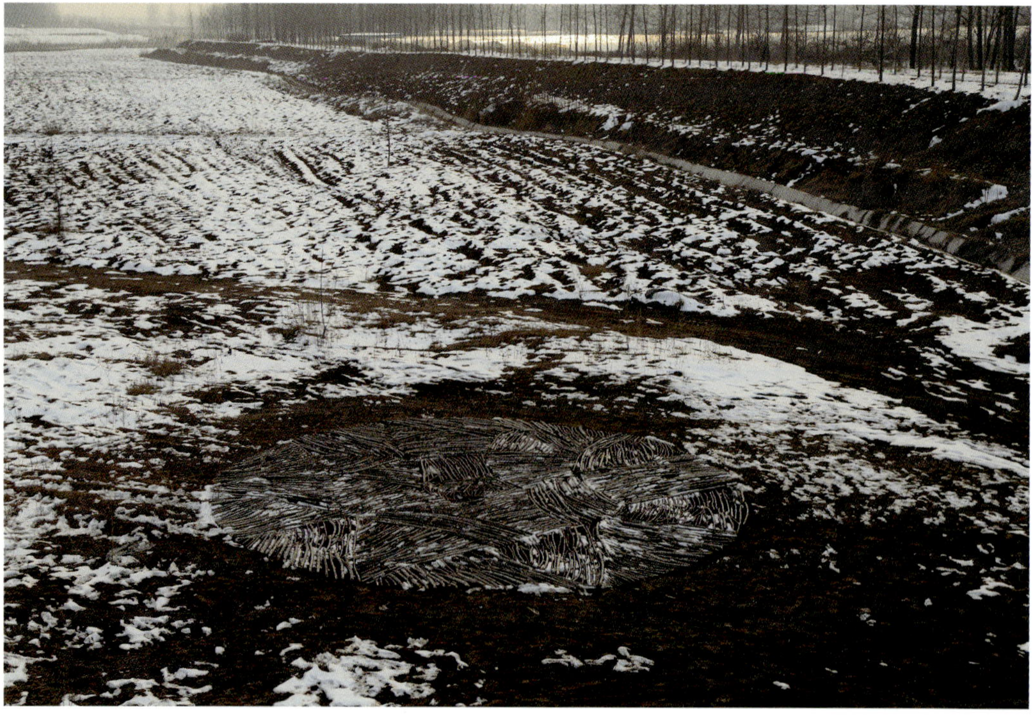

25 February 2013

Dear Charles,

I mentioned to you that Qiuzhuang doesn't have history and future in the last letter. I said it has no history, it doesn't mean that there is no history in Qiuzhuang. It just means that no one recorded its history or cared about it. The old died. The young get old and the children grow up to be the youth. The history of the village was buried in the tombs with the old people as they died. No one is concerned about the future of the village, because now they only care about their life and interest. But speaking of 'now,' we know it's changing all the time.

I like your advice that we should record and compile the history of the village. It will be interesting to work on that. If we can let the villagers know where they come from and where they will go, our work will be very meaningful. Because the past and the future are closely connected but also mutually restricted. This work will be part of the *A Library* project. The archive of the village's history will be displayed in the library.

As for *A Library*, I define it as a public space in the village. We had public life in my childhood. People worked together in the fields and watched outdoor films. There were even acrobatics and opera troupes coming to perform in the village. During the break of harvest season, there were storytellers. In the middle of the 1980s, a market economy replaced public ownership, and the peoples' goal became to get more interest. Some people became rich but some remained poor. Public life gradually disappeared. I want to launch more public activities in the library. Therefore *A Library* plays multiple roles as classroom, cinema, theatre, museum, etc.

My plan to copy the collections of Van Abbemuseum didn't change much. I just want to do my best to have all the works installed in a public space. On one side of the main road, I will put Sol LeWitt's two wall paintings and wall sculptures, Andy Warhol's Mao portraits, Dan Flavin's light installation, Daniel Buren's stripe painting, which I will paint on the fence, and John Körmeling's light installation *HI HA*. Richard Long's *Wood Circle* will be displayed on the ground in an open space. The video of Ulay/Abramović's performance art will be displayed in the grocery store.

The situation of the village is complex and unexpected. According to new city planning, a road extending sixty metres in width will go through the village. More than half the families will have to move, including my family and the library. Many villagers set up new buildings in their yards so as to get more compensation from the government. The future of the village is unknown and the artworks will be removed and gone when the houses are pulled down. But I think the artworks will remain in people's minds and won't be removed from their memory. In principle, I hope that the artworks can stay in the village and fade away in their own ways. Like a man's fate which is unexpected, the road repair and house demolition are not expected and out of the reach of my control. I have to accept these facts. I will record the process of the movement and people's situations as part of my project.

I am still short of money to complete this project. The Dutch consulate responded to me clearly that it will not sponsor this project. I'll discuss with Dadou tomorrow to figure out a way. I hope we can work it out together. But I am determined to finish the project anyway.

If you come to visit the village at the end of April, I think you will see most works of the project.

Take care.

Li Mu

21 March 2013

Dear Charles,

I really appreciate that the Van Abbemuseum collected my four drawings. Thanks to Davide's help, I can continue the *Qiuzhuang Project*.

I met some friends in Shanghai some time ago. They were all discussing my *Qiuzhuang Project*. Here are their views: first of all, the intellectual came back to the village and had the villagers engage in his art experiment. The villagers then became the 'laboratory rat,' which revealed the unequal relation between the artist and the villagers. Secondly, it formed a new culture of colonialism by spreading and permeating the village with Western culture. I think their questions are very interesting. Their views represent the majority of Chinese intellectuals.

A Library has been opened for more than one month. The villagers changed from being very curious about it to getting used to it. Only the children still have enthusiasm for it. On weekends, I turned on the television and played the videos about art. The children here aren't in the habit of reading. They do not cherish the books. Soon the books were creased and stained with dirty fingerprints. Some books were even damaged. The adults came here sometimes. But they were just talking, smoking, and spitting. The librarian was my teacher in elementary school. He is one of the few people who understand my work. Because there aren't many books, his duty is to watch the kids and prevent them from damaging the books. Besides, he also does some cleaning work. When some adults gathered here and talked, he would introduce my work.

We've started the preparation for the book *Qiuzhuang History*, which is the first program under the library project. I started interviewing the old people here. But it's very difficult work, because the history of this village is very vague. It's barely possible to get any documents or information about the time before the Republic of China era. My assistant

Zhong Ming is walking around the village everyday and has taken many pictures.

The weather becomes warm. The willows start to bud. I can feel the spring is coming soon though the village remains grey. It's usually very windy in the spring. The air is thick with dust and noise from the heavy trucks. The wood processing workshops have begun their work. All the adults are busy making money. Before I came to the village, I thought the project was very huge and complex, but now living in the village, I find it's very small.

I've started copying the collections of Van Abbemuseum. I started with John Körmeling's light installation *HI HA*. I was surprised that the workers here never saw that kind of material, so we had to find the similar material and way to make it so as to achieve a similar effect. The copies of Sol LeWitt's wall sculpture (the 'turning ladder') have all been finished and given to some families.

The boss of the aluminium alloy store in the town and his staff spent four days making the fifteen copies. They like it a lot and think it's beautiful. Maybe that's because they made them. One ladder was put on the wall next to *A Library*.

It melded into the surrounding environment very well. But the hostess of the house was very angry. She said that she couldn't see any art in it and it was ugly. The other families put the ladders in the sitting room and the ladders became their storage racks. They put many daily goods and crafts on it. Now the ladders look both functional and nice. A young man even put his wedding photos into the boxes of the ladder. My sister doesn't want to put anything on it, because she thinks it's an artwork and she doesn't want to destroy its original aesthetic beauty. She put it on the wall of the second floor as a kind of decoration.

Zhong Ming is recording my work here, and it's going very well. The villagers have gotten used to the existence of the

camera. We record how the works are born
and how they develop. At the same time
we are recording the villagers' life
situation and their attitudes toward the
art pieces.

I'm looking forward to meeting you in
April 2013.

All my best,

Li Mu

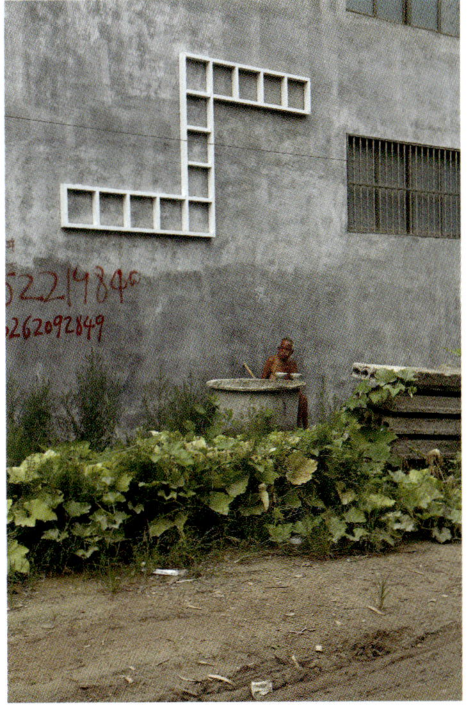

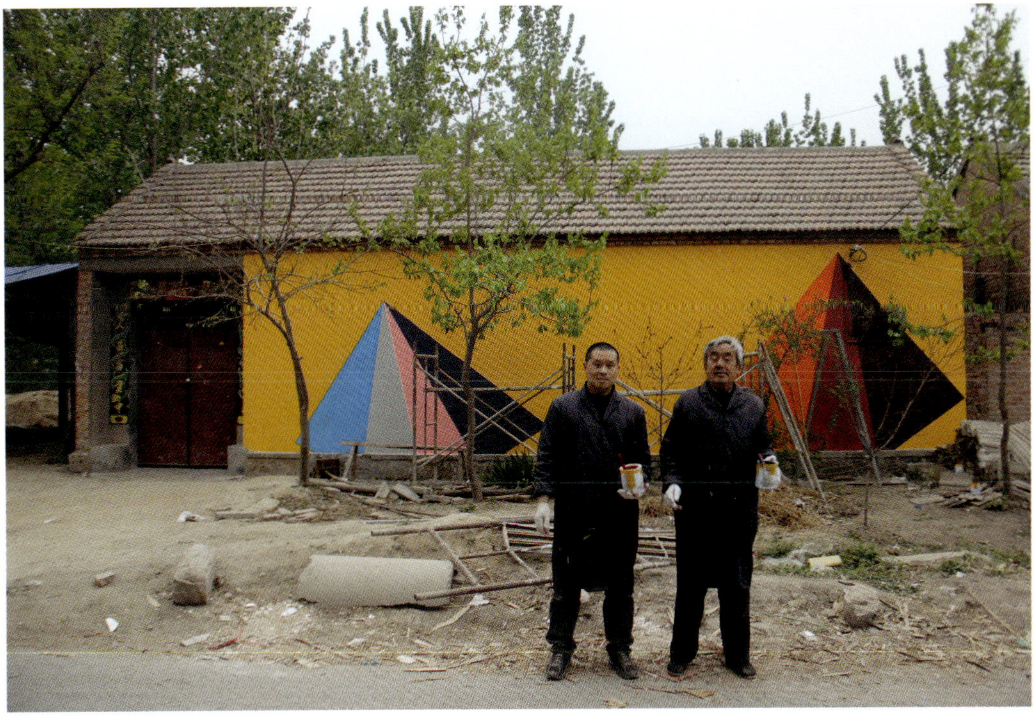

23 May 2013

Dear Charles,

Time flies! It's May now. These days, the seeds of the poplar tree are flying in the air like snow. It's dry and hasn't rained for a long time. The passing trucks throw up dust.

The road repair plan was confirmed. The villagers are speeding up the constructions of temporary buildings before the evaluation of their houses so as to get more compensation. This plan was launched by the government. The villagers know clearly that the compensations are very limited. Some households just built up their new houses and are now facing demolition. The government never sent people to solicit their opinions or told them where they could go when the houses are pulled down. People were just speculating about the compensations and wondering about their future. There is no clear response from the government. All they can do is to build more buildings for more compensation. The grocery store's owner Wang Gaoqi is worried. He is facing the loss of his store and house.

I invited Lu Daode, the old painter in my village, to join me in painting the two wall drawings by Sol LeWitt. Lu is seventy now. He is the only painter in the village. He used to paint patterns on furniture and ancient buildings. Now he makes a living by drawing the statue of Buddha. At first he refused me. He said he didn't like Western art. But eventually he accepted my invitation, maybe it's because I emphasized that I would pay him or he was moved by my sincerity.

We cooperated very well and finished the wall paintings very quickly. He was very professional and devoted to his work. He strictly followed Soll LeWitt's sketches and made the copy. We all call him 'master Lu.' He was very happy those days. Every night we drank a lot. We exchanged our attitudes toward art and our art experience. He liked the two wall paintings we worked on and started showing interest in Western art. The villagers gathered around the two paintings but couldn't understand them. Some people tried to express their interpretation of the two paintings. Though they thought the paintings were beautiful, they couldn't accept them because they couldn't read a story out of the paintings.

The two wall paintings are covered with dust now, which fits into the village even better. People have gotten used to them and no longer discuss them.

We held an activity called 'Weekend Cinema' in *A Library*. We played two films on Saturday and Sunday afternoon. The children do not like serious art films. They are more interested in cartoons. At first I complained that they didn't know how to appreciate art, but gradually I started to accept the fact. Because it's their living environment that leads to their ignorance of art. I tried to find good animated films for them. We have more and more children in the 'Weekend Cinema.' Ellen Zweig, an artist and poet from New York came to visit me. She made a Western picnic for the children by using the ingredients here. More than forty children came to the picnic. Some parents were also present. The children communicated with Ellen in their own ways. They were very happy, because it's their first time taking part in a picnic party and spending time with a foreigner.

More children came to *A Library*, but fewer adults visited. On the one hand, they are busy making money and have no time to visit the library. On the other hand, they think it's children's business to learn, not theirs.

My father told Ellen that he was proud of me. When I heard that I felt a warm feeling rushing through my body. My father never understood my art nor supported my art career. There is deep misunderstanding between him and me. I once tried to communicate with him, but it didn't work. My father is experiencing my art creation by watching me work and listening to me. To experience art is very important. It's very difficult to make people accept my ideas without involving them in that art experience. Their doubts and misunderstanding of me is gradually disappearing. They started to accept the library. Because of the artworks, I am building up a new relationship with the villagers.

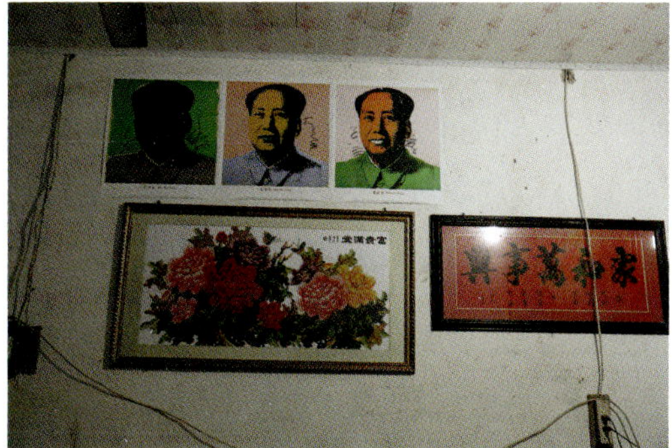 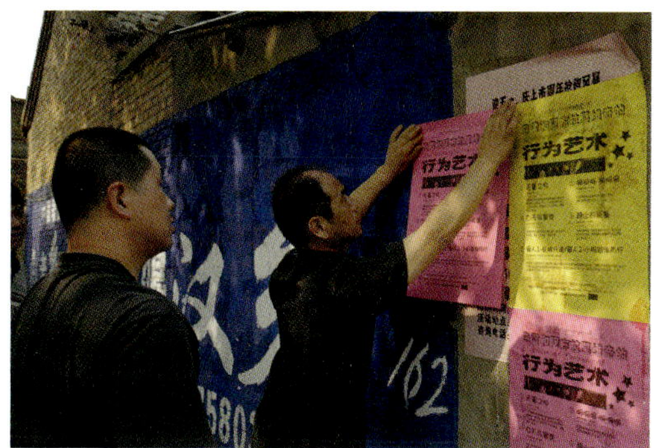

The poster about Ulay/Abramovic's performance art looks like those commercial advertisements we often see on the road. I designed it on purpose to make it look rough and direct, which actually matches the village. We pasted the posters on each intersection and on the walls, having them mixed with those commercial advertisements. The video of Ulay/Abramović's performance art was played in Wang Gaoqi's grocery store. Their performance was shown in this dim room where there was a smell in the air and goods arranged disorderly. To me, this place is the best place to show the video. That performance art seems to belong here. Wang Gaoqi, the owner of the store, watched it almost everyday and he was thinking about its meaning. There is a woman who can't stand the performance cause there was a nude scene. So Wang Gaoqi turned off the video until she left. He turned it on after she left. The villagers kept asking me: What's performance art. They cannot understand why it's art. They suggest that I write down the meaning on the posters.

I printed many Andy Warhol's Mao portraits. My father became nervous when seeing the Mao portraits printed in various colours. He was worried that it would get me in trouble because the government might think I was insulting the former leader. At the same time, the printing house got nervous too. They didn't allow their names to appear on the posters and didn't let me

film the printing process. I know we live under the leadership of the Communist party. The strict political environment made people fear freedom. To protect themselves, they've formed the habit of self-censorship.

I like Warhol's Mao series. I planned to give them to every family in the village. To my surprise, many people didn't like the three portraits. They thought the colours were ugly. They couldn't accept Mao's face in red and blue. It's very interesting that people don't like them after bright colours were added to the picture. But these portraits of Mao are so popular with Western people. The reactions to these Mao portraits in Western countries and China are so different. I know it takes time to get people to accept a new thing. I'm challenging their aesthetic view and their psychological limits. I believe they will eventually appreciate the three Warhol's Mao portraits.

A journalist asked me if art can change society. I said: 'Art is so small and powerless. It's the interest that is driving the society forward. I don't expect that art can change my village. I just hope that these artworks can bring more fun to their lives and leave them with some beautiful memories.'

All my best!

Li Mu

21 August 2013

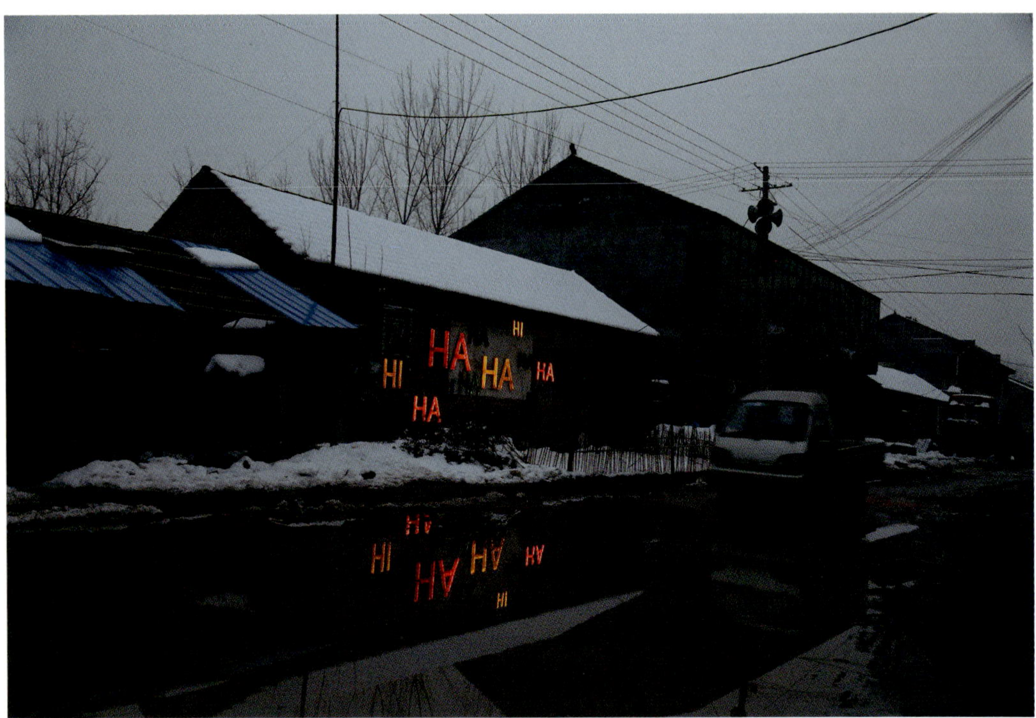

Dear Charles,

It was so hot this summer. There were flies and mosquitos flying all around. And the cicadas were making noise twenty-four hours a day. I couldn't calm down, just like the noisy environment. It has been a long time since the last time that I wrote you a letter. I don't know how to start talking about the things that are going on here.

The persimmon tree grew so fast that its branches and leaves covered most of the wall paintings of Sol LeWitt. People are used to them and don't take a look at them anymore. I know the leaves will fall in the autumn and the wall paintings will appear again.

We made John Körmeling's *HI HA* installation and installed it on the wall opposite the grocery store. Every night, the *HI HA* glittered in the darkness. The villagers gathered at the grocery store and talked to each other. All the people like this piece. Körmeling once told me that he wanted to convey happiness through this work. So I think he succeeded because people here apparently appreciate it. The owner of the house planted beans in front of the installation. Soon the beans crawled over the whole rack and covered most of the installation. When the art is confronted with people's practical interests, it gives way to the latter. Therefore, they can coexist in a harmonious way and enrich the artworks. Because what I care about is the relationship between the art and its surrounding environment, not the art itself.

We also finished Dan Flavin's circle light installation and installed it on the wall of my house. My father's two friends helped with the design and made it. My mother made a red rain curtain. When the dusk falls, my father, like opening a theatre curtain, opens the red curtain to reveal the light. It drew lots of attention from the passersby. They stopped and looked at it. Unlike the original work set in a white box in the museum, this work is set in the environment where there is the mix of earth, noise, crops, and barebacked farmers, which injected vitality to this piece of work. It has melted into the surrounding environment, forming a new landscape.

As the project continues, the copying of works goes more smoothly. On the one hand, it's because I get along well with the villagers and gain their support; on the other hand, it's because the slow pace of working gives them time to digest and accept the works. One villager came to me and asked me if I could paint Sol LeWitt's *Wall Drawing No. 256* in the siting room of his new house. He likes this piece of work. A young man copied the 'ladder' (LeWitt's wall sculpture) and put it on the wall of his sitting room. This is totally out of my expectation. I thought that the Western artworks might produce conflicts when they were set in the village. But in fact, there isn't much conflict. People treated and accepted them in their own way.

It's so hot this summer. I realized the importance of the role of time in the project. So I slowed down the work pace on purpose. I keep reminding Zhong Ming that we are filming the time because we are feeling the passing of time. So we should film the time. All the people, the art pieces, and the entire village are changing. I enjoy the everydayness. Art, like gold, hides in the everyday time.

I planned to complete this project in the first half of the year. But now I have decided to work until the end of the year, around the same time when I started the project last year. Therefore, we have enough time to feel and record the art here and the village. The documentary we will make is not to tell a story but bring people to the space and time behind that story. I don't want the documentary to tell people what happened here. It's a documentary about time. It's an artwork for me.

Many friends from different countries and regions came to visit me. My parents received them warmly. My father was very happy. He is enthusiastic for new things. He learned about the outside world by talking with the visitors. At the same time, he is learning about me through those conversations and understands me better.

The owner set up a shed on that empty open space where we planned to put Richard Long's *Wood Circle*. He did that for more compensation from the government. So I'm still waiting for the right time to do this piece of work. Maybe in the winter when all the leaves fall. Outside of the village, there are fallen branches all over the ground. I want to work with an old woman who is neighbour to the library. She always rides her tricycle to pick those branches for firewood. I realized that art itself is not that important, what is important is that we see something beyond the art. And the things that are beyond art are much richer.

My parents helped me plant a patch of corn in front of the library. I painted Daniel Buren's stripe painting on the fence. The corn grew fast in the air thick with dust. There is thick dust on the leaves, covering the green colour. Many times I wanted to clean the leaves and then take pictures of them, but I told myself that wasn't reality. I wouldn't change them for a beautiful photo.

As the curator of this project, do you have some new opinions or views of the project after following it for so long? Is the project going the way you expected? Have you thought about how we display this project to people? I have almost used up all the funds. Do you know from what channels I can get more funds to complete this project?

When I finished the writing of this letter, the autumn came. And the weather is getting cool.

I'm looking forward to your response. Take Care!

Li Mu

17 November 2013

Dear Charles,

I am sorry I have not written you in such a long time. I left Qiuzhuang more than one month ago, I worked on two shows and a lecture and took care of my wife since she was not feeling well (now she is good, don't worry). And I also worked on the drawings about *Qiuzhuang Project*.

It was winter when I came back to Qiuzhuang.

Qiuzhuang was just like what you see on Facebook: the leaves fell off the branches; the village returned to grey but our artwork's glamour — beautiful colours and flashing lights broke the village's grey. We can feel the vitality of the village. I can find the vitality in the artworks if not among the brilliant village children.

I could look at the village from a distance when I was away. I mentioned to you that this project was about time. At first, we recorded the village like a tourist: we filmed a funeral, the celebration of a baby's birth, a wedding, people working in the wood workshop, people working in the field. We filmed rain, sunsets, and wind. After several months, we found nothing to record; it's like we have recorded everything. Later, people invited us to film them at funerals and weddings, but we were weary of this work. But now, I realize that the time we talked about just embodied these repeated things. People repeated the same work as they went through the seasons. Someone passed away, someone was born, the village went through hundreds of years, even thousands of years. It looks like everything is in repetition, but which thing is really is being repeated? Each time is different; every time is new. We start recording the village and the artworks with these learnings in mind.

I have to stop the work on 'Qiuzhuang History' after some interviews. I haven't enough time to work on it as I focus on copying the artworks and other things around *Qiuzhuang Project*. I cannot get more

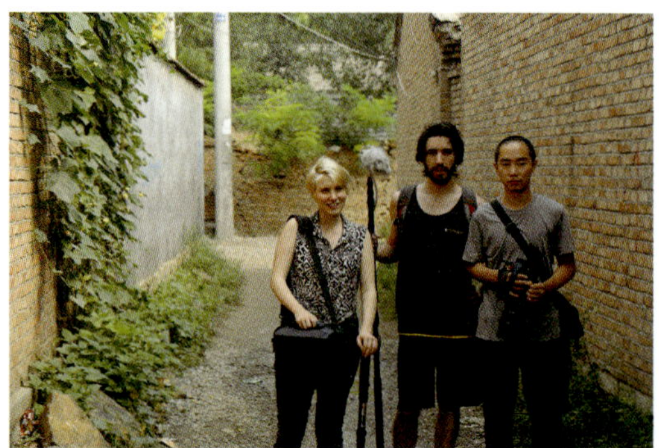

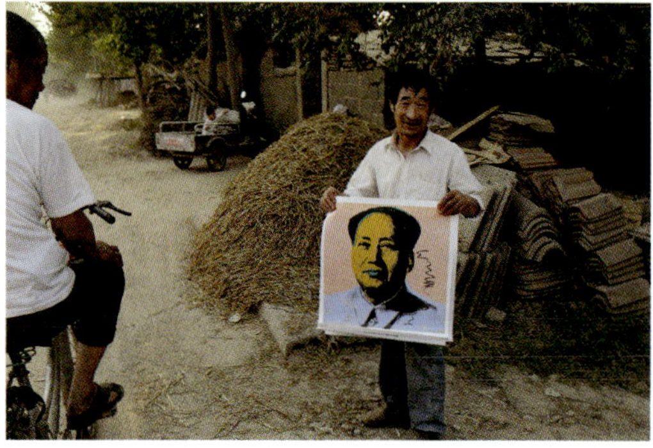

from the interviews: the village's vacancy before Minguo (1900), its blurry situation before new China (1949). I do not know how to work and how to continue it. Recently I found the *Fengxian County History* and read it. I think I can find some information in it. I will work on it when I finish copying the artworks close to the Spring Festival.

We have filmed nearly 300 hours of video and we have several thousand photos—these are for a documentary and exhibition that include video and photographs. I will work on them after the Spring Festival. It will take more than half a year. I am being invited to introduce *Qiuzhuang Project* in several exhibitions and lectures. So I keep thinking about how to face the new place and new audience when the project left Qiuzhuang. What is my experience of Qiuzhuang? How can I use this experience? I'm like a bridge between Qiuzhuang and the outside. They are connected by the bridge.

I planned to make a talking performance with Na Yingyu in AM ARTSPACE in Shanghai at the end of this month. We will talk about the finance of *Qiuzhaung Project*. The account and statistics will be presented to the public as the project's extension.

How can we put the project in Van Abbemuseum? Can we display the copies in the museum together with the originals? What's the relationship between them? Can we display the big images of *Qiuzhuang Project* in the corner and public space in Eindhoven as the artworks were dispersed in the village? Can we present these different documentary materials in the museum from me, Na Yingyu, and Sari (we will share the all videos tapes)? Can we make a publication around a series of articles, talks, letters, and diaries?

I am confronted with the problem of the library. My father started to think that it's not important to the village because so few people came to library, he cares about the money going into the library. I know the library has a small number of readers since I was out of village. I hope the library can stay next year until the house has to be demolished to make way for the new road.

My family gave me more help when I came back, but it still strongly restricted my freedom and independence. I must leave them for a period of time so that they can take a break and get some air.

The villagers still talk about the road and the demolition. We did not receive any notice from the government.

All My Best,

Li Mu

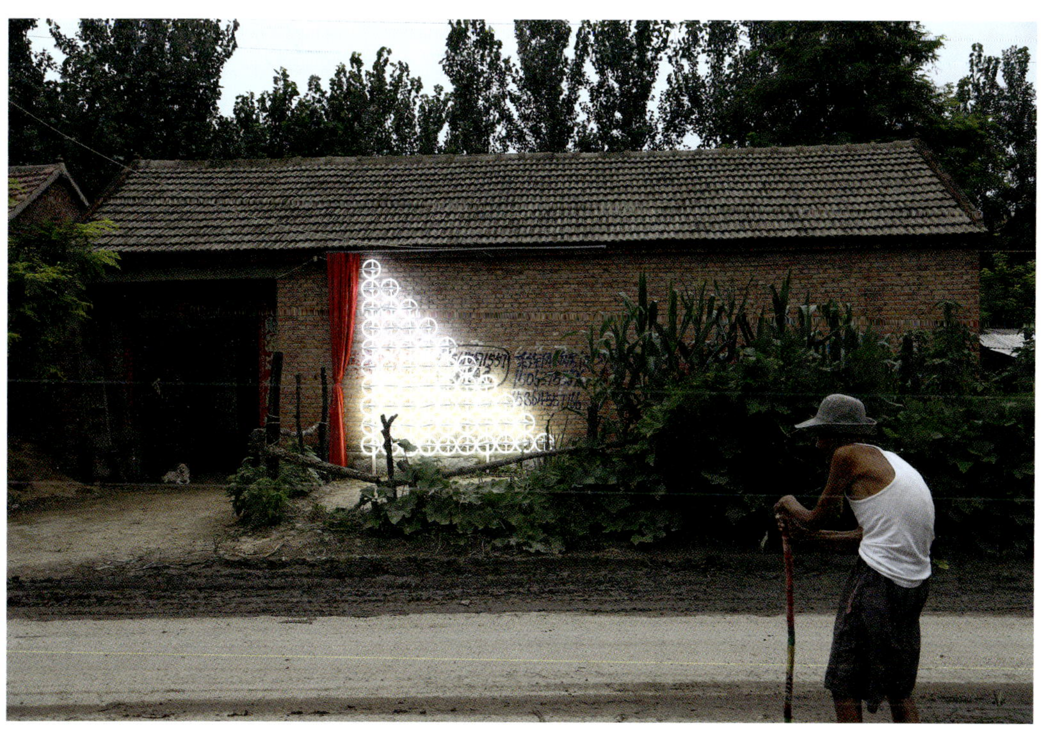

26 February–11 March 2014

Dear Charles,

I just reviewed the seven letters I wrote to you earlier. When I sent you the first letter, this project had not even started. With excitement and worries, I expressed the idea that no matter how complicated and broad this project will be, it must get the 'temperature' from people. This whole project should be concentrated on people and their stories. It's been one year since I discussed this idea with you, and I have finished most of my work on this project in the village. (I copied ten pieces of artworks from Van Abbemuseum, and presented them in the village.) I no longer worry about whether I lose people's 'temperature' or not. Because so many people participated in this project in different ways, and they brought so many stories into this project. And I began to re-ponder the questions I asked myself in the first letter: What did I gain from this project during past year's work? And have I found my direction and goal in my career?

Winter in Qiuzhuang is extremely cold. Though the weather here is better than it is in the North, we don't have a heating system. The only way people can make themselves warm is to wear as many clothes as they can. I put on the cotton trousers my mother made for me and wear cotton gloves to protect my hands from chilblain. After the Chinese New Year, there was a very heavy snow, which I have been expecting for a long time. All the trash and other chaotic scenes were covered by the snow, and the village turned into a place where one can only experience in a fairytale. Unfortunately, it got even colder after the snow began to melt, and my hands are full of chilblains again.

I finished Carl Andre's *Twenty-fifth steel Cardinal* before the Spring Festival. I went to the steel market searching for the proper material I could use for this installation. One of the workers cut a whole piece of steel into twenty-five squares at my request. Both the owner and workers at that store were very curious about how I was about to turn those pieces into an artwork. I told them I will just put them on the ground, then it is done, and art is created.

I planned to put this installation in the living room of one of my uncle's newly renovated houses. But he could not finish the renovation work by then. Thus, I had to put it in the courtyard of my father's house. He couldn't understand why these steel cardinals can be seen as art, since in his opinion, they're neither beautiful nor useful. However, both my mother and he gave me a hand on the installation of this work. The floor was not so flat, so I first put a layer of sand on it to make it more even. On the sand, I put all the steel cardinals and arranged them according to their texture on the surface.

After I took some pictures, my father started to take all his birdcages out of the room and placed them on the steel cardinals. Twenty-five birdcages on twenty-five steel cardinals. He lit a cigarette and enjoyed his work for a while. At that time, he was satisfied. He asked me with a smile on his face: 'Is this art?' I answered: 'Yes, it is installation art.'

During the Spring Festival, he found an interesting function for the cardinals: they can make the sound of fireworks louder and clearer. On the other side, the fireworks would leave some marks on the surface and create new textures for the steel.

After several rains, the steel became rusty, and finally turned into a khaki colour from its original blue-grey, and then an earthly red.

Richard Long's *Wood Circle* was arranged at the end of *Qiuzhuang Project*. I don't know why I made this arrangement, but I think this work is difficult to accomplish. I picked an empty space for it when I started to think about it. But someone put up a shed there, and I could not wait any longer for him to spare the space. So I had to find another place outside of the village, where every inch of land was covered by crops and trees. Finally I got available land on a bank of a big river. Because all the crops couldn't survive there, it was left empty for ages. I guess that Long created his work in a similar environment.

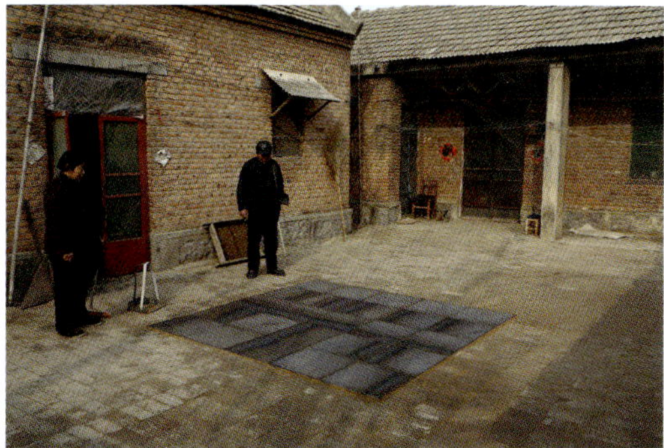 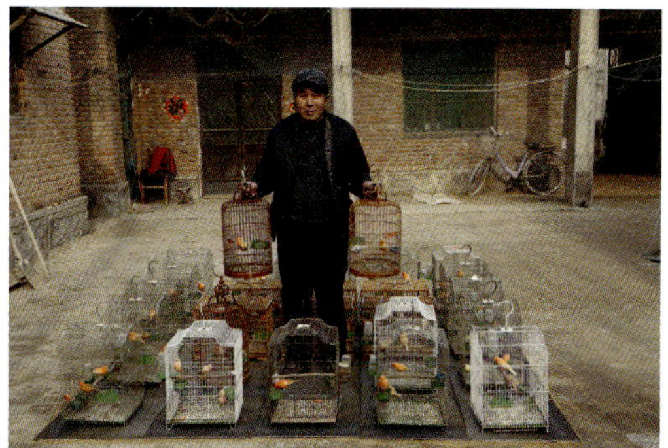

My aunt and my parents helped me with *Wood Circle*. We worked for the whole afternoon to collect and sort out all these branches from the poplars and apple trees. We finished the work next morning. There was a lot of snow on the bank, so we placed the branches on the snow directly. As the snow melted away, all the branches were then visible on the ground.

Wood Circle was installed somewhere close to the village, but just outside of it. As a result, it seems like this was a presentation of the work by all the people in my village. However, the branches are organized in a very orderly way, whereas the village looks messy and chaotic. We were worried that some people would take those branches away and use them as firewood. So I went there everyday to check if *Wood Circle* was still there in its original shape. I was hoping it would stay there through spring, summer, autumn, and winter.

My parents are really happy that I finished all the works in this one year. Even though their misunderstandings and confusions bothered me constantly, they are among the ones who helped me the most during the whole process. They offered me the most generous support without any conditions.

We shot 350 hours of video over the 13 months and we decided to edit these in the style of diary: one day is one chapter, with all the chapters making the whole documentary. As I agreed with my friend and the editor, Na Yingyu, we will present the engaged people and their stories to a wider audience, based on the documentary as well as other videos taken by my assistant Zhong Min. These materials will tell people what happened in the village during the last year. It's not a breathtaking novel or lyric poem. It's like prose. In this way, we can avoid just telling a simple story. Instead, we will be able to give everyone a chance to express themselves. They are not a group of villagers with the same tags on them, but individuals with distinguishable personalities which make every one of them special and different from others.

A year ago, my mind was full of fears and uncertainties when I came back to visit my grey-coloured village. I didn't know what was going to happen for the coming year and how I could possibly handle all the difficulties and problems I could not even anticipate. Neither did I have an idea as to how to deal with people's ignorance, selfishness, and greediness. It was like having a huge empty bag on my shoulders, and I was concerned that I could not put anything in that bag in a year. One year later, I stood on the village's road, and I looked at these colourful wall drawings and installations, and people I am getting really familiar with. This feeling of being lost and sadness did not conquer me. The empty bag is now filled with ideas and

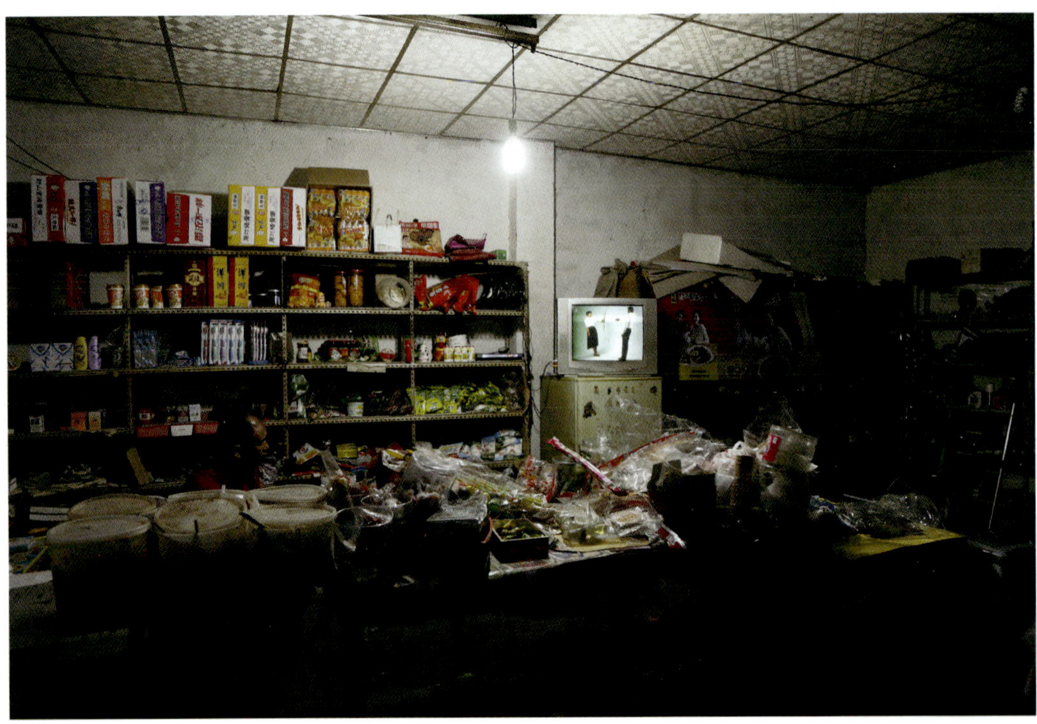

stories, and it is so heavy, but I just
don't know where should I go next. All of
a sudden, I am full of gratefulness in
my heart, to the village, to the people,
whether they are generous or selfish.

For the whole year, I stayed away from
Shanghai and all those art talks,
lectures, and debates there. However, I
still managed to keep good work status
and built a relationship with a wider art
world. But when I was about to finish this
project in the village, this sentiment
that I could not find my way came back to
me again. I realized that this is how my
art career will be like: a career where
you can never know for sure what's coming
next. I left my job at an art institute
only because I cannot bear the feeling of
knowing exactly what's going to happen in
five or ten years. But now, when I am faced
with uncertainties ahead, I am slightly
frightened. But, this is what I choose,
this is my art career!

Now, both my assistant and I have left
Qiuzhuang. *A Library* is still open in
the village and managed by Mr. Wei. The
dismantlement work of the bridge near
the entrance of the village is about to
start. Soon enough, they will begin to
maintain the road, and *A Library* will have
to be closed. We need to find another place
after the maintenance, and reopen the
library.

I had a dream last night: Mr.Wei was
sitting on the back of my electric
bicycle, we travelled all the way from a
flat asphalt road to a bumpy country road.
The electric bicycle was running out of
power, so I had to ride it very difficultly
at the front.

My mother also told me that she was faced
with fears all the year long. I know I
caused lots of trouble for her, and it is
time I leave her and give her a period of
peace. My father is still wondering if I
can make some money out of the works in
this project. I told him affirmatively that
they are going to make lots of money, they
are very valuable.

All my best,

Li Mu

Essay
George Yúdice

Static Gallery's Architecture of Flows as Extradisciplinary Investigation

Noodle Bar and Paul's KIMCHI Co. are two complex art projects-cum-business enterprises that operate both within and without art institutions: the Noodle Bar was installed at Static Gallery in Liverpool in 2008 and Paul's KIMCHI Co. was commissioned for the exhibition *Confessions of the Imperfect, 1848–1989–Today* from November 2014 to February 2015 at the Van Abbemuseum in Eindhoven.

They are part of what I would call Static's practice of interpolative dissemination,[1] meaning that an apparently 'non-art' supplement is inserted into a (museological or other institutional) process, in turn generating often troubling repercussions in other areas (journalism, media, law, public policy, policing, urban zoning, etc.) and rhizomatically transmuting into yet further projects in other venues. Since its opening in 1995, Static has created many projects that can be characterized in this way; however, I will begin my discussion with the most significant antecedent of the Noodle Bar: the Press Corps.

As former co-director Becky Shaw tells it, Static 'responded to the 2004 Liverpool Biennial by performing a heist and naming ourselves as the official host of the Press Corps.'[2] They did this by issuing a press release that 'commandeered,' so to speak, the administration of the press services for the biennial, with a return address at Static Gallery. Static also sent out invitations to art journalists, offering them lodging and meals, hospitality services, and space and communications facilities for their work. The ability to transform the gallery into a press corps, partitioned off so that the 'public' could not gain access to it, is part of Static's signature practice; it is not an accommodation to an exhibition, but the conceptual and performative practice itself:

> It was important that we designed and built a space that could operate outside of public funding by incorporating studios to rent, a cafe/bar, and a large multi-use space for space hires, video/film shoots, etc. Although the building serves these financial objectives, the design was made on concepts of public/private space as

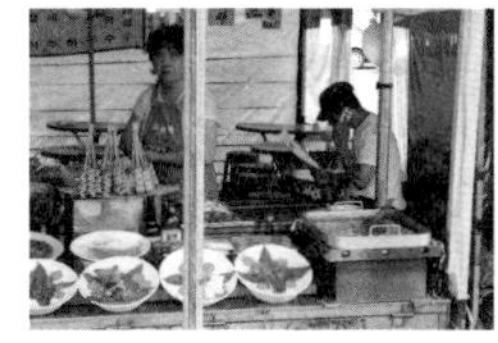
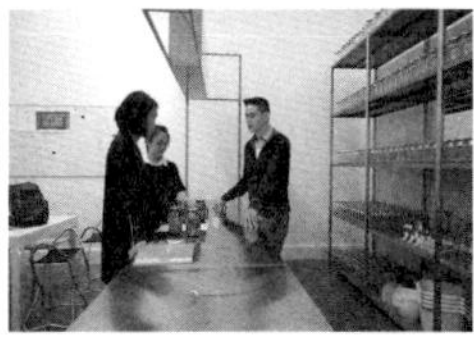
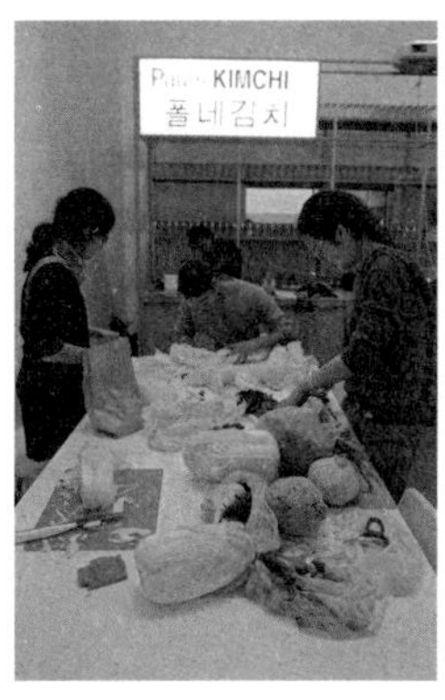

Fig 1 Paul Sullivan, Noodle Bar, 2008, C-print, 25.4 x 15.2 cm
Fig 2–3
Paul's Kimchi Co., workshop Local Seasonal Kimchi Experiment, Van Abbemuseum, Eindhoven, 10 and 11 January 2015

---

1   Static Gallery's practices are planned, designed, and carried out by its director and co-director, currently Paul Sullivan and John Byrne, respectively. Until 2005, Becky Shaw was co-director and actively involved in several projects mentioned in this essay. Others collaborate in these projects but the directors are the mainstays.

2   Becky Shaw, e-mail to Paul Sullivan, Stephen Wright, and John Byrne, 31 July 2013. The Liverpool Biennial has presented festivals in 1999, 2002, 2004, 2006, 2008, 2010, 2012, and 2014. For Static's contribution to the 2004 edition see Liverpool Biennial Independents 2004 Archive, www.newfolder.co.uk/independents2004/independent/citycentral/staticlarge/static.html.

stated above but also ideas of citadel/community and trade. The new building within the building has been made entirely of dry timber/boarding/exposed services in order to allow quick transformations/expansions/deconstructions to take place.[3]

As will become evident further on in this piece, their physical architectural practice extends to interventions into processes, like the biennial process, or to a test of the limits of the processes set in place by other institutions.

One of those processes is the circulation and convertibility of celebrity. The directors were particularly interested in how the press release worked with respect to celebrity: 'What Static found in "Press Corps for Liverpool Biennial 04" was that the press release played a major role in leading and directing subsequent debate around the show.'[4] Static also made available to journalists a range of reviews and writings on the biennial; they sought to measure the impact of these reviews and the VIP treatment in journalists' reports. In his reflection on the publicity value of the press release and the promotional materials' racy images of Yoko Ono's breast and pubis (from her biennial project *My Mummy Was Beautiful*) that were plastered all over town and which in turn multiplied attention from the press and broadcasters, Byrne concludes that in a world of proliferating biennials, the recourse to celebrity provides saliency to a place, even if, as in the case of Ono, as John Lennon's widow, the connection to Liverpool's specificity is specious.

What Static get at in their intervention into the circuitry of celebrity and publicity is what Marxist geographer David Harvey has called the 'art of rent.' In classical economics, the basic market forces of supply and demand determine value. But as Harvey argues, there are other forces that can affect price and the rent that is derived from a commodity. For example, uniqueness, which is a property traditionally

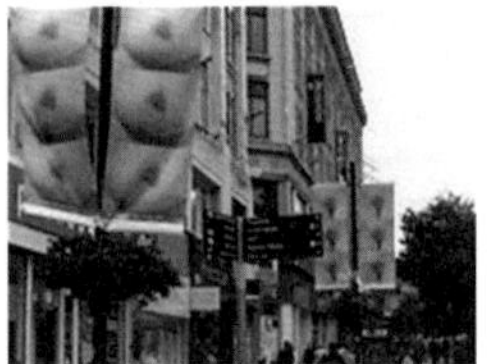

Fig 4　Yoko Ono, *My Mummy Was Beautiful*, 2004, contribution to the 2014 Liverpool Biennial International Exhibition, Liverpool

---

3　Sullivan, e-mail to Wright, Shaw, and Byrne, 11 July 2013.
4　Rene Zechlin, Paul Sullivan, and John Byrne, 'Damien Hirst: One Night Only,' 2014, https://johnmichaelbyrne.files.wordpress.com/2014/02/damien-hirst-one-night-onlly-jb.pdf, p. 8.

attributed to art before the Duchampian and Conceptualist turns. This construal of uniqueness 'forms the basis for monopoly price,' Harvey tells us.[5] He exemplifies how the specifying value of aesthetics is produced with an analogy to the wine industry. Robert Parker, a renowned wine taster whose verdicts can determine the price of wine, 'ranks wines on a scale according to his own distinctive taste.'[6] His opinion can trump the materially based uniqueness claims of territory and 'domaine' taken up and legalized by French wine producers.

Harvey writes that Parker and other wine tasters have invented an aesthetic language 'in which wines are described in terms such as "flavor of peach and plum, with a hint of thyme and gooseberry."'[7] Taste or aesthetics, and the cultural capital that is generated in learning them, are an alternative way to produce uniqueness that enables monopoly rent. But so also are publicity and celebrity, particularly if it is attached to place—even spuriously as Byrne opines regarding Ono's link to Liverpool. Celebrity was also the convertible capital that Static tapped in the exhibition *Damien Hirst: One Night Only* (2005) in which they tested and confirmed that what draws attention (both of the media and the public) is the star quality of an artist, more so than the aesthetic value of her or his art. Static timed the opening of this exhibition of a single £50 print by Hirst one hour after the opening of a Vito Acconci retrospective at Foundation for Art and Creative Technology (FACT), also in Liverpool; when most of the public moved from FACT to Static, they were able to confirm that Hirst's celebrity value was greater than Acconci's.

It could be said that celebrity, like other forms of value-endowment (cultural capital, intellectual property, etc.), flows through conduits of convertibility, which are structured in institutional arrangements (of the media, educational and cultural institutions, policymaking, and

---

5   David Harvey, 'The Art of Rent: Globalization, Monopoly and the Commodification of Culture,' Socialist Register 38 (2002), http://socialistregister.com/index.php/srv/article/view/5778/2674#. VZhmEPlViko, p. 95.

6   Ibid., p. 99.

7   Ibid., p. 100.

enforcement agencies like the WTO and WIPO, etc.).
What I most appreciate about Static's projects is this
chameleon-like ability to simulate forms of value that
travel along these conduits and cause disruptions. Indeed,
Sullivan once told me that he is an architect of flows, or
perhaps it would be more accurate to characterize him as
a *hackitecht* who infiltrates, rearranges, and/or unsettles.

Byrne uses the metaphor of the Trojan Horse in
reference to Static's repeat performance of the Press
Corps for Artist Forum International, Seoul and the
Gwangju Biennale, both in 2006. Given the notoriety—
a convertible value, to be sure—that Static's Press
Corps earned in Liverpool, the Gwangju curatorial team
invited them as artists to set up the Press Corps office
(something that the Liverpool Biennial never did),
and at the same time as members of the press.[8] 'As
a result of the hybrid artist/press position that Static
began to occupy, they were able to embed themselves
as a kind of Trojan Horse within Gwangju Biennale
06—using their unlimited access to provide materials
that questioned both art world, press world, and their
increasingly symbiotic/exploitative relationships.'[9]

I am reminded of one of Allan Kaprow's modes of
artists' work in the shift to what he called unart: 'work
in unrecognizable, i.e., non-art, modes but present the
work in recognizable art contexts, e.g., a pizza parlor in
a gallery.'[10] Indeed, the Press Corps as a form of non-art,
placed within an art institution is in that spirit. But it was
not clear in Kaprow's essay regarding performance (un)art
of the 1960s and 1970s, what kind of heuristic work it did
in an art setting. Kaprow was interested in the relationship
to experience of work that did not necessarily have to take
place within the frame of art, and indeed that should take
place outside it. What we see in Static's projects is a bit
different: the surfing of the financial, publicity, institutional

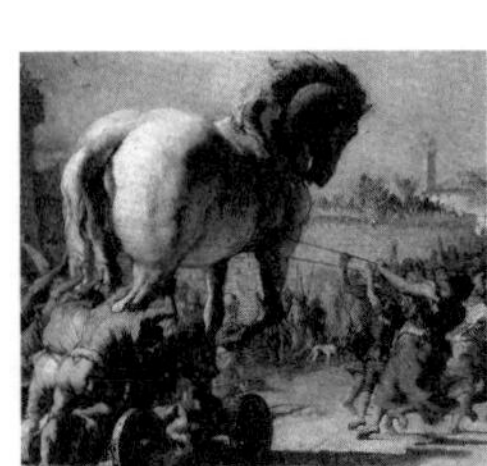

Fig 5 Giovanni Domenico
Tiepolo, *The Procession of
the Trojan Horse in Troy*, 1773
(detail), oil on canvas, 39 x 67
cm, National Gallery, London

---

8   Static even had Paddy Power bookmakers run bets on whether or not the Liverpool Biennial would
invite them as artists to the next edition.
9   Zechlin et al., 'Damien Hirst: One Night Only,' p. 9.
10   Allan Kaprow, *Essays on the Blurring of Art and Life*, ed. Jeff Kelley (Berkeley: University of California
Press, 1993), p. 175.

flows in which a poster or a Press Corps necessarily
is involved is made visible, although not discursively
analyzed as in academic discourse. Nor is Static's work
like the institutional critique one finds in Hans Haacke's
work or in second generation institutional critics like
Andrea Fraser, for whom the frame of art is inescapable.
For Static, the frame is more ambiguous and there is no
finger pointing; that is, the effectiveness of the project
is not based on the smug disclosure of the dubious if not
deplorable underpinnings of the art institution (museum,
gallery, biennial, etc.) while nevertheless living off and
gaining cultural capital in that institution. Rather, it gets
involved in the problems that arise due to its interpolations
into the flows, constituting a learning experience. In
this sense, it is more like another project that Kaprow
reviews: Raivo Puusemp's *Beyond Art — Dissolution of
Rosendale, N.Y.* (1975–1977), which eschewed recognition
as an *art* project and is described later in my text.

While the Press Corps, like the Noodle Bar and Paul's
KIMCHI Co. that I will discuss below, are not exactly
akin to Puusemp's project, they do share the relative
unconcern for a project's measure of artistic value in the
art world. I make this connection despite the fact that
Static seeks to insert these enterprises into art venues
such as biennials and museum exhibitions. In my view that
insertion is not made for the sake of valuation (Harvey's
rent) but rather for heuristic purposes: to examine the
relations that art institutions have with others. That is,
rather than flee the institution Static puts that institution
on the same plane as a range of others, seeking to learn
how it operates in a necessarily relational world. To get
a better sense of why Static's projects are not garden
variety iterations of avant-gardist or conceptualist non-
art-inserted-into-art-settings, it will be helpful to review
Kaprow's account of the move from artlike art to lifelike
art in his *Essays on the Blurring of Art and Life* (1993).

The argument is familiar: several generations of
artists who attempted to get beyond art ultimately only
manage to 'enlarg[e] the range of usable genres.' Aside

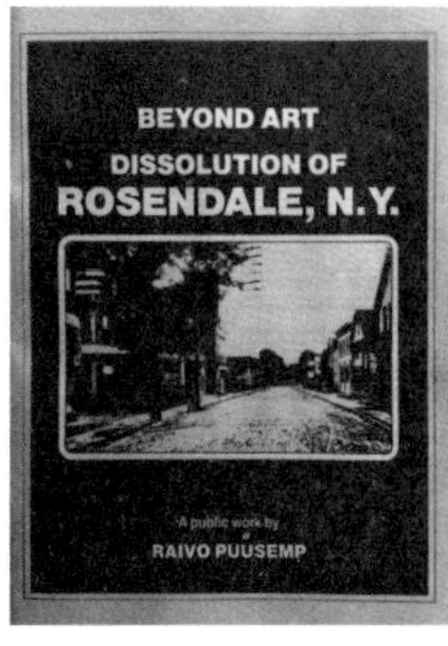

Fig 6   Raivo Puusemp, *Beyond
Art: Dissolution of Rosendale,
N.Y.: A Public Work,* 2013

from conventional artists who 'work within recognizable art modes and present the work in recognizable contexts,' Kaprow focuses on: those who exhibit some selection of non-art, such as factory sounds, and insert them into recognizable art settings; those who take non-art sites like garages or forests as art venues (museum, gallery) with minimal engagement with the surrounding environment; and those who proto-conceptually transform an everyday event—such as people crossing the street—into contemporary art. For Kaprow, to get beyond the performative force of the frame of art entails relinquishing that system of value: 'work[ing] in non-art modes and non-art contexts but ceas[ing] to call the work art, retaining instead the private consciousness that sometimes it may be art, too.'[11]

Kaprow takes Puusemp's *Dissolution of Rosendale, N.Y.* as exemplary of this last mode of work. Puusemp managed to sidestep the issue of enlargement of the frame of art by merging all the parts of the project into a 'whole situation,' in which not only is that frame unmentioned but also in which a multiplicity of frames (political, economic, environmental, urban, etc.) come together, as in 'real life.' Indeed, Kaprow reviews Puusemp's project in an essay entitled 'The Real Experiment' (1983). In this piece, experiment refers not only to planned projects but also to experience, which does not happen in only one dimension or frame. Kaprow distinguishes four aspects of the framing, which operate in an 'unusual' manner if our reference is the art world: the genre or issue at hand, the setting, the participants, and the purpose. This displacement (or rather re-emplacement) enables the project to fully merge into the surroundings, in such a way that it 'doesn't really exist by itself.'[12]

In the mid-1970's, Puusemp, a conceptual artist living in Rosendale Village, ran for mayor as an unstated 'artwork in the form of a political problem.'[13] Looking at the

---

11　Ibid.
12　Ibid., p. 211.
13　Ibid., p. 209.

situation in terms of Kaprow's framing aspects: the issue
at hand was the many problems of the village, including
bankruptcy, environmental blight, and potential dissolution
into the larger township of the same name; the setting
was the geopolitical circumstances of Rosendale and the
county; the public-participants were the townspeople,
who feared losing their community; and the purpose
of the project was therapeutic—to solve the problems.
Puusemp won the election and put to work his skills as
a 'Conceptual artist [with a] theory of social behavior
in mind, [which] he applied … in day-to-day human
terms.'[14] He ameliorated many of the problems and led
the townspeople in a process which culminated in the
dissolution of the village and its incorporation into the
township, thus solving other fiscal and taxation issues.
At that point he resigned as mayor and moved away, took
on a different career and never practiced art again.

Kaprow emphasizes what we might consider the
metaphysical holism of lifelike art practice, which restores
'the possibility of the practice of art as a practice of
enlightenment.' In this sense, 'lifelike art can be, for
therapy and meditation, a bridge into daily affairs.'[15] Thus
he concludes the essay in which Puusemp's project
is exemplary. But one can see it in other ways. My own
proclivity is to see it as a form of research that has a set of
methods for making visible the architecture of flows, to use
Sullivan's metaphor, or hitherto unperceivable structures,
to cite Puusemp himself in his reflection on his tenure
as mayor or Rosendale. 'Deliberate changes in political
structure don't just happen,' he argued. 'They are planned
and occur because they seem inevitable. To make changes
seem inevitable requires a clear structure and a systematic
process.' This is a point that philosopher and art theorist
Stephen Wright stresses in an essay on Puusemp:
Puusemp went from observing physical relationships to
observing and becoming engaged in social relationships,

---

14 Ibid., p. 210.
15 Ibid., p. 218.

the function of the artist in both cases being, as he put it at the time, to define 'structure where one was not evident before.'[16] Wright's interest is in the predictability of the ensuing steps once one makes evident a given process—he calls this the 'predictable innovation principle'—and in Puusemp's disenchantment with the productivity of repeating what has already been discovered. We have here a real life version of Melville's character Bartleby, whose famous declaration 'I would prefer not to' has fascinated literary critics and philosophers, and which for Deleuze, as for Wright, endows the unartist and unart with ambiguous imperceptibility—it becomes an (un)art without qualities.[17] Indeed, for Deleuze, it is precisely the relinquishment of qualities and particularities (which for him may generate violence and idiocy) that enables a new community of the heterogeneous, a 'patchwork of nations.'[18]

I would not go so far as to make these claims about Static's projects—at least not yet—although I take the notion of producing art without qualities as consistent with Static's practice of exploring the flows and contradictions of the multiple frames that they bring together. It is in this sense that I would like to mine another vein in Kaprow's discussion of non-art or lifelike art: it can be thought of as inquiry, research, thus 'reliev[ing] the artist of inspirational metaphors, such as creativity, that are tacitly associated with making art.' It is worth quoting this insight at length:

> Basic research is inquiry into whole situations—for example, why humans fight—even if, like art, they are elusive and constantly changing. What is basic research at one moment becomes detail work or

---

16 See Stephen Wright, 'An Art Without Qualities: Raivo Puusemp's "Beyond Art: Dissolution of Rosendale. N.Y.,"' northeastwestsouth.net, 11 September 2013, http://northeastwestsouth.net/art-without-qualities-raivo-puusemps-beyond-art-dissolution-rosendale-ny, p. 4.

17 In Herman Melville's short story 'Bartleby, the Scrivener: A Story of Wall Street' (1853), the eponymous clerk deflects his employer's will not exactly by refusing but by affirmatively asserting—'I prefer'—a negation—'not to.' What Bartleby enacts is a radical relinquishment of any action that may save him, although there is definitely a will or a willfulness in his renunciation. I sense something similar in Static's negotiations with the city administration, as we see, detailed further on in this essay. Gilles Deleuze, 'Bartleby; or, the Formula,' in *Essays Critical and Clinical*, trans. Daniel W. Smith and Michael A. Greco (Minneapolis: University of Minnesota Press, 1997), p. 74 and Wright, 'An Art Without Qualities,' p. 4.

18 Deleuze, 'Bartleby,' p. 85 and p. 89.

something trivial at another; and seeking what is worth researching at a particular moment is where the guesswork comes in. My hunch about art is that a field that has changed in appearance as fast as it has must also have changed in meaning and function, perhaps to the extent that its role is qualitative (offering a way of perceiving things) rather than quantitative (producing physical objects or specific actions).[19]

Indeed, one of the events organized by Static in a decommissioned airport in Cork, Ireland in 2011— *Terminal Convention*—was characterized by its curator, Peter Gorschlüter, deputy director of the MMK Museum für Moderne Kunst, Frankfurt am Main, as, among other things, a kind of investigation: 'Artists have the capacity to [organize materials that] condense, anatomize, and represent symbolically complex social and historical processes.'[20] It is in this sense—of practice-based research—that in the rest of this essay I would like to comment on Static's Noodle Bar and Paul's KIMCHI Co.

But first a few words about the project's coming into being. As explained earlier, on the basis of the infiltration of the Liverpool Biennial by Static's Press Corps, the curators of the Gwangju Biennale invited Static as artists and as a press service reprise of the project—*mutatis mutandis*— for the 2006 edition of the biennial. As explained on Paul's KIMCHI Co. website, it was on this visit that 'Paul Sullivan—founder of Paul's KIMCHI Co.—fell in love with Korean cuisine, in particular KIMCHI.' The website gives a pithy account of the establishment of the Noodle Bar in Liverpool and its expansion to Eindhoven as a franchise:

After introducing Korean cuisine and Kimchi to Merseyside via a small pop-up Noodle Bar at Static Gallery, Liverpool between 2008/09, Sullivan dreamed of setting up a small Kimchi making facility

---

19 Kaprow, *Essays on the Blurring of Art and Life*, p. 177.
20 From author's notes on the introductory presentations at *Terminal Convention*, Cork City, 17 March 2011.

that would be dedicated to perfecting traditional Korean Kimchi recipes and introducing them to as many people as possible outside of Korea.

This dream has now come true and Paul's Kimchi Co. was established in Liverpool/UK in October 2014 and its first franchise will open at the world famous Van Abbemuseum, Eindhoven, Holland from the 22 November 2014–22 February 2015.[21]

Given that the website is promotional—it explains what kimchi is, gives its history, the nutritional value of its ingredients, invites the public to a Korean gastronomic feast, provides tips on visiting Korea, accompanied by full colour photos of various dishes worthy of a cuisine magazine—it says nothing about the Noodle Bar or Paul's KIMCHI Co. being art projects. Nor does it go into the complications of creating a restaurant and a production company in art institution settings, or contracting foreign workers in the UK. However, a Static Gallery webpage announces a film that provides the details of the negotiations, the contracts, and creation of the Noodle Bar as an art project inspired by Manet's *A Bar at the Folies-Bergère* (1882) 'to examine the strategy of using an artwork as a device to mirror or reflect the human condition,' meaning by this, as is explained subsequently on the webpage, that it 'explores enticement, migration, immigration, adventure, planning, exploitation, betrayal, voyeurism, food, trade and globalisation.'[22]

The practice-based research character of the project comes into relief in the film, *Noodle Bar (Edit 1)*, which was shown at the Van Abbemuseum installation in 2014–2015. The text reproduced in the film, as well as Static's directors' comments on this and other projects, is replete with such verbs as explore, examine, interrogate, test, etc. Static's negotiations with Ssamzie Corporation, an art gallery and studio complex in Seoul, to set up a

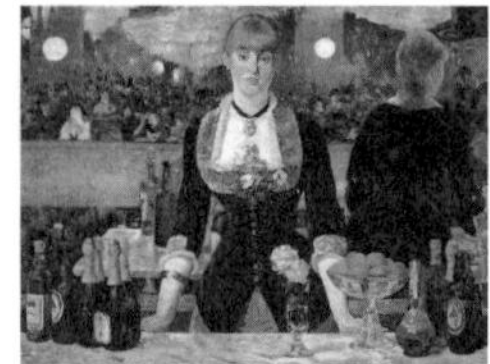

Fig 7   Edouard Manet, *A Bar at the Folies-Bergère*, 1882, oil on canvas, 96 x 130 cm, Courtauld Collection, London

---

21   'About Paul's KIMCHI Co.,' Paul's KIMCHI Co., www.paulskimchico.com/?lang=en.
22   'Noodle Bar,' Static, www.statictrading.com/?p=574.

partnership for the Noodle Bar, was also the occasion to 'explor[e] Migration, Immigration and Planning Control, but the wider idea was to also set up trade relationships and opportunities between the two organisations and their two cities' (see 00:20:13–00:20:23 in the film). What characterizes all of Static's projects are the problems in carrying out projects that have multiple framings: artworks that are illegal businesses that contract foreign labour, and so on. It is as if the projects were crafted in such a way as to mine the faults between the multiple framings.[23] Indeed, Byrne writes that Noodle Bar,

> offers a means to test the terms and conditions of how it simply does not fit, or function and why? Is it an artwork? A business? A hybrid? A montage? A bricollage? Or simply a meaningless replay of bloodless and endless postmodern difference? Who owns it, who made it, how does one activate it—why does it sit so uncomfortably in a Museum like a relic of the future awaiting the energy of re-activation? How could one own it? Account for it, script it, give sense to its borders, commodify it, re-purpose it, condone it or simply make it complicit with the cultural remnants that already litter the disillusioned Western psyche of art and culture?[24]

The various framings often get knotted, as when Static cannot get work permits for the Korean operators of the Noodle Bar, who leave within three weeks, and who had gotten visas instead as artists to work on a restaurant/art project, for which city council planning permits had not been gotten, which in turn led to an eviction notice, which if not heeded would jeopardize arts funding from that very same city council. Everything seems to have been done to run into further problems. If we compare this project with Puusemp's *Dissolution of Rosendale, N.Y.*, we understand

---

23 In a manner similar to Melville, Static seems to dwell on and delve into the fault, regardless of concerns with conventional productivity.
24 Sullivan and Byrne, Noodle Bar/Paul's Kimchi Co. Proposal for Strategy Meeting, e-mail from Sullivan to author, Van Abbemuseum, Eindhoven, 26 February 2015.

that the purpose was not to solve the problems, but to administer the business in such a way as to ensure the generation of contradictions.

Although the reprise of the project at the Van Abbemuseum, now as a slicker Paul's KIMCHI Co., also ran into problems (the franchise did not materialize and two students ran only two workshops), the kimchi sold well. However, the labour relations were not worked out, something that would go without saying in a formal business enterprise:

> Having said that, the economies of working with the students again raised some interesting relationships between art and labour, as the kimchi that the students produced for the opening on the 22 Nov was speculative in that it was sold at the Van Abbemuseum shop for a 60/40% deal (60% to Paul's KIMCHI Co.), the materials were funded by the Van Abbemuseum as part of the production budget but all other workshops were to be funded by sales of KIMCHI … but there was ambiguity about where any profits went, direct to Paul's KIMCHI Co. to be redistributed to the students or to be paid direct to the students.[25]

Unlike the tangle of problems that arose in the case of Noodle Bar in Liverpool in 2008/2009, Paul's KIMCHI Co. did not generate problems for the Van Abbemuseum. Had the museum accepted Static's proposal to create a franchise, Static would have insisted on a three-month lease within one of the galleries, something that might have posed legal problems similar to those experienced in Liverpool. It might be said that the museum declined to play along in enabling some of the problems that characterized the original Noodle Bar, but by doing so they also unleashed some of the heuristic value of the project. This is what Sullivan means by the following comment:

---

25 Paul Sullivan, e-mail to author, 7 June 2015.

> What the project started to unravel was some of
> the complex relationships that develop through the
> commissioning and design of exhibitions and the
> difficulties that arise when a project like Paul's KIMCHI
> Co. is inserted into an orthodox museum structure.'[26]

As I mentioned at the beginning of this essay, Static's
projects have a tendency to transmute into other projects
in other venues. Static proposed to the Van Abbemuseum
curators that the institution invest in a percentage of the
Paul's KIMCHI Co. brand, but they recommended instead
that it transmute more directly into a research project:

> What we find, however, interesting in your practice
> has not so much to do with this preservation of an
> 'object,' but much more in the type of practice-based
> research, which offers an intriguing perspective on the
> contemporary moment in how it organises its economy,
> architecture/city and the position of art within this.
> The project addresses this 'minefield' in a very
> interesting manner … .
>   Instead of investing in Kimchi&Co, we would
> like to explore the possibility to invite you to work
> as researcher on both Noodle Bar and Kimchi&Co,
> allowing also some budget to develop the project
> further, but with an objective that you would focus
> on developing the documentation. We would need
> to work out of the conditions for this research, but
> the end result should be a form of presenting the
> research surrounding Noodle Bar and Kimchi&Co.[27]

What the curators of the Van Abbemuseum call practice-
based art research involves the heuristic or discovery
dimension of art practice. The heuristic, as I understand
it, is not something that puts itself at the service of a
practice; it ensues, rather, from the 'capacity to [organize

---

26 Ibid.
27 Steven ten Thije, e-mail to Paul Sullivan, 14 May 2015.

materials that] condense, anatomize, and represent symbolically complex social and historical processes,' as voiced by Gorschlüter in the context of *Terminal Convention*. It is a dimension inherent in art practice, just as the epistemic, the aesthetic, or the ethical are also dimensions of a practice. None of these dimensions can be separated out for they are inherent in the structure of the practice. Of course, as we have seen in the case of Static, they can be made to contradict or conflict with each other. Something is learned in the process.

For the purposes of Static's projects, I am less interested in the academic institutionalization of practice-based art research. In an influential essay, art theorist Henk Borgdorff defines it as follows:

> Art practice qualifies as research if its purpose is to expand our knowledge and understanding by conducting an original investigation in and through art objects and creative processes. Art research begins by addressing questions that are pertinent in the research context and in the art world. Researchers employ experimental and hermeneutic methods that reveal and articulate the tacit knowledge that is situated and embodied in specific artworks and artistic processes. Research processes and outcomes are documented and disseminated in an appropriate manner to the research community and the wider public.[28]

I am more interested in the way in which philosopher, anthropologist, and cultural theorist Néstor García Canclini approaches it in his book written in 2010 and translated in 2014 as *Art Beyond Itself: Anthropology for a Society without a Story Line*, where he argues for an expanded heuristic in contemporary art because, he tells us, art is no longer only in museums and galleries but has migrated to other areas (media, fashion, social action, investment

---

28 Henk Borgdorff, *The Debate on Research in the Arts: Sensuous Knowledge 2* (Bergen: Bergen National Academy of the Arts, 2006), www.pol.gu.se/digitalAssets/1322/1322713_the_debate_on_research_in_the_arts.pdf, p. 18.

funds, urban revitalization, new technologies, security, recovery programs for at-risk youth, etc.). Globalization is accompanied by this relative exit from the autonomous fields posited by social theorist Pierre Bourdieu, and art can be examined for the semiotic traces of that transit, the different contexts in which it operates, its reception by viewers/participants.[29] 'By upsetting the usual relations between public and private, between cultural experimentation and economic performance, the slow economy of artistic production fulfills the public function of encouraging us to rethink what the impetuous economy of the symbolic industries imposes as public, fleeting, and forgetful.'[30] Much can be learned by 'being near the works and nimble in following their trajectories.'[31] The literal translation of the original Spanish title is 'Society without a Story Line: The Anthropology and the Aesthetics of Imminence'—its subtitle highlighting the imminence or unfinished character of social life. In heuristic terms, it could be said that what García Canclini gets at is a far-reaching exploration of what scientist and philosopher Charles Sanders Peirce called abduction, 'the process of forming an explanatory hypothesis … the only logical operation that introduces a new idea.'[32]

Interruption via artistic means has its correlate for García Canclini in broader cultural and social movements such as indigenous, feminist, environmental, and other movements, which have both hegemonic and anti-hegemonic aspects. But he advocates going beyond this poetics and the

---

29 Following Max Weber, Pierre Bourdieu perceives modernity as characterized by the emergence of fields—arts, education, politics, law, etc.—that are relatively autonomous of a determining (Marxist) infrastructure defined in economic and class terms. For Bourdieu, there are internal rules to these fields (e.g., the rules of valuing art), which have to be learned in order to compete therein, under conditions of unequal distribution of artistic, cultural, educational, political economic, or other capital (capital being precisely the result of successfully deploying the rules). The processes of globalization and other factors have led theorists to focus on the increasing muddling of boundaries among fields such that the rules become inoperative. Indeed, in the case of art, it is this inoperativeness which is increasingly valued, as is evident in Static's practice. In other words, does Bartleby's relinquishment become a means to (aesthetic) productivity? For an explanation of the theory of fields, see Pierre Bourdieu, *The Field of Cultural Production* (Cambridge, UK: Polity, 1993).

30 Néstor García Canclini, *Imagined Globalization*, trans. George Yúdice (Durham, NC: Duke University Press, 2014), p. 179.

31 Néstor García Canclini, *Art Beyond Itself: Anthropology for a Society without a Story Line*, trans. David Frye (Durham, NC: Duke University Press, 2014), p. 178.

32 Charles Sanders Peirce, 'Harvard Lectures on Pragmatism: Lecture VI,' 1903, in *Commens: Digital Companion to C.S. Peirce*, www.helsinki.fi/science/commens/terms/abduction.html.

possibilities of interruption to a politics of intermediation. This politics of intermediation reproduces neither the hegemonic control by governments, large business enterprises, or large NGOs, nor the Deleuzian option for a nomadism that eludes control. Not to speak of the naiveté of Internet enthusiasts who believe that the distributed networks of the web have eliminated intermediaries simply because people get to upload their own content, or that the conceptual harnessing of these networks ushers in the rather vague and wistful 'communism to-come' of political philosopher Antonio Negri.[33]

A strategy for remaining relevant in the era of globalization means developing the capacity to mediate a range of concerns, perhaps something along the lines of Puusemp's mayoralty in Rosendale, NY, but also Static's interventions in/creation of the tangle of frameworks that characterize the various realities in which their projects are inserted. At times, Static has claimed that there is no outside the institution of art, the celebrity circuit or the media hype. But when one examines their projects one sees that their experiments 'don't exhaust themselves inside … , but rather, extend elsewhere,' as cultural theorist Brian Holmes writes in 'Extradisciplinary Investigations: Towards a Critique of New Institutions.'[34] Like García Canclini, Holmes understands that such projects 'can no longer be unambiguously defined as art,' precisely because they move across disciplines—as in Static's case: immigration, planning, zoning, policing, etc.—and involve many different kinds of actors, not only artists.

Holmes emphasizes the transformative, political aspect of this transversality: 'the real critical reserve of marginal or counter-cultural positions—social movements, political associations, squats, autonomous universities—which can't be reduced to an all-embracing institution.' But this is only one particular kind of transversality, one which seeks political effectiveness. There are other possibilities, from

---

33 Antonio Negri, *Time for Revolution*, trans. Matteo Mandarini (New York: Continuum, 2003), p. 144.
34 Brian Holmes, 'Extradisciplinary Investigations: Towards a New Critique of Institutions,' *Transversal* (January 2007), http://eipcp.net/transversal/0106/holmes/en, p. 4.

collaboration with diverse communities, particularly those at a remove from hegemonic Western cosmology, thus enabling a multiply orchestrated intermediation of different knowledges, to the kinds of examinations or investigations in which Static is involved. In this regard, I think it is useful to reexamine Sullivan's disciplinary formation as an architect-turned-designer and intermediary of flows. He brings a spatial sensitivity to the intermediation that is not that common in other contemporary art practices. Indeed, Sullivan began his practice as an architect of flows because of his disenchantment upon graduating from architecture school, at which point he founded Static:

> For me there's something called an architecture profession which didn't do much architecture and there was something called architecture, which was possible but not under the rules of the profession, of planning controls, of building controls, of insurance companies, of quangos, of community groups, of politicians and more. With this in mind I looked at the possibilities for a means of architectural production that bypassed these authorities/agencies as I saw them as barriers.[35]

This entails reimagining infrastructures outside of the designed gallery space in locations such as redundant and/or refurbished industrial or commercial/civic spaces or even decommissioned airports. He has pointed out that as the proliferation of artists working in social non-object based practice continues, architects and new gallery commissioners are left with somewhat of a design problem.[36] Of course, the issue is compounded when the practices are collaborative and involve actors positioned in different disciplines and social spaces. Architectural—or hackitectural—design is necessarily one of flows, and is one way of understanding an (un)art without qualities. In Press Corps, the Noodle Bar, and Paul's KIMCHI Co.,

---

35 Paul Sullivan, e-mail to Stephen Wright, 7 November 2013.
36 Paul Sullivan, e-mail to author, 5 June 2014.

one can witness precisely this kind of design, not only in the physical space, but more importantly in the relations among the different spheres or frames in which the projects necessarily take place: institutions, municipal regulatory bodies, labour regulations, contract law, etc.
I use the term hackitectural because Static mediates, or better yet, torques those frames, yielding different values and insights from what may otherwise go unnoticed, such as a food producing venue in a museum or gallery that is not necessarily recognized as art. Whether we call it art or not, the trick is to recognize the complex design at work.

The author would like to thank Ana Longoni for thinking through with me art as practice-based research.

Collective Difficulty, Feminist Interventions

Tamms Year Ten and Socially Engaged Art Praxis

Christina Aushana

The Tamms Correctional Center—a supermax prison facility dedicated to solitary confinement—has been closed since 2013, but the aftershocks of its existence continue to resonate in a network of embodied dimensions: in the new goals of the mothers of the prisoners, in the stories from prisoners that reached beyond its walls, and in the organizing work of Laurie Jo Reynolds.

Over the past seven years, Laurie Jo has helped organize the all-volunteer coalition of prisoners, poets, artists, men formerly incarcerated in the Tamms Correctional Center, advocates, and—perhaps most central to the project—the women who have shared in the struggle alongside her. This coalition, called Tamms Year Ten (TY10), launched multiple campaigns calling for the reform and later the closure of Tamms supermax, and, as the story goes, they were successful. However, metrics of success seem ill-equipped and the closing of Tamms itself is not the 'end of the story.'

It might be tempting to assume Laurie Jo's leadership position in this network of volunteers and imprisoned men; indeed, her Southern drawl and easy confidence seem to echo the embodied and rhetorical styles of proud Southern matriarchs who have helmed kith and kin. To engage in this poetic metaphor, however, is to mischaracterize the work of TY10. At the intersection of these lives imbricated in the infrastructures and emotional landscapes of incarceration is not one master narrative, but a confluence of many stories. It is, importantly, not a story about Laurie Jo, either. These stories illustrate the messy intersection of care and difficult work enacted among women on the 'outside' of prisons, men in prison, and in the aesthetic responses to the structural forces at play. It is a processual kind of work, and a feminist labour of love, literally. The vignettes that follow bear this affective weight.

Wednesday, 8:50 pm: Janice 'Cookie' Burnom—a long-time anti-Tamms activist— searches for a single text message while sitting across from me on an indoor balcony above patrons conversing over salt-rimmed margarita glasses, seemingly oblivious to the tiny circle of women huddled in a corner of this Mexican restaurant. Having been invited to this fundraiser for Illinois Governor Pat Quinn, alongside Cookie, Laurie Jo and the three other women from TY10, we spend little time regarding the present and its figures moving about in black suits. Instead, Cookie's flip-style mobile phone orients us toward the past. Laurie Jo mentions that she is putting together a visual timeline for an upcoming gallery showing of TY10; she is asking different volunteers about the most memorable moments from the past few years campaigning for the closure of the Tamms Correctional Center. In response, Cookie has found her desired text message and regards our small gathering: 'How could I ever forget? I still remember getting your text message that night, Laurie Jo, saying that the governor agreed to close Tamms. Lord, I just started crying!'

In the convergence of both past and present, Cookie's eyes fill with tears. We are silent, and the chatter of politicians vying for supremacy in their conversations floats above us, disconnected and disinterested. These tears are complicated, for Tamms's closure did not, *could* not, liberate her brother—a story for another time, in another mode. Laurie Jo reaches out to hold Cookie's hand, and I work to hold my tears behind the levy that is the lip of my lower eyelids. This affective difficulty is interrupted when Governor Quinn, having made his initial rounds to greet supporters, stops by our circle. Laurie Jo, without skipping a beat, engages in what could only be described as an embodied shift: she springs up, shakes the governor's hand, and gestures for Cookie and the others to speak with him. Over the clatter of clicking heels and clinking glasses, the governor and Laurie Jo parlay over her upcoming trip oversees for an artist residency in the Netherlands; he insists she must stay and she assures him she will return in time to continue her support of his campaign. Laurie Jo's easy demeanour seems rare in the realm of state politics writ large. In this restaurant filled with seasoned politicians, it is clear that her straightforward sincere approach to working with and *beside* those who write legislation and operate inside of carceral systems disrupts the traditional tactics of both artists and activists.

There is no denying Laurie Jo's aesthetic and conceptual rigor, found both in the collaborative project *Photo Requests From Solitary* (2010) and in her past installations and films. I meditate on the ways in which she navigates the supposed

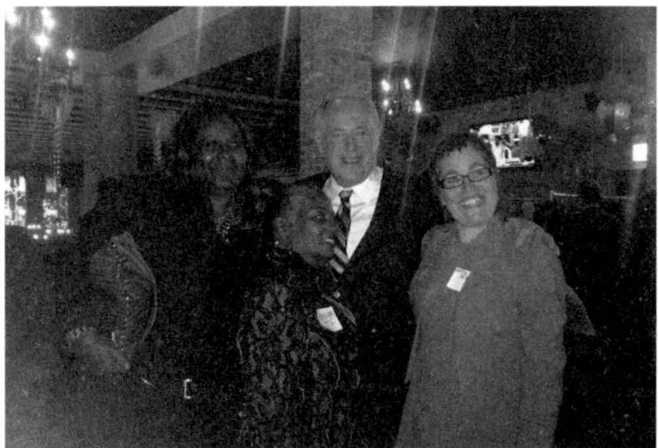

Fig 1   Celebration of
Governor Quinn's birthday

boundaries between her activist commitments and her legibility as an artist. Legibility across different realms provides both affordances and constraints. After our first full day attending two meetings and a memorial service for a an ex-prisoner, Laurie Jo, Melinda, and I found a moment of sedentary respite from the hectic back-and-forth to dwell on the material stakes operating at this intersection between art, activism, and the politics of free labour.

Monday, 5:45 pm: Sitting in one of Chicago's many pub-style restaurants, Laurie Jo speaks frankly about the difficulties of navigating the liminal zones of artistic production and an activist mode; indeed, it is the first time since meeting her that she acknowledges her work within the parlance of art-making. Many of her scheduled weekly and monthly commitments involve hours of unpaid preparation: multiple PowerPoint presentations, phone calls to coordinate with the TY10 women, and endlessly scrolling spreadsheets. With the utmost sincerity, allow me to reiterate: Laurie Jo's spreadsheets are legendary. Not only are they rigorously maintained, they are aesthetic works of art— meticulously colour-coded boxes and little pixels in perfect alignment. They are also a principle figure in the matrix of organizational labour

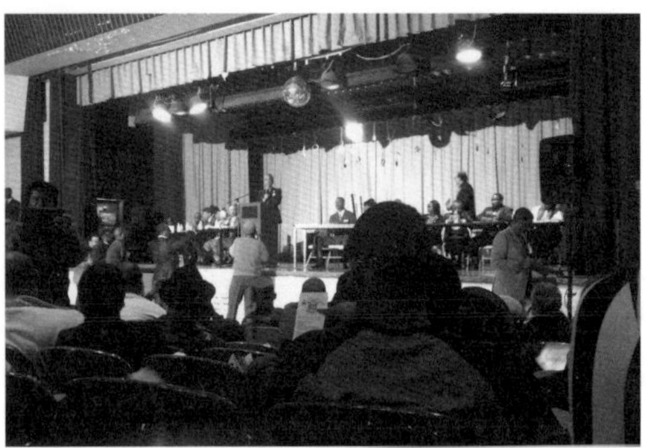

Fig 2   Chicago Town Hall Meeting to address gun violence
Reverend Al Sharpton hosted a town hall meeting at Hyde Park
Academy, sponsored by the National Action Network, aimed at
discussing and ending gun violence in Chicago. Speakers lined
up and spoke for more than two hours. Chicago, Illinois.
December 19, 2013.

that illustrates how navigating the limitations
of time, both inside and beyond the mechanics
of the spreadsheet, is a collective practice
performed by both Laurie Jo and TY10 volunteers.

Thursday, 7:40 pm: We are sitting in a town
hall meeting hosted by Al Sharpton and the
National Action Network in Chicago's Hyde Park.
Reginald 'Akkeem' Berry, Sr., a former Tamms
inmate, stands at the front of a crowded high
school auditorium. He speaks quickly into a
microphone about his work with gang-affiliated
youth in the local community, a concerted effort
to guide a future generation of Chicagoans while
improving public spaces through brick-and-
mortar improvement projects. His message is
clear: youth should lay down guns in favour of
laying down bricks—an intimate engagement
with soil over the imagined 'cold' distance
between fired bullets. He speaks quickly, and
the cant of his speech is lyrical yet tinged
with a grave sincerity: a call to material action
amidst other impassioned voices and pleas
for change in 'our community.' Sharpton nods
impassively, but after an hour of questions and
comments from community members, he seems
withdrawn. Moments afterward, we are standing
together near the high school's entrance, and
Akkeem regales us with tales of sentimentality

and difficulty. His eyes smile as he regards
Laurie Jo; here is one of the few women who
fought tooth and nail for the closure of TY10,
Akkeem left many close friends behind when
he was released from prison and he was very
invested in the struggle to help get them out.
I find myself romanticizing this narrative, but
must ground this tendency in a solemn fact:
Akkeem stands before me, a suit made of fine
taupe wool and gold finery accenting his tall
frame, while other men fill a row of cell blocks
many miles away—burnished cuffs of steel
their state-sanctioned adornments. Though
Akkeem is the first Tamms survivor I was able to
meet, the *Photo Requests From Solitary* project
continues to operate as a material connection
to these other men, voices, and desires.

Reflecting on traditions of critical feminist
scholarship, I dwell on difficulty in the context of
TY10 as a significant component in performing
an intersectional analysis. Like the emotional
and physical labour women from TY10 engage
in, 'doing' intersectional work is difficult work
as well: time consuming, challenging, and,
sometimes, unpopular in particular academic
disciplines. It is often a messy attempt to reach
out and hold onto cross-cutting social and
cultural forces long enough to make sense of
the structures of domination and exclusion that
complicate lives—both inside of prison and
those on the supposed periphery. Difficulty is
always necessarily embodied, and this is how
I understand it in relation to the structures at
play that shape interactions between Laurie Jo,
TY10 volunteers, and prison officials, to name
but a few relational intersections. Difficulty isn't
a disembodied metaphor: it is blood, sweat, and
tears. Difficulty, as a through line in this text,
is also embodied in the many different roles
Laurie Jo must navigate in relation to TY10.

Sociocultural and political markers do not
necessarily restrict Laurie Jo to any category
or primary method of engagement. Rather,
the promiscuous movement between and
across activities and methods suggests
something more profound about her activist
ethos and the work of TY10: the flexibility of
social practice is necessarily unbounded,

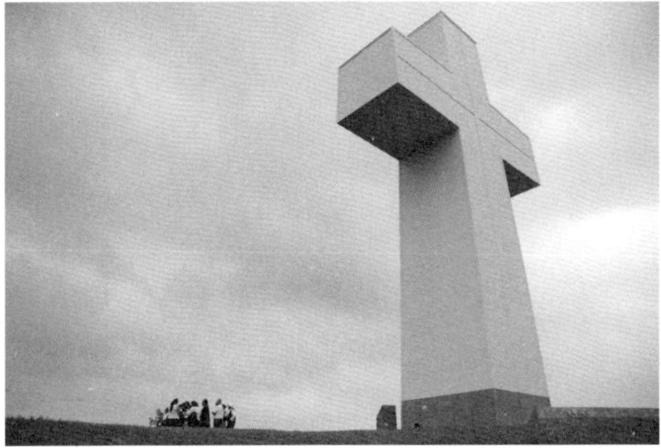

Fig 3 Prayer Vigil at Bald Knob Cross
'Photo Requests from Solitary' was one of many projects launched
by Tamms Year Ten to build up publicity for the campaign. The
men in Tamms were invited to request a photograph of anything in
the world, real or imagined. The resulting requests were touching
and often surprising. They included: the sacred mosque in Mecca,
comic book heroes locked in epic battle, Egyptian artifacts, Tamms
Year Ten volunteers, and a brown and white horse rearing in
weather cold enough to see its breath. Willie Sterling III asked for a
photograph of a vigil at Bald Knob Cross on top of a hill in southern
Illinois to pray for his deliverance from Tamms and to be granted
parole. Tamms Year Ten caravanned down to the cross, held a
litany of songs and prayers, and celebrated with a dinner. The next
day, they drove family members to visit loved ones at the prison.
Sterling was transferred from Tamms, and on 27 July 2012 he was
given parole after thirty-six years in prison.

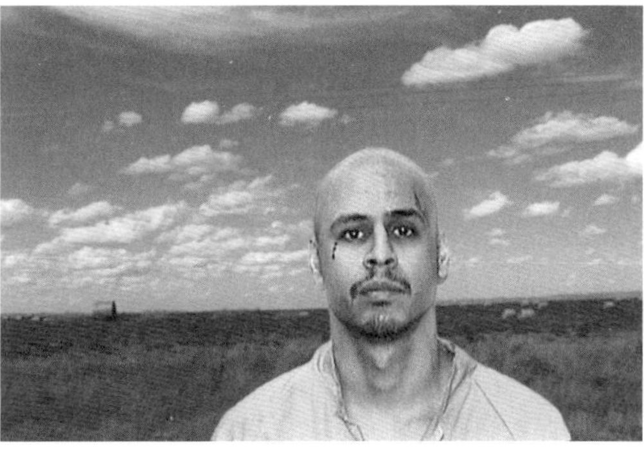

Fig 4 Myself with blue sky background
Several men asked for photos of themselves, taken from their
online Department of Corrections photos, to give to their families.
Robert wanted his picture to have an alternate background. He
wrote, 'If you can place my picture on another background, nothing
too much please. Something simple like a blue sky with clouds or
a sunset in the distance would be fine.' Robert also said, 'I want
to extend my love to you, for you, as you have already done for me.
Because genuine, authentic true love is when you do for others
just because you can, and you hold no preconceived notion that
you will be getting anything in return.'

and thus open to the interstitial spaces,
modes of language, and strategies that
make this fluidity and mobility possible.

Discourses of 'doing time' in a correctional
facility are thickly and intimately constitutive
of this configuration of women, carceral
bureaucracy, and the politics of 'bare life'
in the system of imprisonment.[1] Notions of
giving time, taking time away from prisoners,
navigating the institutional time of prison
schedules, finding time to commute to visit a
correctional facility, and the difficulty of making
time when seemingly in short supply were
expressed in conversations with mothers of
the incarcerated and in speaking with Laurie
Jo. These reorientations of time experienced
by the volunteers of TY10 have been shaped by
the incongruence between the isolating spatial
practices of prisons and the difficult spaces
that these women must make for themselves
across shifting sites: borrowed conference
rooms where they meet with prison officials to
plea on behalf on their loved ones, temporary
gallery spaces that serve as a home base for
their campaign materials, and in the in-between
spaces of hallways and corners of restaurants.

TY10 members remain closely connected,
in the most poetic and embodied way, to the
personal times that men negotiate in prison.
Institutional time may structure bodies according
to a political economy of schedules, but shared
temporalities between TY10 volunteers and
incarcerated men—activists as well within this
paradigm—illustrate the nuances of living with
and in spite of incarceration.

1 See Giorgio Agamben, *Homo Sacer: Sovereign Power and Bare
Life*, trans. Daniel Heller-Roazen (Stanford, CA: Stanford University
Press, 1998).

Time Spent

Melinda Guillen

Five days may not seem like a long enough time to develop a firm grasp of any particular durational project. But that is not the goal of this text. Nor is it the aim of the experimental writing and research project that art historian Grant Kester and curator Lucía Sanromán presented me with.

For it I flew to Chicago, with my co-researcher Christina Aushana, to research artist Laurie Jo Reynolds and the Tamms Year Ten campaign (TY10). I should start with my own critical stakes. Much of my interest in socially engaged practice has been the critical methodologies with which we assess these practices and the positions we take in their analyses. Rather than attempt to invent a new model of criticism, I've often returned to the tenets of feminist art criticism from the 1970s. The ideas of figures such as Arlene Raven and Lucy Lippard and the larger feminist social movement, in which the notion of dialogic exchange—what we now call 'dialogical aesthetics'—seem to share a direct relationship to feminist consciousness-raising strategies. Renowned black feminist theorist bell hooks reflected on the process of consciousness-raising, noting that, 'In small groups, individuals do not need to be equally literate or literate at all because the information is primarily shared through conversation, in dialogue which is necessarily a liberatory expression.'[1]

The shared theoretical relationship between feminist consciousness-raising and dialogical processes informs the two elements of Laurie Jo's practice that I reflect on here: the artist

---

1   bell hooks, *Talking Back: Thinking Feminist, Thinking Black* (New York: South End Press, 1989), p. 24.

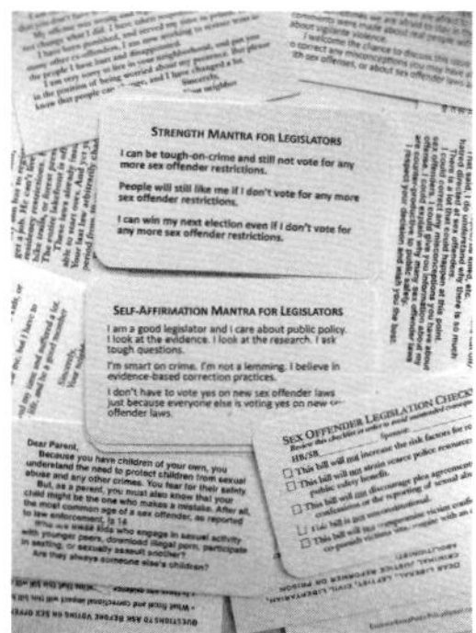

Fig 5   Laurie Jo Reynolds, *Legislative Mantra Cards and Calling Cards*, 2009–present
Rather than implementing policies proven to reduce sexual violence and abuse, our lawmakers can't resist tough-sounding laws that will help them win reelection. Legislators often admit these bills are wrong, but they can't resist voting for them. These mantra cards encourage them to fight this addiction: 'I can be tough-on-crime and still not vote for any more sex offender restrictions. People will still like me if I don't vote for any more sex offender restrictions.' These calling cards, fashioned after those used by deaf people on subways, and in homage to Adrian Piper, were made to prompt dialogue about the stresses of being on a public registry. One starts, 'Dear Friend, I am a sex offender. I know you did not realize that when you…' Another begins, 'Dear Neighbor, I know you recognize me from the sex offender registry…'

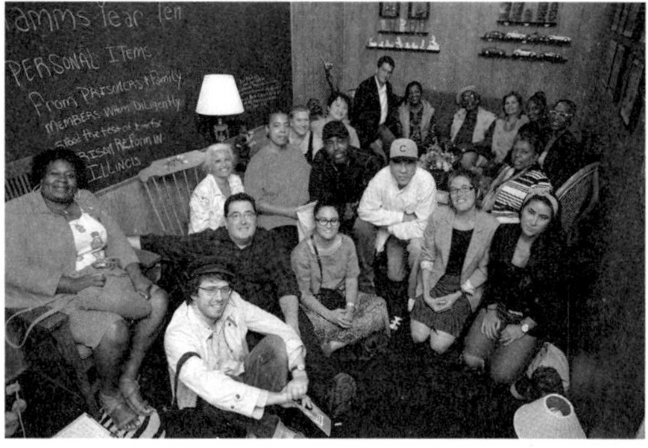

Fig 6   Tamms Year Ten Family Room
The 2013 closing of Tamms supermax prison in southern Illinois marked a major victory for Tamms Year Ten (TY10), the volunteer grassroots legislative campaign initiated by men in Tamms, their families, and artists. That year, TY10's primary goal was to re-elect Illinois Governor Pat Quinn who closed the Tamms supermax, three other prisons, abolished the state's death penalty, 'banned the box,' and signed several 'Second Chance' bills. Returning to the space in the Sullivan Galleries at the School of the Art Institute of Chicago that housed their TY10 Campaign Office (which served as the hub of the 2012 closure efforts), family members and men formerly incarcerated in Tamms created a living room out of furniture and objects from their home. After the 4 November election, the family members used the gallery as a meeting site to access the past, establish closure for TY10, and make plans for the future.

as facilitator (and its inherent problems) and the dialogical labour of the TY10.

During my first week in Chicago, Laurie Jo was invited by the Family Justice Center at Northwestern University's School of Law Building discuss the 'non-traditional forms of organization' that she has used to pursue prison reform, so that the centre could consider new strategies for their major area of focus: juvenile incarceration issues. While Laurie Jo has a lot of such meetings on her schedule, the centre is doing groundbreaking work to advocate for youth who have been given life sentences, and some of the TY10 mothers fit into this category. So this group is a particular favourite of the campaign. This high level of code-switching is central to the dialogical function of Laurie Jo's work. It is part of what constitutes her reputation as a dynamic and savvy organizer.

Laurie Jo's art practice is primarily dialogical and she is able to navigate various social and political realms, be it talking on the phone to wardens in Illinois area prisons or advising advocacy groups and lobbyists. It is precisely her identification as an artist that makes the large and successful network of TY10 possible. It was apparent to me that while various officials, advocacy groups, and non-profits are restricted to their respective mission statements, board interests, and other institutional and political commitments, Laurie Jo 'the artist' can advance the goals of TY10 by creating allies and supporters among these comparably stagnant organizations and institutions, with which she is affiliated. As an artist, she is independent of the institutional hang-ups experienced by many advocacy groups and can remain responsive with her tactics. This ability is further enhanced

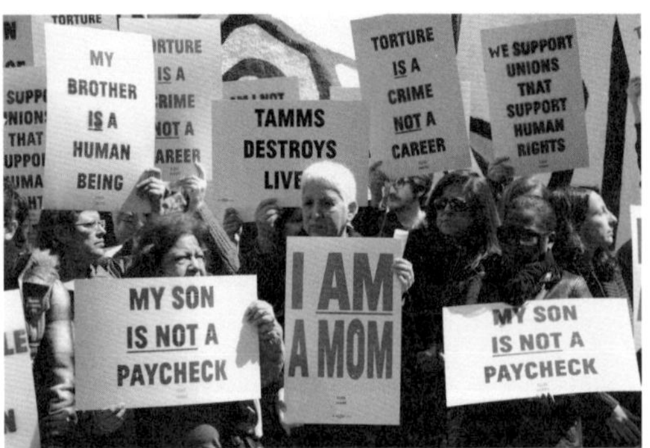

**Fig 7   Mothers of Men in Tamms Supermax at the
I AM A MOM March**

Mothers of men in isolation at Tamms supermax protest the guards
union AFSCME for supporting a prison condemned by international
human rights monitors. Their signs are based on the 'I AM A MAN'
placards first used by striking AFSCME sanitation workers, whom
Martin Luther King, Jr. supported just before he was assassinated
in Memphis in 1968. The mothers said that closing Tamms is
about human dignity, not jobs, and reiterated King's message that
workers' rights and human rights are inseparable. They marched
to AFSCME headquarters on 4 April 2012, the 44th anniversary
of King's death, and told the crowd, 'Human suffering cannot be
the basis of the southern Illinois economy.' Geneva Mullins, Rose
Sifuentes, and Brenda Smith are pictured in the front. Their sons
spent nine, eight, and fourteen years respectively in isolation at
Tamms before Governor Quinn closed the prison.

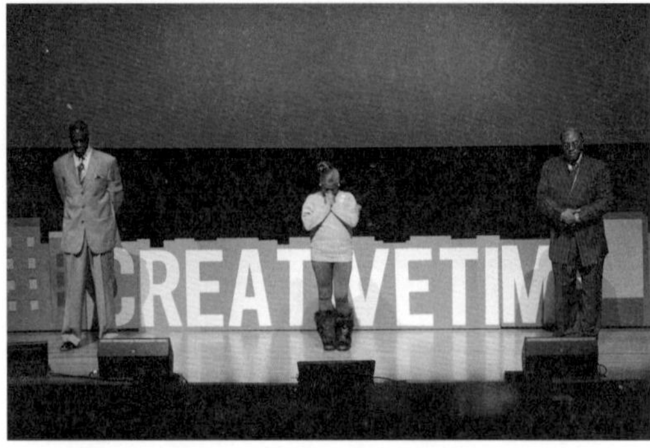

**Fig 8   Performance at the Creative Time Summit: Art,
Place & Dislocation in the 21st Century City. New York City,
October 25, 2013**

In 2013, four TY10 members, Reginald 'Akkeem' Berry, Sr., Darrell
Cannon, Laurie Jo Reynolds, and Brenda Townsend accepted the
Leonore Annenberg Prize for Art and Social Change at the Creative
Time Summit. At the event, the two former Tamms prisoners and a
mother of a prisoner performed a unforgettable act of endurance:
Darrell and Akkeem stood on stage one minute for each year they
were in solitary at Tamms, and Brenda stood for her son. The men
walked away after eight and nine minutes; Brenda was on stage
for fourteen. In prison, in political struggle, and in performance,
the medium is time.

by prevailing notions of the 'neutrality' (or the unthreatening nature) of artists in general, and is central to what enables Laurie Jo to advance the goals of TY10 among its expansive network.

However, we should remember that Laurie Jo herself is an art worker and is subject to the same systems of valuation presently placed on artistic production within the larger schema of opaque economic distribution and precarious labour in art economies. I'd like to consider the break between the 'behind-the-scenes' work (traditionally referred to as 'process') in her practice and the public face of her presence at meetings, lectures, and rallies (or the 'performance' or 'encounter') as an example of a feminized form of labour. After a meeting at Northwestern University, Christina and I sat down with Laurie Jo as she looked at the schedule for the following day. We were amazed by how often she is in communication with various people throughout the day, and asked her how she keeps track of not only the e-mails and phone calls but also their outcomes, as they come to affect the overall goals of the campaign. On her laptop, she pulled up a meticulously colour-coded spreadsheet document, with various names, dates, and multiple other columns and casually joked, 'My art is spreadsheets.' This spreadsheet and other necessary organizational elements in dialogical practices are seldom recognized as a crucial component. Laurie Jo's labour for TY10 is uncompensated. When she advises other non-profits, she effectively allows her own energies and inspiration to be appropriated by these institutions, at her own expense. This tendency toward 'free consultation' is not entirely dissimilar to the art world's propensity

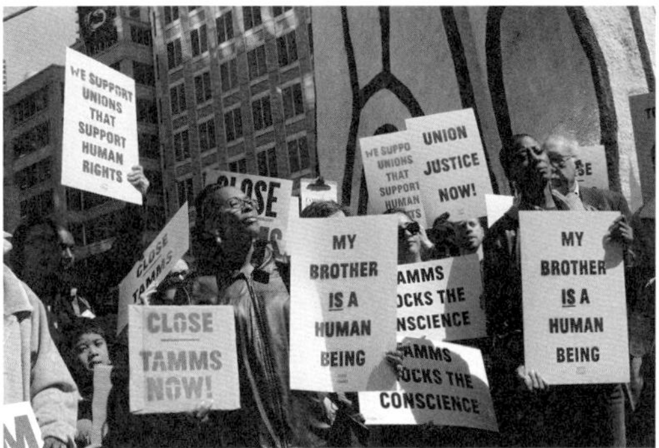

Fig 9 **Sisters of Men in Tamms Supermax at the I AM A MOM March**

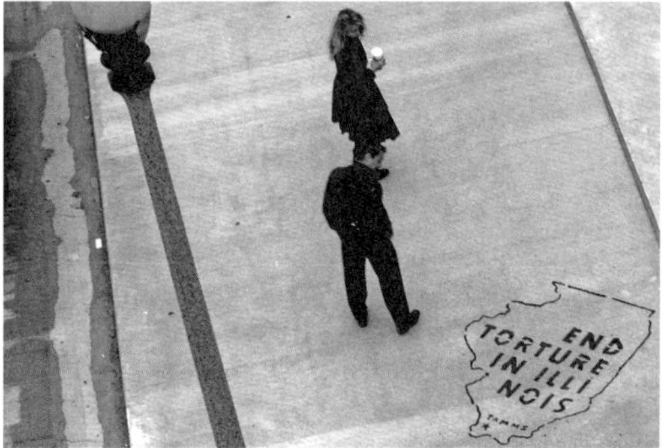

Fig 10 **Mud Stencil Campaign**
Two people passing by are drawn to look at a mud stencil outside the Modern Wing of the School of the Art Institute of Chicago, part of a tactical media project for Tamms Year Ten led by Nicolas Lampert and Jesse Graves to publicize the torture at Tamms. Teams of activists travelled to the city with buckets of mud and tagged walls and sidewalks with the statement 'End Torture in Illinois.' No permission was asked or given for this eco-friendly graffiti. The action brought national and local press attention to the legislative effort.

for artistic labour to be uncompensated in the name of 'exposure.' Perhaps what also leads us to overlook this type of work critically, I wonder, is the failure to recognize its inextricable ties to administrative forms of labour, particularly secretarial and other feminized forms of work within post-war institutional structures.

These forms of feminized labour in socially engaged practices can challenge our own investment in the single, glorified culminating moment of success in a given project—the closure of Tamms Correctional Center in this case—revealing instead an ongoing gradual process that can not be valorized into a single moment. The closure of the prison facility was undoubtedly the goal of the entire campaign and presently, Laurie Jo is working with her collaborators to envision a new set of goals and issues to address going forward. However, it is

unlikely (or perhaps unreasonable to expect) that such a monumental accomplishment is on the horizon again for TY10. What is necessary here, is to not simply move away from the compulsion to only validate practices by paradoxically reducing them to a singular spectacular moment, or that which we perceive of as 'concrete change.' Instead, we need to rethink our own understanding and evaluation of what are typically perceived as banal details, like follow-up phone calls and spreadsheets. It's necessary for us to begin to recognize these minutiae as crucial aspects of a complex mode of cultural production and personal transformation through participation and social progress.

The fact that Laurie Jo's practice can be understood, in part, through the concept of feminized forms of labour is not to suggest that she, as an artist, does not possess art world

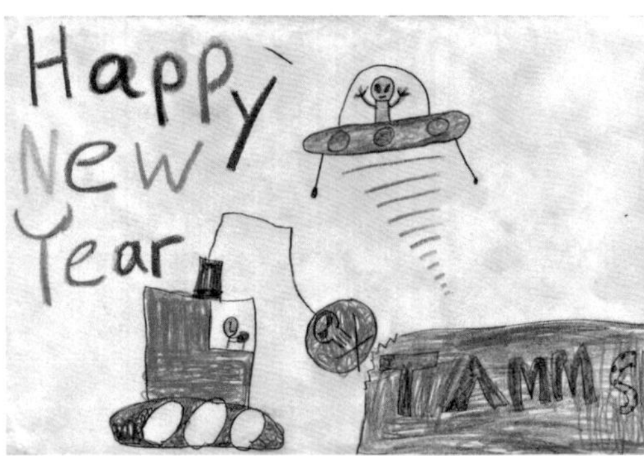

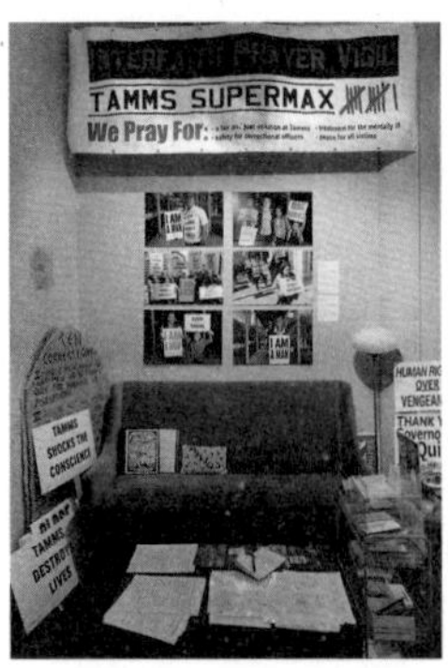

Fig 11 Drawing of Tamms Supermax being destroyed by a wrecking ball with aliens overhead
This drawing was made by a boy whose father was held in Tamms as he anticipated the closure of the supermax. Once it closed, Tamms Year Ten sent a copy of the drawing as a New Year's Day card, signed by volunteers, to each man transferred from Tamms to other prisons. The response was tremendous.

Fig 12 Tamms Year Ten Campaign Office
In 2012, the School of the Art Institute of Chicago exhibition *Tamms Year Ten Campaign Office*, in the Sullivan Galleries, served as the hub for the campaign to close the supermax. The office contained all the files and ephemera from the then five-year-long political battle and was the site of an active campaign. Volunteers met and worked around the clock while gallery visitors stopped by to observe, ask questions, and even sit down and help.

influence. In 2013, she received the Leonore Annenberg Prize for Art and Social Change from Creative Time, in addition to exhibition and residency commitments. I want to emphasize Laurie Jo's leverage of the resources offered to her specifically to further the larger goals of the TY10 campaign. Thus, when offered a show of photographs at the Sullivan Galleries in 2012, she instead organized an exhibition called the *Tamms Year Ten Campaign Office* and essentially became an artist-in-residence. Making the ongoing organizational process of the TY10 campaign indistinguishable from what would otherwise take the form of a stand-alone exhibition-as-archive, Laurie Jo used her position as an artist to expand the exhibition platform and have the School of the Art Institute of Chicago (SAIC) serve as the hub for the ongoing efforts of the TY10 campaign. This included storing and exhibiting all the files and ephemera from the then five-year-old project. Most notably, the SAIC site became the organizational meeting space for the campaign volunteers, many of whom were mothers of Tamms inmates and others who were students at SAIC. Making the SAIC the central hub of the project while regular gallery visitation hours were maintained revealed, at least in part, the unremitting nature of the work required to sustain the TY10 campaign for Laurie Jo and her collaborators.[2]

---

2   This 'art site' was such a small part of my visit to Chicago that I do not wish to give it more weight than is necessary despite it seeming most relevant in this context.

Freehouse

Radicalizing the Local

Jeanne van Heeswijk (ed.)

AFRIKAANDERWIJK

Afrikaanderwijk is a neighbourhood in the south of Rotterdam, the Netherlands. It is in the Feijenoord district of the city, and is traditionally working class. It was one of the first neighbourhoods in the Netherlands to have a majority of residents with an international background, primarily consisting of Turks, Moroccans, Surinamese, and Antilleans. Since the Netherlands' first race riots took place in the Afrikaanderwijk in 1972, it has received special municipal and national attention. The Afrikaanderwijk will go through a vast transformation in the coming years. Two adjoining new neighbourhoods with mainly middle class housing will change the demographics of the community: Parkstad, with 1,200 new dwellings, two new schools, facilities, parks; and Katendrecht, a mix of self-built housing and apartments for sale.

THE QUESTION IS: HOW TO REVITALIZE THE AFRIKAANDERWIJK IN SUCH A WAY THAT LOCAL INHABITANTS WILL NOT BE DISPLACED?

NEIGHBOURHOOD FACTS 2008	NEIGHBOURHOOD FACTS 2014
9,400 INHABITANTS	8,300 INHABITANTS
79% NON-DUTCH ORIGIN	85% NON-DUTCH ORIGIN
29% BELOW POVERTY INDEX (11% IN NL)	29% BELOW POVERTY INDEX (11% IN NL)
48% SOCIAL SECURITY UNEMPLOYED PENSION	55% SOCIAL SECURITY UNEMPLOYED PENSION
84% RENT, SOCIAL HOUSING	85% RENT, SOCIAL HOUSING
33% IS YOUNGER THAN 23 YEARS	37% IS YOUNGER THAN 23 YEARS

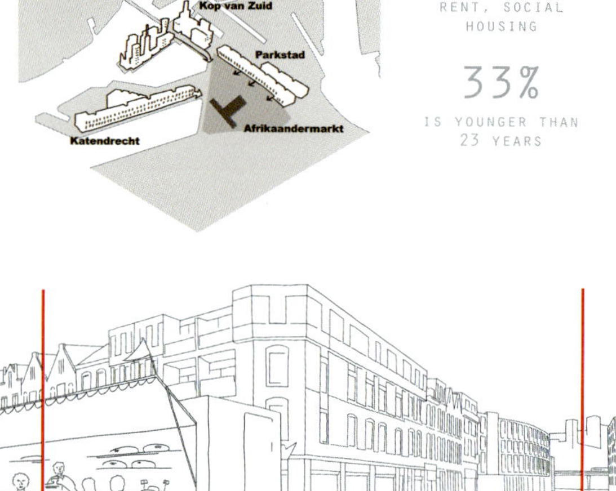

PAGE 21   PAGE 24

DIMINISHING PUBLIC FUNDS

In the last two years, public investment in the Afrikaanderwijk has significantly diminished, partially as a result of administrative and political crises.

2006–2011

PACT OP ZUID was a joint investment programme of the local and national governments, housing corporations, and educational and medical institutions. It aimed at increasing the attractiveness of Rotterdam South, striving to improve the social, economic, and physical characteristics of the area. In a massive allocation of funds, the intention was to invest € 1 billion over 10 years. The programme lasted for 5 years.

January 2012

NATIONAAL PROGRAMMA ROTTERDAM ZUID 'replaces' Pact op Zuid after criticism that it focused too much on physical issues at the expense of social issues. Without its own budget, it requests relevant stakeholders to collaborate and put forward funds.

January 2012

Housing corporation **VESTIA** loses about € 2.6 billion in financial speculations, one of the biggest speculation losses ever worldwide. Being the largest property owner in the area, many planned investments in the neighbourhood were halted or cancelled altogether.

298

FREEHOUSE
RADICALIZING LOCAL PRODUCTION

Since its inception in 1998, Freehouse has created space for encounter, both literally as well as metaphorically. It stimulates local inhabitants and shop-keepers, youngsters, artists, and designers to exchange knowledge, experience, and ideas. The connection of cultural with economic capital results in co-productions that mutually benefit participants socially, and economically. The resulting products also make the underlying cultural process visible. Inspired skill can powerfully lead people's development. Unfortunately, Rotterdam does not always take the creative potential of its inhabitants seriously, especially in the south of the city. From 2008 onward, Freehouse has applied its approach to the Afrikaanderwijk. Economic growth is aimed at through cooperative cultural production. And inclusive urban development is achieved through community participation and self-organization.

As the neighbourhoods surrounding the Afrikaanderwijk are being redeveloped with the addition of middle class dwellings, Freehouse worked toward making the existing inhabitants share in the economic benefits of the redevelopment. Despite diminishing public funds for the Afrikaanderwijk, Freehouse has been able to intensify its activities and to grow its organization. It tested new plans for the market and the area through 450 small-scale interventions and successfully set up 5 communal workshops. As a result, the neighbourhood and its market are becoming a vibrant community again and the area was put on the map as a lively spot for cultural production, both nationally and internationally. In order to secure the accumulated capital and qualities for its inhabitants, Freehouse developed a skill-based neighbourhood co-op that continued its work in 2014.

NEIGHBOURHOOD AS URBAN LABORATORY

The micro scale of the neighbourhood offers us the urban laboratory of our time. The micro urbanisms that are emerging within small communities across the city, in the form of non-conforming spatial and entrepreneurial practices, are defining a different idea of density and land use. By putting forth counter forms of urban and economic developments that thrive on social encounter, collaboration, and exchange, new economics and social institutions will emerge within communities.

2008–2014
450
MARKET & SHOP INTERVENTIONS

5
COMMUNAL WORKSPACES

2008–2014
50
SKILL-BASED JOBS

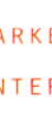

PAGE 25   PAGE 28

July 2012
Urban stage **DE NIEUWE OOGST ROTTERDAM** closes its doors after the Rotterdam Council for Art & Culture recommends the municipality discontinue its funding. This platform for music, culture, and exchange opened less than a year before.

January 2013
KOSMOPOLIS ROTTERDAM, an Afrikaanderwijk-based foundation that produces cultural events, closes its doors due to the cancelation of municipal funds. It focused on contemporary diversity, transculturalism, and polyphony in the public debate and the heritage of the future. Their closing brought to an end significant investments and employment in the neighbourhood.

February 2013
The Parliament decides that **MUNICIPAL DISTRICTS** will be abolished, as part of centralization and economization of local governments. In March 2014, the Feijenoord district council closed down and was replaced by a district manager.

October 2013
SONOR, an organization of neighbourhood counsellors, closes its branch in the Afrikaanderwijk.

June 2013
The fall of the **FEIJENOORD DISTRICT COUNCIL**, of which Afrikaanderwijk is part. Administrators are forced to step down. A subsequent investigation blames the 'diseased administrative culture.'

NEIGHBOURHOOD KITCHEN

The goal of the Neighbour-hood Kitchen is to highlight the Afrikaanderwijk as an area where home cooks make the best dishes and unique co-operations are possible between inhabitants and shopkeepers. In keeping production local, the social and economic inde-pendence of the inhabitants and shopkeepers is actively stimulated. As such, the Neigh-bourhood Kitchen forms an important link in shaping the area's image.

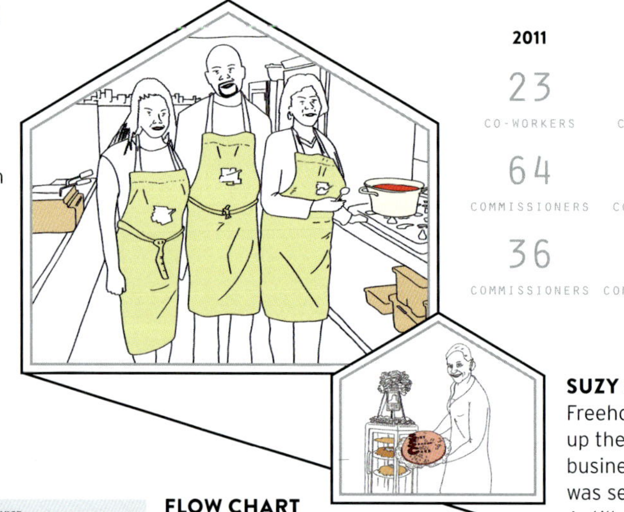

2011	2012	2014
23	12	70
CO-WORKERS	CO-WORKERS	CO-WORKER
64	77	100
COMMISSIONERS	COMMISSIONS	COMMISSION
36	38	42
COMMISSIONERS	COMMISSIONERS	COMMISSION

SUZY SEASON CAKE

Freehouse helps locals set up their own skill-based business. Suzy Season Cake was selling home-baked Antillean pastry and where possible collaborated with th Neighbourhood Kitchen. Suz closed her shop in 2012, due to personal reasons.

FLOW CHART

Superuse Studios mapped in a Material Flow Analysis (MFA), all actors and processes involved in the development of the product Dukkah dip of the Neighbour-hood Kitchen. Lines and arrows indicate streams of material, knowledge, and money. MFAs of regular products are more linear and result in less local value.

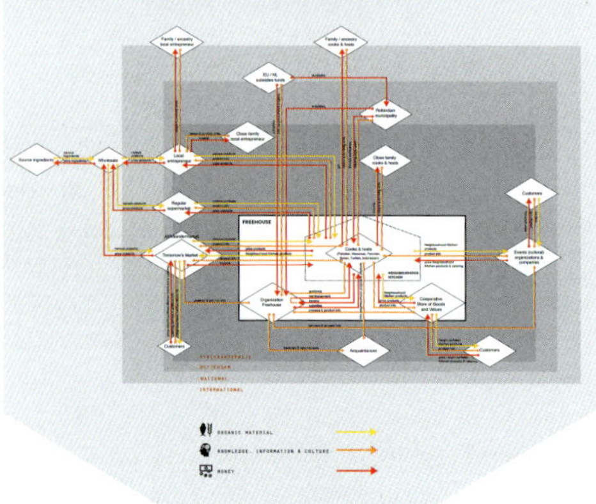

NETWORK RELATIONS

This network map shows the interactions between individuals or groups that are involved with the Neighbourhood Kitchen. A significant amount of knowledge and skills is shared between employees of diverse cultural backgrounds. This is typical of Freehouse's approach and enriches those involved both personally as well as professionally.

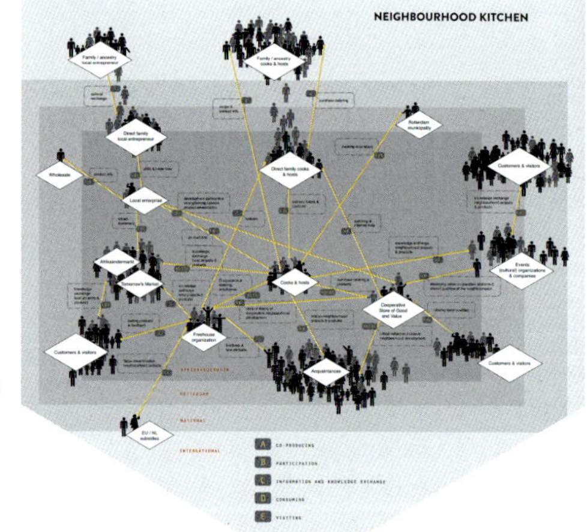

In 2006, the 'Special Measures Law on Metropolitan Problems' came into effect. Drafted on the explicit request of Rotterdam in order to prevent underprivileged non-Western minorities from moving into designated problem areas, it is nationally known as the **'ROTTERDAM LAW.'** It formally allows the municipality to deny housing permits to newcomers in 'fragile' neigh-bourhoods based on an income requirement or on previous 'unwanted' or criminal behaviour. The law has only been implemented in five neighbourhoods nationally, all in Rotterdam South. The Afrikaanderwijk is one of them.

ROTTERDAM LAW

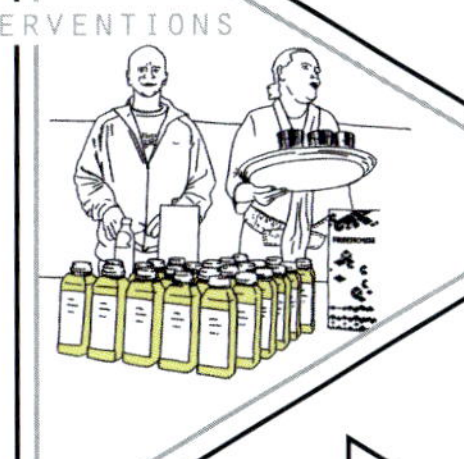

STYLING
Freehouse assisted market stallholders with alternative forms of presentation of products and styling of stalls.

EXPERIMENTS WITH LOCAL PRODUCTS
The production of freshly prepared food and products, produced by local people is a valuable contribution to what the market currently has to offer.

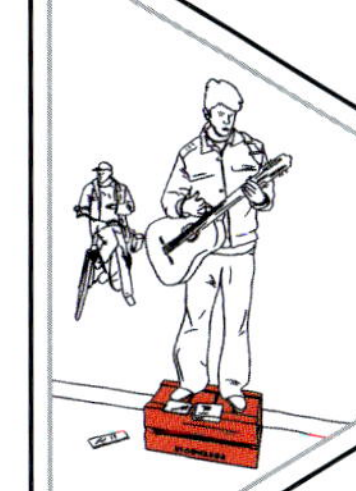

SPEAKERS' CORNER
Historically, a market was not only a place for commerce but also had a social and political function. Speakers' corner is a spot to meet and to exchange thoughts.

BRANCH SELECTION AND CLUSTERING
The arrangement of stalls determines the attractiveness of a market to a large degree. An attractive entrance, clear routing, and clustering of products are important. Between stalls with edibles, food can be prepared and eaten in a collective food court. Between stalls for textiles and clothes, new designs can be displayed on a catwalk.

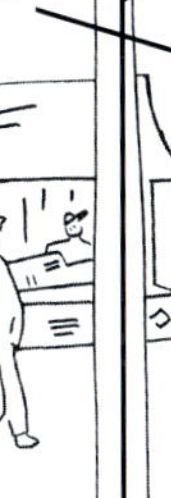

STACKING OF RULES, SHRINKING MARKET

In a time of massive, global financial deregulation, an invisible net of (frequently conflicting) rules and regulations has been set down in the Afrikaanderwijk. Effective rezoning left a lot of empty shops in the area and surveilance increased. The market used to be growing, but now it is shrinking, mainly as a result of these (primarily) municipal interventions.

On a **DISTRICT AND MUNICIPAL LEVEL**, outdated market regulations, a poorly functioning branch list (subdividing all products in groups with quota per group), impractical stall dimensions, and an unattractive market layout have resulted in an impoverished quality and range of products. Moreover, regulations differ per permit holder: original rights pertain-ing to the permit on the day of issue are inalienable, even if the market regulations change afterward. Furthermore, the Local General Ordinance allows the municipality to police the area in ways that would be unconstitutional elsewhere.

On a **NATIONAL LEVEL**, the 'Rotterdam Law' allows the munici-pality to ban underprivileged newcomers from moving to this stigmatized neighbourhood.

On a **EUROPEAN UNION LEVEL**, an upcoming prohibition to preserve products with ice, conflicts with local restrictions on the use of cooling trucks, which is a threat for the continuity of the sale of meat and fish on the Afrikaandermarkt.

SHOP WINDOW PAINTINGS
In cooperation with local shop owners visual artist Bruce TMC painted custom-made messages, highlighting the importance of motherhood on their windows.

NEW PRODUCTS
The existing product range on the market was expanded with quality goods, biological products, and crops from farms in the vicinity of the city.

VENDING CARTS
Tomorrow's Market welcomes the most beautiful and well-equipped vending carts. Small and big.

PRESENTATION PLATFORM
The Afrikaandermarkt misses a central gathering point around which the market can be oriented and where the market and neighbourhood can present itself.

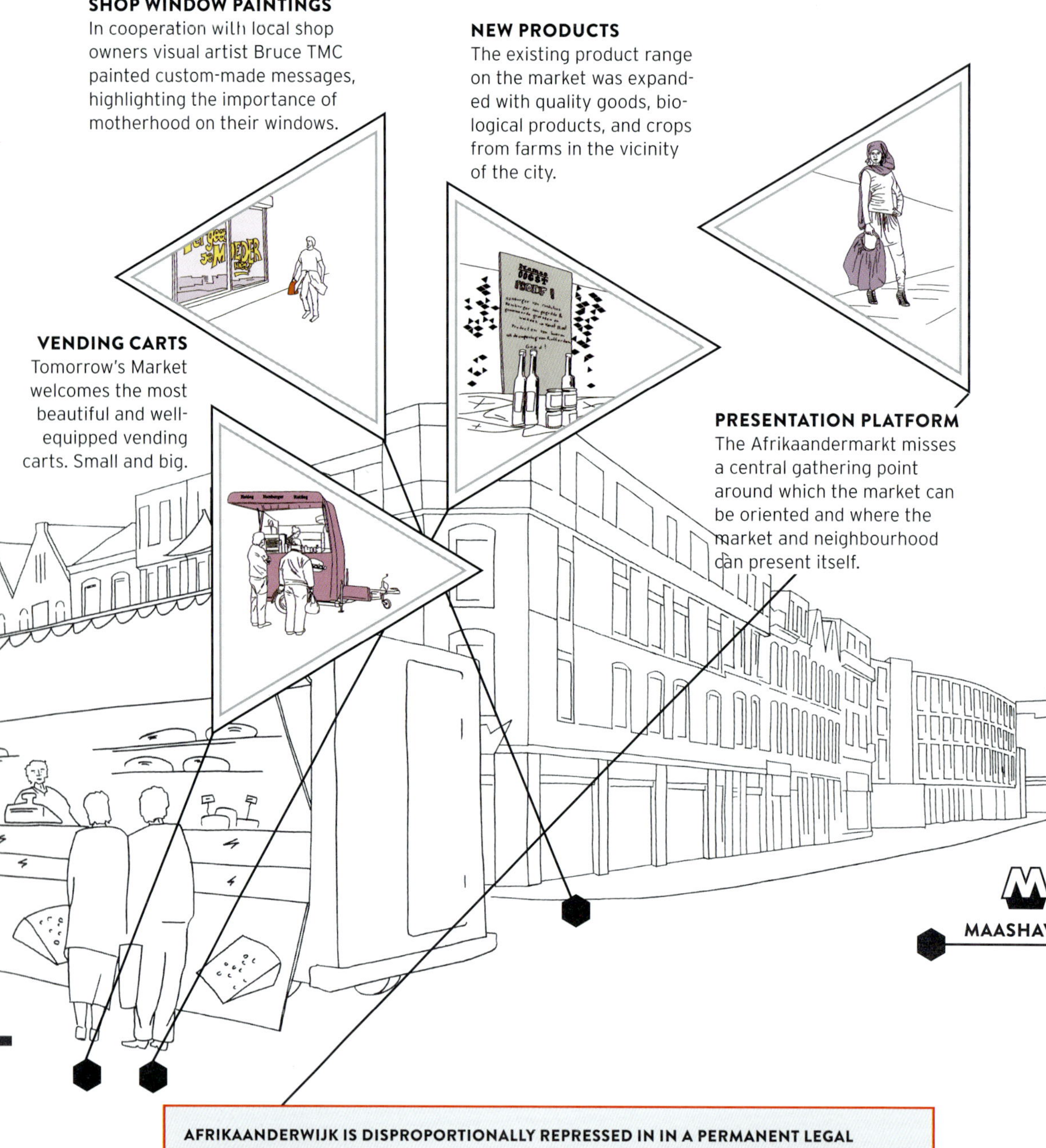

AFRIKAANDERWIJK IS DISPROPORTIONALLY REPRESSED IN IN A PERMANENT LEGAL STATE OF EXCEPTION

Rotterdam is a national leader in policing its inhabitants and the Afrikaanderwijk is one of its main focus areas. Since 2001, efforts have steadily increased. Hundreds of **SURVEILLANCE CAMERAS** now tape the city non-stop, including the Afrikaandermarkt. First, the municipal **NEIGHBOURHOOD SECURITY INDEX** officially established the Afrikaanderwijk as a 'problem area.' It became one of the so-called **NEIGHBOURHOOD SECURITY AREAS**, where special security measures are allowed, such as **PREVENTIVE BODY SEARCHING** (stop and search).

STOP AND SEARCH POLICY

292

TOTAL AMOUNT OF STALLS

STALL TYPE

WEDNESDAY   SATURDAY

157   127

KRAMERIJ*

63   124

CONSUMPTION

40   5

FLOWERS AND PLANTS

14   17

BAKING

9   10

FISH

10   9

STREET VENDORS

AFRIKAANDERMARKT

Since 1964 the Afrikaandermarkt has been held on the Afrikaanderplein, the centre of the Afrikaanderwijk. Wednesday and Saturday are market days and they attract about 15,000 visitors a day. It now has 292 stalls.

PROBLEMS

The Afrikaandermarkt originally had a regional function but it has lost its attraction. It now only serves the surrounding neighbourhoods, whose inhabitants have a small budget for shopping. Meanwhile, markets lost the price war to cheap supermarkets. Since people with higher incomes hardly go to markets anymore, it may be tempting to focus on attracting wealthier customers for the survival of the market. The question is: How can the market create a more diverse product range and strengthen its vendors' livelihoods while embracing its new clientele?

OPPORTUNITY

The market and neighbourhood cannot do without each other. On market days turnover is great according to the shopkeepers. When the market was temporarily moved to neighbouring Katendrecht, one third of shop owners were forced to close their businesses. With the influx of migrants to the Afrikaanderwijk, many new products were introduced, including exotic spices, colourful textiles, olives, nuts, and fish from Asia and Africa. And in order to survive and provide a livelihood, there is an urgent need to continue to diversify the range of products on the market and present them in a more attractive way. Nevertheless, the authorities tend to adhere to a more nostalgic vision of a traditional Dutch market, instead of accommodating the potential of this diverse mixture.

4,000

RIDES 2012

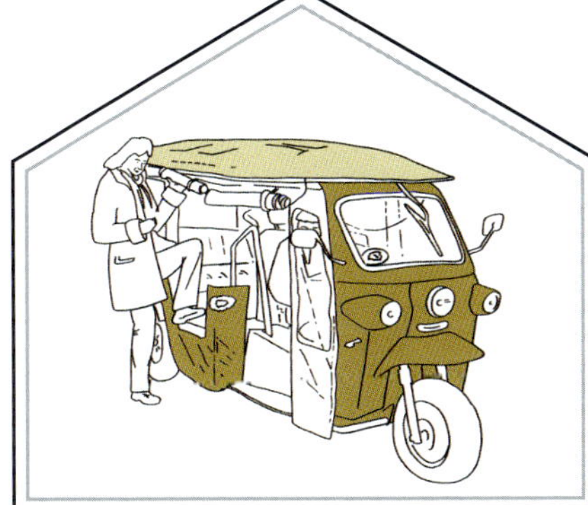

FAST FLEX FEIJENOORD

The FFF is a cooperative project that provides a cheap, local, electric transport service during market days. This environmentally friendly and service-oriented transportation was developed in cooperation with Bemobi and foundation FLEX. The Tuk Tuks offer an alternative to parking problems, walking around with heavy groceries, and noisy delivery mopeds. The project is now functioning as a fully independent offspring in Feijenoord.

AMBIGUOUS AND RIGID ENFORCEMENT STIFLE INNOVATION

The municipal approach to the market is characterized by control and enforcement. Once the Market Master used to be a market vendor selected from amongst peers, now he or she is a civil servant with a background in control and enforcement. Five different agencies currently enforce laws, rules, and regulations. Their differing interpretations make enforcement ambiguous. As a result, vendors limit their experiments in fear of losing their precious vending permit after three fines.

1. **CITY SURVEILLANCE** (enforces market regulations, branch list, market layout)
2. **NEIGHBOURHOOD POLICE** (law enforcement)
3. **MUNICIPAL POLICE** (law enforcement)
4. **REGIONAL POLICE** (law enforcement)
5. **TAX POLICE** (financial control)

Enforcement can also be excessively rigid. A permit holder needs to be present in the stall at all times. Fines have occasionally been given when people were away for a lunch break. The city surveillance has also removed musicians and public speakers.

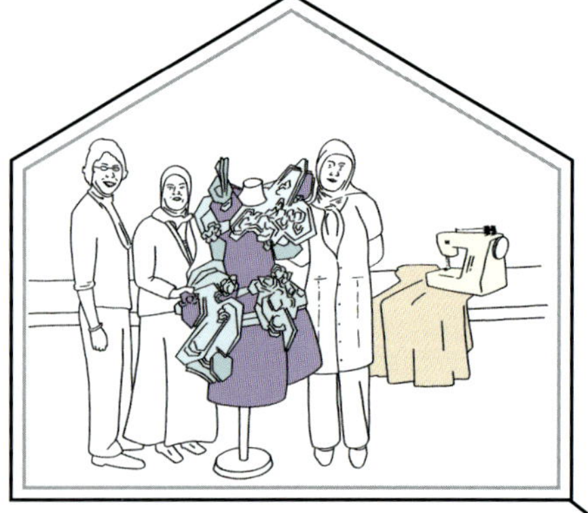

NEIGHBOURHOOD WORKSHOP

In the Neighbourhood Workshop fashion production is combined with design and education. Amateurs and professionals collaborate and exchange skills. Local inhabitants have knowledge of materials and master techniques that are important and interesting for contemporary designers. By actively using this knowledge, these techniques will be passed on and preserved for the future. Participants are involved in the whole production process, from design to end product.

2011	2012
31	21
CO-WORKERS	CO-WORKERS
38	33
COMMISSIONS	COMMISSIONS
22	21
COMMISSIONERS	COMMISSIONERS

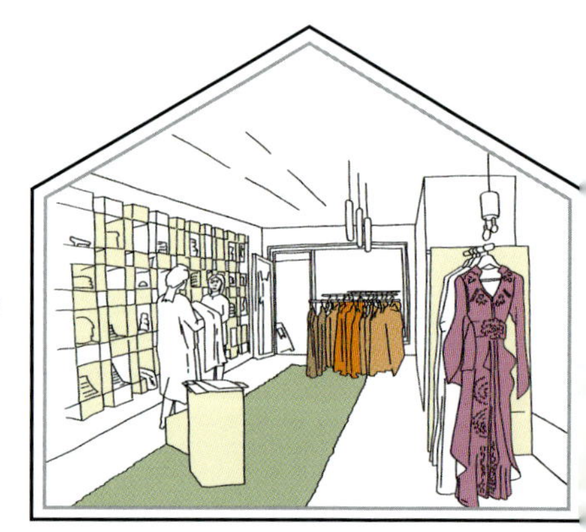

NEIGHBOURHOOD STORE

The Neighbourhood Store is a cooperative shop where products of local designers and craftsmen are presented. This approach is based on the store-in-store concept, using temporarily empty locations. It's attractive for local makers to offer their products to a wide range of people and to test the response to their product.

32

LOCAL MAKERS 2012

LOCAL ADDED VALUE

The value chain of the T-shirt of the Neighbourhood Workshop shows how this product accumulates value through its production process. Step by step, from raw material to end product, every party involved adds value. A sizable amount of value is actually gained from within the neighbourhood (see gray).

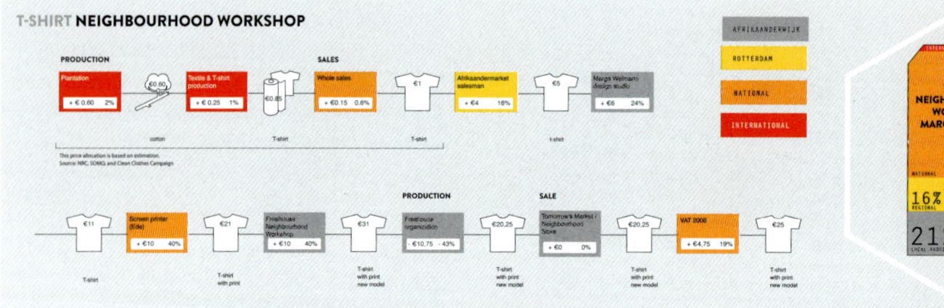

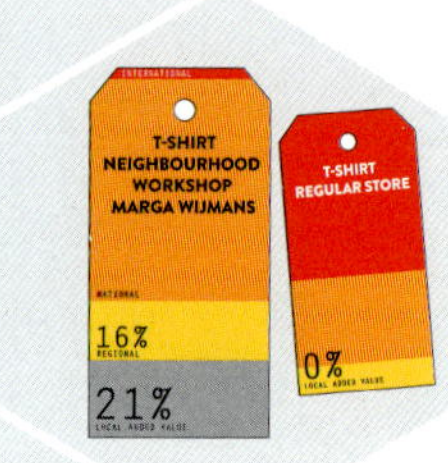

IN SPITE OF MANY VACANT STALLS, MARKET ACCESS IS SEVERELY RESTRICTED

In spite of an estimated 30% of vacant stalls during autumn and winter months, there has been a waiting list of 300 to 400 market vendors who want a place on the market, a serious mismatch of supply and demand. This inhibits a more diversified product range needed for a healthy, prosperous market.

IT IS VERY DIFFICULT TO GET A GUARANTEED PLACE IN THE MARKET

The easiest way to get a guaranteed position in the market was by inheritance. Some prospective vendors have married into families of vendors deliberately to get this secured position. It usually takes 6–15 years to get a fixed spot and market vendors tend to be vendors for life. Since many newcomers are migrants, they are kept from the market disproportionately.

IT IS HARD TO BE ASSIGNED A MARKET STALL FOR A VENDOR

The municipal branch list has over-determined product categories into subcategories and only allows for a limited amount of stalls per

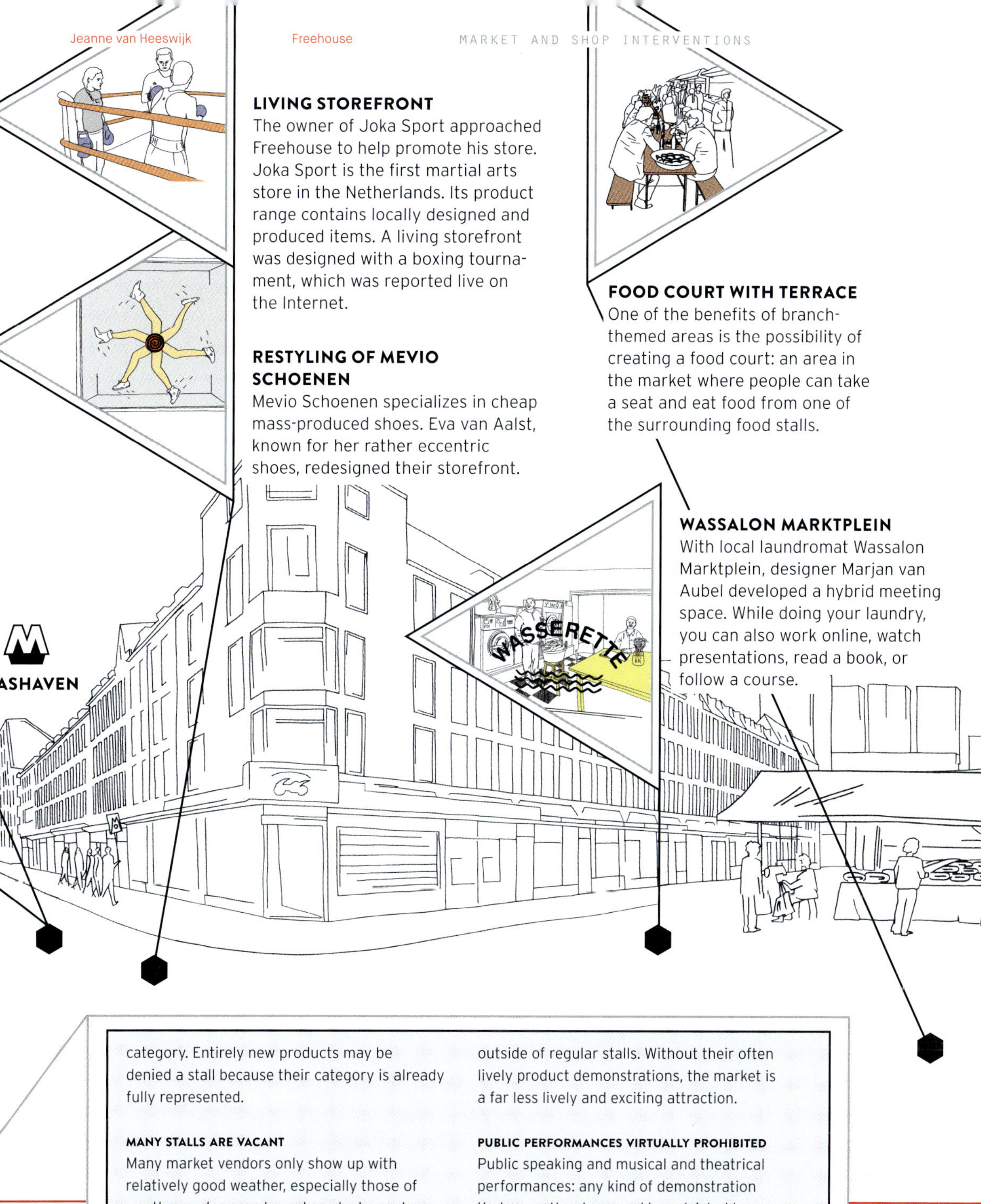

LIVING STOREFRONT

The owner of Joka Sport approached Freehouse to help promote his store. Joka Sport is the first martial arts store in the Netherlands. Its product range contains locally designed and produced items. A living storefront was designed with a boxing tournament, which was reported live on the Internet.

RESTYLING OF MEVIO SCHOENEN

Mevio Schoenen specializes in cheap mass-produced shoes. Eva van Aalst, known for her rather eccentric shoes, redesigned their storefront.

FOOD COURT WITH TERRACE

One of the benefits of branch-themed areas is the possibility of creating a food court: an area in the market where people can take a seat and eat food from one of the surrounding food stalls.

WASSALON MARKTPLEIN

With local laundromat Wassalon Marktplein, designer Marjan van Aubel developed a hybrid meeting space. While doing your laundry, you can also work online, watch presentations, read a book, or follow a course.

category. Entirely new products may be denied a stall because their category is already fully represented.

MANY STALLS ARE VACANT
Many market vendors only show up with relatively good weather, especially those of weather and season bound products, such as ice cream. Vacant stalls are very unattractive and disliked by visitors and vendors alike.

PLACES FOR STREET VENDORS ARE VERY LIMITED
There are very limited (and diminishing) places for street vendors who sell their products outside of regular stalls. Without their often lively product demonstrations, the market is a far less lively and exciting attraction.

PUBLIC PERFORMANCES VIRTUALLY PROHIBITED
Public speaking and musical and theatrical performances: any kind of demonstration that may attract a crowd is restricted to places allocated to vendors, in fear of unsafe congestion. Permits for street musicians have not been granted for years, as there is no application form for such a permit anymore. See 'ban on public assembly' as well.

MOVING INTERVENTION

Freehouse organized catwalk fashion presentations in the market. This was extremely difficult due to the regulations. In order to bypass the 'ban on public assembly' a playful presentation was made. For the presentation of *MO* Magazine* a group of models paraded through the market. A straight line of beautifully dressed boys and girls, accompanied with a megaphone shouting: 'Don't stop, keep moving!'

SERVICES

Services in combination with products were added to the market. For example, in a stall selling scarves, the latest styles of wearing the hijab were demonstrated. And a repair service was added to a stall selling secondhand clothing.

SMALL INDIVIDUAL TERRACES

Possibility to have a quick bite next to a market stall that sells food.

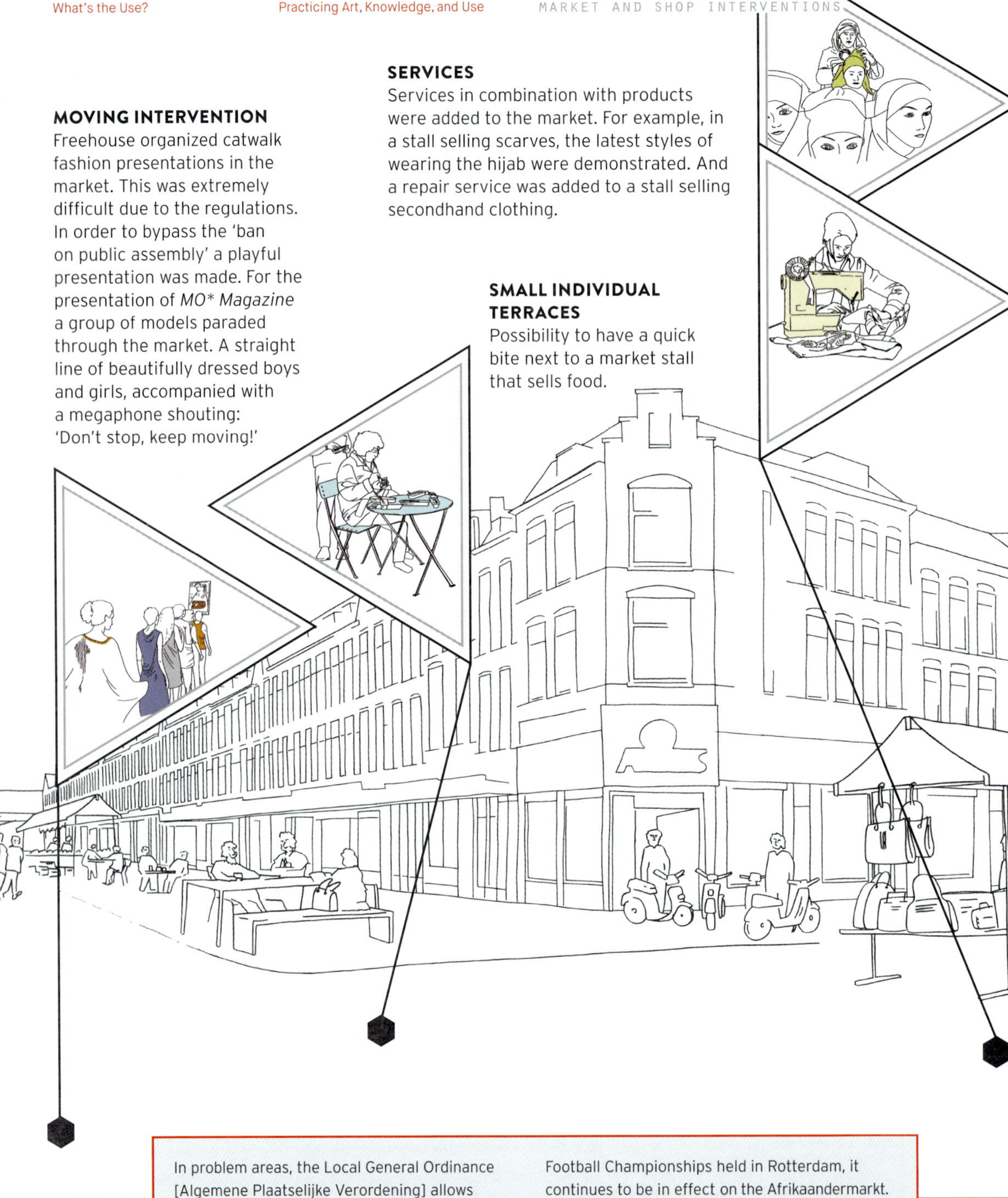

In problem areas, the Local General Ordinance [Algemene Plaatselijke Verordening] allows municipalities to proclaim a **BAN ON PUBLIC ASSEMBLY**. Originating from the 2000 UEFA European Football Championships held in Rotterdam, it continues to be in effect on the Afrikaandermarkt. Although previously legitimated by anti-hooliganism, it is now enforced due to anti-terrorist concerns.

BAN ON PUBLIC ASSEMBLY

TOMORROW'S MARKET

Tomorrow's Market is a detailed live sketch of a possible future for the market, devoting more attention to the quality of goods, introducing new local products and services, and styling and forms of presentation in stalls including cultural expressions and public speaking. Tomorrow's Market has designed prototypes of improved market stalls, a renewed market organization as well as a considerable rearrangement of the available space while negotiating the altering of legislation. Daily small-scale interventions continue to test and advocate a more inclusive market. From 2008 to present, over 400 tests were done. Also 5 future market scenarios on a 1:1 scale where shown.

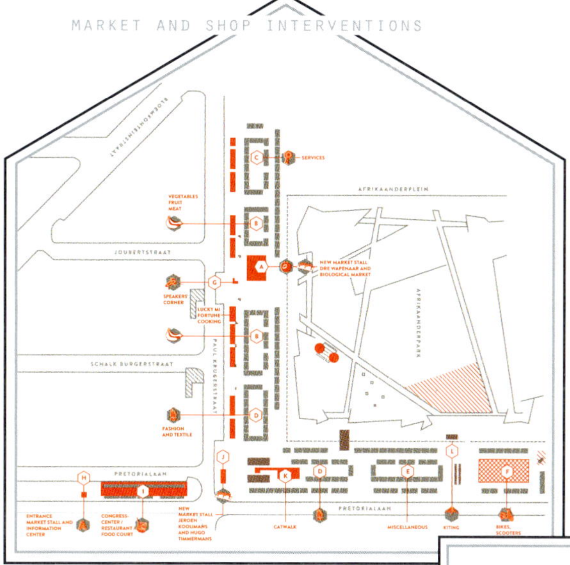

MARKET COUNCIL

In 2009 Freehouse set up a Market Council by gathering all stakeholders involved in the market for the first time: the municipal district of Feijenoord, Rotterdam's municipal surveillance, market vendor association CVAH, and market vendor association VETRA. The council meets regularly and proposes and negotiates improvements in order to settle conflicting regulations and push for creative breakthroughs.

**MARKET
COUNCIL**

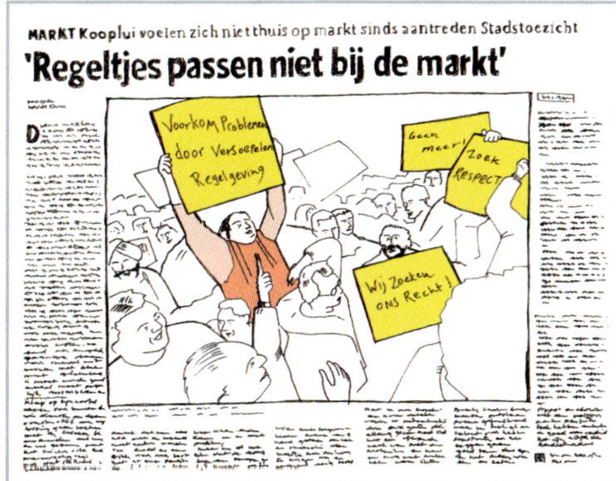

Petty rules do not fit the market.

IN SPITE OF RICH CULTURAL DIVERSITY, PRODUCT RANGE IS RESTRICTED

The municipal branch list restricts the product diversification that is needed in order to provide for one's livelihood and create a vibrant and flourishing market. The neighbourhood's rich variety of cultures, particularly in food and textiles, is seriously under-represented.

ONLY ONE PRODUCT PERMIT PER STALL

Vendors are not allowed to have more than one permit per stall. Selling fruit or vegetables falls into a different product branch from preparing them. As a result, vendors of oranges are not permitted to prepare a fruit salad or sell freshly pressed orange juice. Yet this would be efficient and yield higher margins. Likewise:
- A vendor of women's clothes cannot sell bras as well because they fall into a different product category.

- Many product demonstrations are also not allowed, since for demonstrating products you need a 'street vendor permit': a vendor of household products is not allowed to give a demonstration of cleaning pans with sponges.

FIXED NUMBER OF STALLS PER PRODUCT CATEGORY

The municipal product branch list limits the number of stalls per product category. This effectively blocks new products and services within existing branch categories. For example, vintage clothing, biological fruits and vegetables, or locally produced products are not independent product categories. Even though they would attract different customers, new vendors cannot enter the market with these products, as the maximum amount of stalls for clothing and vegetables has already been reached.

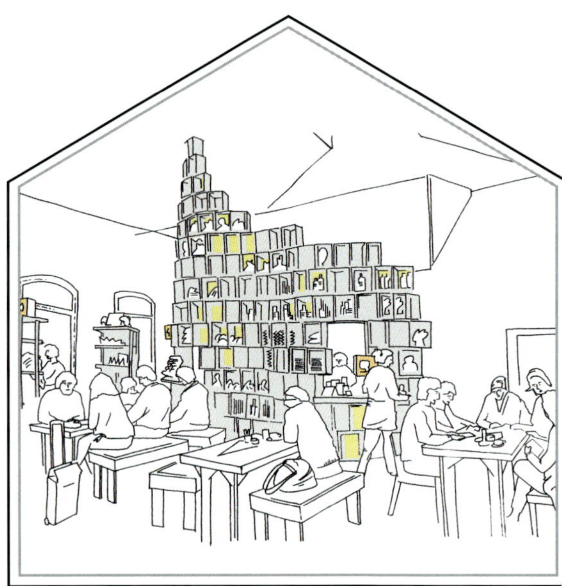

THE NEIGHBOURHOOD AS A COOPERATIVE DEPARTMENT STORE

An approach to conceptualize the neighbourhood with all its shops and services as one single 'department store' on the scale of a neighbourhood. Stakeholders and interested parties connect as co-producers to create a larger understanding of public space in the area. Together, they make the Afrikaanderwijk a thriving community.

WIJKWARENHUIS.NET

Wijkwarenhuis.net is an online platform that for the first time represents all shops in the Afrikaanderwijk. The site is designed as a digital warehouse where visitors can find shops by product category or location. Shopkeepers have their own storefront to promote special products and services and there is also a possibility to add a webshop.

COOPERATIVE STORE OF GOODS AND VALUES

From 2013/14 the Cooperative Store of Goods and Values was a meeting place for production, presentation, sale, services, and knowledge exchange. The starting point was the quality already present in the area. It became the heart and brain of alternative economical, social, and cultural development in the south of Rotterdam. Located in a vacant monumental building, in the centre of the community, it formed a network of cultural producers, production spaces, shops, and active inhabitants. This cooperative organization combined a market space, a knowledge centre, and a shopping mall. It was a neighbourhood service centre and information point at once and marked the start of the Afrikaanderwijk Cooperative.

Although the effect of the 'Rotterdam Law' on neighbourhoods has not been properly researched, an amendment is currently being drafted in parliament. It will extend the current maximum application in an area from 8 to 20 years, a severely prolonged legal '**STATE OF EXCEPTION**.' The municipal ambition to be on the frontier of enforcement is exemplified in slogans such as **ROTTERDAM PERSEVERES** and **CLEAN, WHOLE AND SAFE**.

STATE OF EXCEPTION

THE WORLD AROUND THE SQUARE

Social designer Pablo Calderón developed a movable stage, transforming the Afrikaanderplein into a big open-air cafe. Initiated by Bar 't Tapperijtje, different bars hosted a musical performance ranging from Dutch to Caribbean. During the day the audiences blended into one mixed group that followed the music. The local government normally has a very strict policy on bars and cafes. Surprised by this positive initiative of the bar owners, it authorized the event.

REDESIGN OF MARKET STALLS

Four new prototypes of market stalls were designed and tested to influence the future market layout and retail opportunities. In collaboration with market vendors, Jeroen Kooijmans and Hugo Timmermans designed a foldable stall made from polyester, that is highly suited as a kiosk as well. Dré Wapenaar designed a series of stalls that can collectively span the entire market.

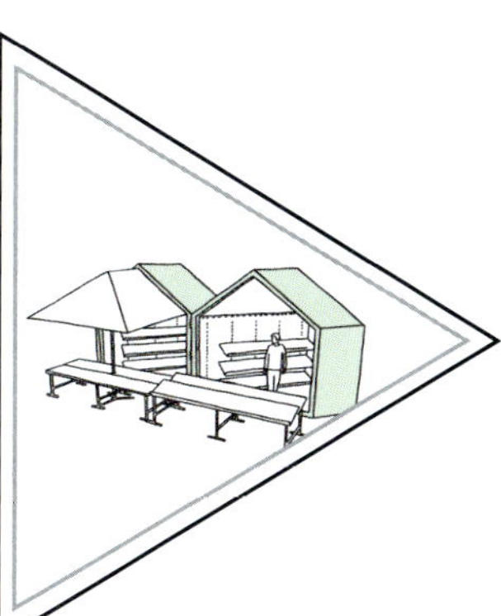

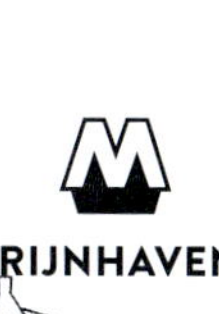

A PLACE TO SIT

By rearranging the position of the stalls, seats were created on the existing concrete guards that protect the trees.

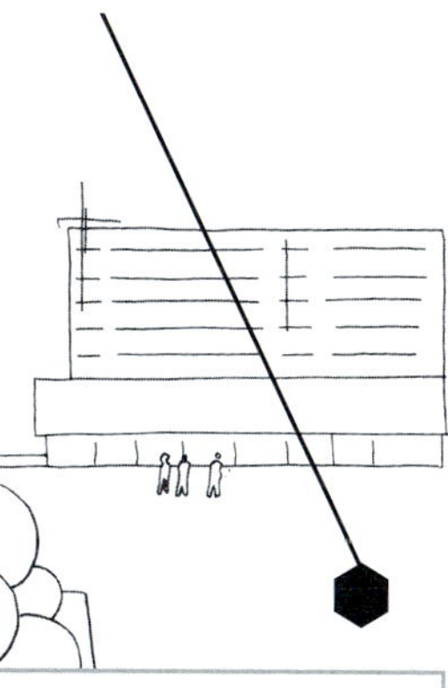

RIGID USE OF SPACE THREATENS SALE OF FISH AND MEAT

RESTRICITVE STALLS

Stalls can only be 5 metres long. Almost a century ago, the municipality awarded a lifelong contract to the family supplying the stalls on the Afrikaandermarkt. Vendors are only allowed to distinguish their stalls from others on the inside. Covering the stall with another material is not permitted. Ambulatory trade thrives with spontaneity, but vendors are not allowed activity outside of their stalls. On a sunny day, they cannot place products, mannequins, or chairs along their stall.

LIMITS ON TRUCKS RESTRICT PRODUCT RANGE

Some branches, such as the food branches, are under-represented on the Afrikaandermarkt. Apart from the designated plots for baking products, no food production vans are allowed. A standard corner plot can house a van of maximum 6 metres, banning the vast majority of market vans from the market. Small trucks are simply inefficient.

BARRED FISH AND MEAT

EU regulations will increase the number of products that have to be sold from vans and trucks. For example, selling fish and meat on ice will not be permitted from 2015 onward. This means they will have to be sold from cooling trucks. However, a stall is only 5 metres long and a vendor may only occupy one adjoining stall if it has been left vacant, creating a temporary vending space of 10 metres. Recently a very limited number of plots of 10 metres have been allocated, however, an efficient cooling truck is about 11.5 metres or longer. As a result the continued sale of fish and meat is under threat.

FREEHOUSE IN THE AFRIKAANDERWIJK 2008–2014

Freehouse renegotiated various urgencies in the area and created urban unions. New forms of commonality came into being through setting up chains of collective production. A process of social, economical, and cultural activities that moved on several scales and made the different informal practices of the everyday emergent, while re-rooting them into stronger networks. It was called Radicalizing the Local. By creating conditions for collaborative production, it allowed individual makers to pool resources and legitimize their informal businesses. The work on knitting stronger networks into urban unions and its cultural capabilities necessitated a new organizational (and economical) form on the scale of a neighbourhood rather than that of interest groups.

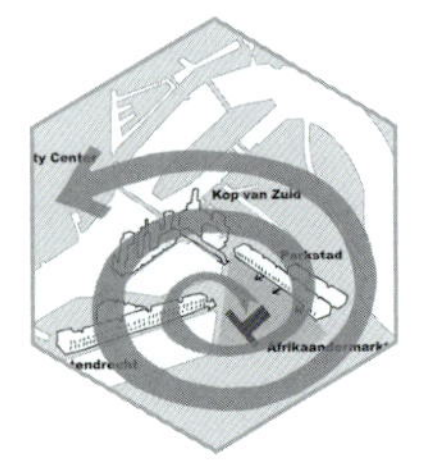

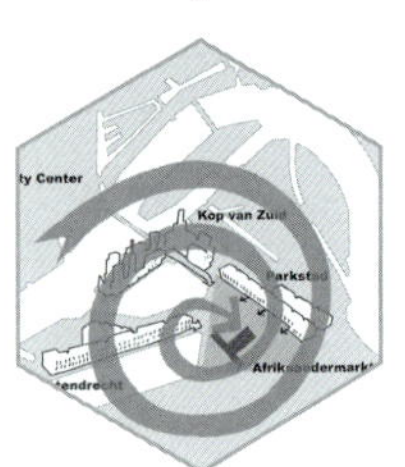

DRAWING FINANCIAL FLOWS INWARD

The extraction of financial capital for social, intellectual, affective values. Top: normal situation, outward spiral. Bottom: desired state, inward spiral.

Aetzel Griffioen | demeent.org

culture, craftmanship, action, enterpreneurial, profit, conflict, work, collective, demonstration, information

---

DEVELOPED SPACE, SERVICES, AND COLLABORATIONS

The Afrikaanderwijk Cooperative applies a self-organized approach in order to make use of all the currently untapped talents and resources that are present in the neighbourhood. Since the start in 2014 it set up several services and activities to generate work, space, and stipulate cost-effective deals for its members. The various activities can be categorized in space, services, and collaborations.

ENERGY COLLECTIVE – SERVICE

In cooperation with Essent the Afrikaanderwijk Cooperative launched an energy collective that realizes substantial savings for businesses in the neighbourhood. At present the first businesses have signed a collective energy contract in order to save operating costs. Simultaneously the cooperative also examines how to supply individual households so more people take advantage of collective buying power.

SCHOON – SERVICE

Cleaning service **SCHOON** ensures that cleaning work that normally is outsourced to companies elsewhere is 'insourced' and carried out by members of the WORKERS CO-OP. The Afrikaanderwijk Cooperative facilitates new jobs and guides starters entering the job market. Currently SCHOON is commissioned by Vestia Feijenoord to clean housing block vestibules in the neighbourhood.

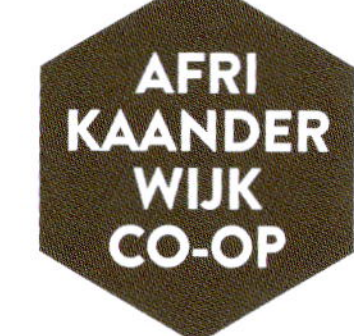

AFRIKAANDERWIJK COOPERATIVE

Those who look at neighbourhoods in large cities solely through a financial lens (with economic indicators) might only see backwardness, poverty, crime, and other threats. The Afrikaanderwijk Cooperative, however, sees the advantages of a diversity of cultures, inhabitants, and shopkeepers, each with their own talents, knowledge, and skills. Based on a long-term Freehouse presence in the area the Afrikaanderwijk Cooperative knows the power of local communities and small organizations in which open learning and work go together. In 2014 Freehouse decided to hand over the task of collective production to to a custom-made organizational form: a cooperative on the scale of a neighbourhood. An umbrella organization that brings together workspaces with shopkeepers, local makers, social foundations, and the market organization.

The cooperative creates opportunities through the provision of skill-based labour, training, services, and products to enhance the self-organizing ability while trying not to waste talent and human capital. It stimulates sustainable local production, cultural development, knowledge exchange, and entrepreneurship, combined with shared responsibility and participation. The result is a self-organized and self-run body that continues to create local, self-produced economic opportunities, leverage political power to shift policy, and negotiate economic advantages. It also develops local skills and self-certifications, strengthens resilient intercultural networks, and tries to create a radical form for self-governance of an area and reinvest profits directly into the local community.

ORGANIZATIONAL DIAGRAM

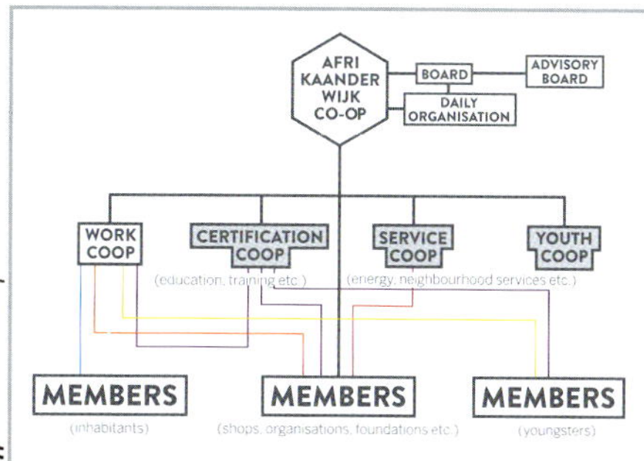

FINANCIAL FLOW

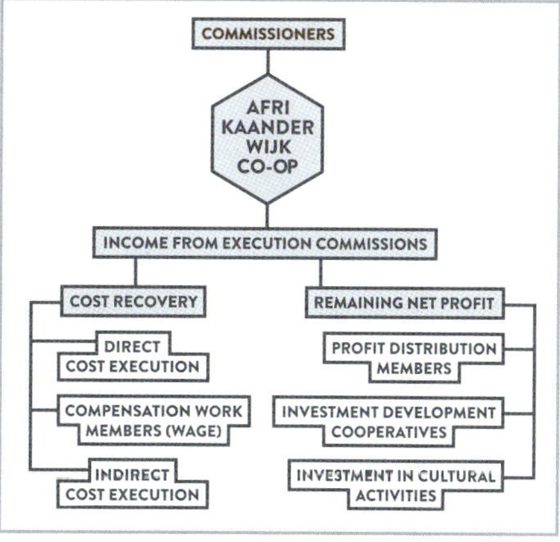

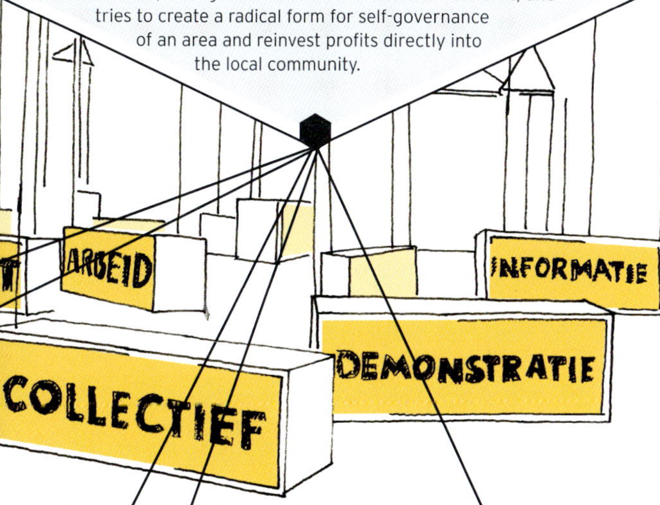

■ SAMEN & ANDERS — COLLABORATION

In the upcoming years Laurens living and care centre Simeon and Anna transforms from a building solely for the elderly, to a place where different groups live together on a reciprocal basis. Called Samen & Anders, it will also house small-scale shopkeepers that serve both inhouse residents, neighbours, and passersby. The cooperative develops the details and tests partnerships for this new care concept.

■ HOME COOKS FEIJENOORD — COLLABORATION

Co-op member the Neighbourhood Kitchen and DOCK Feijenoord set up a meal service for elderly, sick, and disabled people. In Home Cooks Feijenoord professionals and volunteers prepare meals in people's homes. Healthy food, talent development, and combating loneliness go hand in hand. As project partner the cooperative provides management assistance and Het Gemaal as location for communal dinners.

■ A NEIGHBOURHOOD COMMON — SPACE

Het Gemaal (an old pumping station transformed into a restaurant) is now turned into a public place for the neighbourhood. A place for meetings, where presentations and production come together. With committed users, as the Neighbourhood Kitchen and several partners that pay rent, it is ensured that this significant building is free as a central location for local programming activities and knowledge sharing.

From Freehouse to Neighbourhood Co-op:
The Birth of a New Organizational Form

'The co-op's main challenge is to be exceedingly aware of how it changes and why. It must always be questioning what agendas are driving it forward and whether it is living up to its values. And because it is self-produced, the vast diversity of cultures, education levels, economic classes, and individual agendas it encompasses must also be self-critical and reflective. This kind of culture, the culture of a neighbourhood that is organized through cooperative methods, can only be built through millions of conversations, millions of interactions, crossing paths, and working together millions of times. It is an intricate dance with no end, the prospect of a self-run organization that can be focused and reliable, flexible and expansive. The importance of slow learning and cumulative change through an open and long-term process, is a difficult commitment for communities to retain in the face of the urgency, and even desperation that characterize the ongoing struggle for the right to live well.'

Sue Bell Yank
Yank, 'From Freehouse to Neighborhood Co-op: The Birth of a New Organizational Form,' *FIELD: A Journal of Socially-Engaged Art Criticism* 1, no. 1 (Spring 2015), pp. 139–168, http://field-journal.com/issue-1/yank.

I think that utility is a very important tactical term to force open a discussion about why autonomy might be important.

Quote
Charles Esche, *Use,
Knowledge, Art, and History*
→ **See p. 414**

Art as such, as autonomous production, is both a symptom and possibly part of the cure—even if the notion of a useful knowledge and a useful art persists in being hard to match up or might match in some unexpected and damaging ways as well.

Quote
Adrian Rifkin, *Really, Something?*
→ **See p. 68**

Reflexions on Arte Útil (Useful Art)

Tania Bruguera

The natural impulse of artists is to try to understand the things surrounding them and to share the questions they ask themselves and the answers they find with others.

The idea of Arte Útil is to imagine, create, develop, and implement something that, produced in artistic practice, offers people a clearly beneficial result. It is art because it is the elaboration of a proposal that does not yet exist in the real world and because it is made with the hope and belief that something could be done better, even when the conditions for it to happen might not yet be there. Art is the space in which you behave as if conditions existed for making things you want to happen, happen; and as if everyone agreed with what we suggested, though this might not yet be the case—art is living the future in the present. Art is also to make people believe, though we know we might not have much more than belief itself. Art is to start practicing the future.

Arte Útil has to do with understanding that art, only as a proposal, is not enough. Arte Útil goes from the state of proposal to that of real application. It has to do with understanding that proposals coming from art must reveal the next step and be applied, must leave the sphere of what is unattainable, of desired impossibility, to be part of what exists, of the real and functional sphere: to be a feasible utopia. Although Arte Útil may be like a '*pilot*' or '*beta*' programme, where participants can experience how it feels to live in the world that is being proposed, it must be launched as something real. It should |be shown to and shared with those who may make it work in the long term, that is, for people who derive benefits from the proposal and might enable it to have a more permanent state or existence. Art made as Arte Útil does not have a planned obsolescence; on the contrary, it is a proposal others may 'retake' and continue without any further intervention by the artist. Artists suggest its potential life: some projects are imagined as short and specific; in others there is a desire for the work to have repercussions on people and for society to appropriate it. Arte Útil has nothing to do with consumption, but with making something happen.

Arte Útil is transforming affection into effectiveness.

For Arte Útil, failure is not a possibility. If the project fails, it is not Arte Útil. Artists have the challenge of finding forms in which their proposal might actually work; this is not impossible to achieve. So, the means through which art is made do not depend on a capricious ideal of the artist, but on the limits imposed by what can really be achieved and up to what point the reality of what has been dreamed can be pushed. Therefore, the limits of an Arte Útil project are determined by the relationship with the people for whom it is made and the transformations in the conditions within which the work is made. The perfect moment appears when the project is already in movement, when the people for whom it is made understand it, when they expropriate it from the artist and make it theirs. Arte Útil is involved in the life of people and it is to be expected that it becomes part of it.

Arte Útil has no relationship with a view that falsely sees the good in everything; it rather believes in people's possibility to grow. Artists doing social art are not chamans, magicians, healers, saints, or mommies. They are nearer to teachers, negotiators, behaviour builders, or social structures. Arte Útil functions directly with/in reality. Arte Útil has a different society in mind.

Arte Útil is a form of practicing social art. It is a socially consistent (artistic) material which functions as an entrypoint for the audience. With excessive frequency we hear about the barrier existing between the work of art and the non-informed audience for which access to the work is impossible. The usefulness of the work for the audience is, from my point of view, the key to solving this barrier of communication and interest by the non-informed/non-initiated audience in contemporary art. It is a displacement of the use of resources as metaphors, allegories, and others; it is an entry into understanding the idea of the work by using usefulness as a system to interpret and appreciate the work.

If you work in Arte Útil, what can be more gratifying than to see your idea incorporated into the daily life of people? Or to the social programme of a city? Or to nuances in the vocabulary of the individuals? I believe this is the natural place for Arte Útil works which reach the higher level of popularity and effectiveness. Just as images based on visual art at times have lives similar to parts of shower curtains, tea cups, or T-shirts, for socially committed art, popular distribution should be society itself, civic institutions, civic behaviour—the daily life of people. Arte Útil should be part of everyday life; it should be a daily exercise in creativity.

This text is an edited version of Tania Bruguera, 'Reflexiones sobre el Arte Útil,' in *ARTE ACTUAL: Lecturas para un espectador inquieto*, ed. Yayo Aznar and Pablo Martinez (Madrid: CA2M Centro de Arte Dos de Mayo and Dirección General de Bellas Artes del Libro y de Archivos Comunidad de Madrid, 2012), pp. 194–197, www.ca2m.org/en/readings-for-an-edgy-viewer. Translated by the author.

Annie Fletcher in Conversation
with Tania Bruguera

Arte Útil and Actioning Desire

The following conversation took place over Skype between artist and initiator of Arte Útil Tania Bruguera and Van Abbemuseum curator Annie Fletcher who was part of the curatorial team of the *Museum of Arte Útil*. In the conversation, which took place some eighteen months after the *Museum of Arte Útil* closed its doors, Bruguera and Fletcher reflect on the relevance of Arte Útil today, the original motivations of the project, and its manifestation at the Van Abbemuseum. The conversation is prefaced by Bruguera's 'Reflexions on Arte Útil (Useful Art),' written in 2012 and the first text in which she introduces the term Arte Útil.

Annie Fletcher (AF) For a talk I gave recently in The Hague looking at the future, I found myself reading Franco 'Bifo' Berardi. Bifo was part of the autonomy movement in Italy in the 1970s and wrote this wonderful book *After the Future* (2011). In it he insists that we have to think after the future, to forgo this libidinal urge toward progress and all the promises embedded in modernism's relationship with the future. Bifo's position is that it's over; it's collapsed. We are in a deeply fractured moment and we have to release ourselves from the desire and imaginary promise of the future. We are at a point of psychic, physical, ecological, and financial collapse and that is a depressing thought. But it might be a really important one. He says that all bets are off, that we need to re-categorize things. So I wonder: Is that the urge of your concept of Arte Útil, to deal with the catastrophe of now? Is that where the thinking came from, that this sense of disaster is too important to forego, that we have to work on it somehow?

Tania Bruguera (TB) I think it has to do with the sense that we, as artists or cultural workers, or whatever we want to call ourselves, should recuperate. We have the right to have a social impact. We need to react to the many different forms of institutionalization through which we have been living, the most dangerous being the institutionalization of hope. We need to ask: Who's in charge of saying what can and cannot be done? Who's in charge of letting you even think you can or can't change something? So I think it is more about reminding ourselves of the responsibility to keep thinking we can do something and to value that capacity. In Arte Útil this manifests itself as a battle against the endless discourse we have had for over a century about the meaning and the use of art. What is art for? A lot of people have focused on why one makes art today, the sentiments behind it, or the aesthetics of it. The questions of Arte Útil are more direct: What is the objective? Why do you need art? It is a collective question, not a personal question. Hannah Arendt in the essay collection *The Promise of Politics* (2005) talks about the differences between Socrates and Plato and how the former decided to be a philosopher who was only dealing with the abstraction of philosophy, while the latter said, 'no, no, philosophy can be a tool that we can use to have a better society.' So I feel like transferring that approach to art.

The other point of Arte Útil is to explore the role artists and producers play. Art has been co-opted by the entertainment and finance industries. Now art is just another product of financial value. But this is relatively new. It's like trying to go back to the past in order to go forward. That was why it was so important to make the Arte Útil archive, to recuperate examples and highlight that this has been a preoccupation for many years. But it has not been a mainstream preoccupation—it's almost an alternative history that we wanted to map.

AF So you are refusing all the values that the institution of art—or certainly modernist art—has historically insisted on: originality, autonomy, and progress?

TB Yes, and the professionalization of practice.

AF Interesting. Berardi's analysis of the last thirty years is that this unfettered, heavily futurized capitalism has devastated us cognitively, psychically, and organizationally. This has been most strongly felt in terms of solidarity, with even the most simple forms of collectivity and community being dismantled. Our desire, language, all of these things have been incrementally affected. Are you thinking about pulling away from the highly professionalized and marketized space of art today, and recuperating it in relation to life itself?

TB Well, at the very least it is a way to avoid the fatality of not being able to do anything. One of the problems we are facing right now is that everything is too huge. Part of what makes us think we cannot change the world is that everything is so humongous. Corporations are so big. Everything seems proportionally, abusively big. How can you fight that? It's vital that Arte Útil is small scale so it can be flexible, adapt, that it cannot be regulated. That's why it is always about initiation, by an initiator. Because if the project is good, then it should develop on a bigger scale, a social scale, and adapt accordingly. The role of the artist in Arte Útil is just coming up with these other proposals, other ways of thinking and sharing them. Then it grows to the size it needs to be.

AF So, the creativity, the artistic thinking is in the initiation if you like?

TB It's about how we reframe illusion, how we reframe desire, and how we think the power of desire.

AF Looking back at when we were first discussing Arte Útil, I think we were frightened of indulging in the image. We wanted to avoid the seduction of symbolism and metaphor. We wanted to define Arte Útil as beneficial and its utility and pragmatics were vitally important. But I would love to ask you again about the power of the image. Certainly when I saw what you were doing in Cuba last year with the attempted restaging of *Tatlin's Whisper*[1] you negotiated something different, perhaps more complex, in relation to desire and the political impact of encouraging the imagination of an alternative. I wonder, have you changed your position against symbolism?

---

1 In Bruguera's original performance *Tatlin's Whisper* (2009) at the Havana Biennial, the artist set up a stage and open mic so people could spend one minute speaking on a subject of their choice. It was a temporary platform for free speech that is normally denied Cuban citizens. On 17 December 2014, Bruguera wrote a letter to Raúl Castro, Barack Obama, and Pope Francis in reaction to the restoring of diplomatic relations between the United States and Cuba, demanding freedom, democracy, and equality in Cuba. She proposed to Castro to exhibit *Tatlin's Whisper #6 (Havana Version)* at the Plaza de la Revolución, the central square in Havana and site of revolutionary speeches, in order that the people of Cuba could voice their opinion of this historic moment. Bruguera was not allowed to stage the performance. Soon after the platform #YoTambienExijo [I Also Demand] was created. With this platform a (social) media campaign was planned to restage *Tatlin's Whisper #6* on 30 December. The Cuban government arrested Bruguera, along with Angel Santiesteban and Danilo Maldonado, 'El Sexto,' before Bruguera could activate the performance. Subsequently, Bruguera and others were charged with incitement of public disorder, resistance of police, and incitement to commit a crime. She then had her passport confiscated, was under regular police surveillance, and had little access to legal advice. After an eight-month legal battle with the Cuban government she returned to New York. During that time *Tatlin's Whisper #6* was performed in museums, galleries, and public spaces all over the world as an act of solidarity with Bruguera and others arrested.

What is your relationship to that now? I wondered
whether you separated those activities of imaginative
speculation versus art as a tool for yourself.

TB No, actually. In Arte Útil they come together. In
Arte Útil you need to harness desire into a specific
context or set of circumstances. You put desire in
motion and you allow yourself the opportunity to
make your desire reality. So if you are compelled to
act, against immigration laws in the EU for example,
you need to find the tools with which to outsmart
them, to go around them. So there's no feeling of
guilt or regret, which you necessarily have in more
representational modes of working.

AF Or nostalgia?

TB Nostalgia, anxiousness, anger too, you see a lot in
art because these are also human feelings. What I like
about Arte Útil is that it is about putting desire
on track, into action. And that's why the image is
interesting for me. There is an image in Arte Útil,
but it is not a visual image; it is an emotional
image. It situates you very differently emotionally.
What is created is an ethical image. That is why I
came up with the idea of 'Aes-ethics.' I wanted to
think about how aesthetics work through ethics. How
can it move you in a way that you are thinking: Is
this even correct? What should I do? You are put
in a kind of ethical conundrum. But it also has a
critical element, because Arte Útil is not a problem-
solving practice. It is about how you could propose a
different outcome but also rethink ethics and the way
we are in the world.

AF So is Arte Útil made with a desire to be
transgressive but indeed 'productively' transgressive
and transformational? I am interested in the emotional
aspect because that gives Arte Útil another dimension
that I am not sure we got to in our analysis at the
time.

TB I think it is a practice that goes beyond self-criticality, where the affect of the work is often to make you feel guilty as a citizen due to your impotence to affect change. Rather, Arte Útil aspires to a productive criticality of the system. So if you address the banks, you look at debt—that's the point you are critiquing. But you propose an alternative. You are not just saying this could be done better, that's the neoliberal approach. The suggestion is that you should be doing things differently because the system is what doesn't work. It's trying to get to the cause of things. A lot of art is just about the effects. For me this impulse to expose is not enough.

Pa

Exhibit

Insti

Part 3
...ing and ...uting

Exhibiting and Instituting

Introduction
Steven ten Thije

Arte Útil, useful art, or socially engaged art, are types of art that seek to have an impact or use in the social, political sphere. For this type of art the exhibition is merely one stage in a process that reaches beyond the framework of art and its traditional presentation models. What then precisely is the role or function of the exhibition in these types of art projects? Art's engagement or use is not only dependent on the work itself, but is as much determined by the context and how it is presented. It is the nature of the exhibition itself that can determine if art is perceived as a solipsistic object concerned only with itself and its internal history, or whether the work stimulates a visitor to become socially or politically active or engaged. Identifying the role of the exhibition in relation to art's use thus cuts two ways. The texts brought together in this section reflect each side and as such open up both the issue of how to present socially engaged art and how art can be presented in a socially engaged manner.

When trying to understand why the exhibition is such a central and yet complex entity in discussing art's use, what first becomes clear is that the essential conflict is not so much art's usefulness or autonomy, but how what appears useless from one perspective can be considered extremely important and useful from another. What appears out of place or invisible in everyday life, taken into the concentrated environment of an exhibition, can appear relevant and visible. Kimchi can be merely a traditional Korean dish, or it can be the lens through which the contemporary reality of global trade and cultural cross-pollination becomes visible for analysis, as happened in Paul's KIMCHI Co. (2015) presented in *Confessions of the Imperfect, 1848–1989–Today* (Van Abbemuseum, 2015).[1] Within the format of an exhibition this dynamic between use and useless or visible and invisible, is often negotiated through the distinct historicity of the exhibition space. That which was relevant and is now forgotten can be remembered and made visible again in an exhibition.

Only how this remembering is evaluated can differ enormously. As Nick Aikens points out in his essay, from its first modern inception in the Louvre, the museum, as main site for the exhibiting of art, was critiqued for its conservative temporality and ridiculed as a 'graveyard for art' by the splendid early critic of the museum Quatremère de Quincy. In the museum the art exhibited was relieved from its use in the strange temporality that is so alien to everyday life. Jesús Carrillo makes a similar statement in his contribution when referring to Jean-Luc Godard who critiqued the museum along similar lines in the later twentieth century by filming people running through the Louvre to demonstrate the ultimate contradiction between the slow time of the

---

1   See also George Yúdice analysis of Paul's KIMCHI Co. in this reader, pp. 266–285.

museum and the speed of modern culture and its most intimate medium: film. To understand the possibilities of the contradictory temporality of the exhibition space therefore is key to formulating the potential of exhibitions.

It is this contradictory temporality that is its biggest asset. In the space of the exhibition it is possible to take a step back from the maelstrom of everyday life, allowing a fresh perspective on what was previously unseen and unthought. This can open up a new understanding of what is deemed obvious and makes it possible to name those experiences that are present but silent. Carrillo also discusses how the Museo Reina Sofía in Madrid has recently worked to make this possible within the tense landscape of contemporary Spain, still haunted by the recent memories of the Franco dictatorship. Creating a public space to allow for such careful evaluation of what is self-evident, and what is unsaid is of profound importance. My own text addresses the temporality of the museum from another angle, by digging out an episode in the history of exhibition making: the innovative work by museum director Alexander Dorner in the 1920s in Hannover. The text addresses the complex temporality of the museum through the anthropological art theory of Alois Riegl, which was an important source for Dorner's early museum experiments.

The contradictory temporality, however, also comes with a risk. Aikens opens up the debate more directly toward recent experiments and debates around useful art. In his text he revisits the problem from another angle by pointing out the immanent danger of alienated abstraction that also can be the result of the separation produced in aesthetic experience within the museum space. Taking his cue from the *Museum of Arte Útil*, which he co-curated, he thinks through the limits of the museum model, which can be found in harmless representation of social and political conflict without any incentive to actually engage, and analyses possible counter measures. This is further explored in the case study by Lucía Sanromán, who presented socially engaged art projects in the exhibition *Citizen Culture: Artists and Architects Shape Policy* (Santa Monica Museum

of Art, 2014). In her essay she also focuses on the participatory art of Suzanne Lacy. Zdenka Badovinac offers another case study to unpack the complex dynamics between exhibition space and public space, pointing out how in the exhibition *1:1 Stopover* (Moderna galerija, 2013–2014), which she curated, artist and curator had to rethink their position when presenting artistic practice that seeks to have a direct impact in the social, political sphere. In a discussion between Charles Esche, director of the Van Abbemuseum, and Manuel Borja-Villel, director of Museum Reina Sofía, the strategy to embrace the notion of use is addressed critically. Esche advocates that a foregrounding of 'use' or 'Arte Útil' helps to break the dominant modernist context in the Netherlands, while Borja-Villel counters that the rhethoric of use and the desire of artists to realize immediate effects makes it vulnerable for neoliberal cooptation as it can join the call for efficiency.

The section ends with a series of texts that dig into the structure of the exhibitions central to this publication. Liam Gillick adds to this an artist's perspective, reflecting on the exhibition design he delivered for the exhibition *Confessions of the Imperfect*, whereby he developed an experiential frame based on the structure of barricades to negotiate the conflict between the exhibition space and beyond. Tania Bruguera in the second part of an interview with Annie Fletcher engages directly with the ideas and difficulties when developing the *Museum of Arte Útil*. ConstructLab and others reflect the structure of the *Museum of Arte Útil* exhibition and its particular production process. Subtramas describe their contribution to *Really Useful Knowledge*, which consisted out of shaping the mediation programme to inspire active self-reflection and not only the passive consumption of knowledge. Finally the section concludes with a roundtable including curators Nick Aikens, Annie Fletcher, Alistair Hudson, Steven ten Thije, and curatorial collective What, How & for Whom/WHW comprised of Ivet Ćurlin, Ana Dević, Nataša Ilić, and Sabina Sabolović. The discussion maps out both the differences and overlaps in the exhibition projects that are the central source of inspiration for this publication.

Essay
Nick Aikens

Beyond the Exhibition?

A SPECULATION ON HOW THE MUSEUM MIGHT BE PUT TO USE

When speculating on how museums today might be put to use, two inter-dependent contexts should be considered. The first is the premise that the modern museum, a European construct first embodied in the Louvre (Paris, 1793), needs to be rethought in light of our present conjuncture.

In Europe this is felt through the dying embers of social democracy, the subsequent shift in the public's relationship to the state and notions of the public, and the need for new forms of politics that are defined outside market or managerial spheres. Such a moment calls for a change in how the museum engages with different forms of civil society, so that it might mediate positions and subjectivities emerging out of this conjuncture. Secondly, it is informed by a consideration of artistic practice and a corresponding political subjectivity that are defined by their relationship to use or what theorist Stephen Wright has termed the 'politics of usership.'[1] When brought into the institution this politics of usership, which is in part a response to current conditions, reveals some of the fundamental characteristics, suppositions, and limitations upon which museum display (and modern aesthetic experience) is based. Forcing us to look beyond questions of display, their theoretical and pragmatic methodology ask deeper questions about how the institution might allow different inputs and impulses to speak through it. How might such a process lay the ground for new forms of relations between the museum and civil society to emerge?

Let's begin by considering the exhibition *Museum of Arte Útil* at the Van Abbemuseum, which was the catalyst for this reflection and within which many of the contradictions and potentials of this predicament can be found. Initiated by artist Tania Bruguera, the exhibition was centred around an archive or inventory of over 200 projects which aimed to identify and track artistic practices that had notions of use, usership, or use-value at their core. It saw artistic thinking as a tool, as the Spanish word *útil* implies, with which to intervene in social reality.[2] The archive, which lives online,[3] begins in the early nineteenth century with the early labour-exchange project *Cincinnati Time Store*.[4] It runs up

---

1   See Stephen Wright, *Toward a Lexicon of Usership* (Eindhoven: Van Abbemuseum, 2013), p. 2.
2   For a more in-depth description of the exhibition see Nick Aikens, 'The Use of History and the Histories of Use: Museum of Arte Útil and Really Useful Knowledge,' Alter Institutionality, L'Internationale, 13 January 2015, www.internationaleonline.org/research/alter_institutionality/14_the_use_of_history_and_the_histories_of_use_museum_of_arte_til_and_really_useful_knowledge.
3   See www.arte-util.org.
4   See www.arte-util.org/projects/cincinnati-time-store.

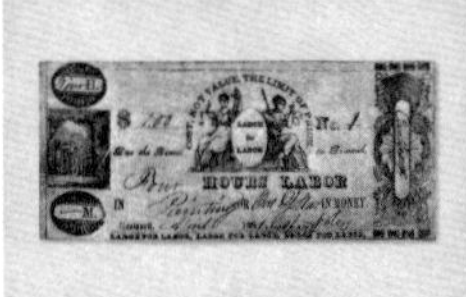

Fig 1 Labour exchange project *Cincinnati Time Store*, 2015

until the present day serving as a means to inventorize or track how artistic thinking has been used to negotiate perceived failings in existing social or political structures. This could mean setting up an alternative pedagogical project such as the *Public School*[5] or proposing a whole new conception of the state as in NSK's State in Time.[6] Presented through a series of groupings, such as 'Use it Yourself,' 'A-legal,' or 'Institutional Repurpose,' the extended display of the archive went in tandem with a series of live projects in the galleries such as Apolonija Šušteršic's *Light Therapy* or Grizedale Arts's *Honest Shop*.

Fig 2 A discussion, meeting, or workshop that took place within the *Museum of Arte Útil*. Discussion in Apoloijna Šušteršič's *Light Therapy Room*, 2014

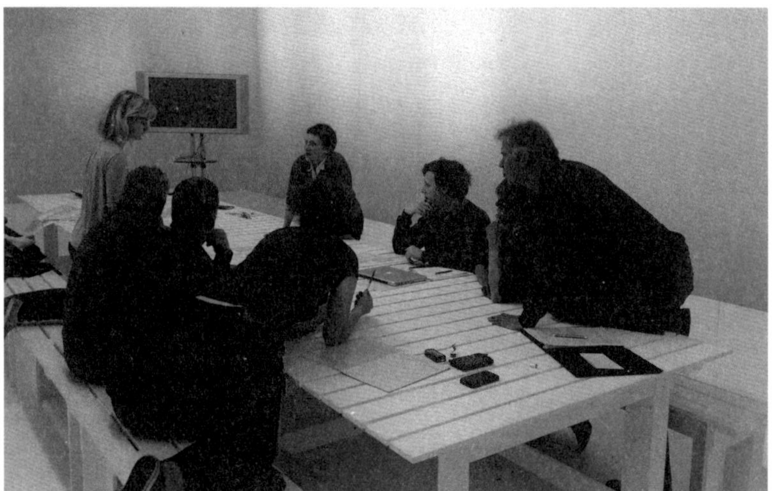

Alongside these projects the museum invited the public to 'use' the museum. As a result well over a hundred different discussions, meetings, and workshops took place within the galleries ranging from city council policy meetings to students from the Eindhoven Design Academy who were using the archive room to generate ideas for new social design projects in the city.[7] All of this was housed within an elaborate scenography, conceived as a 'Social Power Plant' that aimed to draw on the knowledge generated

---

5   See www.arte-util.org/projects/the-public-school.
6   See www.arte-util.org/projects/state-in-time-or-nsk-state.
7   See the *Museum of Arte Útil* calendar http://museumarteutil.net/calendar.
See constructLab, 'Understanding the Social Power Plant' in this publication, pp. 436–441.

within the archive and the activities in the museum for 'fuel' to generate projects outside. The conception of the exhibition aimed to both track a history of practices and turn the museum itself into a site of usership.

The rhetoric of the Arte Útil project is deliberately polemic, defined as it is through a set of criteria and insisting on the role art should play in upsetting entrenched systems of power or market logic. Yet its presence in the institution (Van Abbemuseum) highlighted a wider issue: that the art museum and specifically the format of the exhibition is not yet able to accommodate the type of political approach this works speaks to.[8] Even though the *Museum of Arte Útil* sought to shift the notion of use onto the institution in an attempt to open itself up to different constituents, the exhibition format determines that the institution presents its knowledge to a listening and predominantly passive audience. Similarly, the exhibition format itself is complicit in a wider form of conditioning—both on the artworks it represents and the subjects it addresses. While this has been increasingly interrupted in recent years through project-based exhibitions where galleries are momentarily hijacked as sites for discussion, production, or pedagogy— becoming 'part community centre, part laboratory and part-academy' as was the case with the *Museum of Arte Útil*—they remain as interventions within the conceptual framework and architecture of the exhibition.[9] What needs to be addressed is how the question of usership can be applied more holistically to the museum.

8   The notion of what constitutes Arte Útil was arrived at via a set of criteria that was formulated by Tania Bruguera and curators at the Queens Museum in New York, Van Abbemuseum in Eindhoven, and Grizedale Arts in Coniston. Arte Útil projects should: 1) Propose new uses for art within society; 2) Use artistic thinking to challenge the field within which it operates; 3) Respond to current urgencies; 4) Operate on a 1:1 scale; 5) Replace authors with initiators and spectators with users; 6) Have practical, beneficial outcomes for its users; 7) Pursue sustainability; and 8) Re-establish aesthetics as a system of transformation. See www.arte-util.org/about/colophon.
9   Charles Esche, 'Beyond Institutional Critique: Modest Proposals Made in the Spirit of "Necessity is the Mother of Invention,"' in *Bik Van der Pol: With Love from the Kitchen* (Rotterdam: NAi Publishers, 2005), pp. 22–26.

I. From Representation to Use

In *Toward a Lexicon of Usership*, commissioned as part of the *Museum of Arte Útil*, and republished in this reader, Wright opens by defining what he sees as the 'emergence of a new form of political subjectivity: that of usership.'[10] Tying the notion of usership to the onset of 2.0 culture and user-generated content he sees the political category of usership as challenging three 'deeply entrenched conceptual edifices in contemporary society: *spectatorship, expert culture and ownership*.' Importantly, these three poles are what have defined the modernist aesthetic experience, as detailed in the writings of Immanuel Kant, the eighteenth-century philosopher to which Wright directs most of his fire. He sees Kant's notions of 'disinterested spectatorship' and 'purposeless purpose' as being the bedrock upon which art has, through the course of modernism, increasingly turned in on itself, serving only as a means of reflection and limiting its traction in the real, writing:

> The former [purposeless purpose] imperative was to ensure art's universality, preserving it form the realm of use and utilitarian interest, enabling it to freely embody what he rather nicely called 'aesthetic ideas,' which could be the object of knowledge. But Kant realised that he somehow had to protect this objective dimension of art as knowledge from the slippery slopes of subjective appreciation, even while explicitly acknowledging that art was something that could only be apprehended subjectively. ... Hence his second, complementary brainchild, 'disinterested spectatorship'. It would be difficult to overstate the almost fantastic robustness of this conceptual arrangement that accounts for its extraordinary longevity.[11]

Wright's position is that a politics of usership, and its

---

10 Wright, *Toward a Lexicon of Usership*, p. 3.
11 Ibid., p. 20.

emergence in new forms of artistic practice, overturns
Kant's two major contributions to our understanding
of—or relationship to—aesthetic experience. It insists on
those who engage with art as being neither disinterested
nor spectators. Rather, going one step past Jacques
Rancière's 'emancipated spectator,' as engaged users.

Importantly, Wright also posits that our understanding
of artistic practice should be gleaned not through
a reflection on abstract notions that it may conjure
up, but rather through its use. Here Wright draws on
the writings of Ludwig Wittgenstein and specifically
his idea of 'meaning through use' presented in the
Philosophical Investigations.[12] Wittgenstein uses the
analogy of a toolbox containing multiple tools, positing
that we should only arrive at an understanding of the
meaning of language when we consider its application,
or the use of the tools. When considered abstractly (as
isolated words on a page) language, and by inference
philosophy at large, becomes devoid of meaning.

For art what this approach entails is a turn away from,
or reliance on, representation as the primary mode of
aesthetic operation. Specifically, the modernist tradition
of representation turning in on itself as self-referential,
representing not something with which it engages, but
representation itself. This self-referential representation
can easily become a mode of abstraction, which cannot
be put to use and therefore no meaning can be gleaned
from it. The move away from representation (or the
'de-activation of art's aesthetic function') leads to
what Wright identifies as a range of art practices that
take place on what he terms a 1:1 scale. These are not
scaled down versions, prototypes, or representations
of that which artists seek to address, but the things
themselves. He writes: 'Though 1:1 scale initiatives
make use of representation in any number of ways, they
are not themselves representative of anything. …

---

12 P.M.S. Hacker and Joachim Schulte, eds. and trans., *Philosophical Investigations*, 4th edition
(Oxford: Wiley-Blackwell, 2009).

1:1 scale practices are both what they are and propositions of what they are.'[13] If artistic practice is no longer representative or scaled, how are we to discern what is art from what is not? Further still, if art projects are being played out on a 1:1 scale, 'in the real,' how can they (physically or conceptually) find a place in the museum?

Important examples of 1:1 user-based practices are Laurie Jo Reynolds's *Tamms Year Ten* (TY10) and Jeanne van Heeswijk's *Freehouse*. Reynolds' TY10 programme was a multi-year campaign to close a maximum-security prison in Illinois. Rather than functioning as a critique of the systems of solitary confinement or under-representation for prisoners, TY10 was a political, activist campaign initiated by Reynolds and subsequently a whole team of volunteers with the intent of closing the prison, which in 2012, it succeeded in doing. Speaking to Reynolds, who as part of the *Museum of Arte Útil* spent two months in the Van Abbemuseum, was revealing; she understood TY10 as an art project, rather than as solely an activist campaign. Firstly, she said its definition as an art project could be found in its ambition and seemingly unrealizable aims. Only when conceived as art could the scale and ambition of what she was trying to do be considered. Similarly, when considering the time-based, relational aspect of TY10, the dialogic, durational mode of Reynolds's art practice becomes clear. This is a campaign that is understood through complex, emotionally laden notions of time and relations. However, throughout the project, the line between political activism and artistic project was barely discernible to the naked eye. Rather, it was, as Wright writes in relation to 1:1 scale practice 'informed by artistic self-understanding, not framed as art.' This redefinition of art through self-understanding allows us to escape the often reductive discussion of what is or isn't art and instead allow us to think more productively about how much art a project contains,

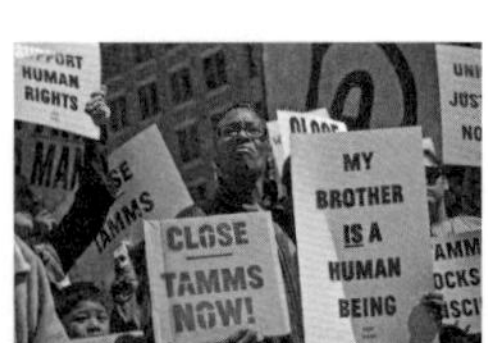
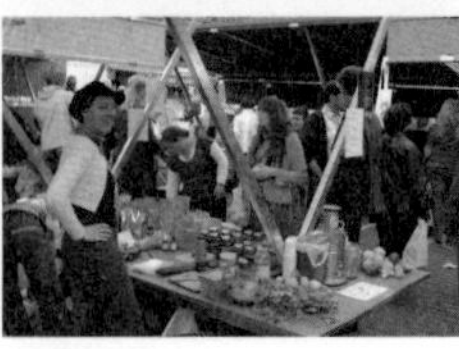

Fig 3　Laurie Jo Reynolds, *Tamms Year Ten*, 2012
Fig 4　Jeanne van Heeswijk, *Freehouse*, Rotterdam, 2008

13　Wright, *Toward a Lexicon of Usership*, p. 3.

or what Wright names the 'co-efficient of art.'[14]

In the Netherlands, Van Heeswijk's *Freehouse* has seen the artist work in the Afrikaanderwijk district in Rotterdam since 2009. She has instigated a series of initiatives and commercial enterprises (a clothes studio, shop, cafe, and community centre as well as working with stall owners on the local market) that draw on the skills of the community, many of whom are migrants, and serving as a direct challenge to the mass gentrification which the neighbourhood is undergoing. The result has been the foundation of a workers' co-operative that is in a position to lobby the city government in relation to its members (who are all local traders and residents) and that has the capacity to challenge existing political or economic interests. In this sense it is an example of a form of civic organization that can shape new political positions.

What these two projects share are artists working with different constituency groups, users of the projects, over long periods of time to challenge entrenched systems. They rely on the artist relinquishing their role as sole author (rather they become organizers or orchestrators of a larger workforce) and they take place on a 1:1 scale. Importantly, they signal emergent forms of civil society that have the capacity to both challenge existing structures or put forward alternatives.

Returning to Wright, what he does so effectively in his lexicon is to link this type of artistic thinking to what he sees as a 'broader usological turn' in society. Wright sees this as being ushered in by the disintegration of long-held collective political frameworks. In Europe this is most visible through the long decline of social democracy, which has relied heavily on consensus and representative democracy. Within this long decline, larger, more structured forms of political representation such as trade unions, have waned dramatically. Usership, as a mode of political action is interesting precisely because it steps outside (or simply doesn't have time for) consensus

---

14 Ibid., p. 13.

or political representation. It speaks directly through its users. Similarly, users like the hacker community for example are not to be found in state institutions or academies but in the cracks of civil society. Further still (and perhaps unfortunately), usership does not purport to offer a grand political narrative, rather it is simply implemented within existing systems, as with TY10 or *Freehouse*. Indeed, what is interesting about Wright's notion of usership is that it is not articulated collectively, but visible through its application and the manner in which it intervenes in the contexts where it is found.

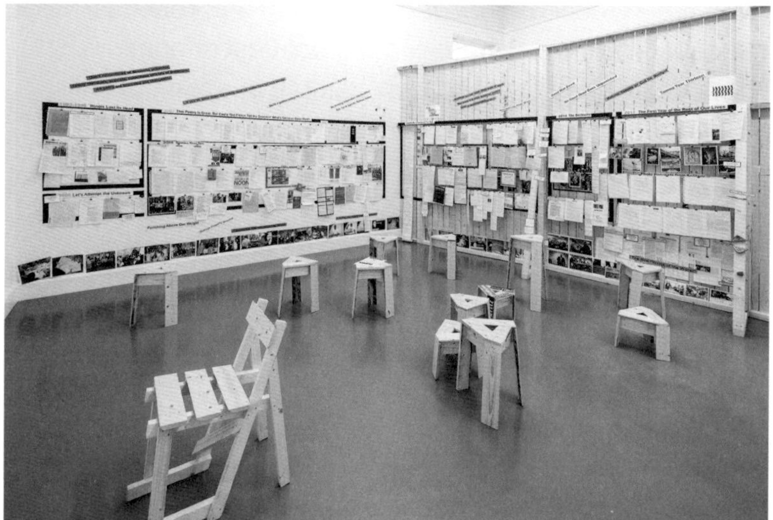

Fig 5   Laurie Jo Reynolds, *Tamms Year 10*, archival installation at the Museum of Arte Útil, Van Abbemuseum, 2014

II: Distance of Display

The prospect of the institution aligning itself with such methodologies and political approaches is appealing. Indeed it was one of the motivations for initiating the *Museum of Arte Útil* and including TY10 and *Freehouse* as major contributions to the exhibition. Yet, the very concept of a *Museum of Arte Útil* and the presentation of such projects presents an inherent contradiction: namely by bringing projects and ways of working that happened in the field, on a 1:1 scale and often over long periods into the museum, they become frozen, subject to institutional capture and modes of presentation. The format of the exhibition, where projects are represented through photographs, documents, or accounts of activities that happened elsewhere, brings into sharp relief questions surrounding display, context, and the framing of the museum. The exhibition format instigates a fundamental—even ontological—shift in the reading of a project. They inevitably lose their status as 1:1 practice. They are reframed, 'de-fanged' as Wright would say, as representational art. The mode of translation that takes place when projects are presented in the museum, such as the elaborate cartographic installation that Van Heeswijk used to represent *Freehouse* or the detailed archival presentation of TY10, can allow for different relations and time frames within a project to be mapped. But the people and contexts involved inevitably become flattened by their presence in the museum. The result is twofold: returning to Wittgenstein, we are unable to understand their meanings as we are unable to grapple fully with their use. Their defining characteristic as user-based practices—how they draw on multiple inputs and necessarily mutate and unfold—is codified through representational systems, be they maps, archives, or photographs. In some respects this critique could be seen as specific to the type of projects that Arte Útil is engaged with. However, the way in which the context formed by museum display informs how artworks are understood can be seen as one of the founding critiques of museum and exhibition practice.

What are the implications for the museum if it is to think beyond the distance of display? This question is not to renounce the exhibition but rather to acknowledge what a move beyond it might mean, both pragmatically and theoretically. In his book *Museum Memories: History, Technology, Art* (1999)[15] literary scholar Didier Maleuvre, begins by recounting the criticisms that accompanied the opening of the Louvre—one of the first public museums—in Paris in 1793, articulated particularly in

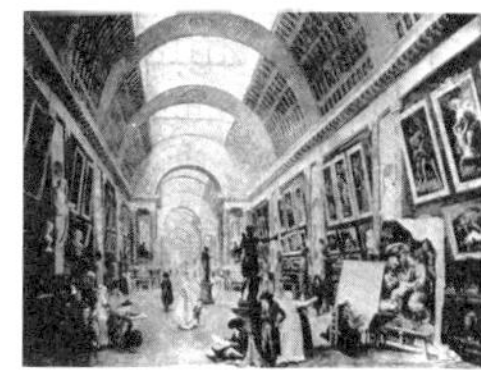

Fig 6   Hubert Robert, *Refurbishment project of the Grande Galerie of the Louvre*, 1796, oil on canvas, 115 x 145 cm, Musée du Louvre, Paris

---

15   Didier Maleuvre, *Museum Memories: History, Technology, Art* (Redwood City, CA: Stanford University Press, 1999).

the writings of the influential Quatremère de Quincy.[16] Maleuvre notes that at the heart of his critique was the argument that artworks should be seen in their original context for their true meaning to be understood. 'An art work without its original context vanishes,' he writes.[17] For De Quincy, the 'social dictates' as Maleuvre calls them, are the most pressing thing when understanding the work of art—its publicness, its authenticity, and he even goes so far as to point to its 'use' writing: 'I need to find them useful, in order to find them beautiful.'[18]

Contemporaneous to De Quincy's critique of the Louvre is the introduction of Kant's notions of the 'disinterested spectator' and 'purposeless purpose' which, Wright would argue, were both set up to empty the aesthetic experience of notions of use and subjectivity.[19] Viewed from this perspective, the primary philosophical and experiential ingredients of the modern museum experience was one that sought to create distance, both literal and conceptual, between the work of art and the world at large. Fast forward over two hundred years and the problems encountered by the display of user-based practices is not entirely new.

For Kant and subsequently many others this distancing is what allows artworks and their contexts to be meaningfully mediated and for a political space to be formed. Indeed, Maleuvre sees De Quincy's critique and insistence on 'art's entrenchment in immanence' as a far more potent neutralizing factor than the context of the institution.[20] If they are unable to reflect on the culture out of which they sprung, they have no critical traction. Hegel is the figure who is crucial in articulating that the work of art only in fact appears once it abstracts itself from the framework of what he describes as 'empirical immediacy.'

---

16 The influential artist, art historian, and then director of the Académie des Beaux-Arts (1816–1839), Quatremère wielded huge influence as a cultural actor and commentator in late eighteenth, early nineteenth-century Paris.
17 Maleuvre, *Museum Memories*, p. 32.
18 Ibid.
19 Significantly, Wright's argument doesn't acknowledge that this emptying out was seen by Kant as a means to distinguish the private interest from the common good, which would serve as a prerequisite to engage with the latter.
20 Wright, *Toward a Lexicon of Usership*, p. 33.

Maleuvre recounts: 'Hegel reveals that what Quatremère holds to be the very heart of the artwork, its original context, is actually merely incidental. Where the artwork once belonged is a comparatively superficial matter, Hegel claims.' It is the move into the museum that allows a mediation on the artwork and its context to take place.

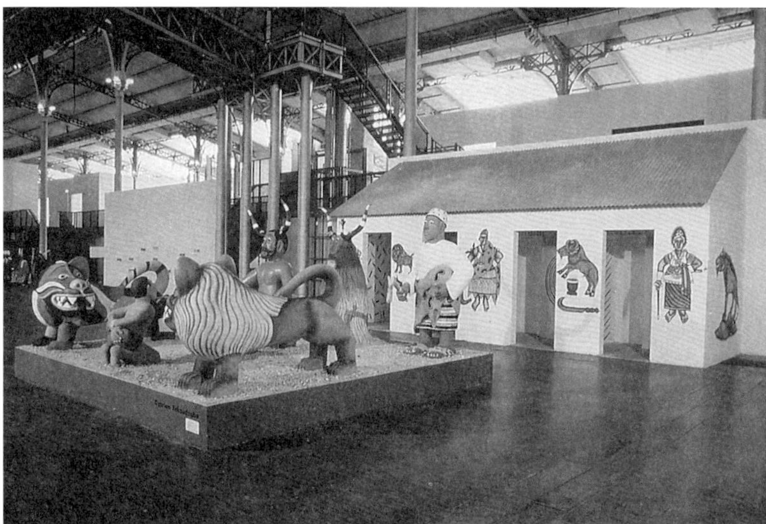

Fig 7   Exhibition view *Magiciens de la terre*, curated by Jean-Hubert Martin, La Grande Halle, Parc de la Villette, Paris, 1989

Yet when one thinks how the space of the museum has evolved into the architecture of the modernist white cube, the potential of the distancing of display becomes subsumed within a context and political formation all its own—namely that of a modernist, Western construction with a specific mode of conditioning, both of the art it presents and the subjects it speaks to. This becomes most explicit with the Western museum's move to incorporate artworks form the so-called 'global south.' Think of the de-contextualizing move made by the curators of *Magiciens de la terre* at the Centre Pompidou, Paris in 1989, for example, who purported to present artworks from outside the West next to their European and American counterparts on an equal footing, giving primacy to the materiality and formal quality of the objects themselves.[21] Such a strategy took place within the framework of the white cube or its moving image counterpart, the black box, meaning the cultural context of the work of art becomes determined not through understanding the origins out of which it came, but through its colonial capture in the museum. Museum framing, far from opening up new readings and political potential, freezes its contents. Returning to Maleuvre, such a freezing is indicative of the contradiction of museum display: 'Museums are paradoxical: they shelter restlessness but in doing so, they build a home around it.' He goes on:

> The museum thus manifests modern culture in the grip of a capitalist dynamic of historical production. Museums replicate the tensions of capital, with its fits of accumulation and expenditure, stockpiling and liquidation: museums preserve culture in a permanent state of rootlessness, that is they choose rootlessness as the principle by which to conserve culture. In capitalism as in the museum, rootlessness turns into a principle, into permanent impermanence.[22]

Such a position is a worrying indictment, yet the contradiction is persuasive. For if we accept the 'paradox' of culture's rootlessness within the museum and that this 'replicates' the tensions of capital, the supposed political or interpretive potential afforded by the space of the museum and the distance of display seems increasingly untenable. Viewed in this light, the contradiction inherent within a *Museum of Arte Útil* is indicative of a wider paradox implicit within museum display: that museum display mirrors capitalist conditioning. The task today would appear to be how to foster, rather than conserve, a condition of restlessness?

21　See Pablo Lafuente, 'Introduction: From the Outside In—"Magiciens de la Terre" and Two Histories of Exhibitions,' in *Making Art Global (Part 2): 'Magiciens de la Terre' 1989*, Lucy Steeds et al. Exhibition Histories Series (London: Afterall, 2013), pp. 8–23.
22　Maleuvre, *Museum Memories*, pp. 38–39.

III. Toward a Museum of Usership

How then to accommodate fluid approaches that themselves seek to confront or escape institutional and market capture? How to open up the institution to the modes of working and relations instituted in projects like TY10 or *Freehouse*? A first step would appear to be to engage in notions of usership outside the rubric of the exhibition. This is not to denounce the format but, rather like Wright's notion of the 'deactivation of art's aesthetic function,' let it recede into the background. Such a move would serve to re-calibrate the modes of address within the museum, collapsing the distance inherent within display. Similarly, it would mean accepting that the roles assigned to those entering the museum are put in a state of flux. As writer Jesús Carrillo points out, it would need to move beyond a definition of the viewing, visiting, or using subject through its sense of lack 'in contrast with the luminous subject defined by the Enlightenment.'[23] In this way the museum would need to insist on not speaking to a predefined subject but as functioning as a space for different voices to emerge and be articulated.

Such a dissolution of roles could be extended to the relationships the museum has into different parts of civil society. This emphasis on an engagement with broader parts of civil society, what David Forgacs, editor of *The Antonio Gramsci Reader: Selected Writings 1916–1935* (2000) has defined in relation to the Italian political theorist's use of the term, as 'the sum of social activities and institutions which are not directly part of the government, the judiciary or repressive bodies' would see the museum as a site for different constituents to come together.[24] Such a move would mean that the institution would shift from representing or hosting a project like Van Heeswijk's *Freehouse*, to seeing how the museum itself could foster and accommodate different users that are part of civil society, allowing micro-political

---

23 See Jesús Carrillo, 'Museos del Sur' in this reader, pp. 346–355.
24 David Forgacs, ed., *The Antonio Gramsci Reader: Selected Writings 1916–1935* (New York: New York University Press, 2000), p. 420.

activity to speak through the space of the institution. Importantly, understanding what Wright terms 'users' as similarly constituent parts of civil society would, following Gramsci, allow the museum to create a public space for 'sphere[s] in which a dominant social group organizes consent and hegemony.'[25] This group could use the museum to 'organise their opposition' and create a site where 'an alternative hegemony can be constructed.'[26] Such a move might allow for the as-yet unarticulated collective wishes of Wright's users to coalesce and structure a collective position. That coming together was pointed to in the *Museum of Arte Útil* with the invitation for different user-groups to 'use the museum.' Yet bound by the temporal and spatial construction of the exhibition, these relationships were inevitably blocked by not having the space they needed to evolve and form positions or by being framed through the context of an exhibition.

The drive to allow the space for relationships between the museum and its users to emerge is a binding feature of many of the partners of the L'Internationale confederation, a pan-European project involving museums and universities that sees one of its aims as exploring how institutions in the twenty-first century might open up to different constituencies. One clear example is the collaboration between Museo Reina Sofía in Madrid and Fundación de los Comunes, also in Spain. The Fundación, which was formed as a network of cultural groups, activists, and intellectuals in the wake of the financial crisis, has been working with Museum Reina Sofía since 2012, looking specifically at the central problems in political organization and agency outside the representational sphere. One of the main outcomes of this relationship has been the open source document 'Charter for Europe.'[27] The charter attempts to map a new direction for Europe 'proclaiming

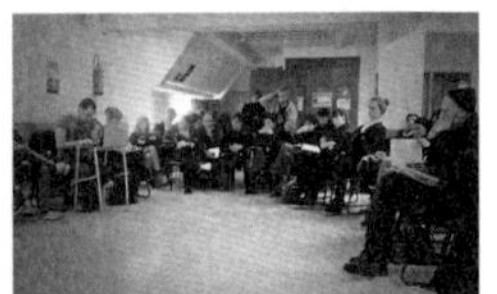

Fig 8 *Democracy*, workshop during the event *The New Abduction of Europe*, February 27-28th and March 1, 2014, MNCARS, in the Museo Reina Sofía, Madrid, 2014

---

25 Ibid.
26 Ibid.
27 See 'Charter for Europe, 1.2,' Real Democracy, L'Internationale, 5 September 2014, www.internationaleonline.org/research/real_democracy/8_charter_for_europe_1_2. The charter was written as the outcome of the large scale 'encounter' titled 'The New Abduction of Europe,' Museo Reina Sofía, Madrid, 27 February–1 March 2014.

without any doubt that the only way to make democracy real is for us all to become its protagonists—all of us who inhabit the European space, all of us who cross it, all of us who experience it.'[28] As a model for how the museum might work toward accommodating emerging political subjects and energies to counter existing hegemonic structures, the 'Charter for Europe' is a compelling example. Significantly, this collaboration has been fostered outside the constraints of exhibition making and without preconceived goals linked to museum programming.

The mode of working between Reina Sofía and Fundación de los Comunes operates as a genuine platform for the museum to serve as a site to rethink the state. Here it chimes with what theorist and writer Gerald Raunig has called for when he has argued for the museum to play a lead role in re-imagining state structures within the dying remains of European social democracy. Calling on the museum to disrupt what he sees as the flatness of neoliberal society he writes:

> [T]his implies no less than newly inventing the state, specifically because and while it still rudimentarily functions. Or rather: it implies inventing a new form of state apparatus while the old one still exists. This re-invention of the state apparatus from below can only succeed as re-territorializing the institution, if it is tried out from many different sides, in small contexts, in a micro-measure, and in radical openness to questions of organisation.[29]

Raunig's proposal is bold. Yet it speaks explicitly to the necessity to think beyond the museum's role of critiquing the status quo and addressing subjects through their sense of 'lack.' Or, as Raunig states, a move 'from the critique of the institution in the direction of instituting.'[30]

---

28 Ibid.
29 Gerald Raunig, 'Flatness Rules: Instituent Practices and Institutions of the Common in a Flat World,' in *Institutional Attitudes: Instituting Art in a Flat World*, ed. Pascal Gielen (Amsterdam: Valiz 2013), pp. 172–173.
30 Ibid., p. 176.

It demands, in line with notions of usership, a shift in emphasis and redirection of resources to pursuing different forms of civic engagements that foster subjectivities through the museum and are not defined by it. It calls for the museum to operate as a space of contestation and negotiation where new 'consents' and 'hegemonies,' as defined by different forms of civil society, could emerge.

If such initiatives could be meaningfully maintained it would point us toward Raunig's call to open up the museum, allowing them to become what he terms 'institutions of the common.'[31] This, in turn, would usher in Raunig's additional layer of potential in the 'common': 'the common as the self-organization of social co-operation' or 'the political project of instituting the common.' Raunig's understanding of the common as 'the concatenation of singular currents, of the re-composition of multiplicity' offers a means with which to imagine how the museum might go beyond the distancing mechanisms of display.[32] It suggests a potential thaw in the freezing of 'restlessness' that Maleuvre saw as mirroring the processes and currents of capitalism. It speaks to a fluid, uncontainable proximity between subject and institution, pointing toward a reconfiguration in the way in which the museum relates and accommodates different forms of political subjectivity, modes of usership, and parts of civil society.

Any such move demands that we think beyond formats of display or the event cycle of institutional programming. Returning to the *Museum of Arte Útil*, as a four-month exhibition it can now be seen as a catalyst for a reflection on how the museum might work with different constituents in more expanded, meaningful ways. For if the exhibition succeeded in representing an alternative history of artistic thinking via the Arte Útil archive, as a mode of accommodating such thinking, it only began to open itself

---

31 Raunig here draws on Michael Hardt and Antonio Negri's positioning of the common as not only 'the common wealth of the material world' (the earth's natural resources) but encompassing what he calls 'those results of social production that are necessary for social interaction and further production, such as knowledge, languages, codes, information, affects and so forth Michael Hardt and Antoni Negri, *Commonwealth* (Cambridge, MA: Belknap, 2000), p. viii, cited in Raunig, 'Flatness Rules', p. 169.
32 Ibid., p. 170.

up to the types of fluid currents that Raunig identifies. It served as an exhibition of usership, somewhat short of its scaled-up museum-wide version. Significantly, its presentation in the format of an exhibition could be seen to have replicated, rather than challenged, the capitalist dynamic much of the project's rhetoric sought to oppose.

The museum is now embarking on a new phase of working with different local constituent groups and mediating Arte Útil, beyond the frame of the exhibition in collaboration with different independent and institutional partners. Working locally, we will partner with social designers, artists, curators, and organizations over extended time periods and without fixed outcomes. A first step is the mapping of practices that address issues and urgencies specific to Eindhoven, before thinking how the museum could foster such practices. These constituent groups will require time, resources, and space to form their own position, both in relation to the topics they wish to address, as well as toward the institution itself. It will involve the museum resisting the need to define (both to itself and its funders) the outcomes of such processes, which must therefore remain unknown. Yet if it is successful it offers the possibility for different constituent groups to coalesce and form new subject positions, a collective usership emerging through the civic space of the institution. Then the museum might yet serve as a site to oppose, not replicate, the political and cultural constraints of our current conjuncture.

Essay
Jesús Carrillo

Museos del Sur

In 1964, Minimalism was taking its first steps and Jean Tinguely was showing his self-destructive machines around the world. Significantly, it was also in that year that Jean-Luc Godard's characters in *Bande à part* ran through the endless galleries of the Louvre in nine minutes, closing down the old time of museums—theatrical, empty, and baroque—and opening up the new time of contemporary experience.

This time required new narratives, architectures, and subject positions. Yet Godard's prophecy, with its Futurist and Situationist overtones, would not be fulfilled—at least not in the way he had imagined; we need only consider the historical drift following '68, and the subsequent postmodern turn.

The so-called 'end of history' inferred in Godard's film implied both the impossibility of projecting ourselves into the future, as Godard's characters wished, but also the tendency to mimic and remediate old-fashioned models, to make pastiche the dominant form of dealing with the past. Museums flourished as providers of this commodified version of history and art. In 1983 museum designer and artist Rémy Zaugg stated that museums' obligation as guardians of the autonomous condition of artistic experience should be understood as part of this regressive and narcissistic turn—especially if we consider the context of the market ideology dominating, and still dominating, the art world and its institutions.

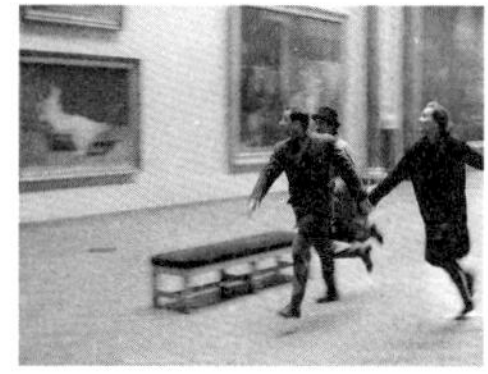

Fig 1 Jean-Luc Godard made the characters of *Bande à part*, 1964

Despite the different waves of new and critical museologies, and the current credence given to interactive and participatory models, museums still perform a bourgeois mise-en-scène. The autonomous beholding of artworks in the museum was one of the most perfect rituals of the enlightened public sphere. By means of aesthetic judgment individuals became conscious of their nature as autonomous subjects, and as members of a political community, a republic of free men. Anachronism is a consubstantial feature of the contemporary museum experience. The museum—including that of contemporary art—is generally recognized by people as an archaic dispositive, even if such archaism might increase its appeal both as a quality touristic product and its authority and power. The contemporary ritual of the museum visit to a great extent imitates the bourgeois public sphere as pastiche, spectacularized, and ready for easy consumption, bearing the ideological mission of presenting it as the apex of the civilization process, once devoid of its emancipation promises.

Yet there is also the possibility to use such anachronisms to reveal the dystopic condition of the present and the need to imagine new public spheres in which to articulate contemporary struggles. In *Une visite au Louvre*, released in 2004, the filmmaker duo Straub-Huillet (Danièle Huillet and Jean-Marie Straub) recovered the slow tempo of aesthetic vision that their colleague Godard had discarded forty years earlier. They did it, however, by making its anachronistic nature explicit: with their camera they enacted the analytic gaze of a young Cézanne beholding the paintings of the great masters displayed in the Louvre, at the threshold of the avant-garde. They seem to say that the terms of contemporary vision are incommensurable with those of the museum, and that only by means of a temporary *décalage* [shift] might it be possible to bind the eyes and the bodies of visitors to the patterns of attention and rhythms required by the sequence of framed images.

In order to 'see' the paintings by Veronese, Ingres, or Delacroix as they are displayed in the Louvre, we should become aware of a subject position alien to our contemporary experience. The absorbed and analytic gaze solicited by the museum should be referred to through fictions—literary, cinematographic, and theatrical mediations which activate our imagination. The scope of these fictions does not need to be the ideological alienation of visitors, nor the production of exciting simulacra, nor the provision of adequate settings for the rituals of new elites. Quite the opposite: the anachronistic and theatrical dispositive of museum displays may have the power to incite in passersby an exceptional degree of 'Brechtian consciousness' of their own gaze. With this they might make visible the shades cast by their own physical, biographical, and political bodies upon any persona they are asked to incarnate. In Straub-Huillet's film, an invisible feminine voice 'recites' the impressions of Cézanne over the images of the paintings, preventing us from identifying with the eye of the artist. The first images contrast the slow pace of Cézanne's gaze with

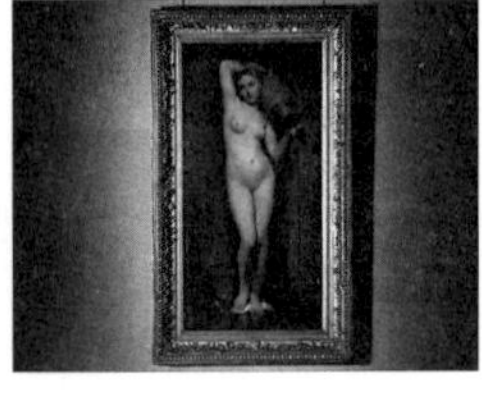

Fig 2 Straub-Huillet, *Une visite au Louvre*, 2004, screen capture

the intense Paris traffic, underscoring the vacant space of the contemporary 'public.'

Pointing to that vacant space, and the need to perform a position upon time, past, present, and future, was particularly urgent in the case of the Museo Nacional Centro de Arte Reina Sofía in Madrid when Manuel Borja-Villel's team, which included myself, started in 2008. On the one hand, the institution's peripheral position within the hegemonic narratives of modernity resulted in a provincial and colonial image of its collections, according to which any local artistic process appeared as an imperfect version of movements that had emerged elsewhere. The biographical approach to Spain's diasporic artists: Miró, Picasso, and Dalí only reinforced the subaltern temporality defined either by an anxiety of lack or a nostalgia of loss. On the other hand the museum was haunted by the ghosts of a recent past seized by decades of dictatorship, and constrained by the subsequent institutionalization of the avant-garde during the democratic transition that brought about a normative and canonical narrative. The only instance in which history and the autonomous development of avant-garde art crossed paths was with Picasso's *Guernica* (1939), placed as the totem in the centre of the museum, absorbing and solving all traumas and conflicts.

The financial crisis since 2008, which in Spain is also institutional, made the recovery of a *hic et nunc* [here and now] urgent so that the museum might project a recognizable point of view, shaking off the historiographical inertias, breaking silence, and shedding light on dead angles. It was essential to provide the visitor with the possibility to face and recognize the contingencies of our uncertain times. This involved taking a position on the stage and rehearsing a new voice in a play that is always unfinished and facing an audience whose expectations were still unknown. The notion of *Museos del Sur*, as proposed by the director of the museum,[1] linked the

---

1   See http://elpais.com/diario/2008/12/20/babelia/1229731569_850215.html.

consideration of these dilemmas to a radical rereading of global modernity, in which the imperial eye of the museum had, as a necessary counterpart, the gazes of the subaltern, always fragmentary, contingent, performative, and resilient.

The methodological implications of this 'Southern' model had already been rehearsed in a previous project, *Desacuerdos* begun in 2002 but which was constrained by the Spanish context.[2] Taking philosopher Jacques Rancière's reference as a point of departure, *Desacuerdos* brought together cultural institutions, activists, artists, and researchers within an experimental project, multiple and dysphonic, which intend to set up narratives against the grain of the official history of the Spanish democratic transition. *Desacuerdos* explored the possibility of locating a counter-hegemonic voice within the institution through a process of conflict and negotiation, as well as the forms of historicization related to the dissonant nature of the project. The activist, artist, and theorist Marcelo Expósito, proposed an epistemological break with canonical histories by politically rebinding the dispersed fragments of the past and the present in a diagrammatic and performative action of storytelling, which, he said, 'may allow [us] to understand the way artistic artifacts bear the traces of their specific historical condition.'[3] The notions of montage and 'variable eye,' taken from film theory were easily transferrable to the notions of mise-en-scène and theatricality used by the museum.

The first curatorial movement toward a Museo del Sur would be to break the hegemony of the abstract present imposed by the museum, triggering a dense time awareness which would encourage visitors to locate themselves in their hic et nunc in order to deal with a range of multiple and diverse chronologies: the time of looking, the parallactic distance with regard to the

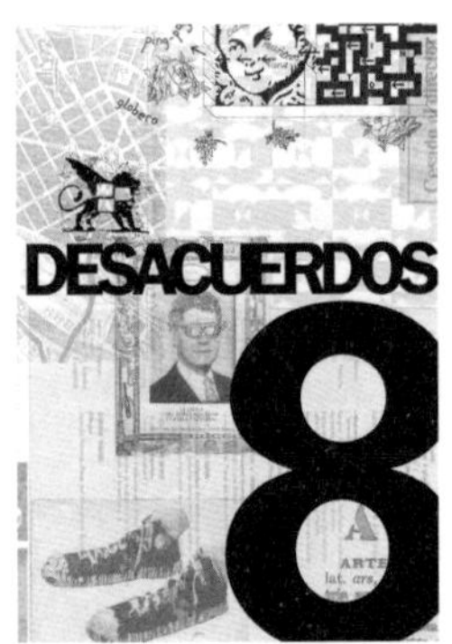

Fig 3   Cover of the magazine *Desacuerdos. Sobre arte, políticas y esfera pública en el Estado español* no. 8

2   *Desacuerdos* consisted of a series of seminars, exhibitions, and publications from 2003 to 2005. The project has continued as a journal under the title *Desacuerdos: Sobre arte, políticas y esfera pública en el Estado español*.

3   Marcelo Expósito, 'Diferencias y antagonismos: Protocolos para una historia política del arte en el Estado español,' *Desacuerdos: Arte, políticas y esfera pública en el Estado español* no. 1 (2004), p. 115. Translation by author.

different strata of the past, the specific time and space of the artworks, the sequences, and the before, then, and after. The museum *should become* a heterochronic space where the polarity between a blind now and a reified past is broken into many pieces, suggesting many possible times, contradictory and overlapping and activating the frictions attached to the politics of memory.

The appeal of the original artistic object, the historical document, and the vintage photograph should be carefully used in order to avoid replacing the literal experience of time with an auratic, reverential distance, conveyors of reified images of the past. The staging of the objects as part of a situation, a crossroads in which different determinations and accidents, subjectivities, and wills converge, and not as monuments of a closed temporality, or as beads of a rosary infinitely repeated, has the power to provide the visitors with an intense perception of their own historical time and their role as agents within an open temporality.

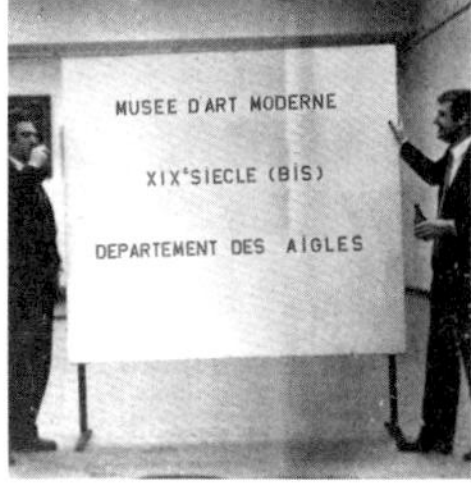

Fig 4 Marcel Broodthaers, *Musée d'Art Moderne, Département des Aigles*, 1975, mixed media

To explore the multiple registers of the artwork became an essential tool in this sense: the material, iconic, formal, poetic, historic, biographic, documental, and so on, outlining some atop others, without ever suppressing them completely in each specific mise-en-scène, as if conducting an orchestra. The versatile nature of the artistic artifact multiplies the narrative and expressive resources available while transmitting a sensation of lightness and openness to the visitors. They are no longer constrained to recognizing the sameness as well as closed and auratic nature of the artwork, but are exposed to their capacity to be vehicles of difference and transformation within an emancipation process.

As a good narrator, this voice should awake expectations, provoke tensions, offer paradoxes and riddles, reveal mysteries, and suggest possible drifts. It should change registers, rehearsing that 'variable eye,' moving from direct speech to detached historical analysis, from sharing intimacy to shouting a manifesto aloud. This voice should activate the minds of the visitors without absorbing their imagination completely, or blocking their capacity to judge, the stimulation of which should be the main goal of the museum.

Finally, 'the voice' of the museum should be modulated in order to reveal its contingent and located nature, thus suspending the fiction of an autonomous artistic truth only waiting to be institutionally displayed. It needs to appear as part of a communicative action which links narrator and recipient within a process of producing meaning. This voice should not be identified with that of the 'author,' a singular voice that would replace one figure of authority (the abstract canon of art history) with that of an exceptional individual. The goal would be to incarnate the voice of a narrator who speaks from a collective and plural 'us' that seeks the complicity of the 'listeners,' creating the conditions for them 'to speak up.'

Who is this 'us'? It cannot be named in terms of identity. It is not the nation, but it is neither 'the human kind.' It congregates around the storytelling, becoming a community of listeners or viewers which feel their commonality when being addressed in a specific time and a specific space, very much as in *The Canterbury Tales*.

Even if we, the team at the museum at this time, choose not to speak to the affluent class, nor to an undifferentiated mass of tourists, it is true that we still address a subject defined in terms of lack, a disempowered subject, imagined in relation to or in contrast with the luminous subject defined by the Enlightenment. It is the subject inflicted upon by the alienating conditions and struggles of late capitalism who, with the aid of the museum would become aware of the ideological nature of the system we live in, starting with the art world and the museum itself (institutional critique).

To an extent, our task is then to provide critical tools to understand a system which we may not have the capacity to change. Would we be ready to deal with a new kind of subject not defined by deprivation but by expectations and desires which go beyond the apparent 'immanence' of current capitalism? Would we be ready to deal with a subject that is already experimenting with other forms of organization and producing its own imaginaries? What if the South started making sense of the world beyond and without our mediations? Could the museum still be a suitable scenario for the performance of this new subjectivity? This is very much an open question.

If undertaken this would probably be a radically different sort of theatricality. As noted above, the rituals of the modern museum identified the subject of the public sphere with the individual who walked and looked surrounded by other anonymous and autonomous bodies and looks, like ours, without having any business, any competition, or any conflict.

Our favourite artists in the museum are those who, like Michelangelo Pistoletto, Marcel Broodthaers, or Godard, questioned the disposition of bodies and spaces defined by capitalist disciplinary society, back in the 1960s. To raise awareness of the alienating nature of such dispositions was never enough. In the last decades there have been very few occasions on which leaving that trench and going out into the open air seemed feasible, monopolized as it was by 'no places' or 'junk spaces.' We are all familiar with museums that did this, becoming similar to airports or shopping malls.

The ground has lately, however, been drastically modified by the *puissance* of new articulations of minds, bodies, and affections with hegemonic claims. In the Arab Spring(s), with the Spanish indignados, and the different forms of the Occupy movement, people did not see themselves any longer as 'protesters' or anti-system, but as central political subjects.

Our critical invocation of the spectres of the modern public sphere need to be negotiated now with a 'political body' which is still in process, but demands to be recognized. It is not enough anymore for them to occupy, precariously, spaces and structures that they considered to be obsolete. They are already imagining new forms of institutional organization and devising strategies to take power. According to Antonio Negri's intervention in the 'New Abduction of Europe' conference earlier this year, a new 'constituent' process may be starting, full of uncertainties and ambivalences.[4] The most repeated claim of the Spanish indignados *'que no nos representan'* not only denounces the crisis of existing institutions but proclaims the upcoming of a new political subject demanding different forms of mediation.

This situation affects the very basis of the museum, since this subject does not have any desire to be the consumer of our cultural products, or the user of our services, as defined either by marketing strategies or by sophisticated specialists. The museums, heirs of the Enlightenment and the compromises of the bourgeois revolutions of the nineteenth century, are urged to strategically suspend their established institutional authority and provide the conditions for a negotiation, a scenario in which the personae of the new play can rehearse their voices.

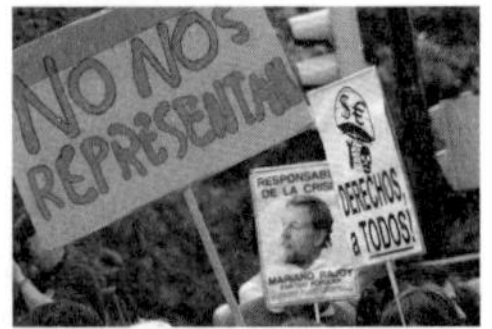

Fig 5 12-M-15-M anti-austerity marches in Madrid in May 2012

4 'The New Abduction of Europe: Debt, War, Democratic Revolutions,' conference, co-organized by Fundación del los Comunes and Museo Nacional Centro de Arte Reina Sofía, Madrid, 27 February–1 March 2014, www.museoreinasofia.es/en/activities/new-abduction-europe.

The museum *should become* a heterochronic space where the polarity between a blind now and a reified past is broken into many pieces.

Quote
Jesús Carillo,
Museos del Sur
→ **See p. 351**

We wanted to allow history to unfold in the now, to proclaim it as not being finished and defined and test it for the present.

Quote
What, How & for Whom,
Really Útil Confessions
→ **See p. 463**

Essay
Steven ten Thije

The Time of Display, the Display of Time

ALOIS RIEGL, ALEXANDER DORNER, AND THE CHANGING HISTORICITY OF MUSEUM DISPLAYS

This text deals with the influence of the Viennese art historian Alois Riegl on German curator Alexander Dorner's museum displays and notion of art history.[1] Such scholarly excursion might seem somewhat out of place in a reader dealing with the question of art and its use and far away from the concerns of the exhibition *Confessions of the Imperfect, 1848–1989–Today*, which I co-curated together with Alistair Hudson at the Van Abbemuseum and which is one of the exhibitions that inspired this publication.

---

1   In the text I use 'museum display' for collection presentations and 'exhibitions' for temporary exhibitions. When discussing the space I use 'museum room' instead of 'museum gallery' to avoid any confusion with commercial galleries.

Yet the concerns that inform this research are very close to the questions central to this book overall.

The main concern of *Confessions* was to map an alternative art history taking its cue from John Ruskin and his particular manner of understanding art as useful. Hudson's essay in this reader outlines this objective very well (see pp. 32–47). However, to present this alternative history, we could not only focus on art and use as such, but needed to present a scenario *about* use. In the end we were telling a story and therefore needed to reactivate the possibility of the museum to present a history through a display. What type of art history informed this display and what kind of strategy would we use to present the narrative? These were key questions we had to deal with.

To then turn to the work of Riegl and Dorner might still be surprising. Why not explore an art historian and curator who might be closer to the narrative presented in *Confessions* like Ruskin? The truth is that I personally arrived at the question of art and use through studying the work of Dorner, and later Riegl. It was by trying to understand the value of the historical narrative in museum display and even more widely in the field of exhibition making that the terrain of art and use opened up for me. This interest first led me to the early twentieth-century reform in German museums and the work of Dorner. It was Dorner's generation who broke through the aristocratic hull of the museum, used by experts or rich dilettantes, and transformed it into a useful tool for educating the masses. In Dorner's own words: 'The main quality and activity of an art museum should not be directed primarily on the *collecting* of artworks, but on what it *does* with its collection.'[2] The two questions I asked myself in response to this change were, first, why did they consider presenting a legible art history to a layman's public to be important, and, second, how did they believe that they could actually achieve this? In this text, working backward, I hope that

---

2   Dorner quoted in Tobias Wall, *Das unmögliche Museum: Zum Verhältnis von Kunst und Kunstmuseen der Gegenwart* (Bielefeld: Transcript, 2006), p. 204.

by shedding light on the second question, we can hint at the first. Whereby I will return again to *Confessions* and how it relates to what was uncovered in my research.

The Historicity of Museum Displays

Art exhibitions, especially in museums, always inspire a historical reading. The historicity of museum displays, however, has changed over time. In the nineteenth century there was a quite clear division of roles, whereby the salons and for instance in Paris the Palais du Luxembourg would present the works of living artists for the public to judge for its merit.[3] Museums, such as the Louvre, presented those works that left the earthly competition and entered the permanent mausoleum of eternal beauty. This understanding is quite beautifully symbolized in the architecture of the Altes Museum in Berlin by architect and painter Karl Friedrich Schinkel, who placed a circular space with a dome in the middle and a ring of sculptures at the edge, altogether acting as a symbol of eternal perfection.[4]

In the early twentieth century this clear division between living artist and canon was disrupted. Especially in Germany, where a group of young museum directors inspired by the innovative work of the older art historian and curator Wilhelm Bode in the Kaiser-Friedrich-Museum in Berlin, started to introduce a new type of exhibition practice.[5] The new style of collection display approached the museum room as an aesthetic unity, which allowed the works to be perceived in a concentrated manner by using a sober display strategy. Rejecting both the salon hangings whereby works were crammed floor to ceiling on the wall, and the period room, in which works were presented under presumed 'authentic' conditions, the new style of display focused on maximizing the effect of the work on the viewer. In this sense these displays can be understood as

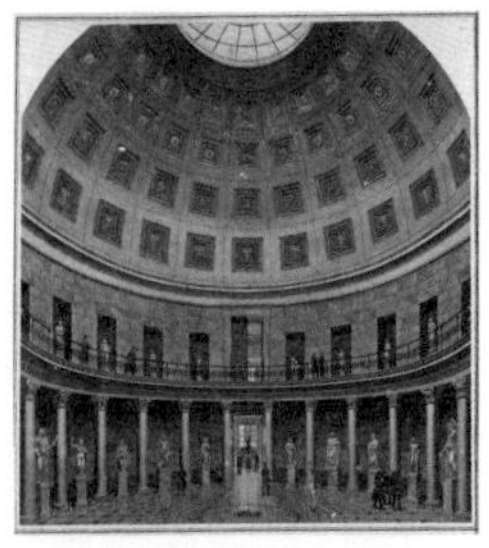

Fig 1   Carl Emanuel Conrad, Rotunde in der Farbgebung des 19. Jahrhunderts (Rotunda in 19th century-colouring), water colour

3   See Jesús Pedro Lorente, *Cathedrals of Urban Modernity: The First Museums of Contemporary Art, 1800–1930* (Aldershot, VT: Ashgate, 1998).

4   A good discussion of the formation of the Altes Museum appears in James J. Sheehan, *Geschichte der deutsche Kunstmuseen: Von der fürstlichen Kunstkammer zur modernen Sammlung*, trans. Martin Pfeiffer (Munich: C.H. Beck, 2002), pp. 113–128.

5   See Alexis Joachimides, *Die Museumsreformbewegung in Deutschland und die Entstehung des modernen Museums 1880–1940* (Dresden: Verlag der Kunst, 2001).

the first predecessors of the White Cube exhibition model that became so hegemonic in the later twentieth century. Even if the motives that inspired this transformation were diverse and conflicting, many strategies developed in this period are still used today.[6] To establish a genealogy of current exhibition strategies the early twentieth century remains an important period to revisit.

This innovative moment in the history of exhibition making has been quite well researched.[7] However, what perhaps has not been explored with as much rigour is the manner in which new art historical theories have affected museum display. What kind of understanding of art and history and the relation between the two informed these displays? Alexis Joachimides, a museum historian who wrote one of the most comprehensive and detailed accounts of this transformation, does emphasize the importance of the professionalization of art history for the German museum reform movement, but then doesn't go into detail on which art historical theory influenced which display strategy.[8] Art historian Charlotte Klonk, who wrote another impressive study on this subject, focuses strongly on the psychology of perception and colour theory in these early displays, which is very relevant and accurate, but leaves out some important aspects of the art historical theories that helped form these museum displays.[9] The influence of Riegl on Dorner is one of these moments of cross-pollination between art history and innovative forms of museum displays, which is worthwhile to explore further. The recent studies of historian Michael Gubser into the concept of history in Riegl's work, shed

---

6   See especially the first chapters of Charlotte Klonk, *Space of Experience, Art Gallery Interiors from 1800 to 2000* (New Haven: Yale University Press, 2009), pp. 1–134.
7   Notably in ibid. and Joachimides, *Die Museumsreformbewegung*.
8   Joachimides, *Die Museumsreformbewegung*, pp. 24–30.
9   Klonk, *Space of Experience*, pp. 50–133.

new light on the relationship between the two.[10] What makes the relation between them especially important for this investigation is the fact that Riegl's approach to art history inspired a much more educational, and perhaps one could even say 'useful' museum display.

Alois Riegl and the Anthropological Historicity of Art

Alois Riegl was an art historian who considered himself and his generation as standing at the beginning of a new chapter in the discipline.[11] He understood his immediate predecessors, the art historians of the late nineteenth century, as marking the second phase of the discipline, which was deeply positivist and primarily preoccupied with the fieldwork of establishing chronologies. Before that, the first generation of dilettante art historians, especially Georg Hegel, had practiced a more synthetic model, integrating the whole history of art in a coherent development of Spirit. Riegl understood himself and his generation of art historians to be introducing a third phase in the history of the discipline that would be able to integrate again within the positivist method a sense of the synthetic form of historiography of the first phase. He took from the first generation the idea that art should be understood as one element of the general development of mankind, yet he took from his immediate predecessors the desire to allow art itself to speak, instead of considering it a mere expression of some more fundamental notion as Spirit. Only through the detailed study of art itself could one arrive at more generic insights.

At first sight Riegl's general understanding of history is rigorous, if not absolutist, positivist. For him time knew only one direction: forward. As he stated in the

---

10 Within both Joachimides's and Klonk's study Dorner is somewhat of a side figure, even if Klonk in particular discusses him in greater detail. Recently Sandra Karina Löschke wrote closely about the relationship between Riegl and Dorner. However, she does not go into the specific aspect of the notion of history used by the two and this is what I want to focus on here. Sandra Karina Löschke, 'Material Aesthetics and Agency: Alexander Dorner and the Stage-managed Museum,' in 'Immaterial Materialities,' ed. Sandra Karina Löschke and Desly Luscombe, *Interstices* 14 (2013), special issue. See also Michael Gubser, *Time's Visible Surface: Alois Riegl and the Discourse on History and Temporality in Fin-de-Siècle Vienna* (Detroit: Wayne State University Press, 2006).

11 Wolfgang Kemp, 'Alois Riegl, 1858–1905,' in *Altmeister Moderner Kunstgeschichte*, ed. Heinrich Dilly (Berlin: Dietrich Reimer Verlag, 1990), pp. 37–62.

introduction of his study on the late-Roman art industry: 'the development [of artistic form] does not only know no regression, it even knows no pause.'[12] He broke with the well-established tradition that considered time as following annual seasons, whereby regressive periods of fall and winter would be superseded by moments of rebirth identified as spring or summer. Instead in his most influential books—*Late Roman Art Industry* (1901) and *The Group Portraiture of Holland* (1902)—he goes to great pains to uncover the progressive element in artistic movements, which his contemporaries deemed regressive.[13]

Even if normally qualified as 'formalist,' Riegl's particular approach to art history could also be described as a form of anthropological positivism. His analysis of the development of artistic forms was quite different from the traditional comparisons with standards of 'good taste' or transcendental principles of beauty. He more mapped an anthropological development of different modes of human interaction with the world and the role artistic or aesthetic sensibility played within it.[14] At each moment in history human beings deploy certain techniques to decode their sense impressions and these techniques translate in the forms used in human production, be they tools, buildings, artworks, or even written text. Instead of focusing on masterpieces alone, he therefore deployed a more cultural form of art history. Formulated in quite extreme terms in a text on the modern *Denkmalkultus,* he stated that each document and artifact shaped by man is 'formed' and as a result is linked to the field of aesthetics.[15] Not that each artifact is equally valuable from

---

12 Alois Riegl, *Spätrömische Kunstindustrie* (Darmstad: Wissenschaftliche Buchgesellschaft, 1973 [1927]), p. 10.

13 See Riegl, *Spätrömische Kunstindustrie* and Alois Riegl, *Das Holländische Gruppenporträt* (Vienna: Druck und Verlag der Österreichischen Staatsdruckerei, 1931).

14 The term 'aesthetic' is complicated in this discussion. I use it not to refer to the academic study of 'beautiful' form, or as a 'logos' of beauty, but to describe the study of human experience and to stress that Riegl was not only interested in an ontological analysis of the artistic forms as material thing, but also in the epistemological function of artistic forms on the viewer. This resonates with Wolfgang Kemp's suggestion to see Riegl as one of the first to write a history of reception. Kemp, 'Alois Riegl,' pp. 54–56.

15 Alois Riegl, 'Der moderne Denkmalskultus, sein Wesen und seine Entstehung,' in *George Dehio, Alois Riegl: Konservieren, nicht restaurieren: Streitschriften zur Denkmalpflege um 1900*, ed. Ulrich Conrads (Braunschweig: Friedrich Vieweg & Sohn, 1988), p. 44.

an artistic perspective, but there is no absolute divide between art and non-art. More importantly he stated in this text that the value of this artistic shape could not be measured by a timeless standard (i.e., 'good taste' or 'transcendental principles'), but that each point in time knows its own aesthetic sensibility.[16] Aesthetics or art was one domain of the general historical development of mankind. Riegl, however, remained convinced that art represented its own field of activity and as such demanded its own method of analysis. In his study of the late Roman art industry he introduced one of his most cryptic terms to define this relative independent developmental trajectory of art as the own 'will' of art: *das Kunstwollen*.[17]

The function of this independent artistic volition within the human subject thereby was understood in quite epistemological terms as being part of how humans use their senses to make sense of the world. Riegl situated art as a bridge between the material and spiritual being of man, a division reminiscent of Hegel whereby Spirit referred to the conceptual echo of the material world.[18] These two fields—Spirit and matter—were continuously negotiated in time, and art or aesthetic sensibility played a profound role in this exchange. Identifying forms and patterns through experiencing the world and then organizing and reproducing them in a new material form was one of the primary actions to arrive at understanding.

The formal patterns that would mark an artistic style or a particular artistic volition are developed out of the

---

16 Ibid., p. 46.

17 *Kunstwollen*, or artistic volition is probably the most debated term within Riegl's art historical method. Wolfgang Kemp makes it a central part in his text, but it resurfaces in most publications on Riegl. Dorner also wrote an early text on the concept, responding to an earlier publication by Erwin Panofsky, with whom he studied in Berlin. Dorner thereby picked up on the developmental quality of Riegl's notion, critiquing Panofsky's neo-Kantian reading that favoured a timeless ahistorical foundation for an apriori framework which would frame any historically determined Kunstwollen. I've written about this in '"Eeuwige theorie" tegen "historische praktijk": Alexander Dorner en Erwin Panofsky in gesprek of Alois Riegl "Kunstwollen,"' in *Étant Donné: Frank Reijnders en zijn meesterzetten: een liber amicorum*, ed. Marta Gnyp and Margriet Schavemakers (Amsterdam: G&S Publishers, 2011), pp. 63–74. See also: Erwin Panofsky, 'Der Begriff des Kunstwollens,' in *Aufsätze zu Grundfragen der Kunstwissenschaft* (Berlin: Verlag Bruno Hessling, 1974), pp. 29–43; Alexander Dorner, 'Die Erkenntnis des Kunstwollens durch die Kunstgeschichte,' *Zeitschrift für Ästhetik und Allgemeine Kunstwissenschaft* 16 (1920), pp. 219–222; and Kemp, 'Alois Riegl,' pp. 49–51.

18 See especially Gubser, 'Rhythm and Temporality in Problems of Style and Late Roman Art Industry,' in *Time's Visible Surface*, pp. 190–202.

ongoing effort of humans to order the constant flow of visual impressions. By linking series' of impressions through the identification of patterns that reoccurred, people arrive at forms that they then start to recreate. This process is temporal in nature as the main action is to align and organize different sense impressions that have occurred over a period of time. The historicity of art is thereby situated in the primordial historicity of experience itself, as it is only through time that different experiences can be compared and rhythms can be identified.

This understanding of history as immanent to the process of human comprehension then also casts a different light on academic art history. Instead of writing a history of art as autonomous entity, Riegl's history of art is more one chapter in the overall history of the development of man, which focuses on the particular ways in which human beings have deployed very different strategies to identify patterns in the physical world and transform them into reproducible shapes. In *Late Roman Art Industry* he for instance shows how earlier Greek and Roman artists use a haptic strategy, whereby the form was arrived at by tracing the outline of things with one's hands. In the late Roman period this strategy was superseded by an optical strategy that produced forms and images by analyzing optical impressions. The somewhat crude looking reliefs of this period for instance deliberately make use of shadows that combined with the physical material create an optical image in the eye. Analyzing these kinds of shifts in aesthetic strategy and understanding how they link to a general development of art and human understanding for Riegl is the primary objective of academic art history. In the words of Gubser: '[For Riegl] artworks allow viewers in the present to grasp past constructions of temporality different from their own—grasp them not as utterly foreign, but as both familiar and distinct.'[19]

---

19 Ibid., p. 202.

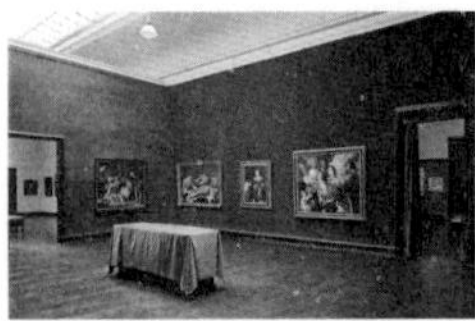

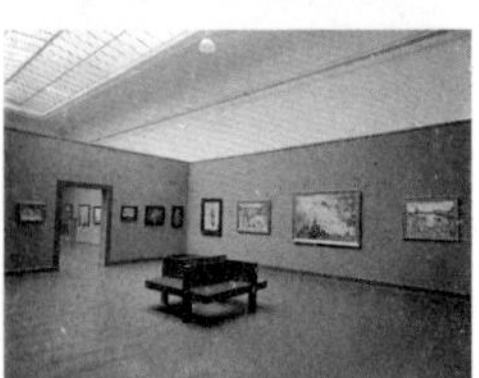

Fig 2 Room for Flemish Baroque art in the Provinzialmuseum Hannover after its reorganization by Alexander Dorner, Hannover, 1920s
Fig 3 Custom-designed bench in the room for Expressionist art in the Provinzialmuseum Hannover after its reorganization by Alexander Dorner, Hannover, 1920

Alexander Dorner's Atmosphere Rooms and the Abstract Cabinet

Riegl's insights have had quite interesting repercussions in the museum displays of Alexander Dorner, who was for some time a 'staunch partisan' of the Viennese art historian.[20] After being appointed director of Provinzialmuseum Hannover in 1925 he undertook a quite monumental effort to bring the very diverse collection of artworks and ethnographic objects together in one synthetic display.[21] The collection in Hannover was a typical nineteenth-century chaotic conglomerate of very different collections which were donated to the city and kept together as a multifaceted cultural treasure, without much desire for a unifying narrative. Riegl's art historical theory offered an effective frame to bring this diverse material together in one display for more than one reason. Firstly, Riegl's anthropological art history was helpful in organizing a collection, which next to artworks also held ethnographic objects. Secondly, it was also helpful to developing an effective display itself. Riegl's study *The Group Portraiture of Holland* appears to have been especially useful.[22] Dorner developed what he coined *Atmosphäreräume* [atmosphere rooms] which were designed to 'bring together' (he uses the German *zusammenfassen*) different works in one display.[23] The manner in which they did this is very similar to Riegl's analysis of Dutch Baroque art.

In the atmosphere rooms Dorner brought unity to a display of works from a single period through a wall tapestry with a colour that connected the different works. In the collection catalogue published alongside this installation he thereby explicitly noted that these

20 Alexander Dorner, *The Way Beyond 'Art'* (New York: New York University Press, 1958), p. 15. On Dorner's relationship to Riegl see also Samuel Cauman, *Das lebende Museum: Erfahrungen eines Kunsthistorikers und Museumsdirektors* (Hannover: Fackelträger-Verlag, 1960 [1958]), pp. 28–37.
21 On Dorner's work in Hannover see: Dorner, *The Way Beyond 'Art,'* pp. 16–19; Cauman, *Das lebende Museum*, pp. 50–123; and Wall, *Das unmögliche Museum*, pp. 204–214.
22 This is addressed in Löschke, 2015. I myself have published on this topic in: Steven ten Thije, 'A Space Beyond Dualism: On Alois Riegl's influence on Alexanders Dorner's "atmosphere rooms,"' in *Kritische Szenografie: Die Kunstausstellung im 21. Jahrhundert*, ed. Kai-Uwe Hemken (Bielefeld: Transcript, 2015), pp. 411–417.
23 Alexander Dorner, ed., *Katalog der Kunstsammlungen im Provinzialmuseum zu Hannover* (Berlin: Klinkhardt & Biermann, 1930), p. XII.

rooms should not be understood as period rooms, but function as a means to comprehend the coherence in a specific period.[24] In this sensitivity Dorner seems to follow a general preoccupation of curators at the time to use colour in a very explicit way to create contrast or synthesis in gallery displays. His particular historical approach to these colours, however, appears to have been directly influenced by his familiarity with the work of Riegl.[25]

Dorner's use of colour shows especially a great structural similarity to the manner in which Riegl analyzed the work of Rembrandt. This can be demonstrated quite clearly when looking at Riegl's analysis of *The Anatomy Lesson of Dr. Nicolaes Tulp* (1632).[26] After a quite straightforward analysis of the composition of the painting, Riegl identifies the real innovation of Rembrandt in his particular subdued colour scheme and use of shadows, which allows things to optically blend into one another. In the painting Rembrandt is able to introduce a sensation whereby the material bodies of the doctors do not appear so much as closed entities, but more as moments of 'contraction' with the space in-between as moments of '*détente.*'[27] For Riegl this blurring of boundaries between the doctors and the space in-between has profound signification and demonstrates a general blurring and becoming dynamic of the relation between subject and object.

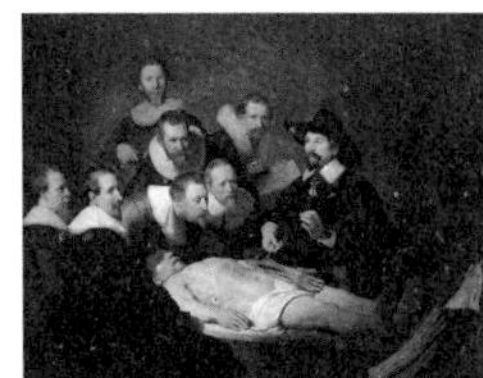

Fig 4 Aloïs Riegl's analysis of Rembrandt's *The Anatomy Lesson of Dr Nicolaes Tulp* (1632), 1902

Dorner's atmosphere rooms had a similar effect by choosing a colour specific to the period, which allowed the different artworks to optically be drawn together. The ambition of Dorner thereby is informed by an equally profound and complex rethinking of the position of the visitor to the museum. Even if also present in the atmosphere rooms themselves, to understand Dorner's objective it is helpful to look into one of his

---

24 Ibid.
25 Klonk, *Space of Experience*, p. 117.
26 Riegl, *Spätrömische Kunstindustrie*, pp. 187–189; see also Ten Thije, *Kritische Szenografie*.
27 In Riegls' words: 'so sollte in gleicher Weise auch der Freiraum bloss eine quantitative, nicht mehr eine qualitative Unterbrechung zwischen den Figurenkörpern bilden.' Riegl, *Spätrömische Kunstindustrie*, pp. 187–188.

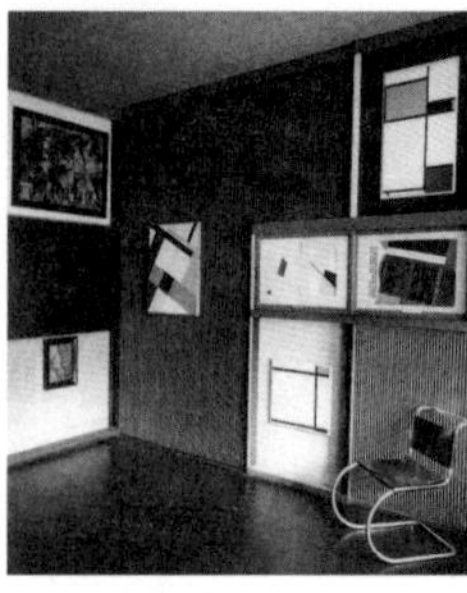

Fig 5 The *Abstract Cabinet* at the Provinzialmuseum Hannover built by El Lissitzky at the invitation of Alexander Dorner, showing works by Piet Mondrian, Ludwig Mies van der Rohe, and others, Hannover, 1927–1928

most adventurous commissions in relation to this: El Lissitzky's *Abstract Cabinet* (1927–1928).[28] Dorner came to this remarkable commission through his desire to also develop a distinct environment for the newest form of art—abstract art—in relation to which he was one of the few museum curators who decided to follow the more mechanical look of Bauhaus and Constructivist art instead of the more popular Expressionist art.[29] First, Dorner had commissioned Theo van Doesburg to design a display in which to exhibit the most recent innovations in the field of fine art. Disappointed by Van Doesburg's design Dorner turned to Lissitzky of whom he had seen a remarkable gallery design for an exhibition in Dresden. One of the strongest features of this gallery was that the walls were covered by thin metal slates, each placed perpendicular to the wall, painted white on one side, and black on the other. When walking through the room, this creates a strong, flickering sensation, reminiscent of the much later Op Art. Combined with interactive exhibition elements, which allowed the viewer to shift paintings in and out of view, the display in all possible ways drew the passive viewer into the active position of a participant and enactor.

In his later study, which offers an abbreviated history of art, provocatively entitled *The Way Beyond 'Art'* (1958), Dorner is explicit in linking the dynamic features of the *Abstract Cabinet* to a general shift in position of the subject. The last phase of Western civilization introduces 'a new unity [which] lies beyond spirit and matter.'[30] Renaissance art according to Dorner had been based on a static conception of space as a coherent and empty container best represented using the technique of linear perspective.[31] The perspective image, based on rational,

---

28 A good analysis of this installation is from Maria Gough, 'Constructivism Disoriented: El Lissitzky's Dresden and Hannover *Demonstrationsräume*,' in *Situating El Lissitzky: Vitebsk, Berlin, Moscow*, ed. Nancy Perloff and Brian Reed (Los Angeles: Getty Research Institute, 2003), pp. 77–125.
29 Klonk, *Space of Experience*, pp. 113–120.
30 Dorner, *The Way Beyond 'Art*,' p. 105.
31 It is interesting that both students of Riegl, Dorner and Panofsky wrote substantial texts on linear perspective. Even if beyond the scope of this text, it is interesting to compare Panofsky's essay on perspective as symbolic form with Dorner's analysis of linear perspective. See Erwin Panofsky, 'Die Perspektive als "symbolische Form,"' in Panofsky, *Aufsätze zu Grundfragen der Kunstwissenschaft*, pp. 99–168.

mathematical rules, was thereby considered a purely spiritual double of the material world. This means that in this period there was a clear hierarchy between the eternal spiritual domain of the subject and the transient material zone of the object. For Dorner this emphasis on immutable ideas was broken in the most recent developments in abstract art. This art started to incorporate a composite subject, which is both a physical, material human being and a spiritual being. This demonstrates itself in the structure of the abstract work, playing deliberately with changing perspectives, which required physical movement of the body of the viewer. Dorner for instance analyzes an *Abstract Composition* by László Peri from 1923, who uses several conflicting perspectives in one image, which forces the subject to deliberately switch from one perspective to the other.[32] The *Abstract Cabinet* thereby functions as a radical 3D version of this strategy, constantly visually poking the viewer to be aware of how his or her own movements produce different experiences.

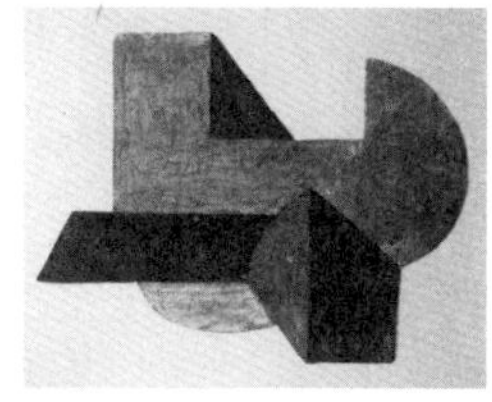

Fig 6 László Peri, *Space Construction VI*, 1922–1923

Dynamic Unity: Limits to Dorner's Model

Dorner's particular understanding of art history had a great impact on his understanding of the museum institution as such. Following Riegl's more anthropological sentiment, Dorner too was less focused on art for art's sake, and more considered the museum as an educational, cultural institution. In the display Dorner tried to make comprehensible the evolution of what he termed 'visual communication' as part of the human condition. The proper title of his study, as he notes, should have been: 'the decline of the species of visual communication called "art" and the origin of a new species of visual communication.'[33] In his museum visitors were not educated into fixed categories of good taste and eternal beauty, but are made aware of the ever-changing structure of experience and how in different periods, different visual strategies

---

32 Dorner, *The Way Beyond 'Art,'* pp. 107–110.
33 Ibid., p. 15.

have been deployed to make sense of the world.[34]

This post-'art' perspective inspired Dorner to think radically in a manner rarely done within the history of museums and museum display. At the end of *Way Beyond 'Art,'* he makes a passionate plea to let go of all the static claims of the past to be a treasure chest for eternal and immutable ideas and to embrace the dynamic nature of the present moment.[35] Only by starting from the contemporary moment and casting aside any false academic virtues of the historian to wait until 'the situation of modern art has become clarified,' can the museum be a constructive force. In his own bombastic language: 'an important factor in the urgently needed integration of life and in the unification of mankind on a dynamic basis.'[36] This approach would even allow the museum to be more 'easy to establish for it would depend much less than the current type on quantitative accumulation, i.e., wealth.'[37]

Dorner in this radical vision opened the door for a type of museum institution which is profoundly different from the major museum for modern art of today, still tied as they are to what art critic Clement Greenberg so elegantly called an 'umbilical cord of gold.'[38] Dorner was not interested in fetishizing priceless originals. Earlier using facsimile photocopies of paintings in an exhibition, challenging the public to see which is which, he had experimented trying to make way for using new technology to fulfill the demonstrative function of the museum.[39] He sought to break loose from the notion of the museum as a treasure chest and wanted to establish the museum as a dynamic 'powerhouse' or *'Kraftwerk,'* which transforms the museum into a relentless engine

---

34 Ibid., p. 147.
35 Ibid., pp. 146–148.
36 Ibid., p. 148.
37 Ibid.
38 Clement Greenberg, 'Avant-Garde and Kitsch,' in *Art and Culture: Critical Essays* (Boston: Beacon Press, 1961), p. 8.
39 Dorner had organized an exhibition in 1929 in which the public was challenged to discriminate high-quality facsimile copies from originals. See especially Alexander Dorner, 'Original and Facsimile,' in *Photography in the Modern Era: European Documents and Critical Writings, 1913–1940,* ed. Christopher Phillips (New York: Metropolitan Museum of Art, 1989), pp. 151–154.

for the perpetual development of mankind.[40]

Inspiring as these ideas might still be today, there is perhaps one element in his vision which would feel problematic to the contemporary curator or museum director: his explicit affirmation of the autarkic author position of the director and curator. In his vision the museum would eventually 'rely primarily upon the imagination and leadership of its staff.'[41] Within Dorner's practice this meant, as architecture historian Sandra Karina Löschke demonstrates, that the exhibition is composed as a smooth, manipulative script, which shows great similarities to the almost irresistible logic of the flow of cinema—the most important propaganda technology of the early twentieth century.[42] Dorner's education of his public on the idea of perpetual change, as a result had a quite peculiar, almost totalitarian twist to it. Change you must! is the dictum of the display. Just as in Riegl's understanding of history, which knew no regression or pause, Dorner takes the visitor on a journey in which there is no way back. In Dorner's terms: 'We exist solely as improvers of our heritage.'[43]

This also points towards a slight discrepancy in Dorner's own logic. In his displays he aspired to convey the specificity of different worldviews, by adding a hue, which would draw the exhibits together and demonstrate the unity of a particular period. This logic, as shown above, however, itself draws from an aesthetic strategy of a specific historical period, namely Dutch Baroque. This period act as a threshold between the earlier phase in which artists pursued static representations of immutable concepts and Dorner's own contemporary moment in which change and transformation were central. Yet by placing the entire history of art in a framework that already inspired a mild dynamic relation between subject and

---

40 In *The Way Beyond 'Art,'* Dorner himself uses the term 'powerhouse.' In German the term 'Kraftwerk' is used, which translates as 'power station.' The definition of what sense the museum should be a powerhouse remains slightly vague. He simply states: 'a kind of powerhouse, a producer of new energies.' Dorner, *The Way Beyond 'Art,'* p. 147.
41 Ibid., p. 148.
42 See Löschke, 'Material Aesthetics and Agency.'
43 Dorner, *The Way Beyond 'Art,'* p. 147.

object, the viewer was offered not a sequence of different worldviews and their respective sentiments, but a kind of a roller coaster ride of them joining body and mind in the present. Using one's own physical body and its movements through the museum, the visitor was asked never to stop or go back, but to accept that all that was build up to, was also superseded by the present, which consumed it completely.

In this sense the dynamism celebrated by Dorner was contained within the singular narrative of the museum director/curator, who acted as the necessary, unifying subtext to allow the visitor to experience the possible multiple perspectives. What he was not able to conceive was the ghostlike survival of past times within the present, as analyzed, for instance, by his contemporary Aby Warburg.[44] The latter tried to trace, in photographic collages in his *Mnemosyne Atlas* (1924–1929), 'ur-shapes' that haunted us from the past and instead of evolutionary celebration, required more therapeutic reconciliation. However, it is also clear that within the museum culture of the early and mid-twentieth century, the museum was (and mostly still is) an authoritative space that relied heavily on powerful author-directors. Warburg's delicate and eccentric historical method might recently have inspired several interesting exhibition projects and rethinking of curating, the mid-twentieth century resonated more with the notion of 'powerhouse.'[45]

Epilogue
The great merit of Dorner's museum vision is his profound embrace of 'change' as a leading principle. Instead of educating people on a fixed canon of eternal beauty, people were invited to consider themselves part of a dynamic process. This process then wasn't conceived of in mere theoretical terms, but was grounded in an almost physiological analysis of art, following Riegl's empirical,

---

44 Described and analyzed very carefully in Georges Didi-Huberman, *Das Nachleben der Bilder*, trans. Michael Bischoff (Berlin: Suhrkamp, 2010).
45 I'm thinking especially of the exhibition curated by Didi-Huberman himself: *Atlas: How to Carry the World on One's Back?*, Museo Nacional Centro de Arte Reina Sofía, Madrid, 26 November 2010– 28 March 2011.

positive study of artistic form. Even if perhaps the authoritarian position he left for the curator is problematic, the approach that systematically tried to link both the formal analysis of artworks and aesthetic shapes with the development of human society, is something to reconsider today. An exhibition, in a museum or elsewhere, is a sensuous entity and its main ability is to direct attention to specific issues by shaping experience. If exhibitions are to perform a function in society, understanding also the formal component of this exhibition as an intricate part of what it is meaning and seeking to make this meaning explicit in theory is an important exercise.

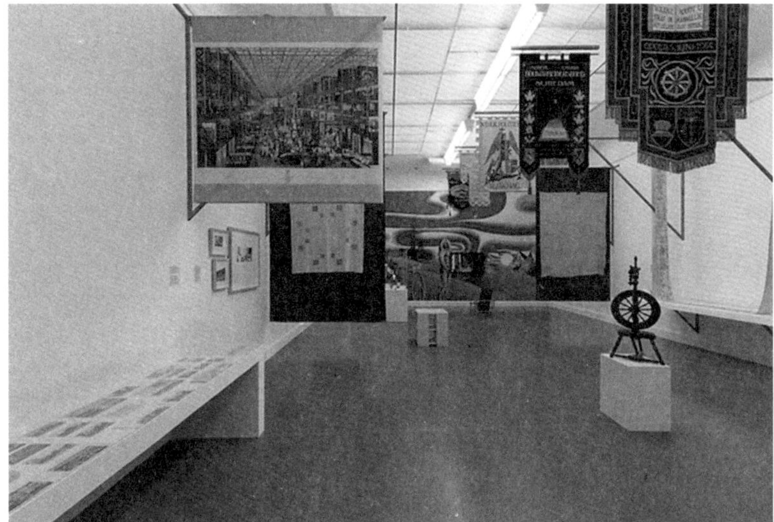

Fig 7 Exhibition view *Confessions of the Imperfect: 1848–1989–Today* at the Van Abbemuseum, 2014–2015. 'Barricade of Vista': including banners from the Dutch trade unions and Jeremy Deller's film *So Many Ways to Hurt You: The Life and Times of Adrian Street*, 2010.

For *Confessions of the Imperfect*—the exhibition which developed organically in parallel to this research and combined elements of Ruskin with Dorner's strategies (with a hint of Warburg)[46]—we took up Ruskin's focus on use and his approach to the museum's rooms as classrooms for education and practice. Only the exhibition

---

46 The continuous action by Alexandra Pirici and Manuel Pelmuş, *Public Collection of Modern Art* (2015) in the centre of the exhibition played especially with the Warburgian idea of 'afterlife' of images. Everyday during the exhibition for four hours (leaving only two hours a day without the ongoing action) performers would enact or embody collection of artworks. In the bodies of the performers shapes of artworks from the past survived and hinted at the constant migration between past forms and contemporary bodies.

itself was not merely a tool shop, but also presented a history of art and its use. The aesthetic method used to build this narrative was designed by Liam Gillick, and operated more or less as an inversion of Dorner's strategy to 'bring together.' Gillick described the design as a series of 'barricades,' in this sense literally emphasizing the possibility to place things apart or set up an obstacle between experiences that invited a conscious linking of things. He hoped to break a sense of autopilot in how the exhibition could be perceived.[47] These obstacles were very diverse and used different strategies. There were banners hanging from the ceiling, mimicking a theatre coulisse, as 'barricades of sight,' or a wooden beam was suspended running diagonally through the space above the visitors, with speakers built in. This created a 'barricade of discourse' in one room.

The history that was presented was not a progressive story of 'improvement.' It more mapped various ways in which aesthetic practices take part in the formation of the social, political, and economic sphere. The 'barricades' functioned as an explicit in-between hoping to create a different dynamic in the exhibition experience. Instead of the curators providing a coherent background—as with Dorner's coloured walls—which would frame material in a singular story, the framing device was an explicit addition. The suggestion was that Gillick and we as curators provided a conscious formal experiential path from one work to the other, which the visitor had to negotiate in full awareness of being manipulated. The exhibition played with a double 'background' using the traditional, white-walled space of the museum, as the surface for another background of sensual barricades. Perhaps one can potentially understand it as an attempt to improve Dorner's own model, creating an even more intense dynamism between the two backgrounds and the works offering the viewer multiple perspectives to navigate between.

---

47 See Gillick. 'The Barricade Has Fragmented and Multiplied' in this reader, pp. 424–427.

Essay
Lucía Sanromán

No Blood/ No Foul

ON THE REPRESENTATION AND REINVENTION OF SOCIALLY ENGAGED ARTWORKS

Operating outside traditional mechanisms of evaluation, interpretation, display, and distribution developed around the object of art, the exhibition of socially engaged artworks should be understood against two frames of reference.

The first is offered by the artwork itself, which is conditioned by several factors within and outside the field of art, including those provided by the artist's own parameters and her social and aesthetic aims. Functioning across disciplines in specific social contexts, participatory and engaged art projects are often conceived to not primarily exist within art institutions, but rather vitally address the world at large, expanding the canons of artistic practice toward specific uses and, frequently, active political agendas. The second frame of reference that bears consideration is the state of museum practice today. Museums, galleries, and kunsthalles, and associated educational programmes are increasingly challenged to address socially engaged works through commissioning, exhibition display and, more and more, collecting.

These considerations were foremost in my curatorial conceptualization for the exhibition *Citizen Culture: Artists and Architects Shape Policy*, organized by the Santa Monica Museum of Art (SMMoA)—a non-collecting institution with a history of exhibiting experimental California-based artists since its inception in 1988.[1] The exhibition opened in September 2014 after more than two years of intensive research and discussion with participants about the display of their works and the implications of this. It included the work of seven artists, architects, designers, creative thinkers, and collectives who have reshaped policy and legislation, while intervening in the delicate ecologies of public life by combining artistic and political processes. There were art projects by the Argentinian collective Ala Plástica (Silvina Babich and Alejandro Meitín), the lobbying platform and artwork Tamms Year Ten (2008–present), a new commission by artist Tania Bruguera, as well as an installation by renowned social practitioner Suzanne Lacy. These were displayed next to a model by architect Michael Maltzan and a collaboration between designer and theorist Teddy Cruz, urban planner

---

1   *Citizen Culture: Artists and Architects Shape Policy* was researched and curated by the author and on view at the Santa Monica Museum of Art, Los Angeles, California from 13 September–13 December 2014.

Alejandro Echeverri, political scientist Fonna Forman, and graphic designer Matthias Goerlich. A fulcrum point of the project was the graphic diagram and conceptual map about the political work of former Mayor of Bogotá Antanas Mockus designed by artist Futuro Moncada. During his time in office (1995–1997 and 2001–2003) Mockus— appropriating methodologies from performance art, theatre, and game theory—redefined the terms by which legislators engage with citizens to implement public policy.

Fig 1 Antanas Mockus with Futuro Moncada, Cultura Ciudadana Infographic, 2014, vinyl on wall

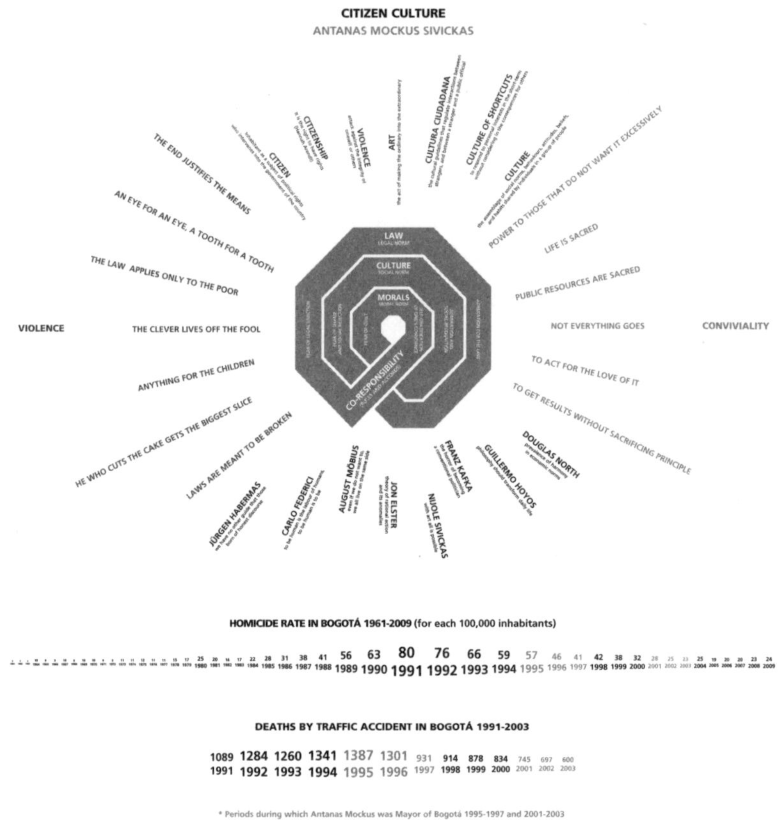

Citizen Culture researched and presented in an exhibition format the growing arena of social practice that seeks to redress specific political problems from prison reform to citizen participation to immigration and environmental policy to socially responsible urban development. It purposefully grouped together a variety of disciplines both conceptually and physically in the galleries at SMMoA in order to clarify their overlaps, areas of tension, and shared strategies. A fundamental observation resulting from this exercise is that these projects share a deeply held commitment to the implementation of long-term policy projects; they do this specifically through catalyzing the role of art and culture—and more abstractly aesthetics—as detonators of change. These projects propose that art and culture might thereby not only reshape legal systems and urban codes, but work toward the reconfiguration of the very psyche of citizens. In this regard, these projects inherit from the historical avant-garde a belief in the power of art to radically transform subjectivities through heightened aesthetic experience, but now extended to the field of ethics.

Suzanne Lacy's participatory artwork *No Blood/No Foul* (1996–1997) is presented as a primary case study here to expand and develop these two frameworks and better understand the matches and mismatches between socially engaged 'useful' artwork and the mechanisms of display and knowledge production at work in art institutions today. For the purposes of *Citizen Culture*, 'use' was defined by a project's efficacy in addressing specific political challenges within the context of government—in other words, projects that enter the systems of lobbying, organizing, and communications that operate at the level of municipal or state government.

In 1995, Lacy was on a team that initiated a youth policy initiative sponsored by then progressive Mayor of Oakland Elihu M. Harris and Councilwoman Sheila Jordan. The initiative sought to improve the relationship between the youth and the civic institutions and services dedicated to them, while instituting new and consistent funding sources to better the lives of marginalized urban youth. *No Blood/No Foul* took place from 1995 to 1996 and was one part of an effort to engage young people, ages thirteen to twenty-five, and communities in the writing and passage of the Oakland Youth Policy. This was part of a citywide response to the rise in homicide rates in the 1990s—identified as a public health crisis—and the growing criminalization of urban youth of colour among other issues. For six months leading up to the drafting of the Oakland Youth Policy, Lacy, her collaborators, the involved Oakland youth as well as members of the local police, participated in committees and workshops, to create initiatives to present for funding to the city council.

On Wednesday 5 June, 1996, from 7 to 9 pm at Club One health club in the Oakland City Center shopping complex, the participatory performance and media event *No Blood/ No Foul* matched the skills of the youth team, 'Da Rebels,' against the police team, 'Da Rollers,' in a fast-paced game of streetball. The game included sports commentators that mixed the rules of the game, pre-recorded interviews with the players, a half-time dance presentation, and original soundtracks. Over the course of the event, youth referees replaced adult referees for the second quarter, followed by no referees as in streetball, and for the last quarter the audience voted in place of referees. Murals by local graffiti artists surrounded the court in the trendy health club where that night treadmills were replaced with bleachers; youth reporters interviewed the crowd and telephones were connected to a hotline for audience response to the proposed Oakland Youth Policy. Designed to reflect the consensual nature of the law, and allowing the community to learn and contribute, *No Blood/No Foul* was presented two nights before the policy was put to a vote by the city council and allowed the community to learn about and contribute to the policy. The performance received extensive television coverage and was attended by the mayor and city council who subsequently passed the Oakland Youth Policy and put it on the general ballot where it was also passed, providing US $180,000 for a youth-to-youth granting program, per year.[2]

No Blood/No Foul is part of The Oakland Projects (1991–2001), a series of public art-collaborative works, authored and directed by Lacy, and organized in conjunction with

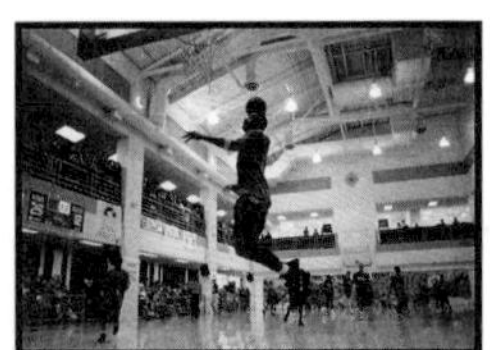

Fig 2 Suzanne Lacy, *No Blood/ No Foul and the Oakland Youth Policy*, 1995–1996

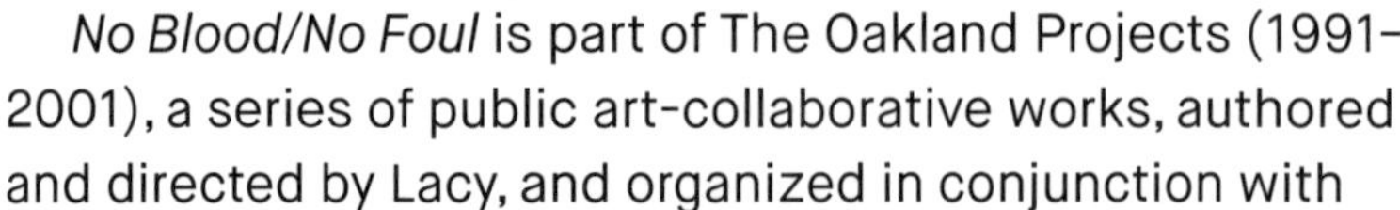

2   Specific information is gathered from interviews with the artist and research into her personal archive, and from the project website www.suzannelacy.com/the-oakland-projects. *No Blood/No Foul* is a streetball term to indicate that 'if there is no blood, there is no foul.'

youth and adult collaborators under the acronym TEAM
(Teens + Educators + Artists + Media Makers). Seven
interlinked projects took place from 1991 to 2000 and
were created through pedagogical and performative
processes that included workshops and classes for youth
and police, media interventions, institutional programs,
and policy development. Averaging two years each, they
had a variety of artistic forms and outcomes including
performance, video, and installation. In their entirety, the
projects constitute one of Lacy's most extensive and
in-depth explorations of what she has termed 'new genre
public art.'[3] This artwork, and the projects in general,
allowed Lacy to experiment with methodologies for the
inclusion of artists in politics and civic life, saying:

> Working together, artists and activists intervened
> in a cultural image war, deconstructing advertising,
> pornography, entertainment, and even visual art.
> Simultaneously, they created models of interdisciplinary
> engagement between artists and government officials,
> public institutions, activists, and the media, often
> drawing them into action on the issues. They created
> the possibility of a public ritual space for the emotive
> and cathartic expression of the private experience.[4]

Mapping social relations and contexts, understanding
communications strategies, addressing efficacy, and
unfolding time signatures are just some of the unorthodox
elements that need to be taken into account when
exhibiting artworks such as *No Blood/No Foul*. These same
elements are also key to how we write about and interpret
them. As theorist Grant Kester has pointed out, there still
remains a lag in the elaboration of writing and criticism
tools appropriate for what he refers to as 'field-based'
practice—works of art that not only emerge from discourse
but that, laying claim to a variety of disciplinary tools and

---

3   See Suzanne Lacy, ed., *Mapping the Terrain: New Genre Public Art* (Seattle: Bay-Press, 1995).
4   Suzanne Lacy, *Leaving Art: Writings on Performance, Politics, and Publics, 1974–2007* (Durham, NC:
Duke University Press, 2010), p. 106.

agendas outside the discourse of art, are seriously embedded within the various registers that constitute a specific social arena.[5] Kester calls for a careful recalibration of the tools of the art historian and theorist in addressing the critical interpretation of such works, one that is expansive and borrows from ethnographic, sociological, and anthropological models of field research, while also relying on political science, among other disciplines. This hybrid disciplinary approach should also be applied toward the presentation and display of such work in an exhibition format. To this end, *No Blood/No Foul*, as an existing model, allows us to develop better tools to interpret and describe these types of art projects while also unfolding the issues that arise from their presentation and display in exhibition formats.

Representation as Negotiation of Time and Space

Careful unpacking of the processes of production of Lacy's socially conditioned dialogical art, involved mapping the specific networks and relationships articulated through its development with a view to understanding the wider context within which it operated. Central to *No Blood/No Foul* is the condition of time, which may be the most important and constitutive difference among artworks whose meaning is captured through single moments of auratic experience. These moments are often ignited by the encounter with an object—as opposed to artworks—whose meaning is established through long-term participation in real-time discourse in social arenas and in negotiation of specific issues. *No Blood/No Foul* established specific plans for social interaction in the form of teaching curricula that resulted in a well-conceived communication strategy for the dissemination of the information collected and created throughout its development. Finally, the presentation of this project also brought to the fore the necessity to create tools to measure outcomes and assess their impact

---

5   See Grant Kester, 'The Device Laid Bare: On Some Limitations in Current Art Criticism,' *e-flux journal* 12, no. 50 (2013), www.e-flux.com/journal/the-device-laid-bare-on-some-limitations-in-current-art-criticism.

a posteriori, in this case twenty years after its production.

Lacy conceived *No Blood/No Foul* as a total, time-based participatory artwork with many temporalities and rhythms.[6] Like other related works, this is a piece with varied shifts in modes of engagement, layered with pedagogical methodologies and communication strategies. There are also multiple degrees of visual representation, all of which, together, constitute the work of art. The subsequent display of such a complex social artwork in an exhibition presents significant challenges. There are, however, representational formats that can provide some guidelines: the presentation of archival and vestigial materials in social-documentary-based exhibitions; the creation of a new installation; artworks utilizing archival and new material; the recreation of key public moments or performances from the original artwork, following increasingly widespread methodologies in the re-staging of performance art and its subsequent acquisition for collections as a set of instructions or 'stage directions'; and the creation of a new interpretation of the work which may or may not include a re-engagement with specific social and performative aspects of the project.

The question of how to represent, display, and collect her short- and long-term discursive artworks has become increasingly important, as Lacy explained in February 2013:

Since around 2007 I have been thinking about the notion of reconstructing, recreating, re-presenting performance from the 70s and 80s. By now theorists are parsing the language and most performance artists of my generation have adopted a position on these issues. Museums are trying to figure out what precisely they are collecting that represents these works. This type of inquiry—what is it, why, shape/ form, transience, etc.—is fundamental to the origins of performance in the 70s. ... My personal thoughts about recreation is that in general I am not interested

---

6   *No Blood/No Foul* (1996) was initially a collaboration with Jacques Bronson, Chris Emerson, Unique Holland, Annice Jacoby, Chris Johnson, Officer Terrence West, Frank Williams, Stan Hebért, and Mike Shaw.

in strictly 'recreating' a performance and the only time I seriously considered it was when we first began talking about recreating *The Crystal Quilt* in Turbine Hall at Tate Modern several years ago. Since my work evolves out of a profound engagement with context and particular and specific people, the idea of recreating an artwork merely as a theatrical event is uninteresting, particularly as my work is not really 'theatrical' in a sense that it can be extractable and re-performed.[7]

The first *re*-presentation of *No Blood/No Foul* came relatively soon after the performance, when Lacy and TEAM collaborators were invited to participate in an exhibition titled *ATOPIC* that took place in Tokyo in the fall of 1996.[8] Exhibited in a large warehouse, the art installation was focused on a full-size basketball court with hoops and game markings, delimited by a chain-link fence that symbolically referred to the prison system and the internal borders that mark the lives of minority youth in the United States. On the face of the chain link a series of monitors presented looped editions of video interviews with youth and police. Their installation stimulated discussion with youth about their relationships to authority. Graffiti murals along the sides mimicked the layout of the original performance.

Nearly twenty years later, at SMMoA, the discussion of what to present in the gallery shifted in response to several factors. Firstly, the space being allotted to Lacy's installation in *Citizen Culture* was significantly smaller and the work had to be integrated into a thematic group exhibition sharing the same gallery space. More importantly, the discussion about youth policy and the criminalization of youth that had been front and centre in the mass media and politics of the mid-1990s, had not been resolved—since that period it had actually

---

7   Suzanne Lacy, 'Suzanne Lacy: Silver Action: Performance Recreation,' Tate Blog, 20 February 2013, www.tate.org.uk/context-comment/blogs/suzanne-lacy-silver-action-performance-recreation.
8   Suzanne Lacy, 'Descriptions: No Blood No Foul: Project Summary,' https://theoaklandprojects.wordpress.com/no-blood-no-foul-1995-96.

regressed. *Citizen Culture* opened to a dramatic increase in the cases of racially motivated police brutality in the US. So while in 1996 Oakland was experimenting with participative youth policy to lower violence levels, incarceration numbers, and relations between youth and police, statistics indicate that by 2014 the criminalization of youth and people of colour is the norm.[9]

As a result, the constraints of Lacy's new installation for *Citizen Culture* were set by the spatial and temporal distance between Santa Monica in 2014, and the context within which *No Blood/No Foul* was created in Oakland in 1996. In terms of the political context, in 2014 it is widely tolerated that youths of colour are criminalized and incarcerated; this is matched by a loss of trust in government to implement real social change, something that gives this project today renewed urgency. Spatially Lacy addressed these complexities by proposing the concept of 're-investigation' as her preferred representational strategy—an alternative to either installation or archival manifestation. With 're-investigation' she proposes an a posteriori representation of the work firmly planted in the original context and intention through research, but reformulated for the current moment.

Lacy expanded on these ideas while explaining *Silver Action* (2013), a new performance commissioned by the Tate Modern created in response to their exhibition of the video piece and quilt installation of *The Chrystal Quilt*, her seminal 1985–1987 performance:

> So I did *Silver Action* not as a completely 'new' work but as a form of re-investigation. How does a situation from 1985 in America get translated through the lens of 2013 in the UK? The social and political context has changed, but some core issues remain similar—and of course different … . In each of these new works I investigated new themes as well as evolutions in the

---

9   From 1998 to 2008 the number of people incarcerated in the United States quadrupled from 500,000 to 2.3 million; of these African American men, women, and youth made up 58% of all prisoners.

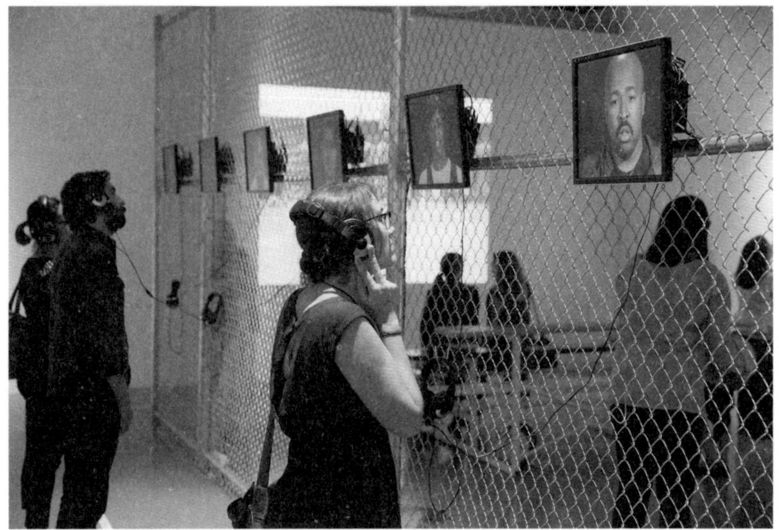

form/schools of art, in the context of the same public issues; what changed, what remains—in art and life. As a result in each case I freely borrow from the iconography of the earlier work and indeed even deliberately refer to it. In *Three Weeks in January*, for example, I made a choice to keep the map itself as the performative core of the work, to emphasize the 'body' as recipient of violence, and as the fundamental element of agency.[10]

The 're-investigation' of *No Blood/No Foul* presented in *Citizen Culture* was dated '1996, 2014'—the comma between the numbers expressing the relationship between two parallel dates of creation rather than the beginning and end implied by a dash. Lacy chose to present three distinct new works, tied to the 1996 process, to re-present the work: the first is titled *No Blood/No Foul Installation: The Fence* and consists of a thirty-foot-long and eleven-foot-high prefabricated chain-link fence with eight monitors hung on its face. Reedited video interviews of the series *Cops and Kids*, originally taped as part of the research and outreach program for the project, are looped and play contiguously. Her decision to have this work open her

---

10   Lacy, 'Suzanne Lacy: Silver Action.'

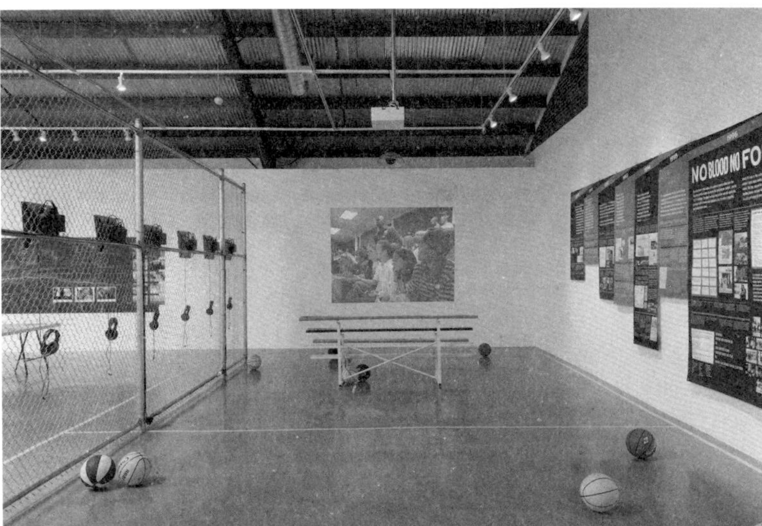

Fig 4 Suzanne Lacy, *No Blood/ No Foul Installation: The Game*, 1996, 2014

installation is a statement of the importance of the police and teenagers who participated in the workshops and were interviewed throughout. It also highlighted the continued relevance of the material in the context of today's violent relationship between youth of colour and police in the US. The second work in the series is titled *No Blood/No Foul Installation: The Game* and consists of painted bleachers with vinyl text, and a new edition of the original video of the performance of streetball that took place on 5 June 1996.

While the two pieces represent a reconceptualization of existing video material in new media installation formats, the third new work produced is a reinvestigation in the sense described by Lacy: new research in the form of a timeline that maps the evolution of youth policy from 1990 to 2000. This timeline presents selected historical events, youth-related statistics, scholarly observations, and quotes by project participants, establishing a broad and decade-long context for The Oakland Projects, from 1990 to 2000. Composed of vinyl banners and basketballs, *No Blood/ No Foul Installation: Timeline* is dated, only, with the year 2014. It was created to give a longer history and context to the struggle of gaining youth rights for people of colour in the US and to show that another political solution is possible if alternative forms of thinking in government are

Fig 5 Suzanne Lacy, *No Blood/ No Foul Installation: Timeline*, 2014

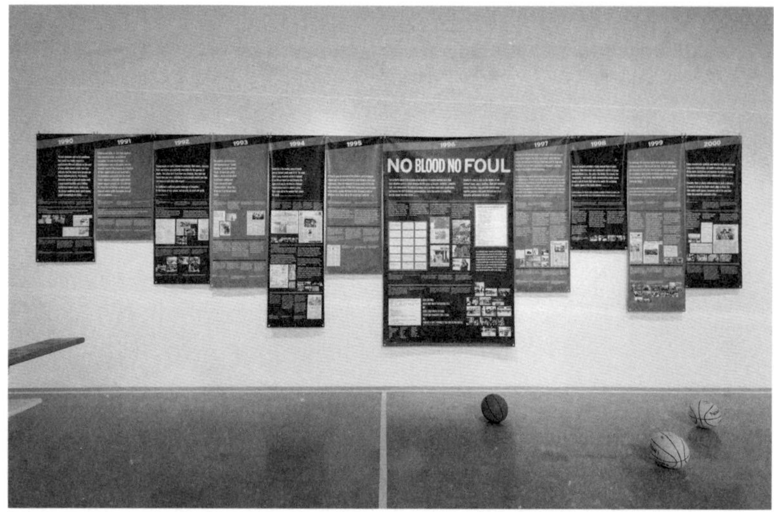

encouraged. More than positioning herself as a curator or interpreter of her own work, Lacy addresses the concept and function of 'reinvestigation' as a form of access for this work. It utilizes existing archival material but more importantly it is a collage that makes present and visible the content of Lacy's dialogical performance through the process of the project—namely negotiation and interaction with government officials, teachers, police, and youth.

A very important aspect of Lacy's exercise in representation is providing an appropriate art historical framework within which to place her work. 'While I have no problem with others doing re-creations,' she has written, 'my personal interest is in "revisiting" certain ideas and in how the experience, information, context, and meaning of early performance art is communicated in terms of art history.'[11]

The experience of art—objects, video, sound, or even certain kinds of performance—and its display often counts on its separation from that which it represents through the mechanism of the exhibition itself. The exhibition format can articulate art's relationship to the history of the field, thereby investing the works on view with artistic autonomy from other fields of human activity. In this regard, the museum often functions as the outer

---

11 Ibid.

physical envelope that demarcates—with the use of material infrastructure—the limits of that which is art, and of artistic experience, from the world. Socially engaged, useful artworks draw on very different strategies to establish their claims as 'art.' Foremost amongst these is the enunciation by an artist that this activity, apparently no different from other disciplines and areas of life, is indeed their artwork. This gesture expands the canon toward discourse, social interaction, and, as in *No Blood/No Foul*, legislation and policy. While the object of art is legitimized by being displayed in a museum, the action and discourse that gives form and content to socially engaged artworks is most often pushed into the realm of art by being products of an artist's activity. This recalls a Duchampian legacy that effectively removes the need for an object as auratic detonator of aesthetic experience.

This transition from everyday life to art that is initiated by Lacy's will to author actions (not objects), recalls a different art historical genealogy: feminist art of the 1960s, California Conceptualism, institutional critique, and specifically Allan Kaprow's writings and teaching on the blurring of art and life.[12] In addition, her performance-based and pedagogical, socially engaged work of that period parallels, by her own analysis, the 'Legislative Theatre' practices of theatre director, writer, and politician Augusto Boal, which he developed while serving in Rio's City Council from 1993 to 1997 and, unbeknownst to Lacy, experimenting with methods and processes close to those used in *No Blood/No Foul*. 'While Kaprow clearly gives permission to include all subject matter as relevant,' Lacy clarifies, 'it is in Boal's work that we find evidence of a highly refined aesthetic of social justice in operation, one that informs and deepens the critique of feminist performance art.'[13]

Such genealogy places Lacy's work in tension with a more mainstream history of contemporary art and

---

12   In 1971 Lacy joined the visual arts program at California Institute of the Arts (CalArts), under the direct mentorship of Judy Chicago and Allan Kaprow.
13   Lacy, *Leaving Art*, p. 278.

exhibition practices. This work is produced as a direct reaction to urgent social issues, and often implicitly critiques the elitist connotations and limits of the traditional exhibition space. Social practitioners like Lacy are extremely sensitive to the semantic changes that are wrought upon their process-based work as it is translated into a representational format for an object-focused exhibition display. As such, they often question whether this kind of reformulation puts the integrity of their work at risk. In the case of *No Blood/ No Foul* at *Citizen Culture*, considerations about the work's representation entailed inquiry into how the project could function as a means to do further research on the topic today, as well as vital outreach to a new generation of police and youth.[14] However, over the course of the project it became increasingly clear that to truly experiment with the museum as an extension of the public sphere was beyond the staffing and financial possibilities of the institution. Art institutions are often strongly enmeshed in a history dedicated to the object, its interpretation and display. Many are therefore ill-equipped to implement complex public programmes that require the expansion of its staffing in multiple disciplines such as community organizing or social work, or trans-institutional collaborations with social services organizations, universities, civic groups, and individuals.

These types of projects are often a challenge to or even imply a breakdown of the model of autonomy on which the status of the artwork and the museum depend. Instead, these projects introduce processes that reformulate the museum as a platform for activities and social interactions that have measurable impact and efficacy in the world including: transforming the museum into a space for discourse where the public sphere, public policy, and even new civic personae can be defined and performed. Although more art institutions

---

14 SMMoA's education department and its director Asuka Hisa created a dynamic outreach program, including a memorable series where teenagers from a local high school gave public tours to groups of local police officers and many others.

are experimenting with what this might be these aims
remain well beyond their traditional mandate to care
for, interpret, and present artworks to varied audiences,
which is the historical purpose of curatorial and
education departments in normative art institutions.[15]

For such complex and multivalent work, its
presentation in a museum implies a significant form of
artistic legitimation. More and more artists are using art
institutions, and the figure of the artist itself, as a platform
from which to engage in politics. But such legitimation
can put into question the political intentions of the
artists who lead these complex enterprises, sometimes
diminishing their political efficacy in government by
being perceived as a gesture, a form of mimicry of the
social and the political for the consumption of the art
world. Conscious of this, *Citizen Culture* aimed to draw
on Santa Monica's sociopolitical landscape to offer
fertile ground to pilot programs. Myself, the education
curator, and the director each hoped this would lead
to greater discussion and dissemination of the ideas,
political proposals, and prototypes presented, and
in turn influence the civic fabric of Los Angeles.

While the exhibition showed examples of successful
legislative projects, *Citizen Culture* as an interpretative
apparatus aimed to formulate an alternative and specific
art history, drawing relations, similarities, and differences
between projects in art, urbanism, and government
policy. For example, *No Blood/No Foul* has elements in
common with the lobbying platform Tamms Year Ten
(2008–present) organized by artist Laurie Jo Reynolds,
with Tania Bruguera's *The Francis Effect* (2014), and
with Ala Plástica's *Evidence: Oil Spill in the Río de la Plata*
(1991–2014). Different in format, each project aims to
address a specific issue through the activation of social
networks, appropriating methodologies and strategies
from community organizing to establish social and political

---

15 Examples of these institutions are Van Abbemuseum (Eindhoven, Netherlands), Queens Museum
(New York City), Museo Reina Sofía (Madrid), and Museo Universitario de Arte Contemporáneo (Mexico
City).

solutions. Each begins by defining a specific problem and moves in the direction of its resolution; they often establish a series of actions that work within existing structures in the social and political arena, such as working with city government in the case of Lacy's project, or with environmental law in the case of Ala Plástica's. Alliances with organizations within and outside art are also essential to their success and utility. The projects advance toward measurable outcomes by engaging in communication campaigns that are intrinsic to their artistic intention. In all of them, lobbying gives form to an artistic practice whose outlines are often dissolved in the shifting field of the social. This implies the elaboration of tools by which outcomes can be measured as part of an artistic platform. For example, in the case of *No Blood/No Foul* the fact that it was ratified by city council two days after the public event was a great mark of success. Equally important was the allocation of specific funding to marginalized youth of colour for uses determined by them—something that was pioneered by this project and which remains to this day.

Together with the other projects in *Citizen Culture*, Lacy's reinvestigation of *No Blood/No Foul* allowed for significant elaboration and investigation of the specific histories that inform this work and others like it. They propose alternative narratives to mainstream art history, but perhaps more importantly new ways to rethink the possibilities of impacting the social and political sphere through art. *Citizen Culture* also constituted a serious exercise in generating display formats to make visible this kind of work in the present moment. Lacy's artwork consistently challenges us to review our definitions of what art is and how to experience it in proposing a topological continuum between past and present, object and action. This continuum extends to what happens within the exhibition space and outside the art institution, reminding us, yet again, of the urgency to create new civic selves to shape the present.

Essay
Zdenka
Badovinac

Using Art as Art

HOW TO EMANCIPATE WORK THROUGH ART

The art of duration, which here I call 1:1 art, is a form of art that precisely because of its temporal dimension, its persistence in a specific real-life situation, includes as directly as possible a social experience. Duration is something that would seem possible to capture in an exhibition only through documentation, and it appears there is not much that can be done apart from this.

I propose, however, that we start thinking about the exhibition not as a space where various combinations of artworks, or their documentation, archives, etc., end up, but as a temporal entity, a moment in the duration of 1:1 artworks.

Not long ago I devoted an exhibition to this idea—*1:1 Stopover*,[1] in which I put forward the question: Where is art in fact located? Or putting it differently: Where, within the time span of 1:1 art, do we find the most art? I should say at once that I do not equate the notion of 'duration' with the time of the presentation of the artist or the art, as is typical, say, of a large part of contemporary performance, including, most famously, the exhibition by Marina Abramović: *The Artist Is Present*, at the Museum of Modern Art in New York in 2010. Duration is something that, in essence, is bound to the contingencies of life and not merely sustained by the abilities of the artist or institution. I did not, in fact, want to call *1:1 Stopover* an exhibition, in the sense of a presentation of finished works, but instead used the word 'stopover' to underscore that the project was part of a time frame that went beyond the set dates of the show. In the case of the ongoing art of duration, an exhibition can capture a work of this kind only somewhere in between, in the midst of its lifespan.

Theorist Stephen Wright describes 1:1 art as art with a double ontology; he mentions, in this regard, works that take the form of web archives, libraries, restaurants, etc. Their primary ontology is the thing they are (that is, web archives and so on), but they also have a secondary ontology in the artistic propositions of these same things.[2] Wright notes that if these works want to be accepted as art, they must also be realized as art within an institution

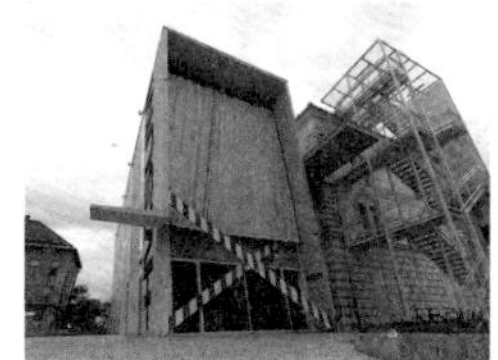

Fig 1 Azra Akšamija, *Museum Solidarity Lobby*, 2013

---

1   *1:1 Stopover*, 17 October 2013–12 January 2014, Museum of Contemporary Art Metelkova (MSUM), Ljubljana, curated by Zdenka Badovinac, produced by Moderna galerija and Maska. Participants: Azra Akšamija; Julieta Aranda and Anton Vidokle; Jože Barši; Walter Benjamin presents *The Collection, the Museum and History*; Cittadellarte – Fondazione Pistoletto and Michelangelo Pistoletto; Domestic Research Society; IRWIN; Isola Art Centre; Janez Janša, Janez Janša, and Janez Janša; Kontekst Kolektiv; Trevor Paglen; Marko Peljhan; Tadej Pogačar; Marjetica Potrč; Marija Mojca Pungerčar; Raqs Media Collective; Marko Sančanin; Igor Štromajer; Apolonija Šušteršič; and Dragan Živadinov::Dunja Zupančič::Miha Turšič.
2   Stephen Wright, '& then you disappear,' *Dear Art*, exh. cat. Moderna galerija (Ljubljana, 2012), p. 24.

that affirms what art is and is not. He wonders whether art has any possible alternative to this institutional capture, to its realization as part of an event, and whether it would then still be possible to describe the work as art. He finds a solution in the escapes that constantly occur within art and represent, not its ultimate horizon, but its modus operandi.

Let's imagine that 1:1 art is everything that happens during the duration of this art and is, in fact, the entirety of the project. The art, then, is considerably more than what we can see at an exhibition. It is precisely this durational aspect and, even more, it is the potential the work contains, which is spread by various interactions beyond its time frame and, indeed, beyond the frame of the project itself.

Wright wonders if it is possible that art is 'no longer … a minority practice, but rather something practised by the majority,' which appears with varying degrees of intensity in different contexts.[3] Here he is essentially speaking about users of art, which means everyone who is involved with art in any way: artists, viewers, owners, experts, etc. Within the possible museum, as Wright sees it, all these people make up a community of users.[4] Such a museum is no longer dependent on the mediational role of the curator but on the community of users' collective negotiations about the meaning and boundaries of the language they use.

1:1 art, in particular, may be understood as a laboratory for creating a community of users, where different forms of knowledge come into play and where expert knowledge is no longer always given primacy. One of the nerve points of these projects, in fact, is that the role of the artist remains, to a large extent, the traditional one. Most of these projects, indeed, are signed by artists under their own names, or by art groups and platforms where the artist still takes the leading role. Not least of all, these works appear regularly in exhibitions, museums, on the art market, etc., and are the subject of discussions within the art field. Clearly,

---

3   Ibid., pp. 28–29.
4   Stephen Wright spoke about this in his talk 'Making Way for Usership,' *CIMAM 2013 Annual Conference: New Dynamics in Museums: Curator, Artwork, Public, Governance*, Museo de Arte Moderno de Río de Janeiro, 12–14 August 2013.

then, the art of duration remains part of the separate sphere of art and wants to be recognized as such. So we must ask ourselves: In what way does this art differ from all other kinds of art? Let's consider this question more closely by looking at some examples from *1:1 Stopover*.

One of the projects we wanted to present was Marija Mojca Pungerčar's *Socialdress – Power to the People*, which had just been exhibited at the small Alkatraz Gallery in Ljubljana. Alkatraz operates as part of the Metelkova City Autonomous Cultural Centre, in the immediate vicinity of the Museum of Contemporary Art Metelkova (MSUM), where *1:1 Stopover* was held. By agreement with the artist and the director of Alkatraz, the project was to be included in a slightly modified size. But this did not happen because before the scheduled transfer of the project could take place, all of the objects in the Alkatraz exhibition were stolen. In the end, then, we exhibited at MSUM only documentation from the show. The objects stolen from Alkatraz included different textile products for the home with embroidered slogans from the recent anti-government protests in Slovenia; they had been made by unemployed women in a free workshop organized by Pungerčar. There the artist taught (mostly) women the crafts of sewing and needlepoint to give them useful knowledge and skills that might make their lives easier in the future. She included their works as part of her exhibition.

The workshop was held at RogLab, a container space set up next to the former Rog bicycle factory, which for over a decade has been squatted by various groups of artists and activists. RogLab was created as a pilot project for the future use of the factory, which is planned as a home for cultural industries. The current users of the factory building feel completely excluded from these plans, despite the fact that, for many years now, they have invested their creative energies in the space. And it appears to have been the Rog activists who stole the objects from the Alkatraz exhibition—as a sign of protest against the treatment they have received and the lack of regard for their presence including on the part

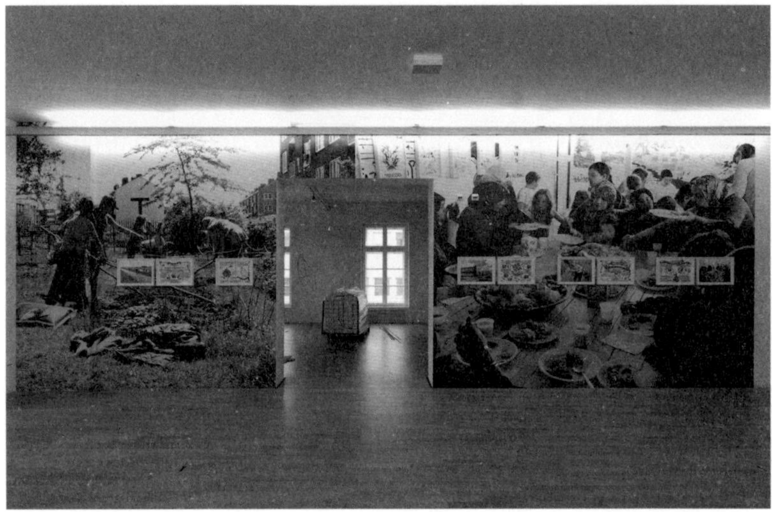

Fig 2 Marija Mojca Pungerčar, *Socialdress – Power to the People*, 2013

of Pungerčar. More precisely, the objects were stolen by a masked group who left flyers on the ground that said: 'We will not be the backhoe that tears down Rog.' The group later sent out an expanded statement, which described the event as a political performance. This was followed by a number of discussions, most of which condemned the thieves and described the artist as the victim of a criminal act. The act was also criminalized by the artist herself, who called the police and gave them an assessment of the value of the stolen objects.

At *1:1 Stopover*, along with documents from the Alkatraz show, I included my own curatorial statement, which focused on the question of what, in fact, had been stolen. I said I doubted whether the art of the project was concentrated wholly in the vanished objects and drew attention to the project's participatory nature. I stressed that artists who create 1:1 projects must expect that once the project is underway they might no longer be able to fully control it. Pungerčar had described her project as connective, as bringing together a community, but she had overlooked the fact that the Rog activists were part of this community and, as such, she had left them out. By declaring their theft to be a political performance they hoped to start a public discussion about the controversial plans for the future

centre for creative industries in the former Rog factory,
plans that completely excluded the current users of
the space. After all that had happened, we at MSUM
tried to contact the activists from Rog to offer them a
space for debate, but our invitation went unanswered.

How, then, can art of duration, with all its unforeseen
interactions, be included in the existing exhibition model?
The only thing left to the institution, it seems, is to follow
the double status of 1:1 art by, on the one side, exhibiting
things the artist produces in connection with the project
while, on the other, monitoring and reacting to all that is
generated by this art as it occurs. Now let's look briefly
at two other projects from *1:1 Stopover*; each of them,
in its way, defines the relationship between the artist
and the community for whom the project is intended.
At *1:1 Stopover* Marjetica Potrč presented the project *The
Cook, The Farmer, His Wife and Their Neighbour* (2009),
in which she collaborated with the collective Wilde
Westen (composed of a cultural producer, a sociologist,
two architects, two designers, and an artist), and a local
community in Amsterdam's Nieuw-West district. The
project centred on the creation of a community garden
and a community kitchen in a disused building. Based
on the artist's proposal, the garden and kitchen gave
neighbourhood residents the opportunity to connect
with each other more easily and, in this way, to reflect
collectively on the concept of public space and their own
community as well. Potrč notes that it is important to be in
direct contact with the community and, in this connection,
writes about 'the four principles of participatory design':

> Listening to and talking with residents before making
> a definite plan; involving the community in the
> decision-making and design processes; involving the
> community in the construction process; transferring
> the responsibility for the developed project to the

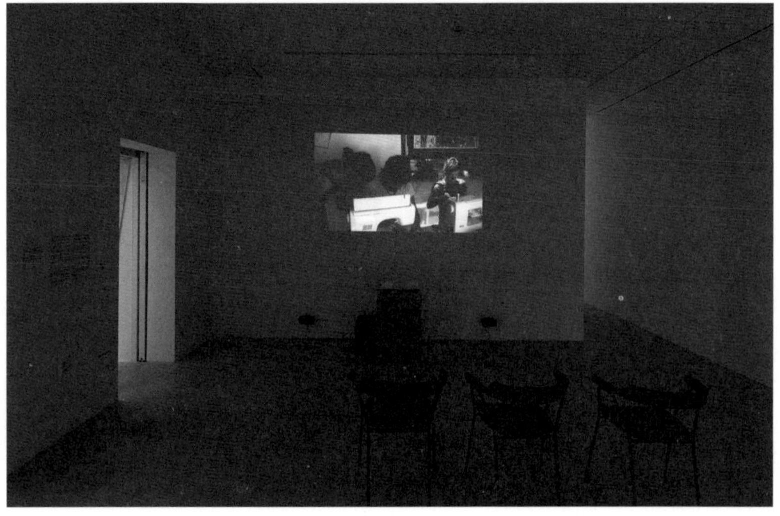

Fig 4 Marjetica Potrč, *Hope After Modernity: The Story of the Residents of Amsterdam's New West*, 2009. Based on the on-site project *The Cook, The Farmer, His Wife and Their Neighbour*, 2009

community in order to leave behind a sustainable work that benefits the community in the long term.[5]

Potrč views her art as connected with the future of the city, which she sees not in plans made 'from the top down' but in small sustainable communities based on an exchange of knowledge and experience. With changes to the concept of public space, which Potrč defines as 'shared space,' art itself, she says, also changes. Thus, for instance, the large public sculptures of the second half of the twentieth century, which were based on formal relationships, are today replaced by an art that prefers researching and proposing different relations in the community. Potrč does not merely describe these relations; she also intervenes in them and with the community conceives improvements and shapes a vision for a different kind of city. She connects and confirms the validity of her community-based projects on the basis of various artistic, urbanistic, and architectural traditions. Thus, in her drawings we find many observations about the failure of modernist designs as well as quotations from various sources of local

5   Potrč often cites these principles when discussing her on-site projects. See, for example, the introduction to *The Soweto Project* (2014), which she did with her students from the Design for the Living World class at the University of Fine Arts in Hamburg, http://designforthelivingworld. com/2013/04/15/soweto-the-soweto-project/.

knowledge, which she offers for reflection on a different culture of living. The form of her drawings follows the concept of notebooks and quick field sketches or can recall spontaneous diagrams for some public presentation. Take for instance her drawing *Notes on Participatory Design* (2011), in which she writes at the beginning, 'Start of the project,' and at the end, 'Project is completed.' Between these two defined points there is a straight black line, which signifies linear objective thinking, the kind of thinking that adheres to a plan and gets quick results. But there is also a red curving line, which rises and dips around the black line; this second line signifies 'thinking in outliers': subjective thinking, 're-routing,' which takes more time but gets better results. Potrč's community-based projects deal with relations that the community members themselves are experiencing and trying to change; in her works, the artist attempts to universalize these relations, or rather, seeks to create an artistic proposal based on combinations of broader civilizational experiences and different kinds of local knowledge.

If Potrč begins with an actual community in an Amsterdam neighbourhood, there are also examples of 1:1 art that connect to more utopian traditions. As part of *1:1 Stopover*, the IRWIN group showed a film they made in collaboration with the director Igor Zupe on the occasion of the First NSK Citizens Congress in Berlin. In 1992, the collective Neue Slowenische Kunst (NSK), which had been founded in 1984, transformed itself into the NSK State in Time and started issuing passports; to date, they have acquired some 15,000 citizens from all over the world. The most active core of these citizens have organized themselves and become independent of the NSK groups. They formed their own website and, in 2010, staged the Berlin congress, where they held discussions about the state as an abstract artistic idea in relation to the status of the contemporary state in general and about the future of the state, all in relation to NSK art. The art of NSK and, of course, the NSK State in Time itself are the connecting elements of this community

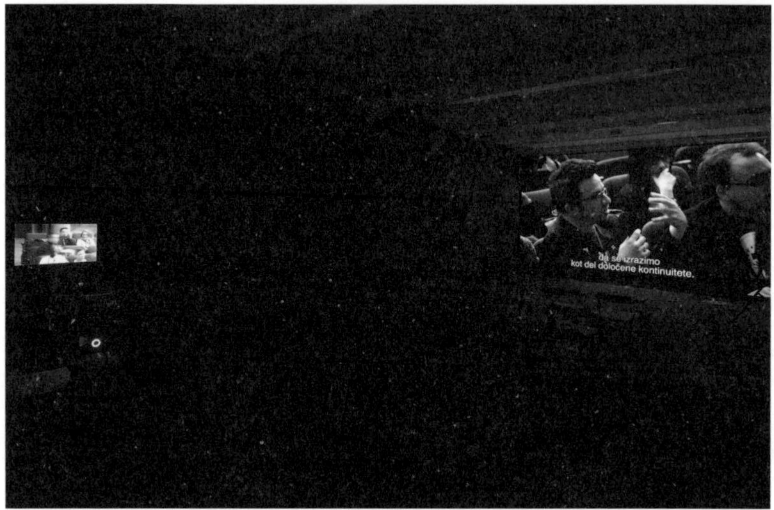

Fig 3 Irwin, film (in collaboration with Igor Zupe) and video document about the First NSK Citizens' Congress held in Berlin in October 2010

and serve as a kind of map through which its members investigate the world. We can understand the NSK State in Time as a new place of meeting for a community.

In the nation-state this place of meeting is usually a language and culture based on a seemingly unproblematic continuity; in the NSK state, however, this role is served by an art that deconstructs this ideology of harmony without conflict. In the NSK project, a community was formed not around some common social concerns, but around the desire for a more general definition of commonality, one that was not linked to any ideology nor any pragmatic motive. *1:1 Stopover*, however, was not presenting the community of NSK citizens but rather an art project by the IRWIN group. From the very beginning of the collective, IRWIN have been the chronicler within NSK, and now they had also become the chronicler of the NSK State in Time. IRWIN and Zupe's film about the congress tried to capture the dynamics between the NSK citizens, especially in their expression of different, sometimes even opposing, positions on the common theme of the state, but also on NSK art as a meta-narrative, as the historical and conceptual frame of their community. The traditional relationship between a community and art was, it seems, turned on its head: instead of a community supporting its art, now the art was providing

an infrastructure that allowed the community to function.
Here, of course, it is worth noting IRWIN's support went
so far as to obtain funding for the Berlin congress.

From the three projects I have described we can conclude
that they still move strictly within the field of art and,
in this sense, are also 'signed' as original projects. But
all three have the potential to help solve the problems,
and even contribute to the functioning, of a particular
community. The measure of the success of these projects
might be found in the consistency of their relations with
the community.

If 1:1 art seeks to make an impact on reality, we must
naturally ask: Why does it still strive to achieve this impact
as art? We might say that art today is developing a rhizome
in concert with other fields in the heterogeneous reality—
social activism, urbanism, science, and nature. But it can
only perform its part in the rhizome as a different kind of
practice, that is to say, as art. This idea sounds contrary to
an entire century of efforts to unite art and life. But that is
not entirely true; we need to remember that life is no longer
the same life it used to be: today life has become equal to
work. The new technologies have substantially contributed
to a blurring of the lines between work time and private
time, between life and work, and so also between work and
art. Today the dominant modes of production are imitating
art and imposing their own concepts of creativity on us.
We could say that capitalism has alienated the notion of
creativity from us and it is now art's task to redefine it. But
the most effective way for art to do this is to present itself
not as something completely different from production,
but as the production process itself. And this is just what
1:1 art tells us. Not only that artists are collaborating
with different communities in alternative economies
and cultures of living, but also that they are becoming
their own producers. It is in no way surprising that most
of the artists in *1:1 Stopover* operate within some sort of
self-organized work platform, such as artist-run spaces
or some other kind of non-governmental organization.

Let's consider another example from the show. One of the trio of artists, each of whom have the same name Janez Janša, is the director of the non-profit production and publishing house Maska, which co-produced the exhibition with us. The Moderna galerija had collaborated with Maska once before, on the production of the exhibition *Arteast Collection 2000+23* (22 September–22 October 2006), which among other things included fifty proposals for artworks that our museum was supposed to purchase in the year 2023. In *1:1 Stopover*, therefore, we included an 'archive-reminder' of the *Arteast* project, in other words, both an archive and a reminder to artists that they should provide us with information about the current state of their works-in-progress. In *1:1 stopover*, then, Janša was present in the role of co-producer, or rather in the redefined role of co-producer, which included his artistic proposal for horizontal collaborations with our institution to work out current artistic issues, such as a new way to conceive the creation of a museum collection.

It appears we're living in a topsy-turvy world: artists have tackled the role of producer, while commerce has assumed the form of art. Philosopher Giorgio Agamben writes about the musealization of the world, about how the crucial value today is exhibition-value.[6] We are valuable only to the degree that we are able to turn ourselves into an image that satisfies the needs of capital. Evidently, the avant-garde demand to unite art and life has in the end been realized by capital, not by art. So today, the only truly radical demand of art seems to be the demand to be separated from life—from a life that has become work, and from work that is equated with a creativity that has been robbed of all independent expression. Creativity has been relocated to a special sphere of capital, which

---

6   Agamben here relies on Walter Benjamin's concept of 'exhibition-value' [*Ausstellungswert*], which designates the transformation experienced by the artwork in the period of technological reproduction. 'Nothing better characterizes the new condition of objects and even the human body in the era of fulfilled capitalism. Into the Marxian opposition between use-value and exchange-value, exhibition-value introduces a third term, which cannot be reduced to the first two. It is not use-value, because what is exhibited is, as such, removed from the sphere of use; it is not exchange-value, because it in no way measures any labour power.' Giorgio Agamben, *Profanations* (New York: Zone Books, 2007), p. 90.

is, as Agamben notes, in a sense, a holy sphere and so must again be profaned. If we translate this idea into our context, we can say that art must be given a new use, not to make it equal with all other profanation, but to use it as a pure means, again, following Agamben—as a pure mediator in the creation of new kinds of social relations.[7] 1:1 art is based on various relations in which various roles are intertwined, but here there can never be any full equation between artist, curator, and member of this or that community. The only way it is possible to use art is as art.

We also exhibit it as such, whether or not we realize that it can never be captured in its entirety, in all of its duration, which can never be fully demarcated. And these unmarked remnants represent the potential of new interactions, which neither curators nor artists can entirely control. And this, it seems, is where we find the answer to our dilemma, namely that curators as well as artists must renounce our ambition to have total knowledge and control of our projects, for only in this way is it possible to consider 1:1 art and the presentation of 1:1 art outside the traditional roles of art and exhibition-making.

7 Ibid.

A Conversation between Charles Esche
and Manuel Borja-Villel

Use, Knowledge, Art, and History

This conversation took place during a L'Internationale confederation meeting in Ljubljana (22–24 June 2015).[1] It touches on the differences in approach and practical application of the two museum directors Charles Esche and Manuel Borja-Villel, and their institutions' respective programmes at the Van Abbemuseum, Eindhoven and Museo Nacional Centro de Arte Reina Sofía, Madrid. Both museums recently staged exhibitions that directly concerned use, knowledge, art, and history: *Really Useful Knowledge* in Madrid, and the *Museum of Arte Útil* and *Confessions of the Imperfect, 1848–1989–Today* in Eindhoven.[2] More than this, however, both museums strive to experiment with forms of exhibition and collection display, as well as to investigate the role of modern and contemporary art institutions. Moderated by Nick Aikens, Esche and Borja-Villel here expand on the relationships between use, knowledge, and history and how these concepts inform modes of working within the institutions and their recent exhibitions or public programmes.

Moments of Danger

<u>Charles Esche (CE)</u> For me, these three terms—use, knowledge, and history—are meaningful in relation to a certain analysis of the contemporary moment. I am interested in genealogies in general, but only insofar as they inform the present moment, or open up ideas that seem excluded by the current consensus. If we take history, then my approach is not about accounting for what was but seeing what is important in what cultural critic Walter Benjamin calls the 'moment of danger,' that is, whatever threatens or calls out for urgent attention.

If I have to describe that moment in my own terms, based on my Northwest-European provincialism, I would say the biggest moment of danger in the present remains the collective failure to come to terms with the big economic and technological changes that began in the 1980s. This is best illustrated by the year 1989, when the World Wide Web was born, the Berlin Wall came down, and real existing communism died. That's the historical moment that made our present possible—made some things thinkable again and changed what we might call the 'common sense' of society.

In my first years at the Van Abbemuseum from 2004 to 2010, I was constantly shocked by how little impact these changes had on the way knowledge was organized in the Netherlands and, in my field, the modernist assumptions about art and artistic quality. There seemed to me a false idea in Western Europe generally that a more or less unbroken continuity flowed from 1945 through the social changes of 1968 to the early

---

1 L'Internationale is a confederation of six modern and contemporary art institutions: Moderna galerija, Ljubljana; Museo Nacional Centro de Arte Reina Sofía, Madrid; Museu d'Art Contemporani de Barcelona (MACBA), Barcelona; Museum van Hedendaagse Kunst Antwerpen (M HKA), Antwerp; SALT, Istanbul and Ankara; and Van Abbemuseum, Eindhoven. L'Internationale works with complementary partners such as: Grizedale Arts, Coniston, United Kingdom; Liverpool John Moores University, Liverpool; Stiftung Universität Hildesheim, Hildesheim; and University College Ghent School of Arts, Ghent along with associate organizations from the academic and artistic fields. The confederation takes its name from the workers' anthem *L'Internationale*, which calls for an equitable and democratic society with reference to the historical labour movement.
2 *Really Useful Knowledge*, curated by What, How & for Whom/WHW, Museo Reina Sofía, Madrid, 29 October 2014–9 February 2015; *Museum of Arte Útil*, initiated by Tania Bruguera, Van Abbemuseum, Eindhoven, 7 December 2013–30 March 2014; and *Confessions of the Imperfect, 1848–1989–Today* curated by Steven ten Thije and Alistair Hudson, Van Abbemuseum, Eindhoven, 22 November 2014–22 February 2015.

twenty-first century. In this way, what I saw as
the 'moment of danger' was and is still failing to
significantly reshape the histories that are generally
shared and that create a common belief in why society
is the way that it is. From my point of view, this
misunderstanding of how the world had changed in
1989 was also contributing to how fundamental social
realities were subsequently perceived, such as climate
change and growing inequality, themselves the result
of the globalism heralded by the Internet and the
death of communism. While such a misunderstanding
was not universally shared, it was and remains very
widespread, to the extent that all change has become
threatening according to some liberal European
thought.

One of the ways that I would use to describe this
position of ignoring the fundamental changes of
the past twenty-five years in my field is 'hardcore
modernist.' By that I mean an unyielding application
of modernist value systems regarding ideas of quality,
artistic autonomy, and even style. It's a position
that is most easily caricatured by Dutch art schools
where students are taught autonomous art, as though
such a thing can be taught. It would seem a basic
truth, even in modernist terms, that autonomy has to
be taken not given and that it cannot be circumscribed
within a curriculum. By incorporating such an
important social concept as autonomy within the state
education system, it is made more or less meaningless,
and art itself becomes something without effective
social value, or without 'use,' to bring in our third
term. The last thing such an understanding of art
would need would be for art to matter in society and
change not only imagination but concrete conditions on
the ground.

So, increasingly I came to see the programme
at the Van Abbemuseum as a way to challenge the
inadequacies of a hardcore modernist position to
describe how art could play a role in post-1989
society and contribute to the looming fight for
sustainability and equality. The idea I had at the
beginning was to celebrate deviance from consensus
in the museum and to offer a different way of
functioning as an institution. Over time the idea
of utility as a problematic but stimulating term
arose, something that countered modernist autonomy
but didn't imply full instrumentalization. Utility
has a long tradition going back to eighteenth-

century philosopher David Hume and his ideas on the relationship between morality and utility. I believe it is worth exploring again through art, as perhaps the most quintessentially non-utilitarian thing. So, I hope you see here a trajectory from Benjaminian ideas of history through breaking down modernist understandings of knowledge, to the fraught concept of use and utility. In terms of programmes, you can see this line unwinding in signature group exhibitions such as *Forms of Resistance: Artists and the Desire for Social Change from 1871 to the Present* and *Be(com) ing Dutch*,[3] in the new version of the museum collection displays called *Once Upon a Time*, and in chronological exhibitions, especially the *Museum of Arte Útil* and *Confessions of the Imperfect*.

It is important to add here, that much of my thinking was shaped by Manuel Borja-Villel and his programmes at Museu d'Art Contemporani de Barcelona (MACBA). The way he developed an understanding of a museum as a place to gather, to test out ideas, and to discuss social alternatives, while making important art exhibitions, was very influential in what I tried to do in Eindhoven.

In Defence of Uselessness

Manuel Borja-Villel (MBV) Obviously we live in a period that is characterized by being a permanent present without historical roots or links. No doubt, this has to do with new technologies and the virtual disappearance of any space/time border or barrier (of course this 'freedom' is mostly of money, not of people). We live in a 24/7 society in which technology keeps us constantly alert as to what will happen every 5 minutes. This means that we lose a sense of history, a sense of future, and of time passing over the long term. We don't live this infinite present willingly, I don't think there is a conspiracy behind it at all, but clearly it represents a great change, almost a revolution in the way humans perceive themselves and their position in relation to each other and to time.

---

3 *Forms of Resistance: Artists and the Desire for Social Change from 1871 to the Present*, curated by Will Bradley, Phillip van den Bossche, and Charles Esche, 22 September 2007–6 January 2008 and *Be(com)ing Dutch*, curated by Charles Esche and Annie Fletcher, 24 May–14 September 2008 (both Van Abbemuseum, Eindhoven).

What we might do as a response is to think in the long term. There are forces that have focused their power and interest on money and material benefits and these have largely been the strongest forces in society. But there have also been a few movements where the important thing is that the human being builds a better society. The irony is that mostly the second, weaker tendency ends up saving the stronger one by helping humanity survive the crises where the focus of money and power usually leads. But, beyond these long-term processes, we can ask what has been happening in the last thirty years that makes it a specific historical period. One thing is obviously the technical revolution that facilitates the infinite present, but also this revolution emphasizes how the author disappears and the receiver or navigator becomes a co-author. Then, it is clear that the forces in the world have global impact but that the nation-state still forms our identity and our means of governmentality. It's a very strange situation. In a way we cannot talk any longer about for instance a Spanish or a Scottish political subject; things are both bigger and smaller than that. Yet it is still our main way of navigating the world and understanding ourselves. So, in a way, we live in a world that is not ours but to which we have to relate—a global world. Finally there is the digital field where people are no longer active but interactive. Everyone does things all the time. But their activity is too often nonsense. It is useless in the sense that it would help to improve the world or change it a little for the better. This is not what most of our activity is doing—it's not good for the world but it is mostly very good for business.

So, people in our position need to ask: What is the role of culture and art in all of this and what is our role politically? On the one hand, museums play a significant role in intellectual and art discourse. This was not always the case. In the 1940s, art discourse was generated by critics or gallerists and intellectual discourse was confined to the universities. Through artists like Michael Asher in the late 1960s, things started to change and the museum as institution became a site to discuss and to critique. Artists like Asher, Marcel Broodthaers, or Hans Haacke started to reflect on the ruins of the museum, in a way because they saw what was coming, that is, the loss of the museum as a site of general

Enlightenment education and knowledge. Museums like the Louvre or British Museum were born with the ideals of the Enlightenment and, however dark, colonial, and problematic Enlightenment values proved, they offered a promise of a bourgeois public sphere where values and education could be shared collectively by a limited number of enfranchised people. Now, instead of widening that franchise or recognizing the dark side of Enlightement values and modifying them, they were ignored and undermined. In their place, museums have become sites of total consumption. Already in the 1980s, Haacke wrote about museum directors being replaced by managers as a symptom of the absorption of culture by economy and management. Since that time in the 1980s, museums have become a kind of machinery for other things: tourism, embezzlement, state politics.

In these circumstances, we are working with tools that are basically no longer ours in that museums are already something else. We are in a world that is changing and our content-centred approach is basically anachronistic. Now, I would also say that the most radical art of the last thirty years is kind of anachronistic, perhaps with some exceptions related to art around new technologies. This art and our institutions then exist within a context and a public that are basically consumers who think they know what they want. Most importantly, they are a radically different political subject to the ones artists and museums spoke to during modernism. In modernity, the artistic avant-garde was connected to a political avant-garde and they were both working on the idea of sharing knowledge and education. Artists did this through developing a language that would allow a relative autonomy. The problem was how to create a language that drew on different sources but could still represent oneself. In this way the workers' movement and the avant-garde artists used photography, film, or collage to represent themselves because those used popular media and not the bourgeois language and culture of painting. Today, we don't need to look for a language of our own to represent ourselves. The problem is that language is co-opted almost from the beginning. It is no longer autonomous but rather empty. In this situation, art and the art institution have to understand that there is a political dimension to art and the art institution and that it relates to a place and specific struggles. For instance, if people are being expelled from a neighbourhood near the museum, the institution has to talk to them, you cannot pretend they don't exist. For this exchange to be meaningful, you have to be there. It's very difficult to be a kind of biennial artist, moving from one place to another or exporting your political actions and holding leftist salons. Secondly, you need aesthetic experience in a true space of exchange that does not distract you every five minutes. This means talking to the other and creating a space which is relational. In that sense, I have doubts about the idea of usefulness. If art is to be anything today it has to create outflows of meanings and favour new forms of understanding and relationships. Being 'useful' is something else.

I have lots of problems with the notion of Arte Útil. I think basically one of the problems is that its advocates don't take into account the materiality of the work of art and what it does in the world. It is important to understand that you can never predict the results of a work of art or whether it will have a use-value in the future that is unknown today. It also seems silly to me to think that just by making an exhibition which includes political content you are doing a political action. An exhibition can change the perception of the world, and that could be political, but then it should be analyzed politically. I am concerned about some kind of fashionable leftism around the idea as well, when art is easy to co-opt or to become the very thing that it fears being. As you know, I have worked with Hans Haacke and Krzysztof Wodiczko and I absolutely support what they do. These artists are often included in the Arte Útil category, but to me their production does not fit that artistic trend. First of all, because the work's conditions of production are incorporated into that same work. This is quite important as, also referring to Benjamin, art cannot be critical if it does not reflect upon its own conditions of production. And I don't see that happening in most of the so-called Arte Útil.

Secondly, and this is a consequence of the first point, artists like Haacke and Wodiczko are fully aware of the place their work occupies within the art system. When Haacke, for instance, denounced real estate speculation in an exhibition which we organized at the Reina Sofía a few years ago, he did it from the point of view of the role art had in the art system.[4]

---

4 Hans Haacke, *Castles in the Air*, Museo Reina Sofía, Madrid, 15 February–23 July 2012.

Similarly, Wodiczko designs the *Homeless Vehicle* not to produce a prototype which will solve our social problems, but to provoke impossible situations, moments of difficult 'digestion' by any well-intentioned spectator.[5] Wodiczko is not a reformist. Can anybody imagine a city populated by homeless people carrying their vehicles from one place to another? This is not Utopia, it is rather a nightmare from which we might want to wake up.

In today's society, art has to be valueless because the moment it has value you forget its other qualities. Value means that it will be bought and sold, turned into a communicational commodity, and then every political aspect of the work will be totally empty. So I think art has to be useless in the sense that it should have a structure that almost makes it impossible to be absorbed by the industry of communication, makes it impossible to be absorbed by the market. I will give you some examples of artists that work in that dimension, James Coleman for one. Of course, he has a system of distribution and there are people that buy his things, but the work is basically made so that you can do very little with it: you cannot use it for advertising, it is complicated to sell it at auction. In different ways, the same is true for Broodthaers or Asher. All their works have something intrinsic that makes it very difficult to absorb into the system and that's essential for me. Another route toward valuelessness departs from a more political point of view. I am thinking as much about art as the art institution and any cultural or educational practice that becomes difficult to absorb because it keeps changing.

My big problem with Arte Útil is the ahistorical use of words here. I don't think it is possible to persuade people anymore. It's a kind of nostalgia for educational ideas from the past. People are consumers now, you cannot tell them anything because they don't care or they will not listen. We run museums and we know when tourists come this type of practice doesn't work. The other problem is that the artists might also be cynically using politics to promote themselves. I think you have to be very careful.

---

5 Krzysztof Wodiczko's *Homeless Vehicle* project (1988) consists of a series of prototype vehicles providing shelter for the homeless.

Useful Art or Beyond Abyssal Thinking?

CE I think we are products of our own environments and one of our abiding concerns is history in historical times. Yet, we see these things quite differently as well and that might come from the North-South difference. Being from the absolute core of Western Europe, from the place the United States most needed to have on its side after the Second World War, gave us huge confidence over three generations in our story of the world. That might have been less true in Spain during the same period. Part of what I do today, in an art historical and museological sense, is to try to shake that confidence. One way to do that is to combine contradictory ideas that are used ahistorically or outside art's traditional frame of reference. Now, of course, the *Museum of Arte Útil* is an initiative of Tania Bruguera from Cuba, so maybe my geographic essentialism is overdone, but clearly Manuel and I differ in our relation to history and it makes us trust different artistic practices I think. The *Museum of Arte Útil* is one in a whole series of attempts to rewrite history in light of the present and therefore to disobey historical 'rules.' These are not alternatives to the historical narrative but a series of other parallel and coexisting versions, as I think was very clear from seeing the *Museum of Arte Útil* and then *Confessions of the Imperfect*, which covered the same chronology in very different ways. That kind of agonism within the museum excites me and I am not so sure that our public do not see it and are not drawn in. My experience, in a much smaller museum than Reina Sofía with few tourists, is that over time and by following different exhibitions and collection displays some people have become more interested and understanding of what we are doing.

I also think that utility is a very important tactical term to wake up the sleeping spirits of autonomy and to force open a discussion about why autonomy might be important in a Dutch situation where the vast majority of art is state sponsored. Until very recently, and still today, many artists are dependent on the state system and at the same time claim their own absolute autonomy in conversations. That seemed to me quite absurd and in need of a little provoking, so Tania's initial idea served a very local problematic. If we continue speaking of the local situation and the differences across Europe, then it is important to remember that capitalism, at least the idea of the stock holding company, was born in Amsterdam and that colonial extraction was financed through the Netherlands. That means that the origins of neoliberalism are Dutch and they are encoded by a certain religious and environmental tradition that has been exported around the world to places that do not necessarily have much instinctive understanding of it. That sense of ownership of capitalism is of course something which also gives Dutch society a very deep, rooted confidence that, in today's world, can seem inappropriate. Arte Útil in this context might be understood differently than in Spain or in Cuba and it is important to acknowledge that.

On the other hand, I am very sympathetic to your critique of salon radicalism and ineffectual leftism. I do doubt the extent to which the art world can carry its claims to political correctness given the deep engagement of the oligarchy and the way so much art seems to decorate the appallingly unequal status quo. However, in those circumstances I think that group and subject exhibitions such as the *Museum of Arte Útil* or *Confessions of the Imperfect* offer a different kind of resistance to what you find in Coleman and Broodthaers. The works themselves might be commodified later but at that moment they are placed within a narrative that is not easily dismissed. For instance, I took it as a great compliment when the director of the White Cube Gallery said that our last São Paulo Biennial was 'not for an art mogul like him.'[6] In that way, the framing of work, its curatorial treatment if you like, can help it to resist a little longer I think.

MBV I agree with this idea of different histories in different parts of Europe or European America. I think it would be important to add a warning that this kind of plurality can also be neoliberal in that it can remove all perspective. Uncritical pluralism can just become another set of choices where you have no sense of reality, like in a supermarket or shopping mall.

---

6 *How to (…) things that don't exist*, curated by Galit Eilat, Charles Esche, Nuria Enguita Mayo, Pablo Lafuente, and Oren Sagiv, 31st São Paulo Biennial, 6 September–7 December 2014.

CE But there should be a difference between singular pluralities and different chronologies that in themselves form a coherent narrative. In that way you provide touchstones and tools for comparison.

MBV Yes, for sure, but I would also want to add something else that is very important and is summed up by sociologist Boaventura de Sousa Santos as 'beyond-abssal thinking.'[7] De Sousa Santos proposes not only a type of knowledge which is against the homogenization and universalism of modern culture and in favour of plurality, but also one that believes that an ecology of knowledge can only be based on the fact that all knowledge is always inter-knowledge, a knowledge based on the relationship and antagonism of ideas. It is not just a derivative form of knowledge as it could be just a general pluralism, but a break with Western forms of acting and thinking. To think critically today means to think from the perspective of the other and, therefore, to question our own position, even if this position is plural. It is not only that there are different stories but that there is a chasm between them that makes them irreconcilable. So it is not just about difference by itself. This element of the abyssal is crucial.

CE I agree and I think that is there in our projects, again in the complexity of the narratives that makes them irreconcilable.

MBV Good, I agree. But if we look at some of the tendencies of Arte Útil, for example, there are other elements that worry me. One is that there seems to be a promise of happiness, this idea that by doing something, you have a happy, consensual community, whereas I think critical art is always negative. As said, this would be the case of Wodiczko's *Homeless Vehicle*. Its 'utopian' design and the reality of society can only be reconciled in abyss. Secondly, I don't think art needs to work on a large scale. Take a fundamental modern author like Stéphane Mallarmé and his most influential poem, *Un coup de dés*, written

---

7 See Boaventura de Sousa Santos, 'Beyond Abyssal Thinking: From Global Lines to Ecologies of Knowledge,' *Review* 1 (2007), pp. 45–89, www.ces.uc.pt/bss/documentos/AbyssalThinking.pdf.

in 1897 but only published in 1914. His original
constituency, his readers, was a very small group
of people. Yet, the poem's ultimate influence is so
profound that it is considered by many as the starting
point of the modern space. Ideas like his may be small
but the circles gradually widen. Mallarmé addressed
his texts 'à qui veut,' to whoever wants to receive
them. That does not mean that he did not want to reach
out to other people, but just that he did not want
to do it indiscriminately. It's what Mallarmé called
restrained actions that slowly gather force.

CE I still think you are characterizing Arte Útil too
narrowly. But let's take another historical period
that is perhaps closer to our own time: the 1920s.
There were moments where artists were aligned with big
causes and political revolution, where art did have a
purchase on social change. Do you think that time was
a complete exception?

MBV The 1920s and 1930s are closer to us today. In a
way, you could say that the Second World War and the
promise of social democracy were the exception because
it feels like we are returning to that earlier state.
This period saw the first popular movements and artists
working directly for new political constituencies such
as El Lissitzky or Alexander Rodchenko. What is maybe
more interesting for us is the way that work was later
taken by institutions such as MoMA in New York and
normalized within a canonical art narrative. Perhaps
we can learn something from this process. Museums need
to think how to create the conditions to reflect on
popular culture again.

I am tired of art institutions, artists, critics,
curators, and directors complaining about lack of
government money. People are suffering again, losing
their jobs and their homes. Artists sometimes come to
me to complain about why the museum doesn't care about
them, doesn't buy their work, and so on. But we are
all precarious now, given the current crisis that is
not going away soon. Of course, there are no museums
without artists but there are also no museums without
the doorman or the bricklayer. The museum belongs to
society and to the public and it is our job to create
a space of agony where people can contribute with what
they know. When it works, the museum creates not only

knowledge, but also a will to learn, a will to have freedom, a will to get together and create a community of affection through learning together. This process should not be about results. It needs to be open but also opaque and complex. I think Arte Útil as an idea misses this element. It can too easily become about sharing communication.

I think the museum's potentiality lies in being anachronistic. We have a chance because, in a way, what we do has no real value. We should be uncomfortable, not in a masochistic sense, but as a space that requires agency to function. After the crisis, after the 15-M Movement and the Arab Spring and everything else, we need to rethink the public space, in the sense that architect Aldo van Eyck, artist Constant, and many others did: as a place where people can come together and rethink the world. We have to learn and relate to how movements organize themselves and to rethink the meaning of the public and popular. This is what *Really Useful Knowledge* was about.

CE I think *Really Useful Knowledge* was important but still it is for me complementary to the *Museum of Arte Útil* or *Confessions of the Imperfect*, rather than antagonistic. If we take the materiality and layout of the exhibitions, we can find some physical resonances that are important. All three exhibitions were built as tools to explore a narrative, and tool is close to utility. Also, a tool requires a user in order to be activated and agency, as you say, in order to make it function. So Arte Útil implies a user and his/her agency as much as it implies the idea of usefulness for me. But I also want to defend Stephen Wright's idea of usership here.[8] I'm thinking of a project like that of Apolonija Šušteršič where she uses light therapy to create a meeting room inside the museum that can be reserved and where another kind of pervasive energy would be present, allowing different kinds of conversations and even decisions.[9] During the Arte Útil exhibition, the room was used quite

---

8 See Stephen Wright, 'Toward a Lexicon of Usership' in this reader, pp. 468–487.
9 Apolonija Šušteršič's *Light Therapy Room*, first created for the Moderna Museet, Stockholm in 1999, was conceived for the *Museum of Arte Útil* to increase communication and social interaction, drawing on the benefits of ultramarine light. The public could use the light therapy room for meetings, discussions and workshops. The project was realized in collaboration wit Eindhoven-based organizations Light & Health Research Foundation (SOLG) and Philips Lighting.

frequently for meetings of the city council or local businesses. I heard testimony that the atmosphere of the meetings was different—not only because of the light but also for taking place in a museum, thereby changing the dynamic of the gatherings in quite abstract ways. Yet the physicality of the experience was important and the users took responsibility for adjusting to their new environment, or at least for being conscious that abnormal discussions were possible. There wasn't a circumscribed outcome to the meeting but what seemed to me an almost spiritual shift that allowed a different agency to exist. It changed people's preconceptions of what a museum might be in a direction I think we both would support. The same happened with Grizedale's *Honest Shop* I believe.[10] So, in this sense, I want to stay with Arte Útil and continue to build the archive and think through it in the museum. It has really opened up the use and purpose of the museum. In a different way, this happened partially in the classroom settings of *Confessions of the Imperfect*. Both experiences have led us to repurpose some of the exhibition rooms in the museum.

The other point I want to make reinforces what you are saying. One of the great challenges that we have as a state or local government institution is to redefine our relationship to the state itself. This touches on how to communicate with new social movements. One of the great falsehoods of social democracy was that the state is on society's side and we need to rely on it rather than be suspicious and interrogate it regularly. We have seen the retreat of the state in the last thirty years, but no real critique of it from the left or on the part of public interest. There is the developing notion of the commons of course but no clear sense of what institutions of the commons will look like and how they can survive economically. I think usefulness, utility, and usership will be crucial terms in developing a museum of the commons for instance. They will not replace your ideas of anachronism, the abyssal, and difficulty, but they will parallel them. It will help us to refocus on the public and serving their interests rather than the interests of the state or its political agents.

---

10 The *Honest Shop*, initiated by Grizedale Arts, was part of the *Museum of Arte Útil*. The project, initiated in Conniston, UK, was a village *shop* selling homemade produced articles or products on an *honesty* basis.

MBV You mentioned therapy and I would say that most therapists would not recommend light therapy so probably it is not useful in my understanding. Also, I wonder how you do therapy in a museum. It is a place to walk through or about, to get lost in, but not a place for therapy that implies a continuous relationship with a patient. Secondly, the state: I agree with you, but two other things I think are important. If we look at degraded communities, they have had support from priests in the distant past, later from state social workers and now you have some artists going to those communities. In the end, you wonder whether we are not just facilitating privatizations. Then I would add another element of this failure of the state, which is where we started in fact. The large, holistic nation-state with its language community etc., is a big part of our identity. Even though we know that the state and our language are constructions and that one is not better than the other, we still need it to locate ourselves and where we come from. However, this castle protecting our identity has become an empty shell; it's a castle of cards and another way in which we face an abyss between two conditions: the global economy and our personal identity.

CE I feel in the end, we come quite close to each other in that the necessity of exposing things that are irreconcilable is shared. I also think we are both looking for small victories if you like—examples where art shows what is possible if the common sense were different and agency of the public activated. I see that more in repurposing an historical lineage in a Benjaminian sense and you in the idea of the abyssal from De Sousa Santos. It's an important difference and one we should keep talking about.

Usership is operative only in the here and now—it has no transcendental horizon line.

Quote
Stephen Wright, *Toward a Lexicon of Usership*
→ **See p. 486**

Art is living the future in the present.

Quote
Tania Bruguera, *Reflexions of Arte Útil*
→ See p. 316

The Barricade Has Fragmented and Multiplied

Liam Gillick

The location of the barricade has moved. The focus of resistance has shifted away from the main event. The barricade has multiplied and adopted new forms. What looks like a barricade is often a deception— a barrier and crowd control tool that is set up by those who are in control in order to keep protestors confused and contained.

In Britain the technique known as 'kettling' involves the police keeping demonstrators within their supposedly chosen zone of protest. In opposition to traditional and ineffective techniques of 'crowd dispersal' such as the calamitous efforts in Ferguson, Missouri, kettling keeps protestors tightly packed, often at the heart of the action, preventing people from leaving or moving. When the G20 meets in some zone near a golf course at a resort or controlled leisure environment, the barricades are now set many kilometres from the centre of action. Multiple barricades are erected, not by the protestors but by the forces of order. There is little way of knowing if these barricades are located to deceive or to confuse, they are at least out of sight to all but a few cameras and an impotent band of traditional protestors.

All of this is a long way from the famous image of a barricade finely draped with cinema posters on the streets of Paris in 1968. The erection of a barricade against the charging agents of order has become a faded memory for most. And replaced—at best—with the image of a group hastily upturning a car, remaining fluid, moving along, shifting fast, and attempting to avoid the placement and control of space that occurs with the erection of authorities' barriers.

In Western Europe we are now used to this reconfigured demonstration. A vanguard of young, primarily male, balaclava-hooded mobile forces move toward any symbol of corporate consumption. Banks, Starbucks', car showrooms—all are targeted for maximum media attention. Ecstatic showers of glass are combined with perfect facades for temporary expressions of anarchistic marking. Meanwhile, the rump of the demo are driven like cattle into the illusion of a place of free dissent—'kettled' in a central

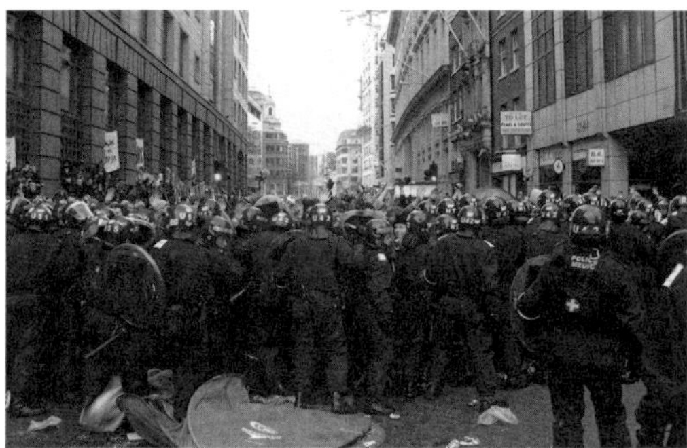

Fig 1 Riot police kettle protesters at the Camp for Climate action, part of the 2009 G20 London summit protests

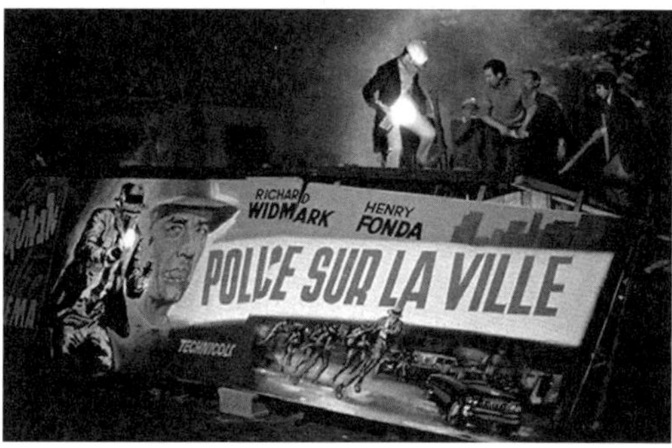

Fig 2 Bruno Barbey, 24 May 1968, Rue de Lyon, Paris, barricade made out of movie posters

zone until they beg to be let out peaceably.

The barricade has fragmented and multiplied. The transfer of the barricade from the protestor to the 'forces of order' is well documented. It has prompted new mobile tactics and attempts to redirect focus. But none of this is effective in a society that has created multiple barricades—some of which are transparent, some of which are self-generated yet out of control.

For *Confessions of the Imperfect, 1848–1989– Today* at the Van Abbemuseum in Eindhoven, I used various models of contemporary and historical barricades as a framing method for an exhibition that documents and reflects upon the two great soft revolutionary moments of European history: 1848 and 1989. I used the term 'soft' not to suggest lack of pain or struggle but to point toward these key events as moments where territory and authority shifted. There were moments of violence, but primarily these events involved the ceding of territory to a broad set of aspirations rather than sustained insurrection. My focus was on the implications of 1989 in relation to the barricade as a form for today's

society; I used the barricade as a structural motif—starting with the street blockades of the 1840s intended to disrupt the cavalry charge, through to the surveillance culture of today, where the personal computer is constantly under attack. Sometimes visible as a framing device in the museum, at other times the barricade was virtual—providing a soundscape or reminiscent of the improvised barricades that take the form of stores and libraries as constructed by the various Occupy movements. From confrontation to irritation the barricade became the backdrop to the content and a history of discontent in a state of dynamic flux.

Twenty-five years on it is hard for some to remember the degree of anxiety that was building in the months leading up to the first breach of the Berlin Wall. The sense of imminent state violence was palpable. For many, especially on the left, the feeling that some trigger may be pulled or button pressed mitigated the sense of anticipation born by the breakdown of the Iron Curtain. Memories are skewed. Margaret Thatcher—still held up by many as some kind of

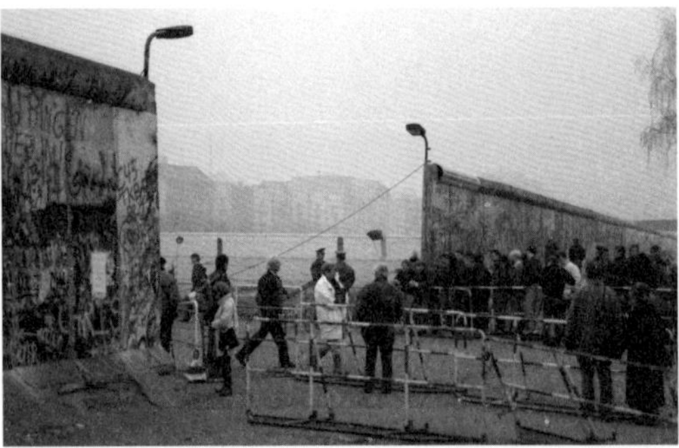

Fig 3   The Potsdamer Platz
crossing, seen from West Berlin
into East Berlin, opened days
after the first breach of the
Berlin Wall in November 1989

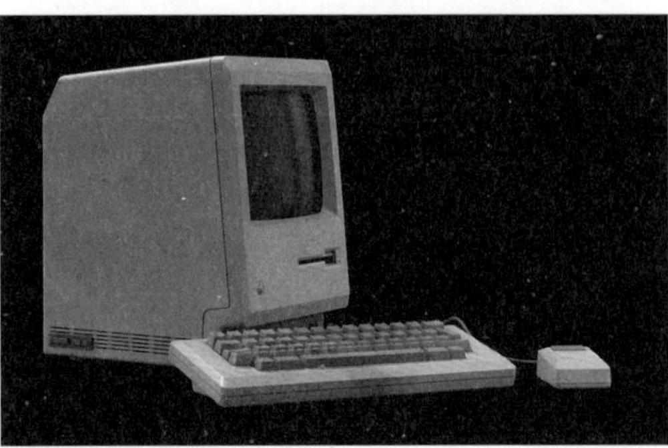

Fig 4   The Apple Macintosh
512 K

beacon of liberty—counselled against the fall of the wall, stating to Mikhail Gorbachev in 1989, 'We do not want a united Germany, this would lead to a change to postwar borders, and we cannot allow that because such a development would undermine the stability of the whole international situation and could endanger our security.' Yet the Berlin Wall fell regardless of political anxieties at the centre of power. And I argue that the image of an institutional barricade being pulled down—first by Berliners and then by those who had constructed the wall in the first place—led to a proliferation of state-controlled temporary barricades and a consequent rejection of the barricade as a form by the remainder of the old left and other new activist groupings.

1989 was the beginning of new development in the potential for electronic communication. The first functional yet expensive Apple computer, the Macintosh SE/30, was released that year. PCs were already proliferating in offices, homes, and governments. The first peripheral computing fortunes were made from the sale of anti-virus software. Even at that point there was a consciousness that the computer was a potential point of surveillance and take-over despite the fact that it was later revealed that most viruses were exaggerated to promote sales of anti-virus software.

Yet fear was widespread. The computer user began a process of producing firewalls and barricades around their vulnerable system. The notion that one is under threat from an unseen enemy who can gain access to everything and remotely steal and destroy your identity. This awareness coincided with increasing mobility on the part of protestors. Barricades in their traditional form had become traps carefully constructed by security forces as a form of human holding pens—the barricade fragmented and multiplied rather than functioning as a refuge or hindrance. Barricades took on new forms in a world of limitless control. Movement and disguise became the new barricades. Masked runners cloaking their identities became the latest attempt to block out order, repression, and identification.

Annie Fletcher in Conversation
with Tania Bruguera

Exhibiting and Instituting Arte Útil

Annie Fletcher (AF) In the roundtable discussion in this section a group of curators discuss exhibiting and use. Alistair Hudson says something really interesting: 'If we were idealistic about Arte Útil there would not be any exhibition at all and all these projects would operate on a 1:1 scale in the museum.'[1] I know this thought is very close to your heart…

Tania Bruguera (TB) I agree 100 percent. Because you remember how troubled I was that we were actually having an exhibition.

AF Sure, by making an exhibition with practice, and thereby mainly trying to function beyond representation out in the world as it were, we were faced with the museum's inadequacies and habits of representation all the time.

TB That was a tactic though. We wanted to show the legitimacy of the discourse, the kind of archeology behind it, which I think is extremely important. But here, there were a lot of challenges when we found out that there were other artists like Pino Poggi, who had named the movement of Arte Útil.[2] So we had to deal with precursors, which were not out when we were trying to identify a history and a set of criteria. These became contradictions and frictions that we had to deal with in a very positive way.

AF Absolutely, looking back at the *Museum of Arte Útil,* the show was really dynamic, exploratory, and significant. But it had conceptual holes. Those erasures, failures, and overlaps were productive and we knew it. We knew we were trying to articulate many impossible things. That is what excites me most about curating and staging an encounter. I think your insistence on the political nature of making the history visible and strategically using the museum's

---

1 Alistair Hudson referencing the 1:1 entry in Stephen Wright's lexicon in 'Really Útil Confessions: A Conversation between Nick Aikens, Annie Fletcher, Alistair Hudson, Steven ten Thije, and What, How & for Whom/ WHW' in this reader, pp. 448–465.
2 See Pino Poggi, *Arte Util, Arte Utile – Konzepte – Bücher – Environments – Aktionen – Modelle* (Munich: Silke Schreiber, 1986).

position in relation to power and visibility was fascinating. You were repurposing the museum.

TB It was important for me to be clear that this was not a fantastical egotistic idea. It was not a capricious artist coming up with a new movement for the sake of making a comment about art history, but a serious endeavour, trying to show that there is a whole history of artists who work in this way, yet they are normally invisible to the museum. We were doing an activist show in terms of art history by demanding the inclusion of this practice in the history of art. It was not a passive exhibition—it was a demand to art historians: 'Hey! Why haven't you looked at all these things that are here, they are being documented.'

AF Yes in the roundtable What, How & for Whom/WHW remark on the tension between exhibiting and historicizing activist practices in their exhibition *Really Useful Knowledge* at the Museo Nacional Centro de Arte Reina Sofía, Madrid from 29 October 2014 to 9 February 2015. You are also talking about the relationship between representation, politics, and activism, and how this is historicized in the museum. It's not about measuring it in terms of success or failure—the act of negotiation is equally a part of the intellectual project.

TB I think for me one very important part of the show was the fact that the archive is going to be maintained by the museum, and disseminated by a variety of different people, like Gemma Medina Estupiñán and Alessandra Saviotti are doing with *Broadcasting the Archive*.[3] I think this is not about buying the work. It's about the role of the museum as the keeper of this knowledge and the distributor of the knowledge, like we are doing right now, and I'm very grateful for that.

---

3 Broadcasting the archive is an independent project conceived by Gemma Medina Estupiñán and Alessandra Saviotti and supported by the Mondriaan Fund to emancipate the usership around the Arte Útil archive. www.arte-util.org/broadcasting-the-archive-a-year-long-project-by-gemma-medina-estupinan-and-alessandra-saviotti.

AF One of the more productive challenges for us has been to try to conceive of museum visitors as users, people who engage with Arte Útil and who benefit from it. So the relationship to art is completely different from that of the traditional spectator. It meant we started to think in a much more elaborate way about the public as constituents. We have a constituency who can, if you think about the political roots of the term, not only have a beneficial relationship with the museum, but negotiate the stakes, even decide what is beneficial and what is not. This power relationship is potentially transformative and it's one of the long-term ways in which we are trying to imagine the museum differently.

TB Yes, to give the audience a role, not a passive role where they come to absorb what is displayed. This is the distinction with 'participatory' art. What you have then is a kind of client role where your services are rendered. After these services are rendered they leave, they do not have the potential to affect how a moment, project, even a whole institution, might evolve. In the case of users or constituencies it is more about what you can bring and how the institution opens itself up to those different inputs. It's also a much longer term and more invested relationship.

AF I suppose the idea of participation is that it's active and in motion. But it's passive motion.

TB Exactly, touching a button in an installation does not mean you have the right to change the course of the work. In the case of Arte Útil there is a generosity in a way that through your involvement you might change the outcome of the work. There is also trust. In the art world we have developed a classist relationship with our audiences. We feel above our audiences.

AF Yes, the relationship remains quite paternalistic. When Stephen Wright grappled with ideas of what using might mean he talked about misuse, that institutions and experts (people like me), despite the rhetoric, are actually terrified of misuse.[4]

> **TB** We are all trained to be afraid of it; it is about pleasing the client, whether the client is an audience member, a collector, or an institution. This is the consequence of relentless professionalization. Arte Útil goes against that. It also champions, to a certain extent, non-skilled art in that the processes and strategies do not need high levels of artistic training. And that gives people the feeling that they can intervene.

AF It redresses the balance a little bit. I listened recently to a forecast on the future of creativity by artist and activist Manuel Beltrán. He was saying that one of the strongest and most sustainable movements will be peer-to-peer creativity. The resources you and the archive are pulling together with Arte Útil might be forecasting that too.

> **TB** Yes, but it cannot fall into a false populism. How can one bring the knowledge, in all of its complexity, so it can be shared without being simplified? I have worked with people who were barely literate but immensely knowledgeable. Their experience and knowledge is developed in the field. They don't have the 'sophistical globalized view' that contemporary art exists in. They were very happy to do Arte Útil because they understood the complexity immediately.

AF When we made the decision to look at the notion of strategy, we decided not to categorize projects in relation to geography or time. You were the one who identified this. What we needed to use for the recalibration of this history was actually your idea of 'strategy.' There are extraordinary strategies being deployed all the time by human beings to survive, live, and work, and that are flexible,

---

4 See Stephen Wright, 'Toward a Lexicon of Usership' in this reader, pp. 468–487.

creative, radical, and proven through use—whether
it's a creative moment, an artistic moment, or an
intellectual moment. And I think it's important to
understand Arte Útil through strategies—the tactics,
but also the impulses that are behind the work. So the
idea of 're-purposing institutions,' which was one of
the strategies, reveals a particular relationship to
how Arte Útil practitioners work with organizational
frameworks, or 'A-legal' allows us to understand how
certain projects operate in grey areas of the law.

TB I think what Arte Útil has just begun to explore
is the need to understand that art is not only about
exposing or making visible a problem. Arte Útil is
trying to propose something more. It's saying, 'Yes,
we do visualize the problem but we don't stay there.
We want things to be proven through use, we want to
implement things in reality.' I feel like now we
are in a moment that art has to step forward. We
have so many resources on hand as practitioners. Not
economically speaking, but in terms of the attention
it receives, certain artists' capacity to use and
think beyond existing frameworks and the way we insist
on more than what is given to us. What Arte Útil does
is put all of these resources into use. And it must be
implemented!

AF I like that idea of art being slightly disabled,
not fulfilling it's fullest potential. But it's a heavy
burden.

TB Well, it's good you say that because the *Museum of
Arte Útil* was criticized as if it was absolute or a
totalitarian argument. But we have never said that
Arte Útil is the *only* way. It is among a variety of
options. What we propose is the right for this to be
part of the conversation in art, because it seems that
when things are useful or they go beyond this kind of
traditional way of seeing art, then they are dismissed
as not art. We want to say, 'Okay, we agree that
everything else exists but there can be another way.'

AF I remember artist Xavier Fourt from Bureau d'Études
said the essence of the *Museum of Arte Útil* was
trying to show the productivity of the movement. I
think he was right. That energized us in making the
exhibition. It was a political act which goes back to
how we deployed the museum. Do you feel like you are
preparing for a moment of change? We have identified
why the museum and modernism are not useful to us
anymore or what artistic practices we can ally with.
So we are in a moment that we are recalibrating.

TB Things are changing in society. Today, there is a
proliferation of social movements, citizens demanding
to have more power to change things. So it feels
inappropriate to have a relationship to art that is
inherited from modernism but has nothing to do with
the world we are living in now. I feel that one of the
aims of Arte Útil is to see what kind of art we can do
for this new kind of society. It's not about negating
what already happened. But we need to recalibrate
history. What kind of art goes with this? What kind of
art corresponds to new social thinking and political
behaviour?

AF You said you have two other formats in which you
want to realize or think about Arte Útil. Can you tell
me more about what they are?

TB I have a three-phase plan! The first was to make
the *Museum of Arte Útil*, so as to historically stamp
the movement and to challenge the structure of the
museum. I imagine the second phase of the project to
be developing a 'non-institutionally-based project,'
so doing it within a different time frame, appropriate
to how projects unfold and users engage with them. The
third one will be more archival: how to document the
projects and the processes as they unfold. Those are
the three phases: history, doing it in real time and
real space, and keeping the memory of it alive.

Understanding the Social Power Plant

constructLab

Design as a Tool

The design and scenographic conception of the *Museum of Arte Útil* was developed in collaboration with constructLab, a collaborative group of architects, designers, and intellectuals among others including Alexander Roemer, Bureau d'Études, and Collective Works.

Unlike the conventional architectural process in which the architect designs and the builder builds, in constructLab's projects, concept and construction are brought together. The construction site is the context in which the project can be enriched by unexpected opportunities that happen on site. For the *Museum of Arte Útil*, constructLab introduced the notion of the Social Power Plant, conceiving the physical space of the museum as a site for collaborative, generative action that can be taken into the outside world. Working on site for two weeks, a team of twelve designed and built the physical spaces of the rooms. Their collaborative and spontaneous approach with artists and museum employees created a synergy that resulted in a collective work in which others felt comfortable to intervene and to use as they saw fit.

Understanding the Social Power Plant

A museum can become a social power plant when users, curators, artists, and museum employees come together to create different forms of agency that serve different values: the pollination of a culture of commons, struggle against private interests, and the use of a social decision process.

Arte Útil projects are the resources used by the Social Power Plant which then processes and reactivates them to make proposals for use in local situations.

A social power plant transforms society via different modes of operation:

– An incubating process produces the basis for social transformation by repurposing use. In the *Museum of Arte Útil*, this process takes form through a game that reemploys Arte Útil projects as prototypes or models for local situations.

– A generating process is the fabric for social self-organization. It operates through a boiler (discussion, debate) and by using social batteries (common resources). In the *Museum*

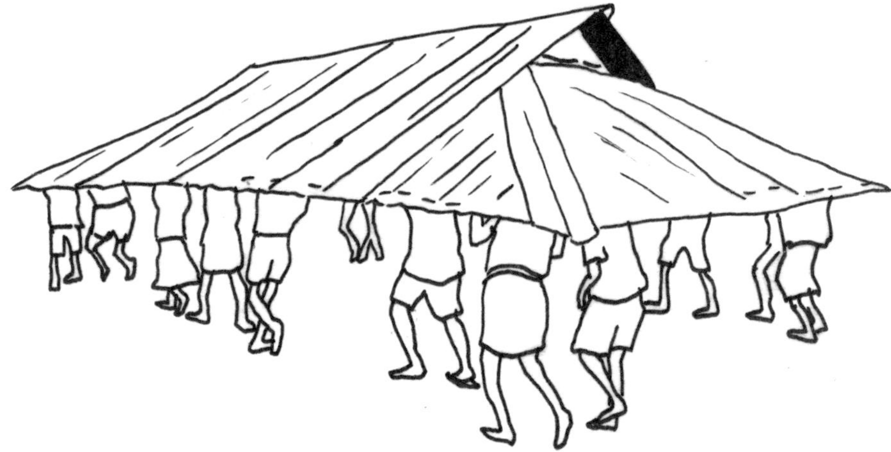

Fig 1 constructLab, museum
as power plant, 2014

of Arte Útil, this process takes form, before the exhibition, through the multiple discussions and social decision processes between curators, artists, and employees.

- A disrupting process stops or hijacks contested social uses, social functions, or existing organization. It operates through disjunctors, surprises, or breakers. In the *Museum of Arte Útil*, this process takes form within the contradiction between institutional constraints (making an exhibition in a classical way, refusing some projects which challenge the legitimacy of the museum, and reproducing standard ways the museum produces a scenography) and the desire of the artists to implement new operations in the museum (for example, employing illegal refugees for the installation of the exhibition to give them a legal status).

- A catalyzing process is produced through the aggregation of the three preceding operations. In the *Museum of Arte Útil* this process takes the form of the exhibition itself.

- A pollination process operates by emulating or amplifying an incubating, a generating, or

a disrupting process. The pollination process is a tool whereby the other processes to be empowered. In the *Museum of Arte Útil* it takes form when an Arte Útil project is realized in Eindhoven.

- A transmuting process includes models, prototypes, or simulations which, through concepts, images, or constructions make proposals for new uses or social practices. In the *Museum of Arte Útil*, this process takes form if the Van Abbemuseum becomes a Museum of Arte Útil permanently.

**Tools to enter the process of
the Social Power Plant:**
The *Museum of Arte Útil* as a social power plant is a place of resources, research, and production. The ideas presented are part of a debate, without a clear nomenclature. Some prototypes are in process but can be challenged in the Room of Controversies.

The scenography gives a condensed view of the global approach adopted in this exhibition:

- The white walls of the institution presents projects extracted from the Arte Útil archive.

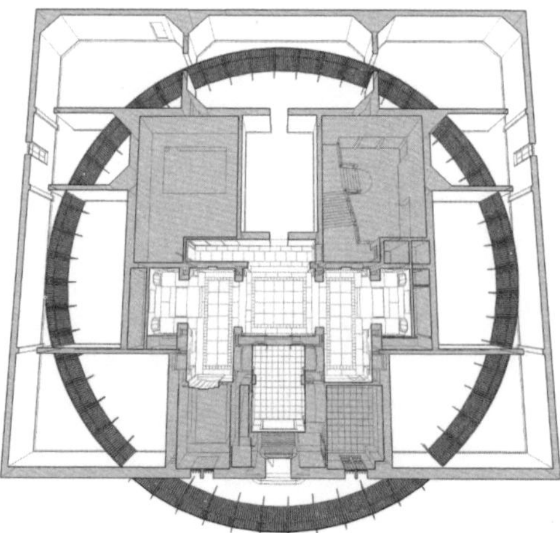

— The wooden wall of the Social Power Plant is a
display in progress with the possibility to add
documents or images during the exhibition.

— These two approaches (institutional and
Social Power Plant) are articulated in each
room through seven strategies such as 'Use
it Yourself' and 'Institutional Repurpose.'

— The archive in the central room is the heart
of the Social Power Plant. It is articulated
with a map and a game.

— The map of the Social Power Plant in the
archive room presents case studies which
are disseminated through time and space.
They are all part of a global social power plant,
which works together to transform societies.

Some Reflections on Collaboration
What would a 'Museum of Arte Útil' look and
feel like? Is the architecture and constraints of
a museum compatible with the notion of Arte
Útil? What are the politics involved in a genuinely
collaborative process where different agendas
(personal, political, institutional) are at play?

These were the questions that drove the
process of building the *Museum of Arte Útil* at
the Van Abbemuseum in Eindhoven. For the
collective constructLab, who were invited
to conceptualize and build the scenography
of the exhibition, it involved working with
the Van Abbemuseum curators and artist
Tania Bruguera for a year in the lead up to
the exhibition. The first phase took the form
of a workshop in the summer of 2013 and
resulted in the conception of the Social
Power Plant, the framework within which to
understand how the project might work—both
spatially and conceptually. These ideas were
brought together in the accompanying text,
which outlines not only how we understood
the social power plant as a model, but how
the different spaces of the museum served
different functions, oscillating between sites
of presentation, contestation, and production.

Rather than reformulate those ideas here, it
seems more important to reflect on a second,
equally important but arguably more complex,
component: the negotiation that needs to take
place between the different actors involved
in realizing, conceptualizing, and delivering
a project like this. The dynamics within any
collaborative process are complicated. This
complexity is amplified when you combine
an artist's proposition, such as Bruguera's

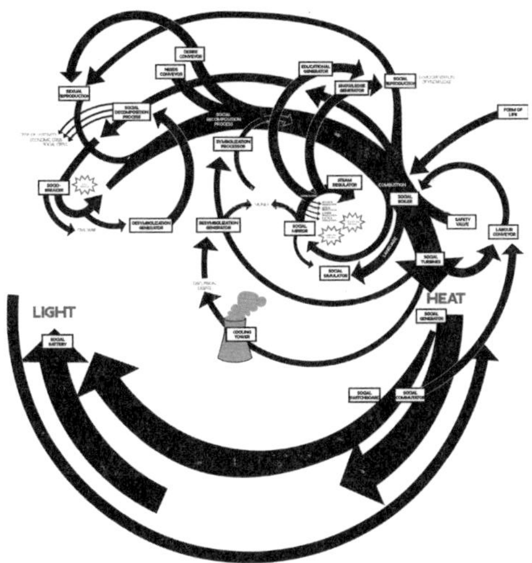

notion of Arte Útil (which will understandably entail ideas of how a project might work), a museum infrastructure that has its own working methodologies and procedures, a curatorial team who wish to construct an exhibition experience that generates a certain narrative history, and a collective such as constructLab, that is itself composed of different artistic, intellectual, and political impulses. The coming together of these different positions and agendas in a temporary collective, such as the one that we formed, is where the politics of a project lies: how decisions are arrived at collectively, how people stand for a position or mode of working, or how the realities of a project might not meet its ambitions and what response you give. The way in which these questions are negotiated during the fleeting yet intense period of collective work is where the nature of collaboration is revealed.

For the *Museum of Arte Útil* this entailed a constant process of negotiation, trying to understand and communicate different inputs. On the one hand, constructLab respected the work and research carried out in the construction of the archive and Bruguera's history in working with the ideas of Arte Útil. Yet its role was to bring a different type of knowledge to the project—one that responded to the context of the museum and the exhibition site. The assignment was to transform this knowledge into a spatial scenography and a process of working, adding a layer to the project that could not be found in the archive or more conventional notions of museum display.

constructLab's process of working means that many of the design decisions happen during the build. Similarly, each member of the lab is invited by Alexander Roemer for a specific project as they bring with them a distinct skill set that is applied in different ways, whether that is design, graphics, or woodwork. Whilst we had settled on structural components such as the large circular wall that ran through the galleries and the curators knew which groupings of projects would be presented in each room, how each of the rooms would be spatially brought together could only happen when we were in the galleries, working with different members of the team, responding to the spaces as we stood in them. The decision to have a central architectural form in the circular wall provided a structure for the members of the collective to feed off and work against, allowing different spatial propositions to emerge within a unified whole. Yet, such a way of working goes against the machinery of the museum, which would

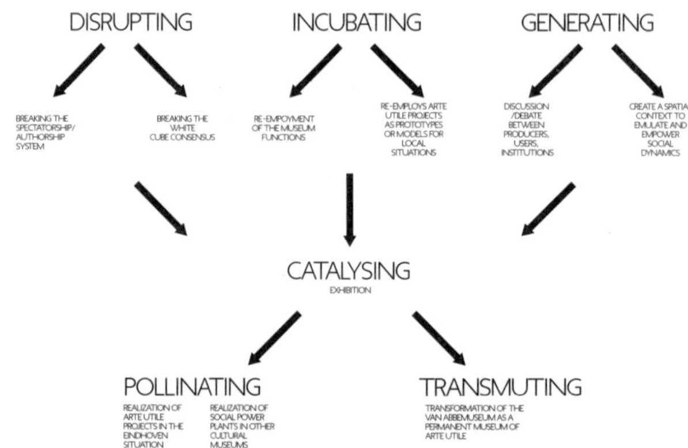

normally have detailed plans and sketches in place for the execution of an installation. It unsettles the methodologies of the institution and takes it out of its comfort zone. The move away from a centralized plan also disrupts the museum's hierarchy as there is no clear authorial voice—whether that is from an artist, designer, curator, or technician. This was a way of working that chimed loudly with the core aims of Arte Útil.

How a working methodology upsets or challenges an existing system reveals itself in the implementation of new protocols, no matter how small they may appear. In the *Museum of Arte Útil* there were two clear examples of this: the first was having the workshop in the gallery, meaning that the production site of the museum was brought out from behind the scenes into the public spaces of the museum. The second was the insistence on having a communal lunch in the central room of the exhibition with all members of the collective and curatorial team. Whilst such decisions may seem small, they directly challenge the museum to think about its working practices and how space and time are allocated to the people who work there. More importantly, they allowed for social, artistic, and institutional boundaries to blur and for different modes of working to be introduced. The effects

of this are never immediately discernible, yet how they impact the museum and how it views its own working practices will emerge over time.

While the aim of these protocols was to flatten conventional modes of working and frameworks, horizontality in any working situation is hard to achieve, especially when there is intense time pressure. Decisions need to be made quickly. Presumptions can take place, there are often heated discussions and subsequently trust, confidence, and friendships are tested. As such, collaboration can be a messy affair. You are forced to consider how you approach the collaborative process, what your own position is, and what your motivations are for making a particular decision. This constant reevaluation and self-reflexivity is exhausting, but it lies at the heart of collaborative work.

Members of the constructLab for the *Museum of Arte Útil*:
Nick Aikens, Tania Bruguera, constructLab (with Alexander Roemer, Bureau d'Études, Collective Works, and others), Annette Eliëns, Charles Esche, Annie Fletcher, Gemma Medina and Alessandra Saviotti, Johanna Dehio, Patrick Hubmann, Licia Soldavini, Samuel Boche, Gonzague Lacombe, Julien Courtial, Manu Macaigne, and Maria Hofmann.

Conversing the Action, Narrating History, Eliciting the Present

Notes on Artistic Mediations
and Practices Outstripping the
Museum's Usual Functions

Subtramas (Diego del Pozo,
Montse Romaní, Virginia Villaplana)

Since 2009, the Subtramas (Diego del Pozo, Montse Romaní, and Virginia Villaplana) artistic collective has been conducting artistic research and production that explores the interface between audiovisual, radical pedagogy, collaborative practices, and social activism.[1]

Based on this ongoing investigation's discursive guidelines, the What, How & for Whom/WHW curatorial collective invited us to take part in the exhibition *Really Useful Knowledge* at the Museo Nacional Centro de Arte Reina Sofía in Madrid.[2] Our response was undertaken in two directions.

First, we presented the semantic diagram we call 'Anagrammatic ABC,' which reviews the potential for collaborative practices in the field of audiovisual production.[3] Second, we developed mediation and public programmes in conjunction with the exhibition. For this purpose we devised an installation called *Four Questions for a Usefulness to Come*, which served as the starting point for each of the itineraries in the mediation programme, and also provided a central hub for activities we organized throughout the duration of the exhibition. Both programmes were aimed at exploring and reinforcing the exhibition's ability to function as an apparatus for (co)learning.

The mediation programme was based on four different routes through the exhibition, which could be easily followed by the public

---

1   We find relevant Hito Steyerl's considerations on the resistance function of artistic research as a form of knowledge production conducted by artistic practice. See Hito Steyerl, "An Aesthetics of Resistance? Artistic Research as Discipline and Conflict," *Transversal* (January 2010), http://eipcp.net/transversal/0311/steyerl/en.
2   The exhibition took place from 28 October 2014–9 February 2015.

3   'Anagrammatic ABC' along with all the project materials can be consulted online at http://subtramas.museoreinasofia.es/es/anagrama.

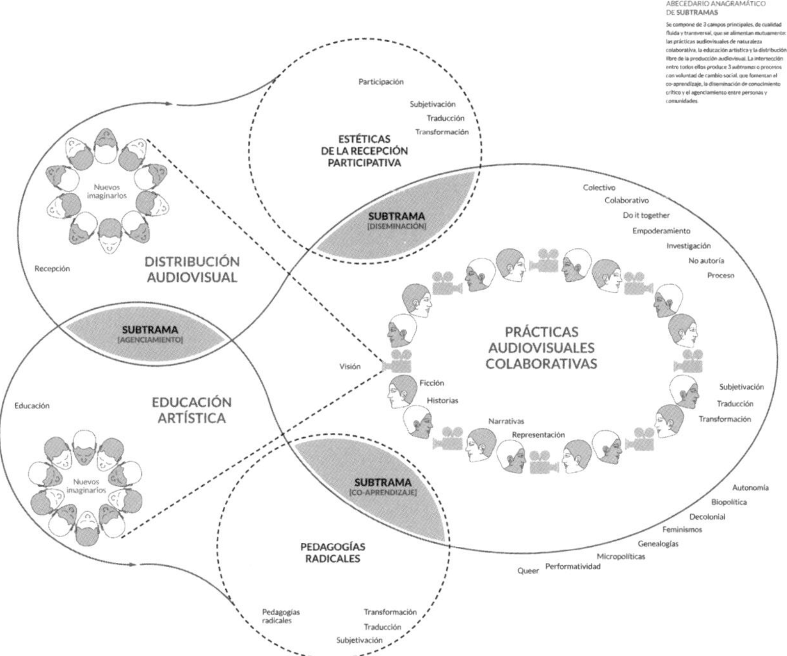

Fig 1 Subtramas
Anagrammatic Alphabet

thanks to the corresponding leaflets. Each of the itineraries detailed tours through a specific selection of works that were meant to elicit a certain reflective or performative dynamic, to be individually or collectively enacted by the viewers. Each of the four routes was guided by one of these questions: Why is learning together useful? How could we energize our imagination to envision a form of non-capitalist-managed happiness? What sort of learning arises from social movements? What sort of politics can be triggered by images?

The intensive work of Silvia Zayas and Eduardo García[4] as route mediators contrasted the conventions of standard, commentary-driven guided tours, resorting instead to Subtramas-inspired methodologies that seek to create conditions where viewers become political subjects comprising new kinds of publics.[5] The aim of the programme—which we felt we came a long way to achieving it—was to engage the audience in rich debates and discussions on the issues raised by the exhibits. For example, 'walking assemblies' formed in a kind of sustained collective performance whereby the public took the leading role in sharing (and questioning) learnings generated by other learnings. Events appeared to shift the terms of enunciation and listening into new frames that critically replied to institutionally authorized knowledge, resituating listener and speaker within the same plane of resonance, but

---

4 Silvia Zayas is an artist and performer and Eduardo García is a freelance curator and cultural mediator.

5 Here we found inspiration in Elizabeth Ellsworth's ideas on *modes of address* in visual culture. Against prevalent structuralizations of the mode of address in audiovisual communication, Ellsworth sees the mode of address in education as performative rather than merely communicative, allowing space for viewers to become aware of themselves, the world and others. See Elizabeth Ellsworth, *Teaching Positions: Difference, Pedagogy and the Power of Address* (New York: Teachers College, 1997).

¿POR QUÉ ES ÚTIL APRENDER JUNTOS?

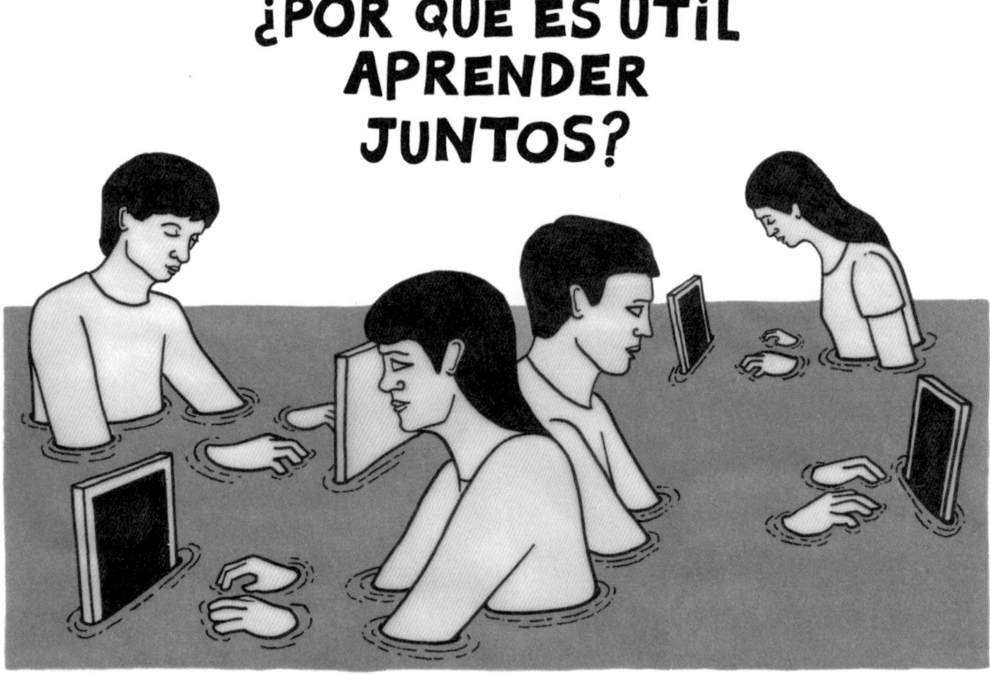

Fig 2 Why is learning together useful?

bound by mutual interpellation. It thus seemed possible to learn how to break the indifference-contract through which we are commonly shaped into consumers-viewers-citizens, and to grasp how our connection with others is affected by what we know or fail to know, and how other people's knowledge also affects us in turn.[6] A key objective for us was to observe the cross-currents of knowledge and affect between viewers in each itinerary (who were supposed to be strangers to one another), and how their viewpoints might be altered, or their imagination might open up to new possibilities.

'No nos representan' ('they don't represent us' or 'there's no representing us')—the rallying cry of the 15-M Movement or Indignados against neoliberal austerity policies in crisis-ridden Spain—referred to 'representation' in the full, multifarious sense of the term, and not merely in the narrow confines of electoral politics.[7] For us the need for a thorough rethinking and overhauling of democratic institutions also extends to cultural institutions, due to the new centrality of culture in postindustrial capitalism. As we know, the map of cultural centres and museums created in Spain between 1982 and 1995 played a central role in the reconceptualization of the nation-state in times of capitalism's global financial hegemony. The museums were caught between the responsibility to provide cultural capital to a democratic citizenry, and their own assimilation into the culture of spectacle. According to this, the nature of the museum has proved to be performative: it was structured

---

6 Marina Garcés, *Un mundo común* (Barcelona: Edicions Bellaterra, 2013), p. 92.

7 The occupation of squares in cities all over Spain in May 2011 was one of the main sources of inspiration for the birth of the Occupy Wall Street movement in New York City a few months later.

¿QUÉ PUEDEN ACCIONAR POLÍTICAMENTE LAS IMÁGENES?

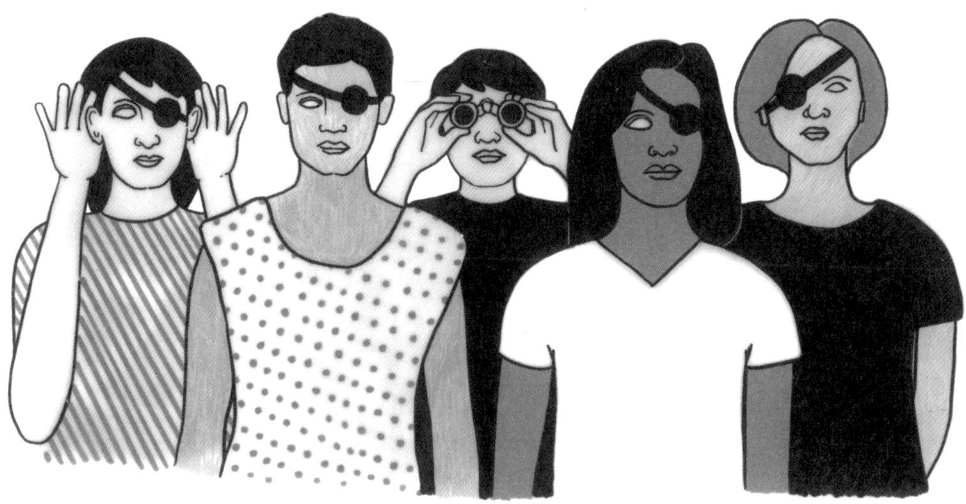

Fig 3 What sort of politics can be triggered by images?

by devices regulating our behaviour, our reflection, and our habits, no less than our experience of exhibitions and space itself.

The need to work for a new democratic institution seems to be urgent. How to overcome the museum's failure to enunciate representation of the citizen? How is it possible to open up spaces where subjects can re-appropriate their own power to produce behaviour and actions in different situations within the museum?

Given that *Really Useful Knowledge* focused on artistic practices in opposition to capitalism, we felt the urge to experiment with *instituent* processes seeking to rethink the museum's own institutional nature. In this regard, the programs we organized were aimed at questioning the museum's institutional operation along with the exhibition itself as the museum's privileged locus of 'mediation.' For this purpose, we held long discussions that sought a deeper understanding with

(and between) different departments within the museum (exhibitions, public activities, education, and communication) as well as other collectives that we invited to take part in the project. Although the Museo Reina Sofía has its own programme of public activities, including lectures and debates, it was crucial for us to go beyond the subaltern status of said activities and to move them—for the first time at this museum—from the lecture hall to the exhibition space, attempting to dismantle hegemony and legitimacy of the latter within the institution.

Drawing on our 'autonomy' as artists, we established a network of connections with certain social and cultural collectives from across Spain that form a kind of decentralized constellation of resistance (some of them committed to the struggle against EU- and IMF-imposed austerity policies). With their collaboration we planned and carried out a series of activities within and around the exhibition that

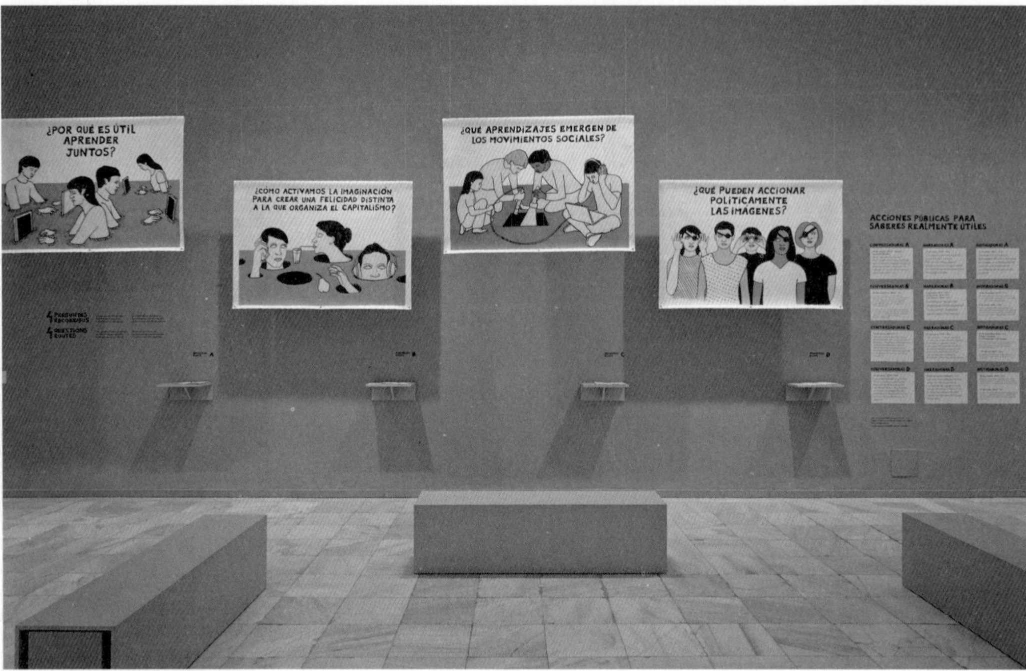

Fig 4 View of the Subtramas installation 'Four Questions for a Usefulness to Come'

were *museum-producing* rather than *museum-produced* or *museum products*. Under the rubric 'Actions on Really Useful Knowledges,' we thus managed to (albeit temporarily) bring the common, direct expressions of popular sovereignty into the museum.

There were three types of activities: conversational, narrational, and instigational. Each category included four activities related to the above-mentioned guiding questions:

Conversational activities comprised a series of dialogues on the collective production of knowledge and experiences—and the ensuing conflicts and repercussions of this. Participants included: WHW in dialogue with representatives from the Museo Reina Sofía exhibition and public programme departments; independent publishers association *Contrabandos* (Spain) in dialogue with open, collaborative library *Bookcamping* (Spain); collectives *Esta es una*

Plaza! (Madrid), *El Patio Maravillas* (Madrid), *La Casa Invisible* (Málaga), and *Observatorio Metropolitano de Barcelona* (Barcelona); and *Las Lindes* (CA2M, Móstoles, Madrid) and *Cine sin Autor* collective (Madrid) in collaboration with the Museo Reina Sofía's educational department.

Narrational activities began with a public reading of texts on the decolonization of knowledge, history, and desire. Participants included: artists' collectives *Declinación Magnética* (Bilbao/Madrid) and *Somatecxs* (Madrid); feminist and queer groups coordinated by activist Fefa Vila; and anonymous people who read a series of entries from Museo Reina Sofía's incidents reports and suggestions sheets.

Participants in **instigational activities** drew on their own self-representation strategies and methodologies to recount achievements connected with current social struggles.

446

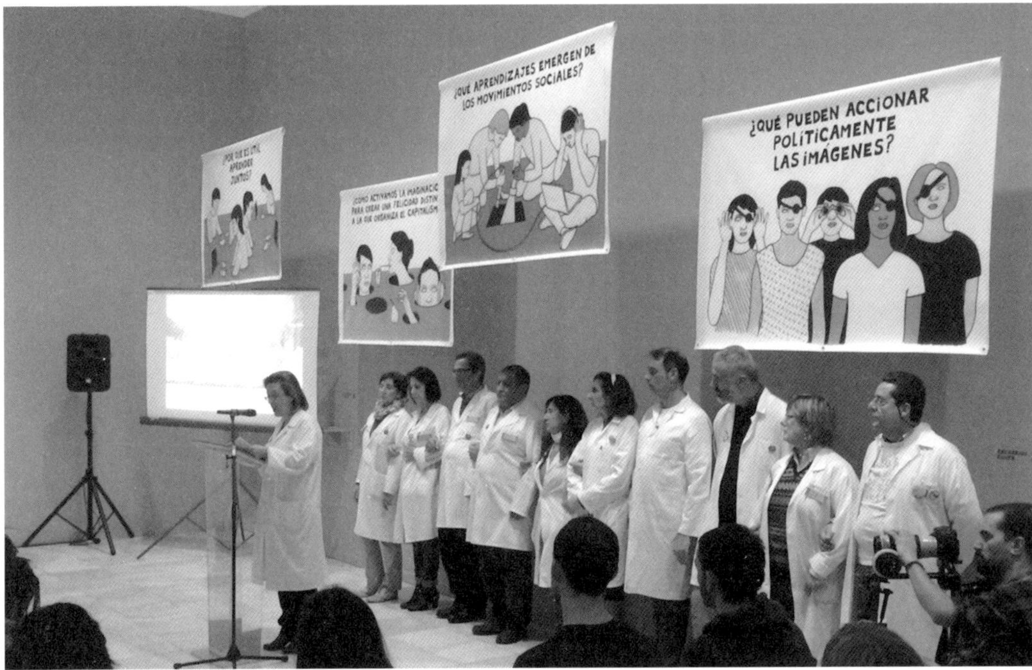

Fig 5 View of the performance by Marea Blanca [White Tide] within the Subtramas installation space

Groups included: movement in support of public education *Marea Verde* [Green Tide] (Madrid); movement in defence of public healthcare *Marea Blanca* [White Tide] (Madrid); (pro-universal healthcare) platform *Yo Sí, Sanidad Universal* (Madrid); domestic workers' collectives *Senda de Cuidados* and *Territorio Doméstico* (Madrid);[8] and *Peninsula* (Spain) postcolonial theory & research group.

In an effort to break down stereotypes of the 'working class,' Jacques Rancière wrote that accelerations, delays, and gaps determined by the system forced proletarians who were 'secretly in love with useless things' to experience a fragmented time. The first step in their emancipation was to re-appropriate that fragmentation of time and create forms of subjectivity that would allow them to live at a pace other than that dictated by the system. Contemporary forms of precarious and intermittent work now appear very similar to this experience of the useless.

We connected notions of non-specialized, nonfunctional, non-capitalizable aspects of time—drivers behind *Really Useful Knowledge*— to the communal learning among social movements and groups that turn their back on individualization processes. 'Actions on Really Useful Knowledges' tested out a different type of usefulness which could contribute to changing social structures—*uselessness* as a kind of usefulness that is still to come.

8　These are autonomous grassroots movements and organizations operating outside the institutional umbrella of officially sanctioned trade unions, which many in Spain believe to be discredited as traditional political parties. The emergence of these post-union movements can be seen to be part of the 'crisis of representation' in the country after May 2011 (translator's note).

A Conversation between Nick Aikens,
Annie Fletcher, Alistair Hudson, Steven ten
Thije, and What, How & for Whom/WHW

Really
Útil
Confessions

In April of 2015, the curators involved in the *Museum of Arte
Útil, Confessions of the Imperfect, 1848–1989–Today*, and *Really
Useful Knowledge* exhibitions met to consider use (in its different
guises) in relation to artistic practice, knowledge production,
and exhibition making.[1] This conversation took place on the
occasion of a presentation of the Arte Útil archive at
Gallery Nova, Zagreb.[2]

The Museum of Arte Útil

<u>Nick Aikens (NA)</u> The Arte Útil project came out of a
proposal by the artist Tania Bruguera. Tania had been
working with the idea of Arte Útil for some years,
teaching it as a course in Havana. When we invited
her to do a solo exhibition at the Van Abbemuseum,
she was working on a long-term project with Immigrant
Movement International at the Queens Museum in New
York and was thinking a lot about the notion of Arte
Útil. So, rather than propose an exhibition of her
own work, Tania challenged us to create a *Museum of
Arte Útil*. The premise of Arte Útil lies in art's
ability to respond to specific urgencies. It aims
to wrench the notion of artistic practice, quite
polemically, away from the autonomy prescribed to it
by Western modernism and to think instead how art can
be used as a tool in the world to affect change. We
consciously opted to use the Spanish word *útil* rather
than 'useful' as it has the connotation of a tool or
device. So we were interested in looking at moments
when individual artists, communities, or collectives
had found ways to intervene in the world when existing
structures be they the government, market, or other
institutional frameworks have failed. It is about how
artistic thinking can offer imaginative strategies to
counter these failures.

Creating a *Museum of Arte Útil* was an attempt to
construct a history of this kind of thinking and
working. The primary means by which we did this was
through the creation of an archive or 'inventory' of
projects from the early nineteenth century to today,
allowing us to track this history. We wanted to use
the museum's capacity as a generator of history to

---

1 *Confessions of the Imperfect, 1848-1989-Today* curated by Steven ten
Thije and Alistair Hudson, Van Abbemuseum, Eindhoven, 22 November 2014-
22 February 2015; *Really Useful Knowledge*, curated by What, How & for
Whom/WHW, Museo Nacional Centro de Arte Reina Sofía, Madrid, 29 October
2014-9 February 2015; and *Museum of Arte Útil*, initiated by Tania
Bruguera, Van Abbemuseum, Eindhoven, 7 December 2013-30 March 2014.
2 Initiated in 2013, the Arte Útil archive is a growing archive of
over 200 case studies that imagine, create, and implement beneficial
outcomes by producing tactics that change how we act in society.
Case studies have been compiled by researchers at Van Abbemuseum,
Eindhoven and Queens Museum, New York, as well as by Tania Bruguera,
international correspondents, and through open call. As a collaboration
between Van Abbemuseum and curatorial collective What, How & for Whom/
WHW, the archive was presented at Gallery Nova, Zagreb (27 March 2015-
16 May 2015) with new projects by initiative Kulturni Lift, artist
Dina Rončević, and working group k.r.u.ž.o.k. The archive is available
at http://museumarteutil.net/archive.

tell a different story about how artistic practice has developed.

Of course by bringing this archive—and the polemic of Arte Útil—into the museum, the question of what was useful, flipped onto the museum. How can a museum itself be 'útil'? What types of processes and projects could take place within the museum that would allow us to bend its physical and conceptual architecture, which was constructed to display and mediate objects? Similarly, what happens to the projects that you are presenting when you extract them from their context and transfer them into the white cube of the museum space? This brought into focus many further questions about the limitations and possibilities of display and the dynamics at play when mediating between artistic practices, the institution, and your public. For us a central one became: What reconfiguration of these three elements needs to take place?

Confessions of the Imperfect, 1848–1989–Today

Steven ten Thije (StT) *Confessions of the Imperfect, 1848-1989-Today* stemmed from the same observation as the *Museum of Arte Útil*—namely, art's complicated relation to use in modern times. But in some sense *Confessions* walked the other way. Where the *Museum of Arte Útil* was explicitly formulated in terms of its use in society, *Confessions* looked more into the tradition of modern art itself and sought for moments where art itself was considered 'useful.' For this we turned to John Ruskin who we recognized as an established and classic aesthetic thinker, somebody who played a role in promoting early modern art, while simultaneously being quite explicit about the modern aesthetic having a 'use-value' in society. The projects and works that were presented in *Confessions* therefore focused more on how aesthetic practice itself was deemed useful, or how it was folded into everyday practice and was even considered a vital component of it.

Alistair Hudson (AH) In this there was also an element of looking at history, looking at the use of history itself, to see how we understand our socio-cultural narratives and *útilise* them to come up with solutions

to our present. When we started to develop these ideas
we looked at the dominance of the Kantian paradigm
with which we all struggle—a beautifully constructed
system that has ultimately lead us to the market model
of art from which we need to escape. In *Confessions*
we were analyzing the instances when art pushed in a
different direction and rereading the moments that
created current concepts, institutions, and languages
in need of revision.

The problems we face today are, for the most part,
programmed or written at the end of the eighteenth
century and there is very much a convergence here
when we look back to that moment, in the search for
other perspectives and agendas. In particular we can
reintroduce the voice of Ruskin, who at that time was
campaigning against the mechanical and instrumental
dehumanization of society. Equally we can cite the
Mechanics' Institutes, originating in the early
nineteenth century to offer a holistic education
for the emerging industrial workforce. This movement
was both instrumental and altruistic. The Institutes
drove enterprise and technical knowledge, whilst
also providing the conditions for the emancipation
of society through education and democracy, creating
the crucible for unions, cooperatives, women's rights,
and 'Really Useful Knowledge.'

Looking again at these histories, these are the
stories we tell ourselves to help us understand the
world around us, our subjectivity, and make informed
decisions about where we should be going. Both the
Museum of Arte Útil and Confessions present human
stories, of art working in life, making real contributions to the development of society.

However, there is a difficulty in narrating this
through exhibition making because these stories are
not linear in time and are created in a very different
language—primarily understood through the doing and
the texture of lived experience that is often lost
in text and image.

Really Useful Knowledge

What, How & for Whom/WHW (WHW) *Really Useful Knowledge* also
foregrounded historical experiments and perspective
and insisted on learning from them. At the same time
it tried to show us that what we learn from them and
how we translate those experiences into the present
is up to us.

We came across 'really useful knowledge' through
informal conversations with a friend and political
scientist in Zagreb, who pointed to the term as used
in early nineteenth-century England. The workers'
movement used it to designate self-organized workers'
education in subjects like economy, politics, history,
and philosophy as opposed to 'useful' education in
applied sciences, engineering, and such, provided
by capitalists. The workers' movement then was
interesting as a point of departure in defining
useful knowledge against useless knowledge. It was a
reaction against the instrumentalization of knowledge
through its strict promotion in the application to
capitalistic production, while also addressing the
class consciousness that governed workers' self-
education and decisions to organize different types of
education. We wanted to look back to these initiatives
of the early nineteenth century to see where we are
now, where the incessant privatization of knowledge
and imposed limitation on access to education has
brought us. The title is a reminder that the struggle
for access to knowledge and its definition has been
part of workers' emancipation since the beginnings of
capitalism. And now when results of years of social
and political reforms are crumbling we again need to
reassess these issues and reclaim universal access to
education.

We started to look into these questions from the
position of a major national museum in Madrid, Spain,
the Museo Nacional Centro de Arte Reina Sofía. We took
into account the museum collection. It is in many ways
exemplary in its decisive politicization of national
art history in relation to the Spanish Civil War and
colonial history, and in its art historical dialogue
with international tendencies primarily defined through
the prism of 'Western' art history. We were wondering
what kind of knowledge we could bring from socialist
and post-socialist geographies, underrepresented in
the collection. As these were some starting points

for our research, this process also meant that we
tried to make an exhibition which would bring forward
our position defined by the break up of Yugoslavia
and experiences of the past twenty-something years.
And also to include intensities of the political and
economic transformations that Croatia as an example of
post-socialist transition and post-war normalization
could offer. We looked into resonances of similar
troubles, xenophobia, nationalism, the rise of right-
wing tendencies, the erasure of the historical
experience of socialism, and the general closure of
social commons, including education, all of which are
certainly not specific to Croatia.

Methodology

NA With the *Museum of Arte Útil* the question of
methodology was present from the start. By naming
Arte Útil we had to decide what could be classified
as 'Útil' and what couldn't. We came to the idea of
creating a set of criteria through which we could
analyze projects. Looking at artistic practice through
criteria is completely counter-intuitive. Yet museums
and exhibitions constantly codify and categorize
artistic practice, often in opaque ways. We wanted to
bring this to the forefront and make it transparent.
The criteria aimed to address what we felt were the
key characteristics of this mode of working: projects
that were 'initiated' not 'authored,' that involved
'users' not 'spectators,' that took place on a 1:1
scale over a long period of time etc., etc.

In the construction of the archive we worked with a
series of correspondents from different parts of the
world who suggested projects that might be suitable
for the archive. We also had two researchers and
worked very closely with the Queens Museum at the

time conducting the *Arte Útil Lab*.[3] The final stage
was to issue an open call asking the public to submit
projects for inclusion in the archive. Once we had
gathered all of these different case studies a group
of us looked at them in relation to the criteria and
this is how the archive was formed. We have since
added many more projects—some of which we have come
across ourselves, others which have been suggested to
us. The next major methodological question was how to
present these projects in the museum. Should we group
them geographically, chronologically, or whatever?

Annie Fletcher (AF) I remember the break-through moment
being when we decided to group the works through
strategies. It was Tania's idea and it allowed us to
think much more tactically about the work and the
exhibition. So we had strategies such us 'Use it
Yourself,' 'Institutional Repurpose,' 'A-legal,' or
'Legislative Change.' Looking at the archive in this
way meant you could read different contexts and time
periods in relation to one another in fascinating
ways. So, through the lens of art and the law in the
room 'Legislative Change,' Augusto Boal's Theatre of
the Oppressed, a radical theatre group working in
Brazil in the 1950s could be read in relation to the
Yirrkala bark petitions (1963), which were key legal
documents in the fight for land rights for Indigenous
Australians.

The focus on strategy also allowed us to foreground
the impulse behind these projects. What was it that
they were driving at? What was their desire for the
project? These are things that you can't get from more
rigid forms of categorization and curating.

Alongside this we had what we called three
'analysis' rooms. These punctuated the strategies
and allowed us to speak from a sort of meta-level if
you like. The first was the 'The Room for Propaganda,

---

3 The *Arte Útil Lab* ran from 17 February–2 June 2013, Queens Museum,
New York. Originally conceived by Tania Bruguera, the *Arte Útil Lab* was
curated by Adrianne Koteen, Prerana Reddy, and Diya Vij. The *Lab* was not
an exhibition, but rather an investigative space. Key to the *Lab* was an
extensive public programme that tested Arte Útil against a series of
hypotheses. The *Lab* hosted four 'Hypotheses Panels' and 'Working Groups'
for practitioners and artists discussing and producing examples of Arte
Útil throughout the time the Lab was open, with a final presentation
of reports from the working groups. The four public workshops tested
hypotheses critical to formulating the principals of Arte Útil including
questions of aesthetics, ethical responsibility, sustainability,
reproducibility, and accessibility under the sections: Aest-ethics:
Moral Aesthetics in Arte Útil; Access & Replication Mechanisms; Project
Ecosystem Management; and Usefulness as Ideology.

Legitimation and Belief.' This was Tania's room!
The second was the 'Room of Controversies,' where we
created a space to discuss many of the more sticky
issues that some of this work gives rise to. And the
third was the 'Archive Room,' where people could look
at all 200 projects.

AH Maybe it is interesting to talk about the wall
that ran through the galleries of the museum. As an
exhibition device it seemed at odds with the premise
of Arte Útil in that it felt largely symbolic or
representative. If we were idealistic about Arte
Útil there would not be any exhibition at all and all
these projects would operate on a 1:1 scale in the
museum. There would be a shift from the museum being
a representational institution to being an activated
institution.

NA Yes, but we were interested in generating—and
representing to a certain extent—a history. We wanted
to make that history legible for the museum's users
whilst also outlining the deficiencies of the museum
in accommodating this way of working. Within that the
question of scenography, of creating an exhibition
experience, became crucial. We needed to break with
the white cube conceptually and physically, and the
wall did just that. It also served as part of a larger
conceptual proposition by constructLab, the designers
of the exhibition, who conceived the museum as a
'Social Power Plant' within which the wooden wall
functioned as a kind of turbine to generate ideas.

AF We were very conscious of the limits of the
exhibition. At the time a lot of work had been done
in the Lab in Queens around where the aesthetics of
this work takes place—and it's clear it's not in the
gallery. It's in the field. And in many respects I
think we were a little too afraid of the image.
     But we decided on working with three registers in
which the work could be experienced. The first took
place on the white walls of the museum, where we
presented a selection of projects from the archives,
corresponding to the room strategy. Here we worked
with artists to think about how to represent their
work, through graphics, photos, text, or installation.

This resulted in some really interesting translations of the projects, like Laurie Jo Reynolds's archive display which she developed having spent six weeks working in the gallery. The second was through a series of live projects such as Grizedale Arts's *Honest Shop* or Apolonija Šušteršič's *Light Therapy Room*, for example, which people could use in the space. The third was the archive itself and interviews with practitioners and people involved through which we tried to mediate the stories behind the works.

Importantly, we tried to make a clear distinction between the static space of the white walls, the interventionist space of the wooden wall (where people were invited to leave traces of activities), and the active space of the galleries where projects unfolded.

AH The use of the wall and the scenography of the *Museum of Arte Útil* did influence the way we thought about *Confessions* and how we presented it. The issue of the wall kept coming back and eventually mutated into the barricade as a key motif or device. The point being that the wall is a symbolic representational thing that we come up with in our heads to symbolize a division between haves and have-nots, the good guys and bad guys, knowledge and uncertainty. Yet in reality it is the working in and around these walls where change really takes place, beyond the symbolic if you like and within daily use. Here we can bring in a different line of thinking through Ruskin and his commentary on architecture and nature. In opposition to a divisive, mechanistic, industrial tool fragmenting and compartmentalizing society and knowledge, we can take from Ruskin's 'ecological' devices, learned through nature as a truer representation of how the world works. Applied to the barricade, this expands the line into a very complex matrix of interconnecting systems and that is where the battles are fought, less through opposing positions but a whole shifting matrix of usership and interdependency. Of course this can be applied to natural systems in a very scientific way but can also be applied to history, art, and aesthetics.

This idea of the physical barricades of the nineteenth century mutating into a *Barricade of Discourse*, a *Barricade of Digital Data*, or a *Barricade of Light* reflects the truth of complexity and perhaps then becomes a better tool to devise a way forward.

It also starts to effect the way we think about history itself, not as a linear process but an ever-present matrix in a perpetual present in which there are multiple histories that weave themselves through our consciousness. For example, we could say we are still living in the age of Richard III. Despite the fact he died in 1485, the recent events and rituals surrounding his discovery and reburial have created a historical narrative anew that is quite different from the one we inherited.

StT It is also important to note that this idea to use the barricade in this manner came from artist Liam Gillick. It was good to work with Liam, because he has a great sensibility for modern art. This was necessary in order to make this quite delicate argument that read, to a certain degree, modern art history against the grain. Especially within the Van Abbemuseum, whose basis is a profoundly modern if not modernist collection of Western art. We needed to find a form that would extend a helping hand to our public who have been 'educated' in looking and appreciating modern art.

The other thing that was important to the barricade structure for me was that it worked as a tool to make explicit the double temporality of the exhibition. On the one hand the exhibition presents a history as a story. On the other it offers a series of experiences that have duration. In other words there is the time of the exhibition visit and looking at the works, next to the abstract time of a historical narrative that is told. The barricade helped to link the two by showing that history itself is always a history of divisions, which first needs to appear before it can be negotiated. They can appear as the classical barricade of 1848, but also less explicitly as different languages, or being able to see things because they are placed in the light, while other things are not. Both history and the experience of the works in the exhibition are built on this activity of linking two things that exist apart. Perhaps this is also what I see as one of the most profound things aesthetics do: allow things to coexist by developing forms of affinity between them.

Another source that inspired the exhibition was Eric Hobsbawm's *The Age of Capital* (1975), which deals with the period 1848-1875. What the book

argues and demonstrates is that the 'Springtime of
Peoples' celebrated as the first decades of democracy
in Europe, with spin-offs all over the globe, was
in fact much more a 'springtime of capital.' The
transfer of power in the mid-nineteenth century that
took place did not follow the path from aristocracy
and the Church to 'the people,' but much more to the
rich upper-class merchants. The modernist history of
'high' art and especially its institutions like the
museum and art market, are part of this transfer as
gatekeeper systems for organizing entry into the upper
echelons of society. The basis for this system and
its institution were situated in a genuine attempt
to understand the affects of certain forms of art or
craft and how they supported communal life. In the
exhibition we focused on a variety of practices and
art projects, which play with this affect of modern
art, design, and architecture in shaping everyday
life.

WHW In that respect for us it was important to look
into this opposition between 'high' and 'popular' art
and how it is embedded in a broader understanding of
art. We considered this especially in light of the
colonial past, where the division between high and low
or popular art was part of the colonial project and
still defines our understanding of art. We showed a
number of works that rely on craft and use traditional
methods of art to problematize the very understanding
of art.

For example, Partisan art: an archive of art
produced in Slovenia during the revolutionary
antifascist struggle of the Yugoslavian nations in the
Second World War, based on the set-up of the permanent
collection of the Moderna galerija Ljubljana. Used
as a form of resistance, Partisan art is specific as
it was popular art in terms of its social effects.
It also used the aesthetic language of high art,
not exclusively of course, but often enough. This
apparent contradiction between aesthetic language and
the demands of popular mobilization is what makes
it interesting for current debates on the role of
art in political struggles. Partisan art was a huge
mobilization tool that through its inclusiveness,
radical openness, and strong educative thrust
reconfigured the whole notion of art. But the claim of
Partisan art was not that it would change the world

by making art, nor even by making art with a different aesthetic language or exclusively through that. The claim was that the role of art is to contribute to political struggles and that political struggles change the world. Partisan art was made in a specific moment of anti-fascist mobilization and revolutionary social transformation that accompanied liberation struggle during the Second World War. Its position is especially instructive now when there is a pressure on art to change the world irrespective of the actualities of political struggles.

Important also was the context of the Museo Reina Sofía, whose collection has a precise political position. We wanted examples like Partisan art to be in dialogue with it, to add different positions that could extend the dialogues in both time and space. It was also about contemporary positions, for example, in relation to the roles of the digital media and technology. It was interesting to go into the process of discussing with the museum the project of *Public Library*—whether they would fund production of something for illegally scanning books available online, books situated in an anarchist commune outside Barcelona, with only a little note on the process and link to the website available at the exhibition.

It is kind of a risky decision for an institution to make. The same goes for *Autonomy Cube*, Trevor Paglen and Jacob Appelbaum's project [see pp. 240-247] which provided a public Internet connection that could be used for sending encrypted information, which is still a grey area in terms of being legal or illegal.

It would be interesting to also talk about the scandal with the little box of matches by Mujeres Públicas, an Argentinean feminist collective that has been working in Buenos Aires for a long time. They work with various public actions connected to gender issues. A pressing topic they continuously deal with is the fact that abortion is illegal in Argentina (and throughout South America). Within the exhibition Mujeres Públicas presented an installation based on the material (posters, leaflets, and matchboxes) with pro-choice propaganda that they distribute during demonstrations. A lot of this material criticizes the Catholic Church given its heavy support of the prohibition of abortion. The part of the work that incited a call for censorship was a matchbox with an image of a burning church and the inscription: 'the only church that illuminates is the one that burns.'

This is a quote from Pyotr Kropotkin appropriated by Buenaventura Durruti, an anarchist killed during the Spanish Civil War. Due to the museum's fire regulations the matches were not accessible within the exhibition space, so we couldn't distribute them (which Mujeres Públicas had proposed). We did not want to emulate the gestures of demonstration within the museum anyway. As a kind of absurdly exaggerated white cube display we showed them as a valuable sculpture inside a closed glass box. The metaphorical fire they started was not on our minds when we decided to include them.

The day immediately after the opening, there were e-mails of complaint in the museum's general e-mail inbox, and soon after the petitions were begun asking the matches and other materials from Mujeres Públicas's installation be removed. As the story was blown up by the tabloids and right-wing media, the petition to remove the works gathered many signatures. The museum completely stood by the artists and by us as curators and they took all the heat caused by the matches.

It is interesting to note that *Public Library* and *Autonomy Cube* are in fact much more provocative with respect to the functioning of the institution than the matchbox with the text from the nineteenth century. But this particular text within the museum context and trajectory of popular art and discussions on what kind of responses images can bring—not necessarily intellectual but more intuitive, emotional behaviour, and so on obviously sparked something, though not in the way we hoped for. It was read as an invitation to burn the churches and manipulated for purposes of 'cultural war.' The 'weight' of this little project and the lack of public discussion surrounding *Public Library* and *Autonomy Cube* are interesting to take into account when thinking about the impact and usefulness of certain artistic approaches.

The Public as Active User

NA In terms of media reaction the *Museum of Arte Útil* had one quite banal, descriptive review from the press. We thought the position we were taking would provoke a response. Perhaps the fact that we didn't have images that people could read and respond to meant people didn't know what to do with it. The media response emphasizes the power of images.

AH Also people are programmed to exhibit certain behaviours. The public expect to use the museum to see or consume images on the whole and when they don't get them it is quite difficult, unless you become a user. If you want to change how the museum works, you would also need to change people's ideas of a museum and you can't suddenly expect everybody to come to the museum to do a 'cheese workshop.' You have to encourage people to do that because they will not naturally do it given their default behaviour, which is to be a spectator.

NA We used blunt tactics in the *Museum of Arte Útil*. When people entered the museum they were asked if they wanted to be a spectator or a user. This was the clearest way we could try and initiate this shift. Spectators had to pay to enter the museum and users could 'use' it for free. And this worked. We also opened up the spaces of the museum for 'use.' Anyone could book rooms for free. We had an extraordinary response. You would walk through the museum and see the city council holding a policy meeting in the *Light Therapy Room* one day and then the next there would be a workshop on hacking. That level of activity was really energizing for thinking through what the museum can be. But it also made us realize we need to think more strategically about what that offer is.

WHW To engage the viewer not only by offering images to contemplate and react to in different ways, we invited the collective Subtramas [see pp. 442–447] to think about different possibilities for mediating the exhibition. They worked with different groups of activists to engage the audience and devise different uses of the museum as an institution. They found their own way to follow our intention in proposing correspondences and associations that take history not as a linear projection but as happening at the same time and as a source from which we can build to position ourselves in the present moment in relation to education.

461

NA We decided to invite a group of designers, constructLab [see pp. 436–441] to work with us on the show. We were very conscious of the fact that we needed to think about how to translate this work—and its history—into a spatial and aesthetic experience. They worked on the scenography of the show but also on communication and mediation. It was vital not only to alter the physical spaces but communicate that what we were proposing was also a behavioural and conceptual shift in how people interact with the institution. In wanting to mediate the ideas through an exhibition you have to construct an exhibition experience.

WHW Of course there are problems when you come to the representation of an artwork or an idea, nevertheless we believe these kinds of experiments are necessary and not to be judged in terms of failure or success but negotiation.

Useful, Útil, or Really Useful?

NA I'm interested in the differences in position between the three exhibitions. The *Museum of Arte Útil* insisted on art performing a function as a tool, *Really Useful Knowledge* did, at times, insist on art's right to be useless.

Within this difference in approach, the role of discourse and critique seems critical. The *Museum of Arte Útil* and *Confessions* to a certain extent offered alternatives rather than critiques of existing systems, power structures, whatever they might be. The proposition of the *Museum of Arte Útil* and in some way *Confessions* was to go beyond a mode of critique. *Really Useful Knowledge* explored the political potential of critique, seeing the knowledge that was generated out of such discourse as allowing different forms of resistance to take place.

AH But in the *Museum of Arte Útil* it is rarely clear-cut who is using who, where the agendas really lie. There aren't that many art practices that fit the precise description of Arte Útil, it's more a question of to what extent, and do we discard all art that lies

outside this boundary? Consequently I have started to
think through the logic of usership in aesthetics: how
we could think of art and usefulness being part of a
sliding scale, of degree. This is for me one of the
most liberating things emerging from Stephen Wright's
work on the 'Lexicon of Usership' [see page 468-487].
Which is that it isn't like something is or is not
art, more to what *degree* something is art. In such a
system there is a way that leads us through to the
thought of art as being useful, but not restricting it
purely to the set of urgent practices defined by our
criteria. In one way or another everything is useful
to someone, somewhere, somehow, or even at some other
time, even misused. So the question remains how we
would make a holistic matrix within which all art
is encompassed, all human activity, within which a
certain co-efficient of activity is defined as more or
less useful, more or less artful, and so on.

WHW In Partisan art that we mentioned before, which
was made during intensified political struggles,
the question is: Where can you take this political
struggle in the present revisionist political climate
and how can you claim that history not only as anti-
fascist, but as communist? How can you go with it
beyond the museum and yet at the same time state
the place of the museum as a rightful space for
free discussions on those issues? In that sense it
is important to keep this space of art free to do
whatever it wants—engaging politically, yet being a
space for experiment and failure, and not necessary
for providing results.

We were much more intuitive than tactical, and in
certain instances we were criticized for taking things
out of historical context. But it was important to
us to show that images work, also when you take them
out of their historical background. Images work even
if you do not know what they are about. We wanted to
allow the viewer to have a more active position, to
allow history to unfold in the now, to proclaim it
as not being finished and defined and test it for the
present.

StT One thing I notice listening to us, but also
being involved now for several years in the museum
confederation L'Internationale, is how different

European regions also invite different strategies.
I believe the contemporary political culture in
Spain has a strong discursive character and is really
a battle of ideas. In Northern Europe, on the other
hand, neoliberalism has saturated both left and right
to such a degree that it is very difficult to have an
ideological discussion. Within the North *Confessions*
and to some degree the *Museum of Arte Útil* try to
stimulate people to understand the things they do
every day as potentially political. In this sense
I believe we all try to work with the political
potential of art, but depending on our context,
this sometimes results in very different types of
exhibitions either being more practice- or discourse-
based.

NA A good example is Jeanne van Heeswijk's *Freehouse*
project in Rotterdam, presented in this reader. Here,
the politics happen through her relationship with the
market, the cooperative she sets up with them and
which is then handed over to them. She talks about
'radicalizing the local.' Hers is a deeply political
agenda but it is achieved through pragmatism and
day-to-day decisions. That is where micro-political
activity happens rather than on a discursive,
rhetorical level.

StT Yes, I think that's a great example. I don't notice
an absolute divide between a more discursive-based
strategy and one that is more practice-based. I even
think it is important to overcome this opposition
somewhat. Wright, for instance, is quite negative
with respect to Jacques Rancière's *The Emancipated
Spectator* (2009) and its reevaluation of passive
contemplation and distance; Wright argues for a much
more active and user-based approach. Yet, I don't
think Rancière's analysis is the problem; I even
find it more detailed in describing the political
nature of aesthetical experience than Wright's
proposal. However, where I agree with Wright is on
his observation that the current culture surrounding
art anaesthetizes any political possibility of art.
I think that we all try to find a form for our project
that cancels out the ways in which art is turned into
a meaningless spectacle and liberates its political
potential. Something that seems especially important

today, in for instance the variations of 'occupy'
happenings, is the development of new forms of
political action. These also use a certain aesthetic
energy, but it needs to be mediated carefully in the
context of a museum so as to keep it vibrant and not
fossilize it into a commodity of 'high' art.

Appe

ndix

Toward a Lexicon of Usership

Stephen Wright

'…since we can neither think nor even name art without appropriate terms, retooling our conceptual vocabulary has become a crucial task, one that can only be undertaken by fostering terminological cross-pollination with other avenues of human activity.'

Emergent concepts (underpinning usership)

Conceptual institutions to be retired

Modes of usership

'the cause and origin of a thing and its eventual usefulness, its actual employment and place in a system of purposes, lie worlds apart; whatever exists, having somehow come into being, is again and again reinterpreted to new ends, taken over, transformed, and redirected by some power superior to it; all events are a subduing, a becoming master, and all subduing and becoming master involves a fresh interpretation, an adaptation through which any previous "meaning" or "purpose" are necessarily obscured or even obliterated.'
Friedrich Nietzsche, *On the Genealogy of Morals*, II, 12
—

The past several decades have witnessed what might be described as a broad *usological* turn across all sectors of society. Of course, people have been using words and tools, services and drugs, since time immemorial. But with the rise of networked culture, users have come to play a key role as producers of information, meaning and value, breaking down the long-standing opposition between consumption and production. With the decline of such categories of political subjectivity as organized labour, and the waning of the social-democratic consensus, *usership* has emerged as an unexpected alternative—one that is neither clear cut nor welcomed by all. For usership runs up against three stalwart *conceptual edifices* of the contemporary order: *expert culture*, for which users are invariably misusers; *spectatorship*, for which usership is inherently opportunistic and fraught with self-interest; and most trenchantly of all, the expanding regime of *ownership*, which has sought to curtail long-standing rights of use. Yet usership remains as tenacious as it is unruly. The cultural sphere, too, has witnessed a shift. Turning away from pursuing art's *aesthetic function*, many practitioners are redefining their engagement with art, less in terms of *authorship* than as users of artistic

competence, insisting that art foster more robust use values and gain more bite in the real.

Challenging these dominant conceptual institutions feels disorienting, however, as the very words and concepts one might 'use' to name and clarify use-oriented practices are not readily available. All too often, user-driven initiatives fall prey to lexical capture by a vocabulary inherited from modernity. Yet no genuine self-understanding of the relational and dialectical category of usership will be possible until the existent *conceptual lexicon* is retooled. This requires both retiring seemingly self-evident terms (and the institutions they name), while at the same time introducing a set of emergent concepts. In the spirit of usership this may be done best by *repurposing* the overlooked terms and modes of use, which remain operative in the shadows cast by modernity's expert culture.

1:1 scale

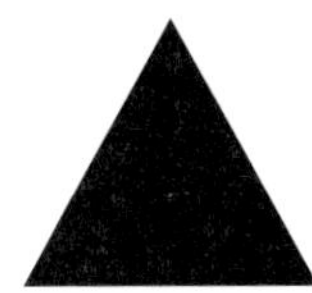

'use the country itself, as its own map'
Lewis Carroll, *Sylvie and Bruno Concluded* (1893)
—

Art and art-related practices that are oriented toward usership rather than spectatorship are characterized more than anything else by their scale of operations: they operate on the 1:1 scale. They are not scaled-down models—or artworld-assisted prototypes—of potentially useful things or services (the kinds of tasks and devices that might well be useful if ever they were wrested from the neutering frames of artistic autonomy and allowed traction in the real). Though 1:1 scale initiatives make use of representation in any number of ways, they are not themselves representations of anything. The usological

turn in creative practice over the past two decades or so has brought with it increasing numbers of such full-scale practices, coterminous with whatever they happen to be grappling. 1:1 practices are both what they are, and propositions of what they are.

Scaling up operations in this way breaks with modernist conceptions of scale. By and large, the art of the twentieth century, like so many post-conceptual practices today, operated at a reduced scale; art was practiced as both other than, and smaller than, whatever reality it set out to map. In his 1893 story, *Sylvie and Bruno Concluded*, Lewis Carroll tells of an impromptu conversation between the narrator and an outlandish, even otherworldly character called 'Mein Herr,' regarding the largest scale of map 'that would be really useful.'

'We very soon got to six yards to the mile. Then we tried a hundred yards to the mile. And then came the grandest idea of all! We actually made a map of the country, on the scale of a mile to the mile! ... It has never been spread out, yet ... the farmers objected: they said it would cover the whole country, and shut out the sunlight! So now we use the country itself, as its own map, and I assure you it does nearly as well.'

A book could be devoted to unpacking that pithy parable! Were the farmers right, do maps (embodiments of the will to make-visible) constitute ecological threats? Every light-shedding device will also inevitably cast shadow, and a map (or any representation) is also a light-occluding device. But whatever it may mean to 'use the country itself, as its own map,' and however it may be done, one thing is sure: it provides an uncannily concise description of the logic of art on the 1:1 scale—as good a description of many usership-oriented initiatives as any on hand.

Notorious for creating tales full of mesmerizing warps in the fabric of space and time, Carroll undercuts some of the fundamental

assumptions about scaled-back representation: its role as surrogate, its status as an abstraction, and its use as a convention that references the real to which it is subordinate. The 'grandest idea of all'— that is, producing a full-scale representation—turned out to be useless... And this is precisely the pitfall of so many politically motivated art initiatives today: they remain squarely within the paradigm of spectatorship. Mein Herr's map, replaceable as it is by the territory it surveys, raises questions about what happens to representation when, at its limit, it resembles its subject so closely as to confound the distinction between what is real and what is not. It evacuates the mapping event altogether. The territory is neither mapped nor transformed in any way. And yet, used 'as its own map,' all is transformed. In this case, the representation not only refuses to be subordinate to its subject, it is also interchangeable with it, and even superior, as Carroll slyly suggests. The ontological discontinuity between map and land—and by extension, between art and whatever life form it permeates—disappears as soon as the territory is made to function on the 1:1 scale as its own self-styled cartography. What are the conditions of possibility and usership of a land's cartographic function, the *becoming-map* of the land-scape?

Or more simply, what do 1:1 practices look like, when they start to use the land as its own map? Well they don't look like anything other than what they also are; nor are they something to be looked at and they certainly don't look like art. One might well describe these practices as being positively 'redundant,' as enacting a function already fulfilled by something else— as having, in other words, a 'double ontology.' Yet in many cases, being burdened with an ontology (let alone a double one!) seems to be just exactly what they are seeking to escape from. Certainly they are intent on eluding ideological and institutional capture, and the kind of defanged representation to which it leads; but that does not describe the full thrust of these projects. They seem to be seeking to escape performative and ontological capture as art altogether. It is certainly possible to describe them as having a double ontology; but it may be more closely in keeping with their self-understanding to argue that this is not an ontological issue at all, but rather a question of the extent to which they are informed by a certain coefficient of art. Informed by artistic self-understanding, not framed as art.

Allure

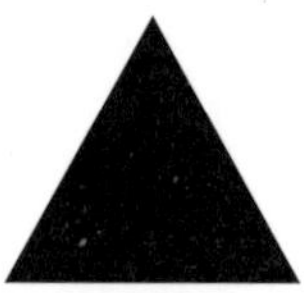

'We need a general term to cover both the comic and charming ways of encountering the sincerity of objects, and the best term I can think of is allure.'
Graham Harman, *Guerrilla Metaphysics. Phenomenology and the Carpentry of Things* (2005)
—

When an art-informed practice is ramped up to the 1:1 scale, deactivating its primary aesthetic function and activating instead its usual or useful function, there's no sure way of seeing it as art. There are certainly no perceptual properties to tip us off once its coefficient of artistic visibility drops to the negligible. To perceive such practices as art requires some supplementary theoretical information, something that lets us know that the initiative, whatever it may be, is both what it is, and a *proposition* of what it is; some external knowledge letting us know that the initiative's existence does not exhaust itself in its function and outcome, but that it is *about* something. It embodies meaning. But what does that knowledge do for our *conception* and even our *perception* of an

activity which itself remains unchanged? However we may wish describe such practices, something definitely happens to our understanding when we see things anew under the aspect of art— either as having a 'double ontology,' simultaneously and inseparably what they are and artistic propositions of what they are; or as having a certain 'coefficient of art,' thus avoiding the issue of art's ontology altogether; or as having an 'infrathin' dimension, to use Marcel Duchamp's cleverly elusive term for an equally elusive dimension. Artworlders invariably assume that our appreciation of something is somehow enriched or augmented, when we learn it is art inspired. Occasionally, though, we hear someone proclaim, upon discovering that some usual activity or service was grounded in artistic self-understanding, that they 'didn't even know it was art,' and find ourselves wondering whether that discovery came as an epiphany or as a let down…

One concept that has been put forward to describe the shift in how we conceive of and perhaps perceive an object or activity once learning of its concealed dimension is that of 'allure,' a term used by Graham Harman. It may seem paradoxical to draw upon the lexicon of Harman's 'object-oriented ontology' in a discussion of relationally defined, usership-oriented social practices; and doubly so in that 'allure' has unabashedly aesthetic overtones. However, speculative realism, with which Harman is closely associated, has done more than any body of thought to challenge Kantian hegemony. On top of which, allure doesn't so much restore art's aesthetic function as allow us see to aesthetics from a new angle.

The 'labour of allure,' writes Harman, involves separating an object from its traits, even as these traits remain physically inseparable from the object. 'Allure,' as he describes it, 'is a special and intermittent experience in which the intimate bond between a thing's unity and its plurality

of notes somehow partially disintegrates.' These notes become sensual objects in their own right, rather than disappearing into the thing to which they belong as happens under ordinary conditions of perception. Allure is not necessarily aesthetic perception but 'whereas normal experience deals solely with surface qualities,' Harman explains, 'allure apparently brings objects directly into play by invoking them as dark agents at work beneath those qualities.' In some way, allure 'connects the upper and lower floors of an object in the manner of a trapdoor or spiral staircase.' Well, that could suit our purposes quite well, could it not? The thing changes not one bit, yet once the trapdoor springs open and the 'dark agents' are on the loose, nothing could be more different.

Artworlds (art-sustaining environments)

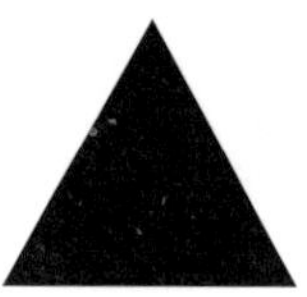

'an atmosphere of artistic theory, a knowledge of the history of art: an artworld.'
Arthur C. Danto, 'The Artworld' (1964)
—

Common sense seems to tell us that we all live in one and the same world. Upholding the conjecture of a plurality of worlds requires a sustained theoretical effort. And yet the consensus around one-worldism has found itself seriously challenged of late: from every quarter, other worlds appear not only possible but far more plausible and desirable than the hegemonic version that continues to pass itself off as the only one. The ontological chauvinism of one-world theory has made some headway into art as well and the mainstream artworld tends to assert a sort of axiological

and ontological superiority over its contenders and counterparts. It doesn't so much deny their existence—art tends to know intuitively and by definition that other worlds are plausible, flattering itself as being one of the more sophisticated launch pads for world multiplication—as it questions their value, saying in effect that though other worlds may be plausible, they're just not much good. However, the past decade has seen an increasing number of art-related practitioners scale up from the production of artworks alone to actively conceiving and developing the art-sustaining environments required if their practices are to thrive, often far from the referenced field of art. Artworlds are the places where art is used and, as such, are fundamental to any usological examination of art and art-related practice.

Assisted readymades and artworld-assisted prototypes

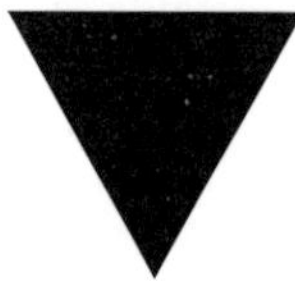

'I realized very soon the danger of repeating indiscriminately this form of expression and decided to limit the production of 'readymades' to a small number yearly. I was aware at that time, that for the spectator even more than for the artist, art is a habit-forming drug.'
Marcel Duchamp, 'Apropos of Readymades' (1961)
—

In a short exposé delivered in 1961, Marcel Duchamp offered some acute insights into the logic of readymades— describing them as highly 'addictive drugs.' In addition to standard readymades, by which usual objects have their use value suspended (as if placed between invisible parentheses) as they are inserted into the performative framework of the artwork, and his farsighted (but uninstantiated) suggestion of *reciprocal* readymades, which restore use value to artworks through their withdrawal from the performative frame, Duchamp briefly describes an intermediary variant. These, he says, are basically standard readymades, except that they have been modified ever so slightly. He calls these 'assisted readymades' (*ready-mades aidés*). It's a nice term—and prescient too; today we have a different name for such deeds and contrivances modestly tweaked by artistic subjectivity: we call them *contemporary art*.

While the assisted readymade has become the addiction of the autonomous artworld, apparently intent on pursuing its logic exhaustively until such time as every commodity on earth has an identical counterpart in the realm of art, it is now rivaled by another trope: the artworld-assisted *prototype*. On the one hand, the prototype borrows the principle of industrial-design characteristic of the readymade but rather than embracing the logic of the multiple, it insists upon its experimental uniqueness. One might say that the proliferation of prototypes in contemporary art production is yet another symptom of an ongoing usological shift; but inasmuch as these prototypes are by no means autonomous but require artworld assistance to function at all, they are above all rather spectacular examples of an attempt to square the conceptual architecture and protocols of autonomous art with emergent intuitions. Such prototypes might indeed be functional, if ever they were freed from their artworld-assistance mechanisms and made available for genuine use.

Authorship

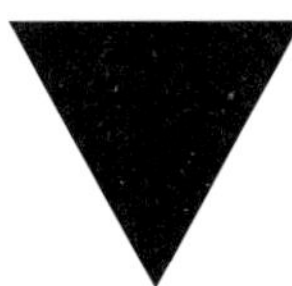

'The possessive quality of modern democratic liberal theory is found in its conception of the individual as essentially the proprietor of his own person or capacities, owing nothing to society for them.'
C.B. MacPherson, *The Political Theory of Possessive Individualism* (1962)
—
With the rise of possessive individualism in seventeenth-century Europe, a previously unheard-of idea began to gain currency—one that today has achieved hegemony—according to which individuals are conceived as the sole proprietors of their skills and owe nothing to society for them, meaning that these skills (and those of others) are commodities to be bought and sold at the marketplace. One of the conventions for packaging those skills is the conceptual institution of *authorship*. People had been using words, notes and pigment to string together tales, tunes and pictures forever, and though history retains the names of some of the more illustrious, it hadn't occurred to anyone that users of words, melodies and colours could somehow lay claim in any meaningful way to some particular arrangement that they had come up with; that they could claim authorship of some particular configuration of otherwise freely circulating marks and noises, and as such regulate other people's use of them. Previously, ideas and sentences, rhymes and rhythms were socially available for all to use (that is, modify, or not, and reproduce). Authorship became the name for stabilizing that semiotic swarm, commodifying it by congealing it around a single name—a signature—as if it owed nothing to the contributive usership of society. What Michel Foucault

famously called the 'authorship function' developed as a way of containing semiotic dispersion around an arbitrary signifier (a proper name).

The twentieth century was not kind to authorship (though by then the institution of authorship had long since triumphed). Psychoanalysis, hermeneutics and post-structuralism amongst many others challenged the idea of a constituent subject underpinning authorship, shifting the locus of production toward the subconscious, the collective, the reader or the viewer... But these critiques, though they deconstructed the notion, paradoxically only strengthened the market value of authorship. Today, authorship continues to function in a sort of holy trinity with objecthood and spectatorship as a mainstay of the mainstream artworld. Indeed, from an investment perspective, authorship has now overtaken objecthood as a monetizable commodity.

However, authorship is facing a challenge from contributive usership. As users contribute content, knowledge, know-how and value, the question as to how they be acknowledged becomes pressing. With the rise of collectively organized art-sustaining environments, single-signature authorship tends to lose its purchase—like possessive individualism in reverse.

Autonomy

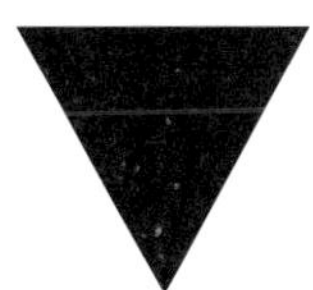

'the watchword of *l'art pour l'art* was always the mask of its opposite'
Theodor Adorno, *Aesthetic Theory* (1970)
—
Autonomy is a tricky term to handle because in the field of art it has come to denote almost the opposite of what it set out to name. Literally, *auto/nomos* means to determine one's own laws. When art

slowly but surely pried open a new social space for itself in nineteenth-century European society, on the basis of aesthetic principles laid out by Kant, Hegel, Diderot and others, it was in the name of giving itself its own laws. Its 'conquest of space,' as Pierre Bourdieu calls it, was about wresting art from the overarching control and hindrance of religious and political authorities, carving out a separate sphere for itself where it could develop in keeping with its own internal logic. This space of autonomous art determined the art of modernity. Of course, the autonomy was only ever relative—but it was effective, and jealously guarded. In fact it still is. Incursions from other fields were repulsed vigorously. Indeed, they still are. This autonomous sphere was seen as a place where art was free from the overcodes of the general economy (its own, utterly unregulated market notwithstanding) and the utilitarian rationality of market society—and as such, something be cherished and protected. This realm of autonomy was never supposed to be a comfort zone, but the place where art could develop audacious, scandalous, seditious works and ideas—which it set about doing.

However, autonomous art came at a cost—one that for many has become too much to bear. The price to pay for autonomy are the invisible parentheses that bracket art off from being taken seriously as a proposition having consequences beyond the aesthetic realm. Art judged by art's standards can be easily written off as, well... *just art*. Of contemplative value to people who like that sort of thing, but without teeth. Of course autonomous art has regularly claimed to bite the hand that feeds it; but never very hard. To gain use value, to find a usership, requires that art quit the autonomous sphere of purposeless purpose and disinterested spectatorship. For many practitioners today, autonomous art has become less a place of self-determined experimentation than a prison house—a sphere where one must conform to the law of permanent ontological exception, which has left the autonomous artworld rife with cynicism.

Coefficient of art

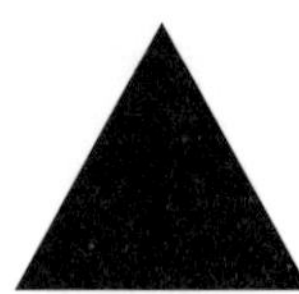

'the coefficient of art is like an arithmetical relation between the unexpressed but intended and the unintentionally expressed'
Marcel Duchamp, 'The Creative Act' (1957)
—

In a famous eight-minute talk called 'The Creative Act,' Marcel Duchamp put forth the idea of a 'coefficient of art,' by which he referred to the discrepancy, inherent in any artistic proposition, between intention and actual realization, setting out to define this gap by a sort of 'arithmetical relation between the unexpressed but intended and the unintentionally expressed.' It is of course this gap that prevents art from being exhausted in the moment of its emergence, conferring on it the potential to evolve through interpretation. Coefficient of art is a nice term, but a strange one too, as if there were something 'unintentionally expressed' in those words—as if it itself had a coefficient of art which was not immediately audible to Duchamp himself. That there might be variable coefficients of art may enable us to understand how art may be construed so as to not fall prey to ontological capture. To speak of 'coefficients of art' is to suggest that art is not a set of objects or events, distinct from the larger set of objects and events that are not art, but rather a degree of intensity liable to be present in any number of things—indeed, in any number of symbolic configurations, activities or passivities. Could it be that art

is no longer (or perhaps never was) a minority practice, but rather something practiced by a majority, appearing with varying coefficients in different contexts? What coefficient of art have we here? Or there? What is the coefficient of art of such and such a gesture, object or practice?

It is a radically deontological conception of art—as socialized competence, rather than performed works. A way of describing art gone fallow, and then to seed; finding itself in a permanent state of extraterritorial reciprocity, having no territory of its own. An unexpected fate, but then, art-historical movement is never lineal; if anything, it seems avunculineal (based not on direct lineage but on the looser inspiration drawn freely from those bearing some family resemblance) moving like the knight on the chessboard, one step to the side for every two forward. Lateral shifts do indeed appear to be taking place on the art field. And though in many ways, if contemporary art seems to be the purview of Duchamp's nieces and nephews, sometimes we may feel more like his orphans.

Cognitive surplus

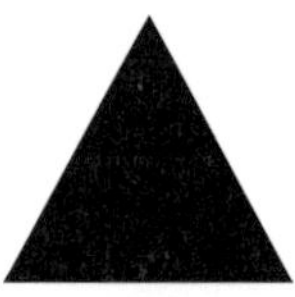

'The atomization of social life in the twentieth century left us so far removed from participatory culture that when it came back, we needed the phrase "participatory culture" to describe it.'
Clay Shirky, *Cognitive Surplus* (2010)
—

The expression 'user-generated content' describes both individual and, more importantly, social acts. No one generate content just for themselves. Insofar as user-generated knowledge creates meaning, and value, it must

be user-shared. Detractors of usership are quick to point to that category's built-in component of self-interest. Yet even as users pursue self-interest, they mutualize uses and produce a kind of usership surplus, building upon and expanding prior uses. In this way, usership is contributive and yields more than the sum of the individual uses that comprise it: sharing all the tools in a workshop allows everyone to benefit both from the use of the tools and (even more so) from the compounding know-how of their collective usership. Call it a utility surplus. When the mode of usership in question involves connecting brainpower—what Gabriel Tarde calls 'intercerebral collaboration'—the type of excess produced is referred to as 'cognitive surplus.'

For instance, when users tag images, texts, sounds or videos, they make those tags available and avail themselves of others' tags in an upward spiral. The rise of contributive usership through new media tools came as something of a surprise; indeed, it could not have been predicted because the possibility of that usership was less determined by the tools themselves than by the desire to gain access to one another. The potential impact of usership-driven cognitive surplus is pretty staggering. Wikipedia, for instance, an extraordinary user-made initiative by any account, has been built out of roughly 1% of the man-hours that Americans spend watching television each year... What makes user-uploaded libraries and film archives and p2p file-sharing arrangements work is usership surplus.

User-aggregated task engines, such as reCAPTCHA (those distorted texts found at the bottom of online registration forms, that one has to retype to reduce spam) produce astronomical amounts of cognitive surplus—that in the case of reCAPTCHA is turned toward transcribing all the books and newspapers prior to 1945, whose print cannot be machine read with reliable accuracy. It is

estimated that some 200 millions CAPTCHAs are solved by humans every day, requiring on average a mere ten seconds of labour time... which, totals some 150,000 hours of unremunerated labour each day. One of the largest factories in the world, driven by inadvertent labour alone. Leaving aside the question as to the universal human value of the tasks into which projects such as reCAPTCHA have yoked internet users, they underscore the prodigious cognitive-surplus potential that aggregated usership embodies. A labour force tantamount to the one required to build the pyramids or put astronauts on the moon—accomplished as the by-product of a primary task! Aggregated usership brings a previously unheard-of potential for cognitive surplus into play, one liable to utterly transform our conception of labour. For now usership has precious little say over the use of its community-generated surplus, and rarely accrues its share of the benefits it produces.

Competence

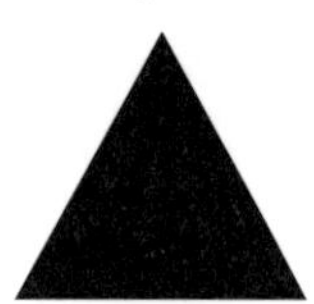

'The difference between linguistic competence and linguistic performance can be illustrated by slips of the tongue, such as "noble tons of soil" for "noble sons of toil." Uttering such a slip doesn't mean that we don't know English but rather that we've simply made a mistake because we were tired, distracted, or whatever. Such "errors" also aren't evidence that you are a poor English speaker... When we say someone is a better speaker than someone else, we are referring to performance, not competence.'
Kristin Denham & Anne Lobeck, *Linguistics for Everyone* (2010)
—

If 1:1 scale, usership-driven practices are not performed

as art, then what will become of art? For all the invaluable insights provided by performance studies, it is clear that performativity has an inherent blind spot, just as any outlook has; and in the wake of the ostentatious and inflationary use of that concept in any number of theoretical sauces, it is 1:1 scale practices which have laid bare its basic aporia. What performativity overlooks is what exactly is being performed—and with respect to art practices leaving the sandbox of art for the social, that can best be called 'competence.' Now after a century of radical deskilling, to speak of artistic competence is to sound suspiciously conservative, if not downright reactionary—at least to the experts policing the field. But competence is not to be confused here with artistic *métier* or skill in the fine arts tradition. In fact it is to be understood as virtually synonymous with *incompetence*, for usership-generated practice is founded on *mutualizing incompetence*. On the face of it, that seems an odd thing to say; but, a competence can only be defined as such from the perspective of a corresponding incompetence. And in effect, it is only because a given incompetence is somehow competence-deficient that it calls a competence to the fore. This is of fundamental importance in situations of collaboration, where art engages in skill sharing and competence crossing with other modes of activity whose domains of competence, and hence of incompetence, are very different. By mutualizing (in)competence, this difference is made fruitful and productive. For instance, as Robert Filliou once famously put it in his equivalency principle, there is in art a fundamental equivalency between the well done, the poorly done, and the not done. Because this 'principle' seems self-evident to art—making it a basic artistic competence—while remaining almost certainly unacceptable to any other field of activity, it goes some way to underscoring

what art per se brings to the table of 1:1 scale practice, once its aesthetic function has been deactivated.

At any event, one can observe a definite tendency amongst contemporary practitioners not to be pressured into constantly performing underlying competences. An analogy can be drawn here with Noam Chomsky's famous distinction between linguistic competence (inherent to all native speakers of a natural language enabling them to distinguish a grammatically coherent speech act from one that is not) and linguistic performance (actualizing that competence in producing speech acts). One can, of course, always perform a competence; but one *need* never perform it for that competence to exist. This gives art particular potency in its contemporary moment of trans-social migration: it can deploy its (in)competences and self-understanding in social settings far removed from art, without ever performing them as art.

This is a huge issue, because it has to do with the socialization of art and the repurposing of existent institutions, both conceptual and physical. Chomsky's insistence on competence has often been criticized as being ahistorical—referring to an inherent, hard-wired attribute—and thus unable to account for change in the way language is actually used or 'performed'. This may not be an insurmountable obstacle, though, inasmuch as competence can also be construed itself as some-thing dynamic, constantly being informed through a kind of feedback loop by developments in performance. What is perhaps most attrac-tive about the idea that competence need never be performed in order to exist is that it draws attention to, and provides an escape route from, an event-centered conception of art—one of the most rarely challenged mainstays of artworld ideology, according to which art is not only made up of events

(exhibitions, publications, production of works) but is itself seen as event. On the one hand, the everyday, here-and-now perspective of usership doesn't allow this privilege. But on the other hand, without those everyday acts of usership and repurposing, there is no way to account for how events actually come about! To put it differently, one might associate event with performance and competence with everyday usership—something largely invisible to the event-focused attention economy but which may actually be the engine of social transformation. It is certainly fair to say that there is an extraordinary amount of art-related competence at work and at play that is simply not being performed—that is, not being captured institutionally and performed as event. The implications for curatorship are obviously immense.

Conceptual edifices

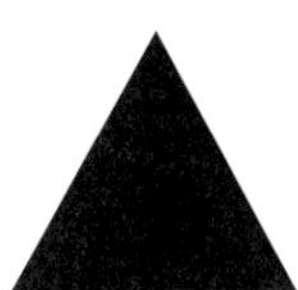

'Just as the reader can make a new book through reading… the user can make a new building through using.'
Jonathan Hill, *Actions of Architecture: Architects and Creative Users* (2003)
—

We dwell in conceptual edifices. They shelter and confine us, with or without our consent, even in the great outdoors. The architecture of these complex, invisible edifices relies on conceptual building blocks repurposed from previous edifices. Though it is rare to be able to point to the architect of any given conceptual edifice, as their users, we are all somehow their co-architects. We use them for our purposes, for without users, they are just empty shells; with time, they come to bear the brunt of usership's wear and tear and ultimately

can no longer contain the uses to which they put. By thwarting purposes, they invite repurposing: with a bit of help from their usership, they inevitably undergo change: an annex is added here, a tunnel and a trapdoor there. But that can only go so far. At some point users tear them down and establish new ones. Needless to say, the conceptual architecture of these edifices very much determines the physical architecture of all society's institutions. Many conceptual edifices of modernity, including Spectatorship, Authorship, the Aesthetic Function of Art, the Nation State and Productivism are showing signs of severe stress and need to be torn down so their constituent parts can be put to new ends.

Deactivate (art's aesthetic function)

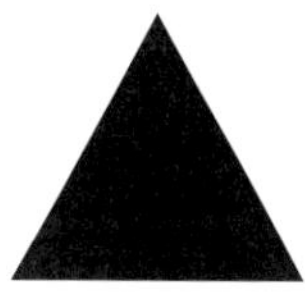

'The creation of a new use is possible only by deactivating an old use, rendering it inoperative.'
Giorgio Agamben, *Profanations* (2007)
—

'Deactivate' is a verb often used by Giorgio Agamben to name the political conditions of possibility for genuine paradigm shifts, which can only happen, he contends, if residual power structures are effectively deactivated. If they are merely displaced or overhauled, their power remains active. To describe the paradigm shifts underway in many contemporary discourse-based and interventionist art practices, investigator Mabel Tapia rightly speaks of the 'deactivation of art's aesthetic function.' It is a stinging formulation, to be sure, but it succinctly captures the radicality of the moment. To say that art's aesthetic function has today been deactivated (and, where still active, has become something of a decoy), is not of course to say that artworks no longer have an aesthetic, or are somehow aesthetic-free—which would be absurd. All sensual things have an aesthetic; that cannot be deactivated. But they do not necessarily have an *aesthetic function*. It was Kant who assigned art an aesthetic function: he did not believe art was functionless, only that it should not be seen as having a purposive or a goal-oriented function, but one which endlessly unfolds in disinterested aesthetic contemplation. As long as that function remains active, art remains outside the realm of usership and can have no operative use value.

Deactivating art's aesthetic function, rendering it inoperative, opens art up— by Agamben's account—to other functions. To a heuristic function, for instance; or an epistemic function. Or the more operative functions of 1:1 scale practices.

But art's aesthetic function is so intimately bound up with many contemporary understandings of what art is that the aesthetic function has become almost ontologized—as if that historically determined (and altogether recent) function were inseparable from art's very mode of being... exactly what Kant had hoped for. This accounts for the reticence amongst some practitioners to envisage the deactivation of art's aesthetic function. Other practitioners, however, have concluded that it is only by deactivating this debilitating, use-precluding function that they can make way for a purposive aesthetics of art; an aesthetics repurposed in the name of usership.

Disinterested spectatorship

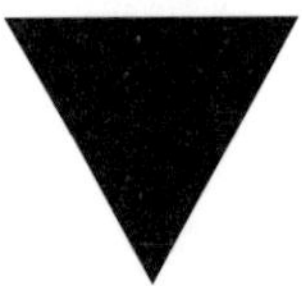

'Kant's view is different: one withdraws to the "theoretical," the onlooking, standpoint of the spectator, but this position is the position of the Judge.'
Hannah Arendt, *Lectures of Kant's Political Philosophy* (1970)
—

Immanuel Kant is the single greatest architect of the conceptual edifice of modern, autonomous art. For all intents and purposes, the conceptual architecture of today's art museums (and, hence, their physical architecture of display) is underpinned by Kant's two intermeshed and brilliantly paradoxical imperatives, formulated at the end of the eighteenth century. On the one hand, he argued, art is characterized by its 'purposeless purpose'; on the other it was geared toward 'disinterested spectatorship.' The former imperative was to ensure art's universality, preserving it from the realm of use and utilitarian interest, enabling it to freely embody what he rather nicely called 'aesthetic ideas,' which could be the object of knowledge. But Kant realized that he somehow had to protect this objective dimension of art as knowledge from the slippery slopes of subjective appreciation, even while explicitly acknowledging that art was something that could only be apprehended subjectively ... Hence his second, complementary brainchild, 'disinterested spectatorship.' It would be difficult to overstate the almost fantastic robustness of this conceptual arrangement— which, of course, is precisely what accounts for its extra-ordinary longevity.

For Kant, an actor in any given situation—or, worse still, a *user*—is not 'autonomous,' and is incapable of theoretical onlooking. As one of Kant's most lucid commentators, Hannah Arendt, points out: 'The standard is the spectator. And this standard is autonomous.' Kant was adamant about these issues, because he felt that if spectatorship fell prey to subjective interest, all was lost. In what can only be described as a pre-Wittgensteinian moment in his *Critique of Judgement*, Kant argued that one could not *say*, before a painting or other artwork, 'this is beautiful *for me*.' For to thus qualify an aesthetic judgement subjectively, *for me*, rather than making a universal claim, was an illicit use of language. Such subjectivity was reserved for issues of preference (Kant mentions Canary wine...), and was precluded from aesthetic judgement that required disinterested spectatorship.

If disinterested spectatorship continues to enjoy strong art-world support, not least of all because it is so entrenched in institutional architecture, it has recently been somewhat up-staged by a not unrelated notion—what Jacques Rancière's refers to as *emancipated spectatorship* ... Seeking to save spectatorship from the inherent passivity to which it has been relegated by such unlikely adversaries as Bertolt Brecht and Guy Debord, Rancière has argued that 'it is in the power of associating and dissociating that the emancipation of the spectator consists ...' Spectators, he claims counterintuitively, know what they see, and know what to do with it, translating and counter-translating in terms of their own experiences. Like *The Emancipated Spectator* as a whole, the argument is enticing, but odd. Does it not stretch the definition, and agency, of spectatorship a notch too far? Genuinely emancipated, spectatorship rolls up its sleeves, as it were, becoming something else altogether, and it may not be unreasonable to name that something else 'usership.' In many respects, *The Emancipated Spectator* reads much better if one replaces 'spectator' with 'user'.

Double ontology

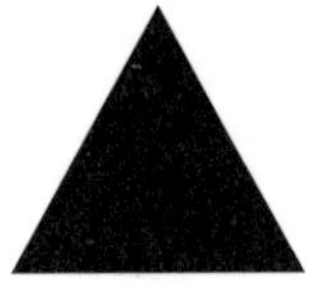

'It was like living a secret life, somehow dishonest, but I felt that to reveal the purpose of the undertaking would compromise the outcome, like the Schodinger's Cat example, where the observance of something changes the outcome.'
Raivo Puusemp, 'Thoughts on Control' (2013)
—

1:1 scale practices operating within a paradigm of usership, actually being what they are— house-painting outfits, online archives, libraries, restaurants, mushroom hunts, whatever— and at the same time artistic propositions of what they are, can be described in different ways, depending on what set of properties (or allure) one wishes to emphasize. They can be described as *redundant*, inasmuch as they fulfill a function, as art, which they already fulfill as whatever it is they are. They can also be said to have a *double ontology*: a primary ontology as whatever they are, and a secondary ontology as artistic propositions of that same thing. The sorts of things Marcel Duchamp once punningly referred to as 'reciprocal readymades.'

Practices with 'double ontologies' do not immediately appear as art, though that is where their self-understanding is grounded. To that degree, at least, they do indeed break with the basic tenets of autonomous art. Whatever its descriptive power, however, the notion of a double ontology has two downsides. Firstly, it is not entirely sure that two ontologies are better than one, even if a double-take of this kind allows for considerable usological and escapological play. In fact, in some ways, it may be twice as cumbersome, and an enormous concession to institutional theory, reinforcing as it does the idea that art has an ontology at all. Secondly, to describe practices in these terms is to make them inherently reliant on performative capture to repatriate them into the art frame—otherwise, their secondary (artistic) ontology remains inert, and not so much disappears as fails to appear in the first place. From the perspective of institutional theory, this is intolerable: what is not performed as art, is not art, and so is lost to posterity. But in another way, that may be precisely the point. To disappear from that ontological landscape altogether in order to gain traction somewhere else.

Escapology

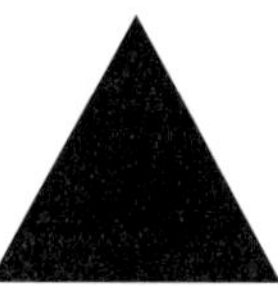

'Escape is all that remains.'
Henri Laborit, *Éloge de la fuite* (1976)
—

Escapology, broadly speaking, refers to the rapidly growing field of empirical enquiry and speculative research into the ways and means, tactics and strategies of escaping capture. Not so much Houdini-style escape from physical bonds (though his methodologies hold metaphorical appeal for both researchers and practitioners as well as for popular culture), as from the more insidious forms of capture in contemporary society that hobble action, desire and thought by cloaking them in often invisible overcodes. Capture may be ideological, encouraging agents to think in terms of categories whose mere existence is their sole merit. Or it may be institutional, framing practices into a sphere of action that determines their specific visibility and forecloses their potential deployment. Ever increasingly, both in the general economy and in the symbolic economies of art and activism, capture may be logistical, subsuming human decision-making and

rationality itself into algorithms. Capture may be epistemic, terminological, but whatever its configuration, escapology is about fleeing its normative clutches. The mode of escapology most widespread in the mainstream artworld has to do with escaping the ontological capture that is the bane of autonomous art practice, whereby actions or objects have their very mode of being (their 'ontology') captured as art; just art. This form of capture relies on that most perversely neoliberal form of capture—operative or performative capture, whereby things are put to work, made to perform. Escapology, in short, is the theory and practice of suspending the operations of all these mechanisms of capture.

Yet escapology is a paradoxical undertaking, and an often-ambivalent science. For obvious reasons, escape itself can neither assert itself for what it is, nor perform itself as escape: it must always appear impossible from the perspective of power, yet at the same time it must be always already under way. Escapology, then, is less the study and implementation of sets of tactics or strategies for avoiding capture, than the acknowledgement of a simple, concrete fact: *escape happens*. This is escapology's *a priori*, and though it seeks to better appreciate the escapological drive in contemporary culture, it does not see escape as a self-conscious attempt to escape *from* something. It envisages escape in terms of offensive retreat; as such, it shares none of the projective logic of an event-driven vision of history. Whereas (left-leaning) art historians and social theorists have conditioned us to think of emancipation, and indeed of art itself, in terms of events—whether past or yet to come—escapology rejects this masculinist perspective as one premised on the luxury of being able to wait for the coming event or to look back on the one which took place. Escapology is the science of the kind of everyday elusiveness, leakage

and doing-otherwise that can really only be described as 'escape' once power structures shift to capture its movement. Ultimately, escapology's examples, those that instantiate its concrete truth, all lie beyond, or behind, the event horizon itself.

In lieu of an example, then, consider this speculative etymology suggestively put forth by a contemporary escapologist. The verb 'escape' is usually thought to derive from the Vulgar Latin *excapare*, from *ex-* ('out') + *capio* ('capture'). It may well be, however, that it comes from the Late Latin *ex cappa*, in reference not to capture at all but to a 'cape' or cloak which remains behind even as the living body which it had clad has slipped away.

Eventhood

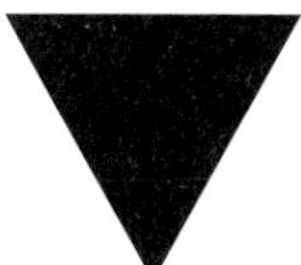

'not infrequently, in these situations, you were really art; it's just that no one noticed'
Mladen Stilinović, *Dear Art* (1999)
—

Eventhood is the horizon line in the spontaneous ideology of much art-historical discourse. Art historians have accustomed us to seeing art in terms of events: artworks, exhibitions, publications, movements... construing art as an irruptive event, penetrating stable appearance with novelty and all the attendant fireworks. But this is a strangely masculinist understanding of art-historical process. To focus on the epiphany of 'events'—and to see art itself as event—rather than on fugitive occurrences, is to foreground particular moments when a set of material, social and imaginary ruptures come together and produce a break in the flow of history. As Dimitris Papadopoulos, Niamh Stephenson and Vassilis Tsianos have argued in *Escape Routes: Control and Subversion*

in the Twenty-First Century (2008), an escapological perspective is inherently different: 'An event is never in the present; it can only be designated as an event in retrospect or anticipated as a future possibility. To pin our hopes on events is a nominalist move which draws on the masculinist luxury of having the power both to name things and to wait about for salvation. Because events are never in the present, if we highlight their role in social change we do so at the expense of considering the potence of the present that is made of people's everyday practices: the practices employed to navigate daily life and to sustain relations, the practices which are at the heart of social transformation long before we are able to name it as such.' In our society of the event, the event itself disappears from view. It becomes the horizon line itself.

Expertise / Expert culture

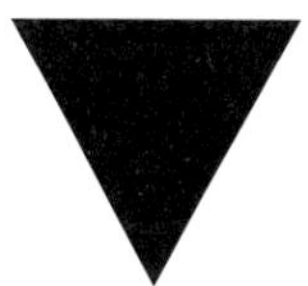

'B's competencies enrich A's competencies if C's incompetencies enrich B's competencies then C's incompetencies change polarity and move to a higher order'
François Deck, 'Reciprocal Expertise' (2004)
—

From the high-minded perspective of expert culture, users' claims are inherently shot through with self-interest. Take the experts of State. On the one hand anxious to uphold their regime of exception with respect to the market-driven private sector, public-sector experts are quick to point out that they serve users, rather than customers or clients; and on the other hand, they are the first to again uphold their exceptional status by stigmatizing users (or consumer advocacy groups) as the Trojan Horse of this same market-driven logic... But the person who takes such and such a bus line every morning at dawn to get to work knows something about that line which no urban planning expert, whose perspective is informed by countless disinterested 'studies,' can simply ever know. This cognitive privilege is user specific.

It is expert culture—whether the editors, the urban planners, the curators—which is most hostile to usership: from the perspective of expertise, *use* is invariably *misuse*. But from the perspective of users, everywhere, so-called misuse is simply... use. In *The Production of Space*, Henri Lefebvre points out a fundamental difference between the cognitive space of usership and the epistemological chauvinism of expert culture.

'The user's space is lived—not represented... When compared with the abstract space of the experts (architects, urbanists, planners), the space of the everyday activities of users is a concrete one which is to say, subjective.'

Of course, this is also what makes usership something of a double-edged sword, which is precisely what makes it interesting to consider, not as an alternative to the supposedly universal category of the 'proletariat,' for instance, but as a way of rethinking the dialectics of collective and individual agency.

Michel Foucault is premonitory in this respect. In his usage, usership at once designates the site where individuals and their comportments and needs are expected, where a space is available for their agency, both defining and circumscribing it; and it refers to the way in which these same users surge up and barge into a universe, which, though accustomed to managing their existence, finds itself thrown off balance by their speaking out as users. In other words—and this is related to Foucault's theory of political action—it is not as if users burst forth in places where they are not expected; rather, the very immediacy of their presence is ambivalent and cannot be reduced to a progressive recognition, nor to a mere cooptation by the powers that be. Governance, control, disciplining devices of all kinds, necessarily generate users whose agency is neither exclusively rebellious nor purely submissive toward an exterior norm. They know they will never be owners; that they will never eliminate that dimension of exteriority from the power relations that impact on them. Users take on those instances of power closest to them. And in addition to this proximity, or because of it, they do not envisage that the solution to their problem could lie in any sort of future to which the present might or ought to be subordinated (very different in this respect to any revolutionary horizon). They have neither the time to be revolutionary—because things have to change—nor the patience to be reformists, because things have to stop. Such is the *radical pragmatism of usership*.

Externalities (positive and negative)

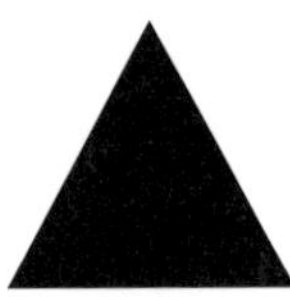

'pollination is but one example of a complex symbiosis underlying the many contributions not based on market exchange'
Yann Moulier Boutang, *The Bee and the Economist* (2010)
—

Externalities are the by-products of usership. Economists define externalities as the inadvertent or indirect benefits or costs that result from a given activity or transaction. Acid rain, for instance, is considered a negative externality of using coal-fired power stations. In calculating the overall social value of that type of energy production, one would have to calculate the intended benefits and the negative externality of being surrounded by dead forests, and so on. One classic example of a positive externality is beekeeping. Beekeepers keep bees primarily for their honey, which accounts only for a modest contribution to the general economy. A spillover effect or positive externality of their activity is the pollination of surrounding crops by the bees (some 80% of all crops are pollinated in this way)—which generates a non-monetized value incommensurably greater than the value of the harvested honey. The implications for usership are tremendous.

Detractors of usership invariably point to its negative externalities. Champions of ownership bemoan the fact that they cannot monetize the positive externalities of their activities that users enjoy for free. But usership is in fact akin to pollination—users are like bees, as it were, producing incalculable externalities. As Yann Moulier Boutang has argued (rather optimistically) in *The Bee and the Economist*, we may currently be transitioning from an 'economy of exchange and production toward an economy of pollination and contribution'—that is, an economy of usership.

Extraterritorial reciprocity

'Always implicated, and yet elusive.'
Maurice Blanchot, *The Infinite Conversation* (1969)
—

What happens when art leaves its 'own' territory? When it moves into situations of collaboration in other territories? When it migrates south, socially and epistemically speaking? All too often, we tend to devote attention to what art does when it gets to whatever new territory it invests, rather than thinking about what happens to the place art left behind. But it is no less important to attend to the fate of art's place of departure than to its point of arrival. Does it not open a kind of invisible void through its often conspicuous absence—taunting culture, the way nature abhors a vacuum? This is the operation of *extraterritorial reciprocity*, a perhaps excessively multi-syllabic way of describing how in leaving its own territory for another, in becoming a 1:1 scale practice, art vacates, in a gesture of reciprocity, a space for other social practices to use. This space, and all that goes with it, formerly reserved for art but suddenly made available to other forms of endeavour, is often a tremendously desirable and useful resource for practitioners from other fields—the very fields where art may have migrated and who repurpose art's vacant space their own use.

It is easy to see what would tempt art to migrate southwards, slipping its moorings and making its way into the shadows of the attention economy; in trading off autonomy for the social; exchanging artworks for practices: the desire to gain traction in the social realm and not find itself, time and again, written off as 'just art.' But the space art leaves behind is a polyvalent one, and the swap may be mutually beneficial. Extraterritorial reciprocity, then, consists of art vacating its convention-be-stowed territory in the artworld, making it available to other activities, in a gesture of reciprocity as it sets up shop in a different domain. This is an art without a territory, which operates in the intersubjective space of collaboration. Yet that 'space' is really no space at all, or only in the metaphorical sense of the term; it is probably more accurate to speak of a 'time' of collaboration and intervention—the time of common yet heterogeneous purpose. But the geographical model, with its cartography of partially overlapping territories, has the advantage of providing a tangible picture of what practitioners of reciprocal extraterritoriality are really after. Constitutive mobility. Elusive implication.

Gaming

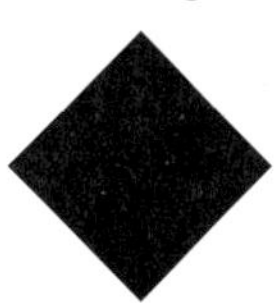

'The bad player sees bluff everywhere, and takes it into account. The good player considers it negligible and follows only the knowledge he has of his cards in hand at any given moment.'
Guy Debord, 'Notes on Poker' (1990)
—

Some would contend that usership is about gaming the system—misusing its intentions to achieve better outcomes. That may be, but insofar as one could also argue the converse (that the system games its usership), the question becomes: is there anything outside gaming? Certainly there are different ways of gaming, but is there anything beyond gaming? Is playing the spoilsport not also a game? It is by no means a moot point, for we know that in language games, for instance, usership alone determines whatever meaning there may be. In *Homo Ludens*, Johan Huizinga argues that what he calls the 'troublesome *only* feeling' (i.e., that it's only a game) is abolished in play. Is that also true for art? The Situationists, who quote Huizinga's remarks on 'just gaming' approvingly, sought to develop a 'superior game' that would be characterized by the disappearance of any competitive dimension—'a bad product of a bad society,' in their eyes. One of the last texts written by Guy Debord is a short treatise called 'Notes on Poker,' a game he played frequently and about which he held highly unorthodox views. Since poker is a game of bluff,

he argued, the good player never bluffs, nor pays any heed to other players' bluffing, but only ever plays his hand. It's hard to say whether the theory has any application in the game of poker; but it provides astounding insight into the game of usership. Spectators see bluff everywhere and take it into account. Users consider bluff to be negligible and follow only the knowledge they have of their means at any given moment. If others bluff, it is of no concern to users. Usership is not beyond gaming; indeed, it's just gaming—but playing for real.

Gleaning

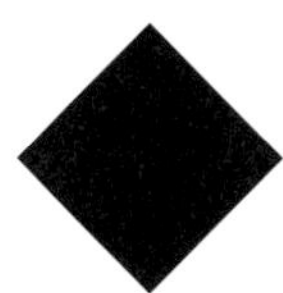

'Leftovers are clusters of possibilities'
Pierre Pons, in Agnès Varda, *The Gleaners and I* (2000)
—

Gleaning has been a customary right to farm products in Europe and elsewhere since the Middle Ages. It refers to both the right and the practice of gathering leftover crops from farmers' fields after they have been commercially harvested or where reaping is not economically viable. Gleaning differs from scrounging in that, unlike the latter, it is legally regulated— it is a common and informal type of usufruct that ensures gleaners a circumscribed right to use (*usus*) others' property and to enjoy its fruits (*fructus*). Because it is specifically regulated (for instance, after thrashing, the collecting of the straw and the fallen grains of wheat is authorized) it is distinguished from pilfering—defined as the offence of stealing fruit or vegetables before they have fallen to the ground. A more subordinate mode of usership than, say, poaching, gleaning is nevertheless significant because it points to historically entrenched rights of common usership over resources found

in private domains. Today, immaterial gleaning is widely practiced by a whole host of art-related practitioners; its agricultural antecedents offer it a haven from encroachment by groups lobbying on behalf of increased intellectual property rights and the foreclosure of the epistemic commons.

Hacking

'What calls for a creative application of the hack is the production of new vectors along which the event may continue to unfold after its initial explosion into social space, and avoid capture by representation.'
McKenzie Wark, *A Hacker Manifesto* (2004)
—

'Hacking' is a great old Saxon word. A hack is a kind of beveled cut with an axe. Not a clean slice, but an oblique chop—opening something up in a way that's not easy to repair. There has been much speculation about when and why the term was adopted by programmers. But the most thought-provoking discussion of what hacking means socially is to be found in *A Hacker Manifesto*, by McKenzie Wark. It is a rare thing, and the measure of genuine intellectual creativity, when a writer is able to develop and deploy a full-fledged, conceptual vocabulary and use it in a sustained way: the writing becomes at once the staging ground and the first application of a new way of talking.

A hacker, in Wark's lexicon, is very different from the image of the super-specialized anarcho-programmer, or criminal subculture, which the term still conjures up for most people; it refers to someone who hacks into knowledge-production networks of any kind, and liberates that knowledge from an economy of scarcity. 'While not everyone is a hacker, everyone hacks,'

writes Wark, suggesting that hacking is really quite akin to usership of knowledge, information, images, sounds and other social resources that one might find useful. In a society based on private-property relations, scarcity is always being presented as if it were natural; but in the contemporary context, where intellectual property is the dominant property form, scarcity is artificial, counter-productive—and the bane of hackers—for the simple reason that appropriating knowledge and information deprives no one else from accessing it. This is a key issue in art-related practice—indeed, Wark talks about hacking as if it *were* an art-related practice—for the system of value-production in the mainstream artworld is also premised on a regime of scarcity, underpinned by the author's signature. Wark hacks his rather unorthodox theory out of Marxism: like Marx, Wark believes human history can be conceptualized in terms of class relations and conflict. Today though, he argues, this conflict is most acute between what he calls the 'vectoralist' class (the class that owns the pipelines, the satellites and the servers, which has come to supplant the hegemony of the capitalist class) and the new productive class that Wark describes as hackers, whose purpose it is to free knowledge from illusions of scarcity. The hacker class, he argues, arises out of the transformation of information into property, in the form of intellectual property.

This is a usefully redescriptive understanding of hacking. And it sheds an interesting light on the Obama Administration's unwavering reaction to the recent Snowden hack, whose shock waves continue to reverberate through global civil society: 'The documents are the private property of the United States Government and must be returned immediately.' As if the hacked documents' ownership were their salient feature! In another way, though, it makes sense to see hacking as a way of turning documents against their owners. In political terms, one might argue that leaking documents is the 'southern' response to the 'northern' privatization of information—southern being understood in an epistemic and political sense. A counterhegemonic gesture, using the information power produced by the adversary—the readymade documents—to tactical advantage. Something that in the hacker milieu is often referred to as 'hack value.'

Hack value is difficult to define and ultimately can only be exemplified. But, by and large, it refers to a kind of aesthetics of hacking. For instance, repurposing things in an unexpected way can be said to have hack value; as can contributing anonymously to collectively used configurations, in the spirit of free software. Steven Levy, in his book *Hackers*, talks at length about what he calls a 'hacker ethic.' But as Brian Harvey has argued, that expression may be a misnomer and that what he discovered was in fact a hacker *aesthetic*. For example, when free-software developer Richard Stallman says that information should be given out freely—an opinion universally held in hacker circles—his opinion is not only based on a notion of property as theft, which would be an ethical position. His argument is that keeping information secret is inefficient; it leads to an absurd, unaesthetic duplication of effort amongst the information's usership.

Idleness (creative and expressive)

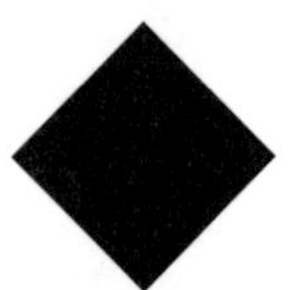

'**Stasis is the new movement.**'
Kenneth Goldsmith,
Uncreative Writing (2011)
—

Can we think of art, not as something that must be performed, but which might well exist as a latent competence, an active yeast or undercurrent beneath the visible field of events, all the more potent in that it remains unperformed? Can we not think of art as capable of a self-conscious, Bartelby-like decision to *prefer not to* (in this case, not to inject competence into the art frame) but instead to bide its time and, perhaps, redirect that competence elsewhere?

Even in its most proactive, productivist moments, there is something profoundly idle about usership. Something slack. It uses what is, what's there. Plagiarism, appropriation, repurposing, patching and sampling, cutting and pasting, then databasing and tagging for reuse—these are the domains of usership's expertise. Translating is a form of usership (of a text, a word, a string of words, an image or a sound): users are translators, transposing what they find in one idiom into another. And while translating can be hard work, it is creatively idle, making do with what is available rather than feeling compelled to add something else.

Imperformativity

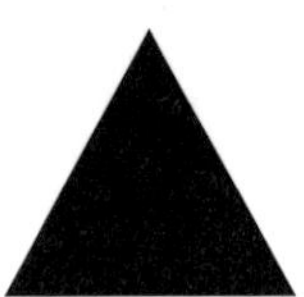

'**aktivnoe strmelenie k nichemu**'
Mit'ki Motto (USSR, 1980s)
—

Usership is characterized by its radical imperformativity. It eschews performative capture. To perform usership would be to spectacularize it—that is, to negate it, to make it into something else. Imperformativity is not usership's horizon, but rather its modus operandi.

Lexicon

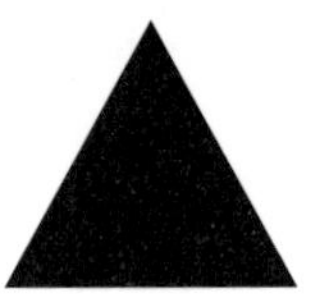

'*Unspeakably more* **depends on what things are called than on what they are. … Only as creators can we destroy! But let us not forget that in the long run it is enough to create new names and plausibilities in order to create new "things".**'
Friedrich Nietzsche, *The Gay Science*, §58 (1890)
—

The powerful conceptual vocabulary inherited from Western modernity presents us with an unusual—indeed, historically unprecedented—paradox. The conceptual toolbox is full; all the word tools are there, and in great shape too. But, somehow, they're not quite the right tools for the jobs at hand; they are the right tools for a job no longer needed—tools calibrated to older conceptual edifices, founded in mainstream artsustaining environments, aligned to practices (before they were even called that) stemming from aesthetic autonomy. And yet, since they are the tools that continue to enjoy the legitimacy of expert culture, their very presence precludes the proper identification of the right job...

Where the crisis of the lexical toolbox's inadequacy becomes excruciatingly obvious, however, is where the continued use of a tool warps, twists and distorts emergent intuitions, forcing contemporary practices into twentieth-century molds. Since we can neither think nor even name art without appropriate terms, retooling our conceptual vocabulary has become a crucial task, one that can only be undertaken by fostering terminological cross-pollination with other avenues of human activity. What we need, perhaps more than anything, is a retooled lexicon. This has nothing to do with drumming up some sort of new expert speak or coining neologisms, and everything to do with repurposing common terms from other lexical fields, other practices of knowledge. The only way to produce a meaningful, user-repurposed wordscape, uninhibited by an overcoded vocabulary, is to listen to the language games of other activities, experimentally importing notional edifices. An extradisciplinary retrofit of sorts, paying heed to the ongoing usological turn in contemporary practice.

Rather than seeing art as the lens through which to consider conceptual migration, it might well prefer to see itself as a host to, and guest of, lexical migrants. If it is to have a useful critical edge, and if it is to challenge invisible norms, naming must be a tool for undoing apparent self-evidences—that 'misty mantle of illusion,' as Nietzsche caustically put it, 'that counts as essential, so-called "reality".' Which is tantamount to wresting 'art' from 'art,' sundering art from itself.

Loopholes

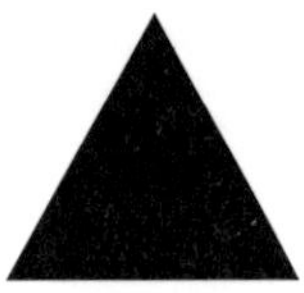

'**Whatever it wins, it does not keep. It must constantly manipulate events in order to turn them into "opportunities".**'
Michel de Certeau, *The Practice of Everyday Life* (1980)
—

Loopholes are the quintessence of usership-instantiated tactics since they offer ways into systems without physically damaging them. Literally, or least historically, 'loopholes' were the narrow vertical windows found in castle walls. The defenders of the castle on the inside referred to them as 'arrow slits,' using them to launch arrows against assailants, who, on the other hand, referred to them as loopholes—the only anchor point for the loop on their climbing rope, and hence the only ready means of gaining entry without breaching or destroying the wall or gate. Thus a loophole in a law—or customary use, institutional convention and so on—often contravenes the intent of the law without technically breaking it. Users have an inherent knack—call it the cognitive privilege of usership—for finding ambiguities in a system which can be used to circumvent its implied or explicitly stated intent. Loopholes are sought out and used strategically and creatively by users, including artists, in all manner of circumstances, including taxation, security, elections, politics, different levels of the legal system and civil liberties.

Artists as users are in a way particularly well equipped to exploit such grey zones inasmuch as one of the reflexes of artistic competence is '*détournement*'—never responding forthrightly to expectations, nor refusing to engage, but rather countering obliquely. Art itself, like the space of autonomy within which mainstream practices operate, is often used as a foil to avoid the legal consequences that would apply to the same action if it were not 'art' or carried out in art's name. Usership-driven art uses loopholes both in the mainstream art system and beyond to circumvent any number of overcodes. The highly paradoxical instrumentalization of artistic autonomy is one widely practiced example.

More consequential forms of loopholing invariably occur in sectors of society where legal norms have failed to keep pace with social need—including migration, mores, ownership issues and various fields of expert privilege—as expressed through the actual usership of available legal instruments. These slackspaces of normative action (sometimes called legal voids) emerge quickly but are swiftly shut down, making loopholing a particularly dynamic mode of under-the-radar operation. Users of such practices know from experience and observation that while it is both fun and possible to

outfox the authorities for a while, once the loophole has come to light, their window of opportunity is already closing and it's time to move on.

Museum 3.0

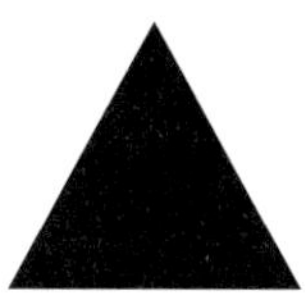

'I leave it an open book'
Macedonio Fernandez, *The Museum of Eterna's Novel* (1925-1952)
—

Museums these days find themselves in the throes of a crisis of self-understanding, hesitating between irreconcilable museological paradigms and userships. On the one hand, their physical architecture of display is very much top down: curatorship determines content which is oriented toward spectatorship. On the other hand, while concerned about protecting their 'vertical dignity,' to the degree that they have tried to keep pace with the usological turn in the field of culture, museums have embraced elements of 2.0 culture. Not in the digital-media sense of the term—we are not talking about some kind of online museum—but insofar as their model of legitimation is at least partially premised on visitor experience, feedback and input. One might argue we have already implemented a 2.0 museum model, we simply haven't acknowledged it yet. Or more precisely, we have usership-dependent museums, integrating elements of user-generated content, without recognizing the contributive usership and its collective input. Museums have so far proved reluctant to make way for usership, both because their physical architecture is geared toward display (not use), but above all because their conceptual architecture would have to be thoroughly revamped in order to make this integration meaningful.

But broader economic developments in society may

soon compel them to take bolder steps. Both from a practical and a theoretical perspective, it seems pointless to continue to bemoan the dismantling of the social-democratic consensus and its public institutions, including museums, by the neo-liberal revolution. This war of attrition can go on indefinitely, but with ever diminishing returns—and entrenchment in a resistencial posture of defending the status quo is a depressing prospect. The moment calls for a bolder strategy. What may be required is to rethink the conceptual architecture of our evolving institutions from a perspective outside the public/private binary—repurposing tools, categories and opportunities inadvertently made available to new ends. Here again the category of usership—a form of collective subjectivity no more governable by neoliberalism than it is palatable to social democracy—comes to mind. In contemporary 2.0 culture, usership generates both content and value; indeed, it is a locus of surplus-value extraction, for it is rarely if ever remunerated. In this respect, 2.0 culture is both a promise, and a swindle. For the time being, 3.0 names the prospect of fulfilling that promise. Though contemporary modes of accumulation have come to rely on usership—making it a category that is unlikely to go away any time soon—it stands opposed to that mainstay of neoliberalism that is ownership. For, simply, users are not owners. Nor are they spectators. But what if the museum made way for usership, actually embedding it in its modus operandi? A museum where usership, not spectatorship, is the key form of relationality; where the content and value it engenders are mutualized for the community of users themselves? Where the usership of museums, like that of languages, produces their meaning? Current scenarios predictions about what 3.0 culture might look like invariably focus on the advent of the 'semantic web' and insinuate that user engagement will somehow

wane in favour of object-oriented content—data talking to data. But this seems excessively ideologically determined, as if users only actively use by default and would really prefer to consume. The offline 3.0 museum, like a kind of walk-in toolbox for usership, could be a place where user engagement—user wear and tear—was explicitly acknowledged as generating value, and as such was entitled to share that value.

Remunerated usership (not financial retribution, perhaps, but in some negotiated form) is tantamount to a cultural revolution, and could only go hand in hand with a politics of usership based on the counterintuitive self-understanding that usership in fact generates value rather than consuming it; for the time being, many users remain grateful not to have to pay for use. When in the 1970s Jean-Luc Godard quipped that television viewers ought to be paid to watch, it was assumed he was sarcastically commenting on the quality of broadcasting. Thirty-five years on, the remark appears utterly premonitory: if usership generates value, it should be remunerated. If it produces surplus value, great! We may be witnessing the end of work as we know it. But that surplus value must be redistributed within the community that produced it, not foster capital accumulation for a rentier class of property owners, who play no useful or productive role in the economy *per se*, but who monopolize access to the use of physical and financial assets and technologies. In *From Capital-Labour to Capital-Life*, Maurizio Lazzarato has recently argued that 'capture, both in creation and realization, is a reciprocal seizure open to the unpredictable and infinite, now that 'creator' and 'user' tend to merge.' All too often, creation and use find themselves radically separated by political economy. But applied to museum usership, they might be made to merge: usership, far from being synonymous with consumption (destruction), spills over into production. Usership is creation socialized, and as such engenders a surplus.

Narratorship (talking art)

'Things happen one way and we tell about them in the opposite sense. You seem to start at the beginning. And in reality you have started at the end.'
Jean-Paul Sartre, *Nausea* (1938)
—

When artistic practice takes place on the 1:1 scale (far from the performative frames of the artworld) how can it be repatriated into the fold of art without betraying its fundamental thrust and use value? In the absence of such reterritorialization, how can we ensure that it not be lost to posterity? How is documentation of the project to be shaken from its state of inertia? Or its residual by-products wrested from their opacity? And their exhibition torn from its mute passivity? In modern times, it was the aesthetic function of art that guaranteed their activation, giving them a voice—ensuring what Michel de Certeau would call their '*prise de parole*.' It was an ambivalent operation, for while it was art's aesthetic regime that authorized them to speak, to mean, no sooner did it do so that retracted that speech in the name of the aesthetic overcode to which they remained subaltern. Today, though, with the deactivation of art's aesthetic function, it is more precisely the document, the exhibition, the proposition itself that seem to call for a gesture to free their potentiality from its latency; now it is they who lay claim to our speech, not the other way round. In other words, the activation of practices that have deliberately impaired their coefficient of specific

visibility cannot be dealt with by a *narrative*, as was supposed by late twentieth-century narratologists, but only through the active agency of *narratorship*.

Narratorship names the vital function of the narrating subject and, as such, opens up a new discursive life for the object (or the document) behind the exhibition's back. The inflationary rise of artists' talks, curated panels, open forums and rap sessions all and sundry has been one of the more marked developments in contemporary art over the past decade—and one of the most significant inasmuch as the need for 'talking art' may be seen as palliating a knowledge crisis. By and large, the tendency has been to integrate talking into the existent conceptual and physical architecture of the artworld; to think of the verbal as a mere enhancement of the visible, rather than perceiving it as a potential alternative to often reifying exhibition structures. Though such narratorship can be adapted to the modalities of visibilization—indeed, anything can—it is worth considering this tendency more closely and ask whether artists talking about their work is not a thoroughly viable and particularly non-reifying way for art to appear in the world—including object-based work. Isn't it invariably more stimulating to hear artists present their work than to have to go and look at their exhibitions? Beyond the trivial explanation that this is because the artist's presence evidences an existential engagement in the work that is not otherwise tangible, it may also reveal that the site of art itself has undergone an historical shift; that art itself is not immediately present, but withdrawn, its coefficient of specific visibility too low for it to be detected and identified as such. One might then contend that in the case of off-the-radar practices, talking art—like the popular musical form of 'talking blues'—is a means of activating a proposition as art. Narratorship as a mode of using art seems to point the

way to a thorough overhaul of how art is apprehended, and where it takes place.

Objecthood

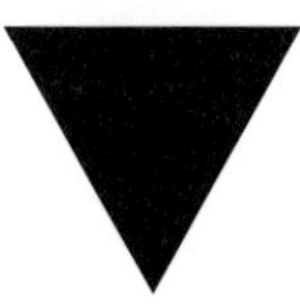

'Perhaps most important, Conceptualists indicated that the most exciting "art" might still be buried in social energies not yet recognized as art.'
Lucy Lippard, 'Escape Attempts' (1997)
—

Objecthood, in a triangulated arrangement with authorship and spectatorship, forms one of the linchpins of the mainstream contemporary artworld. Indeed, a generation ago, it was *the* dominant conceptual institution in art—becoming the target for politicized concept artists who felt that by attacking, and as they put it, 'dematerializing' the reified, fetishized and commodified art object, they could bring down what they saw as a corrupt art system. Though it led to some fantastic art, the assault failed, or more precisely perhaps, succeeded in a perversely unforeseeable way. Objecthood turned out to be a more flexible category than it had seemed (or than it had been). By-products of interventions and snapshots of performances became art objects, as did protocols for immaterial conceptual pieces. And not only did the residual documents become fetishized objects; artistic objecthood itself expanded its purview with documentation and performative capture becoming dominant artistic genres. What had previously been seen as support documents (if indeed they were seen at all) became the object of art. More unexpectedly still, the very characteristics that concept art objected to in objecthood spread to non-objectal artistic experience, once it became clear that it too could be commodified and monetized.

To a large degree, in a kind of zero-sum game, objecthood has now been surpassed by what might be called 'eventhood' as a hegemonic conceptual institution.

Ownership (copyright is not for users)

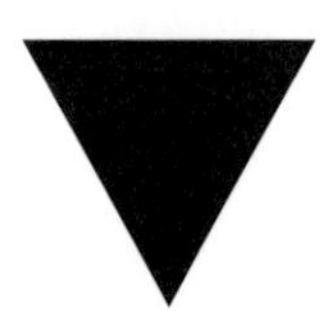

'Theft!'
Pierre-Joseph Proudhon, *What is Property?* (1840)
—

Proudhon's definition of property ownership is at once the most sparing, and unsparing ever proposed. Ownership describes a legal institution that codifies a relationship of exclusivity with respect to an object, or any property construed to be an object, in terms of rights and control. It is made up of complex sets of instruments of regulation and enforcement, and is such a mainstay of liberal ideology that it would enjoy virtually self-evident status in majority opinion were it not for... usership, which challenges its very conditions of possibility by insisting on use value and rights of use.

There isn't much land left to privatize—it's mostly already in the hands of owners—so ownership is now expanding vertically, codifying the notion of 'intellectual property' as fast as it can dream up the arguments and erect the firewalls. But whereas land is, if not scarce, at least finite, privatizing the vertical domain of knowledge requires creating artificial scarcity in the realm of potentially unlimited profusion. And here ownership knows very well the name of its nemesis: usership. Copyright laws and other legal fictions to crack down on p2p and TorrentShare sites, 'premium' (i.e., paid) subscriptions to user-fuelled media like YouTube and other streaming sites, beguiling algorithms for monetizing user-supplied search results by Google, even a special 'photocopillage' tax on photocopy machines. Capitalism is still grappling for a durable model of accumulation for the twenty-first century, but in every case the force to be reckoned with is the same: usership. A category that must by no means be done away with, since it is the locus and agent of surplus-value extraction; but one that cannot be easily governed and whose inherent interests stand opposed to ownership.

Piggybacking

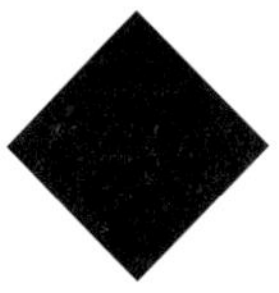

'We lie, as Emerson said, in the lap of an immense intelligence.'
John Dewey, *The Public and its Problems* (1927)
—

Literally, of course, piggybacking refers to carrying a person on one's back or shoulders. By extension, it also refers to transporting something by having it ride on the back of something else—a kind of free ride at no inconvenience to the vehicle since it was going there anyway. Piggybacking has become a widespread mode of usership in the past decade due to the advent of wireless Internet connections. Piggybacking on internet access is the practice of using another subscriber's wireless service without their explicit permission or knowledge. It is a legal and ethical grey zone, regulated in some places, permitted in others. It is a form of freeloading (another nice term), different from parasitism and more akin to a logic of the epiphyte: whereas parasites are the uninvited guests who overeat to the point of endangering the host's food supply, and thereby ultimately imperiling the well-being of the parasites themselves, the epiphyte lives in a negotiated

form of symbiosis with the host. As a form of usership— one very often exploited by art practices operating outside of art-financed domains— piggybacking is akin to reading someone else's newspaper over their shoulder, using a drinking fountain, reading from the light of a porch lamp, that is, benefitting the user at no expense to others. Art practices that use platforms like Skype, for example, as their medium or support might be described as piggybacking off a free and widely used (though often somewhat dodgy) service. In a society whose distribution of resources is so massively and systemically skewed, piggybacking may be seen as a user-driven form of redistributive symbolic justice.

Poaching

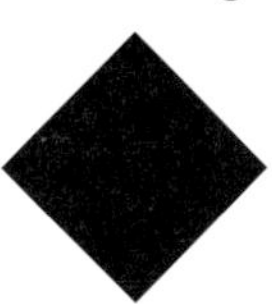

'Everyday life invents itself by poaching in countless ways on the property of others.'
Michel de Certeau, *The Practice of Everyday Life* (1980)
—

Poaching is a particularly evocative mode of usership, drawing attention to some of usership's most salient features. Though it may seem rustic and agrarian, it can also be seen as the rural predecessor to hacking, if the latter is understood and practiced as a form of digital poaching—armed with usb thumb drives, say, rather than snares and guns.

In 2008, ace-hacker Aaron Swartz wrote his 'Guerrilla Open Access Manifesto,' where he argued for the 'need to take information, wherever it is stored, make our copies and share them with the world... We need to download scientific journals and upload them to file sharing networks.' The good news, if Swartz can be believed, is that this is exactly what is happening. Possibly the most interesting passage in the

Manifesto is not where he argues for a principled practice of document sharing amongst users, but where he claims that it's what's occurring anyway:

'Meanwhile, those who have been locked out are not standing idly by. You have been sneaking through holes and climbing over fences, liberating the information locked up by the publishers and sharing them with your friends. But all of this action goes on in the dark, hidden underground. It's called stealing or piracy, as if sharing a wealth of knowledge were the moral equivalent of plundering a ship and murdering its crew.'

Swartz's image of 'sneaking through holes and climbing over fences' draws explicitly on the rhetoric of poaching. Breaches in fences are a recurrent element in its iconography. In most folklore, if not in painterly representation (presumably because of the class bias of its patrons) poachers were widely identified with and celebrated. They were invariably portrayed as one step ahead of the gamekeeper. Traditionally, poaching had nothing to do with the mercenary-style massacre of endangered species with which it has become associated today; it was all about the proactive redistribution of resources, like wood, fruit, fish, game... Legally speaking, poaching is hunting that, for whatever reason, is not allowed. Poaching is one of those 'catch-all' terms for off-the-radar modes of intervention, whereby in the shadow of the night, unauthorized agents (poachers) make stealthy forays behind the enclosures of the owner's land, capture their prey, and withdraw. And in that respect, though born of necessity (the young Marx famously linked the rise of poaching from private woodlots to a rise in unemployment), for those who practice it, poaching has always been a bit of a game— there is a kind of aesthetics of poaching, which distinguishes it from say cattle rustling. Could it be that both the scale and mode of poaching

constitute a useful paradigm, and genealogy, for many contemporary stealth practices whose game are documents rather than venison?

One of the characteristics of poaching is that it is by definition rigorously *imperformative*. A poacher who signs his work, or who *performs* his poach, is no poacher at all—or at least not for long. Poaching inherently withdraws from the event horizon, taking cover in the usual. Events are easy to spot; the usual, on the other hand, is invisible. The subjectivities we are called upon to perform in our prosumer society, though they may appear subversive, are easily read by power. All too often, it seems, we perform our rebellion. As Proudhon put it, in a moment of pre-Foucaldian insight:

'To be ruled is to be kept an eye on, inspected, spied on, regulated, indoctrinated, sermonized, listed and checked off, estimated, appraised, censured, ordered about by creatures without knowledge and without virtues. To be ruled is at every operation, transaction, movement, to be noted, registered, counted, priced, admonished, prevented, reformed, redressed, corrected.'

That's a pretty thorough, and entirely frightening checklist. In *Six Easy Pieces on Autonomy, Dignity, and Meaningful Work and Play*, James Scott refers to a whole realm of what he calls 'infrapolitics,' practiced outside the visible spectrum of what passes for political activity in event-oriented historiography. It is a term that grasps perfectly the imperformative, everyday practice of poaching. Because poaching happens.

'The state has historically thwarted lower-class organization, let alone public defiance. For subordinate groups, such politics is dangerous. They have, by and large, understood, as have guerrillas, that divisibility, small numbers, and dispersion help them avoid reprisal. By infrapolitics I have in

mind such acts as foot-dragging, poaching, pilfering, dissimulation, sabotage, desertion, absenteeism, squatting, and flight. Why risk getting shot for a failed mutiny when desertion will do just as well? Why risk an open land invasion when squatting will secure de facto land rights? Why openly petition for rights to wood, fish, and game when poaching will accomplish the same purpose quietly?'

Profanation

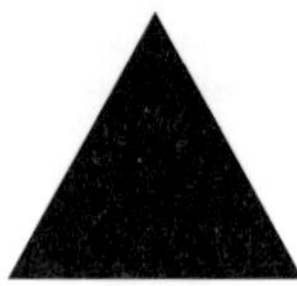

'Once profaned, that which was unavailable and separate loses its aura and is returned to use. Profanation deactivates the apparatuses of power and returns to common use the spaces that power had seized.'
Giorgio Agamben, *Profanations* (2007)
—

Profanation, as Giorgio Agamben defines it, is 'the returning to common usership what had been separated in the sphere of the sacred.' To suggest that profanation instantiates a *return* is of course to imply that common use constitutes the initial state. In Europe today, Agamben is the philosopher who has looked most searchingly into the issue of usership, recently disclosing that the forthcoming final volume of *Homo sacer* will be devoted to the question. That which is sacred is removed from the realm of usership; it is intangible, untouchable, and must not be profaned by consumption. This is true literally and figuratively. Today, as Agamben argues, the usership prohibition has found its place of choice in the Museum, where it is protected by the stalwart institution of spectatorship. Of course the museification of the world is almost total—spectatorship allows its extension far beyond the museum walls to any 'separated dimension where that which is no longer

perceived as true and decisive has been transferred.' It's art, but, well, *it's just art*. This is why in the institution of spectatorship, the analogy between capitalism and religion becomes so evident. And why usership, understood as the reality of using, is a political act: for it repurposes what is used. Repurposing, by transforming former ends into new means, neutralizes the sacred. In this respect, *usership is synonymous with the act of profanation*. The useful, indeed the used in general, is profane.

In his essay on profanation, Agamben both challenges a fundamental proscription of autonomous art and Kantian aesthetics (that art, in essence, must not be profaned... under the threat of ceasing to be art at all) yet also seems to rule out the possibility of something like... 'useful art.' For in the act of artistic profanation, as he sees it, objects do not so much gain *use* value as a kind of *ludic* value... But what about practices that have multiple uses? Can 1:1 scale practices not be conceptualized in terms of profanation—inasmuch as they would seem to embody the very essence of a living form that has become inseparable from life itself?

Purposeless purpose

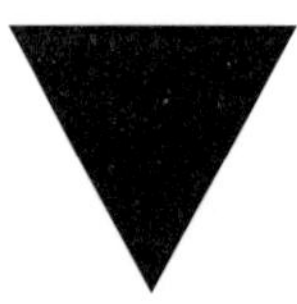

'When artistic objects are separated from both conditions of origin and operation in experience, a wall is built around them that renders almost opaque their general significance...'
John Dewey, *Art as Experience* (1934)
—

Some two centuries ago, through two exceedingly potent, and paradox-laden concepts, Immanuel Kant defined the mechanisms of

capture for autonomous art. Art, Kant argued, is geared toward 'disinterested spectatorship,' through which he introduced the disinterested spectator as the new heroic figure of aesthetic experience. Since everything about that term precludes usership, it dovetailed nicely with Kant's other architectural brainchild: art's 'purposeless purpose'— by which he did not mean that art was useless or without purpose; rather, its usefulness is its uselessness, its purpose is to be purposeless. In a world hell-bent on cost-benefit analysis and utilitarian rationality, this circularity is not without virtue. But it comes at an exceedingly high cost: it deprives art of any purchase, any use-value in the real. To repurpose art and develop a form of purposive aesthetics, then, would require breaking completely with the autonomous sphere of art and the values underpinning it. And this is precisely where we are now with respect to usership-purposed practices: facing the imperative to build a new art-sustaining environment from the ground up.

Reciprocal readymades

'Wanting to expose the basic antinomy between art and readymades I imagined a "reciprocal readymade": use a Rembrandt as an ironing board!'
Marcel Duchamp, 'Apropos of Readymades' (1961)
—

In a late text, Marcel Duchamp set out to distinguish several different types of readymades. Of particular interest in the present context is the genre he punningly described as 'reciprocal readymades.' Anxious, he claimed, 'to emphasize the fundamental antinomy between art and the readymade,' Duchamp

defined this radically new, yet subsequently never instantiated genre through an example: 'Use a Rembrandt as an ironing-board.' More than a mere quip to be taken at face value, or a facetious mockery of use-value, Duchamp's example points to the symbolic potential of recycling art—and more broadly, artistic tools and competences—into other lifeworlds. In that respect, the reciprocal readymade is the obverse of the standard readymade, which recycles the real—in the form of manufactured objects—into the symbolic economy of art. Historically speaking, the readymade is inseparably bound up with objecthood: it refers to a readymade, manufactured object. Yet, it would be reductive to confine the readymade to its objective dimension alone, if only because it provides such a strong general image of the reciprocal logic between art and the real.

In the same way that framing an object in an art context neutralizes it as an object (distinguishing it, as it were, from the mere real thing), can the de-framing of an artwork neutralize it, in reciprocal fashion, as art? This is an important question, and one to which Duchamp was expressly alluding, because it would enable art to produce a use-value. Since Immanuel Kant's influential championing of 'purposeless purpose' and 'disinterested spectatorship' as defining features of our engagement with art, it has been broadly held that art cannot produce use-value. Kant argued in effect that art, unlike design, could not be evaluated and appreciated on the basis of its objective purpose—be it external, regarding the object's utility, or internal, regarding the object's perfection. In so doing, Kant sought to preserve art from the realm of the 'merely useful'; and in our contemporary world where utilitarian rationality and the sort of cost-benefit analysis to which it leads reign supreme, where art is regularly co-opted by such profit-driven, subjectivity-production industries as advertising, to even mention use-value tends to smack of the philistine. Of course one might say that in such a context there is something circular about defending art on the basis of its uselessness alone (or even its 'radical uselessness,' as Adorno put it), for it would seem to suggest there is something very worthwhile and thus useful about something entirely lacking use-value...

At any event, an increasing number of art-related practices in the public sphere cannot be adequately understood unless their primary ambition to produce a use-value is taken into account. In trying to grasp what is at stake and at play in many of the art-informed practices which are, today, self-consciously concerned with generating use-value by injecting artistic skills into the real, it is no doubt useful to anchor their approach in art-historical terms. And perhaps the most straightforward way to understand such works is as attempts to reactivate the unacknowledged genre of artistic activity conceived by Duchamp. For though he never got beyond the speculative phase—never actually putting his thoughts on the reciprocal readymade into practice—Duchamp clearly saw it as a way of 'de-signing' art, of removing the signature by using an artwork to produce a use-value. For it is quite difficult to imagine how an artist-signed artwork (a 'Rembrandt'), put to use as an ironing board, could then be re-signed as an 'artistic' ironing board, at least not within the sphere of autonomous art. Indeed, Duchamp's point was that (until such time as the art-sustaining environment changed substantively) it would revert to non-art status—the price to be paid for acquiring use-value, though it would assuredly be a most uncommon ironing board. With the rise of usership-determined practices, it just may be that after lying dormant so long the reciprocal readymade's time has finally come.

Redundancy

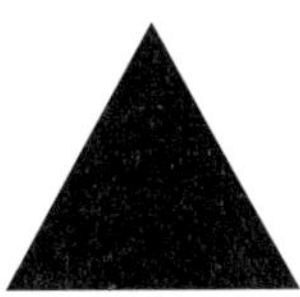

'In other words, art's function as a liberating force is dependent not only on its becoming something other than art but also maintaining its identity as a specific material as well as a symbolic practice.'
Rasheed Araeen, *Art Beyond Art* (2011)
—

Art has become redundant, in every sense of the term. Far from its doom, this may prove to be its salvation. The challenge for this century's art production is to free itself from its economic and social dependency on the institutional-market structure. To do that, it must, from an art-historical perspective, free itself from the conceptual and physical architecture bequeathed upon us by the twentieth-century art economy. Art must find a self-sustaining existence. Perhaps it already has; call it redundancy.

One thing that twentieth-century art could never whole-heartedly commit itself to be was something other than art—subordinating itself, ontologically, to whatever activity or entity it also was. This is a singularly uncoura-geous posture, but art's privileged ontological status enabled it to subordinate all other modes of objecthood and activity to itself. Redundancy means putting an end to art's twentieth-century ontological exception.

So, what is 'redundant' art? It is not possible to define it by what it looks like—it doesn't look, or not look, like art. It looks like what it is: the redundant thing or action. Redundancy ends the charade of artistic autonomy. It is neither more nor less creative or expressive than whatever it also happens to be. Redundant art covers all those activities and passivities, enterprises, initiatives and pursuits, which, though informed

by art and an art-historical self-understanding, are in fact just what they are and what they appear to be. They are redundant only as art.

A redundant system is one that duplicates the same system. Art is not redundant the way in anatomy a second kidney is said to be a redundant organ (the body being able to function with one alone). Art is redundant as an artistic initiative: its artistic ontology is utterly redundant with respect to its primary ontology. Of course twentieth-century art did make regular forays into life systems, life worlds, beyond the porous confines of its autonomous sphere. But it invariably did so as art—at best as a replication—not as a redundant instance of what it also happens to be.

Redundancy is invariably seen as depreciative, a term used to discredit something – be it an activity, phenomenon, object, or utterance – whose function is already fulfilled by something else. However, the notion of redundancy is a highly useful focusing tool in understanding the logic of forward-looking art in the early years of our century. Repurposing redundancy allows us to name in a new way practices that do indistinguishably what is already being perfectly well done in other realms of human activity, and to do it with an entirely different self-understanding. Though redundant, they are by no means superfluous. Today, we see art apparently withdrawing from the world (at least from the artworld); yet upon closer scrutiny, that withdrawal appears more as a merging with the world, a quest for redundancy.

Repurposing

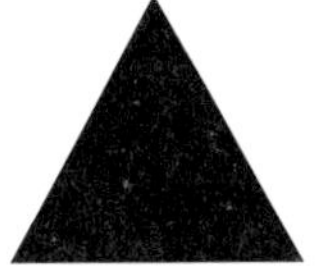

'Remember that bull's head I made out of the handlebars and the seat of a bicycle, which everybody recognized as a bull's head? I'd like to see it metamorphose in the opposite direction. Suppose my bull's head is thrown on the scrap heap. Eventually some guy may come along and say, "Now there's something that would come in very handy for the handlebars and seat of my bicycle..." And so a double metamorphosis would have been achieved.'
Pablo Picasso (1957)
—

There is often a kind of heuristic advantage to frontloading the prefix 're' onto verbs and nouns all and sundry. This is certainly the case with the watchword of usership, 'repurposing'— a term that captures both usership's paradoxical idleness (no need to add anything new) and its transformative dynamic (putting the given to new purposes). In a way, we've already got all the tools and skills we require—they're just not being *used* for the best purposes; we need to wrest them from their original purposes to repurpose them for other tasks. The immediate task at hand is to develop purposive artistic practices.

Slackspace

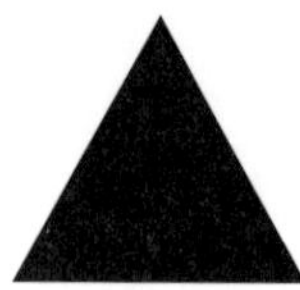

'provide the strength for breaking the rules in the very act that brings them into play'
Michel Foucault, 'Pierre Boulez: Passing Through the Screen' (1982)
—

Slackspace is a technical term in computer science that refers to the under-used or residually-used storage space of file clusters on a hard drive. Typically, computers store files in clusters of a fixed size—for instance, files may be stored in clusters of four kilobytes. If the computer stores a file that is only two kilobytes in a four-kilobyte cluster, there will be two-thousand bytes of slackspace. It's as if the house were bigger when measured on the inside than when measured on the outside! At any rate, in almost any given file (unless its size is exactly divisible by the system's cluster storage size), there is an available space—one that can be used for other purposes. Typically, this slackspace is not empty, but contains leftover information from previously deleted files— making it of great interest to forensic investigators. But hackers often use slackspace as a hiding place for information they wish to conceal, encrypting it—in the strictest sense of the term—in the cluster of an unrelated file. One need not be a conspiracist to see the terrific use-potential of such spaces. Expert culture certainly sees it as 'wasted' space, just waiting to be misused…

However, it is its metaphorical descriptive power which is of interest to us in our contemporary moment of free terminological migration. Slackspace may refer to any similar gap between parts, the wiggle-room between law and custom, the space of play between prescription and actual usership. Slackspace names a vacancy where the imperatives of productivism and conformity are tolerably low; a highly creative space, caught between two norma-tivities (just as a vacant lot is suspended between a defunct usage and an as-yet unrealized one), making it a realm of potentiality. Socially speaking, it is the adaptive space where opportunity effects change. By no means a revolutionary space (it by no means proclaims the overthrow of norms, merely their incessant renegotiation), it is the usual realm of usership.

Though he never uses the term, we derive this understanding of a slackspace as constitutive of usership from Michel Foucault. In the second volume of his *History of Sexuality*, catchily entitled 'The Uses of Pleasure,' Foucault performs a close reading of how *chresis*—the classical Greek term for use or usage— diverged from codified rules; how 'use' names a kind of gap between desire and law— a space of leeway and play never entirely chosen by those who use it, but whose use changes the rules of the game.

Specific visibility (sub specie artis)

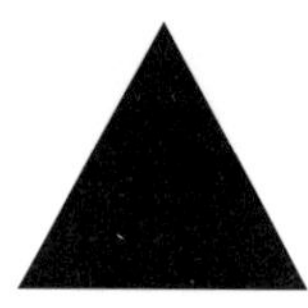

'The one caveat is that it must not be called art.'
Allan Kaprow, *Essays on the Blurring of Art and Life* (2003)
—

In a seminal statement written in 1964, Donald Judd argued that the emerging art of the time could best be described under the heading of 'specific objects.' Close to fifty years on, one might argue that the condition of art today is one of its specific visibility. Judd's 'specific objects' didn't much look like previous art; they were more 'minimal' in many respects; but they weren't invisible, particularly not as art, since the whole point was to frame them as such, thereby provoking a disruptive event of perception within the conceptual and physical architecture of the artworld.

Today, for better or for worse, art has become a question of specific visibility within institutional frameworks, or of specific invisibility without. Yet interestingly, as ever more art eludes those performative frames, the whole issue of art's invisibility becomes dedramatized, as if art were on the cusp of yet another ontological shift, moving from being determined by its coefficient of specific visibility to the coefficient of art it imparts on its host form. Less a question of being, than of intensity. Which of course only augments art's elusiveness, and immunity to scopic capture. It is unsurprising, indeed it is self-evident, that the smaller things get, the harder they are to see. We need magnifying glasses to read fine print, electron microscopes to see virus-size circuitry. Though not visible to the naked eye, small things are not invisible in conceptual terms; just very small. Their 'invisibility', if it makes any sense at all to talk in that way, is a mere function of their scale. In and of itself, this is of no interest for a politics of perception.

What is interesting, and always somewhat surprising, is the invisibility of often very large, even cumbersome, otherwise utterly obvious things; things that elude visual recognition per se despite their 'hyperobtrusive situation'—as Edgar Allan Poe puts it—right before our eyes. This ontological invisibility concerns an entire set of otherwise disparate objects and activities whose specific visibility has effectively been somehow purloined. Now an ontological fate as unique as this does surely raise some conceptual issues; and some key political ones as well. The category of paradoxically invisible, yet otherwise visible things is that of 1:1 artistic practice.

Spectatorship

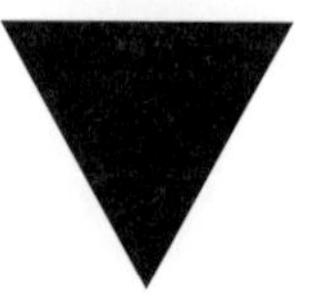

'Do not enrich the spectacle. Diminish it.'
Guy Debord, *Secret Instructions for a Putsch in Culture* (1961)
—

To a still greater extent than objecthood or authorship, spectatorship continues to enjoy almost self-evident status in conventional discourse as a necessary component of any plausible artworld. Indeed, in both popular and learned parlance, there is a tendency to conflate looking at something, and in some cases simply seeing something, with spectatorship. Yet spectatorship is not synonymous with mere viewing; it is a powerful conceptual institution in contemporary societies with a specific history—one whose historical underpinning needs to be unpacked.

The critical sermons of contemporary art are rife with celebration about free and active viewer participation. Yet there is something almost pathetic about such claims at a time when ever more practitioners are deliberately impairing the coefficient of artistic visibility of their activity, beating an offensive retreat into the shadows of the artworld's attention economy, envisaging forms of relationality and usage that fly in the face of the very regime of visibility designated by the collective noun 'spectatorship'. When art appears outside of the authorized performative framework, there is no reason that it should occur to those engaging with it to constitute themselves as spectators. Such practices seem to break with spectatorship altogether, to which they increasingly prefer the more extensive and inclusive notion of usership. Is the current mainstream focus on spectatorship—evidenced by a number of recent theoretical publications (Marie-Josée

Mondzain's *Homo Spectator*, Christian Ruby's *Figure of the Spectator*, or Jacques Rancière's *Emancipated Spectator* being but the most speculative examples)—anything more than a last-ditch effort to stave off a paradigm shift already well underway? The real question, of course, remains: what alternative forms of usership of art are today being put forward to displace and replace it? But to better understand the full implications of this now largely obsolescent institution, it is useful to recall its historical trajectory.

It was Nietzsche, who, in the third essay of his *Genealogy of Morals*, first pointed out how the concept of 'spectatorship' was cunningly introduced into aesthetics in the late eighteenth century by Immanuel Kant in his *Critique of Judgement*, 'unconsciously' making the spectator the new heroic figure of art of the modern era. Nietzsche's own rather conventional proposal—reintroduce the artist as the authentic subject of art—is less interesting than his mordant critique of what is implied by the paradigm shift brought about by Kant. The problem with Kant's aesthetic paradigm, he argues, is that it sets up a conceptual edifice in which 'a lack of any refined firsthand experience reposes in the shape of a fat worm of error. 'That is beautiful,' said Kant, 'which gives us pleasure *without interest*.' Without interest!' One can only imagine Nietzsche's incredulous howl at the very thought... Yet his insight is unassailable: Kant introduced what he called 'disinterested spectatorship' into aesthetics and made it one of the two mainstays of the conceptual (and hence physical) architecture of museums for the two centuries to come. The consequences of Kant's paradoxical brainchild can hardly be overstated, for not only did he introduce a fundamentally passive form of relationality (spectatorship) as the cornerstone of the aesthetic regime of art, he shored it up by insisting on its *désintéressement*—in other words, that it remain exempt

from any possible use, usership or use value. This would be the grounds for art's permanent status of ontological exception throughout the twentieth century.

In *Shipwreck with Spectator*, Hans Blumenberg examines the genealogy of spectatorship, with particular attention to the metaphorical imperative of spectatorship to contemplate the distress of the shipwrecked from a safe vantage point on dry land—metaphorical, that is, of theory's relationship to practice ('*theoria*,' he points out somewhat speculatively, derives from *theoros*, or 'spectator'). It must be said, however, that the advent of Kantian spectatorship had the tremendous advantage of opening up a new space for aesthetic practice—the autonomous field of art. Yet, at the same time—though this would only become obvious two centuries on when art had conquered and fully occupied that space—it tethered art to autonomy and to spectatorship. Today we see cutting edge practices seeking to wrest themselves from spectatorship and the autonomy of art (perceived as shackles rather than opportunities), not in a desire to return to a pre-modern paradigm, but to reactivate a mode of usership that remains forbidden under the regime of spectatorship. It is nevertheless remarkable to see the extent to which the conceptual architecture of contemporary art conventions of display derive from Kantian premises; and to what extent they have been at once normalized through institutional embodiment and naturalized in discourse—even as they are becoming increasingly out of joint with emergent practices.

UIT ('use it together')

'you have to struggle with or deform an engineered social program to practice complex social exchange'
Richard Sennett, *Together* (2012)
—

There is a loathsome expression that has gained currency recently, which refers to taking pride in something, accepting something fully, adapting it to one's purposes, claiming one's due: '*Own it!*' If it appears innocuous, that is only because the ideology of ownership is by now so deeply embedded in the contemporary psyche. The expression is sometimes even applied to public institutions—but rather than users being invited to 'take usership' of their local museum or school through their active involvement ('*Just use it!*'), validation is expressed in terms of 'owning them.' As if ownership were synonymous with pride in, and care of, objects and actions, as opposed to the thoughtlessness and carelessness of usership. This rhetoric of ownership in idiomatic speech is a revealing symptom in our era of cross-the-board privatization.

Although ownership names a relationship to an object based on exclusivity, usership names a far more hands-on mode of engagement. DIY (do it yourself) culture emerged in industrial societies when the division of labour had atomized people's relationship to the production process and ratified expert culture; it was based on taking up and using tools and instruments traditionally reserved for experts. Punk culture took DIY's challenge to expert prerogative a step further—to the level of DIT (do it together). Its watchword has enduring appeal: 'Here's a chord. Here's another. Now let's start a band.' Of course

with the mass availability and usership of digital media, what might be called UIY (use it yourself) culture has become a major form of knowledge and value production. But can one really use alone? Usership is a strangely impersonal collective noun—it doesn't really name a collectivity of users, but it definitely implies multiplicity. '*Séparés, on est ensemble*'—Stéphane Mallarmé's wonderful line from *The White Waterlily*—nicely grasps the mutualization both by affinity and by contagion implied by usership. UIT (use it together) is one way to invite users to consciously build upon this social dimension of usership.

Usology

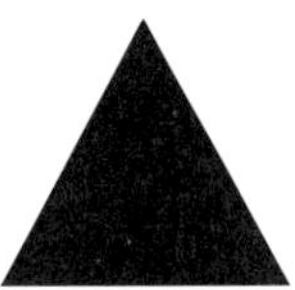

'Pushed to their ideal limits, these procedures and ruses of users compose the network of an antidiscipline...'
Michel de Certeau, *The Practice of Everyday Life* (1980)
—

Usology is an ambulant and approximate science, devoted to the study of uses and modes of usership. Current trends in usological research have tended to focus more specifically on what might be referred to as the 'tactical polyvalence of usages.' The reference here is of course to Michel Foucault's famous formulation regarding the 'tactical polyvalence of discourse,' where he emphasizes the complex and unstable play whereby 'discourse may be at once an instrument and an effect of power, but also an obstacle, a barrier, a hindrance and a starting point for an opposing strategy.' By examining—and accompanying—usership in action, usology is attentive to this constitutive polyvalence. Usership names both what actualizes the function of a space, a building or an initiative and what, in one and the same movement, thwarts that same function. Because this duality is constitutive of usership, it has been the object of particular usological scrutiny. Usology, however, is a far more sweeping field of extradisciplinary enquiry, spanning everything from the history of the ways and means of using to usership's conditions of possibility as put forward in various theories of practice.

Usual (the usual ≠ the event)

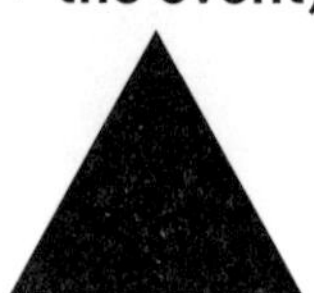

'to think life as that which is never given as property but only as a common use... will demand the elaboration of a theory of use and, moving forward from that, a critique of the operative and governmental ontology that continues, under various disguises, to determine the destiny of the human species.'
Giorgio Agamben, *The Highest Poverty* (2013)
—

A generation ago, the work of Henri Lefebvre and Michel de Certeau persuasively analyzed the goings-on, inventiveness and usership of what has come to be called 'the everyday.' Though it's hard to believe, the everyday has since become a victim of its own unforeseeable success. It has been championed, commodified and framed by spectatorship. For a long time, I considered 'the everyday' to be the environment of usership—the way eventhood is to spectatorship. But it was a poor fit. I couldn't quite figure out what the right concept and the right word might be to name usership's sphere of engagement. I never did figure it out; that's not how language use works. I overheard it one day. A regular stepped up to the bar, exchanged a quick glance with the barman who asked, invitingly, as if confident in what he already knew, *'the usual'*?

Usership

'Don't ask for the meaning, ask for the use.'
Ludwig Wittgenstein (circa 1945)
—

The past two decades have witnessed the emergence of a new category of political subjectivity: that of usership. It's not as if using is anything new—people have been using tools, languages and any variety of goods and services (not to mention mind-altering substances) since time immemorial. But the rise of user-generated content and value in 2.0 culture, as well as democratic polities whose legitimacy is founded on the ability of the governed to appropriate and use available political and economic instruments, has produced active 'users' (not just rebels, prosumers or automatons) whose agency is exerted, paradoxically, exactly where it is expected.

Usership represents a radical challenge to at least three stalwart conceptual institutions in contemporary culture: spectatorship, expert culture, and ownership. Modernist artistic conventions, premised on so-called disinterested spectatorship, dismiss usership (and use value, rights of usage) as inherently instrumental—and the mainstream artworld's physical and conceptual architecture is entirely unprepared to even speak of usership, even as many contemporary artistic practices imply a regime of engagement and relationality entirely at odds with that described by spectatorship. In the artworld and other lifeworlds, it is expert culture—whether embodied in curatorship or formulated by the city hall's design office and other wardens of the possible—which is most hostile to usership. From the perspective of expertise, premised as it is on notions of universality and the general interest, usership is a particularly egregious mode of self-interest. For the expert, to put it bluntly, use is invariably misuse. Usership represents a still more deep-seated challenge to ownership in an economy where surplus-value extraction is increasingly focused on use: how long will communities of use sit by as their user-generated content value, rather than being remunerated, is expropriated and privatized?

Usership is neither revolutionary (usership shares none of the messianic potential attributed to the proletariat) nor is it docile or submissive. It is hands-on, task specific, proximate and self-regulating. And it is operative only in the here and now—it has no transcendental horizonline. We might put it this way: users always and only play away from homegames; they don't have their own field, and just use those that are available available. For one thing, because users know they are not owners, and that whatever their demands, whatever their successes, users know that, no matter what, it will never be all theirs. The challenge is clearly to imagine, and to instantiate, a non-instrumental, emancipated form of usership.

Though usership remains dramatically undertheorized—indeed, the word itself, though immediately understandable, has not been ratified by those indexes of expert culture called dictionaries—there are some compelling philosophical underpinnings that may help to better grasp the concept. The most over-arching is perhaps Ludwig Wittgenstein's user-based theory of meaning in his *Philosophical Investigations*. Wittgenstein argues that in language, all the meaning that there is, and all the stability, is determined by the users of that language, and by nothing else. It seems radically relativistic, yet language usership provides a relative stability of meaning – for the language is used by all, owned by none. It changes, but no one user can effect change; we are, at best, co-authors in the language game of usership. Wittgenstein's insight provides a sort of prism through which to imagine all forms of usership in terms of a self-regulating language game.

So if usership names a category of engagement, of cognitive privilege (if one may call it that), of those whose repurposing of art is neither that of a spectator, an expert nor an owner, then why has art-critical discourse and practice been so reluctant to adopt it? Artworld ideologues speak of 'participation,' often sexing it up with adjectives like 'free' and 'emancipated.' We speak freely of 'art lovers,' but 'art users' smacks of philistinism—which certainly says something about the lingering aristocratic values underpinning contemporary art's ostensibly democratic ethos. Perhaps part of the reason for the artworld's discomfort with usership is that it is an eminently unromantic category. It has none of gusty tailings of hijacking, pirating, *'détournement'* and other such forms of performative high jinks that have become so fashionable in artworldly circles. It may ultimately better name the underlying logic of those operations, but it remains essentially different. Because it is radically imperformative. To perform usership would be to spectacularize it, make it an event—that is, to negate it, to make it into something else. Here the distinction between spectatorship and usership is clearest cut: spectatorship is to the spectacle as usership is to... the usual.

Usership, then, names not just a form of opportunity-dependent relationality, but a self-regulating mode of engagement and operation. Which makes usership itself a potentially powerful tool. In the same way that usership is all about repurposing available ways and means without seeking to possess them, it can itself be repurposed as a mode of leverage, a fulcrum, a shifter, and as such, a game-changer. That newly-purposed ironing board somebody mentioned may be just the war machine we've been looking for. Usership Potemkin.

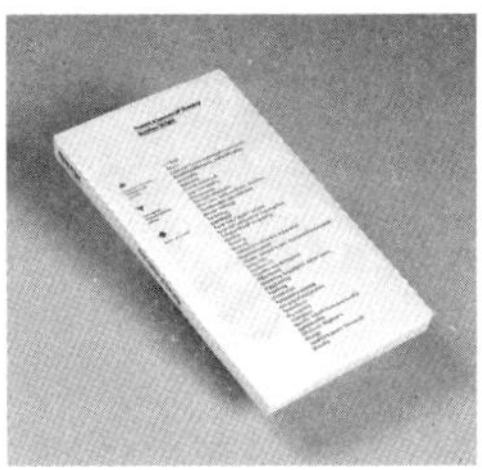

Toward a Lexicon of Usership
was first published on the
occasion of the *Museum of
Arte Útil*, Van Abbemuseum,
Eindhoven, 7 December
2013–30 March 2014,
www.museumarteutil.net

Text: Stephen Wright,
Editors: Nick Aikens and
Stephen Wright,
Text Proofing: Clare Butcher,
Original design: Collective
Works, The Hague

Contributors

Nick Aikens (*1981) is a curator at the Van Abbemuseum in Eindhoven. Recent exhibition projects there include: *Museum of Arte Útil*, 2013; *Positions*, 2014; and *FORWARD!: Ahmet Öğüt*, 2015. He has edited or co-edited a number of publications including *David Maljkovic, Sources in the Air* (2012), *Too Much World: The Films of Hito Steyerl* (2014), *The Company She Keeps, Céline Condorelli* (with Polly Staple) (2014), and *Toward a Lexicon of Usership* (with Stephen Wright) (2013). His writing has been published by *Afterall*, *Flash Art*, *Frieze*, and *L'Internationale Online*, for which he is a member of the editorial board. He has been a faculty member at the Dutch Art Institute since 2012. Aikens lives in Antwerp and works in Eindhoven.

Janine Armin is a writer, editor, and cofounder of Second Culture Press. She is associate editor for *Open!*, and editor for Casco – Office for Art, Design and Theory, Utrecht. Her art writing appears in *Bookforum* and the *International Herald Tribune* and recent books *Social Life of the Record #2: Metal Ideas* (2014) and *Thinking About It* (2014). She lives and works in Amsterdam.

Christina Aushana (*1987) is a performance theorist and PhD student in Communication at the University of California, San Diego. Her current research examines police training facilities and patrol work as sites of performative practices, tracing these engagements with performance from policing to prison reform and incarcerated theater reenactments. As a 2014 Studio for Ethnographic Design Fellow and a recipient of the 2015 Collaboratory for Ethnographic Design (CoLED) summer 2015 research fellowship, Aushana has worked with the prison reform organization Tamms Year Ten, combining this research with a performance-ethnography of police work in San Diego. Aushana is also co-founder of the research collaboratory *Feminist Theory Theater*, a group of readers dedicated to staging feminist theory as an intervention in situated meaning-making in the academy and beyond. Recent exhibitions include *Feminist Theory Theater*, Comm Playground, University of California, San Diego, 2015 and *Senses of Care: Mediated Ability and Interdependence*, gallery@calit2 at the University of California, San Diego, 2014. Aushana lives and works in San Diego.

Zdenka Badovinac is a curator, writer, and the director of the Ljubljana Museum of Modern Art [Moderna galerija] since 1993. She has curated numerous exhibitions presenting both Slovenian and international artists, always dealing with the processes of redefining history and the different avant-garde traditions of contemporary art. Badovinac initiated the first collection of Eastern European art, Moderna galerija's 2000+ Arteast Collection. She has curated *Body and the East: From the 1960s to the Present* at Moderna galerija, Ljubljana in 1998 and travelling to Exit Art, New York in 2001. She continued her curatorial research in 2000 with the first public display of the 2000+ Arteast Collection: *2000+ Arteast Collection: The Art of Eastern Europe in Dialogue with the West* at Moderna galerija, 2000; and with a series of Arteast exhibitions, mostly at Moderna galerija. Badovinac was the Slovenian Commissioner at the Venice Biennale (1993–1997 and 2005), and the Austrian Commissioner of the São Paulo Biennial (2002).

Manuel Borja-Villel (*1957) is the director of Museo Nacional Centro de Arte Reina Sofía (MNCARS) in Madrid since 2008. Together with searching for new forms of institutionality, an important part of his program in the MNCARS is centred on the development and reorganization of the collection, changing the method of presentation of works. Recent exhibitions he has programmed include: *Really Useful Knowledge*, 2014 and *Not Yet, On the Reinvention of Documentary and the Critique of Modernism*, 2015 among others. Borja-Villel lives and works in Madrid.

Tania Bruguera (*1968) is an interdisciplinary artist. Her work has been shown in numerous international museums. From 2002 to 2009 she founded and directed Arte de Conducta [Behaviour Art], the first performance studies programmed in Latin America. From 2003 to 2010 Bruguera was also Assistant Professor at the Department of Visual Arts of the University of Chicago. Since 2014, she has been developing the *Museum of Arte Útil* in collaboration with Queens Museum of Art in New York and Van Abbemuseum, Eindhoven.

John Byrne (*1964) is Senior Lecturer/Researcher in Fine Art at Liverpool School of Art and Design (Liverpool John Moores University, England). Byrne is currently manager and coordinator of 'The Uses of Art: The Legacy of 1848 and 1984' for Liverpool John Moores University and he is also co-director of Static Gallery, an organization for creative production based in Liverpool (England). Byrne is a member of *The Autonomy Project* editorial board, a long-term research project initiated in 2010. He writes regularly for various magazines and journals such as *Third Text*, *Afterall*, and *Open!*. Byrne lives and works in Liverpool.

Jesús Carrillo (*1966) combines his position as head of Cultural Activities in the Museo Nacional Centro de Arte Reina Sofía, Madrid with his academic activity as a professor of history and theory of art in the Universidad Autónoma, Madrid. His published work includes: *Naturaleza e Imperio* (2004); *Arte en la Red* (2003); and *Tecnología e Imperio* (2003). He has also edited the following: *Douglas Crimp: Posiciones críticas* (2005); *Desacuerdos: sobre arte, políticas y* *esfera pública en el Estado español vols. 1, 2 y 3* (2004–2005); and *Modos de hacer: arte crítico, esfera pública y acción directa* (2001).

Christina Clausen (*1987) is an art historian. She studied at the University of Marburg, the Università degli Studi di Padova, and Humboldt University of Berlin. Since 2014 she works as a scientific assistant at the University of Hildesheim. Her research focuses on pictorial representations of architecture, architectural models, and the reception of medieval architecture in the nineteenth century. Clausen lives and works in Berlin.

constructLab (established 1997) is a collective of designers, architects, and artists that experiment with collaborative construction practices, working on both ephemeral and permanent projects. constructLab represents a social method of working from the planning to the execution, from the participants to the public. It is an expression of the need to expand the social interest into the whole process. Relevant projects include the design and construction of the *Museum of Arte Útil*, Van Abbemuseum, Eindhoven, 2013, a project initiated by artist Tania Bruguera.

Tamara Díaz Bringas (*1973) is a curator and researcher. She was the scholarship holder of MACBA's Independent Study Program (PEI), Barcelona (2008–2009) and holds a B.A. in Art History from the Universidad de La Habana (1996). From 1999 to 2009 she was curator and editorial coordinator of the independent project TEOR/éTica, San José, Costa Rica. Her co-curated exhibitions include: *Playgrounds: Reinventing the Square* (with Manuel Borja-Villel and Teresa Velázquez), Museo Reina Sofía, Madrid, 2014; 31 Bienal de Pontevedra: Centroamérica y el Caribe (with Santiago Olmo), Pontevedra, 2010; and *The Doubtful Strait* (with Virginia Pérez-Ratton),

TEOR/éTica, San José, 2006. She has edited several books and written essays for catalogues and publications including *Art Journal*, *Artefacto*, *Tercer Texto*, *Artecontexto*, *Atlántica*, *Art Nexus*, and *Bomb Magazine*. She is a member of the independent research platform *Península. Colonial Processes, Art and Curatorial Practices*. Since 2015 she is a member of the Southern Conceptualisms Network. Díaz lives and works in Madrid.

Georges Didi-Huberman (*1953) is a philosopher, art historian, and teacher at École des hautes études en sciences sociales in Paris since 1990. He has curated about twelve exhibitions in various international museums such as: *L'Empreinte*, Centre Georges Pompidou, Paris, 1997; *Fables du lieu*, Studio National des Arts Contemporains, Tourcoing, 2001; and *ATLAS*, Museo Reina Sofía, Madrid, 2010 which continued till 2011 at the Museum für Neue Kunst, Karlsruhe and the Falckenberg Collection, Hamburg. He has also written about 50 books, including: *Passés cités par JLG. L'Oeil de l'histoire*, 5 (2015); *Essayer voir* (2014); *Sentir le grisou* (2014); *Phalènes. Essais sur l'apparition*, 2 (2013); *L'Album de l'art à l'époque du "Musée imaginaire"* (2013); *Invention of Hysteria: Charcot and the Photographic Iconography of the Salpêtrière* (2003); and *Fra Angelico: Dissemblance and Figuration* (1995) among others. Didi-Huberman lives and works in Paris.

Charles Esche (*1962) is a curator, writer, and the director of the museum of modern and contemporary art Van Abbemuseum in Eindhoven since 2004. Besides his experience in museological institutions, he has been part of the curatorial teams for: 31st São Paulo Biennial, 2014; U3, Moderna galerija, Ljubljana, 2011; Riwaq Biennial, Palestine, 2009 and 2007; Istanbul Biennial, 2005; and Gwangju Biennale, 2002. He is also

a Professor at Central Saint Martins College in London and co-founder of *Afterall Journal* and *Books*. Esche lives and works in Eindhoven.

Annie Fletcher (*1971) is chief curator at the museum of modern and contemporary art Van Abbemuseum, Eindhoven. In 2015 she co-curated a large-scale survey exhibition of Ahmet Öğüt's works titled *Vooruit* and the collection exhibition *A Republic of Art*. In 2014, she worked on the *Museum of Arte Útil*, an initiative by Cuban artist Tania Bruguera. Other projects include solo exhibitions or presentations with Hito Steyerl, Sheela Gowda, David Maljkovic, Jo Baer, Jutta Koether, and Deimantas Narkevicius. She was co-founder and co-director of *If I Can't Dance I Don't Want To Be Part Of Your Revolution* from 2005–2010. She writes on art and curating for various magazines including *Afterall* and *Metropolis M*.

Lara Garcia Diaz (*1986) is an independent art researcher. Her work focuses on the analyses of practices that challenge the boundaries between art and politics, considering alternative modes of empowerment through radical theories and practices of cultural resistance. Since 2014, she collaborates as an assistant researcher at the Van Abbemuseum, Eindhoven. Currently, she is also extending her research on institutional contexts in collaboration with the Research Centre for Arts in Society (Groningen). She has written for publications including *Open!*. She lives in Amsterdam and works between the Netherlands and Spain.

George&Harrison (established 2013) is an Eindhoven-based graphic design studio, founded by Martijn Maas and Maarten Stal. The studio creates projects for clients in the cultural and corporate field—in the form of publications, digital media, and visual identities. The studio focuses on clean, content-driven design that is deprived of any unnecessary noise. It is their aim to create design solutions that balance the desire to connect with individuals on an emotional level. Context, research, and dialogue are key to George&Harrison's approach. Find more of their work on www.georgeandharrison.nl.

Liam Gillick (*1964) is an interdisciplinary and conceptual artist. Gillick deploys multiple forms to expose the new ideological control systems that emerged at the beginning of the 1990s. His work extends into structural rethinking of the exhibition as a form. Gillick's work has been included in numerous exhibitions including Documenta and the Venice and Berlin Biennials as well as in solo museum exhibitions in the following: Museum of Contemporary Art, Chicago; Museum of Modern Art, New York; and Tate Modern, London. Gillick writes on art and curating for various magazines including *Artforum*, *October*, *Frieze*, and *e-flux Journal*.

Melinda Guillen (*1984) is a writer and curator. She holds an MA in Curatorial Practices from the USC Roski School of Art & Design and is currently a PhD candidate in Art History, Theory, and Criticism at UC San Diego. Her current research deconstructs feminist revisionism in American and Argentinian Conceptual Art, feminized forms of labour in social practice, and exposes the gendered binary logic of art and technology discourse. Recent exhibitions include *No Longer Extant: Cayetano Ferrer and Adela Goldbard: Artistic Production and Structural Demolition*, UCSD Structural & Materials Engineering Visual Arts Gallery, San Diego, 2015 and recently edited *Unweave #3: Topologies of the Underground: Metaphors, Extensions and Speculations* (with Elizabeth D. Miller, Mariana Botey, and Tim Ridlen, 2014). Guillen lives and works in Los Angeles and San Diego.

Jeanne van Heeswijk is a visual artist who facilitates the creation of dynamic and diversified public spaces in order to 'radicalize the local.' Van Heeswijk embeds herself as an active citizen in communities, often working in these roles for years at a time. Inspired by a particular current event, cultural context, or intractable social problem, she dynamically involves community members in the planning and realization of a given project. As an 'urban curator,' Van Heeswijk's work often unravels invisible legislation, governmental codes, and social institutions, in order to enable communities to take control over their own futures. Her work has been featured in numerous books and publications worldwide, as well as internationally renowned biennials such as those of Liverpool, Busan, Taipei, Shanghai, and Venice. She is currently the Keith Haring Fellows in Art and Activism at Bard College. In 2012, Van Heeswijk received the Curry Stone Prize for Social Design Pioneers, and in 2011, the Leonore Annenberg Prize for Art and Social Change.

Alistair Hudson (*1969) was appointed director of Middlesbrough Institute of Modern Art (mima) in October 2014. His new vision for mima is based on the concept of the 'Useful Museum' as an institution dedicated to the promotion of art as a tool for education and social change. Hudson was also deputy director of Grizedale Arts in the Lake District, United Kingdom from 2004 to 2014. Recent key projects include: *Confessions of the Imperfect, 1848–1989–Today*, Van Abbemuseum, Eindhoven, 2014–2015; development of the Coniston Mechanics Institute, Cumbria, 2009–2014; *Instituto Mechanicos*, São Paulo Biennial, 2010; *Happystacking*, China, 2008; and *Romantic Detachment*, PS1/MoMA, New York, 2004. Hudson is co-director of the Asociación de Arte Útil with Tania Bruguera and a jury member for the 2015 Turner Prize.

Thomas Lange (*1964) is professor for history and cultural practice of the visual arts at the Institute of Fine Arts and Art Studies at the University of Hildesheim since 2008. Lange was also Assistant Professor at the Art History Institute of the University of Amsterdam from 2003 to 2008. His books include *Das bildnerische Denken Philipp Otto Runges* (2010) and *Dickicht des Materials, Gradnetz des Bildes. Palermo: Bildidee und Werkbegriff* (2000).

Li Mu is a Chinese interdisciplinary artist. He graduated from the Suzhou School of Art and Design in 1995 and the Academy of Art of Tsinghua University, Beijing in 2001. Mu works with different media such as photography, installation, and performance, always challenging his understanding of art and his role as an artist. Everyday life plays an important role in his work. He creates relationships between the environment, the general public, and himself, blurring the boundary between art and life. He has had numerous group exhibitions and solo exhibitions including: *Qiuzguang Project---Sol LeWitt and Lu Daode*, Aurora Museum, Shanghai, 2015; *Confessions of the Imperfect, 1848–1989–Today*, Van Abbemuseum, Eindhoven, 2014; *Cast Accounts/Qiuzhuang*, Project am art space, Shanghai, 2013; *Open Studio Project-FUN ART*, Guangdong Times Museum, Guangzhou, 2012; *Gate Keeper*, Van Abbemuseum, Eindhoven, 2010. Mu lives and works in Suzhou.

Wendelien van Oldenborgh (*1962) develops works, whereby the cinematic format is used as a methodology for production and as the basic language for various forms of presentation. She often uses the format of a public film shoot, collaborating with various participants to co-produce a script and orientate the work toward its final outcome. Solo exhibitions include *From Left to Night*, The

Showroom, London, 2015 and she has participated in group exhibitions and biennials such as: 54th Venice Biennale, 2011; 4th Moscow Biennial, 2011; 29th Bienal de São Paulo, 2010; and 2nd Kochi-Muziris Biennial, 2014. She received the Heineken Award for the Arts from the Royal Netherlands Academy of Arts and Sciences in 2014.

Trevor Paglen (*1974) is a geographer, photographer, and artist. His work deliberately blurs lines between science, contemporary art, journalism, and other disciplines to construct unfamiliar, yet meticulously researched ways to see and interpret the world around us. Paglen has exhibited his work in venues including: Museum of Modern Art, New York; Tate Modern, London; and Walker Art Center, Minneapolis. He has also shown in the 2008 Taipei Biennial and the 2009 Istanbul Biennial among others. He is the author of five books and numerous articles on subjects including experimental geography, state secrecy, military symbology, photography, and visuality. Paglen has received grants and awards from the Electronic Frontier Foundation, Smithsonian, Art Matters, Artadia, San Francisco Museum of Modern Art, LUMA foundation, Eyebeam Center for Art and Technology, and Aperture Foundation.

Manuel Pelmuş has a background in choreography but has worked mostly in the visual arts context over the last two years. Pelmuş represented Romania together with Alexandra Pirici at the 55th Venice Biennale with the acclaimed project *An Immaterial Retrospective of the Venice Biennale*. His recent work has been presented at venues including: Centre Pompidou, Paris and Metz; Bass Museum of Art, Miami; Van Abbemuseum, Eindhoven; Museum M, Leuven; and Hebbel am Ufer, Berlin among others. He was awarded Berlin Art Prize for Performing Arts 2012.

Alexandra Pirici (*1982) is a Bucharest-based artist. She has a background in choreography but works undisciplined, across different mediums, from choreography to visual arts and music. Her recent work with Manuel Pelmuş, *An Immaterial Retrospective of the Venice Biennale*, was exhibited in the Romanian Pavilion at the 55th edition of the Venice Biennale in 2013. Her public space and museum space projects have appeared in venues including: Centre Pompidou, Paris; 12th Swiss Sculpture Exhibition, Biel, 2014; Van Abbemuseum, Eindhoven, 2014–2015; Manifesta 10, St. Petersburg, 2014; Bass Museum of Art, Miami, 2013–2014; and Museum of Contemporary Art, Leipzig, 2013, among others.

Emily Pethick (*1975) is the director of The Showroom, London, a contemporary art space with a focus on collaborative practice. From 2005–2008 she was the director of Casco – Office for Art, Design and Theory, Utrecht and from 2003–2004 she was curator at Cubitt, London. At The Showroom artist commissions include: Wendelien van Oldenborgh, *From Left to Night*, 2015; Ricardo Basbaum, *re-projecting (london)*, 2013; Petra Bauer, *Sisters!*, 2012; Lawrence Abu Hamdan, *The Freedom of Speech Itself*, 2012; and The Otolith Group, *A Long Time Between Suns*, 2009. She has contributed to catalogues and magazines such as *Afterall*, *Artforum*, *dot dot dot*, *Frieze*, and *The Exhibitionist*. She is co-editor of *Cluster: Dialectionary* (with Binna Choi, Maria Lind, and Natasa Petresin-Bachelez) (2014); *Circular Facts* (with Mai Abu ElDahab and Binna Choi) (2011); *Casco Issues XI: An Ambiguous Case* (with Marina Vishmidt and Tanja Widmann) (2008); and *Casco Issues X: The Great Method* (with Peio Aguirre) (2007). Pethick lives and works in London.

Pia Pol (*1985) is deputy publisher at Valiz, book and cultural projects in Amsterdam where she has been working since 2008. She received a BA in English Language & Culture and MA in American Studies from the University of Amsterdam. She has been working in the (art) book trade for over ten years, from bookstores to international distribution and publishing. At Valiz she focuses on production and digital development among many other things. Pol lives and works in Amsterdam.

Laurie Jo Reynolds (*1968) is an artist and policy advocate whose work addresses the harms of the US prison system. She is the organizer for Tamms Year Ten, a legislative campaign launched in 2008 to close the notorious state supermax in Tamms, Illinois, shuttered in 2013 by Governor Pat Quinn. As a 2010 Soros Justice Fellow, Reynolds researched and advocated for best practices to reduce sexual assault recidivism, creating functional and dialogical art to support legislative change. Reynolds is a Creative Capital grantee, a Blade of Grass Fellow, and the recipient of the 2013 Leonore Annenberg Prize for Art and Social Change. She worked on the staff of Governor Quinn's 2014 re-election campaign, and is now Assistant Professor of Public Art, Social Justice, and Media at the University of Illinois at Chicago.

Adrian Rifkin works without a notion medium specifity in order to animate a discourse of images and gestures, of different modes of enunciation. He is a Visiting Professor at Central Saint Martins College, London. Previously he was Professor of Art Writing at Goldsmiths, University of London. His books include *Ingres then, and now* (2000) and *Street Noises: Parisian Pleasure 1900–1940* (1993). He has edited collections such as: *Other Objects of Desire: Collectors and Collecting Queerly* (with Michael Camille) (2001); *About Michael*

Baxandall (1998); and *Voices of the People: The Social Life of 'La sociale' in Second Empire Paris* (with Roger Thomas) (1987). In 2015 a volume of essays and artist pages in dialogue with his work, edited by Dana Arnold, *Interdisciplinary Encounters, Hidden and Visible Explorations of the Work of Adrian Rifkin* was published and in same year Steve Edwards edited a selection of his essays, *Communards and Other Histories*. His website and blog can be found at www.gai-savoir. net. Rifkin lives and works in London.

John Ruskin (*1819; died 1900) was an art critic, social thinker, and political philosopher of the Victorian era. His first written work, *Modern Painters* (5 volumes, 1843–1860) became a study of the principles of art through the defending primarily of Turner's pictures. Later, in *The Seven Lamps Of Architecture* (1849) and *The Stones Of Venice* (1851) he similarly treated the fundamentals of architecture. He was Slade Professor of art at Oxford (1870–1879) and (1883–1884). His later works include *Sesame and Lillies* (1865), *The Crown Of Wild Olives* (1866), and *Fors Clavigera* (1871–1874), concentrating all in the development of a programme of social reform. In the 1870s Ruskin also established the *Guild of St George* to promote the advancement of education and training in the field of rural economy, industrial design and craftsmanship, and appreciation of the arts.

Lucía Sanromán is an independent curator and writer. Her work investigates aesthetics in relation to efficacy in social, participatory, and process-based art practice, focusing on the correlation between art history and theory with disciplines outside of the arts. Sanromán was awarded the 2012 Warhol Foundation Curatorial Fellowship and a 2013 Warhol Exhibition Grant for the exhibition *Citizen Culture: Art and Architecture Shape Policy*, Santa Monica Museum of Art in 2014. She was co-curator with

Candice Hopkins, Janet Dees, and Irene Hofmann of SITE Santa Fe's signature biennial *SITElines.2014: Unsettled Landscapes* and is an awardee of a The Pew Center for Arts & Heritage Fellowship.

Jorinde Seijdel is an independent writer, editor, lecturer, adviser, and art theorist on subjects that are concerned with the topic of art and media in the developing society and its public sphere. She is editor-in-chief of *Open! Platform on Art, Culture & the Public Domain* (formerly known as *Open. Cahier on Art & the Public Domain*) and she has contributed articles to many books and magazines, and participated in many conferences, FORMER WEST among them. In 2011 she published *De waarde van de amateur* [The Value of the Amateur, Fonds BKVB, Amsterdam], about the rise of the amateur in digital culture and the notion of amateurism in contemporary art. From 2010–2012 she was chair on the A PhD in the Arts committee, Fonds BKVB & NWO. She is a member of the Advisory Board Visual Arts & Design (ABKV), Utrecht and the Committee for Art, Design and Architecture at the Dutch Council for Culture (Raad voor Cultuur). Currently, she is theory mentor at Gerrit Rietveld Academie in Amsterdam and a core tutor and program leader at the Dutch Art Institute (MFA ArtEZ) in Arnhem. She lives and works in Amsterdam.

Catarina Simão (*1972) is a Lisbon-based artist, architect and researcher. Simão is known for her essay-like displays using documentation, drawings, and videos incorporating found footage related to African Liberation struggle and also films made in Mozambique just after the Portuguese colonial occupation. Throughout this 'in flux' format she is actually working on the nature of perception and encoded memory built up through image reception and archival concepts. Simão combines art

production with writing and other forms of presenting her long-term research like radio shows, lecture-performances and public talks, film screenings, artists books, and self-publishing. Her artwork has been presented at Serralves Museum, Manifesta 8, Africa.cont, Reina Sofía Museum among other institutions across Europe, New York, Beirut, and Maputo.

Sara Stehr completed her MA in Art History at the Freie Universität Berlin. From 2011 to 2014 she worked as curator of the Kunstverein Wiesbaden and produced a great number of exhibitions and projects with emerging artists from all over the world. In 2012 she co-curated the retrospective of the work of one of the founders of Fluxus, Benjamin Patterson. Since 2014, Stehr is research assistant at the University of Hildesheim. Her research focus is on art and aesthetic discourses from the 1960s until today.

Subtramas [Subplots] is an artistic collective based in Spain, whose members are: **Diego del Pozo Barriuso**, artist, cultural producer, and Associate Professor at the Faculty of Fine Arts of the University of Salamanca; **Montse Romaní**, researcher at the University of Barcelona, involved with projects at the intersection of cinema and visual arts with radical pedagogy and politics; and **Virginia Villaplana**, artist, cultural researcher, and lecturer in the area of Audiovisual Discourse Analysis at the Faculty of Communication & Documentation of the University of Murcia. Since 2009, the collective has been engaged in artistic research and production at the point of convergence of audiovisual production and radical pedagogies, collaborative practices, and social activism. *Subtramas* use visual narratives to explore the extent to which image-based work can help challenge the hierarchies of judgment and productivity that are intrinsic to inherited learning, how far image-based work can review and transform individual experiences and connect them to collective experience, and whether this work fosters a kind of knowledge linked to collaboration that can bring about more democratic forms of communal coexistence. Their website is http://subtramas.museoreinasofia.es/en/anagrama.

Steven ten Thije (*1980) is project leader of the current L'Internationale project *The Uses of Art – on the legacy of 1848 and 1989*. L'Internationale is a confederation of six European heritage institutes focused on modern and contemporary art and culture. In the programme he is active on the Editorial Board of L'Internationale Online (www.internationaleonline.org) and he co-curated *Confessions of the Imperfect, 1848–1989–Today* (22 November 2014–22 February 2015, Van Abbemuseum), together with Alistair Hudson. In the first L'Internationale project on post-war avant-gardes he was part of the curatorial team of *Spirits of Internationalism* (Van Abbemuseum, Eindhoven and M HKA, Antwerp, 2012) together with Charles Esche, Bart De Baere, Anders Kreuger, and Jan De Vree. He is at work on PhD research investigating the complex interplay between curating, art history, and media-history. He was part of the team that organized *Play Van Abbe* (2009–2011) and has published various articles and reviews in publications such as *Exhibiting the New Art, 'Op Losse Schroeven' and 'When Attitudes Become Form' 1969* (2010). He studied art history and philosophy at the University of Amsterdam. He lives and works in Eindhoven.

Astrid Vorstermans (*1960) is an art historian, and worked in various workplaces as publisher, editor, and bookseller, as well as in international book distribution. In 2003 she launched Valiz, a publisher and cultural agency that traces and reacts to developments in contemporary art, architecture, and design in a broad and inventive way. Under the Valiz umbrella she works with a broad network of numerous other professionals in the arts and theory. Vorstermans lives and works in Amsterdam.

What, How & for Whom/WHW (established 1999) is a curatorial collective based in Zagreb and Berlin. Its members are curators Ivet Ćurlin, Ana Dević, Nataša Ilić, and Sabina Sabolović, and designer and publicist Dejan Kršić. WHW organizes a range of production, exhibition, and publishing projects and directs Gallery Nova in Zagreb. Among exhibitions WHW has curated are: *Really Useful Knowledge*, Museo Nacional Centro de Arte Reina Sofía, Madrid, 2014; *Meeting Points 7*, Zagreb, Antwerp, Cairo, Hong Kong, Beirut, Vienna and Moscow, 2013/2014; *One Needs to Live Self-Confidently…Watching*, Croatian pavilion, 54th Venice Biennale, 2011; 11th Istanbul Biennial, *What Keeps Mankind Alive?*, 2009; and *Collective Creativity*, Kunsthalle Fridericianum, Kassel 2005.

Stephen Wright is a Paris-based art writer and teaches the practice of theory at the European School of Visual Arts (eesi.eu). His writing has focused primarily on the politics of usership, particularly in contexts of collaborative, extradisciplinary practices with variable coefficients of art. As an independent curator, he has organized a dozen exhibitions and activations, including: *Escapologies*, Graz, 2012; *Situation Z*, Marseille, 2011; *Plausible Artworlds* (with Basekamp), Philadelphia, 2010; *Recomposing Desire*, Beirut, 2008; *Rumor as Media*, Istanbul, 2007; *Dataesthetics*, Zagreb, 2006; *In Absentia*, Brest, 2005; *The Future of the Reciprocal Readymade*, New York, 2004; and *L'Incurable mémoire des corps*, Paris, 2000, which, focusing on practices with deliberately impaired coefficients of artistic visibility, raise the prospect of an art without objecthood, authorship or spectatorship. He is a founding user of the collective blog n.e.w.s. and international platform IDEA-Z. As an art theorist, his research deals above all with the ongoing usological turn, and current forms of contemporary escapology, in the fields of art and epistemology, examining the conditions of possibility and use of practices which have deliberately withdrawn from the event horizon, necessitating a fundamental reconsideration and repurposing of the conceptual architecture and vocabulary inherited from modernity. In 2013, his *Toward a Lexicon of Usership* was published by the Van Abbemuseum.

George Yúdice is Professor of Modern Languages and Literatures and Latin American Studies at the University of Miami and Director of the Miami Observatory on Communication and Creative Industries. He is also in charge of the Vice-provostship of International and Community Relations for the Universidad de las Artes, Guayaquil, Ecuador. He is the author of books including: *Culturas emergentes en el mundo hispano de Estados Unidos*(2009); *Nuevas tecnologías, música y experiencia* (2007); *The Expediency of Culture: Uses of Culture in the Global Era* (2003); and *Cultural Policy* (with Toby Miller) (2002). He has published over 130 articles on cultural policy, music and audiovisual industries, new media, and rethinking aesthetics in the age of social media. He is on the editorial board of *International Journal of Cultural Policy*.

Index of Names

Index of Works of Art, Exhibitions, Projects, Organizations

Credits of the Images

Nick Aikens 330, 330
Altonaer Museum, Hamburg 101
Ashmolean Museum,
 University of Oxford 36, 44
Christina Aushana 287
Sam Barnett 293
Yael Bartana (or Studio)
 181, 182, 182, 182, 183, 185,
 186, 187, 189, 190, 191
Oded Brosh 187, 187
Tania Bruguera Studio 56
Bureau d'Études for
 constructLab 439, 440
Musée Carnavalet, Paris 46
Courtauld Collection,
 London 276
Peter Cox 336, 373
Adrianne Dues 292
The Farber Collection 54
Tony Favarula 294
José A. Figueroa 51
Grizedale Arts 'Office of
 Useful Art' 40, 124
Lea Hammerstein
 Silverstein 190
Rachel Herman 289
Laura Hsieh 289
Isiah 294
Casey Kelbaugh 292
Soohyun Kim 291
Klassik Stiftung Weimar 106
Kulturhistorisches Museum,
 Magdeburg 99
Kunsthalle Hamburg 33
Musée du Louvre, Paris 337
Magnum Photos 425
Catherine McMillian 293
Futuro Moncada 378
Hans Namuth Estate 125
National Gallery, London 270
Niedersächsisches
 Landesmuseum Hannover
 – Landesgalerie,
 Hannover 366, 366
Trevor Paglen 240
Nadya Pittendrigh 289
Mathias Regan
Laurie Jo Reynolds
 289, 289, 291, 334
Staatliche Museen zu Berlin 94,
 98, 98, 103, 103, 105, 105, 107
Stadtmuseum, Köln 106
Swan Sonnenschein,
 London 79
Tamms Year Ten 289, 334
Tate Britain, London 46

United States Holocaust
 Memorial Museum,
 Washington 190
Universitätsbibliothek
 Heidelberg, Heidelberg 108
José Veigas Archive, Havana 51
Juan José Vidal 51
Virtual Museum of Political Art,
 a private collection by MMAg.
 Dr. Patrick Horvath, M.A.I.S.,
 and Dr. Werner Horvath 189
Cristina Vives 51
Frits Wiarda 426

Acknowledgements

This publication extends the discussions begun during three exhibitions and a conference. It draws on the accumulated knowledge and speculations of the many artists, curators, writers, and institutions involved. Some original exhibition and conference papers reappear here, or have been reworked for this book. These are supplemented by numerous new texts and conversations. The editors would like to give a warm thank you to the contributors of *What's the Use?* and the projects listed below, and all the people, too many to list by name, who made their realization possible. We are incredibly grateful, inspired, and energized by your ideas and dedication.

Museum of Arte Útil
Van Abbemuseum,
Eindhoven, Netherlands
7 December 2013–30 March 2014

Museum of Arte Útil team: Nick Aikens, Tania Bruguera, constructLab (with Alex Roemer, Bureau d'Études, Collective Works and others), Annette Eliëns, Charles Esche, Annie Fletcher, Gemma Medina and Alessandra Saviotti

Initiators: Azra Akšamija, Lara Almarcegui, Artun Alaska Arasli, Joseph Beuys, Augusto Boal, Tania Bruguera, Santiago Cirugeda, Liz Christy, Paulina Cornejo, Eduardo Costa, Critical Art Ensemble, Sean Dockray, Electronic Disturbance Theatre 2.0, Jalila Essaïdi, Claudia Fernández, Daniel Godínez Nivón, Rebecca Gomperts, Grizedale Arts, Núria Güell, Jeanne van Heeswijk, Institute for Human Activities, IRWIN, Djambawa Marawili, Memetro, Mike Merrington, Missdata, NSW Builders Labourers Federation and Victoria Street Resident Action Group, Ahmet Öğüt, Jeannette Petrik, Pivot, Pino Poggi, Bik van der Pol, Provo, Publink, Luca Pucci, Laurie Jo Reynolds, Rolling Jubilee, John Ruskin, Ruben Santiago, Bonnie O. Sherk, Apolonija Šušteršič, Vivireternamente, WochenKlausur, Wooloo Artists from the Yirrkala region Yomango, Stephen Wright, Yao Jui-Chung + Lost Society Document

Confessions of the Imperfect, 1848–1989–Today
Van Abbemuseum,
Eindhoven, Netherlands
22 November 2014–22 February 2015

Curators: Steven ten Thije, Alistair Hudson

Artists: Constant, Jeremy Deller, Fernando García-Dory, Liam Gillick, Renzo Martens, Antoni Miralda, Li Mu, Wendelien van Oldenborgh, Alexandra Pirici & Manuel Pelmuş, John Ruskin, Static and Akram Zaatari
Exhibition design: Liam Gillick

The Uses of Art: History
University of Hildesheim,
Hildesheim, Germany
28–30 November 2014

Organized by Thomas Lange

Contributors: Nick Aikens, John Byrne, Jesús María Carrillo Castillo, Christina Clausen, Juan Cruz, Georges Didi-Huberman, Alistair Hudson, Thomas Lange, Wendelien van Oldenborgh, Alexandra Pirici and Manuel Pelmuş, Srða Popovic, Lena Reisner, Sara Stehr, Steven ten Thije

Really Useful Knowledge
Museo Reina Sofía, Madrid, Spain
29 October 2014–9 February 2015

Curators: What How and for Whom / WHW

Artists: Brook Andrew, Ardmore Ceramic Art, Ariella Azoulay, Hicham Benohoud, Phil Collins, Carole Condé & Karl Beveridge, Chto Delat, Emory Douglas, Núria Güell & Levi Orta, Dmitry Gutov & David Riff [Lifshitz Institute], Danièle Huillet & Jean-Marie Straub, Adelita Husni-Bey, Iconoclasistas, Abbas Kiarostami, Runo Lagomarsino, Darcy Lange, Victoria Lomasko, Marcell Mars, Azzedine Meddour, Mujeres Públicas, Daniela Ortiz, Trevor Paglen, Trevor Paglen & Jacob Appelbaum, Partisan Art, D.A. Pennebaker, Primitivo Evanán Poma & Association of Popular Artists of Sarhua, Hannah Ryggen, Catarina Simão, Mladen Stilinović, Subtramas, Traficantes de Sueños, Lidwien van de Ven, Cecilia Vicuña, Carla Zaccagnini, Želimir Žilnik

Partners

This publication was made possible through the generous support of
L'Internationale,
www.internationaleonline.org

L'Internationale is a confederation of six major European modern and contemporary art institutions and partners. L'Internationale proposes a space for art within a non-hierarchical and decentralised internationalism, based on the values of difference and horizontal exchange among a constellation of cultural agents, locally rooted and globally connected.

This project has been funded with support from the European Commission. This publication reflects the views only of the authors, and the Commission cannot be held responsible for any use which may be made of the information contained therein.

L'Internationale
www.internationaleonline.org

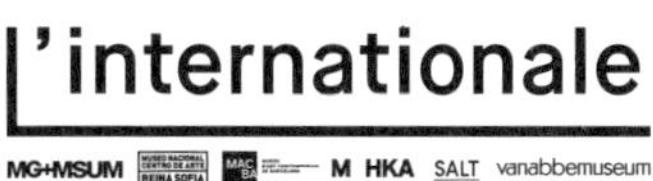

European Union, Culture Programme

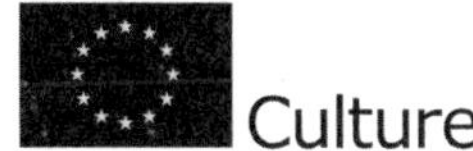

Van Abbemuseum
www.vanabbemuseum.nl

VAN
ABBE
MUSEUM
EINDHOVEN

Stiftung Universität Hildesheim
www.uni-hildesheim.de

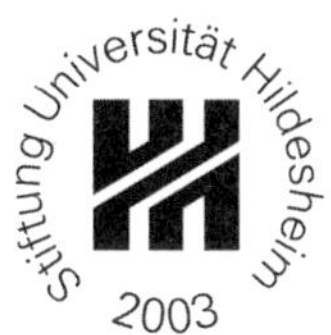

Mondriaan Fund
www.mondriaanfonds.nl

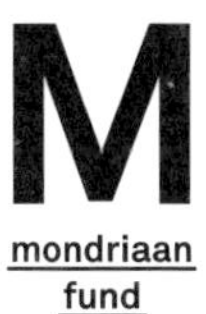

Valiz, book and cultural projects
www.valiz.nl

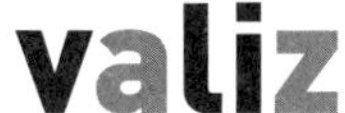

Colophon

Editors
Nick Aikens, Thomas Lange,
Jorinde Seijdel, Steven ten Thije

Contributors
Nick Aikens, Christina Aushana,
Zdenka Badovinac, Manuel
Borja-Villel, Tania Bruguera,
John Byrne, Jesús Carrillo, Christina
Clausen, constructLab, Tamara Díaz
Bringas, Georges Didi-Huberman,
Charles Esche, Annie Fletcher, Lara
Garcia Diaz, Liam Gillick, Melinda
Guillen, Jeanne van Heeswijk,
Alistair Hudson, Thomas Lange,
Li Mu, Wendelien van Oldenborgh,
Trevor Paglen, Manuel Pelmuş, Emily
Pethick, Alexandra Pirici, Laurie Jo
Reynolds, Adrian Rifkin, John Ruskin,
Lucía Sanromán, Catarina Simão,
Sara Stehr, Subtramas, Steven ten
Thije, WHW (What, How & for Whom),
Stephen Wright, George Yúdice

Managing editor
Jorinde Seijdel

Editorial and image research
Lara Garcia Diaz, for the images
assisted by Lotte Schröder

Translation
José Manuel Bueso Fernández
(Subtramas), Zhang Hangya (Li Mu),
Rob Madole (Christina Clausen, Sara
Stehr), Wendy van Os-Thompson
(Georges Didi-Huberman), Nuria
Rodrigues (Tamara Díaz Bringas),
Roopanjali Roy (Catarina Simão)

Text editor
Janine Armin

Proofreading
Els Brinkman

Index
Elke Stevens

Graphic design
George&Harrison
www.georgeandharrison.nl

Production
Valiz, Pia Pol,
Astrid Vorstermans

Lithography and printing
Drukkerij Tienkamp, Groningen

Binding
Stronkhorst Boekbinders, Groningen

Paper inside
Arcoprint Milk
Symbol Freelife Gloss

Paper cover
Sirio Colour Vermiglione E20

Typefaces
Courier New, Dala Floda, Lydian,
Maison Neue

This book has been produced with
best practice methods ensuring
lowest possible environmental
impact, using waterless offset,
vegetable-based inks and FSC-
certified paper.

Publisher
Valiz, Amsterdam in cooperation with
the Van Abbemuseum, Eindhoven
and Stiftung Universität Hildesheim

Amsterdam, Eindhoven, Hildesheim,
2016

Valiz, Amsterdam (NL) www.valiz.nl
Van Abbemuseum, Eindhoven (NL)
www.vanabbemuseum.nl
Stiftung Universität Hildesheim (DE)
www.uni-hildesheim.de

Distribution
BE/NL/LU: Coen Sligting,
www.coensligtingbookimport.nl
CB, www.cb.nl

GB/IE: Anagram Books,
www.anagrambooks.com

Europe/Asia: Idea Books,
www.ideabooks.nl

USA: D.A.P., www.artbook.com

Individual orders:
www.valiz.nl; info@valiz.nl

ISBN 978 94 92095 12 1
NUR 651
Printed and bound in the EU

The editors, authors and the
publisher have made every effort
to secure permission to reproduce
the listed material, illustrations and
photographs. We apologize for any
inadvert errors or omissions. Parties
who nevertheless believe they
can claim specific legal rights are
invited to contact the publisher.